THE *Virgin* ENCYCLOPEDIA OF

THE BLUES

COLIN LARKIN

Virgin

IN ASSOCIATION WITH MUZE UK LTD.

Dedicated To Luther Allison

First published in Great Britain in 1998 by
VIRGIN BOOKS
an imprint of Virgin Publishing Ltd
332 Ladbroke Grove, London W10 5AH

A catalogue record for this book is available from the British Library

ISBN 0 7535 0226 7

Written, edited and produced by
MUZE UK Ltd
to whom all editorial enquiries should be sent
Iron Bridge House, 3 Bridge Approach, Chalk Farm, London NW1 8BD

Editor In Chief: Colin Larkin
Production Editor: Susan Pipe
Editorial and Research Assistant: Nic Oliver
Copy Editor: Sarah Lavelle
Typographic Design Consultant: Roger Kohn
Special thanks to Trev Huxley, Anthony Patterson, Paul Zullo
and all the Klugettes at Muze Inc.,
and to Rob Shreeve of Virgin Publishing.
Typeset by Mean Mr Mustard Studio
Printed and bound in Great Britain by Butler & Tanner Ltd, Frome and London

INTRODUCTION

This new edition proudly bears the Virgin banner. *The Virgin Encyclopedia Of The Blues* is one in the major series of books taken from the *Encyclopedia Of Popular Music*. Other titles already available are:

The Virgin Encyclopedia Of Sixties Music
The Virgin Encyclopedia Of Seventies Music
The Virgin Encyclopedia Of Eighties Music
The Virgin Encyclopedia Of Indie & New Wave
The Virgin Encyclopedia Of Country Music
The Virgin Encyclopedia Of R&B And Soul

The blues is the main artery of rock and pop. Its influence is much greater than is justified by its share of the market. Occasionally a blues album will take the world by storm and sell vast quantities, but sadly John Lee Hooker's *The Healer* has been matched in recent years only by Jonny Lang's *Lie To Me*. However, blues lovers are out there, rock solid in their loyalty and appreciation of a genre that is without doubt popular music's most vital and emotional.

The selections this time have attempted to cover all the historically important artists together with the best of the new wave of talent, both black and white. There are those people who hold the belief that blues has to be black and from the USA. It absolutely does not. When talking to American enthusiasts I am highly flattered to know that many regard the UK as the home of the blues, even though I know differently. What they mean is, if it had not been for the efforts of highly respected British writers such as Paul Oliver, dedicated producers such as Mike Vernon, tireless ambassadors such as Paul Jones (both as performer and broadcaster) and canny record company executives like Bob Fisher, Roger Armstrong and Ted Carroll, the blues would not have the profile it enjoys today. Without UK blues magazines such as *Blues & Rhythm* and *Blueprint*, under the editorship of Tony Burke and Fran Leslie, respectively, we would not be so well informed. Finally, if it had not been for the likes of John Mayall, Graham Bond, Alexis Korner, Rory Gallagher, Brian Jones, Duster Bennett and Peter Green in the 60s, then I and countless others would still be listening to Craig Douglas records.

Much of the original research and many of the entries have been written by blues experts. This book is not for them as they already know far more than is packed into these pages. This book is a solid companion for those who want and will become hooked (or Hookered) on the blues. And you can be black, white or green-skinned to enjoy it. Although our paths rarely cross now, I especially thank Tony Burke and his team, plus the knowledgeable Neil Slaven. Their contributions are still the backbone to this work.

ENTRY STYLE

Albums, EPs (extended play 45s), newspapers, magazines, television programmes, films and stage musicals are referred to in italics. All song titles appear in single quotes. We spell rock 'n' roll like this. There are two main reasons for spelling rock 'n' roll with 'n' as opposed to 'n'. First, historical precedent: when the term was first coined in the 50s, the popular spelling was 'n'. Second, the 'n' is not simply an abbreviation of 'and' (in which case 'n' would apply) but a phonetic representation of n as a sound. The ' ', therefore, serve as inverted commas rather than as apostrophes. The further reading section at the end of each entry has been expanded to give the reader a much wider choice of available books. These are not necessarily recommended titles but we have attempted to leave out any publication that has little or no merit.

We have also started to add videos at the ends of the entries. Again, this is an area that is expanding faster than we can easily cope with, but there are many items in the videography and further items in the filmography, which is another new section we have decided to include. Release dates in keeping with albums attempt to show the release date in the country of origin. We have also tried to include both US and UK titles where applicable.

ALBUM RATING

Due to many requests from our readers we have now decided to rate all albums. All new releases are reviewed either by myself or by our team of contributors. We also take into consideration the review ratings of the leading music journals and critics' opinions.

Our system is slightly different to most 5 Star ratings in that we rate according to the artist in question's work. Therefore, a 4 Star album from Muddy Waters may have the overall edge over a 4 Star album by Sherman Robertson. Sorry Sherman.

Our ratings are carefully made, and consequently you will find we are very sparing with 5 Star and 1 Star albums.

Outstanding in every way. A classic and therefore strongly recommended. No comprehensive record collection should be without this album.

Excellent. A high standard album from this artist and therefore highly recommended.

Good. By the artist's usual standards and therefore recommended.

★★

Disappointing. Flawed or lacking in some way.

★

Poor. An album to avoid unless you are a completist.

PLAGIARISM

In maintaining the largest text database of popular music in the world we are naturally protective of its content. We license to approved licensees only. It is both flattering and irritating to see our work reproduced without credit. Time and time again over the past few years I have read an obituary, when suddenly: hang on, I wrote that line. Secondly, it has come to our notice that other companies attempting to produce their own rock or pop encyclopedias use our material as a core. Flattering this might also be, but highly illegal. We have therefore dropped a few more textual 'depth charges' in addition to the original ones. Be warned.

ACKNOWLEDGEMENTS

Our in-house editorial team is lean and efficient. Our Database is now a fully grown child and needs only regular food, attention and love. Thanks to Susan Pipe; calm and sure as ever. Nic Oliver and Sarah Lavelle our recent full-time discoveries and the blueswailing Roger Kohn's parrot. Our outside contributors are further reduced in number, as we now write and amend all our existing text. However, we could not function without the continuing efforts and dedication of Big John Martland, Bruce Crowther and Alex Ogg. Brian Hogg, Hugh T. Wilson, Spencer Leigh and Robert Pruter continue to supply their specialist knowledge.

Other past contributors' work may appear in this volume and I acknowledge once again; Simon Adams, David Ades, Mike Atherton, Gavin Badderley, Alan Balfour, Michael Barnett, Steve Barrow, John Bauldie, Lol Bell-Brown, Johnny Black, Chris Blackford, Pamela Boniface, Keith Briggs, Michael Ian Burgess, Paul M. Brown, Tony Burke, John Child, Linton Chiswick, Rick Christian, Alan Clayson, Tom Collier, Paul Cross, Bill Dahl, Norman Darwen, Roy Davenport, Peter Doggett, Kevin Eden, John Eley, Lars Fahlin, John Fordham, Per Gardin, Ian Garlinge, Mike Gavin, Andy Hamilton, Harry Hawk, Mark Hodkinson, Mike Hughes, Arthur Jackson, Mark Jones, Max Jones, Simon Jones, Ian Kenyon, Dave Laing, Steve Lake, Paul Lewis, Graham Lock, John Masouri, Bernd Matheja, Chris May, Dave McAleer, Ian McCann, David McDonald, York Membery, Toru Mitsui, Greg Moffitt, Nick Morgan, Michael Newman, Pete Nickols, Lyndon Noon, Zbigniew Nowara, James Nye, Ken Orton, Ian Peel, Dave Penny, Alan Plater, Barry Ralph, John Reed, Emma Rees, Lionel Robinson, Johnny Rogan, Alan Rowett, Jean Scrivener, Roy Sheridan, Dave Sissons, Neil Slaven, Chris Smith, Steve Smith, Mitch Solomons, Christopher Spencer, Jon Staines, Mike Stephenson, Sam Sutherland, Jeff Tamarkin, Ray Templeton, Liz Thompson, Gerard Tierney, John Tobler, Adrian T'Vell, Pete Wadeson, Frank Warren, Ben Watson, Pete Watson, Simon Williams, Val Wilmer, Dave Wilson and Barry Witherden.

Record company press offices are often bombarded with my requests for biogs and review copies. Theirs is a thankless task, but thanks anyway, especially to Alan Robinson of Demon, Sue and Dave Williams at Frontier, Mal Smith at Delta, Darren Crisp of Science Friction, Julia Honeywell at Ace, Murray Chalmers and Laura at Parlophone and Pat Naylor and Nicola Powell at Ryko/Hannibal.

Press offices in general at: A&M, Alligator, Almo, American Recordings (Louise), Arista, BGO (Andy Gray), Blue Note, Bullseye, Chrysalis (Iona), Cooking Vinyl, East West, EMI, Grapevine (Jane), Greentrax, Hightone, Dorothy Howe, HTD, Indigo, Island (Deborah), Koch (Pat), London, MCA (Ted Cummings), Mercury, New Note, Park, Pinnacle, RCA (Sharon), Rounder, Silvertone, Sire, Strange Fruit (Jo), Telarc, Transatlantic, Trauma, Virgin, and all at Richard Wooton's office.

Thanks for the enthusiasm and co-operation of all our new colleagues at Virgin Publishing under the guidance of the over-stretched Rob Shreeve, in particular to Roz Scott who is always amazingly ungrumpy.

To our new owners at Muze Inc., who oil the smooth running of the UK operation and are the business partners I always knew I wanted but never knew where to find. To all colleagues at the office on 304 Hudson Street in New York. In particular to the dedicated Tony Patterson, the perfectly trim Paul Zullo, Steve Figard, Marc Miller and the unceremoniously humble Trev Huxley. And lastly to Dave, Sabra and my most agreeable tin lids; the smile you send out returns to you even when you have de blues.

Colin Larkin, January 1998

ABRAHAMS, MICK

b. 7 April 1943, Luton, Bedfordshire, England. Following a musical apprenticeship in the early 60s with Neil Christian, Dickie Pride and the Toggery Five, guitarist Abrahams made a career breakthrough with Jethro Tull and Blodwyn Pig. He embarked on a largely unsuccessful solo career in 1971. His *Mick Abrahams* and *At Last*, as the Mick Abrahams Band, featured Walt Monahan (bass), Bob Sergeant (keyboards, vocals) and Ritchie Dharma (drums). Abrahams subsequently made a guitar tuition album that eventually outsold his previous catalogue, although he left the music business in 1975. An outstanding player, Abrahams contributed (albeit briefly) to the blues boom of the late 60s, but sadly his career has not matched his undoubted potential. In 1989 it was announced that Abrahams was re-forming Blodwyn Pig, and he now continues to perform with the band and as a solo acoustic blues performer. *All Said And Done* demonstrated a mature musician playing his blend of anglo-blues music with ease. He resurrected Blodwyn Pig in 1993 and released *Lies* using that moniker, presumably a marketing device, as the album was very much a Mick Abrahams project. *One* was a stripped-down blues guitar record, on which Abrahams was able to shine in the musical territory with which he is most comfortable. He continued with more unadulterated blues on *Mick's Back* in 1996.

● ALBUMS: as Mick Abrahams Band *A Musical Evening With Mick Abrahams* (Chrysalis 1971)★★★, *At Last* (Chrysalis 1972)★★★, *Have Fun Learning The Guitar* (SRT 1975)★★★, *All Said And Done* (1991)★★★, *Lies* (A New Day 1993)★★, *One* (A New Day 1996)★★★, *Mick's Back* (Indigo 1996)★★★, *Live In Madrid* (Indigo 1997)★★★.

ACES

Comprising Louis Myers, his brother Dave Myers and drummer Fred Below (b. 6 September 1926, Chicago, Illinois, USA, d. 13 August 1988, Chicago, Illinois, USA), the Aces were Little Walter's backing band in the early 50s (they were often called the Jukes on his records), and were one of the first electric Chicago blues bands to undertake major tours. Their swinging approach was extremely influential. In the 70s they visited Europe, recording accompaniments to blues artists such as Mickey Baker, Willie Mabon and Jimmy Rogers and made albums for Vogue, Black & Blues, and MCM, with special guests including Joe Carter and ex-Muddy Waters guitarist Sammy Lawhorn.

● ALBUMS: *Kings Of Chicago Blues Volume One* (1971), *The Aces With Their Guest* (1975)★★★.

ADAMS, J.T.

b. John Tyler Adams, 17 February 1911, Morganfield, Kentucky, USA. Adams learned blues guitar from his father; moving to Indianapolis in the 40s, he fell in with Scrapper Blackwell, and Mississippian Shirley Griffith, a fellow Chrysler employee who became his closest musical associate. Each accompanied the other, their twin guitars blending as impeccably on Mississippi blues standards such as 'Big Road Blues', as on songster material such as 'Kill It Kid' and 'The Hop Joint'. Adams was recorded in the early 60s, but was heard of little thereafter, although he was reported still to be partnering Griffith at the time of the latter's death in 1974.

● ALBUMS: *Indiana Avenue Blues* (1963)★★★, *Indianapolis Jump* (1976)★★★.

ADAMS, WOODROW

b. Woodrow Wilson Adams, 9 April 1917, Tchula, Mississippi, USA. Although he earned his living driving a tractor in rural Mississippi, Woodrow Adams made enough records to provide us with a fascinating insight into the music of a non-professional Delta blues musician. He learned both harmonica and guitar during childhood, but was 35 years old before he made his first record. In all, he released three singles between 1952 and 1961. The first was an extremely rough, unpolished performance in the Mississippi-based Chicago blues style of the time, but by the time the third was released, there was an attempt to update his sound to a more commercial R&B. None of these records enjoyed any success and Adams was still working on a plantation when researcher David Evans recorded a session with his band in 1967, part of which was later issued on an album.

● ALBUMS: *Lowdown Memphis Harmonica Jam* (1976)★★★.

ADLER, DANNY

b. 1949, Cincinnati, Ohio, USA. This distinctive blues and funk guitarist, singer and composer was noted for his 'Gusha Gusha' music, built around complex rhythms and hard, fatback bass. He initially played piano, influenced by his jazz musician father, but switched to blues guitar on hearing Chuck Berry, Jimmy Reed and local bluesman Lonnie Mack. By 1966, he was regularly jamming (sometimes alongside bass player Bootsy Collins) with Ohio band Albert T. Washington & The Kings. He sat in with Slim Harpo and Amos Milburn, and after moving to California in 1968, he worked behind T-Bone Walker, Solomon Burke and many others. He formed Dr Funk, then in 1970 worked with Elephant's Memory for a short period. Adler moved to London in 1972, gigged with Smooth Loser and recorded with Dave Edmunds and Nick Lowe in 1975. The band Roogalator began to play regularly from September that year, becoming a major attraction on the pub circuit and in Europe, and exemplifying Adler's eclectic musical abilities. He led the Danny Adler Band from 1978, and appeared with both the De Luxe Blues Band and Rocket 88 in the early 80s. In 1989 he 'invented' Otis 'Elevator' Gilmore, a supposedly long-lost Ohio bluesman; Adler in fact passed off his own recordings as those of his discovery, and fooled a major blues reissue label into releasing them. When the hoax was discovered, the album was withdrawn, although white label copies remain in circulation. In 1990 Adler returned home to Ohio.

● ALBUMS: *The Danny Adler Story* (Do-It 1979)★★★, *Gusha Gusha Music* (Armageddon 1981)★★★, with Rocket 88 *Rocket 88* (Atlantic 1981)★★★, *Live* (1982)★★★, *Live Vol. II* (1984)★★★, *The Danny Adler Band* (1988)★★★, with the De Luxe Blues Band *The De Luxe Blues Band* (Blue Horizon 1988)★★★, *Funky Afternoons* (1989)★★★, *MacKinaw City* (1989)★★★, *The Otis 'Elevator' Gilmore Album* (1989)★★★.

● COMPILATIONS: *The Roogalator Years* (Charly 1987)★★★.

AGEE, RAY

b. Raymond Clinton Agee, 10 April 1930, Dixons Mills, Alabama, USA, d. *c* 1990. Contracting polio at the age of fourhh, Agee was left permanently disabled and on crutches. The family moved to Los Angeles a few years later and in 1937 he first sang in public with the Agee Brothers gospel quartet. His next music venture was not until 15 years later, when in 1952 he recorded for Modern, R.K. and Aladdin Records. Thereafter, he recorded prolifically for a number of Los Angeles-based labels, some his own, including Octive, Rayvon, Elko, R&B, Tan, Tridelt, Spark, Ebb and Cash. Many of the sessions featured alto saxophone player Wilbur Reynolds of the Rockin' Brothers. While in Chicago for four months in 1960, he recorded for Monk Higgins' Mar-Jan label before returning west to San Francisco. There he became associated with Bob Geddins, and a number of records, with production by guitarist Johnny Heartsman, appeared on Check and Shirley. He also released records on his own RGA and GRA labels, before signing with Celeste in the mid-60s. Several Celeste singles reappeared on his own Krafton label and some songs appeared simultaneously on both labels. He continued to make singles for Krafton and Fat Back into the 70s before disappearing from the music scene. He is supposed to have returned to singing gospel during the 80s, and is reported to have died in 1990.

● ALBUMS: *Somebody Messed Up* (Krafton 1972)★★★, *Tin Pan Alley* (Diving Duck 1982)★★★, *I'm Not Looking Back* (Mr R&B 1983)★★★, *Black Night Is Gone* (Mr R&B 1984)★★★.

● COMPILATIONS: *California Jump Blues* (Ace 1983)★★★.

AKERS, GARFIELD

b. *c*.1901, Mississippi, USA, d. 1959, Mississippi, USA. Akers was a lifelong friend and partner of Joe Callicott, the two of them taking turns to play lead and second guitar as they sang blues for parties and picnics in north Mississippi's De

Soto County. Callicott was present on the two-part 'Cottonfield Blues', recorded in 1929; Akers was equally impressive on two solo titles cut the following year. His singing and playing are highly rhythmic, with a hypnotic guitar pulse under extended vocal notes. Akers' singing has been said to have the qualities of the field holler, but its lack of decoration belies this; rather it combines danceability with intensity of personal feeling.

● COMPILATIONS: *Son House And The Great Delta Blues Singers* (1990).

ALEXANDER, ALGER 'TEXAS'

b. 12 September 1900, Jowett, Texas, USA, d. 16 April 1954, Richard, Texas, USA. A small, powerful man, Alexander was unusual among rural blues singers on record, in playing no instrument. He worked as a sectionhand when not making his living as an itinerant singer (from about 1923 onwards), and carried a guitar with him in case he should meet a potential accompanist for his resonant baritone. He recorded extensively between 1927 and 1934 with such sophisticated guitarists as Lonnie Johnson and Eddie Lang, whose style dovetailed brilliantly with his artless, structurally unpredictable singing. Other collaborators included the Mississippi Sheiks string band, jazz great King Oliver (a sadly unsuccessful collaboration), and guitarists (and fellow Texans) Dennis 'Little Hat' Jones, Willie Reed and Carl Davis. His songs articulate, as few others do, what life was like for black Texans in a world where poverty and racial oppression were dominant, and the prison system perpetuated slavery. Alexander went to prison in the 40s for singing an obscene song, but it seems likely that he knew prison life even before he came to record, for he sings about it in unusually explicit terms, and many of his blues have the cadences, and sometimes the texts, of worksongs. 'What he talked about, he lived it', said Lowell Fulson, who travelled with Alexander in 1939. A solitary record made in 1950 is rendered almost unlistenable by the combined effects of lack of rehearsal and the syphilis that was soon to kill him.

● ALBUMS: *Texas Alexander Volume 1* (1982)★★★, *Volume 2* (1983)★★★, *Volume 3* (1986)★★★, *Volume 4* (1987)★★★, *Texas Troublesome Blues* (Agram 1988)★★.

ALEXANDER, DAVE

b. Dave Alexander Elam, 10 March 1938, Shreveport, Louisiana, USA. Alexander began to play piano after hearing a record by Albert Ammons on the radio around 1945. His first professional appearance was in 1954; however, he joined the navy at the age of 17, was discharged in 1958 and moved to Oakland, California. He played all over the west coast, but in 1968 was badly wounded in a domestic quarrel and during his hospitalization he started writing his own material. In 1969 he recorded for World Pacific (featuring Albert Collins) and later made two albums for Arhoolie Records. He also recorded with L.C. Robinson. In 1976 he changed his name to Omar Hakim Khayyam and is now known as Omar The Magnificent. A versatile pianist and singer who mixes elements of jazz with his strong blues and boogie-woogie playing, his live show is a capsule of blues piano.

● ALBUMS: *The Rattler* (Arhoolie 1972)★★★, *Dirt On The Ground* (Arhoolie 1973)★★★.

ALLIGATOR RECORDS

'For me the blues is almost like a religious experience, you know - it makes the blind see, the deaf hear, the lame walk.' These are the words of Bruce Iglauer (b. Michigan, USA), whose Alligator label has prospered through its owner's shrewd knowledge of and enthusiasm for the music. After growing up in Cincinnati and studying at Lawrence University in Wisconsin, he moved to Chicago to be nearer the sound of his beloved blues. He initially worked with Bob Koester's Delmark Records as shipping clerk, then business manager, while attending concerts in the evenings. His first discovery was the raw local group Theodore 'Hound Dog' Taylor And The Houserockers, but as Delmark Records required bands with across-the-board appeal, Iglauer started his own Alligator label in 1971 with an inheritance of $2,500. One thousand copies of the Houserockers' debut were pressed as Iglauer began the process of promoting the group to disc jockeys around the country. He then took over the group's management but also released other records such as Big Walter Horton's *Big Walter Horton With Carey Bell* and Fenton Robinson's *Somebody Loan Me A Dime*. Alligator was a one-man operation until 1975, but the following year Koko Taylor's *I Got What*

It Takes was nominated for a Grammy award, the first of several such honours bestowed on her work for the label. Iglauer's next major signing was Texan guitarist Albert Collins who surpassed even Taylor's success with albums such as *Showdown* (1980) recorded with Johnny Copeland and Robert Cray. Other artists were then drawn in from less traditional blues sources, including Professor Longhair, Clifton Chenier (who brought the label its first Grammy award with *I'm Here*), Johnny Winter, Lonnie Mack and Roy Buchanan. For most of these acts Iglauer was executive producer, advising on song selection and arrangements without ever imposing his views. The label helped introduce a new generation of blues artists such as Kenny Neal, Maurice John Vaughan, Tinsley Ellis and the Kinsey Report. A compilation album was released to celebrate Alligator's 20 years in the business in 1991, which was accompanied by a package tour featuring Koko Taylor, Elvin Bishop, Lonnie Brooks, Lil' Ed And The Blues Imperials and Katie Webster.

● ALBUMS: including with various artists *Greatest Hits* (Alligator 1991)★★★★.

ALLISON, LUTHER

b. 17 August 1939, Mayflower, Arkansas, USA, d. 12 August 1997. Born into a family where he was the 14th child of 15, the young Allison worked with his siblings in the local cottonfields. In his youth guitarist Allison sang with a family gospel group and moved to Chicago in 1951, where he attended school with one of Muddy Waters' children. Around 1957 he formed his own band with his brother Grant to work on the west side. They gigged occasionally under the name of the Rolling Stones and later the Four Jivers. After a year the group disbanded and Allison went on to work with Jimmy Dawkins, Magic Slim, Magic Sam, Muddy Waters, Little Richard, Freddie King and others until the mid-60s. In March 1967 he recorded a session for Bill Lindemann, later issued by the collector label Delmark. He toured California, recording there as accompanist to Sunnyland Slim and Shakey Jake Harris. He made his first album under his own name in 1969 and was one of the major successes of the Ann Arbor festivals of 1969 and 1970. In the early 70s he recorded for Motown Records' subsidiary label Gordy and from the late 70s he

spent much of his time in France, living and working, where he had a large and faithful following. He recorded for many labels, usually live albums or studio sessions comprising funk or Jimi Hendrix and Rolling Stones-influenced rock. In the late 80s, following two well-recieved albums, *Serious* and *Soul Fixin' Man*, Allison found his career in ascendance. By the mid-90s he was reaching a peak, winning W.C.Handy awards and experiencing financial success with a bestselling album, *Blue Streak*. This Indian summer of his career was cruelly cut short when in July 1997 he was diagnosed as having lung cancer; tragically, just over a month later, he died. It all happened so quickly that the interviews he had conducted for various magazines had not even gone to press.

● ALBUMS: *Love Me Mama* (Delmark 1969)★★★, *Bad News Is Coming* (Gordy 1973)★★★, *Luther's Blues* (Gordy 1974)★★★, *Night Life* (Gordy 1976)★★★, *Love Me Papa* (Black & Blue 1977)★★★, *Live In Paris* (Free Bird 1979)★★★, *Live* (Blue Silver 1979)★★★, *Gonna Be A Live One In Here Tonight* (Rumble 1979)★★★, *Time* (Paris Album 1980)★★★, *South Side Safari* (Red Lightnin' 1982)★★★, *Lets Have A Natural Ball* (JSP 1984)★★★, *Serious* (Blind Pig 1984)★★★, *Here I Come* (Encore 1985)★★★, *Powerwire Blues* (Charly 1986)★★★, *Rich Man* (Entente 1987)★★★, *Life Is A Bitch* (Encore 1988)★★, *Love Me Mama* (Delmark 1988)★★★, *Let's Try It Again - Live '89* (Teldec 1989)★★, *More From Berlin* (Melodie 1991)★★, *Hand Me Down My Moonshine* (In-Akustik 1992)★★, *Sweet Home Chicago* (1993)★★★, *Soul Fixin' Man* (Alligator 1994)★★★, *Bad Love* (Ruf 1994)★★★, *Blue Streak* (Ruf 1995)★★★, *Reckless* (Ruf 1997)★★★★, *Live In Montreux 1976-1994* (Ruf 1997)★★★★.

ALLISON, MOSE

b. Mose John Allison Jnr., 11 November 1927, Tippo, Mississippi, USA. Allison began piano lessons at the age of five, and played trumpet in high school, although he has featured the latter instrument less frequently in recent years. His music is a highly individual mix of blues and modern jazz, with influences on his cool, laconic singing and piano playing ranging from Tampa Red and Sonny Boy 'Rice Miller'

Williamson to Charlie Parker, Duke Ellington, and Thelonious Monk. He moved to New York in 1956 and worked mainly in jazz settings, playing with Stan Getz and recording for numerous companies. During the 60s Allison's work was much in evidence as he became a major influence on the burgeoning R&B scene. Pete Townshend, one of his greatest fans, recorded Allison's 'A Young Man's Blues' for the Who's *Live At Leeds*. Similarly, John Mayall was one of dozens who recorded his classic 'Parchman Farm', and Georgie Fame featured many Allison songs in his heyday with the Blueflames. Fame's nasal and understated vocal was similar to Allison's, as is Ben Sidran's style and voice. In the 80s Allison saw a resurgence in his popularity after becoming a hero to the new, young audience hungry for his blend of modern jazz. Ultimately, however, his work is seen as hugely influential on other performers, and this has to a degree limited the profile afforded to his own lengthy recording career.

● ALBUMS: *Back Country Suite* (Prestige 1957)★★★, *Local Color* (Prestige 1958)★★★, *Young Man Mose* (Prestige 1958)★★★, *Creek Bank* (Prestige 1959)★★★, *The Transfiguration Of Hiram Brown* (Columbia 1960)★★, *I Love The Life I Live* (Columbia 1960)★★★, *Autumn Song* (1960)★★★, *Ramblin' With Mose* (Prestige 1961)★★★, *Take To The Hills* (Epic 1962)★★, *I Don't Worry About A Thing* (Atlantic 1962)★★★, *Swingin' Machine* (Atlantic 1962)★★★, *The Seventh Son - Mose Allison Sings* (Prestige 1963)★★★, *The World From Mose* (Atlantic 1964)★★★, *V8 Ford* (Columbia 1964)★★★, *Down Home Piano* (Prestige 1966)★★★, *Mose Alive!* (Atlantic 1966)★★★, *Mose Allison* (Prestige 1966)★★★, *Wild Man On The Loose* (Atlantic 1966)★★★, *Jazz Years* (Atco 1967)★★, *Mose Allison Plays For Lovers* (Prestige 1967)★★, *I've Been Doin' Some Thinkin'* (Atco 1969)★★★, *Hello There* (1969)★★, *Universe* (1969)★★, *Western Man* (1971)★★, *Mose In Your Ear* (Atco 1972)★★, *Your Mind Is On Vacation* (Atco 1976)★★, *Ol' Devil Mose* (1976)★★★, *Retrospective* (Columbia 1976)★★★, *That's Jazz* (1976)★★★, *Ever Since The World Ended* (Blue Note 1983)★★, *Middle Class White Boy* (1982)★★, *Lessons In Living* (Elektra 1984)★★, *My Backyard* (Blue Note 1990)★★★, *Sings And Plays* (Fantasy

1991)★★★, *The Earth Wants You* (1994)★★.
● COMPILATIONS: *Mose Allison Sings The Seventh Son* (Prestige 1988)★★★, *Alison Wonderland The Mose Allison Anthology* (1994)★★★, *The Best Of ...* (Sequel 1994)★★★★.
● FURTHER READING: *One Man's Blues: The Life And Music Of Mose Allison*, Patti Jones.

ALLMAN BROTHERS BAND

Formed in Macon, Georgia, USA, in 1969 by guitarist Duane Allman (b. 20 November 1946, Nashville, Tennessee, USA, d. 29 October 1971, Macon, Georgia, USA), the band included brother Gregg Allman (b. 8 December 1947, Nashville, Tennessee, USA; keyboards/vocals), Forrest Richard 'Dickie' Betts (b. 12 December 1943, West Palm Beach, Florida, USA; guitar), Raymond Berry Oakley (b. 4 April 1948, Chicago, Illinois, USA, d. 11 November 1972; bass), Butch Trucks (b. Claude Hudson Trucks Jnr., Jacksonville, Florida, USA; drums) and Jai 'Jaimoe' Johanny Johanson (b. John Lee Johnson, 8 July 1944, Ocean Springs, Mississippi, USA; drums). The above line-up was an amalgamation of the members of several southern-based aspirants, of which the Hour Glass was the most prolific. The latter pop/soul ensemble featured Duane and Gregg Allman, and broke up when demo tapes for a projected third album were rejected by their record company. Duane then found employment at the Fame studio where he participated in several sessions, including those for Aretha Franklin, Wilson Pickett and King Curtis, prior to instigating this new sextet. The Allman Brothers established themselves as a popular live attraction and their first two albums, *The Allman Brothers Band* and *Idlewild South*, were marked by strong blues-based roots and an exciting rhythmic drive. Nevertheless, it was a sensational two-album set, *Live At The Fillmore East*, that showcased the group's emotional fire. 'Whipping Post', a 22-minute *tour de force*, remains one of rock music's definitive improvisational performances. The set brought the band to the brink of stardom, while Duane's reputation as an outstanding slide guitarist was further enhanced by his contribution to *Layla*, the seminal Derek And The Dominos album. Unfortunately, tragedy struck on 29 October

1971 when this gifted musician was killed in a motorcycle accident. The remaining members completed *Eat A Peach*, which consisted of live and studio material, before embarking on a mellower direction with *Brothers And Sisters*, a style best exemplified by the album's hit single, 'Ramblin' Man'. A second pianist, Chuck Leavell (b. Tuscaloosa, Alabama, USA), was added to the line-up, but just as the group recovered its momentum, Berry Oakley was killed in an accident chillingly similar to that of his former colleague on 11 November 1972. Not surprisingly, the Allman Brothers seemed deflated, and subsequent releases failed to match the fire of those first recordings. Their power was further diminished by several offshoot projects. Gregg Allman (who later married Cher twice) and Dickie Betts embarked on solo careers while Leavell, Johanson and new bassist Lamar Williams (b. 1947, Hansboro, Mississippi, USA, d. 25 January 1983 from cancer) formed Sea Level. The Allmans broke up acrimoniously in 1976 following a notorious drugs trial in which Gregg testified against a former road manager. Although the other members vowed never to work with the vocalist again, a reconstituted 1978 line-up included Allman, Betts and Trucks. *Enlightened Rogues* was a commercial success, but subsequent albums fared less well and in 1982 the Allman Brothers Band split for a second time. A new incarnation appeared in 1989 with a line-up of Gregg Allman (vocals, organ), Betts (vocals, lead guitar), Warren Haynes (vocals, slide and lead guitar), Allen Woody (bass), Johnny Neel (keyboards), Trucks (drums) and Mark Quinones (percussion). This much-heralded reunion spawned a credible release: *Seven Turns*. Neel left the band and the remaining sextet made *Shades Of Two Worlds*. Quinones (congas and percussion) joined for *An Evening With The Allman Brothers Band* in 1992. Their 1994 album, *Where It All Begins*, was recorded effectively live in the studio, with production once more by Allman Brothers veteran Tom Dowd. Nevertheless, it is the work displayed on their first five albums that remains among the finest recorded during the late 60s and early 70s, in particular for the skilful interplay between two gifted, imaginative guitarists.

● ALBUMS: *The Allman Brothers Band* (Capricorn 1969)★★★★, *Idlewild South* (Capricorn 1970)★★★★, *Live At The Fillmore East* (Capricorn 1971)★★★★, *Eat A Peach* (Capricorn 1972)★★★, *Brothers And Sisters* (Capricorn 1973)★★★, *Win, Lose Or Draw* (Capricorn 1975)★★★, *Wipe The Windows, Check The Oil, Dollar Gas* (Capricorn 1976)★, *Enlightened Rogues* (Capricorn 1979)★★★, *Reach For The Sky* (Arista 1980)★★, *Brothers Of The Road* (Arista 1981)★★, *Live At Ludlow Garage 1970* (Polygram 1990)★★★, *Seven Turns* (Epic 1990)★★★, *Shades Of Two Worlds* (Epic 1991)★★★, *An Evening With The Allman Brothers Band* (Epic 1992)★★★, *The Fillmore Concerts* (Polydor 1993)★★★★, *Where It All Begins* (Epic 1994)★★★, *2nd Set* (Epic 1995)★★, *Twenty* (SPV 1997)★★.

● COMPILATIONS: *The Road Goes On Forever* (Capricorn 1975)★★★, *The Best Of The Allman Brothers Band* (Polydor 1981)★★★, *Dreams* 4-CD box set (Polydor 1989)★★★★, *A Decade Of Hits 1969-1979* (Polygram 1991)★★★.

● VIDEOS: *Brothers Of The Road* (RCA/Columbia 1988), *Live At Great Woods* (1993).

● FURTHER READING: *The Allman Brothers: A Biography In Words And Pictures*, Tom Nolan. *Midnight Riders: The Story Of The Allman Brothers Band*, Scott Freeman.

ALTHEIMER, JOSHUA

b. *c*.1910, Arkansas, USA. A virtual biographical blank, Altheimer was a pianist of distinction operating on the Chicago blues scene of the 30s. He never had a record issued under his own name but was well known for his work accompanying such artists as Big Bill Broonzy (with whom he worked for three years, 1937-40), Lonnie Johnson, Jazz Gillum, Washboard Sam (Robert Brown) and John Lee 'Sonny Boy' Williamson. Altheimer was not regarded as a great practitioner of boogie styles or display music (although he could certainly rock when required to, but he seldom took a solo), and he was always to be found in a band setting where his reliable and sometimes outstanding rolling piano work was most effective in underpinning some classic blues performances. What little information there is about his life can be found in Broonzy's book *Big Bill Blues* or Paul Oliver's *The Story Of The Blues*.

● COMPILATIONS: *Chicago Blues* (1985).

AMMONS, ALBERT

b. 23 September 1907, Chicago, Illinois, USA, d. 2 December 1949. Ammons began playing piano as a small child and worked in Chicago clubs while still a youth. In the late 20s and early 30s he played in a number of small bands but his real forte was as a soloist. After establishing himself as an important blues piano player in Chicago in the mid-30s, a period that saw him leading a small group at many of the city's top nightspots, Ammons moved to New York City. With Pete Johnson he formed a piano duo, playing in the newly popular boogie-woogie style. In New York Ammons and Johnson appeared at the Cafe Society and occasionally added Meade 'Lux' Lewis to their group to form a powerful boogie-woogie trio. By the mid-40s Ammons had returned to playing on his own, touring the USA before settling back in his home-town, where he died in December 1949. Although best known for his contribution to the briefly popular craze for boogie-woogie, Ammons was one of the outstanding blues piano players. His son, Gene 'Jug' Ammons, played tenor saxophone.
● ALBUMS: *Boogie Piano Stylings* (Mercury 1950)★★★, *King Of Blues And Boogie Woogie, Boogie Piano Stylings* (1950)★★★, *Boogie Woogie Classics* (Blue Note 1951)★★★★, with Pete Johnson *8 To The Bar* (RCA Victor 50s)★★★.
● COMPILATIONS: with Meade Lux Lewis *The Complete Blue Note Recordings Of Albert Ammons And Meade Lux Lewis* (1983)★★★★, *King Of Boogie Woogie* (Blues Classics 1988)★★★★, *Albert Ammons Vols. 1 & 2* (Oldie Blues 1988)★★★★.

ANDERSON, JIMMY

Little biographical information is available on blues harmonica player and vocalist Jimmy Anderson, despite the fact that he recorded as recently as the early 60s. It appears, however, that he was based in Baton Rouge, Louisiana, USA, and all of his records were made for Jay Miller at his studio in Crowley. His records were influenced, almost to the point of impersonation, by the popular Chicago blues singer Jimmy Reed - with the same high-pitched harmonica breaks and nasal whine in the vocals - but despite their derivative qualities, they represent good blues with a contemporary, upbeat sound. One single, 'I Wanna Boogie'/'Angel Please', was issued on Miller's own Zynn label in 1962 and enjoyed some local success, and a further three were leased to Excello Records for wider distribution over the next couple of years. Nothing seems to have been heard from him since then.
● ALBUMS: *Baton Rouge Harmonica* (1988)★★★.

ANDERSON, PINKNEY 'PINK'

b. 12 February 1900, Laurens, South Carolina, USA, d. 12 October 1974, Spartanburg, South Carolina, USA. For much of his life, Anderson was Spartanburg's most famous songster and medicine show huckster. He was 10 when he first learned to play the guitar in open tuning from Joe Wicks. He also earned money as a buck dancer on the streets of Laurens. In 1917 he joined 'Doctor' W.R. Kerr's medicine show, learning every facet of the calling, and stayed with the show, with Peg Leg Sam as his straight man, until it ceased in 1945. When not on the road, he partnered Simmie Dooley, a blind guitarist from whom he learned to tune his guitar and play chords. In 1928 the pair recorded four titles for Columbia Records in Atlanta. One of the songs, 'Every Day In In The Week', also featured on a May 1950 session, recorded while Anderson was performing at the State Fair in Charlottesville, and released in conjunction with titles by another Laurens musician, Blind Gary Davis. Anderson continued to work the medicine shows, teaming up with Baby Tate, until heart trouble forced his retirement in 1957. In 1961 he recorded three albums for Bluesville, each with a theme: blues, medicine show songs and folk ballads. Gradually deteriorating health prevented him from working. An album project for Trix, begun in 1970, was never realized.
● ALBUMS: with Rev. Gary Davis *Carolina Street Ballads/Harlem Street Spirituals* (Riverside 1951)★★★, *Carolina Blues Man* (Bluesville 1962)★★★★, *Medicine Show Man* (Bluesville 1962)★★★, *Ballad And Folksinger* (Bluesville 1963)★★★.

ANTHONY, EDDIE

d. 1934, Atlanta, Georgia, USA. Anthony's raw alley fiddle was an essential component of the Atlanta string band led by Peg Leg Howell, and billed on record as his Gang. Anthony accompanied his gravel-voiced fellow Gang member Henry Williams on the raucous 'Georgia Crawl' and the moving 'Lonesome Blues'. He sawed his way through 'Peg Leg Stomp', 'Turkey Buzzard Blues' and 'Beaver Slide Rag' as a member of the Gang, and, as 'Macon Ed', played a similar repertoire of blues and dance music with the mysterious 'Tampa Joe' (who may have been two different men). Williams died in jail in 1929, and after Anthony died, Peg Leg Howell lost his enthusiasm for performing.

● COMPILATIONS: *Georgia String Bands* (1987)★★★.

ARCENEAUX, FERNEST

b. 27 August 1940, Lafayette, Louisiana, USA. Arceneaux learned accordion in childhood from his father who played in the old French Louisiana style. Over the years, he developed his own distinctive Zydeco sound, more relaxed and easy than that of more dominant figures of the music such as Clifton Chenier, but with considerable appeal, nevertheless. In the 70s he made his first records, with his band Fernest And The Thunders, for Jay Miller's Blues Unlimited label. The increased exposure on this label made his own name more widely known, and he has toured extensively, developing a popular following outside the USA, as well as making several more records. Typically, Arceneaux's sound features crisp and lively accordion work, leading his band through a broad-based repertoire, from traditional French-based dance music to straight blues and New Orleans-style R&B.

● ALBUMS: including *From The Heart Of The Bayou* (JSP 1984)★★★, *Zydeco Stomp* (JSP 1988)★★★, *Gumbo Special* (Schubert 1988)★★★, *Zydeco Blues* (1991)★★★, *Zydeco Blues Party* (Mardi Gras 1994)★★★.

ARCHIBALD

b. Leon T. Gross, 14 September 1912, New Orleans, Louisiana, USA, d. 8 January 1973, New Orleans, Louisiana, USA. With a reputation that rests on his first and only hit, Archibald is best remembered for the impression he made upon younger piano players like Fats Domino, James Booker and Allen Toussaint. Self-taught but influenced by Burnell Santiago, he gained

the nickname 'Archie Boy' during years of playing at parties and brothels. After serving in the army during World War II, he was spotted and signed by Imperial talent scout Al Young. His first release, a two-part version of 'Stack-O-Lee' was an immediate hit, but subsequent records for Imperial and its subsidiary, Colony, failed to maintain his popularity. For many years, he was the resident pianist at the Poodle Patio club, but by the 70s his career was all but over. Nevertheless, his music typified the syncopated piano style with which others achieved more success.

● COMPILATIONS: *The New Orleans Sessions 1950-52* (Krazy Kat 1983)★★★.

ARNOLD, BILLY BOY

b. 16 March 1935, Chicago, Illinois, USA. Arnold first played blues harmonica with Bo Diddley's group in 1950 and became a well-known figure in Chicago blues throughout the following two decades. Among those he accompanied were Johnny Shines and Otis Rush. With a serviceable singing voice and a harmonica style influenced by John Lee 'Sonny Boy' Williamson, Arnold recorded as a solo artist for local labels Cool (1953) and Vee Jay (1955). In 1958 he led a group that included Mighty Joe Young and recorded for Mighty H. However, none of Arnold's records were as successful as the mid-50s hits of Bo Diddley such as 'Pretty Thing' and 'Hey Bo Diddley', to which he contributed the keening harp phrases. The most renowned of Arnold's own tracks is 'I Wish You Would' (VeeJay), which was adopted by British R&B group the Yardbirds, appearing on *Five Live Yardbirds* (1964). During the mid-60s blues boom, he cut an album for Prestige/Bluesville (1964), recorded with pianist Johnny Jones (a 1963 session that remained unreleased for 17 years), and there was also a later album for Vogue. Not forgotten by European blues enthusiasts, Arnold toured there in 1975 as part of the Blues Legends package, when he recorded two albums for Peter Shertser's UK-based Red Lightnin'.

● ALBUMS: *More Blues On The South Side* (Prestige/Bluesville 1964)★★★, *Blow The Back Off It* (Red Lightnin' 1975)★★★, *Sinner's Prayer* (Red Lightnin' 1976)★★★, *Checkin' It Out* (Red Lightnin' 1979)★★★, *Johnny Jones & Billy Boy*

Arnold (Alligator 1980)★★★, *Crying & Pleading* reissue (1980)★★★, *I Wish You Would* mid-50s recordings (1993)★★★, *Back Where I Belong* (Alligator 1993)★★, *Ten Million Dollars* (Evidence 1995)★★★, *Eldorado Cadillac* (Alligator 1996)★★★.

ARNOLD, JAMES 'KOKOMO'

b. 15 February 1901, Lovejoy's Station, Georgia, USA. d. 8 November 1968, Chicago, Illinois, USA. 'Kokomo' Arnold was a left-handed slide blues guitarist who learned the basics of his style from his cousin, James Wigges. After working in steel mills in Illinois and Pennsylvania he became a dedicated fisherman and moonshiner, who looked upon his musical success as an adjunct to 'real life'. Arnold developed an unorthodox method of playing guitar, based on a style that had originally been popular in a few states in the Deep South. He held the instrument flat, using a slide to create an eerie, ringing sound. Unlike the relaxed and often casual approach of many of his contemporaries, Arnold's was an urgent, aggressive style, and he achieved remarkable results with his unusual method of guitar playing and the curiously high-pitched, often unintelligible, singing that accompanied it. Interspersed in these wailings would be sudden bursts of vocal clarity that gave his statements great authority. He gained a reputation that followed him in his travels throughout the northern states in the years after the end of World War I. Arnold did not record until 1930 when he released 'Paddlin' Blues' (a breakneck blues personalization of 'Paddling Madeline Home') and 'Rainy Night Blues' under the sobriquet 'Gitfiddle Jim' for Victor in Memphis. He continued to record throughout the 30s, all his further work appearing on Decca Records. His biggest hit was the double a-side 'Old Original Kokomo Blues' (named after a brand of coffee) and 'Milk Cow Blues', the latter of which he recorded in no less than five numbered versions. It was picked up by other bluesmen and enjoyed a second vogue when it was recorded by rock 'n' rollers such as Elvis Presley and Eddie Cochran in the 50s. With notable exceptions, Arnold's work tended to follow a pattern, but was always enlivened by his powerful slide work and original lyrics. He also added his guitar talents to recordings by Roosevelt Sykes,

Mary Johnson and Peetie Wheatstraw. Arnold ceased recording in 1938 following disagreements with Mayo Williams of Decca Records In the early 60s he made a few appearances in Chicago, during the revival of interest in his brand of folk blues. For all his rather fleeting moments in the limelight, Arnold was an influence on Robert Johnson, who was, in his turn, one of the most seminal of the second-generation blues singers, and whose legacy helped to shape rock music. Arnold died in Chicago in November 1968.

● COMPILATIONS: *Master Of The Bottleneck Guitar* (Document 1987)★★★, *Kokomo Arnold And Peetie Wheatstraw* (Blues Classics 1988)★★★, *Kokomo Arnold And Casey Bill* (Yazoo 1988)★★★, *Kokomo Arnold* 1930-38 recordings (1990)★★★, *Down And Out Blue* (1990)★★★.

AUSTIN, JESSE 'WILD BILL'

b. 1930, Rochelle, New York, USA, d. 22 March 1996. A larger than life bluesman, Austin never lived to achieve the recognition he deserved. A precociously talented child, Austin was taught musical theory in Chicago, but developed his 'hog calling' vocal style on his grandfather's farm. He was primarily influenced by Wynonie Harris, whose 'blues shouting style' Austin attempted to emulate. Illegally visiting one of the New York blues clubs as a teenager, Austin upstaged his idol Harris's show one night, taking the microphone from the ill singer and singing for the rest of the night. Suitably impressed, Harris became Austin's legal guardian and took him out on the road. Austin played piano, drums and bass with Harris's band for eighteen months, as well as writing one of his biggest hits, 'Bloodshot Eyes', before forming The Five Sharps with Eddie and Bobby Buster, the latter of whom gave Austin his nickname following an altercation with Jimmy Witherspoon. Austin then appeared to have achieved his big break backing Percy Mayfield in 1951, but was arrested for draft-dodging and forced to fight in Korea. After his return he did several menial jobs while still playing at weekends, sitting in with jazz musicians including Duke Ellington and Count Basie. It was not until the 90s that Austin finally had his big opportunity, when booking agent Joe Roesch set up his own record company in order to release the singer's material. The release of *Steel Trap* in 1992 was greeted by strong reviews, and, following some extensive self-promotion, reasonable sales. *Baby's Back* cemented his reputation, but Austin died before he could finish work on an eagerly anticipated third album.

● ALBUMS: *Steel Trap* (Roesch 1992)★★★, *Baby's Back* (Roesch 1994)★★★.

AUSTIN, LOVIE

b. Cora Calhoun, 19 September 1887, Chattanooga, Tennessee, USA, d. 10 July 1972. A formally trained pianist and arranger, Austin worked in vaudeville for a number of years. She also led her own band, and in the early and mid-20s, while working as house pianist for Paramount Records, she accompanied many leading blues singers. Tired of touring on the TOBA circuit, she settled in Chicago, where she remained for the rest of her life, working as musical director at a number of theatres. Despite, or perhaps because of, her formal training, Austin was not a good jazz player, either as a soloist or in ensembles, but she displayed a good ear for the needs of singers and always provided a sensitive accompaniment to leading exponents of the blues such as Ida Cox, Alberta Hunter and Ma Rainey.

● ALBUMS: *Alberta Hunter With Lovie Austin And Her Blues Serenaders* (1961)★★★, *Blue Serenaders* (Classic Jazz 1988)★★★.

AZTECS

The Aztecs were formed in Sydney, Australia in 1964. They were initially Billy Thorpe's backing band, but as Thorpe changed his material so did the band, from being a 60s beat dance band to the loudest blues rock band in Australia in the 70s. While the line-up fluctuated, Warren Morgan and Gil Matthews were considered the basis of the band in its latter period (post 1970), co-writing with Thorpe and being responsible for the arrangements. Although generally considered the focal point of the band, Thorpe often played down his leadership role, so much so that the band continued after his retirement. Morgan went on to become John Paul Young's musical director and band leader, while Matthews went into production and record company management. Other significant players to have passed through the band were: Lobby Loyde, Billy Kristian, Vince Maloney, Teddy Toi and Paul Wheeler.

● ALBUMS: *Aztecs...Live* (1971)★★★, *The Hoax is Over* (1971)★★★, *Live At Sunbury* (1972)★★★.

BACON FAT

One of the less renowned groups signed to Mike Vernon's respected UK Blue Horizon label, Bacon Fat are best recalled for the exemplary harmonica work of Rod 'Gingerman' Piazza. A former member of a Californian unit, the Dirty Blues Band, this accomplished musician rivalled Paul Butterfield and Charlie Musselwhite as a leading exponent of the instrument. Buddy Reed (guitar, vocals), Gregg Schaefer (guitar), J.D. Nicholson (vocals, piano), Jerry Smith (bass) and Dick Innes Jnr. (drums) completed Bacon Fat's debut album, *Grease One For Me*. Although they were subsequently augmented by vocalist George Smith, this promising group broke up following the release of their second album.

● ALBUMS: *Grease One For Me* (Blue Horizon 1970)★★★, *Tough Dude* (Blue Horizon 1971)★★★.

BAILEY, DEFORD

b. 1899, Carthage, Smith County, Tennessee, USA, d. 2 July 1982. Bailey suffered from infantile paralysis and although he recovered, he was left with a deformed back and only grew to 4 feet 10 inches. He learned guitar, fiddle, banjo and harmonica from his father and uncle, who were both noted musicians, and by the age of 14, was making a living from playing the har-

monica. He moved to Nashville and, in 1925, he met Dr. Humphrey Bate, a respected harmonica player, who brought him to the attention of the *Grand Ole Opry*. Quite apart from being the *Opry*'s first black artist, Bailey was also its first solo star, although he only received $5 a performance. It was, however, difficult for him to play his self-termed 'black hillbilly' music to white audiences in the south. He recorded for the US labels, Columbia, Brunswick and Victor during 1927-28 but he did not record after that. His best-known work is 'Pan American Blues', which is remembered for its train imitations, and he always appeared smartly dressed in a three-piece suit, matching hat and highly polished shoes. Bailey was dismissed by the *Opry* in 1941, allegedly for refusing to learn new tunes. Bailey, however, maintained that the real reason was racial prejudice. He never forgave the *Opry* for this and was forced to shine shoes for a living. He made a brief television appearance on a blues show in the 60s but he invariably rejected offers he received. There was no other black performer at the *Opry* until Charley Pride. In April 1982, Bailey made his last appearance at the *Opry*, playing 'Pan American Blues' on an old-timers show.
● ALBUMS: *Harmonica Showcase* (Matchbox 1985)★★★.
● FURTHER READING: *Deford Bailey - A Black Star In Early Country Music*, David C. Morton and Charles K. Wolf.

BAILEY, KID

One of the most elusive of Mississippi blues singers, Bailey made one record in 1929, singing in forceful but melancholy fashion, and playing guitar in a style recalling Charley Patton and Willie Brown, with whom he is known to have worked. 'Rowdy Blues', on which Bailey is joined by a second guitarist, bases its accompaniment on Brown's 'M & O Blues'. Remembered as having appeared in many small Delta towns, he also played with Tommy Johnson, and is believed to have died in the 60s.
● COMPILATIONS: *Son House And The Great Delta Blues Singers* (1990).

BAKER, MICKEY

b. McHouston Baker, 15 October 1925, Louisville, Kentucky, USA. After spells in reform school and a children's home, he moved to New York in 1941. He lived on the fringes of the criminal world but took up the guitar and quickly became a virtuoso, equally adept at jazz and blues styles. From the late 40s, Mickey 'Guitar' Baker played on hundreds of recording sessions, accompanying such artists as Ray Charles, the Coasters, Ivory Joe Hunter, Ruth Brown and Screaming Jay Hawkins. Baker occasionally recorded under his own name and in 1956 teamed up with guitarist/vocalist Sylvia Vanderpool. After an unsuccessful version of 'Walking In The Rain', the atmospheric 'Love Is Strange' (co-written by Bo Diddley) by Mickey And Sylvia was a US Top 20 hit on RCA/Groove in 1956. Later singles on Vik and RCA were only minor hits, although the duo contributed to Ike And Tina Turner's 'It's Gonna Work Out Fine' (1961), where Baker's is the male voice answering Tina's. Some of Baker's solo recordings were collected on a 1959 album for Atlantic Records. In the early 60s, he emigrated to Paris and joined the expatriate community of jazz musicians in the French capital. He toured Europe with such artists as Memphis Slim and Champion Jack Dupree, and performed at the 1973 Montreux Jazz Festival. Baker also arranged the strings for Fleetwood Mac's version of 'Need Your Love So Bad' (1968). During the 70s, he recorded several albums in Europe, including two for Stefan Grossman's guitar-instructional label, Kicking Mule.
● ALBUMS: *The Wildest Guitar* (Atlantic 1959)★★★, *But Wild* (1963)★★★, *The Blues And Me* (1974)★★★, *Take A Look Inside* (1975)★★★, *Up On The Hill* (1975)★★★, *Blues And Jazz Guitar* (Kicking Mule 1977)★★★, *Jazz-Rock Guitar* (Kicking Mule 1978)★★★, *Rock A With A Sock* (1993)★★★.

BAKER, WILLIE

Baker's singing and 12-string blues guitar work on his 1929 recordings are heavily influenced by the Atlanta musicians Robert Hicks ('Barbecue Bob'), Charley Lincoln ('Laughing Charley') and Curley Weaver, sharing with them nasal singing, bass guitar work played in open G, and the use of a bottleneck on the treble strings. Baker also shares a repertoire with this group, making it all the more surprising that none of their associates remembered him. He is reported to have lived in Patterson, in south-east Georgia, and is thought to have derived his style from records and personal contact with Hicks, who was known to have visited the area with a medicine show. Some of Baker's recordings are in an older, non-bottleneck style, with a strong ragtime influence. He was last heard of in Miami, Florida, in the mid-60s.

● COMPILATIONS: *Georgia Blues Guitars* (80s).

BALDRY, LONG JOHN

b. 12 January 1941, London, England. Beginning his career playing folk and jazz in the late 50s, Baldry toured with Ramblin' Jack Elliott before moving into R&B. His strong, deep voice won him a place in the influential Blues Incorporated, following which he joined Cyril Davies' R&B All Stars. After Davies' death, Long John fronted the Hoochie Coochie Men, which also included future superstar Rod Stewart, who later joined Baldry in Steam Packet (featuring Brian Auger and Julie Driscoll). After a brief period with Bluesology (which boasted a young Elton John on keyboards), Baldry decided to go solo and record straightforward pop. Already well known on the music scene, he nevertheless appeared an unusual pop star in 1967 with his sharp suits and imposing 6 foot 7 inch height. Composer/producer Tony Macauley and his partner John McLeod presented him with the perfect song in 'Let The Heartaches Begin', a despairing ballad which Baldry took to number 1 in the UK in 1967. His chart career continued with the Olympic Games theme, 'Mexico', the following year, which also made the Top 20. By the end of the 60s, however, the hits had ceased and another change of direction was ahead. Furs and a beard replaced the suits and the neat, short haircut, as Long John attempted to establish himself with a new audience. With production assistance from former colleagues Rod Stewart and Elton John, he recorded a strong album, *It Ain't Easy,* but it failed to sell. After a troubled few years in New York and Los Angeles he emigrated to Vancouver, Canada, where he performed on the club circuit. In the early 90s his voice was used as Robotnik on the Sonic The Hedgehog computer game. After many years a new Baldry album was released in 1993, subtly titled *It Still Ain't Easy.*

● ALBUMS: *Long John's Blues* (United Artists 1965)★★★, *Lookin' At Long John* (United Artists 1966)★★★, *Let The Heartaches Begin* (Pye 1968)★★, *Wait For Me* (Pye 1969)★, *It Ain't Easy* (Warners 1971)★★, *Everything Stops For Tea* (Warners 1972)★, *Good To Be Alive* (GM 1976)★★, *Welcome To The Club* (1977)★★, *Baldry's Out* (A&M 1979)★★, *It Still Ain't Easy* (Stony Plain 1991)★★, *Right To Sing The Blues* (Stony Plain 1997)★★★.

● COMPILATIONS: *Let The Heartaches Begin - The Best Of John Baldry* (PRT 1988)★★★, *Mexico* (Spectrum 1995)★★.

BALL, MARCIA

b. 20 March 1949, Orange, Texas, USA. Born into a musical family, Ball took piano lessons throughout her childhood until she was 14. Her formative years were spent in Vinton, Louisiana, and while at Louisiana State University she played in a blues-rock band, Gum. She also took particular interest in the styles of Fats Domino and Professor Longhair. Moving to Austin in the early 70s, she joined the progressive country group Freda And The Firedogs, along with guitarist John X. Reed. She went solo in 1974 and had a country single released the following year. Her subsequent solo albums combine R&B standards with original songs that draw in elements of blues and country swing. She wrote the title song for *Dreams Come True,* a project that began in 1985 and took five years to bring to fruition with the help of producer Dr. John. Constant touring may have been a factor in the subsequent four-year hiatus before *Blue House* was finally issued in 1994. *Let Me Play With Your Poodle* included songs by Randy Newman and Tampa Red alongside Ball originals.

● ALBUMS: *Circuit Queen* (Capitol 1978)★★★, *Soulful Dress* (Rounder 1983)★★★, *Hot Tamale Baby* (Rounder 1985)★★★, *Gatorhythms* (Rounder 1989)★★★, with Lou Ann Barton, Angela Strehli *Dreams Come True* (Antone's 1990)★★★, *Blue House* (Rounder 1994)★★★, *Let Me Play With Your Poodle* (Rounder 1997)★★★.

BALLEN, IVIN

Ballen formed his 20th Century Records label in Philadelphia during World War II, specializing in a diverse range of music from Jewish humour to gospel. In January 1948, he purchased Sam Goody's Gotham Records and S-G Music Publishing, adding a strong R&B and jazz label to its roster, with artists such as Tiny Grimes, Leo Parker, Jimmy Preston, Johnny Sparrow, Jimmy Rushing and David 'Panama' Francis. In the early 50s, leasing arrangements were made with a network of various independent labels throughout the country - from Washington DC, to New York, Los Angeles, Chicago and Tulsa. The range of styles was enlarged to encompass hillbilly, vocal group R&B and even the down-home blues of Dan Pickett, John Lee Hooker and Eddie Burns. Ballen entered the rock 'n' roll and rockabilly market of the mid-50s, and like many of the small independents found that he could not compete with the big-selling majors such as RCA and Decca. He wound down the label in the late 50s.

BARBECUE BOB

b. Robert Hicks, 11 September 1902, Walton County, Georgia, USA, d. 21 October 1931, Lithonia, Georgia, USA. His older brother Charley (later known as Charley Lincoln), learned guitar first, but Robert seems to have followed soon after, also learning from Curley Weaver's mother Savannah; both brothers played 12-string guitar. Bob moved to Atlanta in 1924, where he worked at a barbecue, which gave him his pseudonym. Here he was heard by a talent scout and made his first records in 1927. This began a successful recording career that lasted just four years but produced over 50 tracks of fine blues. His music is characterized by a heavy, percussive style, often using a bottleneck. His voice is rather rough but can carry a slow blues as well as more up-tempo dance numbers. In 1930, he recorded as part of the Georgia Cotton Pickers, with Curley Weaver and Buddy Moss, and he also appeared as accompanist on Nellie Florence's single 1929 session. Well established as one of the principal figures on the Atlanta blues scene of the time, his career was tragically ended by his death from pneumonia at the age of 29.
● COMPILATIONS: *Brown Skin Gal* (Agram 1978)★★★, *The Remaining Titles* (Matchbox 1987)★★★, *Chocolate To The Bone* (1992)★★★.

BARBEE, JOHN HENRY

b. William George Tucker, 14 November 1905, Henning, Tennessee, USA, d. 3 November 1964, Chicago, Illinois, USA. Tucker worked with John Lee 'Sonny Boy' Williamson and Sunnyland Slim before assuming his new name when he left the south after a shooting incident. He then moved to Chicago, where he recorded a session for Vocalion Records on 8 September 1938. Only one coupling was released and made no impact on the record-buying public. Barbee continued to work on the streets in the company of such men as Moody Jones, until he was drafted into the army in the early 40s. 'Rediscovered', he recorded for Victoria Spivey in 1964 before joining the American Folk Blues Festival for its tour of Europe. This trip was cut short by illness and he returned to the USA only to be involved in a car crash. He was in jail as a result of this accident when he died of a heart attack.
● ALBUMS: *Storyville 171* (1964)★★★.
● COMPILATIONS: *Dance With Daddy G* (See For Miles 1996)★★★.

BARKER, LOUIS 'BLUE LU'

b. 13 November 1913, New Orleans, Louisiana, USA. Barker began her career as a dancer and singer in New Orleans but did not record until 1938 after her move to New York. She is almost certainly the 'Lu Blue' who recorded with Erskine Hawkins in July of that year. Under her own name she continued to record for Decca Records until 1939. She enjoyed a second period of recording activity between 1947 and 1949 with her work appearing mainly on Apollo and Capitol. A band singer of note, she has been cited as an influence on Billie Holiday and Eartha Kitt. Barker's blues were often slyly humorous and marked by a wonderful sense of timing. Married to New Orleans jazz guitarist Danny Barker, she usually worked in his company as well as with many of the great names in jazz, and was still performing in 1977.
● COMPILATIONS: *Red White And Blues* (1980)★★★, *Sorry But I Can't Take You - Woman's Railroad Blues* (1980)★★★.

BARNES, ROOSEVELT 'BOOBA'

b. 25 September 1936, Longwood, Mississippi, USA, d. 3 April 1996, Chicago, Illinois, USA. A self-taught singer, guitarist and harmonica player, Barnes played 'unvarnished gut level blues', strongly influenced by Howlin' Wolf. His first instrument was the harmonica, which he began to play at the age of eight, and he sat in with many of the local blues musicians around Greenville, Mississippi, in the 50s. He formed his first band in 1956 or 1957 and started playing guitar in 1960. In 1964 he moved to Chicago, Illinois, living there until 1971, and then returning two years later to record as a backing musician with the Jones Brothers; these recordings remain unissued. In 1990 Barnes became the first Mississippi-based performer to record an album for the Rooster Blues label.

● ALBUMS: *The Heartbroken Man* (Rooster Blues 1990)★★★.

BARRELHOUSE BUCK

b. Thomas McFarland, 16 September 1903, Alton, Illinois, USA, d. April 1962. On his 1929 debut recording, Barrelhouse Buck sang reflectively, like many St. Louis pianists, but his playing was more percussive than that of his contemporaries. This resulted partly from his experience as a drummer, and partly from a conscious decision to make his style different. By 1934, he had adopted a fierce, growling vocal to match his swinging piano, and perhaps also to compete with his accompanists, drawn from among a rasping fiddler, a clarinettist, and Peetie Wheatstraw's guitar. Together they made exciting dance music, and it is regrettable that Barrelhouse Buck did not record again until shortly before his death, at a hurried session that produced a brief album, marred by an out-of-tune piano.

● ALBUMS: *Backcountry Barrelhouse* (1962)★★★, *St. Louis Piano Styles* (1989)★★★.

BARTHOLOMEW, DAVE

b. 24 December 1920, Edgard, Louisiana, USA. Dave Bartholomew was one of the most important shapers of New Orleans R&B and rock 'n' roll during the 50s. A producer, arranger, songwriter, bandleader and artist, Bartholomew produced and co-wrote most of Fats Domino's major hits for Imperial Records. Bartholomew started playing the trumpet as a child, encouraged by his father, a Dixieland jazz tuba player. He performed in marching bands throughout the 30s and then on a Mississippi riverboat band

led by Fats Pichon beginning in 1939, and learned songwriting basics during a stint in the US Army. Upon his return to New Orleans in the late 40s he formed his first band, which became one of the city's most popular. He also backed Little Richard on some early recordings. Bartholomew worked for several labels, including Specialty, Aladdin and De Luxe, for whom he had a big hit in 1949 with 'Country Boy'. In the same year he started a long-term association with Imperial as a producer and arranger. The previous year Bartholomew had discovered Domino in New Orleans' Hideaway Club and he introduced him to Imperial. They collaborated on 'The Fat Man', which, in 1950, became the first of over a dozen hits co-authored by the pair and produced by Bartholomew. Others included 'Blue Monday', 'Walking To New Orleans', 'Let The Four Winds Blow', 'I'm In Love Again', 'Whole Lotta Loving', 'My Girl Josephine' and 'I'm Walkin'', the latter also becoming a hit for Ricky Nelson. Bartholomew's other credits included Smiley Lewis's 'I Hear You Knocking' (later a hit for Dave Edmunds) and 'One Night' (later a hit for Elvis Presley, with its lyrics tamed), Lloyd Price's 'Lawdy Miss Clawdy', and records for Shirley And Lee, Earl King, Roy Brown, Huey 'Piano' Smith, Bobby Mitchell, Chris Kenner, Robert Parker, Frankie Ford and Snooks Eaglin. In 1963, Imperial was sold to Liberty Records, and Bartholomew declined an invitation to move to Hollywood, preferring to stay in New Orleans. In 1972, Chuck Berry reworked 'My Ding-A-Ling', a song Bartholomew had penned in 1952, and achieved his only US number 1 single.

Although Bartholomew, who claims to have written over 4,000 songs, recorded under his own name, his contribution was primarily as a behind-the-scenes figure. He recorded a Dixieland album in 1981 and in the early 90s was still leading a big band at occasional special events such as the New Orleans Jazz & Heritage Festival.

● ALBUMS: *Fats Domino Presents Dave Bartholomew* (Imperial 1961)★★★, *New Orleans House Party* (Imperial 1963)★★★, *Jump Children* (Pathe Marconi 1984)★★, *The Monkey* (Pathe Marconi 1985)★★, *Heritage* (1986)★★, *Graciously* (1987)★★, *The Spirit Of New Orleans* (1993)★★★.

● COMPILATIONS: *The Best Of Dave Bartholomew: The Classic New Orleans R&B Band Sound* (Stateside 1989)★★★.

BARTON, LOU ANN

b. 17 February 1954, Fort Worth, Texas, USA. In the early 70s, Barton sprang fully formed into the Texas bar-room blues scene. She divided her time between singing with Robert Ealey And His Five Careless Lovers in her home-town, performing with the Dallas band run by Marc Benno (ex-Asylum Choir), and picking up gigs around the Austin clubs, including an early prototype of the Fabulous Thunderbirds. In 1976, Stevie Ray Vaughan chose her to be a member of the Triple Threat Revue, the third being singer/guitarist W.C. Clark. When Clark quit, the band changed its name to Double Trouble. With two strong personalities vying for the spotlight, trouble was, unsurprisingly, not long in coming, and towards the end of 1979, Barton announced that she was joining Roomful Of Blues for a tour of north-west USA. In 1982, Glenn Frey and Jerry Wexler produced her first solo album, *Old Enough*, which was recorded in Muscle Shoals. Unfortunately, her personal habits and the unreliability that they engendered caused Asylum to cancel the tour that had been set up to support the album. Two further albums failed to establish her beyond Austin city limits. Her contributions to *Dreams Come True* remain the best examples of a talent of which the singer Linda Ronstadt has claimed to be frightened.
● ALBUMS: *Old Enough* (Asylum/Antone's 1982/1992)★★★, *Forbidden Tones* (Spindletop 1986)★★★, *Read My Lips* (Antone's 1989)★★★, with Marcia Ball, Angela Strehli *Dreams Come True* (Antone's 1990)★★★.

BASS, RALPH

b. 1 May 1911, New York City, New York, USA. A pivotal figure in the history of R&B, Bass began his career during the 40s, promoting live jazz shows in Los Angeles. He subsequently worked for Black And White Records, producing 'Open The Door, Richard' for Jack McVea, but later left to found several small-scale outlets with releases by Errol Garner and Dexter Gordon. Bass also recorded (Little) Esther Phillips, the Robins and Johnny Otis for the Savoy label, and in 1951

became one of the era's first independent producers through the aegis of the Cincinnati-based King company. Armed with his own outlet, Federal, and its Armo publishing wing, he built an impressive roster of acts around Hank Ballard And The Midnighters, the Dominoes and James Brown, whom Bass signed in 1955 on hearing a demo disc at an Atlanta radio station. Although initially unimpressed by the singer's untutored delivery, King managing director Syd Nathan changed his mind when 'Please Please Please' became a bestseller. Brown remained a Federal artist until 1960 but was switched to the parent outlet when Bass departed for Chess Records. The producer brought Etta James and Pigmeat Markham to his new employers, and in turn, worked with several established acts, including Muddy Waters, Howlin' Wolf and Ramsey Lewis. Bass remained with the label until the mid-70s when its Chicago office was closed. He continued to record R&B acts, the masters from which were latterly compiled on a series of albums under the generic title *I Didn't Give A Damn If Whites Bought It*.

BATTS, WILL

b. 24 January 1904, Michigan, Mississippi, USA, d. 18 February 1956, Memphis, Tennessee, USA. Batts played violin in his father's string band from the age of nine, and was also proficient on guitar and mandolin. Moving to Memphis in 1919, he was a part-time musician, playing in the jug band led by Jack Kelly. His distinctive fiddle playing, equally capable of a punchy muscularity and a languid sensuousness, may be heard behind Frank Stokes on some 1929 recordings, and on a more extensive series made by Jack Kelly's South Memphis Jug Band in the 30s. From 1934, Batts led his own band, and two private recordings from 1954 survive; 'Kansas City' and 'Lady Be Good' testify both to Batts's own versatility and to the continuity of the musical tradition from which he came.

BAXTER, ANDREW AND JIM

b. Calhoun, Georgia, USA. A father and son duo, playing violin and guitar, respectively, the Baxters recorded at four sessions between 1927 and 1929. Their records offer a rare example of an older, more rural, black music tradition in Georgia. While some were blues, notably the gentle and melancholy 'KC Railroad Blues', others such as 'Georgia Stomp' were country dance tunes, similar in many ways to some of the white traditional music recorded around the same time. The latter even included spoken dance calls of the type more usually associated with white country music. Emphasizing this connection, Andrew, the father (who is said to have been half-Cherokee Indian), made one record with the white old-time group the Georgia Yellow Hammers, at the 1927 session.

● COMPILATIONS: *The East Coast States, Vol. 2* (1968).

BEAMAN, LOTTIE

b. *c.*1900, possibly in Kansas City, Missouri, USA. Beaman was one of the first generation of female blues singers to record. Details of her life are sparse, although it is known that her maiden name was Lottie Kimbrough before her marriage to William Beaman in the early 20s. She was billed as 'The Kansas City Butterball', having worked in its bars and taverns as a teenager. Between 1924 and 1929, she recorded in Kansas, Chicago and Richmond, Indiana, sometimes in the company of her brother Sylvester Kimbrough or whistler and singer Winston Holmes. Although not possessing one of the greatest voices she was known and appreciated as a 'moaner' for the quality of despair that she could bring to her blues. Her work was also issued under the names Jennie Brooks, Lottie Brown, Clara Cary, Lottie Everson, Martha Johnson, Lena Kimbrough, Lottie Kimbrough and Mae Moran.

● ALBUMS: *Lottie Beaman (Kimborough) 1924/26 And Louella Miller 1928* (Wolf 1987)★★★.
● COMPILATIONS: *BluesUnion* (AudioQuest 1996)★★★.

BECK, JEFF

b. 24 June 1944, Wallington, Surrey, England. As a former choirboy the young Beck was interested in music from an early age, becoming a competent pianist and guitarist by the age of 11. His first main band was the Tridents, who made a name for themselves locally. After leaving them Beck took on the seemingly awesome task of stepping into the shoes of Eric Clapton, who had recently departed from the 60s R&B pio-

neers, the Yardbirds. Clapton had a fiercely loyal following, but Beck soon had them gasping with his amazing guitar pyrotechnics, utilizing feedback and distortion. Beck stayed with the Yardbirds, adding colour and excitement to all their hits, until October 1966. The tension between Beck and joint lead guitarist Jimmy Page was finally resolved during a US tour: Beck walked out and never returned. His solo career was launched in March 1967 with an unexpected pop single, 'Hi-Ho Silver Lining', wherein his unremarkable voice was heard on a singalong number that was saved by his trademark guitar solo. The record was a sizeable hit and has demonstrated its perennial appeal to party-goers by re-entering the charts on several occasions since. The follow-up, 'Tallyman', was also a minor hit, but by now Beck's ambitions lay in other directions. From being a singing, guitar-playing pop star, he relaunched a career that led to his becoming one of the world's leading rock guitarists. The Jeff Beck Group, formed in 1968, consisted of Beck, Rod Stewart (vocals), Ron Wood (bass), Nicky Hopkins (piano) and Mickey Waller (drums). This powerhouse quartet released *Truth*, which became a major success in the USA, resulting in the band undertaking a number of arduous tours. The second album, *Cosa Nostra Beck-Ola,* had similar success, although Stewart and Wood had now departed for the Faces. Beck also contributed some sparkling guitar and received equal billing with Donovan on the hit 'Goo Goo Barabajagal (Love Is Hot)'. In 1968 Beck's serious accident with one of his hot-rod cars put him out of action for almost 18 months. A recovered Beck formed another group with Cozy Powell, Max Middleton and Bob Tench, and recorded two further albums, *Rough And Ready* and *Jeff Beck Group*. Beck was now venerated as a serious musician and master of his instrument, and figured highly in various guitarist polls. In 1973 the erratic Beck musical style changed once again and he formed the trio Beck, Bogert And Appice with the two former members of Vanilla Fudge. Soon afterwards, Beck introduced yet another musical dimension, this time forming an instrumental band. The result was the excellent *Blow By Blow*, thought by many to be his best work. His guitar playing revealed extraordinary technique, combining rock, jazz and blues styles.

Blow By Blow was a million-seller and its follow-up, *Wired*, enjoyed similar success. Having allied himself with some of the jazz/rock fraternity Beck teamed up with Jan Hammer for a frantic live album, after which he effectively retired for three years. He returned in 1980 with *There And Back* and, now rejuvenated, he found himself riding the album charts once more. During the 80s Beck's appearances were sporadic, though he did guest on Tina Turner's *Private Dancer* and work with Robert Plant and Jimmy Page on the Honeydrippers' album. The occasional charity function aside, he has spent much of his leisure time with automobiles (in one interview Beck stated that he could just as easily have been a car restorer). In the mid-80s he toured with Rod Stewart and was present on his version of 'People Get Ready', though when *Flash* arrived in 1985, it proved his least successful album to date. The release of a box set in 1992, chronicling his career, was a fitting tribute to this accomplished guitarist and his numerous guises (the latest of which had been guitarist on Spinal Tap's second album). Following an award in 1993 for his theme music (with Jed Stoller) for the Anglia TV production *Frankie's House*, he released *Crazy Legs*, a tribute to the music of Gene Vincent. For this, Beck abandoned virtuosity, blistering solos and jazz stylings for a clean, low-volume rock 'n' roll sound, demonstrating once more his absolute mastery of technique. He also made his acting debut, playing Brad the serial killer in *The Comic Strip Presents ... Gregory: Diary Of A Nutcase*.

● ALBUMS: *Truth* (EMI 1968)★★★, *Cosa Nostra Beck-Ola* (EMI 1969)★★, *Rough And Ready* (Epic 1971)★★, *Jeff Beck Group* (Epic 1972)★★, *Blow By Blow* (Epic 1975)★★★★, *Wired* (Epic 1976)★★, *Jeff Beck With The Jan Hammer Group Live* (Epic 1977)★, *There And Back* (Epic 1980)★★, *Flash* (Epic 1985)★★, with Terry Bozzio, Tony Hymas *Jeff Beck's Guitar Shop* (Epic 1989)★★, *Crazy Legs* (Epic 1993)★★★.

● COMPILATIONS: *Beckology* CD box set (Epic 1992)★★★★.

BELL, CAREY

b. Carey Bell Harrington, 14 November 1936, Macon, Mississippi, USA. Bell began to play harmonica after being inspired by the records of Muddy Waters, Little Walter, and Sonny Boy 'Rice Miller' Williams. Carey played with a white C&W band and with his 'stepfather', Lovie Lee. He moved to Chicago with Lee in the mid-50s, and besides picking up harmonica tips from Little Walter and Walter Horton, he also learned guitar from David 'Honeyboy' Edwards, although his main instrument throughout the 60s was bass guitar. He was recorded on Maxwell Street with Robert Nighthawk in 1964, and appeared on a Earl Hooker album in 1968. He quickly recorded his debut album for Delmark, and has appeared on record regularly since, both as leader and accompanist. He had lengthy spells with Muddy Waters and Willie Dixon, and in 1988 he recorded what is claimed to be the world's first ever CD-only issue of a blues album. Besides being rated as one of the leading blues harmonica players, Bell is also a very underrated singer, and he has encouraged many of his children to become blues musicians, with the best-known being Lurrie Bell.

● ALBUMS: *Carey Bell's Blues Harp* (Delmark 1969)★★★, *Last Night* (1973)★★★, with Lurrie Bell *Son Of A Gun* (Rooster 1984)★★★, *Straight Shoot* (Blues South West 1987)★★★, *Harpslinger* (JSP 1988)★★★, *Mellow Down Easy* (Blind Pig 1991)★★★, with Lurrie Bell *Dynasty* (JSP 1990)★★★, *Harpmaster* (JSP 1994)★★★, *Deep Down* (Alligator 1995)★★★.

BELL, EDWARD 'ED'

b. May 1905, Forest Deposit, Alabama, USA, d. 1965. A guitarist who, it has recently been confirmed, also recorded as 'Barefoot Bill' and 'Sluefoot Joe' between 1927 and 1930. Bell stands as the most influential Alabama artist in pre-war blues recordings. With well over three-quarters of his material issued, Bell's 'Mamlish Blues' and 'Hambone Blues' came to define the style of the region and his contemporaries. His influences could still be detected in the 70s recordings of fellow Alabamian, John Lee. The circumstances of Bell's death are shrouded in mystery but it is thought he died in the 60s during a civil rights march.

● COMPILATIONS: *Ed Bell's Mamlish Moan* (1983)★★★, *Barefoot Bill's Hard Luck Blues* (1984)★★★.

BELL, JIMMIE

b. 29 August 1910, Peoria, Illinois, USA, d. 31 December 1987, Peoria, Illinois, USA. A minor figure who made few recordings, Bell was typical of the journeyman musician who plays what he must to earn a living, while harbouring greater ambitions. Beginning violin lessons at the age of 10, he moved on to the guitar, trumpet and trombone before settling on piano. Bell spent his early musical life around St. Louis, where he led a small group in the late 30s, Jimmie 'Lightning' Bell And His Swinging Cats. Prior to that, he had worked with bands such as Earl Van Dyke's Plantation Cotton Pickers and Al Williams' St. Louis Syncopators. In the late 40s, Bell formed the six-piece Gentlemen Of Swing, including Andrew Harris on bass. Harris and guitarist Leo Blevins accompanied him on a 1948 session that produced two singles, one on Aristocrat, the other constituting the third single on the then new Chess label. Although he claimed never to have been a user, Bell was imprisoned twice for possession of heroin. A further three years was served from 1970 for aiding and abetting an abortion. In 1978, he released three singles on his own GDS label, and was imprisoned yet again, this time for possession of counterfeit food stamps. His only album was made up of songs recorded in Shreveport in 1949, along with a 1978 concert at Illinois Central College and material recorded in his own home just before his incarceration.

● ALBUMS: *Stranger In Your Town* (JSP 1979)★★★.

BELL, LURRIE

b. 13 December 1958, Chicago, Illinois, USA. The second son of Carey Bell, Lurrie's musical interests were encouraged from an early age by his father and the guitarist Roy Johnson. By the age of eight Bell was regularly called onstage for guest appearances. In his teens he joined Koko Taylor's band as guitarist. In the 80s he established himself as both a respected bandleader and an in-demand session player, and he toured Europe frequently. He gave up music in 1986, but marked his return three years later with two well-received recordings for the JSP label. Lurrie's soulful, Little Milton-influenced singing and agile guitar playing mark him as a promising prospect and his recent output with

Delmark has demonstrated a much harder, grittier edge.

● ALBUMS: with Billy Branch *Chicago's Young Blues Generation* (L&R 1982)★★★, *Everybody Wants To Win* (JSP 1989)★★★, with Carey Bell *Dynasty!* (JSP 1989)★★★, *Mercurial Son* (Delmark 1995)★★★★, *700 Blues* (Delmark 1997)★★★★.

BELL, MAGGIE

b. 12 January 1945, Glasgow, Scotland. Bell's career began in the mid-60s as the featured singer in several resident dancehall bands. She made her recording debut in 1966, completing two singles with Bobby Kerr under the name Frankie And Johnny. Bell then joined guitarist Leslie Harvey, another veteran of the same circuit, in Power, a hard-rock group that evolved into Stone The Crows. This earthy, soul-based band, memorable for Harvey's imaginative playing and Bell's gutsy, heart-felt vocals, became a highly popular live attraction and helped the singer win several accolades. Bell's press release at the time insisted that she would loosen her vocal chords by gargling with gravel! The group split up in 1973, still rocked by Harvey's tragic death the previous year. Bell embarked on a solo career with *Queen Of The Night*, which was produced in New York by Jerry Wexler and featured the cream of the city's session musicians. The anticipated success did not materialize and further releases failed to reverse this trend. The singer did have a minor UK hit with 'Hazell' (1978), the theme tune to a popular television series, but 'Hold Me', a tongue-in-cheek duet with B.A. Robertson, remains her only other chart entry. Bell subsequently fronted a new group, Midnight Flyer, but this tough, highly underrated singer, at times redolent of Janis Joplin, has been unable to secure a distinctive career and can still be seen on the blues club circuit.

● ALBUMS: *Queen Of The Night* (Super 1974)★★★, *Suicide Sal* (Polydor 1975)★★★.

● COMPILATIONS: *Great Rock Sensation* (Polydor 1977)★★★.

BELL, T.D.

b. 26 December 1922, Lee County, Texas, USA. Bell did not take up blues guitar until his early twenties, after military service. Not surprisingly, the major influence on his style was 'T-Bone' Walker. His band was one of the major attractions of the Austin scene, and backed visiting artists at the Victory Grill, and on tour through west Texas, Arizona and New Mexico. Bell gave up playing in the early 70s when disco made live musicians uneconomical, but resumed in the late 80s in partnership with his long-time associate Erbie Bowser; they were still an impressive team.

● ALBUMS: *It's About Time* (1992)★★★.

BENNETT, DUSTER

b. Anthony Bennett, *c*.1940, d. 26 March 1976. Bennett was a dedicated British one-man-band blues performer, in the style of Jesse Fuller and Dr Ross. He played the London R&B club circuit from the mid-60s and was signed by Mike Vernon to Blue Horizon in 1967, releasing 'It's A Man Down There' as his first single. On his first album he was backed by Peter Green and John McVie of Fleetwood Mac. Bennett also played harmonica on sessions for Fleetwood Mac, Champion Jack Dupree, Memphis Slim, Shusha and Martha Velez. He was briefly a member of John Mayall's Bluesbreakers, and in 1974 recorded for Mickie Most's RAK label, releasing a single, 'Comin Home'. He was killed in a road accident on 26 March 1976 in Warwickshire, England, returning home after performing with Memphis Slim.

● ALBUMS: *Smiling Like I'm Happy* (Blue Horizon 1968)★★★, *Bright Lights* (Blue Horizon 1969)★★★, *12 DBs* (1970)★★★, *Fingertips* (1974)★★.
● COMPILATIONS: *Out In The Blue* (Indigo 1994)★★★, *Jumpin' At Shadows* (Indigo 1994)★★, *Blue Inside* (Indigo 1995)★★★.

BENNETT, WAYNE

b. 1934, Sulpher, Oklahoma, USA, d. 28 November 1992. A skilful blues guitarist, Bennett came to prominence in the mid-50s as a member of Otis Rush's Chicago-based band. From there he was picked by Joe Scott to join the touring and recording orchestra of Bobby Bland. With arrangements by Scott and scintillating solos by Bennett, Bland became the leading live attraction on the chitlin' circuit in the late 50s and early 60s. Bennett's playing also contributed to Bland's numerous hits of the era,

such as 'I Pity The Fool' (1961) and 'Stormy Monday Blues' (1962). During this period, Bennett was also a session player for other Duke/Peacock artists such as Junior Parker and Gatemouth Brown. He left Bland's group in the late 60s and subsequently appeared on records by such blues artists as Buddy Guy, Fenton Robinson, Jimmy Reed and Jimmy Rogers. In 1981, Bennett was named Blues Guitarist of the Year by the National Blues Foundation and in the early 90s he was based in Louisiana performing with Willie Lockett and the Blues Krewe. Bennett died in November 1992 from heart failure, just prior to a scheduled heart transplant operation.

BENOIT, TAB

b. 17 November 1967, Baton Rouge, California, USA. Benoit started out playing classic rock cover versions in local bands. A gifted young guitarist, he was satisfied with this kind of music until a friend played him a copy of a Buddy Guy record. His musical world turned upside-down, Benoit set about recreating Guy's deep-rooted emotion, adopting his style and researching more about the blues tradition. Rejecting a potential career as a pilot, he worked with a brace of Cajun bands, before finding someone receptive to the idea of a white man just out of his teens playing the blues. His first appearance on record placed him in awe-inspiring company - the Justice Records compilation, *Strike A Deep Chord: Blues Guitar For The Homeless*, with his own contributions sitting next to selections from Dr. John, Clarence 'Gatemouth' Brown and Johnny Copeland. His debut album followed in 1993, with contributions from Gregg Bissonette (drums), Steve Bailey (bass) and Paul English (keyboards), and production from Randall Hage Jamail. Although no new ground was broken with his second and third albums he continues to show his dexterity with the Fender Stratocaster and is an asset to the 'white boy' blues genre. *Standing On The Bank* featured a new rhythm section of Greg Rzab (bass) and Ray Allison (drums), borrowed from Buddy Guy; the album was more 'authentic' in feel than his previous efforts.

● ALBUMS: *Nice And Warm* (Justice 1993)★★★★, *What I Live For* (Justice 1994)★★★, *Standing On The Bank* (Justice

1995)★★★ *Live: Swampland Jam* (Justice 1997)★★.

BENSON, AL

b. Arthur Leaner, 30 June 1908, Jackson, Mississippi, USA, d. 6 September 1978, Berrien Springs, Michigan, USA. By the age of seven, Benson was tap-dancing with his father's jazz band, and he went on to work in minstrel shows and to produce musicals. His restless energy led to a number of widely varying jobs, including Chief of Recreation for Jackson's black schools, a railroad cook, probation officer and storefront preacher. His radio career began on Chicago's WGES with a religious programme and then an R&B show that lasted until 1962. In the late 40s and early 50s he started a number of record labels, Old Swingmaster (one of his radio tags), Parrot and Blue Lake, recording such artists as J.B. Lenoir, Sunnyland Slim, Albert King, Willie Mabon and Little Willie Foster. Crash and The Blues each had a brief life during the 60s, releasing material by Magic Sam, Shakey Jake, Johnny 'Big Moose' Walker and others. Benson's flamboyant and self-willed character eventually undermined his status in the black community, although he was active in the civil rights movement, once hiring a plane to drop 5,000 copies of the US Constitution over Mississippi. In later years, he owned a record store in Michigan City before losing both legs due to ill health, which also eventually led to his death from heart failure.

BENTLEY, GLADYS ALBERTA

(aka Fatso Bentley) b. 12 August 1907, Pennsylvania, USA, d. 18 January 1960, Los Angeles, California, USA. A blues singer, pianist and male impersonator, Bentley moved to New York in her late teens to work at various Harlem nightspots, and was soon recording solo for OKeh Records and with the Washboard Serenaders for RCA Victor. In the early 30s, she opened a nightspot, the Exclusive Club, and began arranging and directing her own shows, including the successful Ubangi Club Revue. In the early 40s, Bentley moved to California and started a fresh career as a blues shouter, recording in the style for small independents such as Excelsior, Flame, Top Hat and Swingtime. She was much in demand

throughout the 50s until her death at home of pneumonia.

● COMPILATIONS: one track only *Boogie Blues - Women Sing And Play Boogie Woogie* (1983), one track only *Tough Mamas* (1989).

BENTON, BUSTER

b. Arley Benton, 19 July 1932, Texarkana, Arkansas, USA, d. 20 January 1996. Benton sang in a gospel choir as a youngster, before moving in 1952 to Toledo, Ohio, where he began playing guitar and turned to the blues, influenced by Sam Cooke and B.B. King. Around the end of the 50s he settled in Chicago, where he led his own band and recorded for the Melloway, Twinight and Alteen labels. He owned the Stardust Lounge for some time in the early 70s but spent several years as guitarist with Willie Dixon. Benton had a hit for Jewel Records with 'Spider In My Stew' in the mid-70s, and recordings he made later for Ralph Bass were issued on several labels worldwide. In the 80s he recorded for Blue Phoenix, and despite some serious health problems he continued to perform and record until his death in 1996.

● ALBUMS: *Spider In My Stew* (Ronn 1979)★★★, *Bluesbuster* (Red Lightnin 1980)★★★, *Buster Benton Is The Feeling* (Ronn 1980)★★★, *First Time In Europe* (Blue Phoenix 1985)★★★, *Blues At The Top* (Blue Phoenix 1987)★★★★, *Why Me?* (Ichiban 1988)★★★, *Money's The Name Of The Game* (Ichiban 1989)★★★, *I Like To Hear My Guitar Sing* (Ichiban 1992)★★★.

BETTS, RICHARD 'DICKIE'

b. 12 December 1943, Jacksonville, Florida, USA. Formerly with Tommy Roe's Romans, this exceptional guitarist was also a member of the Second Coming, a Jacksonville group that featured bassist Berry Oakley. Both musicians joined the Allman Brothers Band at its inception in 1969 and Betts' melodic lines provided the foil and support for leader Duane Allman's inventive slide soloing. Allman's tragic death in 1971 allowed Betts to come forward, a responsibility he shouldered admirably on the group's excellent *Brothers And Sisters* album. The country flavour prevalent on several of the tracks, most notably 'Ramblin' Man', set the tone for Betts' solo career. *Highway Call* was released in 1974 but its promise was overshadowed by the parent group's own recordings. Betts formed a new group, Great Southern, in 1976, but their progress faltered when the guitarist was drawn into the resurrected Allman fold. In 1981, Betts formed BHLT with Jimmy Hall (from Wet Willie), Chuck Leavell, Butch Trucks and David Goldflies, but they too were doomed to a premature collapse and the guitarist withdrew from active work. However, in the late 80s Betts was signed to Epic, the outlet for whom Gregg Allman was recording, prompting rumours of a reunion, and Betts was indeed part of the 1989 re-formation of the Allman Brothers.

● ALBUMS: *Highway Call* (Capricorn 1974)★★★, *Dickie Betts And The Great Southern* (Arista 1977)★★, *Atlanta Burning Down* (Arista 1978)★★, *Pattern Disruptive* (Epic 1988)★★.

BIBB, ERIC

b. New York, USA. Based in Sweden, singer-songwriter and guitarist Bibb is, with Corey Harris and Alvin Youngblood Hart, at the forefront of the recent country blues revival. The son of famous 60s folk revivalist Leon Bibb, there was a constant stream of musical visitors to his father's house during his childhood, including Odetta, Pete Seeger, Judy Collins and Bob Dylan. Meeting the cream of the folk revival created a lasting impression on the young Bibb, who first started to learn the guitar when he was eight. Keen to explore different countries, Bibb then left New York to busk and travel in Europe, staying in Paris before moving to Stockholm for 10 years. Returning to New York briefly in the 80s, he finally settled in Sweden with his family. Regular touring with slide guitar player Göran Wennerbrandt built up his live reputation, and he recently supported country blues legend Taj Mahal. He has recorded two albums for the Opus 3 label, with production duties handled by Wennerbrandt. His songs are both social and spiritual, reflecting the influence of the original country blues singers, but tackle modern-day problems and issues rather than lapsing into nostalgic authenticity. After signing to Warner Brothers' Code Blue outlet, Bibb indicated that his new material would reflect a more diverse range of musical influences, which was subsequently borne out by the excellent *Me To You*.

● ALBUMS: *Spirit & The Blues* (Opus 3 1995)★★★, *Good Stuff* (Opus 3 1997)★★★, *Me To You* (Code Blue 1997)★★★.

BIG BAD SMITTY

b. John Henry Smith, 11 February 1940, Vicksburg, Mississippi, USA. Though physically approaching the bulk of Howlin' Wolf and making his reputation on versions of several Wolf classics, Smitty is typical of a generation of blues singers who struggle to find an original voice once their powers of imitation are exhausted. His earliest influences were Lightnin' Hopkins and Lil' Son Jackson, whose music he would pick out on his older brother's guitar. He formed a band with schoolfriend Roosevelt 'Booba' Barnes, playing around Hollandale and into Arkansas. In the 60s, he moved to Jackson where he played alongside Sammy Myers, Johnny Littlejohn, King Edward and Elmore James Jnr. All were recorded by Johnny Vincent, although the results were not officially released until 1981. In his thirties, Smitty took up permanent residence in St. Louis, working with harmonica player Big George Brock and guitarist Bennie Smith. A number of songs were recorded (very badly) for producer James Cotton (not the harmonica player), giving little idea of the power he evinced as a live performer. His debut album, *Mean Disposition*, using the resources of Bennie Smith and harmonica player Arthur Williams, contained the expected songs by Howlin' Wolf and Muddy Waters, as well as Little Milton's 'Lonely Man' and Homer Banks' 'Angel Of Mercy'. His own material suffered by comparison, with the exception of the humorous 'I Didn't Marry Your Family', which indicated the possibility of a talent beyond that so far captured on record.

● ALBUMS: *St. Louis On A High Hill* (JC&E 1988)★★★, *Mean Disposition* (Black Magic 1991)★★★, *Layin' In The Alley* (Black Top 1994)★★★.

● COMPILATIONS: *Going Down To Louisiana* (White Label 1976)★★★, *Genuine Mississippi Blues* (1981)★★★, *St. Louis Blues Today Vol. 2* (Wolf 1992)★★★.

BIG MACEO

b. Major Meriweather, 31 March 1905, Atlanta, Georgia, USA, d. 26 February 1953, Chicago,

Illinois, USA. Big Maceo learned piano while living in a suburb of Atlanta in his early teens. In 1924 he moved to Detroit where he made his name on the local blues scene. In the early 40s, he made a series of classic recordings with the Chicago guitarist Tampa Red. Maceo's piano lends a distinctive toughness and weight to Tampa's records, while the guitarist complements the other's superb sides with his supple and beautifully expressive slide lines. Maceo's 'Worried Life' was a big hit, and has become one of the most covered of all blues songs, while most of the other tracks he recorded for the Bluebird/Victor company are of equal quality. These ranged from the plaintive 'Poor Kelly Blues' to powerful instrumental pieces such as 'Chicago Breakdown'. After a stroke in 1946, his later records failed to recapture the glories of his earlier work.

● COMPILATIONS: *King Of Chicago Blues Piano, Vols. 1 & 2* (Arhoolie 1984)★★★, *The Bluebird Recordings 1941-42* (RCA 1997)★★★★, *The Victor/Bluebird Recordings 1945-1947* (RCA 1997)★★★★.

● FURTHER READING: *Big Maceo: The Art Of Jazz*, Paul Oliver.

BIG MAYBELLE

b. Mabel Louise Smith, 1 May *c*.1920, Jackson, Tennessee, USA, d. 23 January 1972. Maybelle was discovered singing in church by Memphis bandleader Dave Clark in 1935. When Clark disbanded his orchestra to concentrate on record promotion, Smith moved to Christine Chatman's orchestra with whom she first recorded for Decca in 1944. Three years later, Smith made solo records for King and in 1952 she recorded as Big Maybelle when producer Fred Mendelsohn signed her to OKeh, a subsidiary of CBS Records. Her blues shouting style (a female counterpart to Big Joe Turner) brought an R&B hit the next year with 'Gabbin' Blues' (a cleaned-up version of the 'dirty dozens' on which she was partnered by songwriter Rose Marie McCoy). 'Way Back Home' and 'My Country Man' were also bestsellers. In 1955, she made the first recording of 'Whole Lotta Shakin' Goin' On', which later became a major hit for Jerry Lee Lewis. Big Maybelle was also a star attraction on the chitlin' circuit of black clubs, with an act that included risqué comedy as well as emo-

tive ballads and brisk boogies. Leaving OKeh for Savoy, her 'Candy' (1956) brought more success and in 1958, she appeared in *Jazz On A Summer's Day*, the film of that year's Newport Jazz Festival. Despite her acknowledged influence on the soul styles of the 60s, later records for Brunswick, Scepter and Chess made little impact until she signed to the Rojac label in 1966. There she was persuaded to record some recent pop hits by the Beatles and Donovan and had some minor chart success of her own with versions of 'Don't Pass Me By' and '96 Tears'. The latter was composed by Rudy Martinez who also recorded it with his band ? And The Mysterians. Maybelle's career was marred by frequent drug problems which contributed to her early death.

● ALBUMS: *Big Maybelle Sings* (Savoy 1958)★★★★, *Blues, Candy And Big Maybelle* (Savoy 1958)★★★★, *Saga Of The Good Life And Hard Times* (Rojac 60s)★★★, *What More Can A Woman Do?* (Brunswick 1962)★★★, *The Gospel Soul Of Big Maybelle* (Brunswick 1964)★★★★, *The Great Soul Hits Of Big Maybelle* (Brunswick 1964)★★★★, *Gabbin' Blues* (Scepter 1965)★★★, *Got A Brand New Bag* (Rojac 1967)★★★, *The Gospel Soul Of Big Maybelle* (Brunswick 1968)★★★, *The Last Of Big Maybelle* (Paramount 1973)★★★.

● COMPILATIONS: *The OKeh Sessions* (Charly 1983)★★★★, *Roots Of R&R And Early Soul* (Savoy Jazz 1985)★★★★, *Candy* (Savoy 1995)★★★, *The Last Of Big Maybelle* (Muse 1996)★★.

BIG SUGAR

Comprising Gordie Johnson (vocals, guitar), Terry Wilkins (vocals, bass), Al Cross (drums), Kelly Hoppe (saxophone, harmonica), Paul Brennan (drums) and Gary Lowe (bass), Big Sugar were one of the newest sounds to blow out of Canada, combining the blues vocabulary of the Tony D Band with a visionary abandon more akin to the Rheostatics. Leader and mastermind Johnson grew up in Windsor, Ontario, listening to Jimi Hendrix and the music that followed his example. Later, in Toronto, he supplemented that with the music of Charlie Parker and Thelonious Monk, and the ska and reggae he heard in the city's Jamaican clubs. On Big Sugar's debut album, the basic trio was augmented by members of the Bourbon Tabernacle

Choir on a set that combined blues by Skip James, Robert Johnson and Otis Rush with Monk's 'Bemsha Swing' and Henry Mancini's 'Shot In The Dark'. Johnson coarsened the band's approach for *Five Hundred Pounds*, favouring an ambient, open sound reminiscent of Led Zeppelin. Once again, blues suffused the material, sometimes appropriated ('How Many Times' and 'Wild Ox Moan'), at others attributed (Muddy Waters' 'Standing Around Crying' and Al Green's 'I'm A Ram'). Two years after its first release, the album was reissued with obligatory fanfares by the band's new label, which tried to play down the band's obvious inspiration.

● ALBUMS: *Big Sugar* (Hypnotic/Provogue 1992)★★★, *Five Hundred Pounds* (Hypnotic/Provogue 1993)★★★, *El Seven Niteclub Featuring Big Sugar* (Hypnotic 1994)★★★, *Hemi Vision* (A&M 1996)★★★.

BIG THREE TRIO

Willie Dixon, Leonard 'Baby Doo' Caston, Bernardo Dennis and Ollie Crawford (b. December 1917, Mobile, Alabama, USA, d. 1973). Although hindsight has given Dixon the credit, the Big Three Trio was formed and led by Caston. Influenced by Leroy Carr and Walter Davis in his piano playing, Caston also played guitar and helped teach the bass to Dixon. The pair recorded as part of the Five Breezes in November 1940. Dixon also formed the Four Jumps Of Jive with fellow Breezes member Gene Gilmore in 1945. The following year Caston and Dixon teamed up with guitarist Bernardo Dennis to form the Big Three Trio, named after world leaders Roosevelt, Churchill and Stalin. They recorded four titles for Bullet, from which Dixon's 'Signifying Monkey' became their first hit. Dennis was replaced by Ollie Crawford, who had been in the Rhythm Rascals with Caston during the war, and their contract was bought by Columbia Records. Although the band remained popular as live performers and continued to record until 1952, with a 1949 session for Delta also purchased by Columbia, there were no more hits. The group continued until 1956, by which time Dixon's work for the Chess brothers commanded most of his time. A previously unissued version of 'Violent Love' (also issued on OKeh) was issued in 1988 on a Chess box set of Dixon's work. The Big Three Trio were popular with the black middle classes and were thus important as a reflection of their society.

● ALBUMS: *I Feel Like Steppin' Out* (Dr. Horse 1986)★★★, *The Big Three Trio* (Columbia 1990)★★★.

● COMPILATIONS: *Willie Dixon: The Chess Box* (Chess 1988)★★★.

BIG TIME SARAH

b. Sarah Streeter, 31 January 1953, Coldwater, Mississippi, USA. Big Time Sarah's name is at the moment more of a wish than an observation. A blues belter in the style of Big Maybelle and Big Mama Thornton, the power of her voice, trained in church choirs, sometimes disguises her lack of technique and control. She was seven years old when her family arrived in Chicago and within a few years Sarah had taken to singing in blues clubs, helped by the Myers brothers and Magic Slim. A decade later, she had established herself in clubs such as Kingston Mines, Biddy Mulligan's and B.L.U.E.S., and had toured with Sunnyland Slim and Erwin Helfer. Her first recordings were made while on tour in Greece, backed by a band that combined Chicago musicians with locals. John Hammond plays harmonica on the inevitable 'Got My Mojo Working'. Her first American album drew on a similar set of songs, including the title track, 'Undecided', and 'Crying'. In 1989 she formed her own band, the BTS Express. *Crying* was recorded in Germany in 1992, with guitarist Steve Freund and a set of local musicians. *Lay It On 'Em Girls* again had a number of songs in common but was most notable for Willie Dixon's efforts to 'feminise' the lyrics for 'Hoochie Coochie Woman'.

● ALBUMS: with Chicago Blues Skyline *In Athens* (unidentified Greek label 1983)★★★, *Undecided* (B.L.U.E.S. R&B 1986)★★★, *Lay It On 'Em Girls* (Delmark 1993)★★★, *Crying* (CMA Music Production 1994)★★★.

BIG TOWN PLAYBOYS

Often cited as 'the best R&B revival band in Britain', the Playboys were inspired by the increasing interest in R&B that occurred in the late 70s. Originally from the west Midlands, their popularity has survived personnel changes, although pianist and vocalist Mike

Sanchez, whose style is clearly based on that of Amos Milburn, is the obvious frontman. Ex-Savoy Brown and Chicken Shack bassist Andy Sylvester and former leader Ricky Cool were also important figures in the band's history, although the latter left in the 80s. With a large repertoire of 50s R&B songs, a swinging rhythm section and excellent horns, the band are often called on to back visiting Americans, including Little Willie Littlefield, Jimmy Nelson, and Champion Jack Dupree (they recorded with the latter in 1989). By the mid-90s the band had become a permanent fixture on the UK blues circuit and in their own special niche they are unbeatable. The line-up of the band is completed by Steve Walwyn (guitar), Ian Jennings (bass), Mark Morgan (drums), Nick Lunt (saxophone) and Frank Mead (saxophone). They are one of the few bands whose live recordings translate well onto CD and their double set *Off The Clock Live* is highly recommended.

● ALBUMS: *Playboy Boogie* (Spindrift 1985)★★, *Now Appearing* (Blue Horizon/Ace 1990)★★★, *Hip Joint* (Ace 1996)★★★, *Off The Clock Live* (BT 1997)★★★★.

BIG TWIST AND THE MELLOW FELLOW

Big Twist (b. Larry Nolan, 23 September 1937, Terra Haute, Indiana, USA, d. 14 March 1990, Broadview, Illinois, USA) was the lead singer and leader of this R&B big band. He began singing in church in southern Illinois when he was six years old, and in the 50s was drummer and vocalist with the Mellow Fellows, an R&B group. In the early 70s he teamed with guitarist Pete Special and tenor saxophonist Terry Ogolini, and the group had albums released by Flying Fish and Alligator. Their work revealed an approach and breadth of repertoire (including blues, R&B and soul) that was ahead of its time. Big Twist died of a heart attack in 1990, but the group continued, fronted by singer Martin Allbritton from Carbondale, Illinois, and saxophonist-producer Gene Barge on vocals.

● ALBUMS: *Big Twist And The Mellow Fellows* (1980)★★★, with Big Twist *Playing For Keeps* (Alligator 1983)★★★, *One Track Mind* (Red Lightnin' 1982)★★★, *Live From Chicago - Bigger Than Life* (Alligator 1987)★★★, with Martin Allbritton *Street Party* (1990)★★★.

BIGEOU, ESTHER

b. *c.*1895, New Orleans, Louisiana, USA, d. *c.*1935, New Orleans, Louisiana, USA. The light-voiced Esther Bigeou performed and danced in black revues from 1917-30, recording 17 songs for OKeh Records between 1921 and 1923. They are all blues songs, composed by black Tin Pan Alley writers such as W.C. Handy, Richard M. Jones and Clarence Williams, backed by piano or small jazz bands, and typical of the material offered to black theatre audiences of the day. It has not been possible to reconcile a report that she recorded after 1943 with her alleged date of death being 1935.

● COMPILATIONS: *Esther Bigeou* (1991)★★★.

BIHARI BROTHERS

The Bihari family moved in 1941 from Oklahoma to Los Angeles where eldest brother Jules went into business as a supplier and operator of juke-boxes for the black community. The next step was to ensure the supply of suitable blues and R&B recordings to feed the juke-boxes and with Joe and Saul, he founded the Modern Music Company in 1945. As well as recording west coast artists such as Jimmy Witherspoon and Johnny Moore's Three Blazers, the brothers worked with local producers in Houston, Detroit and Memphis who supplied Modern with more rough-hewn blues material by such artists as Lightnin' Hopkins, John Lee Hooker and B.B. King. In 1951, the fourth brother, Lester, set up the Meteor label in Memphis. Meteor was responsible for some of Elmore James's earliest records as well as rockabilly by Charlie Feathers. Other Modern group labels included RPM (for which Ike Turner produced Howlin' Wolf), Blues & Rhythm and Flair. During the early 50s, the Bihari brothers released a wide range of material, even aiming at the pop charts by covering R&B titles from other labels. Among its successes were Etta James's 'Wallflower', 'Stranded In The Jungle' by the Cadets, 'Eddie My Love' by the Teen Queens and Jessie Belvin's 'Goodnight My Love'. The arranger/producer of many Modern tracks was Maxwell Davis. However, by the late 50s, the Modern group turned its attention towards reissuing material on the Crown budget-price label which also included a series of big-band tribute albums masterminded by Davis. After the company found itself in financial difficulties the Biharis released recordings by Z.Z. Hill, Lowell Fulson and B.B. King on the Kent label, but the death of Saul Bihari in 1975 and Joe's departure from the company led to a virtual cessation of recording, and the remaining brothers concentrated on custom pressing at their vinyl record plant. In 1984, the year of Jules Bihari's death, the family sold the catalogues of Modern, Flair, Kent, Crown and RPM. Seven years later, the labels passed into the hands of a consortium of Virgin Records (USA), Ace (Europe) and Blues Interactions (Japan). These companies continued an extensive reissue programme which the Ace label had initiated as licensee of the Modern group in the early 80s.

BISHOP, ELVIN

b. 21 October 1942, Tulsa, Oklahoma, USA. Bishop moved to Chicago in his teens to study at university. An aspiring guitarist, he became one of several young white musicians to frequent the city's blues clubs and in 1965 he joined the house band at one such establishment, Big John's. This group subsequently became known as the Paul Butterfield Blues Band, and although initially overshadowed by guitarist Michael Bloomfield, it was here that Bishop evolved a distinctive, if composite style. Bishop was featured on four Butterfield albums, but he left the group in 1968 following the release of *In My Own Dream*. By the following year he was domiciled in San Francisco, where his own group became a popular live fixture. Bishop was initially signed to Bill Graham's Fillmore label, but these and other early recordings achieved only local success. In 1974, Richard 'Dickie' Betts of the Allman Brothers Band introduced the guitarist to Capricorn Records which favoured the hippie/hillbilly image Bishop had nurtured and investigated his mélange of R&B, soul and country influences. Six albums followed, including *Let It Flow*, *Juke Joint Jump* and a live album set, *Live! Raisin' Hell*, but it was a 1975 release, *Struttin' My Stuff*, which proved most popular. It included the memorable 'Fooled Around And Fell In Love' which, when issued as a single, reached number 3 in the US chart. The featured voice was that of Mickey Thomas, who later left the group for a solo career and subsequently became frontman of Jefferson Starship.

The loss of this powerful singer undermined Bishop's momentum and his new-found ascendancy proved short-lived. Bishop's career suffered a further setback in 1979 when Capricorn filed for bankruptcy. Although he remains a much-loved figure in the Bay Area live circuit, the guitarist's recorded output has been thin on the ground during the last ten years; he has appeared recently on the Alligator label with Dr. John on *Big Fun* and *Ace In The Hole*.

● ALBUMS: *The Elvin Bishop Group* (Fillmore 1969)★★, *Feel It* (Fillmore 1970)★★, *Rock My Soul* (Fillmore 1972)★★, *Let It Flow* (Capricorn 1974)★★★, *Juke Joint Jump* (Capricorn 1975)★★★, *Struttin' My Stuff* (Capricorn 1975)★★★★, *Hometown Boy Makes Good!* (Capricorn 1976)★★, *Live! Raisin' Hell* (Capricorn 1977)★★★, *Hog Heaven* (Capricorn 1978)★★★, *Is You Is Or Is You Ain't My Baby* (Line 1982)★★, *Big Fun* (Alligator 1988)★★★, *Don't Let The Bossman Get You Down* (Alligator 1991)★★★, *Ace In The Hole* (Alligator 1995)★★★.

● COMPILATIONS: *The Best Of Elvin Bishop: Crabshaw Rising* (Epic 1972)★★, *Tulsa Shuffle: The Best Of ...* (Columbia 1994)★★★★.

BLACK ACE

b. Babe Kyro Lemon Turner, 21 December 1907, Hughes Springs, Texas, USA, d. 7 November 1972, Fort Worth, Texas, USA. Black Ace was a blues guitarist from childhood, but his mature style developed after he moved to Shreveport in the mid-30s and met Oscar Woods. In 1937 he recorded six superb blues for Decca, singing in his deep voice and playing fluent, complex slide guitar, his steel-bodied instrument held across his lap and fretted with a small bottle. Ace was a frequent broadcaster on local radio, and made an appearance in the 1941 film *Blood Of Jesus*, but after Army service from 1943, he largely abandoned music; when rediscovered in 1960, however, he had retained all his abilities, and recorded a splendid album.

● ALBUMS: *Black Ace* (Arhoolie 1961)★★★.

● COMPILATIONS: *Texas In The Thirties* (1988)★★★.

BLACK BOB

This pianist was an accompanist on hundreds of blues records in the 30s, mainly for Bluebird, backing Big Bill Broonzy, Jazz Gillum, Tampa Red, Lil Johnson, Washboard Sam and many others. His identity was the subject of years of speculation, for it seemed absurd that the possessor of such a prodigious stride and blues technique should be completely anonymous. Circumstantial evidence suggested that his true name was Bob Alexander, but his immediately recognizable style, percussive yet sparkling and melodious, is very similar to that on an unissued test by Bob Hudson; furthermore, Memphis Slim, when asked if he had known a Bob Hudson, replied, 'Yeah. We called him Black Bob.'

BLACK BOY SHINE

b. Harold Holiday, he was one of what has come to be known as the 'Santa Fe' school of pianists, a loose group of blues artists who played the barrel-houses of south-east Texas in the pre-war years. He recorded in the mid-30s for the Vocalion label, demonstrating a warm singing voice, complemented by a light, rolling, but nevertheless, highly skilful piano style, and the lyrics of his songs, such as 'Brown House Blues', described very evocatively the places to which he had travelled and where he had played. As well as recording on his own, he shared one session with fellow Texans Howlin' Smith and Moanin' Bernice Edwards, although only a few of their tracks were issued.

● COMPILATIONS: *Black Shine Boy* (1989)★★★.

BLACK IVORY KING

b. David Alexander, c.1910, USA. A recording session in Dallas, Texas, in 1937 revealed a reflective pianist and singer, with a simple, direct style related to that of the 'Santa Fe' school, which included Conish 'Pinetop' Burkes and Black Boy Shine. His version seems to be the original of the classic Texas train blues 'Flying Crow', which poeticizes the timetable of a journey from Port Arthur to Kansas City. A topical updating of 'Red Cross Store Blues' into 'Working For The PWA' has a wistful lyricism.

● COMPILATIONS: *The Piano Blues Vol. 11, Texas Santa Fe* (1979), *Texas Piano Styles* (1989), *Running Wild* (HTD Records 1995).

BLACKWELL, FRANCIS HILLMAN 'SCRAPPER'

b. 21 February 1903, North Carolina, USA, d. 7 October 1962, Indianapolis, Indiana. Blackwell was one of the most brilliantly innovative guitarists to work in the blues idiom and his unique style defies categorization, being of a quality close to jazz. He was of Cherokee Indian descent and one of 16 children born to Payton and Elizabeth Blackwell. The details of his childhood are confused but it is known that he was taken to Indianapolis in 1906, and inherited his father's interest in music (Payton was a fiddler). Self-taught on guitar and piano, he began to work as a part-time musician during his teenage years, sometimes straying as far as Chicago but always returning to Indianapolis. In the course of his career he recorded many satisfying and impressive blues guitar solos under his own name, but gained his greatest fame in the company of Leroy Carr. Their piano/guitar duets in support of Carr's warm vocals set the standard for all such combinations throughout the 30s. 'Scrapper' is reported to have been a somewhat difficult and withdrawn man, and his partnership with Carr was sometimes rocky. However, on Carr's death from alcoholism in 1935, Blackwell recorded a tribute to his 'old pal' and largely dropped out of sight. Rediscovered in the late 50s, his new recordings showed that his mastery of the guitar had not diminished, while his blues had become more personal and intense. He was shot by an unknown assassin in 1962.

● COMPILATIONS: *Scrapper's Blues* (Ace 1988)★★★, *The Virtuoso Guitar Of Scrapper Blackwell* (Yazoo 1988)★★★.

BLACKWELL, WILLIE '61'

b. c.1898, USA. Blackwell spent much of his life in Memphis, where he still resided as late as the 70s. Among his early associates were Calvin Frazier (who was reputedly his nephew), step-son Robert Jnr. Lockwood and Robert Johnson. Another musician with whom Blackwell worked in Detroit was Baby Boy Warren. Blackwell was not a particularly inventive musician, but his circle paid keen attention to his original lyrics, and the eight songs he recorded for Bluebird in 1941 (together with two cut for the Library of Congress the following year) are the work of one of the most inventive lyricists in blues. No other singer reflects that hitching a ride would be easier if he knew Masonic hailing signs, or sees World War II as a chance to send his baby son 'a Jap's tooth' to help ease the process of teething! Blackwell was a truly eccentric and unique artist.

● COMPILATIONS: *Walking Blues* (1979)★★★, *Mississippi Country Blues Vol. 2* (1987)★★★.

BLANCHARD, EDGAR

A guitarist and bandleader, Blanchard was a permanent feature of the New Orleans music scene from the 40s to the 60s. By 1947 he was in charge of the resident band at the Down Beat Club on Rampart Street with Roy Brown as one of the vocalists. Blanchard's most well-known band was the Gondoliers. An early version had a two-guitar line-up with Ernest McLean, while in the 60s, the group included Dimes Dupont (alto saxophone), Alonzo Stewart (drums), Frank Fields (bass) and Lawrence Cotton (piano). The band was renowned for its stylistic versatility. Although he frequently played on sessions, Blanchard seldom recorded under his own name. There were singles for Peacock in 1949 and instrumentals for Specialty in the late 50s, including 'Mr Bumps', a tribute to the label's head of A&R, Robert 'Bumps' Blackwell, on which Blanchard duetted with guitarist Roy Montrell. In 1959 he recorded 'Knocked Out' for Johnny Vincent's Ric label, of which he was briefly musical director. His final records were somewhat uncharacteristic raucous blues tracks such as 'Tight Like That'. Made for Joe Banashak's Minit label in the late 60s, they remained unissued until after Blanchard's death in September 1972.

BLAND, BOBBY

b. Robert Calvin Bland, 27 January 1930, Rosemark, Tennessee, USA. Having moved to Memphis with his mother, Bobby 'Blue' Bland started singing with local gospel groups, including the Miniatures. Eager to expand his interests, he began frequenting the city's infamous Beale Street where he became associated with an *ad hoc* circle of aspiring musicians, named, not unnaturally, the Beale Streeters. Bland's recordings from the early 50s show him striving for individuality, but his progress was halted by a stint in the US Army. When the singer returned to Memphis in 1954 he found several of his former associates, including Johnny Ace, enjoying considerable success, while Bland's recording label, Duke, had been sold to Houston entrepreneur Don Robey. In 1956 Bland began touring with 'Little' Junior Parker. Initially, he doubled as valet and driver, a role he reportedly performed for B.B. King, but simultaneously began asserting his characteristic vocal style. Melodic big-band blues singles, including 'Farther Up The Road' (1957) and 'Little Boy Blue' (1958), reached the US R&B Top 10, but Bland's vocal talent was most clearly heard on a series of superb early 60s releases, including 'Cry Cry Cry', 'I Pity The Fool' and the sparkling 'Turn On Your Lovelight', which was destined to become a much-covered standard. Despite credits to the contrary, many such classic works were written by Joe Scott, the artist's bandleader and arranger.

Bland continued to enjoy a consistent run of R&B chart entries throughout the mid-60s but his recorded work was nonetheless eclipsed by a younger generation of performers. Financial pressures forced the break-up of the group in 1968, and his relationship with Scott, who died in 1979, was irrevocably severed. Nonetheless, depressed and increasingly dependent on alcohol, Bland weathered this unhappy period. In 1971, his record company, Duke, was sold to the larger ABC Records group, resulting in several contemporary blues/soul albums including *His California Album* and *Dreamer*. Subsequent attempts at pushing the artist towards the disco market were unsuccessful, but a 1983 release, *Here We Go Again*, provided a commercial lifeline. Two years later Bland was signed by Malaco Records, specialists in traditional southern black music, who offered a sympathetic environment. One of the finest singers in post-war blues, Bobby Bland has failed to win the popular acclaim his influence and talent perhaps deserve.

● ALBUMS: with 'Little' Junior Parker *Blues Consolidated* (1958)★★★, with Parker *Barefoot Rock And You Got Me* (1960)★★★, *Two Steps From The Blues* (Duke 1961)★★★★, *Here's The Man* (Duke 1962)★★★★, *Call On Me* (Duke 1963)★★★, *Ain't Nothin' You Can Do* (Duke 1964)★★★, *The Soul Of The Man* (Duke

1966)★★★, *Touch Of The Blues* (Duke 1967)★★, *Spotlighting The Man* (Duke 1968)★★, *His California Album* (ABC 1973)★★, *Dreamer* (ABC 1974)★★, with B.B. King *Together For The First Time - Live* (MCA 1974)★★★★, with King *Together Again - Live* (MCA 1976)★★★, *Get On Down* (ABC 1975)★★, *Reflections In Blue* (MCA 1977)★★, *Come Fly With Me* (ABC 1978)★★, *I Feel Good I Feel Fine* (MCA 1979)★★, *Sweet Vibrations* (MCA 1980)★★, *You Got Me Loving You* (MCA 1981)★★, *Try Me, I'm Real* (MCA 1981)★★, *Here We Go Again* (MCA 1982)★★, *Tell Mr. Bland* (MCA 1983)★★, *Members Only* (Malaco 1985)★★, *After All* (Malaco 1986)★★, *Blues You Can Use* (Malaco 1987)★★, *Midnight Run* (Malaco 1989)★★★, *Portrait Of The Blues* (Malaco 1991)★★★, *Sad Street* (Malaco 1995)★★★.

● COMPILATIONS: *The Best Of Bobby Bland* (Duke 1967)★★★★, *The Best Of Bobby Bland Vol. 2* (Duke 1968)★★★★, *Introspective Of The Early Years* (MCA 1974)★★★, *Woke Up Screaming* (Ace 1981)★★★, *The Best Of Bobby Bland* (ABC 1982)★★★, *Foolin' With The Blues* (Charly 1983)★★★, *Blues In The Night* (Ace 1985)★★★, *The Soulful Side Of Bobby Bland* (Kent 1986)★★, *First Class Blues* (Malaco 1987)★★★, *Soul With A Flavour 1959-1984* (Charly 1988)★★★, *The '3B' Blues Boy: The Blues Years 1952-59* (Ace 1991)★★★★, *The Voice: Duke Recordings 1959-1969* (Ace 1992)★★★★, *I Pity The Fool: The Duke Recordings Vol. 1* (1993)★★★, *That Did It! The Duke Recordings Vol 3* (MCA 1996)★★★.

BLIND BLAKE

b. Arthur Blake (or possibly Phelps), 1890s, Jacksonville, Florida, USA, d. *c.*1933. One of the very finest of pre-war blues guitarists, Blind Blake is nevertheless a very obscure figure. Almost nothing is known of his early years, but it is reputed that he moved around the east coast states of the USA, as various musicians have recalled meeting him in a number of different locations. It seems likely, however, that he settled in Chicago in the 20s, and it was there that he first recorded for Paramount Records in 1926. Along with Blind Lemon Jefferson he was one of the first black guitarists to make a commercially successful record. Following his first hit, the ragtime guitar solo 'West Coast Blues', he recorded

regularly, producing about 80 issued tracks. It has been argued that Blake should not be described as a blues artist, and indeed his songs range from straight blues, through older traditional-style items such as 'Georgia Bound', to vaudeville numbers such as 'He's In The Jailhouse Now'. Whatever the idiom, his accompaniment was always a model of taste, skill and creative imagination - his notes cleanly picked and ringing, his rhythms steady. His musical talents are perhaps given fullest rein on the stunningly dextrous ragtime solos such as 'Southern Rag' and 'Blind Arthur's Breakdown'. Further superb Blake accompaniments can be heard on the records of other artists such as Ma Rainey and Irene Scruggs, and there is one very memorable duet with Charlie Spand, 'Hastings Street'. As well as his many solo records, he occasionally appeared with a small band. It is likely that he died soon after the demise of Paramount Records in the early 30s, but his influence lived on in the work of eastern artists such as Blind Boy Fuller and others.

● COMPILATIONS: *Ragtime Guitar's Foremost Fingerpicker* (Yazoo 1985)★★★, *The Best Of Blind Blake* (Wolf 1995)★★★, *The Master Of Ragtime Guitar: The Essential Recordings Of Blind Blake* (Indigo 1996)★★★.

BLIND BOY FULLER

b. Fulton Allen, 1908, Wadesboro, North Carolina, USA, d. 13 February 1941. One of a large family, Fuller learned to play the guitar as a child and had begun a life as a transient singer when he was blinded, either through disease or when lye water was thrown in his face. By the late 20s he was well known throughout North Carolina and Virginia, playing and singing at county fairs, tobacco farms and on street corners. At one time he worked with two other blind singers, Sonny Terry and Gary Davis. Among his most popular numbers were 'Rattlesnakin' Daddy', 'Jitterbug Rag' (on which he demonstrated his guitar technique) and the bawdy 'What's That Smells Like Fish?' (later adapted by Hot Tuna as 'Keep On Truckin'') and 'Get Your Yas Yas Out'. At one point in his career he was teamed with Brownie McGhee. In 1940 in Chicago, Fuller's style had become gloomy, as can be heard on 'When You Are Gone'. Hospitalized for a kidney operation, Fuller contracted blood poisoning and died on 13 February 1941. One of the foremost exponents of the Piedmont blues style, there was a strong folk element in Fuller's work. The manner in which he absorbed and recreated stylistic patterns of other blues forms made him an important link between the earlier classic country blues and the later urbanized forms. Among the singers he influenced were Buddy Moss, Floyd Council, Ralph Willis and Richard 'Little Boy Fuller' Trice. (Shortly after Fuller's death Brownie McGhee was recorded under the name Blind Boy Fuller No. 2.)

● COMPILATIONS: *On Down* 1937-40 recordings (Magpie 1979)★★★, *Truckin' My Blues Away* (Yazoo 1979)★★★, *Blind Boy Fuller* 1935-40 recordings (Best Of Blues 1988)★★★, *Blind Boy Fuller And Brownie McGhee* 1936-41 recordings (Flyright 1989)★★★, *East Coast Piedmont Style* 1935-39 recordings (Columbia Legacy 1991)★★★, *I Brought Him With Me* (House Of Blues 1995)★★★, *Get Your Yas Yas Out: The Essential Recordings* (Indigo 1996)★★★.

BLOCK, RORY

b. 6 November 1949, Greenwich Village, New York, USA. American blues singer and guitarist, raised in New York. Her father played classical violin, but at the age of 10, Block started learning to play folk music on the guitar. She later became involved in the burgeoning Greenwich Village folk scene. It was as a teenager that she first heard the blues, and went on to play with such names as Rev. Gary Davis and Mississippi John Hurt; meeting up with Stefan Grossman when she was 13 further encouraged her interest in the music. However, she took a 10-year break to raise her family, and only returned to music in 1975, when she recorded tracks on the small Blue Goose label for an album entitled *Rory Block (I'm In Love)*. This album was re-released in 1989 in a remixed version that omitted two tracks from the original recordings, but included an extra song, 'Blues Again', discovered on the original master tapes. Her first release for Rounder records, *High Heeled Blues*, was co-produced with John Sebastian. She continued in the same vein of recording and performing traditional blues and country blues material alongside her own compositions. The recording of *I've Got A Rock In My* *Sock* featured such luminaries as Taj Mahal and David Bromberg. In 1986, her 19-year-old son, Thiele, was killed in a car accident. The subsequent tribute album, *House Of Hearts*, contained 10 tracks, and all but one were Block originals. *Turning Point*, despite having a bigger production sound overall, did not detract from her earlier blues influences. *Tornado* in 1996 was her most commercial offering to date and was bolstered with some guest 'heavy friends', including Mary-Chapin Carpenter and guitarist David Lindley. Her track record speaks for itself, with her one-time apprehension that a white girl from New York might not sound authentic singing the blues, proving quite unfounded.

● ALBUMS: *Rory Block* (Blue Goose 1975)★★, *High Heeled Blues* (Rounder 1981)★★★, *Blue Horizon* (Rounder 1983)★★★, *Rhinestones And Steel Strings* (Rounder 1983)★★★, *I've Got A Rock In My Sock* (Rounder 1986)★★★, *House Of Hearts* (Rounder 1987)★★★, *Turning Point* (Munich 1989)★★★, *Mama's Blues* (Rounder 1991)★★★, *Ain't I A Woman* (Rounder 1992)★★★, *Angel Of Mercy* (Rounder 1994)★★★, *When A Woman Gets The Blues* (Rounder 1995)★★, *Women In (E)Motion Festival* (Indigo/Tradition & Moderne 1995)★★★, *Tornado* (Rounder 1996)★★★.

● COMPILATIONS: *Best Blues And Originals* (Rounder 1988)★★★★.

BLOOMFIELD, MIKE

b. 28 July 1944, Chicago, Illinois, USA, d. 15 February 1981. For many, both critics and fans, Bloomfield was the finest white blues guitarist America has so far produced. Although signed to Columbia Records in 1964 as the Group (with Charlie Musslewhite and Nick Gravenites), it was his emergence in 1965 as the young, shy guitarist in the Paul Butterfield Blues Band that brought him to public attention. He astonished those viewers who had watched black blues guitarists spend a lifetime trying, but failing, to play with as much fluidity and feeling as Bloomfield. That same year he was an important part of musical history, when folk purists accused Bob Dylan of committing artistic suicide at the Newport Folk Festival. Bloomfield was his lead electric guitarist at that event, and again later on Dylan's 60s masterpiece *Highway 61 Revisited*..

On leaving Butterfield in 1967 he immediately formed the seminal Electric Flag, although he left before the first album's subsequent decline in popularity. His 1968 album *Super Session*, with Stephen Stills and Al Kooper, became his biggest-selling record. It led to a short but financially lucrative career with Kooper. The track 'Stop' on the album epitomized Bloomfield's style: clean, crisp, sparse and emotional. The long sustained notes were produced by bending the string with his fingers underneath the other strings so as not to affect the tuning. It was five years before his next satisfying work appeared, *Triumvirate*, with John Paul Hammond and Dr. John (Mac Rebennack), and following this, Bloomfield became a virtual recluse. Subsequent albums were distributed on small labels and did not gain national distribution. Plagued with a long-standing drug habit he occasionally supplemented his income by scoring music for pornographic movies. He also wrote three film music soundtracks, *The Trip* (1967), *Medium Cool* (1969) and *Steelyard Blues* (1973). Additionally, he taught music at Stanford University in San Francisco, wrote advertising jingles and was an adviser to *Guitar Player* magazine. Bloomfield avoided the limelight, possibly because of his insomnia while touring, but mainly because of his perception of what he felt an audience wanted: 'Playing in front of strangers leads to idolatry, and idolatry is dangerous because the audience has a preconception of you, even though you cannot get a conception of them'. In 1975 he was cajoled into forming the 'supergroup' KGB with Ric Grech, Barry Goldberg and Carmine Appice. The album was an unmitigated disaster and Bloomfield resorted to playing mostly acoustic music. He had an extraordinarily prolific year in 1977, when he released five albums, the most notable being the critically acclaimed *If You Love These Blues, Play 'Em As You Please*, released through *Guitar Player* magazine. A second burst of activity occurred shortly before his tragic death, when another three albums' worth of material was recorded. Bloomfield was found dead in his car from a suspected accidental drug overdose, a sad end to a 'star' who had constantly avoided stardom in order to maintain his own integrity.

● ALBUMS: with Al Kooper and Stephen Stills *Super Session* (Columbia 1968)★★★, *The Live Adventures Of Mike Bloomfield And Al Kooper* (Columbia 1969)★★, *Fathers And Sons* (1969)★★, with Barry Goldberg *Two Jews Blues* (1969)★★, *It's Not Killing Me* (Columbia 1969)★★, with others *Live At Bill Graham's Fillmore West* (1969)★★, *Try It Before You Buy It* (Columbia 1973)★★, with Dr John *Triumvirate* (Columbia 1973)★★★, as KGB *KGB* (1976)★, *Bloomfield/Naftalin* (1976)★★, *Mill Valley Session* (Polydor 1976)★★★, *There's Always Another Record* (1976)★★, *I'm With You Always* (1977)★★, *If You Love These Blues, Play 'Em As You Please* (Guitar Player 1977)★★★, *Count Talent And The Originals* (1977)★★, *Analine* (Takoma 1977)★★, *Michael Bloomfield* (Takoma 1978)★★, *Mike Bloomfield And Woody Harris* (Kicking Mule 1979)★★, *Between A Hard Place And The Ground* (Takoma 1980)★★, *Livin' In The Fast Lane* (Waterhouse 1981)★★, *Gosport Duets* (1981)★★, *Red Hot And Blues* (1981)★★, *Cruisin' For A Bruisin'* (Takoma 1981)★★, *Retrospective* (1984)★★★, *Junco Partners* (1984)★★, *Blues, Gospel And Ragtime Guitar Instrumentals* (Shanachie 1994)★★★.

● COMPILATIONS: *Essential Blues 1964-1969* (Columbia Legacy 1994)★★★.

● FURTHER READING: *The Rise And Fall Of An American Guitar Hero*, Ed Ward.

BLUE HORIZON RECORDS

The Blue Horizon label was founded in February 1965 by brothers Richard and Mike Vernon. The latter was employed as an assistant producer at Decca Records' West Hampstead studio, where he worked with the Graham Bond Organisation, Champion Jack Dupree and Otis Spann. Blue Horizon was initially run from Vernon's Surrey home, in conjunction with the siblings magazine, *R&B Monthly*. The label's first single, 'Across The Board' by Hubert Sumlin, was recorded in Vernon's living room. A further 11 singles ensued, each limited to 99 copies to avoid paying purchase tax. These included material by J.B. Lenoir, Sonny Boy Williamson and Eddie Boyd. Two Blue Horizon albums followed and the Vernon's also instigated two short-lived subsidiary outlets. Purdah featured British acts, including Tony McPhee, John Mayall and Savoy Brown, whereas Outasite followed the pattern of the parent label, mixing master purchases with exclusive recordings. In

November 1969, Mike Vernon entered a national distribution deal with CBS Records. The first release by the 'new' Blue Horizon was 'I Believe My Time Ain't Long' by the recently instigated (Peter Green's) Fleetwood Mac. This innovative, blues-based group was the cornerstone of the label during its early years, providing a British number 1 single with 'Albatross' in 1969. Chicken Shack and Duster Bennett were among the other leading R&B acts signed by Vernon, but the label was of equal importance for its 'Post-war Blues' series, which featured seminal releases by Otis Rush, Magic Sam, B.B. King, Slim Harpo and Lightnin' Slim. Fleetwood Mac left Blue Horizon in 1969, prompting CBS, who sensed the end of the blues-boom, to drop the label the following year. Vernon immediately secured another deal with Polydor Records, but despite continuing the admirable practice of issuing long-lost recordings, Blue Horizon found greater success with contemporary, progressive-styled acts, notably Focus and Jellybread. The label ceased operating in 1972; successful releases were transferred to the parent distributor while the remaining titles were deleted. Vernon then became a highly successful producer, creating hits with the Olympic Runners, Level 42, Bloodstone and Dexys Midnight Runners. However, in 1988 he reactivated Blue Horizon with releases by Dana Gillespie, Lazy Lester, Blues'n'Trouble and the DeLuxe Blues Band.

● COMPILATIONS: *The Blue Horizon Story* 3-CD set (Columbia 1997)★★★★.

BLUE, 'LITTLE' JOE

b. Joseph Valery, b. 23 September 1934, Vicksburg, Mississippi, USA, d. 22 April 1990. Brought up in Tallulah, Louisiana, Blue moved to Detroit in 1951, obtaining work in the car plants. He was drafted into the army in 1954 and served two and a half years in Korea. On his return, having always been attentive to the blues, Joe moved into the music business. He had many singles released on a variety of labels but made his first real impression when 'Dirty Work Going On' was released on Chess in 1966. Subsequently he had albums issued on the Jewel and Space labels before his final two albums appeared on Evejim. 'Dirty Work Going On' was particularly well received. Often judged, unfairly, to be a B.B. King imitator Joe Blue stuck closer to the basics than did his model, and many felt that he pointed to the way B.B. should have gone. Throughout his career on record he made a habit of re-recording certain numbers, as if convinced that he could always improve them. He toured constantly, until just days before his death from cancer.

● ALBUMS: *Blue's Blues* (Charly 1987)★★★, *Dirty Work Going On* (1987)★★★, *I'm Doing All Right Again* (Evejim 1989)★★★.

● VIDEOS: *Devil Got My Woman* (Vestapol Videos 1996).

BLUES, THE

It starts with the sound, the totality of the performance - a sound so unlike anything else that it fascinates from the first hearing, stirring recognition and a sympathy the listener did not know he possessed. The words do not register at first, not, at least, on a conscious level, but the emotion does. The message is often simple, so simple that gradations of meaning only become apparent after the initial intrigue has subsided. The emotion can be palpable, so much so that when set alongside other forms of music, it seems as histrionic as grand opera. You have discovered the blues.

What is the blues? From the title of his autobiography, *I Am The Blues*, the answer ought to be Willie Dixon. And in one sense, that is true. As a studio musician and session supervisor for Chess Records and other Chicago blues labels during the 50s and 60s, Dixon wrote for, and worked with, Muddy Waters, Howlin' Wolf, Otis Rush, Buddy Guy and Little Walter, to name but the most well-known of the city's teeming blues talent. With an ear for assonance that marked the best of his compositions, Dixon averred, 'the blues are the roots and the other musics are the fruits'. Add to that Muddy Waters' 'The Blues Had A Baby And They Called It Rock 'n' Roll', and surely the point is made.

Brownie McGhee also put it succinctly: 'Blues is not a dream. Blues is truth.' John Lee Hooker, interviewed long before his elevation to Grand (and Wealthy) Old Man Of The Blues, said, 'It has more feeling than other music. When I sing these songs I feel them down deep and reach you down deep.' The recently deceased Johnny Shines, an eloquent, if not always grammatical apologist for the blues, was as apposite as McGhee, 'The blues are not wrote; the blues are lived'.

Most appropriately for the status of the blues today, J.B. Hutto delivered this visionary thought: 'The blues will never die because it's the original thing. It's coming back up from where they tried to stomp it down; it's coming back up again and it's gonna get better. Blues will be blues until the world ends.' But just what is the blues?

The blues is both music and the feeling that inspires it. Many scholarly treatises have faltered at the need to be specific. One eminent musicologist wrote a whole book about just one composition, only to admit at its end that, because of the fluid nature of the song's various components and the random approach adopted by its performers, there was no such thing as a definitive performance. Other writers, with a specific axe to grind, subverted their wide-ranging research in order to maintain their own contentions about just one blues singer.

The blues may be truth but there is not just one. There are many truths and all of them pertinent. The clearest analogy to make about the music's origin is to note how often the same scientific discovery is made almost simultaneously in widely separated locations. Music in its many forms, like research, represents the totality of what has preceded it. There came a point in time when the creation of a new musical form within the black communities of America became an inevitability. It was almost as if the blues, like gravity or the genetic code, was just waiting to be identified.

Willie Dixon liked to place the beginning of the blues in the Garden of Eden. Others, less fanciful, pointed to the days of slavery. Booker White had been told by an ex-slave about men and women working in the fields, who would 'sing them songs so pitiful and so long'. Johnny Shines was more graphic: 'Just think of a little child standing at his mother's knee, crying "Mama, take me up". And she can't even look down at him. She's got to look the people in the eye who's gonna sell her and buy her. She can't even reach down and pick him up and nurse him. Now, those people had the blues.' However, the slaves did not know that as the term did not come into common parlance until the last decade of the 19th century, much as the music it described did not coalesce into the predominantly 12-bar format that became its most frequent setting until the first decades of the 20th century.

The story of how the blues came to be what it is, is too long and convoluted to be attempted here. The complex interaction of African and European musical traditions, the way in which European musical instruments and notation were imposed upon, or co-opted into, less formally structured African traditions, happened haphazardly over a century and a half. And, though the phrase has lost its power to impress, and has been reduced almost to cliché, the blues was born out of oppression. To be treated like beasts of burden, casually abused at every opportunity, brutalized to such a degree that family values were totally negated, it is small wonder that the oppressed resorted to a coded behaviour that bound them together and bitterly celebrated their position at the bottom of a social order that barely recognized their existence.

Then again, there were moments when such bitterness could be transcended and spirits could be lifted to exalt existence. Black churches metamorphosed the Christianity that had been imposed upon the slave community into a joyful celebration of the freedom to come. And the blues could provide temporal relief from the harsh realities of black life that not even emancipation could affect.

There were other contributory factors in the emergence of the blues at the dawn of the present century. The momentum of life changed significantly in its first two decades. The unknown was no longer just over the horizon or a day away. Systems of communication brought events in far-off cities into the daily lives of farming communities. The telephone and the telegraph brought instant awareness across the entire continent. The expansion of the railroad system enabled the population to become more mobile.

More importantly for the current narrative, acquisition of musical instruments became easier with the formation of mail-order houses such as the Sears, Roebuck Company. The means to make music, for so long the only form of passive resistance available to black people, was brought within the reach of even the poorest. Sales of guitars boomed. Mobility and portability were the order of the day.

Piano blues flourished alongside guitar blues but inevitably the piano's bulk precluded its easy transportation, making it appropriate for more permanent institutions such as gaming houses and brothels, which often amounted to the same thing. Official indifference to black life meant that such illegal establishments were condoned by the police as long as they remained in the black ghettos of major cities such as St. Louis, Chicago and, particularly, New Orleans.

The last crucial element in the development of the blues was the advent of the phonograph. Recordings of black musical traditions were sparse to begin with, although the Dinwiddie Colored Quartet recorded six single-sided discs of gospel songs in the last days of October 1902. The neon light of blues iconography points to Valentine's Day 1920 as the date on which the first blues record was made. In reality, Mamie Smith's 'That Thing Called Love' was an anodyne pop song, and even the innuendo of 'You Can't Keep A Good Man Down' on the b-side was gentle enough to be lost on those without the tuning apparatus to pick up the signal. 'Crazy Blues', which she recorded six months later, opened a floodgate that released a clutch of 'classic' female blues singers, most of whom already worked in vaudeville.

Inevitably, as 19th century minstrel shows had parodied black musical gatherings, as 'nigger' and 'coon' songs had conveniently distorted and sentimentalized white perceptions of black life, as the instrumental music from New Orleans called 'jass' had been appropriated by white musicians, the blues made its public debut as a performance art that bore only a distant resemblance to the realities that it was meant to reflect.

The dictates of commerce must always exploit the opportunities that are offered. An untapped market for 'blues' music had been identified and the recording industry targeted the black population with avaricious precision. As the 20s progressed, records by Smiths, Bessie, Clara and Mamie, Ida Cox, Lucille Hegamin and Alberta Hunter were eagerly consumed by all levels of the black community.

Companies such as OKeh, Columbia and RCA Victor were joined by a number of smaller, independent labels that were either bought up by the majors or choked off for lack of adequate distribution. In order to feed and foster their profits, the majors cast ever widening nets, sending out talent scouts to summon musicians to their studios in New York and Chicago. In this way, less formal musicians who had never graced a theatre stage had the opportunity to address a wider (and more avid) audience.

One of the first 'country' blues artists to record was Papa Charlie Jackson, who played both banjo and guitar, but favoured the former on his first 1924 releases. The banjo was in fact an American adaptation of an African instrument and, with the violin, was prevalent as the instrument of choice amongst black musicians until the ready availability of the guitar. Jackson was joined within a couple of years by such artists as Blind Blake, Blind Lemon Jefferson and Big Bill Broonzy.

As the 20s progressed, the companies' studio sessions were supplemented by mobile recording teams that criss-crossed the southern states to record musicians performing in regional styles not previously heard outside one town or community. As these records found their way into black homes across America, they sowed the seeds of familiarity that would choke the rich diversity of music that had flourished unchallenged over previous undocumented decades.

Listening to blues recordings of the 20s, that richness is immediately apparent. With even a brief acquaintance, it is possible to identify the spare, extended meters of Texas blues, the churning rhythm and bottleneck vocalization of Mississippi blues, the grace and dexterity of Piedmont blues from the east coast states.

Initially, these records sold predominantly to city dwellers who accepted the music's variety with indiscriminate taste, perhaps remembering the music of their home-town or state. Outside the cities, each artist's recordings sold mainly to the communities familiar with the individual or the style. Sales continued to rise as the 20s were coming to an end. However, even though artists received meagre one-time payments and no royalties, it was just a matter of time before recording costs could no longer be justified by sales.

The 1929 Stock Market crash not only curtailed most blues recording activity, it also created a situation that called for a standardized approach. It was a rationale that would have been imposed in due course, the failure of the money markets only hastened its arrival. As the 30s began, companies like OKeh, Decca, Bluebird and Vocalion pared down their artist rosters to proven talents such as Big Bill, Leroy Carr, Walter Davis, Lonnie Johnson, Memphis Minnie and Tampa Red. Intensive sessions took place over a number of days, with a small group of reliable studio musicians going through the motions while a parade of star names passed before the microphone.

Instead of pursuing a policy of recording little and often, artists were called upon to cut as many as 18 songs at one session. The random brilliance that had been caught a decade before was reduced to a routine proficiency that relied on nuance and contrivance rather than inspiration. In the second half of the 30s, artists like Sonny Boy Williamson and Joe Williams reconnected with the conviction that city-dwelling sophisticates had lost or expunged from their work. However, Williamson quickly acquired the veneer of professionalism, while Williams, the eternal itinerant, shuffled back to the comfort of his independence.

The 30s was also the time of the Great Migration, as farming communities of the southern states were overturned by the arrival of machinery that replaced the gangs of field hands so necessary to cotton farming. Whole families moved to the industrial north, where expanding production called for a larger workforce. Wages were not high by white standards but better than the subtle slavery of the sharecropping system.

These people entered a rigidly delineated social order, as rigorous as that of white society, that did not want to be reminded of its country origins. They wanted their music to reflect their new-found affluence and improved standard of living. It was the era of the big bands of Duke Ellington, Count Basie, Chick Webb and Jimmy Lunceford. Chicago churches vied with one another for the spectacle of their services, the size and skill of their classically trained choirs. Black communities were not necessarily imitating their white counterparts but they were trying to develop a sophistication that at least mirrored the white society of which they could never be a part. The old way of life that was celebrated in country blues had no place in black urban culture.

World War II brought a cessation to recording. War work ensured that industrial cities such as Chicago, Detroit and Pittsburgh remained financial meccas for the black workforce. When the war ended, free enterprise and a ready supply of shellac brought both black and white entrepreneurs into the record business. Men like Syd Nathan, Fred Mendelsohn, Herman Lubinsky, Leonard Chess, the Rene brothers, Art Rupe, the Messner brothers, the Biharis and the Erteguns launched King, Savoy, Exclusive, Specialty, Regal, Aladdin, Modern and Atlantic.

The formulaic fodder churned out by the major companies to replace outmoded traditions was itself no longer what the public wanted. The electric guitar, in the hands of men like T-Bone Walker and Charlie Christian, revolutionized the sound of blues and jazz. The era of the big band came to an end, large orchestras were no longer economically viable for all but the most successful units. Into the void came small six and seven piece bands, led by men such as Joe Liggins, Roy Milton and Johnny Otis, who developed a form of blues-based jump music that they called 'rhythm and blues'.

In Chicago, the sound of amplified slide guitar played by Muddy Waters brought the vitality of Mississippi Delta blues to the city. Amplified guitars and harmonicas swept through the clubs and bars of the city's South Side. Labels like Chess, Chance, Parrot, J.O.B., United and States discovered a host of talent ignored by the larger companies. Released from the straitjacket of formalized sessions, bluesmen such as J.B. Lenoir, Sunnyland Slim, Baby Face Leroy Foster, Johnny Shines, Homesick James and J.B. Hutto followed Muddy's lead.

Chess and its subsidiary, Checker, became the city's leading blues labels with a roster that included Muddy Waters, Howlin' Wolf, Little Walter, Jimmy Rogers, Eddie Boyd and Sonny Boy Williamson; add to that R&B performers like Chuck Berry, Bo Diddley, Etta James and Little Milton. Next in importance during the mid-50s was Vee Jay, with leading lights John Lee Hooker and Jimmy Reed, and a strong gospel catalogue that included the Swan Silvertone Singers and The Staple Singers.

West coast blues tended to be less dramatic. Charles Brown's blues ballads and Amos Milburn's piano boogies were at the forefront of a more relaxed form of blues that entertained rather than confronted its audiences. What country blues there was, was dominated by Lightnin' Hopkins. T-Bone Walker inspired a new generation of bandleading guitarists, including B.B. King and Gatemouth Brown.

As the music proliferated, so its individuality was narrowed down to a small number of influential figures, most of whom have already been mentioned. By the end of the 50s, the torch that T-Bone Walker had lit and B.B. King had carried around the country, was picked up by younger men including Buddy Guy, Magic Sam and Otis Rush. They, in turn, kept their eye on popular music trends, intent upon reaching a wider market place than just the diminishing blues audience. However, having been ignored and marginalized in America for four decades, in the 60s the blues became a major influence on European popular music. British musicians like John Mayall, Eric Clapton and Peter Green, and groups such as the Rolling Stones and the Yardbirds, were at the forefront of a movement that took the music back to an America in need of re-education about its own heritage.

Beginning in 1962, and continuing for a decade, package tours of bluesmen and women travelled throughout Europe. Record labels sprang up in England, France, Italy and Scandinavia to record these musicians, and supply the growing demand for both contemporary blues recordings and reissues of classic recordings from all eras of the blues' development. Blue Horizon was created by producer Mike Vernon, responsible for recording artists such as John Mayall, Savoy Brown, Curtis Jones, Champion Jack Dupree, Eddie Boyd and Otis Spann, to spotlight British blues talent, led by Fleetwood Mac and Chicken Shack, and American bands like Rod Piazza's Bacon Fat.

White Americans, such as Paul Butterfield and Mike Bloomfield, formed bands of their own, and did what they could to promote and encourage the blues among other rock bands. Veteran bluesmen such as Albert King, B.B. King, Muddy Waters and Howlin' Wolf, already heroes to the British bands, took their place alongside their young adherents at venues such as the Fillmore West in San Francisco, the Fillmore East in New York and Chicago's Kinetic Circus.

While Europe was giving the blues a new lease of life, it fell from favour in its own community. Soul music, which combined elements of the blues and mainstream popular music with gospel fervour, provided its audiences with songs that reflected their contemporary concerns in musical settings that were not constrained to reiteration of the past.

With an irony the bluesmen themselves recognized, the blues became more popular on college campuses than it was among their own people. Throughout the 70s, blues artists and their record companies tried to accommodate themselves to the parade of flamboyant musical trends consumed with ever-increasing rapidity by a clamouring public. The traditions that the blues represented were disparaged or ignored in the rush to be 'hip' or relevant. Black pride could not tolerate anything that evoked a subservient past, even though the blues was primarily a music of protest and reaction.

Into the 80s, record companies such as Alligator, Antones, Black Top, Blind Pig, Provogue and Rounder catered to a predominantly white audience with product by both black and white artists. As the decade proceeded, the blues adopted an increasingly higher profile, aided by artists such as Eric Clapton and Stevie Ray Vaughan, who appealed to both blues and rock audiences. Each man took care to use his own success to foster the careers of men like Albert Collins, Buddy Guy and Robert Cray.

Cray and Joe Louis Walker represent a generation of black musicians that includes Kenny Neal, Larry Garner and Jay Owens, who can move between musical genres with ease, developing a repertoire that simultaneously pays homage to the background of the blues while it creates a new dialogue in tune with contemporary concerns. Alongside these men are performers like Charlie Musselwhite, William Clarke, Rod Piazza and Anson Funderburgh, whose command of the blues and respect for its traditions prevent their efforts from slipping into mere pastiche. In addition, there are Terry Garland, Sonny Landreth and the late John

Campbell, all of whom have worked in a traditional blues setting but have chosen to broaden their scope with more original material.

Now, in the 90s, UK companies such as Silvertone and PointBlank are prepared to promote blues records with the same investment and commitment that in the past has been lavished on pop music. The phenomenal success of John Lee Hooker, garnering Grammy awards, gold discs and Top 20 singles in his 70s has meant that the blues is no longer being treated as a train-spotting pursuit, fit only for teenage pensioners in duffel coats. That the Blues is no longer just an American art form is a testament to its power and influence and a guarantee that, in J.B. Hutto's words, 'Blues will be blues until the world ends.'

BLUES BAND

This vastly experienced British blues-rock outfit was put together - initially 'just for fun' - in 1979 by former Manfred Mann band colleagues Paul Jones (b. Paul Pond, 24 February 1942, Portsmouth, England; vocals, harmonica) and Tom McGuinness (b. 2 December 1941, London, England; guitar). They brought in slide guitarist and singer Dave Kelly (b. 1948, London, England; ex-John Dummer Blues Band and Rocksalt), who suggested the bass player from his then-current band Wildcats, Gary Fletcher (b. London, England). On drums was McGuinness's hit-making partner from the early 70s, Hughie Flint (b. 15 March 1942, Manchester, England). Such a confluence of name players brought immediate success on the pub/club/college circuit and, despite the group's humble intentions, recordings followed. *The Official Blues Band Bootleg Album* was literally just that; inability to pay studio bills had forced them to press copies privately from a second copy tape. It sold extremely well, however, and Arista Records soon stepped in, releasing the master recording and issuing four further albums by 1983. The band had split in 1982, but re-formed three years later after a one-off charity performance. Recent releases have placed far more emphasis on original material and augur well for the future. Ex-Family drummer Rob Townsend (b. 7 July 1947, Leicester, England) replaced Flint in 1981. In the 90s the band were still regularly performing even though Jones and Kelly had substantial careers of their own. Jones has become one of the UK's leading blues/R&B broadcasters and Kelly has released a number of solo albums. The latest Blues Band venture is their version of the 'Unplugged' phenomenon, recorded not for MTV, but at the famous Snape Maltings in Aldeburgh, Suffolk. The Blues Band have such a pedigree that even the most stubborn pro-American purist accepts them. Jones alone has made an immense contribution to promoting the blues over four decades.

● ALBUMS: *The Official Blues Band Bootleg Album* (Blues Band 1980)★★★, *Ready* (Arista 1980)★★★, *Itchy Feet* (Arista 1981)★★★, *Brand Loyalty* (Arista 1982)★★★, *Bye-Bye Blues* (Arista 1983)★★★, *These Kind Of Blues* (Date 1986)★★★, *Back For More* (Arista 1989)★★★, *Fat City* (RCA 1991)★★★, *Live* (1993)★★★, *Homage* (Essential 1993)★★★, *Wire Less* (Cobalt 1995)★★★, *Juke Joint Blues* (Ichiban 1995)★★, *18 Years Old And Alive* (Cobalt 1996)★★★★.

● FURTHER READING: *Talk To Me Baby: The Story Of The Blues Band*, Roy Bainton.

BLUES PROJECT

The Blues Project was formed in New York in the mid-60s by guitarist Danny Kalb, and took its name from a compendium of acoustic musicians in which he participated. Tommy Flanders (vocals), Steve Katz (b. 9 May 1945, Brooklyn, New York, USA; guitar), Andy Kulberg b. 1944, Buffalo, New York, USA; bass, flute), Roy Blumenfeld (drums), plus Kalb, were latterly joined by Al Kooper (b. 5 February 1944, Brooklyn, New York, USA; vocals, keyboards), fresh from adding the distinctive organ on Bob Dylan's 'Like A Rolling Stone'. The sextet was quickly established as the city's leading electric blues band, a prowess demonstrated on their debut album *Live At the Cafe Au Go Go*. Flanders then left to pursue a solo career and the resultant five-piece embarked on the definitive *Projections* album. Jazz, pop and soul styles were added to their basic grasp of R&B to create an absorbing, rewarding collection, but inner tensions undermined their obvious potential. By the time *Live At The Town Hall* was issued, Kooper had left the group to form Blood, Sweat And Tears, where he was subsequently joined by

Katz. An unhappy Kalb also quit the group, but Kulberg and Blumenfeld added Richard Greene (violin), John Gregory (guitar, vocals) and Don Kretmar (bass, saxophone) for a fourth collection, *Planned Obsolescence*. The line-up owed little to the old group, and in deference to this new direction, changed their name to Seatrain. In 1971, Kalb reclaimed the erstwhile moniker and recorded two further albums with former members Flanders, Blumenfeld and Kretmar. This particular version of the band was supplanted by a reunion of the *Projections* line-up for a show in Central Park, after which the Blues Project name was abandoned. Despite their fractured history, the group is recognized as one of the leading white R&B bands of the 60s.

● ALBUMS: *Live At The Cafe Au Go-Go* (Verve/Folkways 1966)★★, *Projections* (Verve/Forecast 1967)★★★, *Live At The Town Hall* (Verve/Forecast 1967)★★★, *Planned Obsolescence* (Verve/ Forecast 1968)★★, Flanders Kalb Katz Etc (Verve Forecast 1969)★★, *Lazarus* (1971)★★, *Blues Project* (Capitol 1972)★★, *Reunion In Central Park* (One Way 1973)★★.

● COMPILATIONS: *Best Of The Blues Project* (Rhino 1989)★★★.

BOGAN, LUCILLE

b. Lucille Anderson, 1 April 1897, Amory, Mississippi, USA, d. 10 August 1948. Bogan was one of the toughest female blues singers of the pre-war era. Although not as sophisticated as Bessie Smith, she started to record as early as 1923 and never worked in a true jazz band context. Instead, she utilized a string of gifted pianists, including 'Cow Cow' Davenport, Will Ezell and, particularly, Walter Roland, or a more 'countrified' group featuring guitars and even banjos. After a wobbly first session, her voice deepened, and by 1927 she was into her stride, singing blues exclusively, often from the point of view of a street-walker. She seemed preoccupied with the latter way of life, expressing herself fluently, uncompromisingly and - during one famous session in 1936 - obscenely. Although raised as Lucille Anderson in Birmingham, Alabama, she recorded after 1933 as Bessie Jackson, producing some of her best work between then and 1935 in the company of Roland. She was married at least once, to one Nazareth Bogan, and was the mother of two children. After her own career ended, she managed Bogan's Birmingham Busters, a group organized by her son. In later life she moved to the west coast where she died of coronary sclerosis in August 1948.

● COMPILATIONS: with Walter Roland *Jook it, Jook It* (1970)★★★, *Women Won't Need No Men* (Agram 1988)★★★, with Roland *1927- 35* (1993)★★★, *Complete Recorded Works In Chronological Order Vol. 1* (Document 1995)★★★, *Complete Recorded Works In Chronological Order Vol. 2* (Document 1995)★★★, *Complete Recorded Works In Chronological Order Vol. 3* (Document 1995)★★★.

BOLLIN, A.D. 'ZUZU'

b. 5 September 1922, Frisco, Texas, USA, d. 19 October 1990, Dallas, Texas, USA. One of the legion of guitarists who embraced the innovatory style of 'T-Bone' Walker, for decades Bollin's reputation rested on two records made in Dallas for Bob Sutton's Torch label in 1951/2. He did not take up music until 1947, after service in the US Navy. He received help in his guitar technique from 'T-Bone' himself, while singing with the E.X. Brooks Band in Omaha, Nebraska. His first band, formed in 1949, included jazzmen Booker Ervin and David 'Fathead' Newman, and he also worked with Ernie Fields, Milton (Brother Bear) Thomas and Percy Mayfield. His first record, 'Why Don't You Eat Where You Slept Last Night'/'Matchbox Blues', featured Newman and Leroy Cooper, both later to work with Ray Charles. The second single, 'Stavin' Chain'/'Cry, Cry, Cry', used members of Jimmy McCracklin's band. Both records were later reissued. During the 50s, Bollin worked with Joe Morris and Jimmy Reed before retiring from music at the end of the decade. Apart from two untraced 1954 titles, Bollin did not record again until he was rediscovered in 1988 by Chuck Nevitt, and then recorded the album *Texas Bluesman*, sponsored by the Dallas Blues Society. He toured Europe in 1989 and was in the process of recording a second album at the time of his death. Two titles from these sessions were added to a reissue of the first album.

● ALBUMS: *Texas Bluesman* (Antone's 1991)★★★.

BOND, GRAHAM

b. 28 October 1937, Romford, Essex, England, d. 8 May 1974, London, England. The young Bond was adopted from a Dr Barnardo's children's home and given musical tuition at school; he has latterly become recognized as one of the main instigators of British R&B, along with Cyril Davies and Alexis Korner. His musical career began with Don Rendell's quintet in 1961 as a jazz saxophonist, followed by a stint with Korner's famous ensemble, Blues Incorporated. By the time he formed his first band in 1963 he had made the Hammond organ his main instrument, although he showcased his talent at gigs by playing both alto saxophone and organ simultaneously. The seminal Graham Bond Organisation became one of the most respected units in the UK during 1964, and boasted an impressive line-up of Ginger Baker (drums), Jack Bruce (bass) and Dick Heckstall-Smith (saxophone - replacing John McLaughlin on guitar), playing a hybrid of jazz, blues and rock that was musically and visually stunning. Bond was the first prominent musician in Britain to play a Hammond organ through a Leslie speaker cabinet, and the first to use a Mellotron. The original Organisation made two superlative and formative albums, *Sound Of '65* and *There's A Bond Between Us*. Both featured original songs mixed with interpretations, such as 'Walk On The Wild Side', 'Wade In The Water' and 'Got My Mojo Working'. Bond's own 'Have You Ever Loved A Woman' and 'Walkin' In The Park' demonstrated his songwriting ability, but despite his musicianship he was unable to find a commercially acceptable niche. The jazz fraternity regarded Bond's band as too noisy and rock-based, while the pop audience found his music complicated and too jazzy. Thirty years later the Tommy Chase Band pursued an uncannily similar musical road, now under the banner of jazz. As the British music scene changed, so the Organisation was penalized for its refusal to adapt to more conventional trends in music. Along the way, Bond had lost Baker and Bruce, who departed to form Cream, although the addition of Jon Hiseman on drums reinforced their musical pedigree. When Hiseman and Heckstall-Smith left to form Colosseum, they showed their debt to Bond by featuring 'Walkin' In The Park' on their debut album.

Disenchanted with the musical tide, Bond moved to the USA where he made two albums for the Pulsar label. Both records showed a departure from jazz and R&B, but neither fared well and Bond returned to England in 1969. The music press welcomed his reappearance, but a poorly attended Royal Albert Hall homecoming concert must have bitterly disheartened its subject. His new band, the Graham Bond Initiation, featured his wife Diane Stewart. The unlikely combination of astrological themes, R&B and public apathy doomed this promising unit. Bond started on a slow decline into drugs, depression, mental disorder and dabblings with the occult. Following a reunion with Ginger Baker in his ill-fated Airforce project, and a brief spell with the Jack Bruce Band, Bond formed a musical partnership with Pete Brown; this resulted in one album and, for a short time, had a stabilizing effect on Bond's life. Following a nervous breakdown, drug addiction and two further unsuccessful conglomerations, Bond was killed on 8 May 1974 when he fell under the wheels of a London Underground train at Finsbury Park station. Whether Graham Bond could again have reached the musical heights of his 1964 band is open to endless debate; what has been acknowledged is that he was an innovator, a lovable rogue and a major influence on British R&B.

● ALBUMS: *The Sound Of '65* (Columbia 1965)★★★★, *There's A Bond Between Us* (Columbia 1966)★★★, *Mighty Graham Bond* (Pulsar 1968)★★★, *Love Is The Law* (Pulsar 1968)★★★, - the latter two albums were repackaged as *Bond In America* (Philips 1971)★★★, *Solid Bond* (Warners 1970)★★★, *We Put The Majick On You* (Vertigo 1971)★★★, *Holy Magick* (Vertigo 1971)★★★, *Bond And Brown: Two Heads Are Better Than One* (Chapter One 1972)★★★, *This Is Graham Bond* (Philips 1978)★★★, an edited version of *Bond In America*, *The Beginnings Of Jazz-Rock* (Charly 1977)★★★, *The Graham Bond Organisation Live At Klook's Kleek* (Charly 1984)★★★.
● FURTHER READING: *The Smallest Place In The World*, Dick Heckstall-Smith. *Graham Bond; The Mighty Shadow*, Harry Shapiro.
● FILMS: *Gonks Go Beat* (1965).

BONDS, SON

b. 16 March 1906, Brownsville, Tennessee, USA, d. 31 August 1947, Dyersburg, Tennessee, USA. Unlike many of his contemporaries in the blues field, Bonds lived his whole life in the area in which he was born. By his twenties he had learned guitar, and was playing with other musicians from the same area such as Hammie Nixon and Sleepy John Estes. Between 1934 and 1941, he made several records, first for Decca and later for Bluebird, in which his down-home musical roots were tempered by the commercial blues sound of the period. At his first sessions he was accompanied by Nixon on either harmonica or jug, while at his later ones Estes supported him, a compliment he repaid. He died in 1947 as the result of an accidental gunshot wound.

● COMPILATIONS: *Complete Recordings* (1988)★★★.

BONNER, WELDON 'JUKE BOY'

b. 2 March 1932, Bellville, Texas, USA, d. 29 June 1978, Houston, Texas, USA. Like many blues singers, Bonner's first musical experiences were in singing spirituals as a child. He took up the guitar when he was about 13 years old and began to build up his experience following a move to Houston a few years later. In the mid-50s he was based on the west coast and made his first record for Bob Geddin's Irma label (issued as Juke Boy Barner), playing a driving rhythm guitar and punctuating the vocals with harmonica phrases, a combination that was to become his trademark. On his second record, for Goldband in 1960, he was billed as the One Man Trio. Following this, his musical activity was based entirely around Houston for a few years, until other titles from the Goldband sessions were issued on an album on the Storyville label in Europe. The interest this generated led to further recordings, and albums on Flyright in the UK and Arhoolie in the USA consolidated his reputation. In 1969 Bonner visited Europe. His ability to compose topical blues with thoughtful and imaginative lyrics, coupled with an expressive vocal style and self-contained instrumental accompaniments, made him highly popular with his new audience, and many tours and new recordings resulted. Unfortunately, his success was to be short-lived, and he died of cirrhosis of the liver in 1978.

● ALBUMS: *I'm Going Back To The Country* (Arhoolie 1968)★★★.
● COMPILATIONS: *Legacy Of The Blues Volume 5* (Sonet 1987)★★★, *They Call Me Juke Boy* (Ace 1989)★★★, *The Texas Blues Troubadour* (Home Cooking 1989)★★★, *Juke Boy Bonner: 1960-1967* (Flyright 1991)★★★.

BOOKBINDER, ROY

b. 5 October 1941, New York City, New York, USA. Bookbinder began playing guitar in the early 60s and was initially inspired by Dave Van Ronk. He met Rev. Gary Davis in 1968, ostensibly for guitar lessons, but was travelling with him within a month. Davis regarded Bookbinder as one of his best students. Towards the end of the 60s he recorded for a Blue Goose Records anthology, and in 1970 he made his first full album for Adelphi, dedicated to Pink Anderson, whom Bookbinder brought back into the public eye. The album was extremely well received, with most reviewers commenting on the honesty and individuality of his country blues interpretations. He continues to tour and record (currently for Rounder Records), playing old-time country and hillbilly blues.

● ALBUMS: *Travellin' Man* (Adelphi 1970)★★★★, *Goin' Back To Tampa* (Flying Fish 1971)★★★, *Bookeroo* (1988)★★★, *The Hillbilly Blues Cats* (1992)★★★, *Live Book ... Don't Start Me Talking* (Rounder 1994)★★★.

BOOKER, CHARLEY

b. 3 September 1925, Quiver Valley, near Sunflower, Mississippi, USA, d. 20 September 1989, South Bend, Indiana, USA. While some singers left Mississippi to seek wider recognition, others like Charley Booker remained, their music retaining traditions that urban sophistication expunged. Booker learned the guitar from his father, Lucius, and uncle, Andrew Shaw. Boyd Gilmore was a childhood friend. He moved to Greenville in 1947, playing in drummer Jesse 'Cleanhead' Love's band, and broadcasting over WGVM radio. In January 1952, along with Gilmore and harmonica player Houston Boines, he recorded four titles with Ike Turner, released on the Modern and Blues & Rhythm labels. 'Rabbit Blues', 'Moonrise Blues', 'No Ridin' Blues' and 'Charley's Boogie Woogie', sung in a distinctive voice with natural vibrato, revealed the influence of Charley Patton. Within a year, he recorded in Memphis for Sam Phillips, but the trenchantly rhythmic 'Walked All Night' and 'Baby I'm Coming Home' were not released until 1977. Booker moved to South Bend, Indiana, in 1953, where he remained, rarely performing, until his death in 1989.

BOOKER, JAMES

b. 17 December 1939, New Orleans, Louisiana, USA, d. 8 November 1983, New Orleans, Louisiana, USA. As an exceptionally talented child, Booker studied classical piano, but balanced his virtuosity with blues and boogie learned from Isidore 'Tuts' Washington and Edward Frank. In his early teens he appeared on radio WMRY and formed a band he called Booker Boy And The Rhythmaires. He made his first record for Imperial in 1954; 'Doin' The Hambone' and 'Thinkin' 'Bout My Baby', produced by Dave Bartholomew, led to sessions for Fats Domino, Smiley Lewis and Lloyd Price, among others. Booker made just two more singles during the 50s, 'Heavenly Angel' for Chess and 'Open The Door' for Ace. In 1959 he enrolled at Southern University to study music. A year later, he signed to Peacock and had the only hit of his career, an organ instrumental called 'Gonzo', which reached number 3 in the R&B charts. Further singles such as 'Tubby' and 'Big Nick' failed to achieve similar success. By this point, however, drugs had added to his psychological problems and his work became erratic. In 1970 he served time in Angola State Penitentiary for drug possession. His appearance at the 1975 Jazz Fest led to a recording contract for Island Records. Other records appeared sporadically but his deteriorating mental state and an inability to control his drug problem led to a fatal heart attack.

● ALBUMS: *Junco Partner* (Island/Hannibal 1975/1993)★★★, *New Orleans Piano Wizard Live!* (Rounder 1981)★★★, *Classified* (Rounder 1982)★★★, *Mr Mystery* (Sundown 1985)★★★.
● COMPILATIONS: *Spirit Of New Orleans: The Genius Of Dave Bartholomew* (EMI America 1992)★★★★, *Resurrection Of The Bayou Maharajah* (Rounder 1993)★★★, *Spiders On The Keys* (Rounder 1993)★★★.

BOOZE, BEATRICE 'BEA'

b. 23 May 1920, Baltimore, USA, d. *c*.70s. One of the few female blues guitarists, Bea Booze, aka Wee Bee, was thought to have been the discovery of pianist and talent scout Sammy Price who introduced her to Decca Records in 1942. Despite recording topical numbers such as 'Uncle Sam Come And Get Him' and 'War Rationin' Papa', it was her rendition of the standard 'See See Rider' with which she found fame. Her recording career was short-lived, although she did tour with the Andy Kirk Band in the mid-40s, make one 78 rpm record as Muriel (Bea Booze) Nicholas And Her Dixielanders for 20th Century in 1946, and recorded four tracks for Apollo in 1950. Her last known recordings were with Sammy Price in the early 60s for the Stardust label.

BOP BROTHERS

The Bop Brothers were formed in 1986 by guitarist Jon T-Bone Taylor, a graduate of the Guildhall School Of Music, London, England, whose nickname arose from the similarity of his blues playing to that of T-Bone Walker, and singer Al Eastwood. By 1987 they had been joined by saxophonist Jerry Underwood, bassist Rob Statham and drummer Sam Kelly. However, Underwood subsequently left to work with John Martyn and Kelly found work on the stage show *Ain't Misbehavin'*. Their places were taken by Dick Heckstall-Smith (saxophone, also a member of Colosseum and another graduate of Guildhall) and Louis Borenius (drums). That line-up made their debut in 1995 with *Strange News*, an album recorded at an original valve studio in Chiswick Reach, which included six Eastwood originals. The delay in its recording was attributed to various other projects, including Taylor and Borenius's work with Roogalator and as sidemen with Dana Gillespie.
● ALBUMS: *Strange News* (ABACA/Hotshot 1995)★★★.

BORUM, WILLIE

b. 4 November 1911, Memphis, Tennessee, USA, d. *c*.60s. Borum learned guitar as a child from his father and Jim Jackson, later adding harmonica, on which he learned much from Noah Lewis. He played in the streets in jug bands, and worked in Mississippi with Garfield Akers, Willie Brown and Robert Johnson. In 1934, he accompanied his fellow Memphians Hattie Hart and Allen Shaw on record for Vocalion, performing four tracks of his own that were not released. After serving in the US Army during World War II he continued to play occasionally, but had largely retired from music until a brief return when he was discovered by blues historian/producer Sam Charters in 1961. This resulted in two albums, an appearance in a documentary film, and concerts. He is reported to have died towards the end of the 60s.

● ALBUMS: *Introducing Memphis Willie B* (1961)★★★, *Hard Working Man* (1961)★★★.

BOWSER, ERBIE

b. 5 May 1918, Davila, Texas, USA, d. 15 August 1995, Austin, Texas. Like his partner, guitarist T.D. Bell, Bowser had to wait until old age to be recognized outside his home state. One of nine children, he taught himself to play the piano after his family had moved to Palestine in east Texas. He first played in public with the North Carolina Cotton Pickers and after high school, the Sunset Royal Entertainers. During World War II, he was seconded to the Special Services band and played USO shows throughout Europe and North Africa. Back in Odessa, Texas, in 1947, he was recruited to join T.D. Bell And The Cadillacs and established a long-standing friendship with the band's leader. Moving to Austin, he worked with local bands and played alongside Robert Shaw and Grey Ghost. Given their advanced years, *It's About Time* proved to be a worthy memorial to both Bell and Bowser.

● ALBUMS: *Texas Piano Professors* (Catfish 1987)★★★, *It's About Time* (Black Magic 1992)★★★.

BOY, ANDY

b. c.1906, Galveston, Texas, USA, d. USA. One of a group of Texas blues piano players that included Rob Cooper and Robert Shaw, Boy worked the seaport towns of the southern coast, including Houston and Galveston. His playing has touches of older ragtime styles as well as blues, as can be heard from his excellent accompaniments for the smooth vocals of Houston singer Joe Pullum, but his best work is the set of eight recordings he made for Bluebird in San Antonio in 1937, notably the beautiful 'Church

Street Blues'. He also accompanied Walter Cowboy Washington at the same session. He was last heard of in the 50s, in Kansas City, where he had relocated around the time of World War II.

● COMPILATIONS: *Texas Seaport 1934-1937* (1978)★★★.

BOYD, EDDIE

b. Edward Riley Boyd, 25 November 1914, Stovall, Mississippi, USA, d. 13 July 1994, Helsinki, Finland. Boyd is a half-brother of Memphis Slim and a cousin of Muddy Waters. He spent his early years on Stovall's Plantation but ran away after a dispute with an overseer. Self-taught on guitar and piano, he worked around the south during the 30s, as both 'Little Eddie' and 'Ernie' Boyd, from a base in Memphis, before settling in Chicago where he worked in a steel mill. He was active in music, performing with Waters, Johnny Shines and John Lee 'Sonny Boy' Williamson before he had his first big hit under his own name with 'Five Long Years' on the Job label in 1952. He recorded extensively for Chess Records, having successes with '24 Hours' and '3rd Degree'. He journeyed to Europe during the 'Blues Boom' of the 60s and, considering himself too assertive to live comfortably in the USA, took up residence first in Paris and later in Finland. During this period he appeared with artists as diverse as Buddy Guy and John Mayall and recorded in England, Sweden, Switzerland, Germany, France and Finland. His piano-playing was steadily functional rather than spectacular and his main strength was his ability to put together lyrics that were pithy and acidic. 'Five Long Years' has become a blues standard and features in the repertoires of many singers including Waters and B.B. King.

● ALBUMS: *Legacy Of The Blues Volume 10* (Sonet 1975)★★★, *Rattin' And Running Around* (Crown Prince 1982)★★★, *No More Of This Third Degree* (1982)★★★, *Live* (Storyville 1990)★★★.

BRACEY, ISHMON

b. 9 January 1901, Byram, Mississippi, USA, d. 12 February 1970, Jackson, Mississippi, USA. Bracey's blues had the uncompromising directness both of the aggressive youngster, and of the preacher he eventually became, with little of the melodic decoration and conscious artistry of his associate Tommy Johnson. He learned guitar from the Rev. Rubin Lacey, with whom he played. Bracey was also accompanied by Johnson and others, while performing at black social events around Jackson. It was in company with Johnson that he recorded for Victor in 1928, but they never played together on record. Bracey taking second opposition to Charley McCoy, whose mandolin-like guitar is a perfect foil to Bracey's nasal singing and unadorned guitar playing. A subsequent session for Paramount in 1930 was marred by the unsympathetic clarinet of Ernest Michall. In 1951, Bracey embraced religion and was ordained in the Baptist church; he thereafter steadfastly refused to play blues.

● COMPILATIONS: *Ishmon Bracey* (Wolf 1988)★★★.

BRANCH, BILLY

b. 3 October 1952, Chicago, Illinois, USA. In the late 60s harmonica blues player Branch played with Jimmy Walker, but he first came to public notice at a widely reported and highly controversial 'Battle Of The Harmonicas', hosted and won by Little Mac Simmons (although public opinion held that Branch was the real winner). His initial recording was backing McKinley Mitchell, and the first tracks under his own name were made for Barrelhouse Records in 1975. Branch is now widely regarded as one of the best young harmonica blues players (and a fine singer). In addition to leading the Sons Of Blues, he is an experienced session musician (with Lou Rawls, Saffire, and Johnny Winter, among others) and was part of Alligator Records' 1990 *Harp Attack!* session. Branch is also committed to teaching young people about the blues and frequently plays in schools.

● ALBUMS: with Lurrie Bell *Chicago's Young Blues Generation* (L&R 1982)★★★, *Where's My Money* (Evidence 1996)★★★, *Mississippi Flashback* (1992)★★★, *The Blues Keep Following Me Around* (Verve 1995)★★★.

BRENSTON, JACKIE

b. 15 August 1930, Clarksdale, Mississippi, USA, d. 15 December 1979, Memphis, Tennessee, USA. Credited with making the 'first' rock 'n' roll record, Brenston's career quickly reached a peak as a result and then entered a 25-year decline. He had returned from army service in 1947 and learned to play saxophone from local musician Jesse Flowers. Shortly afterwards, he met Ike Turner who was recruiting for his band, the Kings Of Rhythm. Their local fame prompted B.B. King to recommend them to Sam Phillips in Memphis. Both Turner and Brenston made singles on 5 March 1951 and both were sold to Chess Records, but it was 'Rocket 88' that became a hit, due in part to the distorted sound of Willie Kizart's guitar. Subsequent singles, including 'My Real Gone Rocket' and 'Hi-Ho Baby', failed to reproduce that sound and after two solid years of touring behind his hit, Brenston's career began to languish. He worked in Lowell Fulson's band for a couple of years and then rejoined Turner's Kings Of Rhythm, with whom he recorded two singles for Federal and, in 1961, one for Sue. Brenston recorded one last single, 'Want You To Rock Me', with Earl Hooker's band. He worked for a time in the Shakers, the band of St. Louis bassist Sid Wallace, but by then alcohol was taking hold of his life and was a contributory factor to his fatal heart attack. In an interview, he spoke his own epitaph: 'I had a hit record and no sense.'

● COMPILATIONS: *Rocket 88* (Chess 1989)★★★, with Ike Turner *Trailblazer* (Charly 1991)★★★.

BRETT MARVIN AND THE THUNDERBOLTS

This UK skiffle-cum-blues jug band act was comprised of Graham Hine (guitar, vocals), Jim Pitts (guitar, vocals, harmonica), John Lewis aka Jona Lewie (keyboards, vocals), Pete Gibson (trombone, vocals, percussion), Dave Arnott (drums) and percussionists Keith Trussell and Big John Randall. A group of teachers and pupils from Crawley, Sussex, England, banded together, little knowing that nearly thirty years later they would still be treating audiences to a unique brand of music. Their debut album aroused novelty-based interest, but the unit only enjoyed commercial success after adopting the pseudonym Terry Dactyl And The Dinosaurs. An ensuing single, 'Seaside Shuffle', reached number 2 in 1972, but the Thunderbolts reverted to their original name when subsequent releases failed to repeat its success. Lewie embarked on a solo career following the group's first break-up. Various permutations of this band continue to gig on the club scene where their brand of loose blues and R&B is hugely popular. In not compromising their music they have built a loyal following, and regularly feature onstage, in addition to regular instruments, their own bizarre inventions such as the Zobstick, the Lager Prone and the Electric Ironing Board. In 1993, with Randall now acting as their road manager, the line-up for *Boogie Street* saw the addition of Taffy Davies (vocals, piano, clarinet, mandolin) and Pete Swan (bass).

● ALBUMS: *Brett Marvin And The Thunderbolts* (Sonet 1970)★★★, *Twelve Inches Of Brett Marvin* (Sonet 1971)★★, *Best Of Friends* (Sonet 1971)★★, *Alias Terry Dactyl* (Sonet 1972)★★, *Ten Legged Friend* (Sonet 1973)★★, *Boogie Street* (Exson 1993)★★.

BREWER, 'BLIND' JAMES

b. 3 October 1921, Brookhaven, Mississippi, USA. In the early 60s much of the interest generated by the blues in Chicago was focused on the Maxwell Street open-air market, where musicians could be found playing on the sidewalk with their electric guitars plugged into extensions hired out by local home owners. 'Blind' James Brewer was, by this time, a religious singer who went on to form the Church Of God In Christ, a convocation of local preachers dedicated to working in the Maxwell Street area. Born blind, he had worked as a blues singer since his teenage years, moving from Mississippi to St. Louis before joining Arvella Gray, another well-known street singer, in Chicago. During the 'boom' years of the 60s Brewer found work on the college circuit, appeared on television and had his recorded work issued on such labels as Heritage, Flyright and Testament.

BRIM, GRACE

b. c.1924. One of the few female musicians active on the post-war Chicago blues scene, Brim appeared with her husband John Brim's group, the Gary Kings. At her first recording session in 1950, she played harmonica and sang, demonstrating a pleasant, though not especially expressive, vocal style. Later she took to the

drums, although on at least one record she also sang and played harmonica. Some records appeared under her own name, some as Mrs John Brim, but mostly she played a subordinate role on John's records, and can be heard lending very solid support on his fine topical blues, 'Tough Times', with Eddie Taylor and Jimmy Reed. She continued to play for many years, both with her husband and with other groups, and they appeared together on a single in the 70s.

● COMPILATIONS: *Chicago Slickers* (1981)★★★.

BRIM, JOHN

b. 10 April 1922, Hopkinsville, Kentucky, USA. Born on a farm, Brim played blues guitar from an early age. In the mid-40s, he relocated to Chicago, where he joined the burgeoning post-war blues scene, playing with artists such as John Lee 'Sonny Boy' Williamson, Muddy Waters and later Jimmy Reed. The tough sound of his music placed him firmly in the Chicago style of the day; his vocals were raw and convincing and his guitar-playing rough yet effective. His records, some of which featured his wife Grace Brim singing and playing drums, appeared on a variety of labels, but the best were probably the later 50s tracks, such as 'Rattlesnake' (which was based on Big Mama Thornton's 'Hound Dog' and featured the superb harmonica work of Little Walter), 'Lifetime Blues' and the topical 'Tough Times'. Brim has continued to play, issuing an interesting if rather rough single in the 70s, and a fine half-album of tough Chicago blues in the late 80s. Van Halen's cover of his classic 'Ice Cream Man' led to renewed interest in the late 70s and into the 90s.

● ALBUMS: *Whose Muddy Shoes* (1970)★★★, *Chicago Blues Sessions* (Wolf 1989)★★★, *The Ice Cream Man* (Tone-Cool 1994)★★★.

BROCK, 'BIG' GEORGE

b. Mississippi, USA. Brock's father gave him a harmonica as a Christmas present when he was aged eight. At the age of 12, he sang at a 'fish fry' and later worked in many clubs in his native state. He settled in St. Louis, Missouri, in 1953, and after playing in a club for some time, he took it over temporarily. He subsequently became a bandleader again, working with Ike

Turner, and employed Albert King as his lead guitarist. Brock refused an opportunity to record in 1963, and eventually made his first single in 1990, followed by an album on his own label later the same year. Brock describes himself as 'a low down pure blues singer', strongly influenced by Howlin' Wolf, B.B. King, Muddy Waters, Elmore James and Jimmy Reed. He is the proud possessor of a gold belt, successfully defended in numerous harmonica championships.

● ALBUMS: *Should Have Been There* (1990)★★★.

BROOKS, 'BIG' LEON

b. 19 November 1933, Rabbit Foot Farm, near Sunflower, Mississippi, USA, d. 22 January 1982, Chicago, Illinois, USA. Brooks began playing blues harmonica when he was six years old. His original inspiration was Sonny Boy 'Rice Miller' Williamson, but after moving to Chicago in the 40s he met Little Walter Jacobs, described by Brooks as 'my coach' - a fact obvious to anyone who has heard both men's music. In the 50s, brooks led his own band on a sporadic basis, and supplied accompaniment to Jimmy Rogers, Otis Rush, Robert Nighthawk, and others. He was disillusioned by the changes in the blues in the early 60s and left music until 1976, when he once again began to sing and play in Chicago's blues clubs. He died of a heart attack in 1982.

● COMPILATIONS: four tracks only *Living Chicago Blues, Volume 5* (1980).

BROOKS, HADDA

b. Hadda Hopgood, 29 October 1916, Los Angeles, California, USA. Brooks began taking piano lessons as a young child of four, later studying classical music in Los Angeles and Chicago. In 1945 record executive Jules Bihari, just establishing Modern Records, heard Brooks' playing and signed her. Her first single, 'Swinging The Boogie', was issued in 1945, and Brooks was billed as 'Queen Of The Boogie' (a film of the same name was made in 1947). The follow-up, 'Rockin' The Boogie', set the style for the rest of her career, although the many boogies she recorded - often modern arrangements of classical music such as 'Humoresque' or 'Hungarian Rhapsody No. 2' - were usually backed with fine vocal blues or ballads. Although not trained in the blues, she became

somewhat typecast as a boogie-woogie pianist, and counted Count Basie (who backed her on a single) and actor Humphrey Bogart (who cast her in a film) among her admirers. In 1951 she became the first black woman to host her own television show in California., as well as recording for London and OKeh Records. She toured with the Harlem Globetrotters in her spare time before moving to Australia for most of the 60s. In semi-retirement, she still retains a few choice engagements each year at certain Los Angeles restaurants and hotels. In recent years she has occasionally released material on the small Rob Ray, Alwin and Kim labels, but in the 90s her recorded profile was high with a distribution agreement through Virgin Records. In her 80th year she released a credible album, *Time Was When*.

● ALBUMS: including with Pete Johnson *Boogie Battle* (1977)★★★, *Queen Of The Boogie* (Oldie Blues 1984)★★★, *Romance In The Dark* (Jukebox Lil 1989)★★★, *That's My Desire* (Flair/Virgin 1994)★★★, *Time Was When* (Point Blank 1996)★★★.

BROOKS, LONNIE

b. Lee Baker Junior, 18 December 1933, Dubuisson, Louisiana, USA. Brooks took up the electric guitar while living in Port Arthur, Texas, playing as Guitar Junior with Clifton Chenier and Lonesome Sundown. His first solo record was the local hit 'Family Rules', made for Eddie Shuler's Goldband label in 1957. At this time, he also wrote and recorded 'Pick Me Up On Your Way Down' (with Barbara Lynn on backing vocals) and 'The Crawl', which was revived 30 years later by the Fabulous Thunderbirds. These tracks were reissued on a Charly album in 1984. Guitar Junior moved to Chicago in 1959, recording and touring with Jimmy Reed. He made an unsuccessful single for Mercury ('The Horse') before changing his stage name again, to Lonnie Brooks. During the 60s, Brooks performed in the Chicago area, making singles for Midas, Palos, USA and Chess, where 'Let It All Hang Out' was a local hit. In 1969, he made an album for Capitol Records but his career only began to develop when he toured Europe with Willie Mabon in 1975. There he recorded in France for Black And White and in 1978 he signed to Chicago blues label Alligator. During the 80s, Lonnie Brooks made five Alligator albums, builing up a large following on the Midwest college and club circuit, and made several trips to Europe.

● ALBUMS: *Broke And Hungry* (Capitol 1969)★★★, *Sweet Home Chicago* (1975)★★★, *Bayou Lightning* (Sonet 1979)★★★, *Turn On The Night* (Sonet 1981)★★★, *Hot Shot* (Alligator 1983)★★★, *The Crawl* (Charly 1984)★★★, *Live At Pepper's* (Black Magic 1985)★★★, *Wound Up Tight* (Alligator 1987)★★★, *Live From Chicago - Bayou Lightning Strikes* (Alligator 1988)★★★, *Satisfaction Guaranteed* (Alligator 1991)★★★, *Wound Up Tight* (Alligator 1995)★★★, *Roadhouse Blues* (Alligator 1996)★★★.

● COMPILATIONS: *Deluxe Edition* (Alligator 1997)★★★★.

BROONZY, 'BIG' BILL

b. William Lee Conley Broonzy, 26 June 1893 (or 1898), Scott, Mississippi, USA, d. 14 August 1958, Chicago, Illinois, USA. Broonzy worked as a field hand, and it was behind the mule that he first developed his unmistakable, hollering voice, with its remarkable range and flexibility. As a child he made himself a violin, and learned to play under the guidance of an uncle. For a time, he worked as a preacher, before settling finally into the secular life of the blues singer; after service in the army at the end of World War I, he moved to Chicago, where he learned to play guitar from Papa Charlie Jackson. Despite his late start as a guitarist, Broonzy quickly became proficient on the instrument, and when he first recorded in the late 20s, he was a fluent and assured accompanist in both ragtime and blues idioms. His voice retained a flavour of the countryside, in addition to his clear diction, but his playing had the up-to-date sophistication and assurance of the city dweller. The subjects of his blues, too, were those that appealed to blacks who, like him, had recently migrated to the urban north, but retained family and cultural links with the south. As such, Broonzy's music exemplifies the movement made by the blues from locally made folk music to nationally distributed, mass media entertainment. He was sometimes used as a talent scout by record companies, and was also favoured as an accompanist; up to 1942 he recorded hundreds of tracks in this capacity, as well as over 200 issued, and

many unissued, titles in his own right. His own records followed trends in black tastes; by the mid-30s they were almost always in a small-group format, with piano, and often brass or woodwind and a rhythm section, but his mellow, sustained guitar tones were always well to the fore. Despite his undoubted 'star' status - not until 1949 was it necessary to put his full name on a race record; just 'Big Bill' was enough - the questionable financial practices of the record industry meant that his income from music did not permit a full-time career as a musician until late in his life. After World War II, Broonzy had lost some of his appeal to black audiences, but by this time he had shrewdly moved his focus to the burgeoning white audience, drawn from jazz fans and the incipient folk song revival movement. He had played Carnegie Hall in 1938 (introduced as a Mississippi ploughhand!), and in 1951 was one the blues' first visitors to Europe. He recorded frequently, if from a narrowed musical base, changing his repertoire radically to emphasize well-known, older blues such as 'Trouble In Mind', blues ballads such as 'John Henry', popular songs such as 'Glory Of Love' and even protest numbers, including the witty 'When Do I Get To Be Called A Man'. He became a polished raconteur, and further developed his swinging, fluent guitar playing, although on slow numbers he sometimes became rather mannered, after the fashion of Josh White. Broonzy was greatly loved by his new audience, and revered by the younger Chicago blues singers. In 1955 he published an engaging, anecdotal autobiography, compiled by Yannick Bruynoghe from his letters. It should be noted that Broonzy had learned to write only in 1950, from students at Iowa State University, where he worked as a janitor. Broonzy was a proud, determined man, and a pivotal figure in blues, both when it was the music of black Americans, and as it became available to whites the world over. His reputation suffered after his death, as his later recordings were deemed as having pandered to white tastes. The importance of his earlier contribution to black music was not fully understood. Broonzy was an intelligent and versatile entertainer, and his immense talent was always at the service of his audience and their expectations.

● ALBUMS: *Blues Concert* (Dial 1952)★★, *Folk*

Blues (EmArcy 1954)★★★, *Big Bill Broonzy Sings* (Period 1956)★★★, *Big Bill Broonzy* (Folkways 1957)★★★★, *Country Blues* (Folkways 1957)★★★★, *Big Bill Broonzy Sings And Josh White Comes A-Visiting* (Period 1958)★★★, *Last Session Parts 1-3* (Verve 1959)★★★, *Remembering ... The Greatest Minstrel Of The Authentic Blues* (1963)★★★.
● COMPILATIONS: *The Big Bill Broonzy Story* 5-LP box set (Verve 1959)★★★★, *Memorial* (Mercury 1963)★★★★, *Remembering Big Bill Broonzy* (Mercury 1964)★★★★, *Big Bill And Sonny Boy* (1964)★★★★, *Trouble In Mind* (1965)★★★, *Big Bill's Blues* (1968)★★★★, *Big Bill's Blues* (Epic 1969)★★★, *Feelin' Low Down* (GNP Crescendo 1973)★★★, *Midnight Steppers* (Bluetime 1986)★★★, *Big Bill Broonzy Vol. 1-3* (1986-88)★★★★, *The Young Bill Broonzy 1928-1935* (Yazoo 1988)★★★★, *Sings Folk Songs* (1989)★★★★, *The 1955 London Sessions* (Sequel 1990)★★★, *Remembering Big Bill Broonzy* (Beat Goes On 1990)★★★★, *Good Time Tonight* (Columbia 1990)★★★, *Do That Guitar Rag 1928-35* (Yazoo 1992)★★★, *I Feel So Good* (Indigo 1994)★★★, *Baby Please Don't Go* (Drive Archive 1995)★★★, *Black, Brown & White* (Evidence 1995)★★★.
● FURTHER READING: *Big Bill Blues: Big Bill Broonzy's Story As Told To Yannick Bruynoghe*, Yannick Bruynoghe. *Hit The Right Lick: The Recordings Of Big Bill Broonzy*, Chris Smith.

BROSNAN, MIKE

b. 3 April 1950, Rotorua, New Zealand. Brosnan started playing piano at the age of five, before joining the Derelicts, a Shadows cover band, in the mid-60s (one fellow member, George Barris, continues to play bass with him to this day). The Derelicts later evolved into Nucleus. His first exposure to blues came when Barris played him the debut album by John Mayall's Bluesbreakers. From then on he embarked on a lifelong odyssey of blues discovery. Rev. Gary Davis and Blind Baker were his greatest influences, alongside local musician Carl Wyant whom he met after a spell in the armed forces. He has released a series of albums for his own Flying Kiwi Music Company, which are now distributed through Australian record company Shop Records. Most reveal his trademark penchant for experimentation, frequently employing outside musical influences and welding them to a blues base. His live performances also reveal this affable musician to be fond of extended storytelling breaks between songs.
● ALBUMS: *On A High Wire* (Flying Kiwi 1995)★★★.

BROWN, ANDREW

b. 25 February 1937, Jackson, Mississippi, USA, d. 11 December 1985. A very versatile musician, Brown began playing guitar as a youngster and after moving with his mother to Chicago in 1946, was influenced by Earl Hooker. In the 50s he was associated with Freddie King and Magic Sam, but he also played jazz. He was drafted into the armed services in 1956, and on his discharge settled just outside Chicago. In the mid-60s he recorded for the Four Brothers label; his singles usually coupled an excellent blues with a more commercial side, and he also wrote material for G.L. Crockett. He released a single on Brave in the early 70s, and despite health problems recorded for Alligator, Black Magic and Double Trouble in the years preceding his death from lung cancer.
● COMPILATIONS: *Living Chicago Blues Volume Five* three tracks only (1980)★★★, *Big Brown's Chicage Blues* (1982)★★★, *On The Case* (1985)★★★.

BROWN, ANGELA

b. 1953, Chicago, Illinois, USA. Brown began her musical career by singing gospel music in church and although she was aware of the blues she did not sing them until around 1980, when she played the role of 'Ma' Rainey in the stage musical. Following this, she worked in the numerous Chicago blues clubs, often accompanied by pianists Little Brother Montgomery or Erwin Helfer. Her debut recordings were released by the Red Beans label in 1983, and the first album under her own name was made in 1987 for the German label Schubert. Although she was dubbed 'the Bessie Smith of the 80s', a deserved title given her strong renditions of vaudeville blues material, her powerful voice is also well-suited to more modern blues styles. In the 90s she is a popular attraction at blues festivals all over the world.
● ALBUMS: *The Voice of Blues* (Schubert

1987)★★★, *The 2nd Burnley National Blues Festival* (1990)★★★, *Live* (Acoustic Music 1993)★★★.

BROWN, BESSIE

There were two blues singers operating during the 20s using the name Bessie Brown and biographical details are slim for both. One, known to have worked as a male impersonator and speculated to have been born around 1895 in Cleveland, Ohio, began her career on record in 1925, billed as 'The Original' Bessie Brown - probably indicating a conflict with her namesake who had issued records in the previous year. Just to confuse things further she also used the names Caroline Lee and Sadie Green, the latter also used by popular singer Vaughn De Leath. Brown was married to Clarence Shaw and appears to have retired from show business in the early 30s. Her rival worked on the TOBA circuit with her husband George W. Williams in an act that at one time included a young Fats Waller. Her career on record seems to have been restricted to a brief period on the Columbia label during 1924.
● COMPILATIONS: *Mean Mothers* (1980), *Female Blues Singers Vol. 4* (1990).

BROWN, BUSTER

b. 15 August 1911, Cordele Georgia, USA, d. 31 January 1976, Brooklyn, New York, USA. Brown played harmonica at local clubs and made a few recordings, including 'I'm Gonna Make You Happy' in 1943. Brown moved to New York in 1956 where he was discovered by Fire Records owner Bobby Robinson while working in a chicken and barbecue joint. In 1959, he recorded the archaic-sounding blues, 'Fannie Mae', whose tough harmonica riffs took it into the US Top 40. His similar-sounding 'Sugar Babe' (1961) was covered in the UK by Jimmy Powell. In later years he recorded for Checker and for numerous small labels including Serock, Gwenn and Astroscope.
● ALBUMS: *New King Of The Blues* (1959)★★★, *Get Down With Buster Brown* (1962)★★★, *Raise A Ruckus Tonite* (1976)★★★, *Good News* (Charly 1988)★★★.

BROWN, CHARLES

b. 13 September 1922, Texas City, Texas, USA. Brown's mother died only six months after he was born and he was raised by his grandparents. Despite learning piano and church organ at the insistence of his grandparents while a child, Brown became a teacher of chemistry. In 1943, living in Los Angeles, he realized that he could earn more money working as a pianist-singer. At that time, the top small group in Los Angeles was the Nat 'King' Cole Trio, but when Cole moved on, the Three Blazers, led by Johnny Moore (guitarist brother of Oscar Moore) and whom Brown had just joined, moved into the top spot. By 1946 the band was a national favourite, with hit records including 'Driftin' Blues', and appearances at New York's Apollo Theatre. In 1948 the group broke up although Moore continued to lead a band with the same name, but he was now on his own and virtually unknown as a solo performer. In the early 50s a string of successful records, many featuring his own compositions, boosted his career. Additionally, his work was recorded by such artists as B.B. King, Ray Charles, Sam Cooke, Amos Milburn and Fats Domino, with whom Brown recorded 'I'll Always Be In Love With You' and 'Please Believe Me'. He was heavily influenced by Robert Johnson, Louis Jordan, and especially by Pha Terrell, the singer with the Andy Kirk band. Brown's singing evolved into a highly melodic ballad style that still showed signs of his blues roots. In a sense he has the velvety sound of Cole, encrusted with the tough cynicism of Leroy Carr and Lonnie Johnson. Unlike Cole, Brown's star waned, although he had successful records with songs such as 'Christmas Comes But Once A Year'. One follower was Ray Charles, who modelled his early singing on Brown's and Cole's styles. By the end of the 60s Brown was working in comparative obscurity at Los Angeles nightspots. An appearance at the 1976 San Francisco Blues Festival boosted his reputation, but the pattern remained pretty much unaltered into the 80s and early 90s. He can still be found constantly touring the USA and Europe, providing superb live entertainment, backed by outstanding guitar player/musical director Danny Caron.
● ALBUMS: *Race Track Blues* (50s)★★★, *Mood Music* (Aladdin 1955)★★★★, *Driftin' Blues*

(Score 1958)★★★, *More Blues With Charles Brown* (Score 1958)★★★★, *Music, Maestro, Please* (60s)★★★, *Charles Brown Sings Million Sellers* (Imperial 1961)★★★, *Charles Brown Sings Christmas Songs* (King 1961)★★★★, *The Great Charles Brown* (King 1963)★★★, *Ballads My Way* (Mainstream 1965)★★★, *One More For The Road* (Alligator 1986)★★★, *All My Life* (Round/Bullseye 1990)★★★, *Someone To Love* (1992)★★★, *Blues And Other Love Songs* (1993)★★★, *Just A Lucky So And So* (Bullseye Blues 1994)★★★, *These Blues* (Verve 1994)★★★, *Charles Brown's Cool Christmas Blues* (Bullseye Blues 1994)★★★, *Blues N' Brown* 1971 recording (Jewel 1995)★★★, with Johnny Moore's Three Blazers *Drifting And Dreaming* (Ace 1995)★★★, *Honey Dripper* (Verve 1996)★★★★.

● COMPILATIONS: *Legend* (Bluesway 1970)★★★★, *Driftin' Blues (The Best Of Charles Brown)* (Capitol 1992)★★★, *The Complete Aladdin Recordings Of Charles Brown* (Mosaic 1994)★★★★.

BROWN, CLARENCE 'GATEMOUTH'

b. 18 April 1924, Vinton, Louisiana, USA (some sources give Orange, Texas, where he was raised from the age of three weeks). Brown's father was a musician who taught him to play guitar and fiddle, and during his youth he heard the music of Tampa Red, Bob Wills, Count Basie, and others. He toured the south as a drummer with a travelling show before being drafted into the army. On his discharge he worked as a musician in San Antonio, Texas, where he honed his guitar skills sufficiently to impress Don Robey, who offered him a spot at his club in Houston. It was here that Gatemouth's big break came, when he took over a show from T-Bone Walker, after Walker was taken ill. He was so well received that Robey took him to Los Angeles to record for the Aladdin Label on 21 August 1947. In 1948 he set up his own Peacock label, for which Brown recorded until 1961. Many of these records are classics of Texas guitar blues, and were enormously influential. During the 60s Gatemouth broadened his stylistic base to include jazz and country, best exemplified by his 1965 Chess recordings made in Nashville. These were pointers to the direction in which Brown's music was later to develop. In the 70s

he recorded a mixed bag of albums for the French Black And Blue label (including a Louis Jordan tribute set), a couple of cajun/country/rock hybrids and a good blues album for Barclay Records. In the 80s, Rounder successfully showcased Gatemouth's versatile approach by matching him with a big, brassy band, and he has also recorded for Alligator. In recent years Brown has tended to showcase his fiddle-playing to the detriment of his still excellent blues guitar picking, but he remains a fine singer and an extremely talented instrumentalist, whatever genre of music he turns his attention to. On his recent Verve recordings he has begun to put the fiddle in the background.

● ALBUMS: *The Blues Ain't Nothing* (Black And Blue 1971)★★★★, *Sings Louis Jordan* (Black And Blue 1972)★★★, *The Drifter Rides Again* (Barclay 1973)★★★, *The Bogalusa Boogie Man* (Barclay 1974)★★★, *San Antonio Ballbuster* (Red Lightnin' 1974)★★★, *Cold Strange* (Black And Blue 1977)★★★, *Blackjack* (Music Is Medicine 1977)★★★, *Double Live At The Cowboy Bar* (Music Is Medicine 1978)★★★, with Roy Clark *Makin' Music* (MCA 1979)★★★, *Alright Again* (Rounder 1981)★★★, *One More Mile* (Rounder 1983)★★★, *Atomic Energy* (Blues Boy 1983)★★★, *Pressure Cooker* 70s recording (Alligator 1985)★★★, *Texas Guitarman - Duke-Peacock Story, Vol. 1* (Ace 1986)★★★★, *Real Life* (Rounder 1987)★★★, *Texas Swing* early 80s recording (Rounder 1987)★★★, *The Nashville Session 1965* (Chess 1989)★★★, *Standing My Ground* (Alligator 1989)★★★, *No Looking Back* (Alligator 1992)★★★, *Just Got Lucky* Black And Blue recordings (Evidence 1993)★★★★, *The Man* (Gitanes Jazz/Verve 1994)★★★, *Long Way Home* (Verve 1995)★★★, *Live* 1980 recordings (Charly 1995)★★★, *Gate Swings* (Verve 1997)★★★★.

● COMPILATIONS: *The Best Of Clarence 'Gatemouth' Brown: A Blues Legend* (Verve 1995).

BROWN, DUSTY

b. 11 March 1929, Tralake, Mississippi, USA. A self-taught blues harmonica player, Brown enjoyed a certain amount of success after moving to Chicago in the 40s. He started by sitting in with artists such as Muddy Waters, but soon formed his own band. In 1955, he had a record issued on the local Parrot label (there were also other tracks that remained unissued until over 30 years later), his accompanists featuring, among others, the pianist Henry Gray. Later in the decade, he recorded for Bandera, but again there can have been little commercial success (although, again, a couple of unissued sides have appeared in subsequent years). He gave up attempting to make a living from music until the 70s, when he made a comeback, taking advantage of the renewed interest in the music, in particular from the European market.

● ALBUMS: *Hand Me Down Blues* (1990)★★★.

BROWN, GABRIEL

b. unknown date, probably Florida, USA, d. early 70s, Florida, USA. Apart from the fact that he was the first country blues artist (and one of only very few) to have been recorded in the state of Florida - and this by the Library of Congress, not a commercial record company - virtually nothing is known of the early biography of this singer and guitarist. The Library of Congress sessions were carried out by Alan Lomax and black folklorist and writer Zora Neale Hurston, and produced enough material for a very worthwhile album to be compiled in the 70s. By 1943, Brown had moved north, and was living in Asbury Park, New Jersey. From this base, he seems to have been active on the blues scene in New York and began recording in that year for Joe Davis's record company, chalking up another record by being the first country bluesman to make records in New York after the beginning of World War II. Over the next nine years, he recorded many tracks for Davis, all of which were in a down-home, country blues vein, and featuring only Brown and his guitar. His sound is distinctive, even idiosyncratic, and the material is mostly original. Sometimes, for example in 'The Jinx Is On Me', with its superstitious lyrics and bottleneck guitar accompaniment, the style points back to his southern roots, while at other times it displays an urban sophistication. Brown later returned to Florida, where he drowned in a boating accident.

● COMPILATIONS: *Out In The Cold Again* (1975)★★★, *1943-1945* (1981)★★★, *1944-1952* (Krazy Kat 1984)★★★, *Gabriel Brown And His Guitar* (Flyright 1988)★★★.

BROWN, HENRY

b. 1906, Troy, Tennessee, USA, d. 28 June 1981. Brown moved to St. Louis about 1918, and apart from army service (as a musician) in World War II, he spent his entire musical life there. His economical but highly inventive piano playing usually featured a bouncy, four to the bar chordal bass, and was heard on record both solo and behind a number of St. Louis artists in the 20s and 30s, including Mary Johnson, Alice Moore and the 'gutbucket' trombonist Ike Rodgers. He recorded a superb album in 1960 for Paul Oliver. Thereafter, he was recorded sporadically, but less successfully, until 1974. He had been in declining health for some time before his death in June 1981.

● ALBUMS: *Henry Brown Blues* (1960)★★★★, *The Blues In St. Louis* (1984)★★★.

BROWN, J.T.

b. John T. Brown, 2 April 1910, Mississippi, USA, d. 24 November 1969, Chicago, Illinois, USA. Perhaps best known as a member of the classic Elmore James band that also featured Johnnie Jones and Odie Payne, Brown's quavering tenor saxophone sound was instantly identifiable. His early life is poorly documented but it is known that in his youth he worked with the Rabbit Foot Minstrels and spent time in Memphis before moving to Chicago. In the late 40s, his Boogie Band provided support for sessions by Eddie Boyd, Roosevelt Sykes, St. Louis Jimmy and Memphis Jimmy Clarke. He recorded in the early 50s under his own name, with the addition of such sobriquets as 'Blow It' and 'Nature Boy', for Harlem, United and Premium. 'Black Jack Blues' and 'Dumb Woman Blues' were each recorded twice. Between 1952 and 1960, he recorded and toured with Elmore James, appearing on definitive versions of 'It Hurts Me Too', 'Dust My Broom', 'The Sun Is Shining' and 'I Can't Hold Out'. In the meantime, his own sessions for JOB, Parrot, United and Atomic-H largely remained unissued until the 70s and 80s. In 1964 he played clarinet on a Muddy Waters session, giving some clue as to the origin of his tenor saxophone technique. His final session was in January 1969, when Fleetwood Mac recorded *Blues Jam At Chess* and he backed Jeremy Spencer's Elmore imitations and recorded a last version of 'Black Jack Blues'.

● COMPILATIONS: *Rockin' With J.T.* (Krazy Kat 1988)★★★, *Cool Playing Blues* (Relic 1990)★★★.

BROWN, LEE

Brown was an associate of the Tennessee musicians who accompanied Sleepy John Estes, and whose guitar is heard on Brown's first record. Jimmy Rogers recalled him as an irascible paranoid, and Hammie Nixon, who last saw him in the late 60s, recalls that when they first met as hobos, Brown was on the run from a murder charge. Brown recorded sporadically from 1937-40, and also had two records issued in 1946, making several versions of his theme song 'Little Girl, Little Girl'. He was a limited pianist - his best records are those on which Sam Price plays piano as part of a small jazz band - and his laconic, unemotional singing was perhaps an attempt to emulate the success of Curtis Jones.
● COMPILATIONS: *Lee Brown* (EarlArchives 1987)★★★.

BROWN, LILLYN

b. 24 April 1885, Atlanta, Georgia, USA, d. 8 June 1969, New York City, New York, USA. Brown was in showbusiness from 1894-1934 (at one time billed as 'the Kate Smith of Harlem'), returning for a period in the 50s. A singer, dancer and male impersonator, she added blues to her act in 1908. In 1921 she recorded four titles with her Jazz-bo Syncopators. The music, as her background and the group's name imply, was a hybrid of blues, jazz, and the ragtime-influenced pop of a decade earlier, with 'If That's What You Want Here It Is' being a particularly impressive, spirited performance. In the 50s, she operated an acting and singing school, and from 1956 was secretary to the Negro Actors' Guild, also writing and directing plays for her church as late as 1965.
● COMPILATIONS: *Female Blues Singers B/C* (1990).

BROWN, NAPPY

b. Napoleon Brown Culp, 12 October 1929, Charlotte, North Carolina, USA. Brown began his career as a gospel singer, but moved to R&B when an appearance in Newark, New Jersey, led to a recording contract with Savoy in 1954. A deep-voiced, highly individual R&B singer, he had a number of hits during the 50s, including

'Don't Be Angry' (1955), the Rose Marie McCoy/Charlie Singleton song 'Pitter Patter' (a pop hit in Patti Page's cover version), 'It Don't Hurt No More' (1958) and 'I Cried Like A Baby' (1959). He also made the original version of 'The Night Time Is The Right Time' a 1958 hit for Ray Charles. A prison term kept Brown inactive for much of the 60s. He returned to music with an album for Elephant V in 1969 and recorded gospel music in the 70s with the Bell Jubilee Singers for Jewel and as Brother Napoleon Brown for Savoy. In the 80s, Brown was rediscovered by a later generation of blues enthusiasts. He performed at festivals and recorded for Black Top and Alligator, with guitarist Tinsley Ellis accompanying him on *Tore Up*. Brown also appeared on a live album recorded at Tipitina's in New Orleans in 1988. He recorded in 1990 for Ichiban and for New Moon in 1994 and 1997, although nothing had the power of his work of the 50s
● ALBUMS: *Nappy Brown Sings* (London 1955)★★★★, *The Right Time* (London 1958)★★★★, *Thanks For Nothing* (Elephant V 1969)★★★, *Tore Up* (Nightflite 1986)★★★, *Something Gonna Jump Out The Bushes* (Black Top 1988)★★★, *Apples & Lemons* (Ichiban 1990)★★, *Aw, Shucks* (Ichiban 1991)★★, *I'm A Wild Man* (New Moon 1994)★★, *Don't Be Angry* (Savoy 1995)★★, *Who's Been Foolin' You* (New Moon 1997)★★★.

BROWN, OLIVE

b. 30 August 1922, St. Louis, Missouri, USA. The Brown family moved to Detroit, Michigan, when Olive was three months old, although they often returned to visit St. Louis, where she began singing in church. In the 30s and 40s she sang with many well-known bands (including Todd Rhodes) and recorded for Our World Records in 1948. In the 50s she made a demonstration tape for Don Robey which was released by Ace in 1988; it presented Brown as a typical R&B singer for the time. The following decade Brown appeared on the Spivey and Blues spectacle labels, and in 1973 she recorded as a vaudeville-blues-styled singer for JTP Records. She continues to work in this area.
● ALBUMS: *The New Empress Of The Blues* (JTP 1973)★★★.
● COMPILATIONS: with various artists *Peacock*

Chicks & Duchesses Sing The Blues three tracks only (1988).

BROWN, RICHARD 'RABBIT'

b. *c*.1880, New Orleans, Louisiana, USA, d. 1937, New Orleans, Louisiana, USA. Nicknamed in reference to his small stature, 'Rabbit' Brown made a living in the streets and brothels of New Orleans, singing in a gritty voice and playing fluent guitar that incorporated flamenco runs, string snapping and high-speed bass runs; he also took tourists for rowing boat rides on Lake Ponchartrain. He recorded in 1927, singing early black pop songs, two long and remarkable ballads about the 'Titanic' and a local kidnapping, and the poignant 'James Alley Blues', named after the slum birthplace he shared with Louis Armstrong.
● COMPILATIONS: *The Greatest Songsters* (1990).

BROWN, ROBERT

b. 15 July 1910. Walnut Ridge, Arkansas, USA, d. 13 November 1966, Chicago, Illinois, USA. Brown's numerous pseudonyms included 'Washboard Sam', 'Ham Gravy' and 'Shuflin Sam'. In the increasingly sophisticated world of urban blues of the late 30s, when clarinets, trumpets and saxophones were becoming more popular as the music edged towards R&B, Robert Brown was something of an oddball. He played the washboard, an instrument described as 'semi-legitimate' at best. His strength was his deep, strong voice and his ability to deliver lyrics that were both pertinent to the times and more often than not, humorous. He was a close friend of Big Bill Broonzy, who often joked that Brown was his half-brother, a claim that cannot be confirmed, although they did both come to Chicago from the same rural area of Arkansas. Brown's popularity is emphasized by the fact that he was consistently recorded between 1935 and 1949 by Victor Records and that almost everything was issued. He was a mainstay of a shifting group of musicians centred on A&R man Lester Melrose, which included Broonzy, Tampa Red, Jazz Gillum and Memphis Slim. They often played on each other's sessions and joined together in groups such as the Hokum Boys and the State Street Swingers, thus giving rise to what writer Sam Charters described as 'the Bluebird Beat'. Brown's popularity declined sharply as the 50s arrived and he recorded under his own name for only one more label, Chess in 1953, and one of these records was issued as being by Little Walter. He played on the Spivey recordings made by John Henry Barbee in 1964 but died before he could take advantage of the renewed interest in blues.
● COMPILATIONS: *Washboard Sam* (1965)★★★, *Feeling Lowdown* (1972)★★★, *Hottest Brand Goin'* (Ace 1989)★★★.

BROWN, WILLIE

b. 6 August 1900, Cleveland, Mississippi, USA, d. 30 December 1952, Tunica, Mississippi, USA. An associate of both Charley Patton and Son House, Brown made few recordings of his own and what reputation he has earned is usually through association with other men. The son of sharecroppers, he is supposed to have received guitar tuition from Earl Harris, who also performed the same function for Charley Patton. Around the time of World War I, Brown was partnered by William Moore, and in the following decade, he worked alongside Memphis Minnie as well as accompanying Patton. Along with pianist Louise Johnson and Son House, he accompanied Patton on his third recording session for Paramount in May 1930. Although several masters remain untraced, Brown did record two records, 'M&O Blues' and 'Future Blues', both songs being hoarsely sung versions of Patton themes. He also accompanied Patton, can be heard shouting on Johnson's titles, and almost certainly backed House on a recently located recording of 'Walking Blues', the song later adapted by Robert Johnson. After Patton's death, Brown continued to work with House and the pair, along with Fiddling Joe Martin and Leroy Williams, were recorded by Alan Lomax at Lake Cormorant, Mississippi. Thereafter, he accompanied House when the latter moved north to Rochester, New York, but then returned to the Delta region where he died of a heart attack in 1952.
● ALBUMS: with Son House *Delta Blues* (Biograph 1991)★★★.
● COMPILATIONS: *Masters Of The Delta Blues* (Yazoo 1991)★★★.

BROZMAN, BOB

b. 1954, New York City, New York, USA. Born and raised in the Hudson River Delta, blues musician, author and musicologist Bob Brozman began playing the piano at the age of four, gravitating to guitar by the age of six. Eventually he adopted the National steel guitar in 1968, and from then on developed a keen interest in and long-standing commitment to the blues. At college he undertook a degree in musicology, his thesis a comparative study of Tommy Johnson and Charley Patton that argued that they must have met at some point. Outside of the blues, he also stumbled across Hawaiian National guitar player Solomon Ho'op'i'i of the Ho'op'i'i Brothers, and began acquiring a huge collection of pre-war Hawaiian 78 rpm records. When he discovered that Ho'op'i'i had been influenced by jazz players such as Bix Beiderbecke, it convinced him of the interconnected nature of much modern music: 'For me the real interesting definition of World Music is where the First World and the Third World intersect. Third Worlders use the industrialised world's instruments to create more interesting music than anybody in the industrialised world has.' Since that time he has travelled extensively, documenting his discovery of the musics of several different continents, both academically and also in his own guitar-playing techniques. He is a virtuoso performer in his own right, his skill conditioned by what he estimates as some 11,000 45-minute bar sets played between 1973 and 1980. His love of the National steel guitar has led to his amassing a collection of over 100. Although he maintained a low profile as a performer, that situation changed dramatically in the early 90s when his *Truckload Of Blues* set for Sky Ranch Records achieved massive popularity in France. As a result he was signed to Virgin Records in that country, and released two more highly successful albums, *Slide A Go-Go* and *Blues Around The Bend*.

● ALBUMS: *Truckload Of Blues* (Sky Ranch 1992)★★★★, *Slide A Go-Go* (Sky Ranch 1993)★★★, with the Thieves Of Sleep *Blues Around The Bend* (Sky Ranch 1995)★★★.

BRUCE, JACK

b. John Symon Asher, 14 May 1943, Glasgow, Lanarkshire, Scotland. Formerly a piano student at the Royal Scottish Academy of Music, he was awarded a RSAM scholarship for cello and composition. Bruce has utilized his brilliant bass playing to cross and bridge free jazz and heavy rock, during spells with countless musical conglomerations. As a multi-instrumentalist he also has a great fondness for the piano, cello and acoustic bass, and is highly accomplished on all these instruments. At 19 years of age he moved to London and joined the R&B scene, first with Alexis Korner's band and then as a key member of the pioneering Graham Bond Organisation. Following brief stints with John Mayall's Bluesbreakers and Manfred Mann, Bruce joined with his former colleague in the Bond band, Ginger Baker, who, together with Eric Clapton, formed Cream. The comparatively short career of this pivotal band reached musical heights that have rarely been bettered. During this time Bruce displayed and developed a strident vocal style and considerable prowess as a harmonica player. However, it was his imaginative and sometimes breathtaking bass playing that appealed. He popularized an instrument that had previously not featured prominently in rock music. Dozens of young players in the 70s and 80s cited Bruce as being the reason for them taking up the bass guitar. Upon the break-up of Cream, Bruce released an exemplary solo album, *Songs For A Tailor*. A host of top jazz/rock musicians were present on what was his most successful album. On this record he continued the songwriting partnership with Pete Brown that had already produced a number of Cream classics, 'White Room', 'Politician', 'I Feel Free', 'Sunshine Of Your Love' and 'SWLABR' ('She Was Like A Bearded Rainbow'). Brown's imaginative and surreal lyrics were the perfect foil to Bruce's furious and complex bass patterns. Evocative songs such as 'Theme For An Imaginary Western' and 'The Weird Of Hermiston' enabled Bruce's ability as a vocalist to shine, with piercing clarity.

Throughout the early 70s, a series of excellent albums and constantly changing line-ups gave him a high profile. His involvement with Tony Williams' Lifetime and his own 'supergroup', West, Bruce And Laing, further enhanced his position in the jazz and rock world. A further aggregation, Jack Bruce And Friends, included jazz guitarist Larry Coryell and former Jimi

Hendrix drummer Mitch Mitchell. During this busy and fruitful period Bruce found time to add vocals to Carla Bley's classic album *Escalator Over The Hill*, and Bley was also a member of the 1975 version of the Jack Bruce Band. In 1979 he toured as a member of John McLaughlin's Mahavishnu Orchestra. The 80s started with a new Jack Bruce Band which featured former Bakerloo, Colosseum and Humble Pie guitarist Dave 'Clem' Clempson and David Sancious. They found particular favour in Germany and played there regularly. The ill-fated heavy rock trio BLT formed in 1981 with guitarist Robin Trower and drummer Bill Lordan but disintegrated after two albums; their debut, *BLT*, reached the US Top 40. During the 80s Bruce kept a low profile after having experienced severe drug problems in the 70s. In 1987 the perplexing album *Automatic* appeared. This obviously low-budget work had Bruce accompanied by a Fairlight machine, an odd coupling for a musician whose previous collections had consistently teamed him with highly talented drummers. Much more impressive was 1990's *A Question Of Time* which attempted to restore Bruce's now lapsed career to its former glory. Other than his long-term admirers Bruce has found it difficult to reach a wide new audience. Those that have followed his career understand his major shifts from jazz to heavy rock, but his position in today's musical climate is hard to place. His vocal work accompanied by his emotional piano playing has been his particularly strong point of late. In 1994 he formed BBM, with Gary Moore and Baker. Two parts Cream, the unit might have been more aptly called Semi-Skimmed. This was his most rock-oriented project for many years and clearly showed that Bruce was in sparkling form, fit and well. Bruce remains forever (probably because of Cream) the most renowned and respected of rock bassists.

● ALBUMS: *Songs For A Tailor* (Polydor 1969)★★★★, *Things We Like* (Polydor 1970)★★★, *Harmony Row* (Polydor 1971)★★★, *Out Of The Storm* (Polydor 1974)★★★, *How's Tricks* (RSO 1977)★★★, *I've Always Wanted To Do This* (Epic 1980)★★★, with Robin Trower *Truce* (Chrysalis 1982)★★★, *Automatic* (President 1987)★★, *A Question Of Time* (Epic 1990)★★★, And Friends *Live At The Bottom*

Line (Traditional Line 1992)★★★, *Something Else* (1993)★★★, *Cities Of the Heart* (CMP 1994)★★★★, with Paul Jones *Alexis Korner Memorial Concert Vol. 1* (Indigo 1995)★★★.

● COMPILATIONS: *Jack Bruce At His Best* (Polydor 1972)★★★, *Greatest Hits* (Polydor 1980)★★★, *Willpower* (Polydor 1989)★★★, *The Collection* (Castle 1992)★★★.

BRUTON, STEPHEN

b. Turner Stephen Bruton, 7 November 1948, Delaware, USA. Growing up in Fort Worth, Texas, Bruton benefited from the fact that his father's record store was the focal point for all types of musical activity. Folk music was his first inspiration to play the guitar, but at night he and his brother Sumter listened to the blues on local radio. As a teenager, he and T-Bone Burnett would play early shows at clubs such as the Tracer and the East Side, where he met Delbert McClinton. Moving to Woodstock in 1970, he took a serious interest in the guitar and within a year was offered a job with Kris Kristofferson, whom he had met earlier in Texas. The relationship lasted 15 years, during which time Bruton also worked with McClinton and formed Little Whisper And The Rumors with Glen Clark. That band brought him to Bonnie Raitt's notice and another long-standing musical relationship began. His solo debut album, *What It Is*, reflects the eclecticism of his musical education, combining elements of blues, rock, New Orleans R&B and rockabilly. Bruton continues to work with Raitt and McClinton and also produces other Austin-based artists such as Johnny Nicholas, Loose Diamonds, Chris Smither, Sue Foley, Jimmie Dale Gilmore, Storyville and Alejandro Escovedo. *Right On Time* was a similar eclectic mix but began to highlight the fact that his voice is not as strong as either his guitar playing or his songwriting ability.

● ALBUMS: *What It Is* (Dos 1994)★★★, *Right On Time* (Dos 1995)★★★.

BRYANT, BEULAH

b. Blooma Walton, 20 February 1918, Dayton, Alabama, USA, d. 31 January 1988, New York City, New York, USA. Bryant frequently sang with local church groups before moving to California in 1936 where she heard, and was influenced by, Ella Fitzgerald. After winning a networked radio show amateur contest the following year, she formed her own trio and began making regular appearances on the west coast. In 1945 she moved to New York and began working as a solo artist. Her recording career began in the late 40s on the tiny Do-Kay-Lo label, switching to MGM (many of the masters being provided by Joe Davis), and making a final session for Excello in 1955. Throughout the 50s, 60s and 70s Bryant was used extensively in radio, films and television. She also maintained an exhaustive touring schedule. In 1979 she resumed her recording career with a fine session for Victoria Spivey's label.

● ALBUMS: with Irene Redfield, Millie Bosman *Blues Women* (1985)★★★.

BUCHANAN, ROY

b. 23 September 1939, Ozark, Alabama, USA, d. 14 August 1988. The son of a preacher, Buchanan discovered gospel music through the influence of travelling revivalists. This interest engendered his love of R&B and having served an apprenticeship playing guitar in scores of minor groups, he secured fame on joining Dale Hawkins in 1958. Although Buchanan is often erroneously credited with the break on the singer's much-lauded 'Suzie Q', contributions on 'My Babe' and 'Grandma's House', confirmed his remarkable talent. Buchanan also recorded with Freddie Cannon, Bob Luman and the Hawks, and completed several low-key singles in his own right before retiring in 1962. However, he re-emerged in the following decade with *Roy Buchanan*, an accomplished, versatile set that included a slow, hypnotic rendition of the C&W standard 'Sweet Dreams'. *Loading Zone* was an accomplished album and contained two of his finest (and longest) outings; the pulsating 'Green Onions', which featured shared solos with the song's co-composer Steve Cropper, and the extraordinary 'Ramon's Blues' (again with Cropper). His trademark battered Fender Telecaster guitar gave a distinctive treble-sounding tone to his work. A series of similiarly crafted albums were released, before the guitarist again drifted out of the limelight. His career was rekindled in 1986 with *When A Guitar Plays The Blues*, but despite enjoying the accolades of many contemporaries, including Robbie Robertson, Buchanan was never com-

fortable with the role of virtuoso. A shy, reticent individual, he made several unsuccessful suicide attempts before hanging himself in a police cell in 1988, following his arrest on a drink-driving charge.

● ALBUMS: *Roy Buchanan* (Polydor 1972)★★★, *Second Album* (Polydor 1973)★★★, *That's What I'm Here For* (Polydor 1974)★★★, *In The Beginning* (Polydor 1974)★★★, *Rescue Me* (Polydor 1975)★★, *Live Stock* (Polydor 1975)★★, *A Street Called Straight* (Polydor 1976)★★★, *Loading Zone* (Polydor 1977)★★★, *You're Not Alone* (Polydor 1978)★★, *My Babe* (Waterhouse 1981)★★, *When A Guitar Plays The Blues* (Alligator 1986)★★★, *Dancing On The Edge* (Alligator 1987)★★, *Hot Wires* (Alligator 1987)★★.

● COMPILATIONS: *Early Roy Buchanan* (Krazy Kat 1989)★★★, *Sweet Dreams: The Anthology* (Mercury Chronicles 1992)★★★★, *The Early Years* (Krazy Kat/Interstate 1993)★★★.

● VIDEOS: *Custom Made* (Kay Jazz 1988).

BUCKWHEAT ZYDECO

Founded by Stanley Dural (b. 1947, Lafayette, Louisiana, USA). Dural started his musical career playing piano and organ in local bands around south-east Louisiana. In the late 80s and early 90s, Buckwheat Zydeco emerged as one of the leaders of zydeco music, the accordion-led dance music of southern Louisiana's French-speaking Creoles. Dural, taking the nickname 'Buckwheat', worked with R&B singers Joe Tex, Barbara Lynn and Clarence 'Gatemouth' Brown during the 60s. Following a period playing keyboards in Clifton Chenier's band, he took up accordion and moved to the indigenous sound of zydeco. He formed his own funk band, the Hitchhikers, in the 70s, followed by the Ils Sont Partis Band in 1979. That outfit recorded eight albums for Blues Unlimited, Black Top and Rounder Records before accordionist Dural formed Buckwheat Zydeco. Signed to Island Records in 1987, the group had recorded three albums for the label by 1990, the latter produced by David Hidalgo of Los Lobos. Newcomers to this music should start with the excellent compilation *Menagerie*.

● ALBUMS: *One For The Road* (Blues Unlimited 1979)★★, *Take It Easy Baby* (Blues Unlimited 1980)★★★, *100% Fortified Zydeco* (Rounder

1983)★★★, *Turning Point* (Rounder 1984)★★★, *Waitin' For My Ya Ya* (Rounder 1985)★★★, *Buckwheat Zydeco* (Rounder 1986)★★★, *Zydeco Party* (Rounder 1987)★★★, *On A Night Like This* (Island 1987)★★★★, *Taking It Home* (Island 1988)★★★, *Buckwheat Zydeco And The Ils Sont Partis Band* (Island 1988)★★★, *Where There's Smoke There's Fire* (Island 1990)★★★★, *On Track* (Charisma 1992)★★★.
● COMPILATIONS: *Menagerie: The Essential Zydeco Collection* (Mango 1994)★★★★.
● VIDEOS: *Taking It Home* (Island Visual Arts 1989), *Buckwheat Zydeco Live* (Polygram Music Video 1991).

BUFORD, 'MOJO' GEORGE
b. 10 November 1929, Hernando, Mississippi, USA. Buford began to dabble with the harmonica at the age of 12 while living in Memphis, but he started playing seriously after hearing Little Walter's 'Juke'. He moved to Chicago in 1952 and formed the Savage Boys, a band 'adopted' by Muddy Waters to retain his club residency while he was on tour. Buford recorded behind Joseph 'Jo Jo' Williams in 1959 and in the same year joined Waters' band for the first of several spells. In 1962, Buford left and moved to Minneapolis where he acquired his nickname by fulfilling requests for 'Got My Mojo Working'. While there, he recorded sporadically under his own name until the late 70s. In 1967 he recorded with several of Muddy Waters' sidemen and later played on several of Waters' recording sessions. Buford returned to Chicago in 1978, making an album for Rooster Blues, and in the 80s moved back to Memphis. He has also recorded sessions in Europe for Isabel and JSP Records. Buford's vocals and his approach to blues still remain close to the Waters sound.
● ALBUMS: *Mojo Buford's Chicago Blues Summit* (Rooster)★★★, *State Of The Blues Harp* (JSP 1990)★★★, *Harpslinger* (Blue Loon 1993)★★★, *Juice Machine* (Taxim 1995)★★★, *Still Blowin' Strong* (Blue Loon 1996)★★★★.

BUMBLE BEE SLIM
b. Amos Easton, 7 May 1905, Brunswick, Georgia, USA, d. 1968, Los Angeles, California, USA. Bumble Bee Slim was a blues guitarist, although he seldom played on record; it was as a singer that he recorded prolifically from 1931-37. Leaving home around 1920, he led a itinerant life for eight years before settling in Indianapolis, and later Chicago. As a singer, he was influenced by Naptown's Leroy Carr, and his songs convey a modified version of Carr's bittersweet aesthetic. Easton appears friendly, confiding and philosophical, sometimes bruised by life's adversities, but never crushed by its tragedies. In part, no doubt, this is a reflection of his own personality, but it also typifies the switch from personal expression to performance art of recorded blues in the 30s. His records were very popular; songs such as 'B&O Blues' and 'Sail On, Little Girl, Sail On' fed back into folk tradition, and several were big enough hits to be remade with fresh lyrics, and have 'New' prefixed to their titles. Slim's pleasant personality, the distinguished calibre of many of his accompanists, and the way his blues mirrored black life in the 30s all contributed to his star status. Nevertheless, lack of reward seems to have prompted him temporarily to stop recording in 1937, and to move to Los Angeles, where he had three records issued for black consumption, and released an unsuccessful album aimed at the new white audience, accompanied by cool jazz musicians.
● COMPILATIONS: *Bee's Back In Town* (1962)★★★, *City Blues* (1973)★★★, *Vintage Country Blues* (1976)★★★, *Bumble Bee Slim* (1987)★★★.

BURDON, ERIC
b. 11 May 1941, Walker, Newcastle-upon-Tyne, Tyne & Wear, England. Burdon originally came to prominence as the lead singer of the Animals in 1963. His gutsy, distinctive voice was heard on their many memorable records in the 60s. Following the demise of the latter-day Eric Burdon And The New Animals, it was announced that he would pursue a career in films. By 1970 no offers from Hollywood were forthcoming so he linked up with the relatively unknown black jazz/rock band Nite Shift, and, together with his friend Lee Oskar, they became Eric Burdon And War. A successful single, 'Spill The Wine', preceded the well-received *Eric Burdon Declares War*. In the song Burdon parodied himself with the lyrics: 'Imagine me, an overfed, long-haired leaping gnome, should be a star of a Hollywood movie.' Both this and the

follow-up, *Black Man's Burdon*, combined ambitious arrangements mixing flute with Oskar's harmonica. Eventually the jazz., rock, funk, blues, soul mix ended up merely highlighting Burdon's ultra pro-black stance. While his intentions were honourable, it came over to many as inverted racism. Burdon received a great deal of press in 1970 when he was still regarded as an influential spokesperson of the hippie generation. At the time of Jimi Hendrix's death, he claimed to possess a suicide note, the contents of which he refused to divulge. After parting company, War went on to become hugely successful in the early 70s, while Burdon's career stalled. He teamed up with Jimmy Witherspoon on *Guilty* and attempted a heavier rock approach with *Sun Secrets* and *Stop*. The ponderous Hendrix-influenced guitar style of the last two albums did not suit reworked versions of early Animals hits, and the albums were not successful. In 1980 Burdon formed Fire Dept in Germany, making one album, *Last Drive*. He finally fulfilled his long-standing big-screen ambitions by appearing in the film *Comeback*, albeit as a fading rock star. Throughout the 80s Burdon continued to perform with little recorded output, while experiencing drug and alcohol problems. His 1977 and 1983 reunion albums with the original Animals were not well received. Burdon's popularity in Germany continued, while his profile in the UK and USA decreased. His confessional autobiography was published in 1986. Burdon remains one of the finest white blues vocalists of our time, although ultimately typecast as the man who sang 'House Of The Rising Sun'.

● ALBUMS: as Eric Burdon And War *Eric Burdon Declares War* (Polydor 1970)★★★, as Eric Burdon And War *Black Man's Burdon* (Liberty 1971)★★★, the Eric Burdon Band and Jimmy Witherspoon *Guilty!* (United Artists 1971)★★★, *Ring Of Fire* (Capitol 1974)★★★, *Sun Secrets* (Capitol 1975)★★, *Stop* (Capitol 1975)★★, *Survivor* (Polydor 1978)★★, *Darkness - Darkness* (Polydor 1980)★★, as Eric Burdon's Fire Department *The Last Drive* (Ariola 1980)★★, *Comeback* (Line 1982)★★★ reissued as *The Road* (Thunderbolt 1984), as The Eric Burdon Band *Comeback* new songs from 1982 session (Blackline 1983)★★, *Power Company* aka *Devil's Daughter* new songs from 1982 session (Carrere 1983)★★, as The Eric Burdon Band *That's Live* (In-Akustik 1985)★★, *I Used To Be An Animal* (Striped Horse 1988)★★, *Wicked Man* reissue of *Comeback/Power Company* material (GNP Crescendo 1988)★★, with Robby Krieger *The 1990 Detroit Tapes* (1991)★★, *The Unreleased Eric Burdon* (Blue Wave 1992)★★, *Crawling King Snake* (Thunderbolt 1992)★★, with Brian Augur *Access All Areas* (SPV 1993)★★, *Misunderstood* (Aim 1995)★★.

● COMPILATIONS: War featuring Eric Burdon *Love Is All Around* (ABC 1976)★★, *The Touch Of Eric Burdon* (K-Tel 1983)★★, *Star Portrait* (Polydor 1988)★★★, *Sings The Animals Greatest Hits* (Avenue 1994)★★.

● VIDEOS: *Finally* (Warners 1992).

● FURTHER READING: *Wild Animals*, Andy Blackford. *I Used To Be An Animal But I'm All Right Now*, Eric Burdon. *The Last Poet: The Story Of Eric Burdon*, Jeff Kent. *Good Times: The Ultimate Eric Burdon*, Dionisio Castello.

● FILMS: *The Eleventh Victim* (1979), *Movin' On* (1987), *The Doors* (1990).

BURKES, CONISH 'PINETOP'

Connie Burkes came from the extensive school of blues pianists operating in jukes, lumber camps, and tank towns along the course of the Santa Fe Railroad network in Texas, USA. This sparse information is virtually all that is known about Burke, and comes from the memories of surviving contemporaries. He recorded only once - a six-track session made for Vocalion in San Antonio, Texas, during 1937.

● COMPILATIONS: *The Piano Blues Volume II* (1979).

BURKS, EDDIE

b. 17 September 1931, Greenwood, Mississippi, USA. There was a time when Chicago's Maxwell Street area was referred to by its citizens as Jewtown, and 'Jewtown' Burks was one of the weekend market's most powerful performers. Finance and political correctness have put paid to both names, but Burks remains an eminently listenable and resourceful musician. He obtained his first harmonica at the age of three and received new ones as Christmas gifts in the subsequent years. Despite his family's strong religious tradition, he listened to Rice Miller's

KFFA broadcasts for inspiration. He arrived in Chicago on 27 December 1946 and shortly afterwards gained employment in a steel mill. Although his religious activities kept him from performing blues, he frequented the West Side clubs. When his health forced him to quit the steel mill and his first marriage failed, he devoted himself to music, sitting in with Magic Sam, Freddie King and Howlin' Wolf and taking a residency at the Majestic Lounge. His first single, 'Lowdown Dog', was issued in 1977 and credited to Jewtown Burks, followed by 'Operator' and 'Evelina' on the Cher-Kee label. During the 70s and 80s he worked with Jimmy Dawkins and Eddie Shaw, mostly as a driver. In 1988, he married Maureen Walker, who assisted him in setting up Rising Son (later changed to Rising Son Blues), and in 1991 he released *Vampire Woman*. A year later, an album of Chicago blues standards, *This Old Road*, was recorded live in Rochester, New York. An impressive live performer, Burks has managed to avoid involvement with the corporate blues fraternity.

● ALBUMS: *Harpin' On It* (JSP 1983)★★★, *Vampire Woman* (Rising Son 1991)★★★, *This Old Road* (Rising Son 1992)★★★, *Comin' Home* (Rising Son Blues 1994)★★★.

BURLESON, HATTIE

Burleson was an important figure on the blues scene in Texas, USA; she made a few records, including a tribute to her lover, 'Jim Nappy', but was most significant as an entrepreneur. Based in Dallas, she ran a stable of singers, dancers and musicians that was the mainstay of shows at Ella B. Moore's Park Theater. Along with lesser known artists, Burleson managed Lillian Glinn, and was instrumental in securing recording opportunities for her, and for a good many other Texas musicians, usually ensuring that they recorded her own compositions. Burleson also ran a dancehall and a Marathon dancing rink in Dallas, and her road shows toured throughout the south-west under Jim Nappy's management; even in the mid-50s she was touring in southern Texas with a small show.

● COMPILATIONS: *Texas Blues - Dallas* (1980), *Female Blues Singers B/C* (1990).

BURNETT, CHESTER

(see Howlin' Wolf)

BURNS, EDDIE

b. 8 February 1928, Mississippi, USA. Inspired by John Lee 'Sonny Boy' Williamson and self-taught, Burns was a stalwart of the immediate post-war Detroit blues scene, being first recorded in 1948 by Bernie Bessman. The latter was responsible for giving John Lee Hooker his break and used Burns as a session musician for Hooker in 1949. This session produced four tracks, including the fast shuffle, 'Burnin' Hell', which was notable for Burns's powerful harmonica playing. Throughout the 50s and 60s he periodically recorded for Joseph Van Battle, who either released the material on his own JVB and Von labels or else sold the masters to concerns such as Gotham and Checker. Rarely straying from his home state of Michigan, Burns briefly visited Europe in 1972 under the billing Eddie 'Guitar' Burns, recording an album in London for Action. He returned three years later for a more intensive tour under the 'American Blues Legends '75' banner. Since then Eddie Burns has stayed mostly in Detroit, working day-jobs, playing clubs in the evenings and occasionally appearing at festivals.

● ALBUMS: *Detroit Black Bottom* (Big Bear 1975)★★★, *Treat Me Like I Treat You* (Moonshine 1985)★★★, with John Lee Hooker *Detroit* (Krazy Kat 1987)★★★.

BURNSIDE, R.L.

b. 23 November 1926, Coldwater, Mississippi, USA. Burnside, 'Rule' to his friends, was a keen observer of his neighbour Mississippi Fred McDowell, as well as Son Hibler and Ranie Burnett, and learned from them the modal rhythm-based techniques of the north Mississippi blues. To these he added songs by Muddy Waters, John Lee Hooker and Lightnin' Hopkins heard on the radio. Prior to taking up the guitar, he had moved to Chicago in the late 40s, where he worked in a foundry and witnessed Muddy Waters' music first-hand. In 1950 he returned south and spent the ensuing years doing farm-work by day and playing jukes and house parties at weekends. He was discovered and recorded in 1967 by George Mitchell, and after the release of *Mississippi Delta Blues*, was in demand to appear at festivals in North America and Europe. As well as performing solo, Burnside also leads the Sound Machine, a band that features various members of his large family on guitar and bass, and son-in-law Calvin Jackson on drums. *Bad Luck City* features sons Dwayne and Joseph assisting on a wide range of contemporary material, representative of a typical set played at local clubs such as Junior Kimbrough's at Chulahoma. *Too Bad Jim* was recorded there, in part, and consists of songs played in the older, modal tradition with pupil Kenny Brown on second guitar. These latter recordings prove the enduring strength of Mississippi blues as well as Burnside's eminence as a stirring performer of its intricacies. *A Ass Pocket Of Whiskey* was a highly-praised set recorded with rootsy punksters the Jon Spencer Blues Explosion, while Don Van Vliet (Captain Beefheart) and Ry Cooder replicated the Burnside sound for *Strictly Personal* in 1968. Burnside's 1997 follow-up *Mr Wizard* failed to reproduce the magic.

● ALBUMS: *Mississippi Delta Blues Vol. 2* (Arhoolie 1968)★★★, *Hill Country Blues* (Swingmaster 1988)★★★, *Plays And Sings The Mississippi Delta Blues* (Swingmaster)★★★, *Sound Machine Groove* (Blues Today)★★★, *Mississippi Blues* (Arion)★★★, *Bad Lucky City* (Fat Possum 1991)★★★, *Deep Blues* (Atlantic 1992)★★★, *Too Bad Jim* (Fat Possum 1994)★★★, *A Ass Pocket Of Whiskey* (Matador 1996)★★★★, *Mr. Wizard* (Fat Possum 1997)★★★.

BURRIS, J.C.

b. 1928, Selby, North Carolina, USA, d. 15 May 1988, Greensboro, North Carolina, USA. Burris learned harmonica from his uncle Sonny Terry. He left his farm work in his early 20s and moved to New York, where between 1955 and 1960 he made some recordings with Granville 'Sticks' McGhee, Brownie McGhee and Terry. At the turn of that decade, he moved out to the west coast, eventually settling in San Francisco, where he began to make a name for himself on the local folk-blues scene. A stroke disabled him for some years, but he eventually returned to music, performing regularly and making an album in 1975. His style owed much to Terry's, but he added his own distinctive touches, per-

forming solo, playing bones as well as his harmonica, and sometimes appearing with a wooden dancing doll.

● ALBUMS: *One Of These Mornings* (Arhoolie 1975)★★★.

BURSE, CHARLIE

b. 25 August 1901, Decatur, Alabama, USA, d. 20 December 1965, Memphis, Tennessee, USA. A banjoist from childhood, Burse moved to Memphis in 1928, and joined the Memphis Jug Band on guitar. He quickly imposed his extrovert personality on their music, and seems to have effectively become co-leader with Will Shade. The band's last recordings in 1934 owed much to his scat singing and Fats Waller inspired vocal interjections. The jazz influence is even more marked on the 1939 recordings by Charlie Burse And His Memphis Mudcats, which featured an alto saxophone. He relocated in 1956, and recorded occasionally until 1963, usually in association with Will Shade.

● COMPILATIONS: *American Skiffle Bands* (1958)★★★, *Beale Street Mess Around* (1976)★★★, *Charlie Burse & James De Berry* (1989)★★★, *The Memphis Jug Vol. 2 & 3* (1991)★★★.

BURTON, ARON

b. USA. Having spent 20 years as a landscaper and floral horticulturist for the city of Chicago, blues bassist Aron Burton's day job has led to his becoming the manager of the Garfield Park Plant Conservatory. However, throughout this time he has continued to lead his band at local venues such as the Blue Chicago and B.L.U.E.S. Etcetera in the evenings. One of Albert Collins' original Ice Breakers, Burton backed that artist with his guitar-playing brother Larry on *Ice Pickin'*, Collins' debut for Alligator Records. Burton has also worked on sessions for numerous other Alligator artists, including James Cotton, Fenton Robinson, Lonnie Brooks and Koko Taylor. Other credits include work on Valerie Wellington's *Million Dollar Secret* (1983) and *So Called Friends* (1984) by Johnny Littlejohn - the slide guitarist who married his sister. Burton recorded his debut solo album in 1987 with the backing of Champion Jack Dupree during a three-year stay in Europe. On his return to the USA he found employment on albums by David 'Honeyboy' Edwards and 'Big' Jack Johnson. Both were released on Earwig Records, the label where Burton has become a regular collaborator, writer and arranger. His real breakthrough as a solo performer came in 1993 with the acclaimed *Past, Present And Future* collection, which showcased his maturity as an artist and his deep affinity with blues music.

● ALBUMS: *Usual Dangerous Guy* (1987)★★★, *Past, Present And Future* (Earwig 1993)★★★★, *Not Gonna Worry About Tomorrow* (JSP 1995)★★★.

BUTLER, GEORGE 'WILD CHILD'

b. 1 October 1936, Autaugville, Alabama, USA. Butler was one of the last of the wandering bluesmen. He suffered from the general lack of interest in older musical forms shown by the black record-buying public, yet still managed to make his most prized recordings during the mid to late 60s. His introduction to the blues came via his elder brother Edward (he was one of twelve children) but his imagination was sparked by the recordings of Sonny Boy 'Rice Miller' Williamson, and with a harmonica in his pocket he took to the road. He recorded a single for Shaw Records in Montgomery, Alabama, in 1964, but his real break came when Willie Dixon introduced him to Stan Lewis's Jewel label, which, operating out of Shreveport, Louisiana, was the only label of any size still producing records for the southern juke-box trade. Since that time his output on record has remained limited, although his tough harmonic style has continued to earn him a living.

● ALBUMS: *Open Up Baby* (Charly 1985)★★★, *Keep On Doin' What You're Doin'* (1991)★★★, *Lickin' Gravy* (Rooster Blues 1989)★★★, *Stranger* (Bullseye Blues 1994)★★★.

BUTTERBEANS AND SUSIE

Butterbeans (b. Jody Edwards, 19 July 1895, Georgia, USA, d. 28 October 1967) and Susie (b. Susie Hawthorn, 1896, Pensacola, Florida, USA, d. 5 December 1963, Chicago, Illinois, USA) were one of the most durable teams in black vaudeville. They appeared together from before their marriage in 1916 until just before Susie's death nearly 50 years later. They supported Trixie Smith in 1920 and James Brown in 1959, and headlined their own revues in the late 20s.

Their recordings were miniature comic sketches in song and speech, with Butterbeans always cast as the henpecked, put-upon husband and Susie as the dominant wife, making both sexual ('I Wanna Hot Dog For My Roll') and financial ('Papa Ain't No Santa Claus, Mama Ain't No Christmas Tree') demands. Sometimes backed by top jazz musicians, their performances, though seldom explicitly blues, usually had blues inflections.

● COMPILATIONS: *Butterbeans And Susie* (1960)★★★, *Papa's Got The Mojo* (Bluetime 1989)★★★.

BUTTERFIELD, PAUL

b. 17 December 1942, Chicago, Illinois, USA, d. 3 May 1987. As a catalyst, Butterfield helped shape the development of blues music played by white musicians in the same way that John Mayall and Cyril Davies were doing in the UK. Butterfield had the advantage of performing with Howlin' Wolf, Muddy Waters and his mentor Little Walter. Butterfield sang, composed and led a series of seminal bands throughout the 60s, but it was his earthy Chicago-style harmonica-playing that gained him attention. He was arguably the first white man to play blues with the intensity and emotion of the great black blues harmonica players. Mike Bloomfield, Mark Naftalin, Elvin Bishop, David Sanborn and Nick Gravenites were some of the outstanding musicians that passed through his bands. His now infamous performance at the 1965 Newport Folk Festival gave him the distinction of being the man who supported Bob Dylan's musical heresy by going electric. In 1973 his new venture *Better Days* went on the road to a lukewarm response, and during subsequent years he struggled to find success. Ill health plagued him for some time, much of it caused by aggravating stomach hernias caused by his powerful harmonica playing. Butterfield's legacy remains and much of his catalogue is still available. *East-West* remains his best-selling and most acclaimed work, although the rawness of the debut album also attracts many critical admirers.

● ALBUMS: *Paul Butterfield Blues Band* (Elektra 1966)★★★★, *East-West* (Elektra 1966)★★★★, *The Resurrection Of Pigboy Crabshaw* (Elektra 1968)★★★, *In My Own Dream* (Elektra

1968)★★★, *Keep On Movin'* (Elektra 1969)★★, *Live* (Elektra 1971)★★, *Sometimes I Just Feel Like Smilin'* (Elektra 1971)★★, *Offer You Can't Refuse* (1972)★★, as Better Days *It All Comes Back* (Bearsville 1973)★★, as Better Days *Better Days* (Bearsville 1973)★★★, *Put It In Your Ear* (Bearsville 1976)★★, *North South For Bearsville* (Bearsville 1981)★★, *The Legendary Paul Butterfield Rides Again* (1986)★★★, *Strawberry Jam* (Winner 1995)★★, *Lost Elektra Sessions* (Rhino 1995)★★.
● COMPILATIONS: *Golden Butter - Best Of The Paul Butterfield Blues Band* (Elektra 1972)★★★.

CAGE, JAMES 'BUTCH'

b. 16 March 1894, Hamburg, Mississippi, USA, d. 1975, Zachary, Louisiana, USA. Butch Cage moved to Louisiana following the great 1927 floods, and worked at various menial jobs, entertaining his neighbours at weekend parties and, if they were musicians, playing alongside them. After being recorded in 1959, Cage and his partner Willie B. Thomas were a sensation at the 1960 Newport Folk Festival. Cage had begun his musical career on fife, and was also a respectable guitar player, but his main instrument was the fiddle. He had learned to play the instrument in 1911 from two elderly musicians, and his playing preserved the rasping dissonances of African fiddle music. His repertoire encompassed religious music, blues and popular song, and was an integral part of the life of his community.
● ALBUMS: *Country Negro Jam Session* (1960)★★★, *I Have To Paint My Face* (1969)★★★, *Raise A Ruckus Tonight* (Flyright 1979)★★★.

CALE, J.J.

b. Jean Jacques Cale, 5 December 1938, Tulsa, Oklahoma, USA. This mercurial artist began performing professionally in the 50s as guitarist in a western swing group. With the advent of rock 'n' roll he led his own group, Johnnie Cale And The Valentines, before moving to Nashville late in the decade for what proved to be an unsuccessful career in country music. He subsequently settled in Los Angeles, there joining fellow Tulsa ex-patriots Leon Russell, Carl Radle and Chuck Blackwell. Cale played in bar bands, worked as a studio engineer and recorded several low-key singles before collaborating with songwriter Roger Tillison on a psychedelic album, *A Trip Down Sunset Strip*. Credited to the Leathercoated Minds, this tongue-in-cheek selection has since become a cult favourite.
An impoverished Cale returned to Tulsa in 1967. He remained an obscure local talent for three years but his fortunes changed dramatically when Eric Clapton recorded 'After Midnight', a song Cale had written and released as a single in 1965. 'It was like discovering oil in your own backyard', he later commented. Producer Audie Ashworth then invited him to Nashville where he completed the excellent *Naturally*. The completed tape was then forwarded to Leon Russell, who released it on his fledgling Shelter label. The concise, self-confident album, arguably Cale's best, featured a re-recording of 'After Midnight', as well as several equally enchanting compositions including 'Call Me The Breeze', 'Magnolia' and 'Crazy Mama', which became a US Top 30 hit. His laconic, almost lachrymose, delivery quickly became a trademark, while the sympathetically light instrumental support from veterans David Briggs (keyboards), Norbert Putnam (bass) and Tim Drummond (drums), previously members of Area Code 615, enhanced its intimate atmosphere. *Naturally* created a style from which Cale has rarely strayed and while some critics detected a paucity of ideas, others enthuse over its hypnotic charm. *Really* confirmed the high quality of the artist's compositions. Marginally tougher than its predecessor, it included the R&B-flavoured 'Lies' and featured contributions from the Muscle Shoals team of Barry Beckett (keyboards), David Hood (bass) and Roger Hawkins (drums). While *Okie* and *Troubadour* lacked its

immediacy, the latter contained the singer's own version of 'Cocaine', another song popularized by Clapton, who also recorded 'I'll Make Love To You Anytime' from *Five*. Although Cale has remained a somewhat shy and reticent figure, his influence on other musicians has been considerable. Mark Knopfler of Dire Straits appropriated much of his delivery from Cale's self-effacing style, yet while such devotees enjoyed massive commercial success, the originator entered a period of semi-retirement following an ill-fated dalliance with a major label. Despite the inclusion of the popular 'Money Talks' and the acquisition of Cale's back-catalogue, Cale's two albums for Phonogram, *Grasshopper* and *8*, failed to sell in the quantities anticipated and he asked to be released from his contract. The artist re-emerged in 1989 with *Travel Log*, which was issued on Silvertone, a British independent label. Devotees were relieved to hear little had changed; the songs were still largely based on 12-bar structures, his guitar style retained its rhythmic, yet relaxed pulse, while Cale's warm, growling voice was as distinctive as ever. Cale is an artist who would lose fans if he dared to change and even though the waiting time between each album can be agonizing, he never fails. *Closer To You* and *Guitar Man* were both (fortunately) more of the same and, as usual, faultless musicians gave him support. On the former release ex-Little Feat keyboardist Bill Payne, bassists Tim Drummond and Larry Taylor were featured among the array of names. The Chronicles *Anthology* is an excellent double CD collection.

● ALBUMS: *Naturally* (Shelter 1971)★★★, *Really* (Shelter 1972)★★★, *Okie* (Shelter 1974)★★★, *Troubadour* (Shelter 1976)★★★, *Five* (Shelter 1979)★★★, *Shades* (Shelter 1981)★★★, *Grasshopper* (Mercury 1982)★★, *8* (Mercury 1983)★★, *Travel Log* (Silvertone 1989)★★★, *Ten* (1992)★★★, *Closer To You* (Virgin 1994)★★★, *Guitar Man* (Virgin 1996)★★★.

● COMPILATIONS: *Special Edition* (Mercury 1984)★★★, *La Femme De Mon Pote* (Mercury 1984)★★★, *Nightriding* (Nightriding 1988)★★★, *Anyway The Wind Blows: The Anthology* (Mercury Chronicles 1997)★★★★.

CALL, BOB

Bob Call was a blues pianist, active in Chicago and best known for his accompaniments. He recorded in the late 20s with a number of artists, including Thomas A. Dorsey, Elzadie Robinson, Washboard Sam and James 'Boodle It' Wiggins. Robinson's 'St. Louis Cyclone Blues' was a particularly outstanding recording. He also recorded one single track under his own name at this time, '31 Blues'. Most of his sessions were for Lester Melrose. In 1948, he appeared on record again, one side a piano-led instrumental, the other featuring the vocals of Grant Jones.

● COMPILATIONS: *The Piano Blues, Volume 2* (1977).

CALLICOTT, JOE

b. 11 October 1900, Nesbit, Mississippi, USA, d. 1969, Mississippi, USA. Joe Callicott spent his whole life in the area south of Memphis, and his music has affinities with that of his neighbour Jim Jackson and especially Frank Stokes, with whom he sometimes worked in Memphis. His chief musical associate, however, was Garfield Akers, and it was as Akers' second guitarist that he first recorded in 1929. Callicott's solitary 78 rpm single was recorded the following year, pairing 'Fare Thee Well Blues', from the songster tradition, with 'Travelling Mama Blues', an amalgam of contemporary verses, both sung in a high, forceful voice to a rhythmic accompaniment. Callicott virtually ceased playing in 1959 when Akers died; although he had slowed down somewhat, his guitar rhythms were still metronomic. His voice became gentler, making the sound of his music more akin to that of Frank Stokes (minus the melodic embellishments usually provided by Stokes' second guitar or violin accompanists). Callicott favoured extended performances, but his ability to play in a variety of keys and tunings saves his work from the monotony that might be expected from the steady rhythmic tread, so that the overall effect is gently hypnotic.

● COMPILATIONS: *Deal Gone Down* (1968), *Mississippi Delta Blues, Volume 2* (1968), *Presenting The Country Blues* (1969), *Son House And The Great Delta Blues Singers* (1990).

CAMPBELL, EDDIE C.

b. 6 May 1939, Duncan, Mississippi, USA. Campbell began playing music on a one-string guitar, and later moved to Chicago with his family at the age of seven. He was inspired by Muddy Waters to learn to play seriously, and in the late 50s he was part of the coterie of young, exciting blues guitarists on the city's west side (acquaintances included Magic Sam, Otis Rush, Luther Allison and Willie James Lyons). He played with Johnny Taylor, Koko Taylor, Willie Dixon and Lowell Fulson prior to 1970. He made a few recordings for small, local labels but his debut album in the 70s (featuring Carey Bell and Lurrie Bell) suffered from poor distribution. He did, however, gain international acclaim in 1979 as a member of the American Blues Legends tour. He returned to Chicago, but settled in Europe in 1984 and has since acquired a large following for his style of blues. His original album has benefitted from a complete re-mix and much wider distribution from Rooster Blues.
● ALBUMS: *King Of The Jungle* remixed 1985 (Rooster Blues 1977)★★★, *Let's Pick It* (Black Magic 1985)★★★, *The Baddest Cat On The Block* (JSP 1985)★★★, *Mind Trouble* (Double Trouble 1988)★★★, *That's When I Know* (Blind Pig 1995)★★★.

CAMPBELL, 'LITTLE' MILTON

(see Little Milton)

CAMPBELL, JOHN

b. 1952, Shreveport, Louisiana, USA, d. 13 June 1993, New York. Campbell, a white man, became an authentic-sounding blues singer/guitarist after a serious drag racing accident in 1967, which left him without one of his eyes and a mass of stitches in his face, which became permanently scarred. Prior to this crash, he had been curious about music - his grandmother played lap steel guitar - but he was more interested in being a tearaway. During his lengthy period of recuperation, much of it spent in solitude, he taught himself to play guitar and became devoted to the work of the black bluesmen who had recorded for the local Jewel label in Shreveport; in particular, John Lee Hooker and Lightnin' Hopkins, the latter of whom became his major influence. Leaving school in the late 60s, he became a travelling troubadour, working as the opening act for 'Gatemouth' Brown and Hubert Smith, ultimately relocating to New York where he played local clubs for many years. His recording debut came in 1988, when guitarist Ronnie Earl sent a tape of Campbell to the specialist Crosscut label in Germany. Earl produced his first album, *A Man And His Blues*, but it had little distribution in the USA, and he remained an obscure cult figure until he began working with guitarist Alexander Kennedy. He and Kennedy were opening for Albert King in New York when he was signed by Elektra Records, and in 1991 he released *One Believer*, produced by Dennis Walker (also Robert Gray's producer), and backed by members of both Gray's band and Joe Ely's group. Campbell played solely amplified acoustic guitar, and his songwriting partnership with Walker and Kennedy produced several modern blues classics such as 'Devil In My Closet', 'Tiny Coffin' and 'Take Me Down'. *Howlin' Mercy* consolidated his standing as an important (although cult) figure in the recent blues boom. He died in 1993 prior to undertaking a European tour.
● ALBUMS: *A Man And His Blues* (Crosscut 1988)★★★, *One Believer* (Elektra 1991)★★★★, *Howlin' Mercy* (Elektra 1993)★★★.

CANNED HEAT

This popular, but ill-fated, blues/rock group was formed in 1965 by two Los Angeles-based blues aficionados: Alan Wilson (b. 4 July 1943, Boston, Massachusetts, USA, d. 3 September 1970; vocals, harmonica, guitar) and Bob 'The Bear' Hite (b. 26 February 1943, Torrance, California, USA, d. 5 April 1981, Paris, France; vocals). Wilson, nicknamed 'Blind Owl' in deference to his thick-lensed spectacles, was already renowned for his distinctive harmonica work and had accompanied Son House on the veteran bluesman's post-'rediscovery' album, *Father Of Folk Blues*. Wilson's obsession with the blues enabled him to build up a massive archive blues collection by his early twenties. The duo was joined by Frank Cook (drums) and Henry Vestine (b. 25 December 1944, Washington DC, USA, d. November 1997; guitar), a former member of the Mothers Of Invention. They took the name Canned Heat from a 1928 recording by Tommy Johnson and employed several bassists prior to the arrival of Larry Taylor, an experienced session musician who had worked with Jerry Lee Lewis and the Monkees. Canned Heat's debut album was promising rather than inspired, offering diligent readings of such 12-bar standards as 'Rollin' And Tumblin'', 'Dust My Broom' and 'Bullfrog Blues'. However, the arrival of new drummer Alfredo Fito (b. Adolfo De La Parra, 8 February 1946, Mexico City, Mexico) coincided with a new-found confidence, displayed almost immediately on *Boogie With Canned Heat*. This impressive selection introduced the extended 'Fried Hookey Boogie', a piece destined to become an in-concert favourite, and the hypnotic remake of Jim Oden's 'On The Road Again', which gave the group a UK Top 10 and US Top 20 hit single in 1968. Wilson's distinctive frail high voice, sitar-like guitar introduction and accompanying harmonica have made this version a classic. A double set, *Livin' The Blues*, includes an enthralling version of Charley Patton's 'Pony Blues' and a 19-minute *tour de force*, 'Parthenogenesis', which captures the quintet at their most experimental. However, it was Wilson's adaptation of a Henry Thomas song, 'Bulldoze Blues', that proved most popular. The singer retained the tune of the original, rewrote the lyric and emerged with 'Goin' Up The Country', whose simple message caught the prevalent back-to-nature attitude of the late 60s. This evocative performance charted in the US and UK Top 20, and was one of the highlights of the successful *Woodstock* movie.

In 1969 and 1970 Canned Heat recorded four more albums, including a spirited collaboration with blues boogie mentor John Lee Hooker, and a fascinating documentary of their 1970 European tour. *Hallelujah* boasted one of artist George Hunter's finest album covers. It also featured 'Get Off My Back', which in its day was used by hi-fi buffs to check their systems were in phase, as the cross-channel switching in the mix was outrageously overdone. *Future Blues* marked the arrival of guitarist Harvey Mandel, replacing Vestine, who could no longer tolerate working with Taylor. The reshaped band enjoyed two further UK hits with a cover of Wilbert Harrison's 'Let's Work Together', which reached number 2, and the cajun-inspired 'Sugar

Bee', but they were then shattered by the suicide of Wilson, whose body was found in Hite's backyard on 3 September 1970. His death sparked a major reconstruction within the group: Taylor and Mandel left to join John Mayall, the former's departure prompting Vestine's return, while Antonio De La Barreda became Canned Heat's new bassist. The new quartet completed *Historical Figures And Ancient Heads*, before Hite's brother Richard replaced Barreda for the band's 1973 release, *The New Age*. The changes continued throughout the decade, undermining the band's strength of purpose. Bob Hite, the sole remaining original member, attempted to keep the group afloat, but was unable to secure a permanent recording contract. Spirits lifted with the release of *Human Condition*, but the years of struggle had taken their toll. On 5 April 1981, following a gig at the Palomino Club, the gargantuan vocalist collapsed and died of a heart attack. Despite the loss of many key members, the Canned Heat name has survived. Inheritors Larry Taylor and Fito De La Parra completed 1989's *Re-heated* album with two new guitarists, James Thornbury and Junior Watson. They now pursue the lucrative nostalgia circuit with various former members coming and going. Vestine was allowed to perform when he stuck to soft alcohol and herbal substances (he subsequently died in November 1997). Taylor now has a heart condition, and the band is led by De La Parra.

● ALBUMS: *Canned Heat* (Liberty 1967)★★★, *Boogie With Canned Heat* (Liberty 1968)★★★, *Livin' The Blues* (Liberty 1968)★★★, *Hallelujah* (Liberty 1969)★★★★, *Vintage - Canned Heat* early recordings (Pye International 1970)★★, *Canned Heat '70: Concert* (Liberty 1970)★★, *Future Blues* (Liberty 1970)★★★, with John Lee Hooker *Hooker 'N' Heat* (Liberty 1971)★★★, with Memphis Slim *Memphis Heat* (Barclay 1971)★★, *Historical Figures And Ancient Heads* (United Artists 1972)★★★, with Clarence 'Gatemouth' Brown *Gate's On Heat* (Barclay 1973)★★★, *New Age* (United Artists 1973)★★, *One More River To Cross* (Atlantic 1974)★★, with Memphis Slim *Memphis Heat* (Barclay 1975)★★, *Live At Topanga Corral* (DJM 1976)★★, *The Human Condition* (Takoma 1978)★★, *Captured Live* (1981)★★, with Hooker *Hooker 'N' Heat - Live* (Rhino

1981)★★★, *Kings Of The Boogie* (Destiny 1981)★★, *The Boogie Assault - Live In Australia* (Bedrock 1987)★★, *Re-Heated* (Dali 1989)★★, *Live At The Turku Rock Festival* (Bear Family 1990)★★, *Internal Combustion* (River Road 1995)★★, *Blues Band* (Mystic 1997)★★, *The Ties That Bind* 1974 recording (Archive 1997)★★.
● COMPILATIONS: *Canned Heat Cook Book (The Best Of Canned Heat)* (Liberty 1970)★★★, *The Very Best Of Canned Heat* (1973)★★★, with Hooker *Infinite Boogie* (Rhino 1987)★★★, with Hooker *Hooker 'N' Heat Volume 2* (Rhino 1988)★★, *The Best Of Hooker 'N' Heat* (See For Miles 1988)★★★, *Let's Work Together - The Best Of Canned Heat* (Liberty 1989)★★★, *The Big Heat* (1992)★★★, *Uncanned - The Best Of Canned Heat* (Liberty 1994)★★★★.

CANNON'S JUG STOMPERS

Led by Gus Cannon, the Jug Stompers were the finest and most blues-orientated of the Memphis jug bands, recording for Victor from 1928 to 1930. The permanent members were Cannon himself (playing rushing, syncopated banjo and a fruity, ribald jug) and harmonica player Noah Lewis. Guitarists Ashley Thompson and Elijah Avery passed through the group's trio format in 1928 before vocalist Hosea Woods became the third member. The group blended the light-hearted novelties of the medicine shows with strutting ragtime pieces and deeply emotional blues, particularly when Lewis was providing vocals; Cannon's booming singing was more suited to the extrovert side of their repertoire. Woods died in the 30s, and Avery's subsequent history is unknown; Thompson was still playing in 1971 but died during the mid-70s.
● COMPILATIONS: *Cannon's Jug Stompers* (1974)★★★, *Old Country Blues* (1979)★★★, *The Complete Works* (1989)★★★.

CANNON, GUS

b. 12 September 1883, Red Banks, Mississippi, USA, d. 15 October 1979, Memphis, Tennessee, USA. As a youth, Cannon was a proficient fiddler, as well as a guitarist and pianist, but his main instrument was the banjo. Cannon, whose parents had been slaves, made his first banjo at the age of 12 from a guitar neck and a bread pan. He was taught to play in Clarksdale, Mississippi,

by a musician named Bud Jackson and studied other local players, such as W.C. Handy. It was as 'Banjo Joe' that Cannon appeared on the 'medicine shows' every summer from 1914-29, working as a farm labourer during the winter months. While in Chicago with a medicine show he recorded for Paramount in 1927, with Blind Blake on guitar. Spurred on by the 1927 success of the Memphis Jug Band, Cannon added a coal-oil can on a neck harness to his equipment, and was signed when the Victor label came to Memphis in 1928. Cannon's Jug Stompers recorded annually from 1928-30, producing some of the finest and most bluesy jug band 78s. As fashions changed, Cannon ceased playing the streets for money in 1950, but he kept in practice, and made some recordings for folklorists in 1956 and 1961. In 1963 came an unlikely moment of fame, when the Rooftop Singers had a number 1 hit with 'Walk Right In', which the Stompers had recorded in 1929. He continued to make occasional recordings for friends in the 70s, though naturally, they were of diminishing liveliness. Cannon has since been considered by music historians as one of the links between pre-blues Negro folk music and the blues.
● ALBUMS: *American Skiffle Bands* (1958)★★★, *Walk Right In* (Stax 1962)★★★.
● COMPILATIONS: *Old Country Blues* (1979)★★★, *Gus Cannon* (Collectors Issue 1988)★★★, *Will Shade And Gus Cannon* (1989)★★★, *The Complete Works* (1989)★★★, *Gus Cannon* (Document 1992)★★★, *Gus Cannon & Noah Lewis* (Document 1992)★★★, *The Legendary 1928-1930 Recordings* (JSP 1994)★★★.

CAROLINA SLIM

b. Edward P. Harris, 22 August 1923, Leasburg, North Carolina, USA, d. 22 October 1953, Newark, New Jersey, USA. Little is known about Harris, but it seems that he started his musical career in North Carolina and moved to Newark about the time of his first recordings in 1950. Records followed on three different labels, under four different pseudonyms; Carolina Slim, Jammin' Jim, Country Paul and Lazy Slim Jim. These records are unusual for their time in that many of them feature solo country blues, either in the Carolina style of Blind Boy Fuller, or blatant copies of Lightnin' Hopkins, although all are skilful and convincing performances. At his best, Slim could synthesize his influences to produce a satisfyingly distinctive sound, but unfortunately he did not live long enough to develop a real style of his own.

● COMPILATIONS: *Carolina Blues And Boogie* (Travelin' Man 1985)★★★, *1950-52* (1993)★★★.

CARR, LEROY

b. 27 March 1905, Nashville, Tennessee, USA, d. 29 April 1935. A self-taught pianist, Carr grew up in Kentucky and Indiana but was on the road working with a travelling circus when still in his teens. In the early 20s he was playing piano, often as an accompanist to singers, mostly in and around Covington, Kentucky. In the mid-20s he partnered 'Scrapper' Blackwell, touring and recording with him. Carr's singing style, a bittersweet, poetic interpretation of the blues, brought a patina of urban refinement to the earthy, rough-cut intensity of the earlier country blues singers. Even though he rarely worked far afield, his recordings of his own compositions, which included 'Midnight Hour Blues', 'Hurry Down Sunshine', 'Blues Before Sunrise' and, especially, 'How Long, How Long Blues', proved enormously influential. Although he died young, Carr's work substantially altered approaches to blues singing, and powerful echoes of his innovatory methods can be heard in the work of artists such as Champion Jack Dupree, Cecil Gant, Jimmy Rushing, Otis Spann, Eddie 'Cleanhead' Vinson and T-Bone Walker, who, in their turn, influenced countless R&B and rock 'n' roll singers of later generations. An acute alcoholic, Carr died in April 1935.

● COMPILATIONS: *Leroy Carr (1928)* (Matchbox 1983)★★★, *Blues Before Sunrise* (Official 1988)★★★, *Naptown Blues* (Yazoo 1988)★★★, *Leroy Carr: 1929-1934* (Document 1989)★★★, *Don't Cry When I'm Gone* (Magpie 1990)★★★, *Hurry Down Sunshine: The Essential Recordings Of Leroy Carr* (Indigo 1995)★★★.

CARTER, BIG LUCKY

b. Levester Carter, 1920, Weir, Mississippi, USA. Although he had played spirituals on his grandmother's piano, Carter did not take up the guitar until he was serving in the Pacific during World War II. When he returned to Mississippi, he took instruction from local musicians James Henry and Big Boy Anderson. In 1949, he joined a band that also featured pianist Ford Nelson. In Memphis the following year he joined his cousin, saxophonist Ed Kirby (who worked as Prince Gabe), in his band, the Rhythmaires. He remained with the band (its name having been changed to the Millionaires) for eight years. In January 1957 they recorded a session for Sun Records under his cousin's real name, from which some titles were issued during the 70s. Carter led his own band during the 60s but continued to record with Kirby for Savoy, Westside and Bandstand USA. In 1969 he made two singles for Willie Mitchell's M.O.C. label, one of which, 'Goofer Dust', is regarded as his principal achievement, and on which he was backed by members of Al Green's band, including guitarist Mabon 'Teenie' Hodges. These and two further titles were issued on *River Town Blues* two years later. Although he continued to write and perform, nothing was heard from Carter until his appearance at the 1993 Burnley Blues Festival.

● ALBUMS: *River Town Blues* (Hi 1971)★★★, *River Town Blues Plus!* (Hi 1991)★★★.

CARTER, BO

b. Armenter Chatmon, 21 March 1893, Bolton, Mississippi, USA, d. 21 September 1964, Memphis, Tennessee, USA. One of Henderson Chatmon's many musical sons, Bo Carter was a performing, and occasionally a recording, member of the family band, the Mississippi Sheiks. He played on guitar and violin, but it was as a solo singer and guitarist that he was best known on record. A talented player whose steel guitar provided him with an instantly recognizable sound, he was the first to record 'Corrine Corrina', and could compose sensitive, introspective songs such as 'Sorry Feeling Blues'. However, both his guitar talents and his sensitivity were underemployed on record, where he recorded many tracks with titles like 'Banana In Your Fruit Basket' and 'Please Warm My Weiner' with stereotyped accompaniments. Blindness and changing fashions ended his career in the early 40s, and he died in poverty.

● COMPILATIONS: *Greatest Hits* (Yazoo 1970)★★★, *Twist It Babe* (Yazoo 1974)★★★, *Banana In Your Fruit Basket* (Yazoo 1979)★★★, *Bo Carter* (Yazoo 1982)★★★.

CARTER, GOREE

b. 31 December 1930, Houston, Texas, USA, d. 29 December 1990, Houston, Teaxs, USA. One of a legion of guitarists influenced by T-Bone Walker, Carter's recording career was brief and proscribed by the expectations of the record companies for whom he recorded. Eighteen years old when he made his first records for Samuel Kahl's Freedom label, young Goree had picked up the guitar five years earlier after an older sister had witnessed T-Bone's act at the Bronze Peacock and bought his records. As 'Rock Awhile' and 'My Love Is Coming Down' showed, Carter had mastered his mentor's style, even if he sometimes favoured a coarser guitar tone. Attempts to broaden his style were thwarted by his manager's insistence on emulating T-Bone Walker's example. Further sessions for Imperial, Sittin In With, Jade (as Rocky Thompson), Modern and Coral over the course of the next two years saw little change in the prevailing tenor of his music. A stint in the army and the strain of nursing his ailing mother effectively ended his short career. One further session for Peacock in 1954 remained unissued after he and label owner Don Robey exchanged blows. When he was rediscovered in 1982, he had not played in public for more than a decade.
● COMPILATIONS: *Rock Awhile* (Blues Boy 1983)★★★, *Unsung Hero* (Collectables 1993)★★★, *Let's Boogie* (Collectables 1993)★★★, *Come On Let's Boogie* (P-Vine 1994)★★★.

CARTER, JOE

b. 6 November 1927, Midland, Georgia, USA. In 1952 Carter settled in Chicago and is chiefly known as an Elmore James-styled slide guitarist and singer, although he can also play in a more modern vein. Carter made his only full album for the Barrelhouse label in 1976, although he has had numerous tracks released by JSP, MCM and Red Lightnin'; he also appeared in the BBC Television documentary series *The Devil's Music*. In the late 70s he toured Europe, billed on some appearances as 'Elmore James Junior' and continues to play the clubs around Chicago as one of the city's few remaining slide guitarists in the traditional style.
● ALBUMS: *Mean And Evil Blues* (Barrelhouse 1976)★★★.

● COMPILATIONS: *The Devil's Music* (1976)★★★, *Original Chicago Blues* 1976 recordings (JSP 1982)★★★, *I Didn't Give A Damn If Whites Bought It! Volume One* 1977 recording (1984)★★★.
● VIDEOS: *New Music* (Kay Jazz 1988).

CARTER, VIVIAN, AND JAMES BRACKEN

In 1948, Jim Bracken (b. 1909, Kansas City, Missouri, USA, d. 1972), set up Vivian's Record Shop in Gary, Indiana, named after his radio announcer wife, Vivian Carter (b. 1920, Tunica, Mississippi. USA, d. 12 June 1989, Gary, Indiana, USA). Five years later, the duo started the Vee Jay label to record Chicago's blues and R&B talent. Their first artists were blues singer Jimmy Reed and doo-wop group the Spaniels, whose 'Goodnight Sweetheart Goodnight' was Vee Jay's first R&B hit in 1954. Subsequently, Reed provided a series of 13 chart records between 1955 and 1961. The musical directors of the company were Calvin Carter (Vivian's brother) and Ewart Abner who signed artists such as Dee Clark and the Impressions. During the 50s, Vee Jay also recorded gospel music (Swan Silvertones, Staple Singers) and licensed in R&B material from all over the USA. Pop success followed in the 60s with 'Duke Of Earl' by Gene Chandler and 'Sherry' by the Four Seasons. Then, in 1963, Vee Jay was offered tracks by a new British group who had been turned down by Capitol, the US sister company to their UK label. At first, singles by the Beatles made little impact, but after the onset of Beatlemania, Bracken and Carter had Top 10 hits with 'Please Please Me' and 'Twist And Shout'. The headquarters were briefly moved to Los Angeles but like many other small, locally based labels, Vee Jay could not compete on a national level and its financial affairs were insufficiently supervised by the owners. By 1966 the company was bankrupt. After the collapse, Abner joined Motown while Bracken and Carter ran small labels including J.V. and Ra-Bra.

CASTON, LEONARD 'BABY DOO'

b. 2 June 1917, Sumrall, near Hattisburg, Mississippi, USA, d. 22 August 1987, Minneapolis, Minnesota, USA. More than just a blues pianist, Baby Doo Caston was a musician whose range included popular and light classical music. His early influence and mentor was his cousin Alan Weathersby, who taught him to play guitar at an early age. After several moves they began playing around the Natchez area and were managed by Leonard's mother Minda. Baby Doo took up the piano around 1936 and moved to Chicago, where he heard the likes of Earl Hines, Big Bill Broonzy and T-Bone Walker, but he was most influenced by Leroy Carr. He played with the Five Breezes and his own group, the Rhythm Rascals Trio, before the war found him on a United States Overseas entertainment tour with Alberta Hunter. He worked through China, Burma, India, Egypt, Africa and Europe, a high spot being a command performance for Generals Eisenhower, Montgomery and Zhukov in Germany in 1945. Returning to Chicago, he formed the Big Three Trio with Willie Dixon and Ollie Crawford, with whom he recorded for Bullet, Columbia and OKeh, as well as working as a soloist (recording an album on his own Hot Shot label) and supporting many blues artists. His final job was a long-standing engagement in Minneapolis where he died of heart failure.

● ALBUMS: *Hot Shot* (Hot Shot 1986)★★★, *I Feel Like Steppin' Out* (1986)★★★, *Willie Dixon And The Big Three Trio* (Columbia 1990)★★★.

● FURTHER READING: *From Blues To Pop: The Autobiography Of Leonard 'Baby Doo' Caston*, Jeff Todd Titon.

CAT IRON

b. William Carradine, *c*.1896, Garden City, Louisiana, USA, d. *c*.1958, Natchez, Mississippi, USA. A folklorist's mishearing of his surname resulted in the evocative billing given to this singer and guitarist's only album. Recorded on a single day in 1958, at first he would play only stirring versions of old hymns with slide accompaniment, but later consented to record a number of fine blues, including the important blues ballad 'Jimmy Bell'. Cat Iron made a television appearance that year, but is believed to have died soon afterwards.

● ALBUMS: *Cat Iron Sings Blues & Hymns* (1960)★★★.

CATFISH KEITH

b. Keith Daniel Kozacik, 9 February 1962, East Chicago, Indiana, USA. A blues singer and gui-

tarist, having attended school in Davenport, Iowa, Keith first started listening to blues music on the radio with his father, following fishing trips. However, it was at the age of 15, when he heard 'Death Letter' by Son House, that he was truly bitten by the blues bug. By his late teens Keith was already on the road performing, the nickname 'Catfish' given to him by a friend on a fishing trip in the Virgin Islands. Since his debut release, *Catfish Blues*, for Kicking Mule, Keith has recorded for his own Fish Tail Records label, giving him full artistic control over the end result. Over the years he has developed a highly refreshing style, utilizing acoustic and National steel slide guitar. Apart from his own compositions, he features material by blues greats such as John Lee Hooker, Mississippi John Hurt and Skip James, to name only a few. *Twist It Babe!* featured some inspired acoustic bass from Marty Christensen.

● ALBUMS: *Catfish Blues* (Kicking Mule 1985)★★★, *Paper In My Shoe* (Fish Tail 1991)★★★, *Jitterbug Swing* (Fish Tail1992)★★★, *Cherry Ball* (Fish Tail 1993★★★), *Fresh Catfish* (Fish Tail 1995)★★, *Twist It Babe!* (Fishtail 1997)★★★.

CEPHAS, JOHN

b. 4 September 1930, Washington DC, USA. Cephas was raised in Bowling Green, Kentucky, and learned guitar from local musicians and from records. His music is indebted to Blind Boy Fuller and Eugene 'Buddy' Moss, and his dexterous, slightly anonymous playing shares with them a ragtime-influenced complexity. His singing voice is deep and rather unvaried, and his repertoire eclectic, drawing on both tradition and recordings (including, surprisingly, those of Skip James). Cephas has led a settled life as a civil service carpenter, with music as a sideline; only in the 70s did his talent come to wider notice, when he began to play festivals and to record, at first with Wilbert 'Big Chief' Ellis and, since Ellis's death, with the young harmonica player Phil Wiggins.

● ALBUMS: *Living Country Blues*, Volume 1 (1981)★★★, *Dog Days Of August* (Flying Fish 1986)★★★, with Phil Wiggins *Guitar Man* (Flying Fish 1989)★★★, with Wiggins *Cool Down* (Alligator 1995)★★★.

CHAIN

While blues music in Australia has been limited to a handful of solo performers (Dutch Tilders, Margaret Roadknight, Ian Beecroft) and one or two enduring bands in the state capitals (the Foreday Riders in Sydney; the Others in Adelaide; Southern Lightning in Melbourne; and Union Blues Band in Brisbane), it has never had a high profile, nor enjoyed much chart success. One exception was Chain, who had a nationwide hit with 'Black & Blue' in 1971. The follow-up single reached the charts, although the band was much better known for their extended blues jamming on the live circuit. Chain was formed in Melbourne in 1969 and went through over a dozen line-ups before disbanding in 1974. The best-known line-ups were based around long-serving bassist and drummer Big and Little Goose (Barry Harvey and Barry Sullivan). In 1976 the band recruited singer-songwriter Matt Taylor (b. 12 July 1948, Australia), whose gruff, unsophisticated voice gave the music a readily identifiable sound. The band played and recorded mainly traditional material, with its sound enhanced by renowned blues guitarist Phil Manning. After Taylor left to live on a commune, the band lost much of its mainstream appeal, despite persistent recording and live appearances. Taylor recorded three solo albums, the first capturing his homespun songs and harmonica playing. The Taylor, Manning, Sullivan, Harvey line-up re-formed briefly in 1982, but then, as the others dropped out over the next few years, Taylor replaced them with various Perth hard rock musicians, which subsequently led to Chain's blues sound becoming somewhat diminished.

● ALBUMS: *Live* (1970)★★★, *Towards The Blues* (1971)★★★, *Live Again* (1972)★★★, *Two Of A Kind* (1973)★★★, *Child Of The Street* (1985)★★★, *Australian R&B* (1988)★★★, *Blue Metal* (1989)★★★.

CHARLES, RAY

b. Ray Charles Robinson, 23 September 1930, Albany, Georgia, USA. Few epithets sit less comfortably than that of genius; Ray Charles has borne this title for over thirty years. As a singer, composer, arranger and pianist, his prolific work deserves no other praise. Born in extreme poverty, Charles was slowly blinded by glau-coma until, by the age of seven, he had lost his sight completely. Earlier, he had been forced to cope with the tragic death of his brother, whom he had seen drown in a water tub. He learned to read and write music in braille and was proficient on several instruments by the time he left school. His mother Aretha died when Charles was 15, and he continued to have a shared upbringing with Mary Jane (the first wife of Charles's absent father). Charles drifted around the Florida circuit, picking up work where he could, before moving across the country to Seattle. Here he continued his itinerant career, playing piano at several nightclubs in a style reminiscent of Nat 'King' Cole. Charles began recording in 1949 and this early, imitative approach was captured on several sessions. Three years later Atlantic Records acquired his contract, but initially the singer continued his 'cool' direction, revealing only an occasional hint of the passions later unleashed. 'It Should've Been Me', 'Mess Around' and 'Losing Hand' best represent this early R&B era, but Charles's individual style emerged as a result of his work with Guitar Slim. This impassioned, almost crude blues performer sang with a gospel-based fervour that greatly influenced Charles's thinking. He arranged Slim's million-selling single, 'Things That I Used To Do', of which the riffing horns and unrestrained voice set the tone for Charles's own subsequent direction. This effect was fully realized in 'I Got A Woman' (1954), a song soaked in the fervour of the Baptist Church, but rendered salacious by the singer's abandoned, unrefined delivery. Its extraordinary success, commercially and artistically, inspired similarly compulsive recordings, including 'This Little Girl Of Mine' (1955), 'Talkin' 'Bout You' (1957) and the lush and evocative 'Don't Let The Sun Catch You Crying' (1959), a style culminating in the thrilling call and response of 'What'd I Say' (1959). This acknowledged classic is one of the all-time great encore numbers performed by countless singers and bands in stadiums, clubs and bars all over the world. However, Charles was equally adept at slow ballads, as his heartbreaking interpretations of 'Drown In My Own Tears' and 'I Believe To My Soul' (both 1959) clearly show. Proficient in numerous styles, Charles's recordings embraced blues, jazz, standards and even country, as his muscular reading of 'I'm Movin' On' attested.

In November 1959 Charles left the Atlantic label for ABC Records, where he secured both musical and financial freedom. Commentators often cite this as the point at which the singer lost his fire, but early releases for this new outlet simply continued his groundbreaking style. 'Georgia On My Mind' (1960) and 'Hit The Road Jack' (1961) were, respectively, poignant and ebullient, and established the artist as an international name. This stature was enhanced further in 1962 with the release of the massive-selling album, *Modern Sounds In Country And Western*, a landmark collection that produced the million-selling single 'I Can't Stop Loving You'. Its success defined the pattern for Charles's later career; the edges were blunted, the vibrancy was stilled as Charles' repertoire grew increasingly inoffensive. There were still moments of inspiration, 'Let's Go Get Stoned' and 'I Don't Need No Doctor' brought a glimpse of a passion now too often muted, while *Crying Time*, Charles' first album since kicking his heroin habit, compared favourably with any Atlantic release. This respite was, however, temporary and as the 60s progressed so the singer's work became less compulsive and increasingly MOR. Like most artists, he attempted cover versions of Beatles songs and had substantial hits with versions of 'Yesterday' and 'Eleanor Rigby'. Two 70s releases, *A Message From The People* and *Renaissance*, did include contemporary material in Stevie Wonder's 'Living In The City' and Randy Newman's 'Sail Away', but subsequent releases reneged on this promise. Charles's 80s work included more country-flavoured collections and a cameo appearance in the film *The Blues Brothers*, but the period is better marked by the singer's powerful appearance on the USA For Africa release, 'We Are The World' (1985). It brought to mind a talent too often dormant, a performer whose marriage of gospel and R&B laid the foundations for soul music. His influence is inestimable, his talent widely acknowledged and imitated by formidable white artists such as Steve Winwood, Joe Cocker, Van Morrison and Eric Burdon. Charles has been honoured with countless awards during his career including the Lifetime Achievement Award. He has performed rock, jazz, blues and country with spectacular ease but it is 'father of soul music' that remains his greatest title; it was fitting that, in 1992, an acclaimed documentary, *Ray Charles: The Genius Of Soul*, was broadcast by PBS television. *My World* was a sparkling return to form, and is one of his finest albums in many years, particularly noteworthy for his version of Leon Russell's 'A Song For You', a song that sounds like it has always been a Charles song, such is the power of this man's outstanding voice. *Strong Love Affair* continued in the same vein with a balance of ballads matching the up-tempo tracks; however, it was clear that low-register, slow songs such as 'Say No More', 'Angelina' and 'Out Of My Life' should be the focus of Charles's concentration.

● ALBUMS: *Hallelujah, I Love Her So* aka *Ray Charles* (Atlantic 1957)★★★, *The Great Ray Charles* (Atlantic 1957)★★★★, with Milt Jackson *Soul Brothers* (Atlantic 1958)★★★, *Ray Charles At Newport* (Atlantic 1958)★★★, *Yes Indeed* (Atlantic 1959)★★★, *Ray Charles* (Hollywood 1959)★★★★, *The Fabulous Ray Charles* (Hollywood 1959)★★★, *What'd I Say* (Atlantic 1959)★★★, *The Genius Of Ray Charles* (Atlantic 1959)★★★★★, *Ray Charles In Person* (1960)★★★, *Genius Hits The Road* (ABC 1960)★★★, *The Genius After Hours* (Atlantic 1961)★★★★, *The Genius Sings The Blues* (Atlantic 1961)★★★★, with Milt Jackson *Soul Meeting* (Atlantic 1961)★★★, *Do The Twist With Ray Charles* (Atlantic 1961)★★★, *Dedicated To You* (ABC 1961)★★★, *Genius + Soul = Jazz* (ABC 1961)★★★★★, with Betty Carter *Ray Charles And Betty Carter* (ABC 1961)★★★★, *Modern Sounds In Country And Western* (ABC 1962)★★★★★, *Modern Sounds In Country And Western Volume 2* (ABC 1962)★★★★, *Ingredients In A Recipe For Soul* (ABC 1963)★★★★, *Sweet And Sour Tears* (ABC 1964)★★★, *Have A Smile With Me* (ABC 1964)★★★, *Live In Concert* (ABC 1965)★★★, *Country And Western Meets Rhythm And Blues* aka *Together Again* (ABC 1965)★★★, *Crying Time* (ABC 1966)★★★, *Ray's Moods* (ABC 1966)★★★, *Ray Charles Invites You To Listen* (ABC 1967)★★★, *A Portrait Of Ray* (ABC 1968)★★, *I'm All Yours, Baby!* (ABC 1969)★★, *Doing His Thing* (ABC 1969)★★★, *My Kind Of Jazz* (Tangerine 1970)★★★, *Love Country Style* (ABC 1970)★★, *Volcanic Action Of My Soul* (ABC 1971)★★, *A Message From The People* (Tangerine 1972)★★, *Through The Eyes Of Love*

(ABC 1972), *Jazz Number II* (Tangerine 1972)★★★, *Come Live With Me* (Crossover 1974)★★, *Renaissance* (Crossover 1975)★★, *My Kind Of Jazz III* (Crossover 1975)★★, *Live In Japan* (1975)★★★, with Cleo Laine *Porgy And Bess* (RCA 1976)★★★, *True To Life* (Atlantic 1977)★★, *Love And Peace* (Atlantic 1978)★★, *Ain't It So* (Atlantic 1979)★★, *Brother Ray Is At It Again* (Atlantic 1980)★★, *Wish You Were Here Tonight* (Columbia 1983)★★, *Do I Ever Cross Your Mind* (Columbia 1984)★★, *Friendship* (Columbia 1985)★★, *The Spirit Of Christmas* (Columbia 1985)★★, *From The Pages Of My Mind* (Columbia 1986)★★, *Just Between Us* (Columbia 1988)★★, *Seven Spanish Angels And Other Hits* (Columbia 1989)★★, *Would You Believe* (Warners 1990)★★, *My World* (Warners 1993)★★★★, *Strong Love Affair* (Qwest 1996)★★, *Berlin, 1962* (Pablo 1996)★★★★.
● COMPILATIONS: *The Ray Charles Story* (1962)★★★, *A Man And His Soul* (1967)★★★, *The Best Of Ray Charles 1956-58* (Atlantic 1970)★★★★, *25th Anniversary In Show Business Salute To Ray Charles* (ABC 1971)★★★★, *The Right Time* (Atlantic 1987)★★★, *A Life In Music 1956-59* (Atlantic 1982)★★★★, *Greatest Hits Vol. 1 1960-67* (Rhino 1988)★★★★, *Anthology* (Rhino 1989)★★★★, *The Collection* ABC recordings (Castle 1990)★★★, *Blues Is My Middle Name* 1949-52 recordings (Double Play 1991)★★★, *The Birth Of Soul 1952-59* (Atlantic 1991)★★★★★, *The Complete Atlantic Rhythm And Blues Recordings* 4-CD box set (Atlantic 1992)★★★★★, *The Living Legend* (1993)★★★, *The Best Of The Atlantic Years* (Rhino/ Atlantic 1994)★★★, *Classics* (Rhino 1995)★★★, *Genius & Soul* 5-CD box set (Rhino 1997)★★★.
● FURTHER READING: *Ray Charles*, Sharon Bell Mathis. *Brother Ray, Ray Charles' Own Story*, Ray Charles and David Ritz.
● FILMS: *Blues For Lovers* aka *Ballad In Blue* (1964), *The Blues Brothers* (1980).

CHATMON, SAM

b. 10 January 1897, Bolton, Mississippi, USA, d. 2 February 1983, Hollandale, Mississippi, USA. Guitarist Sam Chatmon was one of the many children of ex-slave fiddler Henderson Chatmon, all of whom were musicians. Besides Sam, Lonnie (as the fiddling half of the Mississippi Sheiks), Bo (as Bo Carter) and

pianist Harry all made recordings in the 30s. In addition, Sam's own son, Singin' Sam, is a bass guitarist. Sam Snr.'s 1936 recordings with Lonnie as the Chatmon Brothers are, not surprisingly, similar to those of the Mississippi Sheiks, who were the one black string band to become major stars on record. When white interest in the blues was aroused in the 60s, Sam proved to be the only member of the family to have survived with his musical faculties intact, and he came out of almost 20 years of musical retirement to perform for the new audience until his death. A strong, somewhat inflexible vocalist, and a fluent, although rather anonymous, pattern picker, Chatmon in his later career played mostly blues, emphasizing the risqué when he was not covering the recorded hits of others. Perhaps more interesting than this side of his repertoire were the minstrel and popular songs of his youth, such as 'I Get The Blues When It Rains' and 'Turnip Greens'. He claimed, with some plausibility, to have composed 'Cross Cut Saw', twice made famous by Tommy McClennan and later by Albert King.
● COMPILATIONS: *The Mississippi Sheik* (1970)★★★, *The New Mississippi Sheiks* (1972)★★★, *Hollandale Blues* (1977)★★★, *Sam Chatmon's Advice* (Rounder 1979)★★★, *Mississippi String Bands* (1989)★★★.

CHAVIS, WILSON 'BOOZOO'

b. 23 October 1930, Lake Charles, Louisiana, USA. 'Boozoo' Chavis was one of the first artists to perform zydeco music in the 50s and enjoyed renewed popularity in the 80s and 90s. Chavis had learned to play accordion and harmonica by the age of nine and performed around Lake Charles while in his teens. In 1954 he was signed to Folk-Star Records by owner Eddie Shuler. Chavis recorded a traditional song, 'Paper In My Shoe' (for which he and Shuler took writing credit), backed by the local Classie Ballou's Tempo Kings. The session marked the first time Chavis had played with a band. The record sold well regionally and was picked up for national distribution by Imperial Records of Los Angeles. Chavis continued to record for Folk-Star and Shuler's Goldband label sporadically through the early 60s, then retreated from the music industry until 1984, when he began performing again in Louisiana. He quickly

became a local favourite and began recording for the small Maison de Soul, Rounder Records and Antones labels.
● ALBUMS: *Lousiana Zydeco Music* (1986)★★★, *Boozoo Zydeco* (Maison De Soul 1987)★★★, *Paper In My Shoe* (Ace 1987)★★★, *La Zydeco Music* (Maison De Soul 1987)★★★, *Live At Richard's Zydeco Dance Hall, Volume One* (Rounder 1988)★★★, *Nathon And The Zydeco Cha Cha's* (1989)★★★, *Boozoo's Breakdown* (Sonet 1991)★★★, with the Majic Sounds *Live! At The Habibi Temple, Lake Charles, Louisiana* (Rounder 1994)★★★, *Hey Do Right!* (Antones 1996)★★★.
● COMPILATIONS: *The Lake Charles Atomic Bomb* (1990)★★★.

CHENIER, C.J.

b. 28 September 1957, Port Arthur, Texas, USA. C.J. is the son of the 'king of zydeco', Clifton Chenier. He began playing saxophone while at school, but grew up knowing little about Louisiana zydeco music, and he spoke English at home. However, he learned quickly when he became a member of his father's band, replacing saxophonist John Hart. He recorded with his father and around 1984 he began to play accordion, graduating to opening shows as his father's health deteriorated. When his father died, he left his accordion to C.J., who has since recorded under his own name and rapidly established himself as a force to be reckoned with in the blues and zydeco market.
● ALBUMS: with the Red Hot Louisiana Band *Let Me In Your Heart* (Arhoolie 1988)★★★, *Hot Rod* (London 1991)★★★, *Too Much Fun* (Alligator 1995)★★★, *The Big Squeeze* (Alligator 1996)★★★.

CHENIER, CLIFTON

b. 25 June 1925, Opelousas, Louisiana, USA, d. 12 December 1987. This singer, guitarist, harmonica and accordion player is regarded by many as the 'king of zydeco music'. Chenier was given lessons on the accordion by his father, and started performing at dances. He also had the advantage of being able to sing in French patois, English and Creole. In 1945, Chenier was working as a cane cutter in New Iberia. In 1946, he followed his older brother, Cleveland, to Lake Charles. He absorbed a wealth of tunes from musicians such as Zozo Reynolds, Izeb Laza, and Sidney Babineaux, who, despite their talents, had not recorded. The following year, Chenier travelled to Port Arthur, along with his wife Margaret, where he worked for the Gulf and Texaco oil refineries until 1954. Still playing music at weekends, Chenier was discovered by J.R. Fulbright, who recorded him at radio station KAOK, and issued records of these and subsequent sessions. In 1955, 'Ay Tee Tee' became Chenier's best-selling record, and he became established as an R&B guitarist. By 1956, having toured with R&B bands, he had turned to music full-time. In 1958, Chenier moved to Houston, Texas, and from this base played all over the south. Although ostensibly a Cajun musician, he had also absorbed zydeco, and R&B styles influenced by Lowell Fulson. During the 60s Chenier played one concert in San Francisco, backed by Blue Cheer, and recorded for a number of notable labels, including Argo and Arhoolie, in a bid to reach a wider audience. 'Squeeze Box Boogie' became a hit in Jamaica in the 50s, but generally his style of music was not widely heard before the 60s. In later life, in addition to suffering from diabetes, he had part of his right foot removed due to a kidney infection in 1979. Although this prevented him from touring as frequently, his influence was already established. *Sings The Blues* was compiled from material previously released on the Prophecy and Home Cooking labels. His son C.J. Chenier carries on the tradition into a third generation of the family.
● ALBUMS: *Louisiana Blues And Zydeco* (Arhoolie 1965)★★★★, *Black Snake Blues* (Arhoolie 1966)★★★★, with Lightnin' Hopkins, Mance Lipscomb *Blues Festival* (1966)★★★, *Bon Ton Roulet* (Arhoolie 1967)★★★, *Sings The Blues* (Arhoolie 1969)★★★★, *King Of The Bayous* (Arhoolie 1970)★★★, *Bayou Blues* (Specialty/Sonet 1970)★★★★, *Live At St. Marks* (Arhoolie 1971)★★★, *Live At A French Creole Dance* (Arhoolie 1972)★★★, *Out West* (Arhoolie 1974)★★★, *Bad Luck And Trouble* (1975)★★★, *Bogalusa Boogie* (Arhoolie 1975)★★★★, *Red Hot Louisiana Band* (Arhoolie 1978)★★★★, with Rob Bernard *Boogie In Black And White* (Jin 1979)★★★, *In New Orleans* (GNP Crescendo 1979)★★★, *Frenchin' The Boogie* (Barclay 1979)★★★, *King Of Zydeco* (Home Cooking

1980)★★★, *Boogie 'N' Zydeco* (Sonet 1980)★★★, *Live At The 1982 San Francisco Blues Festival* (Arhoolie 1982)★★★, *I'm Here* (Alligator 1982)★★★★, *Live At Montreux* (Charly 1984)★★★, *The King Of Zydeco, Live At Montreux* (Arhoolie 1988)★★★, *Playboy* (1992)★★★.

● COMPILATIONS: *Clifton Chenier's Very Best* (Harvest 1970)★★★★, *Classic Clifton* (Arhoolie 1980)★★★★, *Sixty Minutes With The King Of Zydeco* (Arhoolie 1987)★★★★.

● VIDEOS: *King Of Zydeco* (Arhoolie 1988), *Hot Pepper* (Kay Jazz 1988).

CHESS RECORDS

Polish-born brothers Leonard and Philip Chess were already proprietors of several Chicago nightclubs when they bought into the Aristocrat label in 1947. Its early repertoire consisted of jazz and jump-blues combos, but these acts were eclipsed by the arrival of Muddy Waters. This seminal R&B performer made his debut with 'I Can't Be Satisfied', the first of many superb releases which helped establish the fledgling company. Having then secured the services of Sunnyland Slim and Robert Nighthawk, the brothers confidently bought out a third partner, Evelyn Aron, renaming their enterprise Chess in 1950. Initial releases consisted of material from former Aristocrat artists, but the new venture quickly expanded its roster with local signings Jimmy Rogers and Eddie Boyd, as well as others drawn from the southern states, including Howlin' Wolf. Their recordings established Chess as a leading outlet for urban blues, a position emphasized by the founding of the Checker subsidiary and attendant releases by Little Walter, Sonny Boy Williamson (Rice Miller) and Elmore James. Other outlets, including Argo and Specialist were also established, and during the mid-50s the Chess empire successfully embraced rock 'n' roll with Chuck Berry and Bo Diddley. White acts, including Bobby Charles and Dale Hawkins, also provided hits, while the label's peerless reputation was sufficient to attract a new generation of virtuoso blues performers, led by Otis Rush and Buddy Guy. The R&B boom of the 60s, spearheaded by the Rolling Stones and later emphasized by John Mayall and Fleetwood Mac, brought renewed interest in the company's catalogue, but the rise of soul, in turn, deemed it anachronistic. Although recordings at the Fame studio by Etta James, Irma Thomas and Laura Lee matched the artistic achievements of Motown and Atlantic, ill-advised attempts at aiming Waters and Wolf at the contemporary market with *Electric Mud* and *The New Howlin' Wolf Album*, marked the nadir of their respective careers. The death of Leonard Chess on 16 October 1969 signalled the end of an era and Chess was then purchased by the GRT corporation. Phil left the company to run the WVON radio station, while Leonard's son, Marshall, became managing director of Rolling Stones Records. Producer Ralph Bass remained in Chicago, cataloguing master tapes and supervising a studio reduced to recording backing tracks, but he too vacated the now moribund empire. Chess was later acquired by the All Platinum/Sugarhill companies, then MCA, who, in tandem with European licensees Charly, have undertaken a major reissue programme.

● COMPILATIONS: *Chess: The Rhythm And The Blues* (1988)★★★★, *The Chess Story: Chess Records 1954-1969* (1989)★★★★, *First Time I Met The Blues* (1989)★★★, *Second Time I Met The Blues* (1989)★★★, *Chess Blues* 4-CD box set (1993)★★★★, *Chess Rhythm & Roll* 4-CD box set (MCA 1995)★★★★.

● FURTHER READING: *The Chess Labels*, Michel Ruppli. *Chess Blues Discography*, L. Fancourt.

CHICKEN SHACK

Chicken Shack was the product of eccentric guitarist Stan Webb, veteran of several R&B groups including the Blue 4, Sound Five and the Sounds Of Blue. The latter, active between 1964 and 1965, included Webb, Christine Perfect (b. 12 July 1943, Birmingham, England; piano, vocals) and Andy Sylvester (bass), as well as future Traffic saxophonist Chris Wood. Webb and Sylvester formed the core of the original Chicken Shack, who enjoyed a long residency at Hamburg's famed Star Club before returning to England in 1967. Perfect then rejoined the line-up which was augmented by several drummers until the arrival of Londoner Dave Bidwell. Producer Mike Vernon then signed the quartet to his Blue Horizon label. *Forty Blue Fingers Freshly Packed And Ready To Serve* was a fine balance between original songs and material by John Lee Hooker and Freddie King, to whom Webb was stylistically indebted. *OK Ken?* emphasized the guitarist's own compositions, as well as his irreverence, as he introduces each track by impersonating well-known personalities, including UK disc jockey John Peel, ex-Prime Minister Harold Wilson and UK comedian Kenneth Williams. The quartet also enjoyed two minor hit singles with 'I'd Rather Go Blind' and 'Tears In The Wind', the former of which featured a particularly moving vocal from Perfect, who then left for a solo career (later as Christine McVie). Her replacement was Paul Raymond from Plastic Penny. Ensuing releases, *100 Ton Chicken* and *Accept*, lacked the appeal of their predecessors and their heavier perspective caused a rift with Vernon, who dropped the band from his blues label. Friction within the line-up resulted in the departure of Raymond and Bidwell for Savoy Brown, a group Sylvester later joined. Webb reassembled Chicken Shack with John Glassock (bass, ex-Jethro Tull) and Paul Hancox (drums) and embarked on a period of frenetic live work. They completed the disappointing *Imagination Lady* before Bob Daisley replaced Glassock, but the trio broke up, exhausted, in May 1973, having completed *Unlucky Boy*. The guitarist established a completely new line-up for *Goodbye Chicken Shack*, before dissolving the band in order to join the ubiquitous Savoy Brown for a US tour and the *Boogie Brothers* album. Webb then formed Broken Glass and the Stan Webb Band, but he has also resurrected Chicken Shack on several occasions, notably between 1977 and 1979 and 1980 and 1982, in order to take advantage of the band's continued popularity on the European continent, which, if not translated into record sales, assures this instinctive virtuoso a lasting career. In the 90s, Stan 'The Man' Webb was once again delighting small club audiences with his latest incarnation of Chicken Shack.

● ALBUMS: *Forty Blue Fingers Freshly Packed And Ready To Serve* (Blue Horizon 1968)★★★★, *OK Ken?* (Blue Horizon 1969)★★★, *100 Ton Chicken* (1969)★★★, *Accept! Chicken Shack* (1970)★★★, *Imagination Lady* (Deram 1972)★★★, *Unlucky Boy* (Deram 1973)★★, *Goodbye Chicken Shack* (Deram 1974)★★, *The Creeper* (Warners 1979)★★, *The Way We Are* (1979)★★, *Chicken Shack* (Gull 1979)★★, *Roadie's Concerto* (RCA 1981)★★, *Chicken Shack On Air* (Band Of Joy 1991)★★★, *Changes* (1992)★★★, *Webb's Blues* (Indigo 1994)★★★, *Plucking Good* (Inak 1994)★★★, *Stan 'The Man' Live* (Indigo 1995)★★★.

● COMPILATIONS: *Stan The Man* (1977)★★★, *The Golden Era Of Pop Music* (Columbia 1977)★★★, *In The Can* (Columbia 1980)★★★, *Collection: Chicken Shack* (Castle 1988)★★★, *Black Night* (Indigo 1997)★★★.

CHRISTIAN, LITTLE JOHNNY

b. 19 August *c*.30s, Mississippi, USA, d. *c*.1993. Christian sang in a church choir as a youngster, and continued singing gospel music after moving to Chicago in 1951, working and recording with the Highway QCs from 1957-61. In the 60s he worked as a bass player with Otis Rush, Elmore James and others, before joining Jimmy Dawkins as bassist and singer. He formed his own band in the 70s working exclusively as a singer, and recorded several singles in the 80s. Renowned for his soulful vocals, Christian made his debut album for the Chicago-based Big Boy label at the end of the decade.

● ALBUMS: *Somebody Call My Baby* (Big Boy 1989)★★★, *Ain't Going To Worry About It* (Big Boy 1993)★★★.

CLAPTON, ERIC

b. Eric Patrick Clapp, 30 March 1945, Ripley, Surrey, England. The world's premier living rock guitarist will be forever grateful to his grandparents, for they gave him his first guitar. The young Eric was raised by his grandparents Rose and Jack Clapp when his natural mother could not face bringing up an illegitimate child at the age of 16. Eric received the £14 acoustic guitar for his 14th birthday, then proceeded to copy the great blues guitarists note for note. His first band was the Roosters, a local R&B group that included Tom McGuinness, a future member of Manfred Mann, and latterly part of the Blues Band. Clapton stayed for eight months until he and McGuinness left to join Casey Jones And The Engineers. This brief sojourn ended in 1963 when Clapton was sought out by the Yardbirds, an aspiring R&B band, who needed a replacement for their guitarist Tony Topham. The reputation swiftly established by the Yardbirds was largely centred on Clapton, who had already been nicknamed 'Slowhand' by the partisan crowd at Richmond's Crawdaddy club. Clapton stayed for 18 months until musical differences interfered. The Yardbirds were taking a more pop-orientated direction and he just wanted to play the blues. He departed shortly after the recording of 'For Your Love'. The perfect vehicle for his frustrations was John Mayall's Bluesbreakers, one of Britain's top blues bands. It was with Mayall that Clapton would earn his second nickname: 'God'! Rarely had there been a similar meteoric rise to such an exalted position. Clapton only made one album with Mayall but the record is now a classic; on its famous cover, *Bluesbreakers* shows Clapton sitting reading a copy of the *Beano* comic. Between Mayall and his next band, Clapton made numerous session appearances and recorded an interesting session with a conglomeration called the Powerhouse. They recorded three tracks - 'Crossroads, 'I Want To Know' and 'Steppin' Out' - the line-up comprising Paul Jones, Steve Winwood, Jack Bruce, Pete York and Clapton. He was elevated to superstar status with the formation of Cream in 1966, and together with ex-Graham Bond Organisation members Jack Bruce and Ginger Baker, he created one of the most influential rock bands of our time. Additionally, as L'Angelo Mysterioso he played the beautiful lead solo on George Harrison's 'While My Guitar Gently Weeps' for the Beatles' *The Beatles* ('The White Album'). Cream lasted just over two years, and shortly after their demise he was back with Baker, this time as Blind Faith. The line-up was completed by Steve Winwood and Rick Grech. This 'supergroup' was unable to stay together for more than one self-titled album, although their financially lucrative American tour made the impending break-up easier to bear. During the tour Clapton befriended Delaney And Bonnie, decided that he wanted to be their guitarist, and then joined them before the sweat had dried following his last Blind Faith gig in January 1970. He played on one album, *Delaney And Bonnie On Tour*, and three months later he had absconded with three members of the former band to make the disappointing *Eric Clapton*. The band then metamorphosed into Derek And The Dominos. This memorable unit, together with Duane Allman,

recorded one of his most famous compositions, the perennial 'Layla'. This clandestine love song was directed at George Harrison's wife Pattie, with whom Clapton had become besotted. George, unaware of this, invited him to play at his historic Bangla Desh Concert in August 1971. Clapton then struggled to overcome a heroin habit that had grown out of control, since being introduced to the drug during the recording of *Layla And Other Assorted Love Songs*. During the worst moments of his addiction he began to pawn some of his precious guitars and spent up to £1,500 a week to feed his habit. Pete Townshend of the Who was appalled to discover that Clapton was selling his guitars and proceeded to try to rescue him and his girlfriend Alice Ormsby-Gore. Townshend organized the famous Eric Clapton At The Rainbow concert as part of his rehabilitation crusade, along with Steve Winwood, Rick Grech, Ron Wood and Jim Capaldi. His appearance broke two years of silence, and wearing the same suit he had worn at the Bangla Desh concert, he played a majestic and emotional set. Although still addicted, this represented a turning point in his life, and following pleas from his girlfriend's father, Lord Harlech, he entered the Harley Street clinic of Dr Meg Patterson for treatment.

A rejuvenated Clapton began to record again and released the buoyant *461 Ocean Boulevard* in August 1974. The future pattern was set on this album; gone were the long guitar solos, replaced instead by relaxed vocals over shorter, more compact songs. The record was an incredible success, a number 1 hit in the USA and number 3 in the UK. The singles drawn from it were also hits, notably his number 1 US hit with Bob Marley's 'I Shot The Sheriff'. Also included was the autobiographical message to himself, 'Give Me Strength', and the beautifully mantric 'Let It Flow'. Clapton ended 1974 on a high note; not only had he returned from the grave, but he had finally succeeded in winning the heart of Pattie Harrison. During 1975 he maintained his drug-free existence, although he became dependent on alcohol. That same year he had further hits with *There's One In Every Crowd* and the live *E.C. Was Here*. Both maintained his reputation, and since then Clapton has continued to grow in stature. During 1977 and 1978 he released two more major albums, *Slowhand* and *Backless*.

Further single success came with the gentle 'Lay Down Sally' (co-written with Marcella Detroit, later of Shakespears Sister) and 'Promises', while other notable tracks were 'Wonderful Tonight', J.J. Cale's 'Cocaine', and John Martyn's 'May You Never'. Clapton had completely shrugged off his guitar hero persona and had now become an assured vocalist/songwriter, who, by chance, played guitar. A whole new audience, many of whom had never heard of the Yardbirds or Cream, saw Clapton as a wholesome, healthy individual with few vices, and no cobwebs in his attic. Clapton found additional time to play at the Band's historic *Last Waltz* concert.

The 80s have been even kinder to Clapton, with every album selling in vast quantities and being critically well received. *Another Ticket* and *Money And Cigarettes*, which featured Ry Cooder, were particularly successful at the beginning of the 80s. *Behind The Sun* benefited from the firm production hand of Clapton's close friend Phil Collins. Collins played drums on his next album, *August*, which showed no sign of tiredness or lack of ideas. This particularly strong album contained the excellent hit 'Behind The Mask', and an exciting duet with Tina Turner on 'Tearing Us Apart'. Throughout the record Clapton's voice was in particularly fine form. *Journeyman* in 1989 went one better; not only were his voice and songs creditable but 'Slowhand' had rediscovered the guitar. The album contains some of his finest playing and, not surprisingly, it was a major success. Clapton has contributed to numerous artists' albums over many years, including John Martyn, Phil Collins, Duane Allman, Marc Benno, Gary Brooker, Joe Cocker, Roger Daltrey, Jesse Davis, Dr. John (Mac Rebannack), Bob Dylan, Aretha Franklin, Rick Danko, Champion Jack Dupree, Howlin' Wolf, Sonny Boy Williamson, Freddie King, Alexis Korner, Ronnie Laine, Jackie Lomax, Christine McVie, the Mothers Of Invention, the Plastic Ono Band, Otis Spann, Vivian Stanshall, Stephen Stills, Ringo Starr, Leon Russell, Doris Troy, Roger Waters and many, many more. He also appeared as the Preacher in Ken Russell's film of Pete Townshend's rock opera *Tommy*.

Clapton has enjoyed a high profile in recent years with his touring, the Live Aid appearance, television documentaries, two biographies, and the now annual season of concerts at London's Royal Albert Hall. His 24 nights there in 1991 represented a record - such is his popularity that he could fill the Albert Hall every night for a year. As a final bonus for his many fans he plays three kinds of concerts, dividing the season with a series of blues nights, orchestral nights and regular nights. In the 90s Clapton's career went from strength to strength, although the tragic death of his son Conor in 1991 halted his career for some months. During December 1991 he toured Japan with George Harrison, giving Harrison the moral support that he had received more than a decade earlier. *Unplugged* in 1992 became one of his most successful albums (US sales alone were 10 million copies by 1996). On this he demonstrated his blues roots, playing acoustically in relaxed circumstances with his band (including sterling support from Andy Fairweather-Low); Clapton oozed supreme confidence. The poignant 'Tears In Heaven', about the death of his son, was a major hit worldwide. *From The Cradle* was a worthy release, bringing him full circle in producing an electric blues album. Those guitar buffs who mourned his departure from Mayall and despaired when Cream called it a day could rejoice once again. 'God' had returned. Clapton has already earned the title of the greatest white blues guitarist of our time, but he is now on the way to becoming one of the greatest rock artists of the era too. An encouraging thought for a man whose life had all but ended in 1973.

● ALBUMS: three tracks as the Powerhouse with Steve Winwood, Jack Bruce, Pete York, Paul Jones *What's Shakin'?* (Elektra 1966)★★★, *Eric Clapton* (Polydor 1970)★★★, *Eric Clapton's Rainbow Concert* (RSO 1973)★★★, *461 Ocean Boulevard* (RSO 1974)★★★★, *There's One In Every Crowd* (RSO 1975)★★★, *E.C. Was Here* (RSO 1975)★★, *No Reason To Cry* (RSO 1976)★★★, *Slowhand* (RSO 1977)★★★★, *Backless* (RSO 1978)★★★, *Just One Night* (RSO 1980)★★★, *Another Ticket* (RSO 1981)★★★, *Money And Cigarettes* (Duck 1983)★★★, *Behind The Sun* (Duck 1985)★★★, *August* (Duck 1986)★★★, with Michael Kamen *Homeboy* television soundtrack (Virgin 1989)★★, *Journeyman* (Duck 1989)★★★★, *24 Nights* (Duck 1991)★★, *Rush* film soundtrack (Reprise

1992)★★, *MTV Unplugged* (WEA 1992)★★★★, *From The Cradle* (Duck 1994)★★★.
● COMPILATIONS: *Time Pieces - The Best Of Eric Clapton* (RSO 1982)★★★, *Time Pieces Volume II: Live In The Seventies* (RSO 1983)★★★, *Backtrackin'* (Starblend 1984)★★★★, *Crossroads* 4-CD box set (Polydor 1988)★★★★★, *The Cream Of Eric Clapton* (Polydor 1989)★★★★, *The Magic Of ...* (1993)★★★, *Crossroads 2: Live In The 70s* (Polydor 1996)★★★★.
● VIDEOS: *Eric Clapton On Whistle Test* (BBC Video 1984), *Live '85* (Polygram Music Video 1986), *Live At The NEC Birmingham* (MSD 1987), *Cream Of Eric Clapton* (Channel 5 1989), *Man And His Music* (Video Collection 1990), *Eric Clapton In Concert* (Abbey Music Video 1991), *24 Nights* (Warner Music Video 1991).
● FURTHER READING: *Conversations With Eric Clapton*, Steve Turner. *Eric Clapton: A Biography*, John Pidgeon. *Survivor: The Authorized Biography Of Eric Clapton*, Ray Coleman. *Clapton: The Complete Chronicle*, Marc Roberty. *Eric Clapton: The New Visual Documentary*, Marc Roberty. *Eric Clapton: Lost In The Blues*, Harry Shapiro. *Eric Clapton: The Complete Recording Sessions*, Marc Roberty. *The Man, The Music, The Memorabilia*, Marc Roberty. *Edge Of Darkness*, Christopher Sandford. *Complete Guide To The Music Of*, Marc Roberty. *Crossroads: The Life And Music Of Eric Clapton*, Michael Schumacher.

CLARK, DAVE

b. 6 March 1909, Jackson, Tennessee, USA, d. 22 July 1995, Madison, Mississippi, USA. Although not a star of America's R&B period, Clark's work on promotion, spanning 50 years, was central to the music's development. Growing up in Chicago, he graduated from Lane College in Jackson in 1934, then the Juilliard School Of Music in New York five years later. During this period he had already started writing his own compositions, and 'plugged' these for sale to local bands. His first success in this capacity was with Jimmy Lunceford's recording of 'St. Paul's Walking Through Heaven With You' in 1938. He had already established his name in the Chicago music community by starting a jazz column for *Downbeat* magazine in 1934. Having worked in promotion for several small Chicago labels

before the war, after its end he began a contract with Aristocrat Records and its successor, Chess Records. He then joined Star Maid and Ronel Records in 1955. However, much of the time he operated on a piece-work basis, simultaneously pushing records for several companies in a manner that anticipated the later trend for freelance promotion and plugging. By 1954 he had joined Duke/Peacock Records in Houston with whom he would later work exclusively. Playing a large hand in the establishment of such artists as Bobby Bland, Junior Parker and O.V. Wright, Clark stayed with Duke until the early 70s. In this period he also worked as a songwriter, co-writing 'Why I Sing The Blues' (1969) and 'Chains And Things (1970) with B.B. King. He moved to Stax Records in 1971 for five years, working with Little Milton and the Staple Singers. TK Records was his next stop, an association that included promoting such artists as KC And The Sunshine Band and Betty Wright. By now Clark had built up strong loyalties within the music community, and when he moved to Malaco Records in 1980 he was able to attract artists including Z.Z. Hill, Johnnie Taylor, Bobby Bland and Denise LaSalle. While in his 70s, he scored a major success by pushing Z.Z. Hill's blues back to the black radio community, with his album *Down Home* (1982) becoming one of the decade's biggest blues successes. In the 90s his health failed, and he was confined to a nursing home until his death.

CLARKE, WILLIAM

b. 29 March 1951, Inglewood, California, USA, d. 2 November 1996. Clarke began playing harmonica at the age of 16, inspired by the records of Junior Wells and Walter Horton. He turned professional two years later, and by the late 70s had become a well-respected harmonica player and singer on the Los Angeles blues scene. He associated with Smokey Wilson, Shakey Jake Harris, and George 'Harmonica' Smith, with the latter, in particular, being a great influence. Clarke recorded in his own right for the Good Time, Rivera, and Alligator labels, and in 1991 he also paid homage to his roots by playing on an acclaimed Los Angeles blues anthology *Hard Times*, which he compiled and produced for Black Magic Records.
● ALBUMS: *Hittin' Heavy* (Good Time

1978)★★★, *Blues From Los Angeles* (Hittin' Heavy 1980)★★★, *Can't You Hear Me Calling* (Watch Dog 1983)★★★, *Tip Of The Top* (Satch 1987★★★), *Blowin' Like Hell* (Alligator 1990)★★★, *Serious Intentions* (Alligator 1992)★★★, *Groove Time* (Alligator 1995)★★★, *The Hard Way* (Alligator 1996)★★★.

CLAY, W.C.

b. 1927, Jonestown, Mississippi, USA. Along with a number of Mississippi-and Arkansas-based blues artists, Clay played with the *King Biscuit* radio show entertainers, including Sonny Boy 'Rice Miller' Williamson. After 1950, and following Williamson's death in 1965, Clay regularly featured on the show playing Williamson favourites such as 'Keep It To Yourself'. In 1976 he was living in Elaine, near Helena, Arkansas.
● COMPILATIONS: with various artists *Keep It To Yourself - Arkansas Blues, Volume 1* (1983).

CLAYTON, PETER J. 'DOCTOR'

b. 19 April 1898, Georgia, USA, d. 7 January 1947, Chicago, Illinois, USA. Although he recorded a little over a dozen records in as many years (1930-46), his compositions influenced many blues singers, most notably Sunnyland Slim and B.B. King. His distinctive vocals, which usually ended in falsetto 'whoops', have been greatly imitated, but it is as songwriter that he is best remembered. Of his handful of recordings about half a dozen have become blues standards, including 'Hold That Train Conductor', 'Gotta Find My Baby' and 'I Need My Baby', courtesy of B.B. King. He was known as a bizarre character prone to outlandish dressing, performing in bare feet and verging on being alcoholic. However, recordings like '41 Blues', which castigated Hitler and threatened him with a razor, and 'Pearl Harbour Blues', a scathing attack on the 'dirty Japanese', belie this apparent frivolity. In the autumn of 1946, Clayton developed tuberculosis and died in hospital the following year.
● COMPILATIONS: *Gotta Find My Baby 1941-46* (1987)★★★, with Sunnyland Slim *Dr. Clayton And His Buddy 1935-47* (1989)★★★, *Complete Pre-War Recordings 1935-42* (1993)★★★.

CLEARWATER, EDDY

b. Eddy Harrington, 10 January 1935, Macon, Mississippi, USA. Clearwater grew up hearing C&W records and began playing guitar in church after moving to Birmingham, Alabama, when he was 13 years old. He settled in Chicago in 1950 and was playing blues within a few years. Although primarily a powerful blues singer and guitarist in the west side Chicago style, he has also displayed, both on record and stage, a penchant for Chuck Berry-influenced rock 'n' roll, soul, and country. He is a popular performer, both in the USA and Europe and is often seen performing in a spectacular native north American headdress and feathers. He has made numerous recordings for a variety of labels, although it is his very versatility that often results in the failure to satisfy any listener completely, despite the fact that he can perform in almost any musical genre. His cousin is Carey Bell.
● ALBUMS: *The Chief* (Rooster 1980)★★, *Two Times Nine* (Charly 1981)★★★, *Flim Doozie* (Rooster 1987)★★, *Blues Hangout* (Black & Blue 1991)★★★, *Help Yourself* (Blind Pig 1992)★★, *Live At The Kingston Mines, Chicago, 1978* (1992)★★★, *Boogie My Blues Away* (Delmark 1995)★★★, *Mean Case Of The Blues* (Bullseye 1996)★★★★, *Black Night* (Storyville 1996)★.

CLEMPSON, DAVE

b. 5 September 1949, Tamworth, Staffordshire, England. Guitarist Dave 'Clem' Clempson achieved early recognition as a member of Bakerloo, an inventive blues-based trio that completed an excellent album for the Harvest label. In October 1969 he replaced James Litherland in Colosseum with whom he remained for two years. Clempson then joined Humble Pie, whose brand of brash rock contrasted with that of his previous jazz rock employers. *Smokin'* (1972) and *Eat It* (1973) offered his most emphatic work, but by 1975 the quartet was losing its direction. Clempson then formed Strange Brew with bassist Greg Ridely and drummer Cozy Powell, but this short-lived unit dissolved when the latter broke his wrist. Having briefly joined Steve Marriott's All Stars, the guitarist formed Rough Diamond with ex-Uriah Heep singer David Byron. This ill-fated venture collapsed in 1977 with Byron embarking on a solo career. The remaining musicians became known as Champion but Clempson's nomadic path was resumed in 1979 when he departed to join Roger Chapman. During the 80s Clempson played some of his finest work with Jack Bruce and was particularly popular in Germany. In 1994 he was part of *Cities Of The Heart*, the album to celebrate Bruce's 50th birthday. He is one of the most accomplished rock guitarists to emerge from the late 60s blues boom.

CLIMAX BLUES BAND

Originally known as the Climax Chicago Blues Band, this enduring group comprised Colin Cooper (b. 7 October 1939, Stafford, England; vocals, saxophone), Peter Haycock (b. 4 April 1952, Stafford, England; vocals, guitar), Richard Jones (keyboards), Arthur Wood (keyboards), Derek Holt (b. 26 January 1949, Stafford, England; bass) and George Newsome (b. 14 August 1947, Stafford, England; drums). They made their recording debut in 1969 with *The Climax Chicago Blues Band* which evoked the early work of John Mayall and Savoy Brown. Its somewhat anachronistic approach gave little indication of a potentially long career. Jones departed for university prior to the release of *Plays On*, which displayed a new-found, and indeed sudden, sense of maturity. A restrictive adherence to 12-bar tempos was replaced by a freer, flowing pulse, while the use of wind instruments, in particular on 'Flight', implied an affiliation with jazz rock groups such as Colosseum and Blodwyn Pig. In 1970 the band switched labels to Harvest. Conscious of stereotyping in the wake of the blues' receding popularity, the group began emphasizing rock-based elements in their work. *A Lot Of Bottle* and *Tightly Knit* reflected a transitional period where the group began wooing the affections of an American audience responsive to the unfettered styles of Foghat or ZZ Top. Climax then embarked on a fruitful relationship with producer Richard Gottehrer who honed the group's live sound into an economic, but purposeful, studio counterpart. *Rich Man*, their final album for Harvest, and *Sense Of Direction* were the best examples of their collaboration. Richard Jones rejoined the band in 1975 having been a member of the Principal Edwards Magic Theatre since leaving university. The band enjoyed a surprise UK hit single when 'Couldn't Get It Right' reached number 10 in 1976, but the suc-

cess proved temporary. Although they have pursued a career into the 90s, the Climax Blues Band have engendered a sense of predictability and consequently lost their eminent position as a fixture of America's lucrative FM rock circuit. In 1994 the line-up retained only Cooper from the original band, who had recruited George Glover (keyboards, vocals), Lester Hunt (guitar, vocals), Roy Adams (drums) and Roger Inniss (bass). Their live 1994 album, *Blues From The Attic*, however, sounded remarkably fresh for a band that had been gigging for so long.

● ALBUMS: *Climax Chicago Blues Band* (Parlophone 1969)★★, *Plays On* (Parlophone 1969)★★★, *A Lot Of Bottle* (Harvest 1970)★★, *Tightly Knit* (Harvest 1971)★★★, *Rich Man* (Harvest 1972)★★★, *FM/Live* (Polydor 1973), *Sense Of Direction* (Polydor 1974)★★★, *Stamp Album* (BTM 1975)★★★, *Gold Plated* (BTM 1976)★★, *Shine On* (Warners 1978)★★★, *Real To Reel* (Warners 1979)★★★, *Flying The Flag* (Warners 1980)★★★, *Lucky For Some* (Warners 1981)★★, *Sample And Hold* (Virgin 1983)★★, *Drastic Steps* (Clay 1988)★★, *Blues From The Attic* (HTD 1994)★★★.

● COMPILATIONS: *1969-1972* (Harvest 1975)★★★, *Best Of The Climax Blues Band* (RCA 1983)★★★, *Loosen Up (1974-1976)* (See For Miles 1984)★★★, *Couldn't Get It Right* (C5 1987)★★, *25 Years Of The Climax Blues Band* (Repertoire 1993)★★★.

COBBS, WILLIE

b. 15 July 1940, Monroe, Arkansas, USA. As a youngster, Cobbs was deeply involved in gospel music in his local area. He moved to Chicago in 1951, where he received tuition in the blues harmonica from Little Walter. After his national service from 1953-57 he returned to Chicago and recorded (as a singer only) in 1958. In 1961 he made 'You Don't Love Me', now a much-covered standard which has overshadowed Cobbs' musical career. Since the 60s he has been based in the south, recording down-home blues singles (sometimes with backing vocals as a nod to the soul market) for a plethora of small labels, although in 1991 he recorded for Rooster Records.

● ALBUMS: *Down To Earth* (Rooster 1995)★★★.

● COMPILATIONS: *Hey Little Girl* (1991)★★★.

COLE, ANN

b. Cynthia Coleman, 24 January 1934, Newark, New Jersey, USA. Cole is best known for recording the original version of 'Got My Mojo Working' (1957), which Muddy Waters later placed on the charts and practically made his signature song. Her father sang with the family gospel group, the Coleman Brothers, and young Cynthia began singing in her grandfather's church as a child. In 1949, after absorbing the diverse influences of Billie Holiday and Mahalia Jackson, she formed a gospel group with her cousins, the Colemanaires, who recorded for Timely Records in 1953 and 1954. She began a solo career in 1954 under the name of Ann Cole, recording obscure sides for Timely and Mor-Play before switching to Baton Records in 1956. There she had some success with the original versions of two famous blues songs, 'Easy Easy, Baby' (made famous by Magic Sam) and 'Got My Mojo Working'. She had chart success with 'Are You Satisfied' (number 10 R&B) in 1956 and 'In The Chapel' (number 14 R&B) in 1957. After leaving Baton in 1959, her only subsequent hit was for Roulette in 1962, 'House Fun' (number 21 R&B) backed with 'Don't Stop The Wedding' (number 99 pop), the latter an answer to Etta James's 'Stop The Wedding'. Cole suffered a serious accident that eventually resulted in her being confined to a wheelchair, and she returned to performing the spirituals and hymns that were her first inspiration.
● COMPILATIONS: *Got My Mojo Working: Original Baton Recordings: 1956-1959* (Krazy Kat 1984)★★★.

COLEMAN, BURL C. 'JAYBIRD'

b. 20 May 1896, Gainsville, Alabama, USA, d. 28 June 1950, Tuskegee, Alabama, USA. A blues harmonica player who recorded 15 titles between 1927 and 1930, Coleman drew his material from sources as varied as children's playground songs and spirituals. Whatever the source of his nickname, it was unlikely that it related to the birdsong - his singing and playing were rooted in that of the field-holler. His technique was best exemplified by 'No More Good Water', a call-and-response blues, where the harmonica's wailing quality is used as a second voice. It is thought he spent the last two decades of his life as a street musician in Bessemer, Alabama, finally succumbing to cancer at the age of 54. He, and George 'Bullet' Williams, are the only known harmonica players from Alabama recorded in their own right.
● COMPILATIONS: with George 'Bullet' Williams *Alabama Harmonica Kings* (1988)★★★.

COLEMAN, GARY 'BB'

b. 1 January 1947, Paris, Texas, USA, d. 14 February 1994. Coleman remembers hearing blues on record and radio as a child, and recalls his favourites as Jimmy Reed, Muddy Waters, Lightnin' Hopkins, Chuck Berry and Freddie King. He taught himself to play guitar around the age of 11; it remains his main instrument, although he is now a multi-instrumentalist. He has always worked as a professional musician; in 1986 he recorded an album for his own Mr B.'s Records label, which was leased to Ichiban Records who went on to make it a very successful seller. Coleman has since become a major figure at Ichiban, not only with his own contemporary blues records, but also for his work as producer and musician with such artists as Barbara Lynn, Blues Boy Willie, Little Johnny Taylor, and Chick Willis.
● ALBUMS: *Nothing But The Blues* (Ichiban 1987)★★★, *If You Can't Beat Me Rockin'* (Ichiban 1988)★★★, *One Night Stand* (Ichiban 1989)★★★, *Dancin' My Blues Away* (Ichiban 1990)★★★, *Romance Without Finance Is A Nuisance* (1991)★★★, *Cocaine Annie* (Boola Boo 1993)★★★.
● COMPILATIONS: *The Best Of Gary 'BB' Coleman* (Ichiban 1990)★★★.

COLEMAN, JESSE 'MONKEY JOE'

b. c.1906. Little is known about this vocalist/pianist other than that he recorded his first tracks for the Bluebird label in New Orleans in 1935, at a session he shared with Little Brother Montgomery. Thereafter, his work appeared on Vocalion and OKeh, having being recorded in Chicago. He is rumoured to have recorded again in 1961. His somewhat loose piano style and choice of material has given rise to speculation that he may have been from Mississippi.
● COMPILATIONS: *Crescent City Blues (Little Brother Montgomery)* (1975)★★★.

COLEMAN, MICHAEL

b. 24 June 1956, Chicago, Illinois, USA. Coleman came to the blues from choice but not until he had exhausted his taste for Top 40 show bands. It was something of a return, since in his early years he had grown up surrounded by the musicians who congregated for rehearsals with his father, drummer Cleo 'Bald Head Pete' Williams. Consequently, he was playing guitar and bass before his tenth birthday. As well as Top 40 work, he also accompanied Aron Burton and Johnny Dollar to Chicago's North Side to play blues, and in 1975 turned to playing blues full-time. In 1979 he toured Europe with Eddy Clearwater and later, Professor Eddie Lusk. During the 80s Coleman spent a year with Junior Wells and shorter periods with Buster Benton and Jimmy Dawkins. He also worked with James Cotton for 10 years and backed him on his Alligator album, *Live From Chicago - Mr Superharp Himself*. His two solo albums showcase his solid qualities as a forceful guitarist and an effective, if unoriginal, singer. Like many of his contemporaries who work from the same palette of influences, it renders his work entertaining but not individual.

● ALBUMS: with Professor Eddie Lusk *The Great Heavyweights From Chicago* (Black & Blue 1981)★★★, *The New Bluebloods* (Alligator/Sonet 1987)★★★, *Back Breaking Blues* (Wolf 1991)★★★, *Shake Your Booty* (Wolf 1994)★★★.

COLLINS, ALBERT

b. 3 October 1932, Leona, Texas, USA, d. 24 November 1993, Las Vegas, Nevada, USA. Collins was the embodiment of the Texas blues guitar style, using non-standard tuning, and slashing out blocked chords and sharp flurries of treble notes (played without a plectrum) to produce an 'ice-cold' sound from his Fender Telecaster. As a youth he developed his style by listening to fellow-Texan Clarence 'Gatemouth' Brown, Frankie Lee Sims and his own cousin Willow Young. His first singles, released from 1958 onwards on small local labels, were exciting shuffle instrumentals, of which 'The Freeze' and 'Frosty' became blues standards, but it was not until the late 60s that he was confident enough to use his laconic, understated singing voice with any regularity. A series of splendid studio and live albums over the following years extended his basic Texas style across the boundaries of jazz and funk, and established him as a major international blues attraction. His stage shows, which often included a walk through the audience as he played his guitar on its 100-foot lead, were memorable events. Collins heavily influenced the style of Robert Cray, with whom he recorded and helped in his career. During the early 70s there was a lull in his own career when blues experienced one of its quiet periods. *Ice Pickin'* announced his return to the major league, having been signed by Bruce Iglauer to record in Chicago for Alligator. On this album he was supported by the Icebreakers who comprised Larry Burton (guitar), Chuck Smith (saxophone), Casey Jones (drums), A.C. Reed (saxophone) and Alan Batts (keyboards). The album established Collins as a guitarist who could play pure blues, brassy Stax-influenced numbers and out-and-out funk. Further albums with Alligator in the 80s were all excellent showcases, although Collins' strength remained his stage act. Two live albums in the 80s emphasized this; *Frozen Alive* and the excellent *Live In Japan* show him in his element. The version of 'Stormy Monday' on the latter is a joy. For the 1993 compilation Collins chose his favourite past cuts and, with his band, re-recorded them with the help of musicians such as Branford Marsalis and B.B. King. Collins did not possess a great voice and for some, the tone of his Telecaster (against the smoother Stratocaster) was too harsh. What cannot be denied was his remarkable guitar technique, memorable stage shows and a humble and kind manner that left him with few critics. Collins endured his terminal disease with great humility and refused to discuss the severity of his illness; his death at 61 was a cruel shock. He was a major figure of post-50s blues.

● ALBUMS: *The Cool Sound Of* (TCF Hall 1965)★★★, *Love Can Be Found Anywhere, Even In A Guitar* (Imperial 1968)★★★, *Trash Talkin* (Imperial 1969)★★★, *The Complete Albert Collins* (Imperial 1969)★★★, *Alive And Cool* (1969)★★★, *Truckin' With Albert Collins* (Blue Thumb 1969)★★★, with Barrelhouse *Live* (Munich 1970)★★, *There's Gotta Be A Change* (1971)★★, *Ice Pickin'* (Alligator 1978)★★★★, *Frostbite* (Alligator 1980)★★★★, *Frozen Alive!*

(Alligator 1981)★★★★, *Don't Lose Your Cool* (Alligator 1983)★★★, *Live In Japan* (Alligator 1984)★★★★, with Johnny Copeland, Robert Cray *Showdown!* (Alligator 1985)★★★★, *Cold Snap* (Alligator 1986)★★★, *The Ice Man* (Charisma/Point Blank 1991)★★★★, *Molten Ice* (Red Lightnin' 1992)★★★, *Live 92/93* (Pointblank 1995)★★★.

● COMPILATIONS: *The Complete Imperial Recordings* (EMI 1991)★★★★, *Collins Mix (The Best Of)* (Pointblank 1993)★★★★, *Deluxe Edition* (Alligator 1997)★★★★.

COLLINS, SAM 'CRYING'

b. 11 August 1887, Louisiana, USA, d. 20 October 1949, Chicago, Illinois, USA. Sam Collins was raised in McComb, Mississippi, just over the border from his native state, and by 1924 was performing in local barrelhouses at weekends. He was an intermittent partner of King Solomon Hill (Joe Holmes), and shared with him the use of falsetto singing and slide guitar. Holmes was an associate of Willard Thomas, and elements of Thomas's style influenced Collins. Collins was extensively recorded by both Gennett in 1927 and ARC in 1931, but many titles unfortunately remained unissued; it is clear, however, that he played blues, spirituals, medicine show numbers and pop songs - the repertoire of a songster. As a blues guitarist, Collins was not a virtuoso, and by conventional standards he was often out of tune, but he provided a steady beat for dancing, and his bottleneck playing, ranging freely through the treble and bass registers, was an effective foil to his eerie singing, for which one record company billed him as 'Cryin' Sam Collins And His Git-Fiddle' in its advertising. He migrated to Chicago in the late 30s, and died there of heart disease.

● COMPILATIONS: *The Jailhouse Blues* (Yazoo 1991)★★★.

COLOSSEUM

The commercial acceptance of jazz rock in the UK was mainly due to Colosseum. The band was formed in 1968 from the nucleus of the musicians who accompanied John Mayall on his influential album *Bare Wires*. Colosseum comprised Jon Hiseman (b. 21 June 1944, London, England; drums), Dick Heckstall-Smith (b. 26 September 1934, Ludlow, Shropshire, England; saxophone), Dave Greenslade (b. 18 January 1943, Woking, Surrey, England; keyboards), Tony Reeves (b. 18 April 1943, London, England; bass) and James Litherland (b. 6 September 1949, Manchester, England; guitar/vocals). Ex-Graham Bond Organisation members Heckstall-Smith and Hiseman took their former boss's pivotal work and made a success of it. From the opening track of their strong debut, *Those Who Are About To Die Salute You* (1969), with Bond's 'Walkin' In The Park', the band embarked on a brief excursion that would showcase each member as a strong musical talent. Heckstall-Smith, already a seasoned jazz professional, combined with 19-year-old Litherland to integrate furious wah-wah guitar with bursting saxophone. Greenslade's booming Hammond organ intertwined with Reeves' melodically inventive bass patterns. This sparkling cocktail was held together by the masterful pyrotechnics of Hiseman, whose solos, featuring his dual bass drum pedal technique, were incredible. *Valentyne Suite* the same year maintained the momentum, notably with the outstanding Heckstall-Smith composition 'The Grass Is Greener'. As with many great things, the end came too soon, although departing member Litherland was replaced with a worthy successor in Dave 'Clem' Clempson (b. 5 September 1949, England). In order to accommodate Clempson's wish to concentrate on guitar they enlisted Greenslade's former boss in the Thunderbirds, Chris Farlowe. His strong vocals gave a harder edge to their work. Following the departure of Reeves and the recruitment of Mark Clarke, their work took a more rock-orientated approach. The end came in October 1971 with their last studio album, *Daughter Of Time*, quickly followed by *Colosseum Live*. Hiseman and Clarke formed Tempest, but after two mediocre albums Hiseman resurrected the name in the shape of Colosseum II in 1975. The new version was much heavier in sound and featured ex-Thin Lizzy guitarist Gary Moore, future Whitesnake bassist Neil Murray and future Rainbow keyboard player Don Airey. Vocalist Mike Starrs completed the line-up and they progressed through the mid-70s with three albums, before Colosseum II finally collapsed through Hiseman's exhaustion, and his wish to return to his jazz roots. He eventually joined his wife Barbara Thompson, playing jazz with her band Paraphernalia. Colosseum will be remembered for their initial pioneering work in making jazz rock accessible to a wider market. In 1997 the majority of the original band reconvened with Farlowe as vocalist. Although Hiseman had often mooted the idea of a reunion, he stated in 1997 that the time 'seemed right'.

● ALBUMS: *Those Who Are About To Die Salute You* (Fontana 1969)★★★★, *Valentyne Suite* (Vertigo 1969)★★★★, *The Daughter Of Time* (Vertigo 1970)★★, *Live* (Bronze 1971)★★★, *Strange New Flesh* (1976)★★, *Electric Savage* (MCA 1977)★★, *Wardance* (MCA 1977)★★.
● COMPILATIONS: *The Grass Is Greener* (1969)★★★, *Collector's Colosseum* (Bronze 1971)★★★, *Pop Chronik* (1974)★★★, *Epitaph* (Raw Power 1986), *The Golden Decade Of Colosseum* (Nightriding 1990)★★★, *The Collection* (Castle 1991)★★★.

COODER, RY

b. Ryland Peter Cooder, 15 March 1947, Los Angeles, California, USA. One of rock's premier talents, Cooder mastered the rudiments of guitar while still a child. He learned the techniques of traditional music from Rev. Gary Davis and by the age of 17 was part of a blues act with singer Jackie DeShannon. In 1965 he formed the Rising Sons with Taj Mahal and veteran Spirit drummer Ed Cassidy, but this promising group broke up when the release of a completed album was cancelled. However, the sessions brought Cooder into contact with producer Terry Melcher, who in turn employed the guitarist on several sessions, notably with Paul Revere And The Raiders. Cooder enjoyed a brief, but fruitful, association with Captain Beefheart And His Magic Band; his distinctive slide work is apparent on the group's debut album, *Safe As Milk*, but the artist declined an offer to join on a permanent basis. Instead, he continued his studio work, guesting on sessions for Randy Newman, Little Feat and Van Dyke Parks, as well as to the soundtracks of *Candy* and *Performance*. Cooder also contributed to the Rolling Stones' album *Let It Bleed*, and was tipped as a likely replacement for Brian Jones until clashes with Keith Richard, primarily over the authorship of the riff to 'Honky Tonk

Woman', precluded further involvement.

Cooder's impressive debut album included material by Lead Belly, Sleepy John Estes and Blind Willie Johnson, and offered a patchwork of Americana that became his trademark. A second collection, *Into The Purple Valley*, established his vision more fully and introduced a tight but sympathetic band, which included long-standing collaborators Jim Keltner and Jim Dickinson. By contrast, several selections employed the barest instrumentation, resulting in one of the artist's finest releases. The rather desolate *Boomer's Story* completed Cooder's early trilogy and in 1974 he released the buoyant *Paradise And Lunch*. His confidence was immediately apparent on the reggae interpretation of 'It's All Over Now' and the silky 'Ditty Wa Ditty', and it was this acclaimed collection that established him as a major talent. A fascination with 30s topical songs was now muted in favour of a greater eclecticism, which in turn anticipated Cooder's subsequent direction. *Chicken Skin Music* was marked by two distinct preoccupations. Contributions from Flaco Jiminez and Gabby Pahuini enhanced its mixture of Tex-Mex and Hawaiian styles, while Cooder's seamless playing and inspired arrangements created a sympathetic setting. The guitarist's relationship with Jiminez was maintained on a fine in-concert set, *Showtime*, but Cooder then abandoned this direction with the reverential *Jazz*. This curiously unsatisfying album paid homage to the Dixieland era, but a crafted meticulousness denied the project life and its creator has since disowned it. Cooder then embraced a more mainstream approach with *Bop Till You Drop*, an ebullient, rhythmic, yet rock-based collection, reminiscent of Little Feat. The album, which included cameo performances from soul singer Chaka Khan, comprised several urban R&B standards, including 'Little Sister', 'Go Home Girl' and 'Don't Mess Up A Good Thing'. Its successor, *Borderline*, offered similar fare, but when the style was continued on a further release, *The Slide Area*, a sense of weariness became apparent. Such overtly commercial selections contrasted with Cooder's soundtrack work. *The Long Riders*, plus *Paris, Texas* and *Crossroads*, owed much to the spirit of adventure prevalent in his early work, while the expansive tapestry of these films allowed greater scope for his undoubted imagination. It was five years before Cooder released an official follow-up to *The Slide Area* and although *Get Rhythm* offered little not already displayed, it re-established a purpose to his rock-based work. This inventive, thoughtful individual has embraced both commercial and ethnic styles with equal dexterity, but has yet to achieve the widespread success that his undoubted talent deserves. In 1992, Cooder joined up with Nick Lowe, Jim Keltner and John Hiatt to record and perform under the name of Little Village. In the mid-90s he was acclaimed for his successful collaborations with V.M. Bhatt on *A Meeting By the River* in 1993, and with Ali Farka Toure on *Talking Timbuktu* in 1994.

● ALBUMS: *Ry Cooder* (Reprise 1970)★★★, *Into The Purple Valley* (Reprise 1971)★★★★, *Boomer's Story* (Reprise 1972)★★★★, *Paradise And Lunch* (Reprise 1974)★★★★, *Chicken Skin Music* (Reprise 1976)★★★★, *Showtime* (Warners 1976)★★★, *Jazz* (Warners 1978)★★, *Bop Till You Drop* (Warners 1979)★★★, *Borderline* (Warners 1980)★★★, *The Long Riders* film soundtrack (Warners 1980)★★★, *The Border* film soundtrack (MCA 1980)★★★, *Ry Cooder Live* (Warners 1982)★★★, *The Slide Area* (Warners 1982)★★, *Paris, Texas* film soundtrack (Warners 1985)★★★, *Alamo Bay* film soundtrack (Slash 1985)★★★, *Blue City* film soundtrack (Warners 1986)★★, *Crossroads* film soundtrack (Warners 1987)★★, *Get Rhythm* (Warners 1987)★★, *Johnny Handsome* film soundtrack (Warners 1989)★★★, with Little Village *Little Village* (Reprise 1992)★★, *Trespass* film soundtrack (Sire/Warners 1993)★★, with V.M. Bhatt *A Meeting By The River* (Water Lilly 1993)★★★, with Ali Farka Toure *Talking Timbuktu* (World Circuit 1994)★★★★, *Geronimo* film soundtrack (Columbia 1994)★★★.

● COMPILATIONS: *Why Don't You Try Me Tonight?* (Warners 1985)★★★, *Music By ...* (Reprise 1995)★★★.

COOPER, MIKE

b. 1943, England. A singer and guitarist based for most of his years in Reading, Berkshire, England, Cooper was one of the leading lights of the country blues movement in Britain in the 60s. His first bookings came at the Shades cafe, and led to his first recording, *Out Of The Shades*, an EP for the independent Kennet Records label. By now a major advocate of the blues, he established a popular folk/blues club in Reading and was one of the instigators of the Matchbox label, for which he also recorded. There were even rumours that he turned down an offer to join the Rolling Stones. Between 1968 and 1974 he appeared on the Pye, Dawn and Fresh Air labels, and he also contributed guitar work to records by Ian A. Anderson, John Drummer, Stefan Grossman and Heron. His own solo album debut came in 1969 with *Oh Really*, but it was not until the advent of a follow-up collection a year later that he had begun to write his own material. This only gelled fully on the same year's minor masterpiece, *Trout Steel*, a visionary mix of blues and free jazz improvisation. The formula was further refined on *Places I Know*, which was scheduled to have accompanied his collaboration with Reading band Machine Gun as a double album. In the event Dawn/Pye released each record separately and, unsure of Cooper's direction, refused to countenance any further records. Cooper, however, was still under contract, and the two-year recording hiatus this enforced undoubtedly damaged his career. Disillusioned, he travelled to Spain to become a fisherman, until Tony Hall of the Fresh Air production company invited him back to record *Life And Death In Paradise* in 1974. The album allowed his bitterness towards the music industry to surface, preceding another period of seclusion, this time in Heidelburg, Germany. There he liaised with local actors and poets, and was drawn to the underground *avant garde* scene. On his return to England he joined Eddie Prevost's band and also worked with Lol Coxhill. *Live From Papa Madeo* saw him return to the blues, this time rooted in the Delta tradition rather than his previous ragtime-inspired approach. Further musical expansion, with the experimental dance project Tristerio System and world music with Dudu Pukwana, ensued. Truly eclectic, he also flirted with Greek Rembetico and Hawaiian slide guitar music, before forming Receedents with Coxhill and Roger Turner. Now based in Rome, he appears more rarely in England these days, but his staggering tally of over 40 recordings provides as richly varied an output as it is possible to imagine.

● ALBUMS: *Oh Really* (Pye 1969)★★★★, *Do I*

Know You? (Dawn 1970), *Trout Steel* (Dawn 1970)★★★★, *Places I Know* (Dawn 1971)★★★, with Machine Gun *Machine Gun* (Dawn 1972)★★★, *Life And Death In Paradise* (Fresh Air 1974)★★, with Joanna Pyne *Have They Started Yet?* (SAJ 1979)★★, with Lol Coxhill, Dave Holland *Johnny Rondo Duo* (SAJ 1982)★★, *Live From Papa Madeo* (SAJ 1983)★★★, with Ian A. Anderson *The Continuous Preaching Blues* (Appaloosa 1984)★★★, *Uptown Hawaiians* (1987)★★★, with Receedents *Zombie Bloodbath On The Isle Of Dogs* (1991)★★★, with Viv Dogan Corringham *Avant Roots* (Mash 1994)★★★.

COOPER, TRENTON

b. 1923, Hope, Arkansas, USA. This talented blues pianist played in his college orchestra before joining an R&B band led by Jay Franks. The band also featured Nelson Carson on guitar. Cooper also co-wrote Franks's 'Fish Tail'. After 1950 Cooper played in the Drops Of Joy, the popular R&B combo led by Jimmy Liggins. When he was traced by blues historian Jim O'Neal in 1976, he was the director of the Cooperative Education office at the University of Arkansas in Pine Bluff.

● COMPILATIONS: with various artists *Keep It To Yourself - Arkansas Blues, Volume 1* (1983).

COPELAND, JOHNNY

b. 27 March 1937, Haynesville, Louisiana, USA, d. 4 July 1997, New York. A former boxer, Johnny 'Clyde' Copeland was active as a guitarist and singer on the Houston blues scene during the late 50s and 60s. While there is no doubt as to Copeland's blues credentials, throughout the 60s in particular, he laid down a wide body of genuinely top-drawer soul. Although all of his 60s soul tracks appear to have been recorded in Houston (from the 70s onwards, some were cut in Los Angeles), Copeland was a 'label-hopper' supreme. He made numerous singles for such labels as Mercury ('All Boy' 1958), Paradise, Golden Eagle ('Down On Bending Knees') and Crazy Cajun. His version of Bob Dylan's 'Blowin' In The Wind' was issued by New York-based Wand in 1965 and there were later records for Atlantic. The renewed interest in the blues during the 70s brought a recording contract with Rounder, and

Copeland's Nappy Brown-influenced vocals were heard to good effect on a 1977 album with Arthur Blythe (saxophone). He joined the festival circuit, and a rousing performance at Chicago in 1984 with fellow Texan guitarists Albert Collins and Gatemouth Brown led to the Grammy-winning *Showdown!* (1985). This collaboration with Collins and Robert Cray included the Copeland originals 'Lion's Den' and 'Bring Your Fine Self On Home'. Later albums were released by Rounder and included *Bringin' It All Back Home*, recorded in Africa. In 1995 he underwent major surgery following serious heart problems, and a benefit was held for him shortly before his death in 1997.

● ALBUMS: *Copeland Special* (Rounder 1977)★★★, *Make My Home Wherever I Hang My Hat* (Demon 1982)★★★, *Texas Twister* (Demon 1984)★★★, with Albert Collins, Robert Cray *Showdown!* (Alligator 1985)★★★★, *Bringin' It All Back Home* (Demon 1986)★★★, *Ain't Nothin' But A Party* (Rounder 1988)★★★, *When The Rain Starts Fallin'* (Rounder 1988)★★★, *Boom Boom* (Rounder 1990)★★★, *Flyin' High* (1993)★★★, *Catch Up With The Blues* (Verve 1994)★★★, *Jungle Swing* (Verve 1996)★★★, *Live In Australia* (Black Top 1997)★★.

● COMPILATIONS: *Dedicated To The Greatest* (Kent 1987)★★★, *Soul Power* (1989)★★★.

● VIDEOS: *The Three Sides Of Johnny Copeland* (MMG Video 1991).

COPELAND, MARTHA

'An exclusive Columbia recording artist' despite also recording for Victor and OKeh, Copeland was one of the legion of second-string female blues singers of the 'classic' period. She recorded 34 tracks between 1923 and 1928 and demonstrated a good 'moaning' style on occasions with considerable humour. Despite some promotion by Columbia who billed her as 'everybody's mama' she never achieved the popularity of stablemates Bessie and Clara Smith.

CORLEY, DEWEY

b. 18 June 1898, Halley, Arkansas, USA, d. 15 April 1974, Memphis, Tennessee, USA. An interest in music inherited from his father led Corley to a career playing a variety of instruments - including harmonica, wash-tub bass and kazoo - in jug bands in Memphis, from the 20s to the 50s. He played with the famous Memphis Jug Band, and also Jack Kelly's South Memphis Jug Band, although he does not seem to have appeared on any of either group's records. In the 60s and into the early 70s, he was able to take advantage of the revival of interest in blues and related music, making a number of recordings and appearing at several folk festivals, both as accompanist to other artists and in his own right.

● COMPILATIONS: *Mississippi Delta Blues, Volume 1* (1969).

COTTON, JAMES

b. 1 July 1925, Tunica, Mississippi, USA. A guitarist and harmonica player, he learned his blues harp style from Sonny Boy 'Rice Miller' Williamson in Arkansas before returning to Memphis to lead his own group with guitarist Pat Hare. There he recorded 'Cotton Crop Blues' (Sun 1954), with its tough guitar solo by Hare, and backed Willie Nix. Moving to Chicago, Cotton replaced Junior Wells in the Muddy Waters group in 1955. He stayed for five years, contributing harmonica solos to Waters tracks such as 'Got My Mojo Workin'' and 'I Feel So Good'. After performing with Waters at the Newport Jazz Festival in 1960, Cotton began to develop a solo career. He later toured Europe, and recorded for Vanguard, Verve-Forecast, Capitol (where a 1970 album was produced by Todd Rundgren), Buddah (the soul-flavoured *100% Cotton* and *High Energy*, produced by Allen Toussaint), Alligator and Antone's. Although he developed a versatile approach, incorporating jazz and soul elements, Cotton retained his Mississippi blues roots, re-recording an old Sun tune, 'Straighten Up Baby', on his 1991 album for Antone's. Joe Louis Walker and Dr. John bolstered his 1995 album, *Living The Blues*, as Cotton's vocals sounded as dry as sandpaper.

● ALBUMS: *From Cotton With Verve* (Verve 1964)★★★, *Chicago - The Blues - Today!, Vol. 2* (1964)★★★, *Super Harp - Live And On The Move* (Buddah 1966)★★, *Cut You Loose* (Vanguard 1967)★★★, *The James Cotton Blues Band* (Verve/Forecast 1967)★★★, *Pure Cotton* (Verve/Forecast 1968)★★★, *Taking Care Of Business* (1970)★★, *100% Cotton* (Buddah 1974)★★, *High Energy* (Buddah 1975)★★, *High Compression* (Alligator 1984)★★, *Live From Chicago* (Alligator 1986),★★★ *Live At Antone's* (Antone's 1988)★★★, *My Foundation* (Jackal 1988)★★★, *Take Me Back* (Blind Pig 1988)★★, *Mighty Long Time* (Antone's 1991)★★, *Dealing With The Devil* (King Bee 1991)★★, *Live At Electric Lady* (Sequel 1992)★★★, *Living The Blues* (Verve 1995)★★, *Deep In The Blues* (Verve 1996)★★.

● COMPILATIONS: *Three Harp Boogie* (Tomato/Rhino 1994)★★★★, *Best Of The Verve Years* (Verve 1995)★★★.

COTTON, SYLVESTER

Nothing is known about Cotton except what can be gleaned from 18 tracks that he recorded in Detroit in 1948-49 for Bernie Besman's Pan American Record Company. Only three of these were issued at the time (although all have now appeared on album), and one of those was credited to John Lee Hooker when leased to Modern. The other two appeared, properly credited, on a Sensation label 78 rpm release. All of Cotton's recordings featured solo guitar and vocal country blues and were very basic and primitive for the period. It is apparent that he extemporized some songs in the studio, most notably the personal lyrics of 'I Tried'.

● COMPILATIONS: *Detroit Blues Volume 1* (Krazy Kat 1984)★★★.

COUNCIL, FLOYD

b. 2 September 1911, Chapel Hill, North Carolina, USA, d. June 1976, Sanford, North Carolina, USA. Sometimes known as Dipper Boy or The Devil's Daddy-In-Law, Council learned to play blues guitar (and also mandolin) in his youth and played on the streets of his hometown in a small band. In 1937, he was spotted in this location by a talent scout, which led to his making records. Following two sessions in New York, three discs were released, and a later session produced a further two sides that remain unissued. On a number of other records, he played second guitar to Blind Boy Fuller, and his style was in the popular east coast vein associated with that artist. Indeed, some of his records were sub-credited to Blind Boy Fuller's Buddy. He continued to play for many years, although he did not record again.

● COMPILATIONS: *Bull City Blues* (1972)★★★.

COUNTRY JIM

b. Jim Bledsoe, c.1925, near Shreveport, Louisiana, USA. A somewhat obscure character, Bledsoe made several records in Shreveport, in 1949-50. As the pseudonym suggests, his music was down-home country blues, accompanied only by his guitar, a string bass, and occasional drums. His first record was issued on the local Pacemaker label, under the name Hot Rod Happy, but the later ones appeared on Imperial and had wider distribution. A year or so later, he completed a couple of long sessions for the Specialty company, but nothing was issued at the time, although a few sides appeared on albums in the 70s.
● COMPILATIONS: *Country Blues* (1973), *Down South Blues* (1977).

COVEY, JULIAN, AND MACHINE

b. Phil Kinorra, England. Before establishing this blues/progressive rock vehicle, Covey had played with Brian Auger at the outset of his career. The group he recruited around him to form Machine in 1967 included guitarist John Moreshead, formerly of Johnny Kidd And The Pirates and Shotgun Express, bass player John Holliday, keyboard player Peter Shelly and drummer Keith Webb. Other contributors at various points included Jim Creagan, Peter Bardens (later of Family and Blossom Toes) and Dave Mason. Despite their excellent pedigree, the group managed to release just a solitary single for Island Records. 'A Little Bit Hurt', backed by 'Sweet Bacon', was an unspectacular but highly musical effort, but the assembled personnel soon moved on to new duties. Moreshead had the most prominent posting subsequently, working extensively with Aynsley Dunbar.

COVINGTON, BLIND BOGUS BEN

Covington had played banjo and rack harmonica in the streets of Birmingham, Alabama, USA, singing blues and hokum and, as his 1928 record labels indicate, pretending to be blind, though evidently with no great conviction. His most startling number began: 'I heard the voice of a porkchop say, come unto me and rest'. He was a member of a jug band that included Joe Lee 'Big Joe' Williams, although it seems unlikely that this was the Birmingham Jug Band that recorded in 1930. Covington was probably the same man as Ben Curry, who recorded four tracks in 1932.
● COMPILATIONS: *Alabama Jug And String Bands* (1988).

COX, IDA

b. Ida Prather, 25 February 1896, Toccoa, Georgia, USA, d. 10 November 1967. Like many early blues vocalists, Cox's origins are vague and details of the date and place of her birth vary widely. One of the classic blues singers, Cox began her career as a child, appearing on stage when barely in her teens. She made her first recordings in 1923 and for the rest of the decade recorded extensively for Paramount, often accompanied by Lovie Austin. Cox's singing style, a brooding, slightly nasal monotone, was less attractive than that of some of her contemporaries, but there was no denying the heartfelt passion with which she imbued the lyrics of her songs, many of which took death as their text. Among her greatest performances were 'Bone Orchard Blues', 'Death Letter Blues', 'Black Crepe Blues', 'Worn Down Daddy' and 'Coffin Blues' (on which she was accompanied by her husband, organist Jesse Crump). Her accompanying musicians were usually of the highest calibre; in particular, she worked with Tommy Ladnier, whose intense trumpet-playing beautifully counterpointed her threatening drone. Cox toured extensively during the 30s but was absent from the recording studios. In 1939 she was invited by John Hammond to appear at the Carnegie Hall 'Spirituals To Swing' concert, after which she made more records, this time accompanied by several top-flight jazzmen who included Oran 'Hot Lips' Page, Edmond Hall, Charlie Christian, Lionel Hampton, Red Allen and J.C. Higginbotham. In the early 40s Cox again toured with her own shows, but in 1945 she suffered a stroke and thereafter worked only sporadically. She did, however, make a welcome return to the recording studios in 1961. While these final performances inevitably showed the signs of her advancing years, she was still recognizably Ida Cox, 'The Blues Queen'.
● ALBUMS: *Sings The Blues* (London 1954)★★★★, *Wild Women Don't Have The Blues* (1961)★★★, *Blues For Rampart Street* (Riverside 1961)★★★.
● COMPILATIONS: *Ida Cox Vol. 1* (Fountain

1971)★★★, *Ida Cox Volume 2* (Fountain 1975)★★★, *Paramount Recordings* 6-LP box set (Garnet 1975)★★★★.

CRAWFORD, SUGARBOY

b. James Crawford, 12 October 1934, New Orleans, Louisiana, USA. Responsible for one of the two anthems of New Orleans' Mardi Gras festival, Crawford's career was cut short when he was assaulted by a policeman. A self-taught pianist, his career began when he and some schoolfriends started an informal band that came to the attention of disc jockey Dr. Daddy-O. He named them the Chapaka Shaweez, after the Creole title of one of their tunes, which translated as 'We are not raccoons'. He also introduced them to Dave Bartholomew, who produced them as the Sha-Weez for Aladdin in November 1952. A year later, Crawford And His Cane Cutters, featuring a young Snooks Eaglin on guitar, recorded 'Jock-O-Mo' for Checker, which with the Hawketts' 1955 hit, 'Mardi Gras Mambo', helped to define the city's festivities. Further Checker sessions only produced one more single, after which Bartholomew signed Crawford to Imperial. None of his four singles made much impression and he made just three singles between 1959 and 1962, for Jin, Ace and Peacock. He and his band were in Monroe on the way to a gig when the police accused him of drink-driving. In the altercation that followed, he was pistol-whipped about the head; the blow rendered him paralysed for a year and effectively ended his career. In 1965, three high school students called the Dixie-Cups appropriated his finest moment, called it 'Iko Iko' and thereby mugged Crawford a second time.
● COMPILATIONS: *Sugarboy Crawford* (Chess 1976)★★★, *New Orleans Classics* (Pathe Marconi 1985)★★★.

CRAY, ROBERT

b. 1 August 1953, Columbus, Georgia, USA. The popularity of guitar-based blues during the 80s had much to do with the unassuming brilliance of Cray. Although he formed his first band in 1974, it was not until *Bad Influence* in 1983 that his name became widely known. His debut, *Who's Been Talking*, failed because the record label folded (it has since been reissued on Charly). Cray's music is a mixture of pure blues,

soul and rock and his fluid, clean style owes much to Albert Collins and Peter Green, while on faster numbers a distinct Jimi Hendrix influence is heard. The Robert Cray Band features long-time bassist Richard Cousins, Dave Olson (drums) and Peter Boe (keyboards). *Strong Persuader* in 1987 became the most successful blues album for over two decades and Cray has taken this popularity with calm modesty. He is highly regarded by experienced stars like Eric Clapton, who in addition to recording Cray's 'Bad Influence', invited him to record with him and play at his 1989 marathon series of concerts at London's Royal Albert Hall. In 1988 Cray consolidated his reputation with the superb *Don't Be Afraid Of The Dark*, which featured some raucous saxophone playing from David Sanborn. *Midnight Stroll* featured a new line-up that gave Cray a tougher-sounding unit and moved him out of mainstream blues towards R&B and soul. *Some Rainy Morning* was Cray's vocal album: there were no blinding solos to be found, but rather, a mature and sweet voice that prompted Cray to be viewed as a soul singer rather than a blues guitarist. Cray's quartet in the mid-90s featured Kevin Hayes (drums), Karl Sevareid (bass) and Jim Pugh (keyboards). *Sweet Potato Pie* featured the Memphis Horns on a cover version of Isaac Hayes and David Porter's 'Trick Or Treat'
● ALBUMS: *Who's Been Talkin'* (Tomato 1980)★★★, *Bad Influence* (High Tone 1983)★★★★, *False Accusations* (High Tone 1985)★★★, with Albert Collins, Johnny Copeland *Showdown!* (Alligator 1985)★★★★, *Strong Persuader* (Mercury 1986)★★★, *Don't Be Afraid Of The Dark* (Mercury 1988)★★★★, *Midnight Stroll* (Mercury 1990)★★★★, *Too Many Cooks* (Tomato 1991)★★★, *I Was Warned* (Mercury 1992)★★★, *The Score* rerelease of *Who's Been Talkin'* (Charly 1992)★★★, *Shame And A Sin* (Mercury 1993)★★★, *Some Rainy Morning* (Mercury 1995)★★★, *Sweet Potato Pie* (Mercury 1997)★★★★.
● VIDEOS: *Smoking Gun* (Polygram Music Video 1989), *Collection: Robert Cray* (Polygram Music Video 1991).

CREACH, 'PAPA' JOHN

b. 28 May 1917, Beaver Falls, Pennsylvania, USA, d. 22 February 1994, Los Angeles, California, USA. John Creach began his career as a fiddle player upon his family's move to Chicago in 1935. He later toured the Midwest of the USA as a member of cabaret attraction the Chocolate Music Bars, but settled in California in 1945. Creach played in the resident band at Palm Springs' Chi Chi Restaurant, undertook session work and entertained tourists on a luxury liner before securing a spot at the Parisian Room in Los Angeles. He was 'discovered' at this venue by Joey Covington, drummer in Hot Tuna and Jefferson Airplane, and by October 1970 Creach was a member of both groups. His tenure was not without controversy; many aficionados resented this intrusion, but although he left the former group two years later, 'Papa' John remained with the latter act until 1975, surviving their transformation into Jefferson Starship. *Papa John Creach* featured support from many bay area acolytes, including Jerry Garcia, Carlos Santana and John Cipollina, while *Filthy* was notable for 'Walking The Tou Tou', effectively a Hot Tuna master. *Zulu (Playing My Fiddle For You)* marked Creach's growing estrangement from the 'Airplane' family and was his final release on their in-house Grunt label. Successive releases failed to match the profile of those early recordings, but Creach remained an enduring live attraction in Los Angeles throughout the 70s. He was awarded the Blues Foundation's W.C. Handy Award in 1993, shortly before his death.

● ALBUMS: *Papa John Creach* (Grunt 1971)★★, *Filthy* (Grunt 1972)★★★, *Zulu (Playing My Fiddle For You)* (Grunt 1974)★★, *I'm The Fiddle Man* (Buddah 1975)★★, *Rock Father* (Buddah 1976)★★, *The Cat And The Fiddle* (DJM 1977)★★, *Inphasion* (DJM 1978)★★.

CREAM

Arguably the most famous trio in rock music, Cream comprised Jack Bruce (b. John Symon Asher, 14 May 1943, Glasgow, Lanarkshire, Scotland; bass, vocals), Eric Clapton (b. Eric Patrick Clapp, 30 March 1945, Ripley, Surrey, England; guitar) and Ginger Baker (b. Peter Baker, 19 August 1939, Lewisham, London, England; drums). In their two and a half years together, Cream made such an impression on fans, critics and musicians as to make them one of the most influential bands since the Beatles. They formed in the height of swinging London

during the 60s and were soon thrust into a non-stop turbulent arena, hungry for new and interesting music after the Merseybeat boom had quelled. Cream were announced in the music press as a pop group, Clapton from John Mayall's Bluesbreakers, Bruce from Graham Bond and briefly Manfred Mann, and Baker from the Graham Bond Organisation via Alexis Korner's Blues Incorporated. Baker and Bruce had originally played together in the Johnny Burch Octet in 1962. Cream's debut single, 'Wrapping Paper', was a comparatively weird pop song, and made the lower reaches of the charts on the strength of its insistent appeal. This was a paradox to their great strength of jamming and improvisation, each member was already a proven master of their chosen instrument. Their follow-up single, 'I Feel Free', unleashed such energy that it could only be matched by Jimi Hendrix. The debut album *Fresh Cream* confirmed the promise: this band were not what they seemed, another colourful pop group singing songs of tangerine bicycles. With a mixture of blues standards and exciting originals, the album became a record that every credible music fan should own. It reached number 6 in the UK charts. That same crucial year, *Disraeli Gears*, with its distinctive dayglo cover, went even higher, and firmly established Cream in the USA, where they spent most of their touring life. This superb album showed a marked progression from their first, in particular, in the high standard of songwriting from Jack Bruce and his lyricist partner, former beat poet, Pete Brown. Landmark songs such as 'Sunshine Of Your Love', 'Strange Brew' and 'SWLABR' (She Was Like A Bearded Rainbow) were performed with precision.

Already rumours of a split prevailed as news filtered back from America of fights and arguments between Baker and Bruce. Meanwhile, their live performances did not reflect the music already released from studio sessions. The long improvisational pieces, based around fairly simple blues structures were often awesome. Each member had a least one party piece during concerts, Bruce with his frantic harmonica solo on 'Traintime', Baker with his trademark drum solo on 'Toad' and Clapton with his strident vocal and fantastic guitar solo on 'Crossroads'. One disc of the magnificent two-record set,

Wheels Of Fire, captured Cream live, at their exploratory best. Just a month after its release, while it sat on top of the US charts, they announced they would disband at the end of the year following two final concerts. The famous Royal Albert Hall farewell concerts were captured on film; the posthumous *Goodbye* repeated the success of its predecessors, as did some later live scrapings from the bottom of the barrel.

The three members came together in 1993 for an emotional one-off performance at the Rock 'n' Roll Hall Of Fame awards in New York, before the CD age finally recognized their contribution in 1997, with the release of an excellent 4-CD box set, *Those Were The Days*. Two CDs from the studio and two from the stage wrap up this brief career, with no stone left unturned. In addition to all of their previously issued material there is the unreleased 'Lawdy Mama', which Bruce claims features the wrongly recorded original bass line of 'Strange Brew'. Another gem is a demo of the Bruce/Brown diamond, 'The Weird Of Hermiston', which later appeared on Bruce's debut solo album *Songs For A Tailor*. This collection reaffirms their greatness, as three extraordinary musicians fusing their musical personalities together as a unit. Cream came and went almost in the blink of an eye, but left an indelible mark on rock music.

● ALBUMS: *Fresh Cream* (Polydor 1966)★★★★, *Disraeli Gears* (Polydor 1967)★★★★★, *Wheels Of Fire* (Polydor 1968)★★★★, *Goodbye* (Polydor 1969)★★★, *Live Cream* (Polydor 1970)★★★, *Live Cream, Volume 2* (Polydor 1972)★★★.

● COMPILATIONS: *The Best Of Cream* (Polydor 1969)★★★★, *Heavy Cream* (Polydor 1973)★★★, *Strange Brew - The Very Best Of Cream* (Polydor 1986)★★★★, *Those Were The Days* 4-CD box set (Polydor 1997)★★★★★.

● VIDEOS: *Farewell Concert* (Polygram Music Video 1986), *Strange Brew* (Warner Music Video 1992), *Fresh Live Cream* (Polygram 1994).

● FURTHER READING: *Cream In Gear (Limited Edition)*, Gered Mankowitz and Robert Whitaker (Photographers). *Strange Brew*, Chris Welch.

CROCKETT, G.L.

b. *c*.1929, Carrollton, Mississippi, USA, d. 14 February 1967. In the late 50s George L. Crockett was living on Chicago's west side and sitting in as a singer with Magic Sam, Freddie King and others. He made his first record for the Chief label in 1958, later reissued by USA and Checker: 'Look Out Mabel' was a much sought after item in the late 70s, often cited as the original black rockabilly record. In 1965 he recorded the Jimmy Reed soundalike 'It's A Man Down There' for Four Brothers Records and it was the company's biggest hit (a US R&B Top 10 and pop Top 100). There were two less successful singles before Crockett died of a cerebral haemorrhage.

● COMPILATIONS: *Chess Rockabillies* one track only (1978).

CRUDUP, ARTHUR 'BIG BOY'

b. 24 August 1905, Forest, Mississippi, USA, d. 28 March 1974, Nassawadox, Virginia, USA. During the 40s and early 50s Arthur Crudup was an important name in the blues field, his records selling particularly well in the south. For much of his early life Crudup worked in various rural occupations, not learning to play the guitar until he was 32. His teacher was local blueman, 'Papa Harvey', and although Crudup's guitar style never became adventurous, it formed an effective backdrop for his high, expressive voice. Allegedly, Crudup was playing on the sidewalk in Chicago when he was spotted by the music publisher and general 'Mr Fixit', Lester Melrose. Like many others with his background, Big Boy's first recordings were his most countrified; 'If I Get Lucky' and 'Black Pony Blues' were recorded in September 1941 and probably sold largely to the same group of resident and ex-patriot southerners who were buying records by Tommy McClennan and Sleepy John Estes. During the next 12 years he recorded approximately 80 tracks for Victor, including songs that became blues standards. 'Mean Old Frisco' was later picked up by artists as diverse as Brownie McGhee (1946) and B.B. King (1959), and was one of the first blues recordings to feature an electric guitar. He recorded 'Dust My Broom' in 1949 and the following year moonlighted for the Trumpet label in Jackson, Mississippi, under the name 'Elmer James'. Despite attempts to update his sound by the introduction of piano, harmonicas and saxophones, by 1954 Big Boy's heyday was over. When he was contracted to record an album of his hits for Fire in 1962, the project had to be delayed until the picking season was over, Crudup having given up music and gone back to working on the land. Two of Crudup's compositions, 'That's All Right' and 'My Baby Left Me' were recorded by Elvis Presley, who also sang his 'I'm So Glad You're Mine', but it is not likely that Crudup benefited much from this. A second career bloomed for Big Boy with the interest taken in blues by a white audience in the mid-60s, beginning with an album for Bob Koester's Delmark label. This prompted appearances at campuses and clubs in the USA and Europe. It appears likely that Big Boy Crudup gave more to the blues than he ever received in return.

● ALBUMS: *Mean Ol' Frisco* (Fire 1957)★★★★, *Look On Yonders Wall* (Delmark 1968)★★★, *Crudup's Mood* (Delmark 1970)★★★, *Meets The Master Blues Bassists* (Delmark 1994)★★★.

● COMPILATIONS: *The Father Of Rock And Roll* (RCA Victor 1971)★★★.

CRUMP, JESSE

b. 1906, Paris, Texas, USA. A pianist and organist, Crump was touring on the TOBA circuit in his early teens as a singer, dancer, instrumentalist and comedian. His duet recordings with Billy McKenzie are in a vaudeville vein, but he was an excellent blues accompanist, best demonstrated in his many recordings with Ida Cox, to whom he was married for some years. From the late 30s he gave up touring in favour of nightclub residencies, settling first in Muncie, Indiana, and later on the west coast, where he recorded with Bob Scobey's Frisco Band in 1956. By the early 60s, he had effectively retired.

CRUTCHFIELD, JAMES

b. 25 May 1912, Baton Rouge, Louisiana, USA. A self-taught pianist, Crutchfield left home and found work in the saw mills and lumber camps of Louisiana and Texas. In a logging camp in Bogalusa he met pianist Little Brother Montgomery who taught him to play '44 Blues'. In the late 40s Crutchfield moved to St. Louis where he worked in clubs, coming into contact with artists such as Henry Brown and Roosevelt Sykes. Around 1955, Charlie O'Brien, blues fan and policeman, introduced Crutchfield to John Bentley, who included four of his songs in a series of albums devoted to St. Louis jazz and blues pianists. Crutchfield resurfaced in the early 80s, toured parts of Europe and recorded an album for the Swingmaster label in Holland.

● ALBUMS: *Original Barrelhouse Blues* (Swingmaster 1985)★★★.

CURTIS, JAMES 'PECK'

b. 7 March 1912, Benoit, Mississippi, USA, d. 1 November 1970, Helena, Arkansas, USA. Peck Curtis was a blues drummer, whose musical roots lay in playing washboard for medicine shows, with which he travelled throughout the 30s. He also played with the South Memphis Jug Band and later accompanied a young Howlin' Wolf. He is particularly associated, however, with Sonny Boy 'Rice Miller' Williamson, with whom he played for many years on the famous *King Biscuit Time* radio show. In 1952, he made some recordings, but these were not issued at the time (one appeared many years later). In the 60s, he began to work with Houston Stackhouse, and a number of their recordings appeared on albums.

● COMPILATIONS: *Arkansas Blues* (1970)★★★.

DADDY STOVEPIPE

b. Johnny Watson, 12 April 1867, Mobile, Alabama, USA, d. 1 November 1963, Chicago, Illinois, USA. Daddy Stovepipe, named because of his top hat, was an itinerant street musician for most of his long life. He was recorded playing guitar and rack harmonica as early as 1924 and, with Whistlin' Pete, in 1927. A longer series of records with his wife, Mississippi Sarah, singing and playing jug, were recorded in 1931 and 1935, and included 'Greenville Strut', referring to the Mississippi town where they lived. After Sarah's death in 1937, Watson went to Texas playing there with zydeco bands and

Mexican musicians (from whom he learned 'South Of The Border'). From 1948, he resided in Chicago, playing both secular music and gospel on Maxwell Street until shortly before his death.
● COMPILATIONS: *Blues From Maxwell Street* (1961)★★★, *Harmonicas Unlimited* (1986)★★★.

DALE, LARRY
b. Ennis Lowery, 1923, Wharton, Texas, USA. Dale's reputation as a blues guitarist fundamentally stems from the February 1958 session that produced Champion Jack Dupree's Atlantic album, *Blues From The Gutter*, and a handful of records issued under his own name. Leaving his parents' farm when he was 18, he spent the next eight years running a car repair shop in Hungerford, Texas. In 1949 he moved to New York, his wife's home-town, to pursue the same work. Repairing Apollo owner Bobby Schiffman's car led to him winning the Wednesday night talent contest two weeks running. Dale also drove Brownie McGhee and Bob Gaddy to their New Jersey nightclub job, and later joined them onstage, at first to sing and then as an apprentice guitarist. Subsequently, he joined Gaddy in the Houserockers, a partnership that lasted until 1970. His first records for Jax and Groove featured him as vocalist with Paul Williams' band and for Mickey Baker (as Big Red McHouston). Baker played guitar on Dale's singles for Groove, Herald and Ember, but his own proficiency enabled Dale to work on sessions for Cootie Williams and Champion Jack Dupree for Victor, Groove and Vik, as well as on Frankie Lymon And The Teenagers' 'Why Do Fools Fall In Love?' Further singles during the 60s for Glover, Fire, Ram and Atlantic Records failed to make an impression. When interviewed in 1986, Dale was continuing to lead the Houserockers at gigs around New York.
● ALBUMS: *Harlem Hit Parade* (Ace 1987)★★★, *Still Groove Jumping!* (Detour 1987)★★★, *Old Town Blues Vol. 1* (Ace 1986)★★★, *Old Town Blues Vol. 1: Downtown Sides* (Ace 1993)★★★, *Old Town Blues Vol. 2: The Uptown Sides* (Ace 1994)★★★.

DALLAS, LEROY
b. 12 December 1920, Mobile, Alabama, USA. Dallas travelled the south in the 30s and 40s, teaming up for some time with Frank Edwards, and sang in the Chicago streets for a while before settling in New York from 1943. His 1949 recordings for Sittin' In With are in a small group format with Brownie McGhee (with whom Dallas had played guitar and washboard in the 30s) and Big Chief Ellis; they bear little sign of urbanization (indeed his springy guitar rhythms positively countrify 'Jump Little Children, Jump', usually a preserve of blues shouters). By 1962, he had ceased to play professionally, but was still a capable guitarist and a convincing singer. His subsequent whereabouts is unknown.
● COMPILATIONS: *Country Blues Classics Vol. 4* (1966)★★★, *Blues All Around My Bed* (1967)★★★.

DANE, BARBARA
b. Barbara Jean Spillman, 12 May 1927, Detroit, Michigan, USA. Born into a white middle-class family, as a child Dane sang and played piano in Sunday school and also learned to play guitar. From the mid-40s she became involved with the labour, civil rights and feminist movements. She sang folk and jazz, working with Pete Seeger, Kid Ory, George Lewis, Turk Murphy and others, appearing at festivals and on television, and she even hosted her own show in San Francisco. Dane appeared at many prestigious venues and shared bills with distinguished performers, including Louis Armstrong, Memphis Slim, Lightnin' Hopkins and controversial comedian Lenny Bruce. In 1959, she recorded with Earl Hines and toured with Jack Teagarden's band, and continued her high profile on television, radio and in concert, throughout the 60s and 70s. In this time she became increasingly involved in political causes, including demonstrations and marches in support of the civil rights movement and in protest against American military involvement in Vietnam. She concentrated her musical efforts on singing at fund- and consciousness-raising gatherings in America, Spain, Cuba and Italy, and travelled to Vietnam in 1975. Dane's decision to ally her singing to political causes has tended to keep her from the general audience. Her folk-singing has a strong sense of commitment and she is also a convincing singer of the blues. Her records are hard to find but worth seeking out.
● ALBUMS: *Trouble In Mind* (San Francisco

1957)★★★, *Livin' With The Blues* (Dot 1959)★★★, *On My Way* (Capitol 1962)★★★.

DANIELS, JULIUS

b. 1902, Denmark, South Carolina, USA, d. 18 October 1947, Charlotte, North Carolina, USA. Daniels was a guitarist and singer and one of the first black artists in the south-eastern states to record. He effectively represented an older and more localized musical tradition. Although he only made a few records, the music he left behind embraced blues, sacred music and even songs evoking the white country music of the day, all accompanied with light, melodic picking. At his first session, in Atlanta in 1927, he was supported by guitarist Bubba Lee Torrence, and although the latter's contribution was rather low-key, they shared the billing on the resulting records. During his second session later that same year, he used another guitarist, Wilbert Andrews. Both Torrence and Andrews probably came from Pineville, North Carolina, where Daniels lived, but nothing more is known about them.
● COMPILATIONS: with Lil McClintock *Atlanta Blues, 1927-30 (Complete Recordings In Chronological Order)* (Matchbox 1986)★★★.

DARBY, 'BLIND' TEDDY

b. 2 March 1906, Henderson, Kentucky, USA. Born sighted, Darby lost his eyesight in the 20s after moving to St. Louis, where he stayed for the rest of his life. Later in that decade, he learned to play guitar and established himself on the local blues scene. In 1929, he made his first records, and over the next few years made several more for four different labels, including three that were issued under the pseudonym Blind Squire Turner. His plaintive vocals and melodic blues style had the capacity to be quite distinctive, but more often he reflected other popular contemporaries, sounding on occasions like Leroy Carr, or fellow citizen Peetie Wheatstraw. In the 50s, he was ordained as a deacon, and although he made some recordings in 1964, these have not been issued.
● COMPILATIONS: *St. Louis Country Blues 1929-1937* (Earl Archives 1987)★★★.

DARNELL, LARRY

b. Leo Edward Donald, 1929, Columbus, Ohio, USA, d. 3 July 1983, Columbus, Ohio, USA. Darnell began singing in Columbus gospel choirs and started sneaking into local clubs in the early 40s to sing for cash. At the age of 15 he joined the travelling show Irwin C. Miller's Brownskin Models, which he left in New Orleans after being offered a residency at the famous Dew Drop Inn. Something of a heart-throb, he became known as 'Mr Heart & Soul' and secured a recording contract with Regal in 1949, with whom he enjoyed big hits with 'For You My Love' and the two-part 'I'll Get Along Somehow', backed by Paul Gayten's band. Moving to New York in 1950, Darnell's later tracks for Regal, OKeh, Savoy and DeLuxe failed to live up to the early successes. Having made occasional recordings in the 60s for Warwick, Argo and Instant, he retired from popular music in 1969, although he continued to sing for the church and contribute to benefit shows until two years before his death from cancer in 1983.
● COMPILATIONS: *I'll Get Along Somehow* (Route 66 1987)★★★.

DAVENPORT, JED

b. Mississippi, USA. Davenport settled in Memphis, where he performed regularly when not touring with medicine shows. He played guitar, trumpet and jug, but it was on harmonica that he recorded, beginning in 1929 with exciting, highly vocalized versions of 'How Long How Long Blues' and 'Cow Cow Blues'. In 1930, he recorded with his Beale Street Jug Band, which included Kansas Joe and Memphis Minnie, producing 'Beale Street Breakdown', a *tour de force* of harmonica pyrotechnics and ensemble work. A later recording by what was essentially the same ensemble was credited to Memphis Minnie And Her Jug Band, probably as a marketing ploy. Davenport was last seen in Memphis in the 60s.
● COMPILATIONS: *Memphis Harmonica Kings* (1983)★★★.

DAVENPORT, LESTER

b. 16 January 1932, Tchula, Mississippi, USA. Prior to recording his debut album in 1992, Davenport's claim to fame had been as the replacement for Billy Boy Arnold in the Bo

Diddley band, although he proved less adept at improvising on the harmonica over a one-chord vamp. He was five years old when he received a harmonica as a Christmas present; within a few years, he was accompanying his slide guitarist father Neely at weekend suppers. At the age of 14, he joined his older brothers in Chicago. Homesick James lived nearby and he and Snooky Pryor gave lessons to Davenport and his cousin, Otis (later Smokey) Smothers. After sharing gigs with James, Johnny Young and pianist Jimmy Walker, he joined Big Boy Spires' Rocket Four. While with that band, he was asked by Diddley to replace Arnold in his band, and he played on the session that produced 'Pretty Thing' and 'Bring It To Jerome'. He proved his versatility in the early 60s by playing drums with Howlin' Wolf. In the ensuing years, he also drummed for Sunnyland Slim and Junior Wells, as well as organizing his own groups, yet he never abandoned his job as a paint sprayer. He also took up bass guitar and played both bass and drums on the 1979 American Blues Legends tour. In 1987, he joined Big Daddy Kinsey and the Kinsey Report, with whom he worked for six years. *When The Blues Hit You*, using the resources of Sunnyland Slim and John Primer among others, was greeted as a solid but uninspired collection of traditional Chicago blues.

● ALBUMS: *American Blues Legends 1979* (Big Bear 1979)★★★, *When The Blues Hit You* (Earwig 1992)★★★.

DAVIES, CYRIL

b. 1932, Buckinghamshire, England, d. 7 January 1964. Along with Alexis Korner and Graham Bond, the uncompromising Davies was a seminal influence in the development of British R&B during the beat boom of the early 60s. His superb wailing and distorted harmonica shook the walls of many clubs up and down Britain. Initially he played with Alexis Korner's Blues Incorporated and then formed his own band, the All-Stars, featuring Long John Baldry, session pianist Nicky Hopkins and drummer Mickey Waller. Their Chicago-based blues was raw, loud and exciting. Like Bond, he died at a young age, after losing his battle with leukaemia.

● ALBUMS: *The Legendary Cyril Davies* (Folklore 1970)★★★.

DAVIES, DEBBIE

b. Los Angeles, California, USA. Davies had her first guitar at the age of 12 and when *Bluesbreakers*, the John Mayall album on which Eric Clapton played guitar, was released in 1965, she set out to memorize all of Clapton's solos. Intrigued by the names of black blues artists mentioned in his interviews, she discovered the records of Freddie King, Otis Rush and Gatemouth Brown. Her first live gigs were in a club in a northern California college town, where she was able to witness Buddy Guy, Junior Wells, Etta James and Albert Collins in action. After playing in several bar bands, she returned to Los Angeles and auditioned for Maggie Mayall And The Cadillacs, an all-female R&B band that often opened for Maggie's husband John Mayall. Davies met Albert Collins while playing local gigs with Bluesbreaker Coco Montoya. He invited her to sit in at the San Francisco Blues Festival and later offered her a gig with his band. After three years, she left to tour with Jimmy Buffet's harmonica player, Fingers Taylor, before forming her own band. Collins guests on one track of her debut album, which also pays tribute to influences such as Freddie and Albert King. *Loose Tonight* contains more original material, with ample space for her fluent lead guitar. Davies is a confident writer and performer in a field that contains few to equal her.

● ALBUMS: *Live!* (NQD 1992)★★★, *Picture This* (Blind Pig 1993)★★★, *Loose Tonight* (Blind Pig 1994)★★, *I Got That Feeling* (Blind Pig 1997)★★★.

DAVIS, 'BLIND' JOHN

b. 7 December 1913, Hattiesburg, Mississippi, USA, d. 12 October 1985, Chicago, Illinois, USA. Davis taught himself piano after being blinded in 1923, and led his own six-piece band for 15 years from 1938. He professed not to care for blues, but his fame rests on the hundreds of blues accompaniments he recorded during the late 30s and early 40s. Among those who used him were 'Big' Bill Broonzy, Tampa Red and 'Doctor' Peter Clayton. Usually he worked in a small band setting, where his generally unspectacular playing would sometimes show a quiet inventiveness. His self-accompanied 1938 vocal recordings are mediocre, but his back-up work, with its rolling right hand figures, was both immediately recognizable and creatively varied. In the post-war years, Davis was an early visitor to Europe, recording two albums in Paris in 1952, revealing a personal taste for songs such as 'O Sole Mio' and 'Lady Be Good'. Despite his declared preferences his recorded work emphasized blues and boogie, with a smattering of jazz and popular music. Seldom profound (although his song 'No Mail Today' is a beautiful piece of controlled melancholy), Davis was always proficient and professional.

● ALBUMS: *Live In Hamburg* (1974)★★★, *The Incomparable Blind John Davis* (1974)★★★, *Stomping On A Saturday Night* (1978)★★★, with Lonnie Johnson *Blues For Everybody* (1979)★★★, *In Memoriam* (Document 1986)★★★, *The First Recording Sessions* (1992)★★★.

DAVIS, CeDELL 'BIG G'

b. 1926, Halena, Arkansas, USA. An excellent slide guitar and harmonica player Davis performed briefly as a member of the King Biscuits Time entertainers in the early 50s with Sonny Boy 'Rice Miller' Williamson, before joining guitarist Robert Nighthawk's band. In 1961 he moved to Pine Bluff, Arkansas, and continued to work locally and occasionally with Nighthawk, who along with Tampa Red, influenced his slide guitar playing. Because of the effects of childhood polio which denied him the full use of his hands, Davis played the guitar upside down and used a butter knife for a slide. He was last reported to be living in a nursing home in Pine Bluff.

● COMPILATIONS: *Keep It To Yourself, Arkansas Blues Volume 1* (1983)★★★, *Feel Like Doin' Something Wrong* (Demon 1994)★★★, *The Best Of CeDell Davis* (Capricorn/Fat Possum 1995)★★★.

DAVIS, GARY, REV.

b. 30 April 1896, Laurens, South Carolina, USA, d. 5 May 1972, Hammonton, New Jersey, USA. This highly accomplished guitarist was self-taught from the age of six. Partially blind from an early age, he lost his sight during his late twenties. During the Depression years, he worked as a street singer in North Carolina, playing a formidable repertoire of spirituals,

rags, marches and square dance tunes. In 1933, he was ordained as a Baptist minister and continued to tour as a gospel preacher, recording several spiritual and blues songs for ARC in the mid-30s. After moving to New York in 1940, he achieved some fame on the folk circuit and subsequently recorded for a number of labels, including Stinson, Riverside, Prestige-Bluesville and Folkways. *Harlem Street Singer*, released in 1960, was an impressive work, and one that emphasized his importance to a new generation of listeners. Davis taught guitar and greatly inspired Stefan Grossman, and among Davis's other devotees were Bob Dylan, Taj Mahal, Ry Cooder and Donovan. Davis visited the UK in 1964, and returned as a soloist on several other occasions. He appeared at many music festivals, including Newport in 1968, and was the subject of two television documentaries in 1967 and 1970. He also appeared in the film *Black Roots*. His importance in the history of black rural music cannot be overestimated.

● ALBUMS: *Harlem Street Singer* (1960)★★★, *From Blues To Gospel* (Biograph 1971)★★★.
● COMPILATIONS: *Best Of Gary Davis In Concert* (Kicking Mule 1979)★★★, *Pure Religion And Bad Company* (Smithsonian/ Folkways 1991)★★★, *Blues And Ragtime* 1962-66 recordings (Shanachie 1993)★★★, *The Complete Early Recordings* (Yazoo 1994)★★★, *The Complete Early Records* (Yazz 1995)★★★, *O Glory: The Apostolic Studio Sessions* (Edsel 1996)★★★.
● FURTHER READING: *Oh What A Beautiful City: A Tribute To Rev. Gary Davis 1896 - 1972*, Robert Tilling.

DAVIS, JAMES 'THUNDERBIRD'

b. James Houston, 10 November 1938, Pritchard, Alabama, USA, d. 24 January 1991, St. Paul, Minnesota, USA. Schooled in gospel singing as he grew up in the Mobile area, Davis moved into R&B in the late 50s. He was discovered by Guitar Slim, who gave him his nickname after a drinking bout and used him as his 'warm up' singer until Slim's death in 1959. Settling in Thibodeaux, Louisiana, Slim's home-town, Davis toured with Nappy Brown and the Lloyd Lambert Orchestra. He made his recording debut for Duke in 1963, and was persuaded to move to Houston by label boss, Don Robey, who used him to demo songs for Bobby Bland to learn while on tour. His own records went unpromoted, even though 'Blue Monday' and 'Your Turn To Cry' subsequently earned considerable status as blues standards. After working as the opening act for Joe Tex and O.V. Wright, Davis left the business. He was rediscovered in Gray, Louisiana, by Lambert and Black Top boss, Hammond Scott, and recorded *Check Out Time* in the spring of 1988. He also took part in *Black Top Blues-A-Rama*, a live session recorded at Tipitina's in New Orleans with Ronnie Earl and Anson Funderburgh. Plans for a second album were in hand when he collapsed and died onstage at the Blues Saloon in St. Paul, Minnesota.

● ALBUMS: *Angels In Houston* (Rounder 1985)★★★, *Check Out Time* (Black Top 1989)★★★, *Black Top Blues-A-Rama Vol. 3* (Black Top 1990)★★★.

DAVIS, JIMMY 'MAXWELL STREET'

b. Charles W. Thompson, 2 March 1925, Tippo, Mississippi, USA, d. 28 December 1995. After spells as a singer and dancer with touring minstrel shows, and an unissued 1952 recording session for Sun Records, Davis moved to Chicago, playing for tips on Maxwell Street (sometimes outside a small restaurant that he operated there). His guitar playing is dark, complex and vigorous; in its emphasis on bass lines, it is much influenced by his Mississippi neighbour Tony Hollins, and by John Lee Hooker, from whom Davis learned much during a late 40s stay in Detroit. His singing, too, has the brooding, introspective manner of Hooker and other Delta-born blues singers. As well as traditionally based material, Davis incorporated a number of recorded hits into his repertoire, but made them his own by his personal, committed peformances.

● ALBUMS: *Maxwell Street Jimmy Davis* (1965)★★★, *Chicago Blues Sessions Volume 11* (Wolf 1989)★★★.

DAVIS, LARRY

b. 4 December 1936, Kansas City, Missouri, USA, d. 19 April 1994, Los Angeles, California, USA. One of many blues artists to be remembered solely for one early record, Larry Davis continued to make distinctive albums for the contemporary market until his death. Moving to Little Rock, Arkansas, with his father in 1944, he learned to play drums in the school band. His first gig was with harmonica player Sunny Blair, although he was not present on Blair's sessions for RPM and Meteor in 1952. He also played with guitarist Sammy Lawhorn and Gilbert Cables. Fenton Robinson and Charles McGowan visited Little Rock in 1955 and Davis joined their band before moving on to St. Louis. In 1957, Davis, McGowan, Billy Gayles and pianist Ernest Lane travelled to California, working there for a year, and the following year Davis recorded with Robinson for Duke Records in Houston. 'Texas Flood' was his first and best-known recording, followed by 'Angels In Houston' and 'Will She Come Home'. Davis did not record again until the late 60s, cutting Robinson's 'The Years Go Passing By' for B.B. King's Virgo label and completing various sessions from which tracks were issued on Kent and Pieces. Further recordings for Hub City and True Soul in the 70s, on which Davis played guitar, went unnoticed. He was recorded live at J.B. Hutto's St. Louis club in 1980 but the album was only issued in Japan. Davis's first studio album, *I Ain't Beggin' Nobody*, was made in 1988, and in 1992 he recorded *Sooner Or Later*, an album that mixed Southern Soul in the Bobby Bland manner with more straighforward guitar blues.

● ALBUMS: *I Ain't Beggin' Nobody* (Pulsar 1988)★★★, *Sooner Or Later* (Bullseye Blues 1992)★★★.

DAWKINS, JIMMY

b. 24 October 1936, Tchula, Mississippi, USA. Dawkins taught himself to play blues guitar in the early 50s and moved to Chicago in 1957, forming his own band two years later, while also working club dates with bluesmen such as Jimmy Rogers and Magic Sam. Dawkins is an expressive singer and a strong, inventive guitarist, and in the latter capacity he has been called on for recording sessions by many artists from the 60s onwards; Luther Allison, Wild Child Butler, Phil Guy and Johnny Young are only a few in a long list. He has recorded under his own name for many labels, including Delmark, Black And Blue, MCM, Excello, Isabel, JSP and Rumble Records. Dawkins is a quiet man who takes his blues very seriously; in the

early 70s he was a contributor to *Blues Unlimited* magazine, and in the 80s he ran his own Leric label, recording artists such as Little Johnny Christian rather than promoting his own career.
● ALBUMS: *Fast Fingers* (Delmark 1971)★★★, *All For Business* (Delmarl 1973)★★★, *Blisterstring* (Delmark 1975)★★★, *Transatlantic 770* (Sonet 1978)★★★, *Hot Wire '81* (1981)★★★, *Feel The Blues* (JSP 1985)★★★, *Kant Sheck Dees Bluze* (Earwig 1992)★★★, *B Phur Real* (Ichiban 1995)★★★.

DE BERRY, JIMMY

b. 17 November 1911, Gumwood, Arkansas, USA, d. 17 January 1985, Sikeston, Missouri, USA. De Berry was an active if peripheral member of the Memphis blues community from its heyday during the 20s until the early 50s. He grew up in Arkansas and Mississippi before moving to Memphis to live with his aunt in 1927. Teaching himself to play ukulele and then banjo and guitar, he associated with the likes of Will Shade, Charlie Burse, Jack Kelly, Frank Stokes and a very young Walter Horton. While in East St. Louis in 1934, he lost the lower part of his right leg in a train accident. Five years later, he recorded for Vocalion with his Memphis Playboys in a style that updated the hokum music from the earlier part of the decade. Over the next 15 years De Berry spent time in St. Louis and Jackson, Tennessee, returning to Memphis to make radio appearances with Willie Nix and Walter Horton. In 1953 he recorded two sessions for Sun Records; at the first session, he and Horton recorded the classic 'Easy', an instrumental adaptation of Ivory Joe Hunter's 'I Almost Lost My Mind'. The blues ballad 'Time Has Made A Change', with accompaniment from pianist Mose Vinson, came from the second session. In 1972 producer Steve LaVere reunited De Berry and Horton for sessions designed to recreate their earlier partnership, an endeavour that met with little success.
● COMPILATIONS: *Sun Records Harmonica Classics* (Rounder 1989)★★★, with Charlie Burse *Complete Recordings* (Old Tramp 1989)★★★, with Walter Horton *Easy* (Crosscut 1989)★★★, *Back* (Crosscut 1989)★★★.

DEAN, JOANNA

b. Memphis, Tennessee, USA. A raucous hard rock/blues singer in the tradition of Janis Joplin, Memphis singer Joanna Dean sings the blues in a similarly uninhibited style. Club dates soon led to a major recording contract with Polydor Records, who released her debut album, *Ain't Misbehavin'*, in 1988. Widely acclaimed within both blues and hard rock circles, it established Dean as a major new talent. However, for 1990's *Bad Romance* she assumed less high-profile billing behind her backing band of the same name. This collection included a duet with Cinderella vocalist Tom Keifer on 'Love Hurts', as well as heady new original material.
● ALBUMS: *Ain't Misbehavin'* (Polydor 1988)★★★★, with Bad Romance *Bad Romance* (Polydor 1990)★★★.

DEE, DAVID

b. David Eckford, *c*.1942, Greenwood, Mississippi, USA. Dee's family moved to East St. Louis when he was a baby. He sang gospel music when he was 12 years old and after a spell in the services he formed the short-lived vocal group David And The Temptations. In 1968 he began playing bass guitar in his own band, but switched to guitar in 1972, heavily influenced by Little Milton, Albert King, B.B. King, and Eddie 'Guitar Slim' Jones. In 1982 he enjoyed a big local hit with the up-tempo blues 'Going Fishing' on Oliver Sain's Venessa label, which established him as a major figure on the St. Louis blues scene. Edge Records and Ichiban have also released Dee's material.
● ALBUMS: *Sheer Pleasure* (1987)★★★, *Portrait Of The Blues* (1988)★★★, *Goin' Fishing* (Ichiban 1991)★★★.

DEREK AND THE DOMINOS

Eric Clapton (b. 30 March 1945, Ripley, Surrey, England), formed this short-lived band in May 1970 following his departure from the supergroup Blind Faith and his brief involvement with the down-home loose aggregation of Delaney And Bonnie And Friends. He purloined three members of the latter; Carl Radle (d. May 30 1980; bass), Bobby Whitlock (keyboards, vocals) and Jim Gordon (drums). Together with Duane Allman on guitar, they recorded *Layla And Other Assorted Love Songs*, a superb double album. The band were only together for a year, during which time they toured the UK playing small clubs, toured the USA, and consumed copious amounts of hard and soft drugs. It was during his time with the Dominos that Clapton became addicted to heroin. This, however, did not detract from the quality of the music. In addition to the classic 'Layla', the album contained Clapton's co-written compositions mixed with blues classics such as 'Key To The Highway' and a sympathetic reading of Jimi Hendrix's 'Little Wing'. The subsequent live album, recorded on their US tour, was a further demonstration of their considerable potential had they been able to hold themselves together.

● ALBUMS: *Layla And Other Assorted Love Songs* (Polydor 1970)★★★★, *In Concert* (Polydor 1973)★★★.

DETROIT JUNIOR

b. Emery H. Williams Junior, 26 October 1931, Haynes, Arkansas, USA. Junior became interested in music in the mid-40s. In the early 50s, as a pianist and bandleader, he had a residency in a Detroit club where he backed artists such as Rosco Gordon and Amos Milburn, the latter greatly influencing his songwriting. Eddie Boyd took Junior to Chicago, where he teamed up with J.T. Brown and then later with Mac Simmons. From 1960 onwards, Junior recorded singles for many local labels, and his best-known songs were the much-covered 'Money Tree' and 'Call My Job'. In the late 60s and 70s he toured and recorded with Howlin' Wolf and besides recording albums for The Blues On Blues and Wolf labels, he was also part of Alligator's *Living Chicago* series. However, this talented blues entertainer remains under-recorded.

● ALBUMS: *Chicago Urban Blues* (Blues On Blues 1972)★★★, *Turn Up The Heat* (Blue Suit 1995)★★★.

DICKINSON, JIM

b. Little Rock, Arkansas, USA. A prolific guitarist, songwriter and producer, Dickinson grew up with the Delta traditions of jug band music and the blues. Although born in Little Rock, he spent the first nine years of his life in Hollywood and Chicago, before making his permanent home in Memphis. One of his earliest recordings was as singer and pianist on the Jesters' 'Cadillac Man', a hallowed rockabilly single released on Memphis's Sun Records. After attending Baylor University as a student of theater arts, Dickinson became a sideman for artists including Aretha Franklin, the Rolling Stones (on the sessions for *Sticky Fingers*), Arlo Guthrie, Dan Penn, Jerry Jeff Walker, Alex Chilton, Dr. John, Sam And Dave, the Cramps, the Flamin' Groovies, Los Lobos, Steve Vai, Hank Ballard and John Hiatt. He was also a member of the Dixie Flyers session group, alongside Jerry Wexler, as well as local band Mudboy And The Neutrons, with whom he has recorded over a career spanning two decades. His first solo record, 1971's *Dixie Fried*, was produced by Tom Dowd and was widely acclaimed by critics as a definitive statement in contemporary Memphis Delta blues. As a producer he has worked with Mojo Nixon, Ry Cooder, Jason And The Scorchers, the Nighthawks, True Believers, Green On Red and Joe 'King' Carrasco. Arguably his best work in this capacity is represented by the Replacements' *Pleased To Meet Me*, Big Star's *Third* and Toots Hibbert's *Toots In Memphis*. He has scored or contributed to many films, including *Gimme Shelter*, *Crossroads*, *Streets Of Fire*, *The Long Riders*, *Stroker Ace*, *Paris, Texas* and *Brewster's Millions*. Despite his illustrious career, Dickinson is still unable to read music, having suffered from a 'multiple sight' condition from an early age. Dickinson's two sons have also followed him into music, forming a trio, DDT.

● ALBUMS: with Bill Justis Orchestra *Dixieland Folk Style* (Southtown/Monument 1965)★★★, *Dixie Fried* (Atlantic 1971)★★★★, with Mud Boy And The Neutrons *Known Felons In Drag* (New Rose 1980)★★★, *DXPCVI* (New Rose 1994)★★★.

DIDDLEY, BO

b. Elias Bates (later known as Elias McDaniel), 28 December 1928, McComb, Mississippi, USA. After beginning his career as a boxer, where he received the sobriquet 'Bo Diddley', the singer worked the blues clubs of Chicago with a repertoire influenced by Louis Jordan, John Lee Hooker and Muddy Waters. In late 1954, he teamed up with Billy Boy Arnold and recorded demos of 'I'm A Man' and 'Bo Diddley'. Re-recorded at Chess Studios with a backing ensemble comprising Otis Spann (piano), Lester

Davenport (harmonica), Frank Kirkland (drums) and Jerome Green (maracas), the a-side, 'Bo Diddley', became an R&B hit in 1955. Before long, Diddley's distorted, amplified, custom-made guitar, with its rectangular shape and pumping rhythm style became a familiar, much-imitated trademark, as did his self-referential songs with such titles as 'Bo Diddley's A Gunslinger', 'Diddley Daddy' and 'Bo's A Lumberjack'. His jive-talking routine with 'Say Man' (a US Top 20 hit in 1959) continued on 'Pretty Thing' and 'Hey Good Lookin'', which reached the lower regions of the UK charts in 1963. By then, Diddley was regarded as something of an R&B legend and found a new lease of life courtesy of the UK beat boom. The Pretty Things named themselves after one of his songs while his work was covered by such artists as the Rolling Stones, Animals, Manfred Mann, Kinks, Yardbirds, Downliner's Sect and the Zephyrs. Diddley subsequently jammed on albums by Chuck Berry and Muddy Waters and appeared infrequently at rock festivals. His classic version of 'Who Do You Love' became a staple cover for a new generation of US acts ranging from Quicksilver Messenger Service to the Doors, Tom Rush and Bob Seger, while the UK's Juicy Lucy took the song into the UK Top 20.

Like many of his generation, Diddley attempted to update his image and in the mid-70s released *The Black Gladiator* in the uncomfortable guise of an ageing funkster. *Where It All Begins*, produced by Johnny Otis (whose hit, 'Willie And The Hand Jive', owed much to Diddley's style), was probably the most interesting of his post-60s albums. In 1979, Diddley toured with the Clash and in 1984 took a cameo role in the film *Trading Places*. A familiar face on the revival circuit, Diddley is rightly regarded as a seminal figure in the history of rock 'n' roll. His continued appeal to younger performers was emphasized by Craig McLachlan's hit recording of 'Mona' in 1990. Diddley's sound and 'chunk-a-chunka-cha' rhythm continues to remain an enormous influence on pop and rock, both consciously and unconsciously. It was announced in 1995, after many years of relative recording inactivity, that Diddley had signed for Mike Vernon's Code Blue record label; the result was *A Man Amongst Men*. Even with the assistance of Richie Sambora,

Jimmie Vaughan, Ronnie Wood, Keith Richards, Billy Boy Arnold, Johnny 'Guitar' Watson and the Shirelles the anticipation was greater than the result.

● ALBUMS: *Bo Diddley* (Checker 1957)★★★, *Go Bo Diddley* (Checker 1958)★★★, *Have Guitar Will Travel* (Checker 1959)★★★, *Bo Diddley In The Spotlight* (Checker 1960)★★★, *Bo Diddley Is A Gunslinger* (Checker 1961)★★★, *Bo Diddley Is A Lover* (Checker 1961)★★★, *Bo Diddley* (Checker 1962)★★★, *Bo Diddley Is A Twister* (Checker 1962)★★★, *Hey Bo Diddley* (Checker 1963)★★★, *Bo Diddley And Company* (Checker 1963)★★★, *Bo Diddley Rides Again* (Checker 1963)★★★, *Bo Diddley's Beach Party* (Checker 1963)★★★, *Bo Diddley Goes Surfing* aka *Surfin' With Bo Diddley* (Checker 1963)★★★, *Hey Good Looking* (Checker 1964)★★★, with Chuck Berry *Two Great Guitars* (Checker 1964)★★★, *500% More Man* (Checker 1965)★★★, *Let Me Pass* (Checker 1965)★★★, *The Originator* (Checker 1966)★★★, *Boss Man* (Checker 1967)★★★, *Superblues* (Checker 1968)★★★, *The Super Super Blues Band* (Checker 1968)★★★, *The Black Gladiator* (Checker 1969)★★, *Another Dimension* (Chess 1971)★★★, *Where It All Begins* (Chess 1972)★★, *The Bo Diddley London Sessions* (Chess 1973)★★, *Big Bad Bo* (Chess 1974)★★★, *Got My Own Bag Of Tricks* (Chess 1974)★★★, *The 20th Anniversary Of Rock 'N' Roll* (1976)★★, *I'm A Man* (1977)★★, *Signifying Blues* (1993)★★★, *Bo's Blues* (1993)★★, *A Man Amongst Men* (Code Blue 1996)★★.

● COMPILATIONS: *Chess Master* (Chess 1988)★★★, *EP Collection* (See For Miles 1991)★★★★, *Bo Diddley: The Chess Years* 12-CD box set (Charly 1993)★★★★★, *Bo Diddley Is A Lover ... Plus* (See For Miles 1994)★★★, *Let Me Pass ... Plus* (See For Miles 1994)★★★.

● VIDEOS: *I Don't Sound Like Nobody* (Hendring Video 1990).

● FURTHER READING: *Where Are You Now Bo Diddley?*, Edward Kiersh. *The Complete Bo Diddley Sessions*, George White (ed.). *Bo Diddley: Living Legend*, George White.

DIXON, FLOYD

b. 8 February 1929, Marshall, Texas, USA. Aka J. Riggins Jnr., Dixon began playing piano and singing as a child, absorbing every influence from gospel and blues to jazz, and even hillbilly. In 1942 his family moved to Los Angeles and he came into contact with fellow ex-Texan Charles Brown who, sensing Dixon's potential, introduced him to his brand of cool, jazzy night club blues as singer and pianist with Johnny Moore's Three Blazers. When the Blazers split up, Dixon was the natural choice for a substitute Charles Brown, and he made early recordings in the Brown style with both Eddie Williams (the Blazers' bassist) for Supreme and with Johnny Moore's new Blazers for Aladdin and Combo. His own trio recorded extensively for Modern, Peacock and Aladdin labels between 1947 and 1952; later, they played in a harder R&B style for Specialty, Cat and Checker, and in the late 50s and 60s for a host of tiny west coast and Texas independent labels. In 1975 Dixon made a comeback, beginning with a tour of Sweden, and became the first artist to be featured on Jonas Bernholm's celebrated Route 66 reissue label. Dixon was commissioned to write 'Olympic Blues' for the 1984 Los Angeles games.

● ALBUMS: *Opportunity Blues* (Route 66 1980)★★★, *Houston Jump* (Route 66 1980)★★★, *Empty Stocking Blues* (Route 66 1985)★★★★, *Hitsville Look Out, Here's Mr. Magnificent* (1986)★★★, *Wake Up And Live* (Alligator 1996)★★★.

● COMPILATIONS: *Marshall Texas Is My Home* (Ace 1991)★★★.

DIXON, MARY

A native of Texas, Dixon is otherwise a biographical blank. Her five records, made in New York in 1929, include a pop coupling, 'Dusky Stevedore' and 'I Can't Give You Anything But Love', but otherwise are exclusively blues, with interesting lyrics about sex, violence and superstition. They are distinguished by first-class jazz accompaniments. Her powerful singing voice has the distinctive nasal tone of many women from her native state, and her imitation of Bubber Miley's growling trumpet is an arresting gimmick.

● COMPILATIONS: *The Complete Blues Sessions Of Gladys Bentley & Mary Dixon* (Collctors Classics 1988)★★★.

DIXON, WILLIE

b. 1 July 1915, Vicksburg, Mississippi, USA, d. 29 January 1992. At an early age Dixon was interested in both words and music, writing lyrics and admiring the playing of Little Brother Montgomery. As an adolescent, Dixon sang bass with local gospel groups, had some confrontation with the law, and hoboed his way to Chicago, where he became a boxer. He entered music professionally after meeting Baby Doo Caston, and together they formed the Five Breezes, whose 1940 recordings blend blues, jazz, pop and the vocal group harmonies of the Inkspots and the Mills Brothers. During World War II, Dixon resisted the draft, and was imprisoned for 10 months. After the war, he formed the Four Jumps Of Jive before reuniting with Caston in the Big Three Trio, who toured the Midwest and recorded for Columbia Records. The trio featured vocal harmonies and the jazz-influenced guitar work of Ollie Crawford. Dixon's performing activities lessened as his involvement with Chess Records increased. By 1951 he was a full-time employee, as producer, A&R representative, session musician, talent scout, songwriter, and occasionally, name artist. Apart from an interlude when he worked for Cobra in a similar capacity, Dixon remained with Chess until 1971. The relationship, however, was ultimately complex; he was forced to regain control of his copyrights by legal action. Meanwhile, Dixon was largely responsible for the sound of Chicago blues on Chess and Cobra, and of the black rock 'n' roll of Chuck Berry and Bo Diddley. He was also used on gospel sessions by Duke/Peacock, and his bass playing was excellent behind Rev. Robert Ballinger. Dixon's productions of his own songs included Muddy Waters' 'I'm Your Hoochie Coochie Man', Howlin' Wolf's 'Spoonful', Diddley's 'You Can't Judge A Book By Its Cover', Otis Rush's 'I Can't Quit You Baby' (a triumph for Dixon's and Rush's taste for minor chords), and Koko Taylor's 'Wang Dang Doodle', among many others. In the early 60s, Dixon teamed up with Memphis Slim to play the folk revival's notion of blues, and operated as a booking agent and manager, in which role he was crucial to the American Folk Blues Festival Tours of Europe. Many British R&B bands recorded his songs, including the Rolling Stones and Led Zeppelin, who adapted 'You Need Love'. After leaving Chess, Dixon went into independent production with his own labels, Yambo and Spoonful, and resumed a recording and performing career. He also administered the Blues Heaven Foundation, a charity that aimed to promote awareness of the blues, and to rectify the financial injustices of the past. Willie Dixon claimed, 'I am the blues'; and he was, certainly, hugely important in its history, not only as a great songwriter, but also as a producer, performer and mediator between artists and record companies.

● ALBUMS: *Willie's Blues* (Bluesville 1959)★★★, *Memphis Slim & Willie Dixon At The Village Gate* (1960)★★★★, *I Am The Blues* (Columbia 1970)★★, *Peace* (1971)★★★, *Catalyst* (Ovation 1973)★★★, *Mighty Earthquake And Hurricane* (1983)★★★, *I Feel Like Steppin' Out* (1986)★★★, *Gene Gilmore & The Five Breezes* (1989)★★, *Hidden Charms* (Bug 1988)★★★, *The Big Three Trio* (Columbia 1990)★★★, *Blues Dixonary* (1993)★★★, *Across The Borderline* (1993)★★★.

● COMPILATIONS: *The Chess Box* (Chess 1988)★★★, *The Original Wang Dang Doodle - The Chess Recordings & More* (MCA/Chess 1995)★★★★.

● FURTHER READING: *I Am The Blues*, Willie Dixon.

DOMINO, FATS

b. Antoine Domino, 26 February 1928, New Orleans, Louisiana, USA. From a large family, he learned piano from local musician Harrison Verrett who was also his brother-in-law. A factory worker after leaving school, Domino played in local clubs such as the Hideaway. It was there in 1949 that bandleader Dave Bartholomew and Lew Chudd of Imperial Records heard him. His first recording, 'The Fat Man', became a Top 10 R&B hit the next year and launched his unique partnership with Bartholomew who co-wrote and arranged dozens of Domino tracks over the next two decades. Like that of Professor Longhair, Domino's playing was derived from the rich mixture of musical styles to be found in New Orleans. These included traditional jazz, Latin rhythms, boogie-woogie, Cajun and blues. Domino's personal synthesis of these influences involved lazy, rich vocals supported by rolling piano rhythms. On occasion his relaxed

approach was at odds with the urgency of other R&B and rock artists and the Imperial engineers would frequently speed up the tapes before Domino's singles were released. During the early 50s, Domino gradually became one of the most successful R&B artists in America. Songs such as 'Goin' Home' and 'Going To The River', 'Please Don't Leave Me' and 'Don't You Know' were bestsellers and he also toured throughout the country. The touring group included the nucleus of the band assembled by Dave Bartholomew for recordings at Cosimo Matassa's studio. Among the musicians were Lee Allen (saxophone), Frank Field (bass) and Walter 'Papoose' Nelson (guitar).

By 1955, rock 'n' roll had arrived and young white audiences were ready for Domino's music. His first pop success came with 'Ain't That A Shame' in 1955, although Pat Boone's cover version sold more copies. 'Bo Weevil' was also covered, by Teresa Brewer, but the catchy 'I'm In Love Again', with its incisive saxophone phrases from Allen, took Domino into the pop Top 10. The b-side was an up-tempo treatment of the 20s standard, 'My Blue Heaven', which Verrett had sung with Papa Celestin's New Orleans jazz band. Domino's next big success also came with a pre-rock 'n' roll song, 'Blueberry Hill'. Inspired by Louis Armstrong's 1949 version, Domino used his creole drawl to perfection. Altogether, Fats Domino had nearly 20 US Top 20 singles between 1955 and 1960. Among the last of them was the majestic 'Walking To New Orleans', a Bobby Charles composition that became a string-laden tribute to the sources of his musical inspiration. His track record in the *Billboard* R&B lists, however, is impressive, with 63 records reaching the charts. He continued to record prolifically for Imperial until 1963, maintaining a consistently high level of performance. There were original compositions such as the jumping 'My Girl Josephine' and 'Let the Four Winds Blow' and cover versions of country songs (Hank Williams' 'Jambalaya') as well as standard ballads such as 'Red Sails In The Sunset', his final hit single in 1963. The complex off-beat of 'Be My Guest' was a clear precursor of the ska rhythms of Jamaica, where Domino was popular and toured in 1961. The only unimpressive moments came when he was persuaded to jump on the twist bandwagon, recording a number titled 'Dance With Mr Domino'.

By now, Lew Chudd had sold the Imperial company and Domino had switched labels to ABC Paramount. There he recorded several albums with producers Felton Jarvis and Bill Justis, but his continuing importance lay in his tours of North America and Europe, which recreated the sound of the 50s for new generations of listeners. The quality of Domino's touring band was well captured on a 1965 live album for Mercury from Las Vegas with Roy Montrell (guitar), Cornelius Coleman (drums) and the saxophones of Herb Hardesty and Lee Allen. Domino continued this pattern of work into the 70s, breaking it slightly when he gave the Beatles' 'Lady Madonna' a New Orleans treatment. He made further albums for Reprise (1968) and Sonet (1979), the Reprise sides being the results of a reunion session with Dave Bartholomew. In 1991 EMI, which now owns the Imperial catalogue, released a scholarly box-set of Domino's remarkable recordings. Two years later, Fats was back in the studio recording his first sessions proper for 25 years, resulting in his *Christmas Is A Special Day* set. 'People don't know what they've done for me', he reflected. 'They always tell me, "Oh Fats, thanks for so many years of good music". And I'll be thankin' them before they're finished thankin' me!' He remains a giant figure of R&B and rock 'n' roll, both musically and physically.

● ALBUMS: *Carry On Rockin'* (Imperial 1955)★★★★, *Rock And Rollin' With Fats* (Imperial 1956)★★★★, *Rock And Rollin'* (Imperial 1956)★★★★, *This Is Fats Domino!* (Imperial 1957)★★★★, *Here Stands Fats Domino* (Imperial 1958)★★★★, *Fabulous Mr D* (Imperial 1958)★★★★, *Let's Play Fats Domino* (Imperial 1959)★★★★, *Fats Domino Swings* (Imperial 1959)★★★★, *Million Record Hits* (Imperial 1960)★★★★, *A Lot Of Dominos* (Imperial 1960)★★★★, *I Miss You So* (Imperial 1961)★★★, *Let The Four Winds Blow* (Imperial 1961)★★★★, *What A Party* (Imperial 1962)★★★, *Twistin' The Stomp* (Imperial 1962)★★★, *Just Domino* (Imperial 1962)★★★, *Here Comes Fats Domino* (ABC 1963)★★★, *Walkin' To New Orleans* (Imperial 1963)★★★★, *Let's Dance With Domino* (Imperial 1963)★★★, *Here He Comes Again* (Imperial 1963)★★★, *Fats On Fire* (ABC 1964)★★★, *Fats Domino '65* (Mercury 1965)★★★, *Getaway With Fats Domino* (ABC 1965)★★★, *Fats Is Back* (Reprise 1968)★★★, *Cookin' With Fats* (United Artists 1974)★★★, *Sleeping On The Job* (Sonet 1979)★★★, *Live At Montreux* (Atlantic 1987)★★★, *Christmas Is A Special Day* (Right Stuff/EMI 1994)★★★.

● COMPILATIONS: *The Very Best Of Fats Domino* (Liberty 1970)★★★★, *Rare Domino's* (Liberty 1970)★★★, *Rare Domino's Vol. 2* (Liberty 1971)★★★, *Fats Domino - His Greatest Hits* (MCA 1986)★★★, *My Blue Heaven - The Best Of Fats Domino* (EMI 1990)★★★★, *They Call Me The Fat Man: The Legendary Imperial Recordings* 4-CD box set (EMI/Imperial 1991)★★★★★, *Out Of Orleans* 8-CD anthology (Bear Family 1993)★★★★★, *The EP Collection Vol. 1* (See For Miles 1995)★★★★, *The Early Imperial Singles 1950-52* (Ace 1996)★★★★, *The EP Collection Vol. 2* (See For Miles 1997)★★★★.

● FILMS: *The Girl Can't Help It* (1956), *Jamboree* aka *Disc Jockey Jamboree* (1957), *The Big Beat* (1957).

DORSEY, THOMAS A.

b. 1 July 1899, Villa Rica, Georgia, USA, d. 23 January 1993. Often known as the founder of gospel music. Born into a religious family, Dorsey nevertheless shunned sacred music for many years, although it is in that idiom that he was to make the biggest impact. He learned to play piano in his youth, and when he settled in Chicago in 1916 he began to carve out a career for himself on the blues scene there. In the early 20s, he toured as a musician in the Ma Rainey show. Between 1928 and 1932 he recorded extensively as a blues artist under his pseudonym Georgia Tom, as partner to Tampa Red, as part of groups such as the Hokum Boys, and as accompanist to many artists, from obscure figures such as Auntie Mary Bradford and Stovepipe Johnson to big names such as 'Big' Bill Broonzy, Memphis Minnie and Victoria Spivey. Despite the comparative brevity of this period of his career, he was very influential for the quality and variety of his piano accompaniments, and also for one of his best-known records, with Tampa Red, 'It's Tight Like That', a smutty, double-meaning song that was enormously popular and led to a vast number of cover versions, copies and variants. In 1930, he began to compose and publish religious songs, and two years later, at the height of his success as a blues musician, Dorsey renounced this idiom and moved to gospel music, with which he was to stay for the rest of his long career. He joined singer Sallie Martin, and developed a new career with the Gospel Choral Union. His successful blues recording career led him straight into recording gospel songs, dropping the pseudonym Georgia Tom in favour of his own full name. One of his biggest successes, however, has been as a songwriter, and it was when the Heavenly Gospel Singers recorded his song 'Precious Lord' that he really began to make his name in this respect; the song has become one of the best known, and most prolifically recorded, of all black gospel songs. He remained active into a remarkably old age, appearing in a television film as late as the 80s, still preaching and singing.

● ALBUMS: *Georgia Tom* (1989)★★★.
● FURTHER READING: *The Rise Of Gospel Blues: The Music Of Thomas Dorsey In The Urban Church*, Michael Harris.

DOTSON, BIG BILL

An obscure figure, Big Bill Dotson is known only for one record, made around 1952, possibly in Houston, Texas, and issued on the Black & White label. Singing accompanied only by his guitar, his style on this very limited evidence was reminiscent of Lightnin' Hopkins, and indeed, his two tracks have appeared on a Hopkins album, credited to that artist. His vocals were somewhat lighter and his guitar work more rudimentary than those of the more famous artist, but he deserves his own small place in blues history.

● COMPILATIONS: *Blues From The Deep South* (1969).

DOTSON, JIMMY

b. 19 October 1933, Ethel, Louisiana, USA. Dotson began his musical career singing blues at a local juke joint, but later developed his skills to encompass drums and guitar. He played in a band with Lazy Lester, and later with Silas Hogan in a group called the Rhythm Ramblers. Although Hogan was the leader of this group, their first record was made with Dotson on vocals. Two singles were issued on Jay Miller's

own Rocko and Zynn labels under Dotson's name, both in an upbeat R&B vein, quite different from Hogan's down-home blues sound. Dotson lived in Memphis for several years and had another single issued on the Home Of The Blues label, but moved back to Baton Rouge in the early 80s and resumed his career at Tabby Thomas's Blues Box club.

● ALBUMS: *Baton Rouge Blues* (1985)★★★, *Baton Rouge Harmonica* (1988)★★★.

DOUGLAS, K.C.

b. 21 November 1913, Sharon, Mississippi, USA, d. 18 October 1975, Berkeley, California, USA. Baptised with initials only, Douglas came from a strict Baptist family, his father a minister who disapproved of blues. Although interested in the guitar, he did not acquire one until 1936, taking instruction from uncle Scott Douglas and cousin Isadore Scott. Moving to Jackson, Mississippi, in 1940, he met Tommy Johnson, having previously copied his style from records. In 1945, he moved to Vallejo, California, as a government recruit to work in the Kaiser shipyard. He then moved north to Richmond and met harmonica player Sidney Maiden. The pair recorded for Bob Geddins' Down Town label in 1948, Douglas singing 'Mercury Boogie', using a guitar loaned by Lowell Fulson, and Maiden singing 'Eclipse Of The Sun', songs for which each man was subsequently lauded. In 1954, Douglas moved to Oakland and recorded 'K.C. Boogie' for Rhythm, another Geddins label. Two years later, he was recorded at a house party, the resulting performance released as an album on Cook, a New York label. In 1960-61 he was recorded several times by Arhoolie owner Chris Strachwitz, who leased two albums to Bluesville. He also backed Maiden and Mercy Dee on albums recorded at the same time and released on both labels. In the late 60s, he made singles for Galaxy and Blues Connoisseur. His last album featured him with a band that included harmonica player Richard Riggins.

● ALBUMS: *K.C. Blues* (Bluesville 1962)★★★, *The Country Boy* (Arhoolie 1974)★★★, *Big Road Blues* (Ace 1988)★★★.

DOYLE, CHARLIE 'LITTLE BUDDY'

No biographical details are available for Doyle, an obscure, impoverished, blind American street blues singer who, as his name implies, was also a dwarf. He was thought to have been born in Memphis, perhaps at the turn of the century and recorded 10 tracks there for Columbia in July 1939, which were to be a major influence on Detroit bluesman Baby Boy Warren. Other Memphis musicians such as Walter Horton, Will Shade and Furry Lewis claim to have worked with him; Shade and Horton both profess to be the harmonica player on his recordings. Informants report that Doyle probably died in early 1940 but this has never been confirmed.

DR. FEELGOOD

The most enduring act to emerge from the much touted 'pub rock' scene, Dr. Feelgood was formed in 1971. The original line-up included Lee Brilleaux (b. 1953, d. 7 April 1994; vocals/harmonica), Wilko Johnson (b. John Wilkinson, 1947; guitar), John B. Sparks (b. 1953; bass), John Potter (piano) and 'Bandsman' Howarth (drums). When the latter pair dropped out, the remaining trio recruited a permanent drummer in John 'The Big Figure' Martin. Initially based in Canvey Island, Essex, on the Thames estuary, Dr. Feelgood broke into the London circuit in 1974. Brilleaux's menacing personality complemented Johnson's propulsive, jerky stage manner, while the guitarist's staccato style, modelled on Mick Green of the Pirates, emphasized the group's idiosyncratic brand of rhythm and blues. Their debut album, *Down By The Jetty*, was released in 1974, but despite critical approbation, it was not until the following year that the quartet secured due commercial success with *Stupidity*. Recorded live in concert, this raw, compulsive set topped the UK charts and the group's status seemed assured. However, internal friction led to Johnson's departure during sessions for a projected fourth album and although his replacement, John 'Gypie' Mayo, was an accomplished guitarist, he lacked the striking visual image of his predecessor. Dr. Feelgood then embarked on a more mainstream direction which was only intermittently successful. 'Milk And Alcohol' (1978) gave them their sole UK Top 10 hit, but they now seemed curiously anachronistic in the face of the punk upheaval. In 1981 Johnny Guitar replaced Mayo, while the following year both Sparks and the Big Figure decided to leave the line-up. Brilleaux meanwhile continued undeterred, and while Dr. Feelgood could claim a loyal audience, it was an increasingly small one. However, they remained a popular live attraction in the USA where their records also achieved commercial success. In 1993 Brilleaux was diagnosed as having lymphoma and, owing to the extensive treatment he was receiving, had to break the band's often-inexorable touring schedule for the first time in over 20 years. He died the following year.

● ALBUMS: *Down By The Jetty* (United Artists 1975)★★★★, *Malpractice* (United Artists 1975)★★★, *Stupidity* (United Artists 1976)★★★, *Sneakin' Suspicion* (United Artists 1977)★★, *Be Seeing You* (United Artists 1977)★★★, *Private Practice* (United Artists 1978)★★★, *As It Happens* (United Artists 1979)★★★, *Let It Roll* (United Artists 1979)★★, *A Case Of The Shakes* (United Artists 1980)★★, *On The Job* (Liberty 1981)★★, *Fast Women And Slow Horses* (Chiswick 1982)★★, *Mad Man Blues* (I.D. 1985)★★★, *Doctor's Orders* (Demon 1986)★★, *Brilleaux* (Demon 1986)★★, *Classic Dr. Feelgood* (Stiff 1987)★★, *Live In London* (Grand 1990)★★★, *The Feelgood Factor* (1993)★★, *Down At The Doctors* (Grand 1994)★★, *On The Road Again* (Grand 1996)★★★.

● COMPILATIONS: *Casebook* (Liberty 1981)★★, *Case History - The Best Of Dr. Feelgood* (EMI 1987)★★★, *Singles (The UA Years)* (Liberty 1989)★★★, *Looking Back* 4-CD set (EMI 1995)★★★, *25 Years Of Dr. Feelgood* (Grand 1997)★★★★.

DR. JOHN

b. Malcolm John Rebennack, 21 November 1940, New Orleans, Louisiana, USA. Dr. John has built a career since the 60s as a consummate New Orleans musician, incorporating funk, rock 'n' roll, jazz and R&B into his sound. Rebennack's distinctive vocal growl and virtuoso piano playing brought him acclaim among critics and fellow artists, although his commercial successes have not equalled that recognition. Rebennack's musical education began in the 40s when he accompanied his father to blues clubs. At the age of 14 he began frequenting recording studios, and wrote his first songs at that time. By 1957 he was working as a session musician, playing guitar, keyboards and other instruments on recordings issued on such labels as Ace, Ric, Rex and Ebb. He made his first recording under his own name, 'Storm Warning', for Rex during that same year. His first album was recorded for Rex in 1958, and others followed on Ace and AFO Records with little success. In 1958 he also co-wrote 'Lights Out', recorded by Jerry Byrne, and toured with Byrne and Frankie Ford. By 1962 Rebennack had already played on countless sessions for such renowned producers as Phil Spector, Harold Battiste, H.B. Barnum and Sonny Bono (later of Sonny And Cher). Rebennack formed his own bands during the early 60s but they did not take off. By the mid-60s Rebennack had moved to Los Angeles, where he fused his New Orleans roots with the emerging west coast psychedelic sound, and he developed the persona Dr. John Creux, The Night Tripper. The character was based on one established by singer Prince La La, but Rebennack made it his own through the intoxicating brew of voodoo incantations and New Orleans heritage. An album, *Zu Zu Man*, for A&M Records, did not catch on when released in 1965. In 1968 Dr. John was signed to Atco Records and released *Gris Gris*, which received critical acclaim but did not chart. This exceptional collection included the classic 'Walk On Gilded Splinters' and inspired several similarly styled successors, winning respect from fellow musicians, and resulting in Eric Clapton and Mick Jagger guesting on a later album. The same musical formula and exotic image were pursued on follow-up albums, *Babylon* and *Remedies*. Meanwhile, he toured on the rock festival and ballroom circuit and continued to do session work. In 1971, Dr. John charted for the first time with *Dr. John, The Night Tripper (The Sun, Moon And Herbs)*. The 1972 *Gumbo* album, produced by Jerry Wexler, charted, as did the single 'Iko Iko'. His biggest US hit came in 1973 with the single 'Right Place, Wrong Time', which reached number 9; the accompanying album, *In The Right Place*, was also his best-selling, reaching number 24. These crafted, colourful albums featured the instrumental muscle of the Meters, but despite a new-found popularity, the artist parted from his record label, Atlantic, and subsequent work failed to achieve a similar status. During that year he toured with the New Orleans band the Meters, and recorded *Triumvirate* with Michael Bloomfield and John Hammond. The single 'Such A Night' also charted in 1973. Dr. John continued to record throughout the 70s and 80s for numerous labels, among them United Artists, Horizon and Clean Cuts, the latter releasing *Dr. John Plays Mac Rebennack*, a solo piano album, in 1981. In the meantime, he continued to draw sizeable audiences as a concert act across the USA, and added radio jingle work to his live and recording work (he continued to play on many sessions). He recorded *Bluesiana Triangle* with jazz musicians Art Blakey and David 'Fathead' Newman and released *In A Sentimental Mood*, a collection of interpretations of standards including a moody duet with Rickie Lee Jones, on Warner Brothers Records. Despite employing a low-key approach to recording, Dr. John has remained a respected figure. His live appearances are now less frequent, but this irrepressible artist continues his role as a tireless champion of Crescent City music.

● ALBUMS: *Zu Zu Man* (A&M 1965)★★★, *Gris Gris* (Atco 1968)★★★★, *Babylon* (Atco 1969)★★★, *Remedies* (Atco 1970)★★★, *Dr. John, The Night Tripper (The Sun, Moon And Herbs)* (Atco 1971)★★★, *Dr. John's Gumbo* (Atco 1972)★★★★, *In The Right Place* (Atco 1973)★★★, with John Hammond, Mike Bloomfield *Triumvirate* (Columbia 1973)★★★, *Desitively Bonnaroo* (Atco 1974)★★★, *Hollywood Be Thy Name* (United Artists 1975)★★, *Cut Me While I'm Hot* (1975)★★, *City Lights* (Horizon 1978)★★★, *Tango Palace* (Horizon 1979)★★, *Love Potion* (1981)★★, *Dr. John Plays Mac Rebennack* (Clean Cuts 1982)★★★, *The Brightest Smile In Town* (Clean Cuts 1983)★★★, with Chris Barber *Take Me Back To New Orleans* (1983)★★★, *Such A Night - Live In London* (Spindrift 1984)★★★, *In A Sentimental Mood* (Warners 1989)★★, *Going Back To New Orleans* (1992)★★★, *Television* (GRP 1994)★★, *Afterglow* (Blue Thumb 1995)★★.

● COMPILATIONS: *I Been Hoodood* (Edsel 1984)★★★, *In The Night* (Topline 1985)★★★, *Bluesiana Triangle* (1990)★★★, *Mos' Scocious* 2-CD (Rhino 1994)★★★★, *The Best Of ...* (Rhino 1995)★★★★.

● VIDEOS: *Doctor John And Chris Barber, Live At The Marquee Club* (Jettisoundz 1986), *Live At*

The Marquee (Hendring Video 1990).
● FURTHER READING: *Dr. John: Under A Hoodoo Moon*, Mac Rebennack with Jack Rummel.

Dr. Ross

b. Charles Isiah Ross, 21 October 1925, Tunica, Mississippi, USA. Ross had American Indian ancestry. He learned harmonica at the age of nine and was performing with Willie Love and on radio stations in Arkansas and Mississippi in the late 30s. He served in the US Army from 1943-47. His paramedical training there earned Ross the sobriquet of Doctor when he returned to music, leading his Jump And Jive Band and appearing on radio in the *King Biscuit Time Show*. Ross also developed a one-man band act, which he frequently performed in the 50s and 60s. His Memphis recordings for Sam Phillips in the early 50s included 'Country Clown' and 'The Boogie Disease'. In 1954, he moved to Flint, Michigan, to work in an car factory. Ross continued to perform and in 1958 set up his own DIR label. In the early 60s, he benefited from the growing white interest in blues, recording for Pete Welding's Testament label and touring Europe with the 1965 Folk Blues Festival. He returned to Europe during the 70s, recording in London and performing at the Montreux Jazz Festival with Muddy Waters' band.
● ALBUMS: *The Flying Eagle* (1966)★★★, *Dr Ross, The Harmonica Boss* (1972)★★★, *Jivin' The Blues* (1974)★★★, *Live At Montreux* (1975)★★★, *First Recordings* (Reissue 1981)★★★, *Call The Doctor* (Testament 1994)★★★.

Drifting Slim

b. Elmon Mickle, 24 February 1919, Keo, Arkansas, USA, d. 17 September 1977. He was inspired to sing and play harmonica by John Lee 'Sonny Boy' Williamson, whose style he emulated successfully on local radio stations in the 40s. Mickle formed his first band in 1951 and recorded for the Modern/RPM company; he learned to play guitar and drums and worked occasionally as a one-man band. In 1957 he moved to Los Angeles, where he recorded for several small labels (including Elko, E.M., J Gems, Wonder, Magnum and Styletone, using the pseudonym Model T. Slim for the latter),

and in 1966 he made an album for Milestone Records. Poor health prevented him playing many club dates in the 70s; he died of cancer in September 1977.
● ALBUMS: as Model T. Slim *Somebody Done Voodoo The Hoodoo Man* (1980)★★★.

Duarte, Chris, Group

Formed in Austin, Texas, USA, the Chris Duarte Group are John Jordan (bass), Brannen Temple (drums) and band leader Chris Duarte (guitar, vocals). The release of *Texas Sugar Strat Magik* brought immediate acclaim for the band's gritty, intense southern blues sound, with Duarte singled out for his technique. Indeed, in the 1995 *Guitar World* magazine Readers' Poll, he was voted fourth best blues guitarist behind the much more established and esteemed company of Eric Clapton, Buddy Guy and B.B. King. The group's debut was additionally voted fourth best blues album. Duarte has described the band's sound as 'blues based, but it has that loud aggressive edge that punk had. I liked Dead Kennedys, Sex Pistols, Dead Boys, anything that was hard.' The decision to employ producer Dennis Herring, the former Los Angeles session guitarist previously noted for his work with Camper Van Beethoven and Throwing Muses, was also interesting. Afterwards the album was promoted on US touring dates with Buddy Guy.
● ALBUMS: *Texas Sugar Strat Magik* (Silvertone 1994)★★★.

DuChaine, Kent

b. 20 April 1951, Minneapolis, Minnesota, USA. Starting on the ukulele at the age of six, it was always DuChaine's intention to be a musician. As a teenager, he played in a number of groups, even playing bass in a psychedelic band, while he studied slide technique at home. In 1972, he played bass in Aces, Straights and Shuffles with Kim Wilson and the pair also worked as a duo. Wilson moved to Texas in 1974 and DuChaine followed soon after, with a band called Crossroads. In 1989, while living and playing in Alabama, he met Johnny Shines and the pair formed a fruitful working relationship. DuChaine played on several tracks on *Back To The Country*, one of Shines' last sessions. The following year he set up his own label, which bears all the hallmarks of a cottage industry.

Take A Little Ride With Me gives credit to his battered National steel guitar, Leadbessie, and features a song extolling his 1956 Cadillac, Marilyn, in which he lived and toured during the 80s.
● ALBUMS: with Johnny Shines, Snooky Pryor *Back To The Country* (Blind Pig 1991)★★★, *Just Me And My Guitar* (Cadillac 1992)★★★, *Lookin' Back* (Cadillac 1994)★★★, *Take A Little Ride With Me* (Cadillac 1995)★★★, *She's Irresistible* (Cadillac 1996)★★★.

DUKES, 'LITTLE' LAURA

b. 10 June 1907, Memphis, Tennessee, USA. An early start in music led Little Laura Dukes to a lifetime of involvement with entertainment in Memphis. Her father had been a drummer with W.C. Handy's band, but it was a less sophisticated idiom that Dukes chose, playing blues with the jug bands for which that city is so well known. She sang and played banjo and ukelele with the Will Batts Novelty Band, and although they made two recordings in the early 50s, these were not issued until 20 years later. She made some more records with the revival of interest in blues and related music in the 70s, and also appeared in a BBC television series. As late as the 80s, she was still performing in Memphis, at the Blues Alley club, set up to showcase the city's blues talent.
● ALBUMS: *South Memphis Jug Band* (1975)★★★.

DUMMER, JOHN, BLUES BAND

This UK band came into being in 1965, evolving from the Muskrats and the Grebbells, and lasted until the early 70s, surviving numerous personnel changes. The line-up included prominent British blues artists such as pianist Bob Hall, guitarist Dave Kelly and his sister Jo Ann Kelly, Mike Cooper, and Tony McPhee. The band backed touring American artists John Lee Hooker and Howlin' Wolf, and recorded albums for Mercury and Vertigo between 1969 and 1973. Drummer John Dummer went on to work with English pop vocal group Darts in the mid-70s. In recent years all Dummer's albums have become much sought after items in the collectors' market and currently carry very high prices.
● ALBUMS: *Cabal* (Mercury 1969)★★★, *John Dummer's Blues Band* (Mercury 1969)★★★★, *Famous Music Band* (Philips 1970)★★, *This Is John Dummer* (Philips 1972)★★★, *Volume II, Try Me One More Time* (Philips 1973)★★, *Blue* (Vertigo 1973)★★, *Oobleedooblee Jubilee* (Vertigo 1973)★★.

DUNBAR, AYNSLEY, RETALIATION

This unit was formed in 1967 by ex-John Mayall drummer Aynsley Dunbar. Having recorded an informal version of Buddy Guy's 'Stone Crazy' with an embryonic line-up of Rod Stewart (vocals), Peter Green (guitar) and Jack Bruce (bass), Dunbar created a permanent Retaliation around ex-Johnny Kidd And The Pirates and Shotgun Express guitarist, Jon Morshead, Keith Tillman (bass) and ex-Alexis Korner vocalist, Victor Brox. This line-up completed a solitary single, 'Warning'/'Cobwebs', for the Blue Horizon label before Tillman was replaced by Alex Dmochowski (ex-Neil Christian's Crusaders). *The Aynsley Dunbar Retaliation* showcased this superior blues group's self-assurance, with one side devoted to concise performances and the other to freer, instrumentally based workouts. Although it lacked the overall strength of its predecessor, *Dr. Dunbar's Prescription* was another worthwhile album that offered strong original songs and several judicious cover versions. However, the group is best recalled for *Retaliation* aka *To Mum From Aynsley And The Boys*, which was produced by John Mayall. Former Grease Band keyboard player Tommy Eyre was added for this powerful, moody collection on which the unit created some of its finest recordings, including 'Don't Take The Power Away' and 'Journey's End'. In November 1969 Dunbar and Eyre left the group to form Aynsley Dunbar's Blue Whale. A fourth set, *Remains To Be Heard*, was culled from remaining masters and newer recordings by the extant trio with singer Annette Brox, but the Retaliation broke up soon after its completion.
● ALBUMS: *The Aynsley Dunbar Retaliation* (Liberty 1968)★★★, *Dr. Dunbar's Prescription* (Liberty 1968)★★★, *Retaliation* aka *To Mum From Aynsley And The Boys* (Liberty 1969)★★★, *Remains To Be Heard* (Liberty 1970)★★.

DUNBAR, SCOTT

b. 1904, Deer Park Plantation, Mississippi, USA, d. 4 September 1994, Centreville, Mississippi,

USA. Dunbar taught himself guitar as a child, and despite some involvement with a local string band, his music was idiosyncratic and unpredictable, combining seemingly spontaneous guitar playing with a singing style that veers abruptly between normal and falsetto registers; the total performance often seems almost a free-form exploration of the song. Dunbar never travelled more than 100 miles from his rural home, and was further isolated by his illiteracy, which meant that his lyrics were memorized, and often startlingly fragmented. He seldom - and by the 60s, never - played for black audiences, owing to his wife's fear of possible violence. He combined work as a fisherman and guide with playing for tourists, and his repertoire reflected this, with popular tunes substantially outnumbering blues.

● ALBUMS: *From Lake Mary* (1970)★★★.

DUNN, ROY

b. 13 April 1922, Eatonton, Georgia, USA, d. 2 March 1988, Atlanta, Georgia, USA. Dunn was a blues guitarist and singer, who had learned from and played with Georgia artists such as Curley Weaver, Buddy Moss and Blind Willie McTell in the 30s, although he was of a younger generation. This meant that he missed out on recording at a time when his style of music was at its most commercially popular. In his younger days, he sang in a family gospel quartet, the Dunn Brothers, then between the late 30s and early 40s he toured with a series of other gospel groups. In the early 70s, he recorded an album, and appeared at a number of blues festivals. He was also credited as a major source of information and contacts by researchers into the blues of the east coast states.

● ALBUMS: *Know'd Them All* (1974)★★★.

DUPREE, CHAMPION JACK

b. William Thomas Dupree, 4 July 1910, New Orleans, Louisiana, USA, d. 21 January 1992. Orphaned in infancy, Dupree was raised in the Colored Waifs Home for Boys until the age of 14. After leaving, he led a marginal existence, singing for tips, and learning piano from musicians such as Willie 'Drive-'em-down' Hall. Dupree also became a professional boxer, and blended fighting with hoboing throughout the 30s, before retiring from the ring in 1940, and

heading for New York. Initially, he travelled only as far as Indianapolis, where he joined with musicians who had been associates of Leroy Carr. Dupree rapidly became a star of the local black entertainment scene, as a comedian and dancer as well as a musician. He acquired a residency at the local Cotton Club, and partnered comedienne Ophelia Hoy. In 1940, Dupree made his recording debut, with music that blended the forceful, barrelhouse playing and rich, creole-accented singing of New Orleans with the more suave style of Leroy Carr. Not surprisingly, a number of titles were piano/guitar duets, although on some, Jesse Ellery's use of amplification pointed the way forward. A few songs covered unusual topics, such as the distribution of grapefruit juice by relief agencies, or the effects of drugs. Dupree's musical career was interrupted when he was drafted into the US Navy as a cook; even so he managed to become one of the first blues singers to record for the folk revival market while on leave in New York in 1943. Dupree's first wife died while he was in the navy, and he took his discharge in New York, where he worked as a club pianist, and formed a close musical association with Sonny Terry and Brownie McGhee. His own post-war recording career commenced with a splendid series of solo recordings for Joe Davis, on some of which the influence of Peetie Wheatstraw is very evident. More typical were the many tracks with small groups recorded thereafter for a number of labels from 1946-53, and for King between April 1953 and late 1955. As ever, these recordings blend the serious with the comic, the latter somewhat tastelessly on songs such as 'Tongue Tied Blues' and 'Harelip Blues'. 'Walking The Blues', a comic dialogue with Teddy 'Mr Bear' McRae, was a hit on King, and the format was repeated on a number of titles recorded for RCA's Vik and Groove. In 1958, Dupree made his last American recordings until 1990; 'Blues From The Gutter' appears to have been aimed at white audiences, as was Dupree's career thereafter. In 1959, he moved to Europe, and lived in Switzerland, England, Sweden and Germany, touring extensively and recording prolifically, with results that varied from the excellent to the mediocre. This served both as a stamp of authenticity and as a licensed jester to the European blues scene. *One Last*

Time was his final recording session before his death in 1992.

● ALBUMS: *Blues From The Gutter* (Atlantic 1959)★★★, *Natural And Soulful Blues* (Atlantic 1960)★★★, *Champion Of The Blues* (Atlantic 1961)★★★, *Sings The Blues* (King 1961)★★★, *Women Blues Of Champion Jack Dupree* (Folkways 1961)★★★, *Cabbage Greens* (OKeh 1963)★★★, *The Blues Of Champion Jack Dupree* (1963)★★★, with Jimmy Rushing *Two Shades Of Blue* (Ember 1964)★★, *Trouble Trouble* (Storyville 1965)★★★, *Portraits In Blues* (Storyville 1965)★★★, *From New Orleans To Chicago* (Decca 1966)★★★, featuring Mickey Baker *Champion Jack Dupree And His Blues Band* (Decca 1967)★★★, *Champion Jack Dupree* (Storyville 1967)★★, *Scoobydoobydoo* (Blue Horizon 1969)★★★, *When You Feel The Feeling* (Blue Horizon 1969)★★★, *The Incredible Champion Jack Dupree* (Sonet 1970)★★, *Legacy Of The Blues* (Sonet 1972)★★, *Blues From Montreux* (Atlantic 1972)★★, *Rub A Little Boogie* (Krazy Kat 1982)★★, *Junker Blues* ('Travelin'' Man 1985)★★★, *Shake Baby Shake* (Detour 1987)★★★, *Legacy Of The Blues Volume 3* (Sonet 1987)★★★★, *Live At Burnley* (JSP 1989)★★★, *Blues For Everybody* (Charly 1990)★★★, *1945-1946 (The Joe Davis Sessions)* (Flyright 1990)★★★, *Back Home In New Orleans* (Bullseye Blues 1990)★★★, *Forever And Ever* (Bullseye Blues 1991)★★★, *Home* (1993)★★★, *One Last Time* (1993)★★★, *Won't Be A Fool No More ... Plus* (See For Miles 1994)★★★, *The Blues Of Champion Jack Dupree Vol 2* (Storyville 1996)★★★★.

DURST, LAVADA 'DR. HEPCAT'

b. 9 January 1913, Austin, Texas, USA, d. 31 October 1995, Austin, Texas. As a 12-year-old, Durst learned to play the piano in the church. He later claimed his left hand was influenced by Albert Ammons and Meade 'Lux' Lewis and his right by renowned Texas bluesman, Robert Shaw. Durst continued to play in an amateur capacity at house-rent parties and suppers while running recreation facilities in East Austin. His talent for jive talk landed him a job as an announcer at baseball games at Disch Field, which in turn brought him to the attention of the local radio station, KVET. As 'Dr. Hepcat', in 1948 he became the first black disc jockey in Texas, broadcasting six days a week. Programme director Fred Caldwell also owned Uptown Records, for whom Durst recorded 'Hattie Green' and 'Hepcat's Boogie' in 1949. Shortly afterwards he re-recorded the first title for Don Robey's Peacock label. In the late 50s, Durst managed the Chariottes spiritual group, who also recorded for Peacock. He gave up playing music in 1965 when he was ordained as a minister at the Mt. Olive Baptist Church, but returned to the piano a decade later. Durst was unusual for a Texas blues pianist by maintaining a strong left-hand pulse to his blues and boogie improvisations that accompanied his semi-improvised monologues.

● COMPILATIONS: *Deep Ellum Blues* (Documentary Arts 1986)★★★, *Piano Professors* (Catfish 1987)★★★.

DUSKIN, 'BIG' JOE

b. 10 February 1921, Birmingham, Alabama, USA. In the 30s Duskin moved with his family to Cincinnati, Ohio, where he began playing piano, inspired by the records of Roosevelt Sykes, Albert Ammons, and Pete Johnson. During World War II he was drafted into the army and met Ammons, Johnson, and Meade 'Lux' Lewis on USO shows. After demobilization Joe promised his preacher father that he would not play 'the devil's music' while the old man (in his 80s) was still alive; however, he lived to be 104! Duskin's debut album was finally released by Arhoolie Records in 1979 and revealed him as a worthy bearer of the boogie-woogie tradition. Later albums have appeared on the Special Delivery and Wolf labels, and Duskin has also recorded with Dave Peabody and the Blues Band.

● ALBUMS: *Cincinnati Stomp* (Arhoolie 1979)★★★, *Don't Mess With The Boogie Man* (Special Delivery 1988)★★★, *Live* (1990)★★★, *Boogie Woogie Is My Religion* (Back To Blues 1995)★★★, *Down The Road Apiece* 1982 recording (Wolf 1996)★★, *Don't Mess With The Boogie Man* (Indigo 1997)★★★.

DYER, JOHNNY

b. 1938, Rolling Fork, Mississippi, USA. Dyer took up the harmonica when he was seven and as a teenager sat in with Smokey Wilson in a local club. He moved to Los Angeles in January

1958 and formed his own band, the Blue Notes, backing visitors such as J.B. Hutto, Jimmy Reed and Jimmy Rogers. He later formed a duo with George Smith, at that time still working as Little Walter Jnr. He recorded a couple of singles for Shakey Jake's Good Time label before cutting an album, *Johnny Dyer And The LA Dukes*, for Murray Brothers in 1983. Some of the tracks were later issued in Japan by Mina Records. In 1991, William Clarke included him on *Hard Times*, an anthology of contemporary LA bluesmen. Soon afterwards, he formed the Houserockers with guitarist Rick 'LA Holmes' Holstrom, who had previously recorded with Clarke, Billy Boy Arnold, Rod Piazza and Smokey Wilson. *Listen Up* managed to combine Holstrom's Pee Wee Crayton-influenced technique with Dyer's more down-home harmonica playing, including an effective version of Little Walter's 'Blue Midnight'. *Shake It!* added pianist Tom Mahon on a set of original songs that encapsulate the hybrid west coast-Chicago style.
● ALBUMS: *Johnny Dyer And The L.A. Jukes* (Murray Brothers 1983)★★★★, (reissued as *Jukin'* (Blind Pig 1996), with Shakey Jake *Straight Ahead* (Mina 1985)★★★, *Hard Times - LA Blues Authority* (Black Magic 1991)★★★, *Listen Up* (Black Top 1994)★★★, with Rick Holmstrom *Shake It!* (Black Top 1995)★★★,

DYKES, OMAR

b. Kent Dykes, 1950, McComb, Mississippi, USA. The 12-year-old Kent wanted a baseball glove for Christmas and was not impressed by the guitar he received instead. However, he changed his mind, aided by his father's purchase of a Jimmy Reed album. Soon, he was crossing the road to sit in at his local juke-joint, commemorated in the title of his 1993 album, *Courts Of Lulu*. At high school he played Chuck Berry and Bo Diddley songs and listened to the Beatles, the Rolling Stones and the Animals. His band, the Howlers, was formed in Hattiesburg, Mississippi, in 1973; three years later they moved to Austin, Texas, and Dykes turned professional. The band's basic three-pronged approach to music, one part Creedence Clearwater Revival to two parts Theodore 'Hound Dog' Taylor, allied to Dykes' Howlin' Wolf-like vocals, was established with their second album, *I Told You So*. Two albums for

Columbia Records in the late 80s flirted with added instrumentation, but that ended with 1990's *Monkey Land*. Subsequent albums, *Blues Bag* and *Muddy Springs Road*, carry a solo credit and refine the sound. Content to work the southern club circuit and enhance his burgeoning European reputation with regular tours (*Live At Paradiso* was recorded in Amsterdam in September 1991), Dykes has taken pride in being able to survive without overt commercial success.
● ALBUMS: *Big Leg Beat* (Amazing 1980)★★★, *I Told You So* (Austin 1984)★★★, *Hard Times In The Land Of Plenty* (Columbia 1987)★★★, *Wall Of Pride* (Columbia 1988)★★★, *Monkey Land* (Antone's 1990)★★★, *Blues Bag* (Provogue 1991)★★★, *Live At Paradiso* (Provogue 1992)★★★, *Courts Of Lulu* (Provogue 1993)★★★, *Muddy Springs Road* (Provogue 1994)★★★.

EAGLIN, SNOOKS

b. Fird Eaglin, 21 January 1936, New Orleans, Louisiana, USA. Eaglin was left blind after a childhood illness and was given the nickname Snooks after a character in a radio series. He played guitar and sang in Baptist churches before winning a local talent contest in 1947. During the 50s he was a street singer in New Orleans, performing a variety of pop, blues and folk material. However, his first recordings, made by Harry Oster for Folkways and Folk-Lyric in 1958, emphasized the country blues side of his repertoire. He was equally at home in R&B, however, and his 1960 records for Imperial were in this format. During the 60s, Eaglin was a popular artist in New Orleans, where he frequently accompanied Professor Longhair on guitar. Eaglin returned to a 'songster' mix of folk and pop when recorded in 1972 by Quint Davis, and his later records showed a versatility ranging from flamenco to swamp-pop. Eaglin's 80s albums for Black Top were produced by Hammond Scott and included accompaniments from Anson Funderburgh (guitar), Grady Gaines (saxophones) and Sam Myers (harmonica).

● ALBUMS: *Blues From New Orleans Vol. 1* (Storyville 1958)★★★★, *New Orleans Street Singer* (Folkways 1958)★★★★, *Snooks Eaglin* (Heritage 1961)★★★, *That's All Right* (Bluesville 1962)★★★, *Possum Up A Simmon Tree* (Arhoolie 1971)★★★, *Legacy Of The Blues* (1971)★★★, *Down Yonder* (Sonet 1978)★★★, *Baby You Can Get Your Gun!* (Black Top 1987)★★★, *Out Of Nowhere* (Black Top 1989)★★★, *Teasin' You* (Black Top 1992)★★, *Country Boy In New Orleans* (1993)★★★, *Soul's Edge* (Black Top 1995)★★★, *Live In Japan* (Black Top 1997)★★★.

● COMPILATIONS: *Legacy Of The Blues Volume 2* (Sonet 1988)★★★★, *The Complete Imperial Recordings* (Capitol 1996)★★★★.

EALEY, ROBERT

b. 1924, Texarkana, Texas, USA. With each parent belonging to a different church, it was inevitable that Ealey's first singing experience was with a gospel quartet. However, he favoured the music of Frankie Lee Sims, Lightnin' Hopkins and Lil' Son Jackson. At the age of 20, he moved to Dallas, where he could witness artists such as T-Bone Walker first-hand. He had drummed for Lightnin' Hopkins and sung in clubs by the time he moved to Fort Worth, where he worked with 'Cat Man' Fleming and teamed up with guitarist U.P. Wilson to form the Boogie Chillen. In 1967, he formed a band with guitarist Sumter Bruton, Johnny B and Ralph Owens. The following year, Ealey, Bruton and Owens, along with Mike Buck and Freddie Cisneros, formed the Five Careless Lovers, which on occasions also included Lou Ann Barton. The band's residency was the Bluebird, where Ealey remained for two decades before putting his name to two clubs, Robert Ealey's Underground and Robert Ealey's Thunderbird Lounge, both of which quickly folded. His most

recent recordings feature him with some of the guitarists who have passed through his bands, Hash Brown, Sumter Bruton, Jim Suhler, Mike Morgan and Coco Montoya among them. Ealey's talent as a live performer translates fitfully to record, where the inconsistencies of his technique cannot be hidden.

● ALBUMS: *Bluebird Open* (Amazing 1984)★★★, with Edd Lively And The Blues Movers *Got Them Cowtown Blues* (Full Moon 1988)★★, with Joe Jonas, Curly 'Barefoot' Miller *Texas Bluesmen* (Topcat 1994)★★★, *If You Need Me* (Top Cat 1994)★★, *Turn Out The Lights* (Black Top 1996)★★★, *I Like Music When I Party* (Black Top 1997)★★★.

EARL, RONNIE

b. Ronald Earl Horvath, 1953, New York City, New York, USA. Earl was inspired to play blues guitar after seeing Muddy Waters at a club in Boston, Massachusetts, adopting the name Earl because: 'When I used to sit in with Muddy and all those old guys, they couldn't pronounce my last name.' He listed his influences as Robert Lockwood, B.B. King, Magic Sam and T-Bone Walker, among others. Earl quickly graduated to playing clubs around the Boston area, and he also spent some time in Chicago and Texas, backing many touring blues artists. He replaced Duke Robillard in Roomful Of Blues and stayed with them for almost eight years, leaving in the mid-80s to pursue a successful solo career. He has also become an in-demand session guitarist, particularly with Black Top Records. Often referred to as 'Mr Intensity', Earl is rated as one of the finest living blues guitarists.

● ALBUMS: *They Call Me Mr Earl* (Black Top 1984)★★★, *Soul Searching* (Black Top 1988)★★★, *I Like It When It Rains* (Antone's 1988)★★★, *Peace Of Mind* (Demon 1990)★★★, *Surrounded By Love* (Black Top 1991)★★★, *Still River* (Audioquest 1993)★★★, *Language Of The Soul* (Bullseye Blues 1994)★★★, *Blues & Forgiveness - Live In Europe* (Crosscut 1994)★★★, *Blues Guitar Virtuoso Live In Europe* (Bullseye 1995)★★★, *Grateful Heart: Blues & Ballads* (Bullseye Blues 1996)★★★, *The Colour Of Love* (Verve 1997)★★★★.

EASY BABY

b. Alex Randall, 3 August 1934, Memphis, Tennessee, USA. Easy Baby is an accomplished blues singer/harmonica player who was already involved in the west Memphis blues scene before he moved to Chicago in 1956, where he worked with local groups and led his own band for a time. He gave up music for many years, then began singing and playing again in the mid-70s, when he recorded for the Barrelhouse and Mr. Blues labels (with further material recorded for these companies issued by Rooster and JSP). He rarely plays in Chicago clubs nowadays.
● ALBUMS: *Sweet Home Chicago Blues* (1977)★★★.

EDWARDS, ARCHIE

b. 1918, Rocky Mount, Virginia, USA. From a musical family, Edwards' desire to be a guitar player developed out of the Saturday night gatherings his father held at their home during his childhood. As a teenager he learned to sing and play by mimicking the 78s of Blind Lemon Jefferson, Mississippi John Hurt and hillbilly artist Frank Hutchinson. For most of his life he continued with his day jobs, only performing at weekends or evenings at clubs in Washington DC. In more recent years, Edwards has become a great favourite on the festival circuit, having visited Europe in the 80s and recorded for the German L&R label. Together with John Jackson and John Cephas, Archie Edwards represents the continuation of the east coast blues tradition begun in the 30s by Blind Boy Fuller.
● ALBUMS: *Blues N Bones* (Mapleshade 1991)★★★.

EDWARDS, CLARENCE

b. 25 March 1933, Linsey, Louisiana, USA, d. 20 May 1993, Scotlandville, Louisiana, USA. Edwards began playing blues guitar at around the age of 12, when he moved to Baton Rouge. In the 50s and 60s, he was working the same local blues circuit as men like Lightnin' Slim, in bands with names such as the Boogie Beats and the Bluebird Kings. His first experience of recording was in a traditional setting, in sessions for folklorist Harry Oster between 1959 and 1961, with his brother Cornelius and violinist James 'Butch' Cage. Nine years later, he recorded again, this time with a more contemporary sound, and from the mid-80s, when the blues scene revived with the help of Tabby Thomas's Blues Box club, he was playing regularly. In 1990, he recorded his first album, a powerful mixture of acoustic and electric sounds in the swamp blues style. Four years after his death an excellent compilation *I Looked Down That Railroad* was released.
● ALBUMS: *Swamp's The Word* (Red Lightnin' 1991)★★★★, with Henry Gray and Short Fuse *Thibodeaux's Cafe* (Sidetrack 1995)★★★.
● COMPILATIONS: *I Looked Down That Railroad* (Last Call 1996)★★★★.

EDWARDS, DAVID 'HONEYBOY'

b. 28 June 1915, Shaw, Mississippi, USA. Born and raised in the Mississippi Delta country, Edwards played with and learned from such important blues figures as Charley Patton, Robert Johnson and Big Joe Williams. His first recordings were made for the Library of Congress in 1941, a set of typical Mississippi country blues, demonstrating a tense, emotional vocal delivery and considerable skills on harmonica and, particularly, guitar. Ten years later, his first commercial recording appeared on the obscure Texas label ARC, and in the next couple of years he also recorded for Sun Records in Memphis and Chess in Chicago, although nothing was issued at the time. Rediscovered in the 60s in Chicago, Edwards has made several fine albums, encompassing traditional country blues as well as more urban stylings. He has also toured widely, playing in Europe several times in recent years. A fascinating autobiography was published in 1997.
● ALBUMS: *I've Been Around* (1979)★★★, *White Windows* (1989)★★★, *Mississippi Blues: Library Of Congress Recordings* (1991)★★★, *Delta Bluesman* (Indigo 1992)★★★★, *I've Been Around* (Trix 1995)★★★, *The World Don't Owe Me Nothing* (Earwig 1997).
● FURTHER READING: *The World Don't Owe Me Nothing: The Life And Times Of Delta Bluesman Honeyboy Edwards*, David Honeyboy Edwards with Janis Martinson & Michael Robert Frank.

EDWARDS, FRANK

b. 20 March 1909, Washington, Georgia, USA. Raised in St. Petersburg, Florida, Edwards took up guitar at an early age, adding rack harmonica in 1934. He became an itinerant musician, with his home base in Atlanta, where he played with the Star Band, whose members included Leroy Dallas, a long-time associate. In 1941, Edwards recorded for OKeh Records, a session that was set up by *Lester Melrose*, manager of Tommy McClennan, with whom he was travelling at the time. Settling in Atlanta after World War II, he recorded for Savoy in 1949, but the titles remained unissued until the 60s, by which time Edwards himself had stopped playing; rediscovered in the 70s, however, he proved able to recreate his old sound with little difficulty.

● ALBUMS: *Living With The Blues* (1964)★★★, *Sugar Mama Blues* (1969)★★★, *Done Some Travelin'* (1973)★★★, *Chicago Blues* (1987)★★★, *Georgia Blues* (Wolf 1990)★★★.

EDWARDS, MOANIN' BERNICE

b. *c.*1910, Houston, Texas, USA. Bernice Edwards was described by Sippie Wallace as being 'one of the family'; the family in question was Sippie's own renowned Thomas Family of Houston, Bernice being the same age as its most gifted member, the child prodigy Hersal. From another member of the family, Hociel, she learned to play the piano and sing the blues. She remained in Houston when the family moved north and was often in the company of Black Boy Shine (Harold Holliday). When she recorded for Paramount in 1928 these influences were evident in her introspective 'moanin' blues and her piano style. When she attended her third and last session (for ARC in 1935) she was in the company of Holliday and one record was issued by her, Holliday and Howling Smith together. Apart from the fact that she later married and joined the church, little more is known.

● ALBUMS: *The Thomas Family* (1977)★★★.

ELLIOTT, RAMBLIN' JACK

b. Elliott Charles Adnopoz, 1 August 1931, Brooklyn, New York, USA. The son of an eminent doctor, Elliott forsook his middle-class upbringing as a teenager to join a travelling rodeo. Embarrassed by his family name, he dubbed himself Buck Elliott, before adopting the less-mannered Jack. In 1949 he met and befriended Woody Guthrie, who in turn became his mentor and prime influence. Elliott travelled and sang with Guthrie whenever possible, before emerging as a talent in his own right. He spent a portion of the 50s in Europe, introducing America's folk heritage to a new and eager audience. By the early 60s he had resettled in New York where he became an inspirational figure to a new generation of performers, including Bob Dylan. *Jack Elliott Sings The Songs Of Woody Guthrie* was the artist's first American album. This self-explanatory set was succeeded by *Ramblin' Jack Elliott*, in which he shook off the imitator tag by embracing a diverse selection of material, including songs drawn from the American tradition, the Scottish music hall and Ray Charles. Further releases included *Jack Elliott*, which featured Dylan playing harmonica under the pseudonym Tedham Porterhouse, and *Young Brigham* in 1968, which offered songs by Tim Hardin and the Rolling Stones as well as an adventurous use of dobros, autoharps, fiddles and tablas. The singer also guested on albums by Tom Rush, Phil Ochs and Johnny Cash. In 1975 Elliott was joined by Dylan during an appearance at the New York, Greenwich Village club, The Other End, and he then became a natural choice for Dylan's nostalgic carnival tour, the Rolling Thunder Revue. Elliot later continued his erratic, but intriguing, path, and an excellent 1984 release, *Kerouac's Last Dream*, showed his power undiminished.

● ALBUMS: *Jack Elliott Sings The Songs Of Woody Guthrie* (1960)★★★, *Ramblin' Jack Elliott* (Prestige 1961)★★★, *Ramblin' Jack Elliott Sings Woody Guthrie And Jimmy Rogers* (MTR 1962)★★★, *Jack Elliott* (Prestige 1964)★★★, *Ramblin' Cowboy* (1966)★★★, *Young Brigham* (Warners 1968)★★★, *Kerouac's Last Dream* (Folk Freak 1984)★★★, *South Coast* (Red House 1995)★★★, *Me And Bobby McGee* (Rounder 1996)★★★.

● COMPILATIONS: *The Essential Ramblin' Jack Elliott* (Vanguard 1976)★★★, *Talking Dust Bowl - The Best Of Ramblin' Jack Elliott* (Big Beat 1989)★★★, *Hard Travelin'* (Big Beat 1990)★★★, *Ramblin' Jack - The Legendary Topic Masters* (Topic 1996)★★★.

ELLIS, TINSLEY

b. 1957, Atlanta, Georgia, USA. Like many American musicians of his generation, Ellis first took up the guitar at the age of seven, inspired by groups in the British invasion. While playing in rock bands, he took an increasing interest in the work of Howlin' Wolf, Muddy Waters and John Lee Hooker and particularly in guitarists Freddie King, Buddy Guy and Magic Sam. Returning from Florida in 1979, he joined the Alley Cats, a blues band that also featured future Thunderbird, Preston Hubbard. Two years later, Ellis formed the Heartfixers with veteran harmonica player 'Chicago Bob' Nelson. Their debut album helped to make them the city's foremost blues-rock band. With Nelson's departure, the band moved to Landslide. The release of *Cool On It* and their supporting role in Nappy Brown's *Tore Up* brought them attention in America and Europe where they and Brown toured in 1987. By then, Ellis had already determined on a solo career, and while recording *Georgia Blue*, his contract was acquired by Alligator. His subsequent albums have sought to reinvent him in Stevie Ray Vaughan's image, and though he may have the talent to transcend such an identification, he is yet to manifest it.

● ALBUMS: *The Heartfixers* (Southland 1981)★★★, *Live At The Moonshadow* (Landslide 1983)★★★, *Cool On It* (Landslide/Alligator 1986)★★★, *Georgia Blue* (Alligator 1988)★★★, *Fanning The Flames* (Alligator 1989)★★★, *Trouble Time* (Alligator 1992)★★★, *Storm Warning* (Alligator 1994)★★★, *Fire It Up* (Alligator 1997)★★★.

ELLIS, WILBERT 'BIG CHIEF'

b. 10 November 1914, Birmingham, Alabama, USA, d. 20 December 1977, Birmingham, Alabama, USA. A part-time musician, Ellis also worked as a taxi driver, bartender and gambler. His blues piano was rooted in the rolling, hard hitting styles of Birmingham, to which was added a strong influence from Walter Davis. Resident in New York from 1936, he made a few splendid records under his own name in the 50s, and accompanied Tarheel Slim, Brownie McGhee, Jack Dupree and others. Rediscovered in Washington in the 70s, he returned to performing, enthusiastically and with unimpaired skills, until his death.

● ALBUMS: *Big Chief Ellis* (1976)★★★, *Let's Have A Ball* (1978)★★★.

EMBRY, 'QUEEN' SYLVIA

b. 14 June 1941, Wabbaseka, Arkansas, USA, d. February 1992. Embry began playing piano as a child and sang in church choirs, moving to Memphis at the age of 19. In the 60s she settled in Chicago, where she met and married blues guitarist Johnny Embry, who taught her to play bass guitar. In the 70s she worked for several years with Lefty Dizz and she can be seen playing bass and singing one song with his band in the film *Mississippi Delta Blues*. She shared the credit with her husband on an album for Razor Records, was part of Alligator's *Living Chicago Blues* project, and had an album released under the name Blues Queen Sylvia on the German L&R label. A strong singer and fine bass player, *Living Blues* magazine reported in 1985 that she had turned her back on blues and was playing gospel music.

● ALBUMS: Johnny And Sylvia Embry *After Work* (Razor 1980)★★★, four titles only *Living Chicago Blues Volume Six* (Alligator 1980)★★★, as Blues Queen Sylvia *Midnight Baby* (L&R 1983)★★★.

EMERSON, BILLY 'THE KID'

b. William Robert Emerson, 21 December 1929, Tarpon Springs, Florida, USA. Emerson's father was a blues singer and the young Emerson played piano with the Billy Battle Band and other local groups before serving in the forces in 1952-54. On his return, he joined Ike Turner's band in Memphis. Here, Emerson made his first records for Sun which displayed his talent for wordplay and included 'No Teasing Around', the jive-talking 'The Woodchuck' and 'Red Hot', a song later taken up by rockabilly singer Billy Lee Riley and by Bob Luman. He moved to Chicago soon afterwards, playing piano or organ on numerous recording sessions and releasing singles under his own name from 1955-57 for Vee Jay ('Every Woman I Know Is Crazy About An Automobile', later revived by Ry Cooder) and from 1958-59 for Chess ('I'll Get You Too'). There were later records for Mad (1960), M-Pac (the dance craze song 'The Whip',1963) and USA (1963) before Emerson formed his own Tarpon label in the mid-60s. Among his Tarpon singles was 'I Dig The Funky Broadway'.

● ALBUMS: (reissues) *Little Fine Healthy Thing* (Charly 1980)★★★, *Crazy 'Bout Automobiles* (Charly 1982)★★★.

ESTES, SLEEPY JOHN

b. John Adams Estes, 25 January 1899, Ripley, Tennessee, USA, d. 5 June 1977, Brownsville, Tennessee, USA. This influential blues singer first performed at local house-parties while in his early teens. In 1916 he began working with mandolinist James 'Yank' Rachell, a partnership that was revived several times throughout their respective careers. It was also during this formative period that Estes met Hammie Nixon (harmonica), another individual with whom he shared a long-standing empathy. Estes made his recording debut in September 1929. He eventually completed eight masters for the RCA company, including the original versions of 'Diving Duck Blues', 'Poor John Blues' and the seminal, often-covered 'Milk Cow Blues'. These assured compositions inspired interpretations from artists as diverse as Taj Mahal, Tom Rush and the Kinks. However, despite remaining an active performer throughout the 30s, Estes retired from music in 1941. A childhood accident impaired his eyesight and by 1950 he had become completely blind. The singer resumed performing with several low-key sessions for Hammie Nixon, before reasserting his own recording career in 1962. Several excellent albums for Chicago's Delmark label followed, one of which, *Broke And Hungry*, featured a young Mike Bloomfield on guitar. Estes, Nixon and Rachell also made a successful appearance at the 1964 Newport Folk Festival and the three veterans continued to work together until 1976 when Estes suffered a stroke.

● ALBUMS: *The Legend Of Sleepy John Estes* (Delmark 1962)★★★, *Broke And Hungry, Ragged And Hungry Too* (Delmark 1963)★★★, *Portraits In Blues, Volume 10* (1964)★★★, *Brownsville Blues* (Delmark 1965)★★★, *Sleepy Jon Estes* (Delmark 1969)★★★, *Electric Sheep* (Delmark 1969)★★★, *Down South Blues* (1974)★★★, *1929-30 Sessions* (Roots 1978)★★★, *Live In Austria, 1966* (Wolf 1988)★★★, *First Recordings* (1992)★★★, *Broke And Hungry* (Delmark 1995)★★★, *Someday Baby* (Indigo 1996)★★★.

● COMPILATIONS: *The Blues Of Sleepy John Estes '34-'40* (Swaggie 1982)★★★, *The Blues Of Sleepy John Estes '34-'40, Volume Two* (Swaggie 1983)★★★.

EVANS, JOE, AND ARTHUR McLAIN

'The Two Poor Boys' were black, and are reported to have come from Fairmount, in east Tennessee, where whites outnumbered blacks by 12 to one. This goes some way towards explaining the eclecticism of, and the large white influence on, their music. Recorded in 1927 and 1931, they performed blues, but this only constituted about half of their issued titles; they also recorded medicine show material, coon songs, 20s pop, white fiddle pieces such as 'Sourwood Mountain' (transferred to mandolin and guitar), black ballads such as 'John Henry', and a parody of Darby And Tarlton's 'Birmingham Jail'. As well as ranging widely in styles, they featured a remarkable variety of instruments: guitar, kazoo, piano, mandolin, and violin. It is thought that although both men played guitar and kazoo, only Evans played the other instruments.

EVANS, LUCKY

b. 1 May 1937, Estabuchie, Mississippi, USA. Also known as 'Lucky Lopez', Evans was inspired by the singing and playing of his father and began to play the guitar at the age of eight. As a teenager he worked with a band in Milwaukee and then travelled throughout the southern states until 1964 when he settled in Chicago, having joined Howlin' Wolf's band. He worked with many of the city's leading bluesmen in the 60s and made his debut recording in 1967 (only one track was released). He next recorded in 1973, financing the session himself. In 1988, he visited Britain, touring incessantly and slowly establishing a reputation as one of the great, underrated blues singers. He recorded in England for the JSP and Borderline labels.

● ALBUMS: *Chinaman's Door* (Borderline 1988)★★★, *Evil* (Borderline 1989)★★★, *Southside Saturday Night* (JSP 1989)★★★.

EVANS, MARJORIE ANN 'MARGIE'

b. 17 July 1940, Shreveport, Louisiana, USA. Evans was largely inspired by Billie Holiday and

Bessie Smith. She studied education and music at Grambling College. After moving to Los Angeles in her late teens, she began working with Billy Ward's Sextet between 1958 and 1964. She made some unissued recordings for Dore Records in Hollywood in the early 60s and began touring with Ron Marshall's orchestra from the mid- to late 60s. In 1969 she joined the Johnny Otis band, recorded for Epic and extensively toured the USA and the Far East. In 1972 she began touring with Willie Dixon's Chicago All-Stars, and made her first solo recordings for Yambo (1972), United Artists (1973), and Buddah (1974). She was particularly renowned for her powerful live performances at clubs and jazz festivals in the USA and Europe. In recent years she has released two fine albums on L&R Records.

● ALBUMS: *Mistreated Woman* (L&R 8195)★★★★, *Another Blues Day* (L&R 1988)★★★★.

EVANS, TERRY

b. *c*.1944, Vicksburg, Mississippi, USA. Having spent more than a decade as one of Los Angeles' foremost session singers, in recent years Evans has taken firm steps towards a solo career. As a teenager, he sang with a high school vocal group, the Knights, who from time to time sang with the Red Tops, a big band popular in Clarksdale and Jackson and around the Delta. Evans was 22 when he moved to Los Angeles. For several years, he held a day job and at weekends sang in small clubs around South Central LA, including the Cotton Club and the Road Runner. He met Bobby King through a mutual friend and the pair rehearsed together. In 1976, King secured a contract with Warner Brothers and called Evans when Ry Cooder asked for backing singers while recording *Chicken Skin Music*. Both men worked on further Cooder albums and toured with him. When not on tour, Evans gigged locally with his own five-piece group, which formed the basis of the studio band for their two albums. During that time, he also sang on albums by Boz Scaggs, Maria Muldaur, John Fogerty and John Lee Hooker. Evans' debut came about through one of his songs being used on Pops Staples' solo album. Produced by Cooder, it draws on a studio band that includes Frankie Ford, Robert Ward, Jim

Keltner, the Paramount Singers and Cooder himself.

● ALBUMS: with Bobby King *Live And Let Live* (Rounder/Special Delivery 1988)★★★, with King *Rhythm, Blues, Soul & Grooves* (Rounder/Special Delivery 1990)★★★, *Blues For Thought* (PointBlank 1994)★★★, *Puttin' It Down* (Audioquest 1995)★★★, *Come To The River* (Audioquest 1997)★★★.

EZELL, WILL

b. 1896, Shreveport, Louisiana, USA. Ezell had a recording career that lasted from September 1927 to September 1929, and produced a total of 17 tracks including alternative takes. His fame rests not only on his outstanding piano work but on being one of the originators of boogie-woogie. His 'Pitchin' Boogie' was one of the earliest known uses of the term. In his role as 'house pianist' for Paramount Records he supplied musical support for artists such as Lucille Bogan, Blind Roosevelt Graves, Side-Wheel Sallie Duffie and Bertha Henderson and he is also rumoured to have worked for Bessie Smith. Although Ezell was well respected by contemporaries such as Little Brother Montgomery and Cripple Clarence Lofton, he seems to have fallen foul of the great Depression as nothing is known of him after his last appearance in a recording studio in 1931.

● COMPILATIONS: *Pitchin' Boogie* (Oldie Blues 1986)★★★.

FABULOUS THUNDERBIRDS

Formed in Texas, USA, in 1977, the Thunderbirds comprised Jimmy Vaughan (b. 20 March 1951, Dallas, Texas, USA; guitar), Kim Wilson (b. 6 January 1951, Detroit, Michigan, USA; vocals, harmonica), Keith Ferguson (b. 23 July 1946, Houston, Texas, USA, d. 29 April 1997; bass) and Mike Buck (b. 17 June 1952; drums). They emerged from the post-punk vacuum with a solid, unpretentious brand of R&B. Their debut album, *The Fabulous Thunderbirds* aka *Girls Go Wild*, offered a series of powerful original songs as well as sympathetic cover versions, including a vibrant reading of Slim Harpo's 'Scratch My Back'. This mixture has sustained the group throughout its career, although it took a move from Chrysalis Records to the Epic label to provide the success that their exciting music deserved. The Thunderbirds line-up has undergone some changes, with former Roomful Of Blues drummer Fran Christiana (b. 1 February 1951, Westerly, Rhode Island, USA) replacing Mike Buck in 1980, and Preston Hubbard (b. 15 March 1953, Providence, Rhode Island, USA) joining after Ferguson departed. Throughout these changes, Wilson and Vaughan, the brother of the late blues guitarist Stevie Ray Vaughan, remained at the helm until Vaughan jumped ship in 1995. Drummer Buck formed the Leroi Brothers in 1980, while Ferguson went on to forge a new career with the Tail Gators. Although both of these groups offer similar bar band fare, the Thunderbirds remain, unquestionably, the masters. The Danny Korchmar-produced *Roll Of the Dice* was the first album with Kim Wilson leading the band in the wake of Vaughan's departure and showed the new lead guitarist, Kid Ramos, having a difficult job to fill.

● ALBUMS: *The Fabulous Thunderbirds* aka *Girls Go Wild* (Chrysalis 1979)★★★★, *What's The Word* (Chrysalis 1980)★★★, *Butt Rockin'* (Chrysalis 1981)★★★, *T-Bird Rhythm* (Chrysalis 1982)★★★, *Tuff Enuff* (Columbia 1986)★★★, *Hot Number* (Columbia 1987)★★★, *Powerful Stuff* (Columbia 1989)★★★, *Walk That Walk, Talk That Talk* (Columbia 1991)★★★, *Roll Of The Dice* (Private Music 1995)★★.

● COMPILATIONS: *Portfolio* (Chrysalis 1987)★★★★.

● VIDEOS: *Tuff Enuff* (Hendring Video 1990).

FARLOWE, CHRIS

b. John Henry Deighton, 13 October 1940, Islington, London, England. Farlowe's long career began during the 50s skiffle boom when the John Henry Skiffle Group won the all-England championship. He then formed the original Thunderbirds, which remained semi-professional until 1962 when they embarked on a month's engagement in Frankfurt, Germany. Farlowe then met Rik Gunnell, owner of London's Ram Jam and Flamingo clubs, and the singer quickly became a stalwart of the city's R&B circuit. He made his recording debut that year with the pop-oriented 'Air Travel', but failed to secure commercial success until 1966 when his version of the Rolling Stones' song, 'Out Of Time', produced by Mick Jagger, soared to the top of the UK charts. Several minor hits, including 'Ride On Baby' (1966) and 'Handbags And Gladrags' (1967), followed, as well as a brace of pop/soul albums, but Farlowe's intonation proved too craggy for popular consumption. He and the Thunderbirds - which between 1964 and 1967 featured Albert Lee (guitar), Dave Greenslade (organ), Bugs Waddell (bass), Ian Hague (drums) and Jerry Temple (congas) - remained one of the country's most impressive R&B acts, although session musicians were increasingly employed for recording purposes. By 1968 the group had been reduced to a line-up of Farlowe, Lee, Pete Solley (keyboards) and Carl Palmer (drums), but two years later the singer founded an all-new group, the Hill. The venture's sole album, *From Here To Mama Rosa*, was not a commercial success and Chris joined ex-colleague Greenslade in Colosseum. This powerful jazz rock group disbanded in 1971, and having briefly switched allegiances to Atomic Rooster, Farlowe retired from rock to pursue an interest in military and Nazi memorabilia. He re-emerged in 1975 with *The Chris Farlowe Band,*

Live, but has conspicuously failed to find a satisfactory niche for his powerful, gritty voice. Cameo appearances during the 80s on sessions for Jimmy Page engendered the widely acclaimed *Out Of The Blue* and *Born Again*, which together served notice that the singer's feeling for the blues remained intact. Although he gigs infrequently he can still be seen performing in the mid-90s as a support act, and he can still cause goosebumps with his sensational version of 'Stormy Monday Blues'. He rejoined his colleagues in Colosseum in 1996 for a reunion tour and album. Farlowe is blessed with a magnificent voice; with it he should have been a giant.

● ALBUMS: *Chris Farlowe And The Thunderbirds* aka *Stormy Monday* (Columbia 1966)★★★, *Fourteen Things To Think About* (Immediate 1966)★★★, *The Art Of Chris Farlowe* (Immediate 1966)★★★, *The Fabulous Chris Farlowe* (EMI Regal 1967)★★★, *Paint It Farlowe* (1968)★★★, *The Last Goodbye* (Immediate 1969)★★, as Chris Farlowe And The Hill *From Here To Mama Rosa* (Polydor 1970)★★, *The Chris Farlowe Band, Live* (Polydor 1976)★★★, *Out Of The Blue* (Polydor 1985)★★, *Born Again* (Brand New 1986)★★★, *Waiting In The Wings* (1992)★★★, *Lonesome Road* (Indigo 1995)★★★, with Zoot Money *Alexis Korner Memorial Concert Volume 2* (Indigo 1995)★★★.

● COMPILATIONS: *The Best Of Chris Farlowe Vol. 1* (Immediate 1968)★★★, *Out Of Time* (Immediate 1975)★★★, *Out Of Time - Paint It Black* (Charly 1978)★★★, *Greatest Hits* (Immediate 1978)★★★, *Hot Property (The Rare Tracks)* (1983)★★, *Mr. Soulful* (Castle 1986)★★★, *Buzz With The Fuzz* (Decal 1987)★★★, *I'm The Greatest* (See For Miles 1994)★★★.

FERGUSON, H-BOMB

b. Robert Ferguson. In the fallout that succeeded the acquisition of his stage name, Ferguson obliterated all knowledge of his past, beyond the fact that his father was a minister who disapproved of his son playing blues and boogie woogie on the church piano. In later years, another fallout has been masked by a bewildering array of gaudy wigs. He first took the stage at the age of 16, having persuaded Cat Anderson to let him sing with his band. A year later, Anderson hired him. He first recorded as Bob Ferguson with Jack Parker's Orchestra for Derby in 1950. Around this time, manager Chet Patterson suggested he call himself The Cobra Kid, but his 1951 records for Atlas billed him as H-Bomb, as celebrated in 'Rock H-Bomb Rock'. After a single for Prestige, he signed to Savoy and singles such as 'Good Lovin'' and 'Preachin' The Blues' (based on 'Bloodshot Eyes') were full-blown imitations of the Wynonie Harris shouting style. In 1953 he recorded two titles for Specialty that remained unissued for some 40 years. Further singles for Sunset, Finch, Big Bang and ARC failed to sell and his 1960 session for Federal marked the end of his recording career at the time. In recent years, he has made a comeback, but his energetic live performances and outlandish headwear are insufficient compensation for a wayward talent long since spent.

● ALBUMS: *Life Is Hard* (Savoy Jazz 1987)★★★, *Bad Times Blues* (Papa Lou Recordings 1990)★★, *Wiggin' Out* (Earwig 1993)★★.

● COMPILATIONS: *Roots Of Rock'n'Roll Volume 9, The Shouters* (Savoy 1980)★★★★, *Shouting The Blues* (Specialty 1993)★★★★.

FIELDSTONES

A Memphis-based electric band, the Fieldstones play an eclectic repertoire, mixing versions of traditional blues such as 'Dirt Road' and 'Sweet Home Chicago' with more modern material like Little Milton's 'Little Bluebird' and Albert King's 'Angel Of Mercy'. Vocals are shared by guitarist Willie Roy Sanders, formerly of the Binghampton Blues Boys, and drummer Joe Hicks, and vary between the older, brooding, Delta style and an intense, soul-cum-west side Chicago vein. Their enjoyable live performance talents do not always stand up to exposure on albums. However, their music does reflect the Memphis State University's need to release material illustrative of academic research.

● ALBUMS: *Memphis Blues Today* (1982)★★★.

FIVE BREEZES

The group comprised Gene Gilmore, Leonard 'Baby Doo' Caston, Willie Dixon, Joseph Bell and Willie Hawthorne. When pianist/guitarist Caston arrived in Chicago in 1939, he met up with Arthur Dixon and Gilmore, who, like him, wanted to make records. They made a test recording for Mayo Williams of Decca Records but it was fruitless. In the meantime, Dixon had introduced Caston to his brother Willie, a prize fighter with a good bass voice who also played an imitation string bass. They joined with Gilmore and singers Joseph Bell and Willie Hawthorne to form the Five Breezes, performing material that added a bluesier dimension to the Ink Spots repertoire. Each assumed a name: Caston was 'Evening Breeze', Dixon, 'Big Breeze', Gilmore, 'Midnight Breeze', Bell, 'Cool Breeze' (a name he used on post-war records for Bell and Ebony) and Hawthorne, 'Morning Breeze'. The group worked every night of the week at the Pink Poodle, a mob club from which they could not escape. Both Caston and Gilmore recorded for Decca in June 1940 and five months later the Five Breezes cut an eight-title session for Bluebird. The band continued to be successful until America's entry into World War II, when each man went his own way. Gilmore and Dixon, along with guitarists Bernardo Dennis and Ellis Hunter, recorded two singles as the Four Jumps Of Jive for Mercury Records in late 1945, just before Caston, Dixon and Dennis formed the Big Three Trio.

● ALBUMS: *Gene Gilmore & The Five Breezes* (Blues Documents 1989)★★★.

FLEETWOOD MAC

The original Fleetwood Mac was formed in July 1967 by Peter Green (b. Peter Greenbaum, 29 October 1946, Bethnal Green, London, England; guitar) and Mick Fleetwood (b. 24 June 1947, Redruth, Cornwall, England; drums), both of whom had recently left John Mayall's Bluesbreakers. They secured a recording contract with Blue Horizon Records on the strength of Green's reputation as a blues guitarist before the label's overtures uncovered a second guitarist, Jeremy Spencer (b. 4 July 1948, Hartlepool, Cleveland, England), in a semi-professional group, the Levi Set. A temporary bassist, Bob Brunning, was recruited into the line-up, until a further Mayall acolyte, John McVie (b. 26 November 1945, London, England; bass), was finally persuaded to join the new unit. Peter Green's Fleetwood Mac, as the group was initially billed, made its debut on 12 August 1967 at Windsor's National Jazz And Blues Festival. Their first album, *Fleetwood Mac*, released on Blue Horizon in February the following year, reached the UK Top 5 and established a distinctive balance between Green's introspective compositions and Spencer's debt to Elmore James. A handful of excellent cover versions completed an album that was seminal in the development of the British blues boom of the late 60s. The group also enjoyed two minor hit singles with 'Black Magic Woman', a hypnotic Green composition later popularized by Santana, and a delicate reading of 'Need Your Love So Bad', first recorded by Little Willie John. Fleetwood Mac's second album, *Mr. Wonderful*, was another triumph, but while Spencer was content to repeat his established style, Green, the group's leader, extended his compositional boundaries with several haunting contributions, including the heartfelt 'Love That Burns'. His guitar playing, clean and sparse but always telling, was rarely better, while McVie and Fleetwood were already an instinctive rhythm section. *Mr. Wonderful* also featured contributions from Christine Perfect (b. 12 July 1943, Birmingham, England), pianist from Chicken Shack, and a four-piece horn section, as the group began to leave traditional blues behind. A third guitarist, Danny Kirwan (b. 13 May 1950, London, England), was added to the line-up in September 1968. The quintet had an immediate hit when 'Albatross', a moody instrumental reminiscent of 'Sleep Walk' by Santo And Johnny, topped the UK charts. The single, which reached number 2 when it was reissued in 1973, was the group's first million-seller. Fleetwood Mac then left Blue Horizon, although the company subsequently issued *Blues Jam At Chess*, on which the band jammed with several mentors, including Buddy Guy, Otis Spann and Shakey Horton. Following a brief interlude on Immediate Records, which furnished the hypnotic 'Man Of The World', the quintet made their debut on Reprise with 'Oh Well', their most ambitious single to date, and the superb *Then Play On*. This crafted album unveiled Kirwan's songwriting talents and his romantic leanings offset the more worldly Green. Although pictured, Jeremy Spencer was notably absent from most of the sessions, although his eccentric vision was showcased on a self-titled solo album. Fleetwood Mac now enjoyed an international reputation, but it was a mantle too great for its leader to bear. Peter Green left the band in May 1970 as his parting single, the awesome 'The Green Manalishi', became another Top 10 hit. He was replaced by Christine Perfect, now married to John McVie, and while his loss was an obvious blow, Kirwan's songwriting talent and Spencer's sheer exuberance maintained a measure of continuity on a fourth album, *Kiln House*. However, in 1971 the group was rocked for a second time when Spencer disappeared midway through an American tour. It transpired that he had joined a religious sect, the Children Of God and while Green deputized for the remainder of the tour, a permanent replacement was found in a Californian musician, Bob Welch (b. 31 July 1946, California, USA).

The new line-up was consolidated on two melodic albums, *Future Games* and *Bare Trees*. Neither release made much impression with UK audiences who continued to mourn the passing of the Green-led era, but in America the group began to assemble a strong following for their new-found transatlantic sound. However, further changes occurred when Kirwan's chronic stage-fright led to his dismissal. Bob Weston, a guitarist from Long John Baldry's backing band, was his immediate replacement, while the line-up was also bolstered by former Savoy Brown vocalist, Dave Walker. The group, however, was unhappy with a defined frontman and the singer left after only eight months, having barely completed work on *Penguin*. Although not one of the band's strongest collections, it does contain an excellent Welch composition, 'Night Watch'. The remaining quintet completed another album, *Mystery To Me*, which was released at the time of a personal nadir within the group. Weston, who had been having an affair with Fleetwood's wife, was fired midway through a prolonged US tour and the remaining dates were cancelled. Their manager, Clifford Davis, assembled a bogus Mac to fulfil contractual obligations, thus denying the 'real' group work during the inevitable lawsuits. Yet despite the inordinate pressure, Perfect, Welch, McVie and Fleetwood returned with *Heroes Are Hard To Find*, a positive release that belied the wrangles surrounding its appearance. Nonetheless, the controversy proved too strong for Welch, who left the group in December 1974. His departure robbed Fleetwood Mac of an inventive songwriter whose American perspective helped redefine the group's approach.

It was while seeking prospective recording studios that Fleetwood was introduced to Stevie Nicks and Lindsey Buckingham via the duo's self-named album. Now bereft of a guitarist, he recalled Buckingham's expertise and invited him to replace Welch. Buckingham accepted on condition that Nicks also join, thus cementing Fleetwood Mac's most successful line-up. *Fleetwood Mac*, released in 1975, was a promise fulfilled. The newcomers provided easy, yet memorable compositions with smooth harmonies, while the British contingent gave the group its edge and power. A succession of stellar compositions, including 'Over My Head', 'Say You Love Me' and the dramatic 'Rhiannon', confirmed a perfect balance had been struck giving the group their first in a long line of US Top 20 singles. The quintet's next release, *Rumours*, proved more remarkable still. Despite the collapse of two relationships - the McVies were divorced, Buckingham and Nicks split up - the group completed a remarkable collection that laid bare the traumas within, but in a manner neither maudlin nor pitiful. Instead the ongoing drama was charted by several exquisite songs; 'Go Your Own Way', 'Don't Stop', 'Second Hand News' and 'Dreams', which retained both melody and purpose. An enduring release, *Rumours* has sold upwards of 25 million copies and is second to Michael Jackson's *Thriller* as the best-selling album of all time. Having survived their emotional anguish, Fleetwood Mac were faced with the problem of following up a phenomenon. Their response was *Tusk*, an ambitious double set that showed a group unafraid to experiment, although many critics damned the collection as self-indulgent. The title track, a fascinating instrumental, was an international hit, although its follow-up, 'Sara', a composition recalling the style of *Rumours*, was better received in the USA than the UK. An in-concert selection, *Fleetwood Mac: Live*, was released as a stopgap in 1980 as rumours of a complete break-up flourished. It was a further two years before a new collection, *Mirage*, appeared, by which point several members were pursuing independent ventures. Buckingham and Nicks, in particular, viewed their own careers with equal importance and *Mirage*, a somewhat self-conscious attempt at creating another *Rumours*, lacked the sparkle of its illustrious predecessor. It nonetheless yielded three successful singles in 'Hold Me', 'Gypsy' and Buckingham's irrepressible 'Oh Diane'.

Five years then passed before a new Fleetwood Mac album was issued. *Tango In The Night* was a dramatic return to form, recapturing all the group's flair and invention with a succession of heartwarming performances in 'Little Lies', 'Family Man' and 'You And I (Part 2)'. Christine McVie contributed a further high point with the rhythmic singalong 'Anyway'. The collection was, however, Lindsey Buckingham's swan-song, although his departure from the band was not officially confirmed until June 1988. By that point two replacement singer/guitarists, ex-Thunderbyrd Rick Vito (b. 1950) and Billy Burnette (b. 7 May 1953), had joined the remaining quartet. The new line-up's debut, *Behind The Mask*, ushered in a new decade and era for this tempestuous group that gained strength from adversity and simply refused to die. Its success confirmed their status as one of the major groups in the history of popular music. In recent years the release of *The Chain*, compiled by Fleetwood, gave the band greater critical acclaim than it had received of late. In September 1995 Fleetwood self-promoted the excellent *Peter Green's Fleetwood Mac: Live At The BBC*. This was a project that was dear to his heart, as during the promotion it became clear that Fleetwood still has great emotional nostalgia for the original band and clearly regrets the departure of Green and the subsequent turn of events. A month later a new Fleetwood Mac album was released to muted reviews and minimal sales. The addition of ex-Traffic guitarist Dave Mason and Bekka Bramlett (b. 1970, USA, daughter of Delaney And Bonnie) for the album *Time* failed to ignite any spark. The dismal reaction to *Time* must have prompted Fleetwood to reconsider the band's direction. He had made no secret of the fact that he longed for the days of Green and the latter-day line-up of Nicks and Buckingham. Some diplomacy must have taken place behind closed doors because in the spring of 1997 it was announced that the famous *Rumours* line-up had reunited and were recording together. A live album was released in

August on the 20th anniversary of *Rumours*. Bramlett and Burnette formed a country/rock duo in 1997.

● ALBUMS: *Fleetwood Mac* (Columbia/Blue Horizon 1968)★★★★, *Mr. Wonderful* (Columbia/Blue Horizon 1968)★★★, *English Rose* (Epic 1969)★★★, *Then Play On* (Reprise 1969)★★★★, *Blues Jam At Chess* aka *Fleetwood Mac In Chicago* (Blue Horizon 1969)★★★, *Kiln House* (Reprise 1970)★★★, *Future Games* (Reprise 1971)★★★, *Bare Trees* (Reprise 1972)★★, *Penguin* (Reprise 1973)★★, *Mystery To Me* (Reprise 1973)★★, *Heroes Are Hard To Find* (Reprise 1974)★★★, *Fleetwood Mac* (Reprise 1975)★★★★, *Rumours* (Warners 1977)★★★★, *Tusk* (Warners 1979)★★★, *Fleetwood Mac Live* (Warners 1980)★★, *Mirage* (Warners 1982)★★★, *Live In Boston* (Shanghai 1985)★★, *London Live '68* (Thunderbolt 1986)★, *Tango In The Night* (Warners 1988)★★★, *Behind The Mask* (Warners 1989)★★★, *Live At The Marquee* 1967 recording (Sunflower 1992)★, *Live* 1968 recording (Abracadabra 1995)★, *Peter Green's Fleetwood Mac: Live At The BBC* (Fleetwood/Castle 1995)★★★★, *Time* (Warners 1995)★, *The Dance* (Reprise 1997)★★★.

Solo: Danny Kirwan *Second Chapter* (DJM 1976)★★, *Midnight In San Juan* (DJM 1976)★, *Hello There Big Boy* (DJM 1979)★. Jeremy Spencer *Jeremy Spencer* (Reprise 1970)★★, *Jeremy Spencer And The Children Of God* (Columbia 1973)★, *Flee* (Atlantic 1979)★. Mick Fleetwood *The Visitor* (RCA 1981)★, *I'm Not Me* (RCA 1983)★. John McVie *John McVie's Gotta Band With Lola Thomas* (Warners 1992)★. Christine McVie *Christine Perfect* (Blue Horizon 1970)★★★, *Christine McVie* (Warners 1984)★★.

● COMPILATIONS: *The Pious Bird Of Good Omen* (Columbia/Blue Horizon 1969)★★, *The Original Fleetwood Mac* (Columbia/Blue Horizon 1971)★★, *Fleetwood Mac's Greatest Hits* (Columbia 1971)★★★★, *The Vintage Years* (Sire 1975)★★★, *Albatross* (Columbia 1977)★★★, *Man Of The World* (Columbia 1978)★★, *Best Of* (Reprise 1978)★★★, *Cerurlean* (Shanghai 1985)★★, *Greatest Hits: Fleetwood Mac* (Columbia 1988)★★★, *The Blues Years* (Essential 1991)★★★, *The Chain* CD box set (Warners 1992)★★★, *The Early Years* (Dojo 1992)★★, *Fleetwood Mac Family Album*

(Connoisseur 1996)★★, *The Best Of ...* (Columbia 1996)★★★.
● VIDEOS: *Fleetwood Mac* (Warners 1981), *In Concert - Mirage Tour* (Spectrum 1983), *Video Biography* (Virgin Vision 1988), *Tango In The Night* (Warner Music Video 1988), *Peter Green's Fleetwood Mac: The Early Years 1967-1970* (PNE 1995).
● FURTHER READING: *Fleetwood Mac: The Authorized History*, Samuel Graham. *Fleetwood Mac: Rumours 'N' Fax*, Roy Carr and Steve Clarke. *Fleetwood Mac*, Steve Clarke. *The Crazed Story Of Fleetwood Mac*, Stephen Davis. *Fleetwood Mac: Behind The Masks*, Bob Brunning. *Fleetwood: My Life And Adventures With Fleetwood Mac*, Mick Fleetwood with Stephen Davis. *Peter Green: The Biography*, Martin Celmins.

FLOYD, FRANK

b. 11 October 1908, Toccopola, Mississippi, USA, d. 7 August 1984, Memphis, Tennessee, USA. Having spent many of his earlier years travelling the southern states of the USA, playing in carnivals and street shows, Floyd, aka Harmonica Frank, developed a solo guitar and harmonica style much influenced by black country blues. This led to his first recordings - made by Sam Phillips in Memphis in 1951 - being issued on the Chess label, at that time oriented entirely towards a black audience. These, along with later recordings that Phillips issued in 1954 on his own Sun label, in particular 'Rocking Chair Daddy', stand as direct precursors to the first Elvis Presley records, also on Sun, in their mixture of white and black styles, although Floyd saw no such commercial success. In the late 50s, he recorded again for a self-owned label, and there was also an album for Barrelhouse in 1975.
● ALBUMS: *Harmonica Frank Floyd* (Barrelhouse 1975)★★★.

FOLEY, SUE

b. 29 March 1968, Ottawa, Canada. Foley fields a strong sense of rhythm which puts an interesting spin on a Texas shuffle. She took up the guitar at 13, encouraged by her father and three brothers. Two years later, she saw James Cotton and spent the next few years sneaking into clubs to jam with blues bands. At 18 she formed a band of her own and moved to Vancouver, where she developed a guitar style that favoured Earl Hooker, Freddie King and Magic Sam. Her tours took her to the USA and in Memphis she was seen by Clifford Antone, who signed her to his label in March 1990. *Young Girl Blues* featured her regular rhythm team, supplemented by a guest list that included Kim Wilson and Reese Wynans, on a set in which cover versions predominated. There were fewer guests and more original songs on *Without A Warning*, an album that emphasized the confrontational nature of her talent. This was further exhibited on *Big City Blues*.
● ALBUMS: *Young Girl Blues* (Antone's 1992)★★★, *Without A Warning* (Antone's 1993)★★★, *Big City Blues* (Antone's 1995)★★★, *Walk In The Sun* (Antone's 1996)★★★.
● COMPILATIONS: *Antone's Women* (Antone's 1992)★★★.

FORD, ROBBEN

b. Robben Lee Ford, 16 December 1951, Woodlake, California, USA. A jazz, blues and rock guitarist, Robben is the most celebrated member of the musical Ford family. His father Charles was a country musician, and his brothers Patrick and Mark are bluesmen, playing drums and harmonica, respectively. Inspired initially by Mike Bloomfield and Eric Clapton, Ford's first professional engagement was with Charlie Musslewhite in 1970. He formed the Charles Ford Band with his brothers in 1971, then backed Jimmy Witherspoon from 1972-74. He toured and recorded with both Joni Mitchell (as part of L.A. Express) and George Harrison in 1974, the resulting exposure bringing him a considerable amount of session work. In 1978, he formed the Yellowjackets with keyboards player Russell Ferrante and also found time to record a patchy solo debut, *Inside Story*. The early 80s saw him performing with Michael McDonald and saxophonist Sadao Watanabe; in 1986 he joined the Miles Davis band on its tour of the USA and Europe. *Talk To Your Daughter* was a triumphant return to his blues roots, and picked up a Grammy nomination in the 'Contemporary Blues' category. In 1993 he recorded with a new unit, the Blue Line featuring Roscoe Beck (bass), Bill Boublitz (keyboards) and Tom Brechtlein (drums). Ford plays cleanly in an uncluttered style (like Mike Bloomfield), but occasionally with the frantic energy of Larry Carlton.

● ALBUMS: with the Charles Ford Band *The Charles Ford Band* (1972)★★★, *Inside Story* (1978)★★★, with the Charles Ford Band *Reunion* (1982)★★★, *Talk To Your Daughter* (Warners 1988)★★★, *Mark Ford With The Robben Ford Band* (1991)★★★, *Robben Ford And The Blue Line* (1992)★★★★, with Jimmy Witherspoon *Live At The Notodden Blues Festival* (1993)★★★, with the Blue Line *Mystic Mile* (Stretch/GRP 1993)★★★, *Handful Of Blues* (Blue Thumb 1995)★★★★, *Tiger Walk* (Blue Thumb 1997)★★.

● COMPILATIONS: *The Blues Collection* (Crosscut 1997)★★★★.

● VIDEOS: *Highlights* (Warner Music 1995).

FOREHAND, EDWARD 'LITTLE BUSTER'

b. 28 September 1942, Hertford, North Carolina, USA. Born partially sighted but now totally blind, Little Buster is an exceptionally talented guitar player and vocalist. Sharing the same name as Carolina harmonica player Buster Brown, Forehand began singing gospel music on street corners before switching to the electric guitar. Moving to New York in the early 60s, he played at blues clubs with drummer Melvin Taylor, building up a loyal following that enabled him to gradually augment the group with other instruments, including bass, organ, saxophone and trumpet. He recorded sides for Jubilee in the 60s, the most successful of which were 'Looking For A Home' and 'Young Boy Blues', but a mooted album was cancelled. After two sides on the Minit label Forehand was forced to concentrate on live work, steadily building up a strong reputation throughout the 70s and 80s. Recording as Little Buster And The Soul Brothers for the Rounder offshoot Bullseye Blues, he released the acclaimed *Right On Time!* in 1996, earning a W.C. Handy nomination for Best Soul Blues album. Apart from the seasoned originals (some of which dated to an aborted recording session in the mid-80s), the album included a track, 'Whatever It Takes', written by legendary songwriter Dan Penn.

● ALBUMS: *Right On Time!* (Bullseye Blues 1996)★★★★.

FOREST CITY JOE

(see Pugh, Joe Bennie)

FOSTER, LEROY 'BABY FACE'

b. 1 February 1923, Algoma, Mississippi, USA, d 26 May 1958, Chicago, Illinois, USA. A guitarist and drummer, Foster followed the black migration north in the 40s, and worked Maxwell Street and the clubs. Foster's singing was indebted to John Lee 'Sonny Boy' Williamson, and like Williamson he was equally impressive on both up-tempo and slow, intense blues. In 1948, he made his debut on record, singing a riotous 'Locked Out Boogie' and a reflective 'Shady Grove Blues', with Muddy Waters providing guitar. Foster also made fine recordings for JOB with Snooky Pryor, Sunnyland Slim and Robert Lockwood in support; for Parkway Records, he participated in a magnificent session with Little Walter and a contract-jumping Muddy Waters, which constitutes, above all on the two-part 'Rollin' And Tumblin'' a manifesto for the transformation of Mississippi Delta blues in the Chicago ghetto.

● ALBUMS: *Genesis: The Beginnings Of Rock* (1972)★★★, *Blues Is Killing Me* (1983)★★★.

FOSTER, LITTLE WILLIE

b. 5 April 1922, Clarksdale, Mississippi, USA. Foster came to Chicago in 1941, already playing guitar, piano and harmonica. Tutored on the latter instrument by Walter Horton, he played on Maxwell Street, and in a band with Homesick James, Floyd Jones and Moody Jones. Foster recorded two singles in the mid-50s, and 'Crying The Blues', one of the titles, sums up both his emotional singing and his wailing, swooping harmonica. Shortly thereafter, he was shot and semi-paralysed; he improved slowly, and remained able to play and sing, but only rarely in public. Floyd Jones stated that Foster fatally shot a man, and was placed in a mental hospital early in 1974, but as he was photographed in Chicago in September of that year, this information is somewhat doubtful. His debut album came in 1996 and was produced by Bobby Mack, who played the guitar parts. Another example of somebody who should not to have waited until his twilight years to be 'discovered'.

● ALBUMS: *I Found Joy* (Palindrome 1996)★★★.

● COMPILATIONS: *Chicago Blues - The Early 1950s* (1965)★★★, *King Cobras* (1980)★★★.

FRANKLIN, GUITAR PETE

b. Edward Lamonte Franklin, 16 January 1928, Indianapolis, Indiana, USA, d. 31 July 1975, Indianapolis, Indiana, USA. His mother wrote many songs for her lodger Leroy Carr, and Franklin's interest in music developed early, beginning with piano, on which he was as adept as on guitar. His guitar playing was influenced by local musicians Scrapper Blackwell and Jesse Ellery (who recorded as accompanist to Jack 'Champion' Dupree), but he could change his playing completely to fit with an amplified Chicago ensemble. As a pianist, Franklin was, not surprisingly, indebted to Leroy Carr, but on both instruments he was an original and remarkably accomplished musician, who was not recorded to the extent his talent merited.
● ALBUMS: *Guitar Pete's Blues* (1963)★★★, *Windy City Blues* (1975)★★★, *Indianapolis Jump* (1977)★★★.

FRAZIER, CALVIN

b. 16 February 1915, Osceola, Arkansas, USA, d. 23 September 1972, Detroit, Michigan, USA. The Frazier family was large, musical and deeply religious; father Van played fiddle, guitar and banjo, mother Bell played bass, and Lonnie, Rebecca and Johnny all played guitar and mandolin, as did Calvin. By 1922, they lived in South Hobart Place in Memphis, along with cousin Johnny Shines. Nine years later, Shines linked up with Calvin and Johnny, and played for handouts on the Memphis streets. During the early 30s, Calvin also worked with Robert Johnson and James 'Peck' Curtis. In April 1935, Frazier was involved in a shooting incident that forced him to leave town, in company with Johnson and Shines. The trio fled to Canada and found work in religious broadcasting, playing on *The Elder Moten Hour.* Shortly after returning to Detroit, Shines and Johnson moved on, but Frazier stayed, teaming up with guitarist Sampson Pittman. They were recorded in October 1938 for the Library of Congress by Alan Lomax, Frazier revealing a guitar style whose boogie patterns and falsetto vocals echoed Johnson's. During the 40s, he played with Big Maceo, Baby Boy Warren and Eddie

Kirkland, but did not record again until 1952 for Savoy, with pianist T.J. Fowler's band. He also played on sessions by Baby Boy Warren and Washboard Willie. He recorded infrequently during the 50s; 'Lilly Mae', first cut for the Library of Congress, and 'Have Blues, Must Travel' were recorded for Fortune and JVB, the latter also issued by Checker.
● ALBUMS: *I'm In The Highway Man* (1980)★★★.

FROST, FRANK

b. 15 April 1936, Auvergne, Arkansas, USA. Frost's skills encompass keyboards and guitar, but like many other blues artists, he started with the harmonica. He learned much from Sonny Boy 'Rice Miller' Williamson in the mid-50s and appeared regularly with him on the famous radio show *King Biscuit Time.* In 1962 he recorded for Sam Phillips with a band that included guitarist Big Jack Johnson, with whom Frost still plays and records. One single and an album resulted, featuring a very tough and raw, but tight, down-home blues sound, unusual on record at this time. A similar sound emerged from his next sessions in Nashville in 1966, which produced three fine singles and, later, an album on Jewel Records. Subsequently, Frost went back to mainly local performing in the juke joints around his home area in the Mississippi Delta, but has also continued to make records and tour. He has undertaken some highly acclaimed appearances in Europe, and also appeared in the feature film *Crossroads.*
● ALBUMS: *Frank Frost* (Jewel 1979)★★★, *Hey Boss Man* (Charly 1981)★★★, *Ride With Your Daddy Tonight* (Charly 1985)★★★, *Midnight Prowler* (1989)★★★, *Jelly Roll King* (Charly 1990)★★★, with Sam Carr *Keep Yourself Together* (Evidence 1996)★★★.
● FILMS: *Crossroads* (1990).

FULLER, JESSE 'LONE CAT'

b. 12 March 1896, Jonesboro, Georgia, USA, d. 29 January 1976, Oakland, California, USA. A veteran of the tent shows, Fuller fashioned himself a unique one-man band of six-string bass (played with his right foot), a combination of kazoo, harmonica and microphone fixed to a harness around his neck, a hi-hat cymbal (played with the left foot) and a 12-string guitar.

He came to fame in the late 50s as a result of appearances on US television, where he followed Ramblin' Jack Elliot's lionization via his recording of 'San Francisco Bay Blues'. In the 50s he made three albums of original and traditional material and by the mid-60s became the darling of the 'coffee house circuit' after Bob Dylan cited him as one of his influences. Similar success followed in Britain resulting from Donovan's performance of 'San Francisco Bay Blues' on UK Independent Television's *Ready Steady Go* music programme in 1965. Although Fuller's output is meagre his influence is considerable. Eric Clapton provoked renewed interest with his excellent version of 'San Francisco Bay Blues' on his *MTV Unplugged* album in 1992. Original Blues Classics have reissued his albums on CD with the original covers.

● ALBUMS: *Workin' On The Railroad* (World Songs 1954)★★★, *'Frisco Bound* (Cavalier 1958)★★★, *Work Songs Blues And Spirituals* (Good Time Jazz 1958)★★★, *The Lone Cat* (Good Time Jazz 1961)★★★, *San Francisco Bay Blues* (Folklore 1964)★★★★, *Railroad Worksong* (1993)★★★★.

FULLER, JOHNNY

b. 20 April 1929, Edwards, Mississippi, USA. Major Fuller moved his family west to Vallejo, California, in 1935, possibly drawn by work in the shipyards. Johnny was a largely self-taught musician and played guitar, his first interest being C&W music, particularly the songs of Ernest Tubb and Gene Autry. At the age of 15, he was singing in church, later forming the Teenage Gospel Singers, which became the Golden West Gospel Singers. In about 1948 he made solo gospel records for Jackson, and for several years performed every Sunday on stations KWBR in Oakland and KRE in Berkeley. In the early 50s, he learned piano and organ and played blues in a style reminiscent of Charles Brown, but with less sophistication. This was evident on his first record, 'Train, Train Blues', for Bob Geddins' Rhythm label. Subsequent sessions were sold to Flair and Hollywood. His tribute, 'Johnny Ace's Last Letter', leased to Aladdin, became his first success and put him on the package tour circuit for several years. His 1956 single for Imperial, 'Don't Slam That Door', was later covered by Snooks Eaglin. Later records for Irma and Specialty strayed into rock 'n' roll and rockabilly. He spent much of the 60s outside music, returning to the clubs of Oakland and Richmond at the end of the decade. In 1973 he recorded an album, released in Australia, combining new material with older songs such as 'Fools Paradise', 'Bad Luck Overtook Me' and 'Strange Land', with a band that also featured Philip Walker. Further club and festival work continued through the 70s, since which time nothing further has been reported.

● ALBUMS: *Fuller's Blues* (Diving Duck 1974/1988)★★★.

FULSON, LOWELL

b. 31 March 1921, Tulsa, Oklahoma, USA. Blues guitarist Lowell Fulson (whose surname is often mistakenly misspelled Fulsom) recorded steadily from 1946 until the late 70s and still performs regularly on the US and European club circuits. He began his career in his native Oklahoma, performing with string bands and backing country blues vocalist Alger 'Texas' Alexander in the late 30s. During World War II he was stationed in Oakland, California, where he met record producer Bob Geddins. Following his discharge from the US Navy, Fulson recorded for several labels under the direction of Geddins, including Big Town, Down Beat, Gilt Edge and Trilon. His first hit came in 1950 on the Swing Time label when he reworked Memphis Slim's 'Nobody Loves Me' into 'Every Day I Have The Blues'. At that time his 12-piece orchestra included Ray Charles on piano. Also playing with Fulson around this time was tenor saxophonist Stanley Turrentine. Fulson recorded for Aladdin Records in 1953 and then switched to Checker Records, a subsidiary of Chess Records, the following year. His first side for that company, 'Reconsider Baby', was covered by Elvis Presley. Fulson stayed with Checker Records into the early 60s and then moved to Kent Records, who changed the spelling of his name. Among his biggest hits for Kent were 'Black Nights' in 1965 and 'Tramp' the next year. The latter song, co-written with Jimmy McCracklin, was later a hit for Otis Redding and Carla Thomas. In 1968 Fulson signed with Jewel Records and then recorded for a succession of small labels including Crazy Cajun and Granite. By the early 90s his early work often appeared on reissues, while some of his new material was only being released on minor labels, such as France's Blue Phoenix Records. However, in 1993 the artist received five W.C. Handy Awards, and was inducted into the Blues Hall Of Fame, both for himself and his song, 'Reconsider Baby'.

● ALBUMS: *In A Heavy Bag* (Jewell 1965)★★★★, *I've Got The Blues* (Jewell 1965)★★★★, *Lowell Fulson* (Kent 1965)★★★★, *Soul* (Kent 1966)★★★★, *Tramp* (Kent 1967)★★★, *Lowell Fulson Now!* (Kent 1969)★★★, *Let's Go Get Stoned* (1971)★★★, *The Ol' Blues Singer* (Jet 1976)★★★, *Lovemaker* (1978)★★★, *Think Twice Before You Speak* (JSP 1984)★★★ *Blue Days, Black Nights* (Ace 1986)★★★, *I Don't Know My Mind* (Bear Family 1987)★★★, *Baby Won't You Jump With Me* (Crown Prince 1988)★★★, *Back Home Blues* (1992)★★★, *Hold On* (Bullseye 1993)★★★, *River Blues* (1993)★★★, *Them Update Blues* (Bullseye 1995)★★★.

● COMPILATIONS: *Man Of Motion* (Charly 1981)★★★, *Everyday I Have The Blues* (1984)★★★★, *Lowell Fulson 1946-57* (Blues Boy 1987)★★★, *San Francisco Blues* (1993)★★★, *Reconsider Baby* (1993)★★★, *Every Day I Have The Blues* (Night Train 1996)★★★★, *Sinner's Prayer* (Night Train 1996)★★★★.

● VIDEOS: *John Lee Hooker/Lowell Fulson/Percy Mayfield* (1992).

FUNDERBURGH, ANSON

b. 15 November 1954, Dallas, Texas, USA. Funderburgh played blues guitar with local bands and in 1981 recorded with the Fabulous Thunderbirds. He later formed his own band, the Rockets and signed to blues revivalist label Black Top in 1984. Funderburgh's guitar pyrotechnics made the group a favourite at blues festivals, where they often performed with veteran harmonica player Sam Myers (b. 1936, Mississippi, USA). Myers also featured on Funderburgh's studio releases, and in 1997 the partnership celebrated their tenth anniversary together with a tour of the UK. In 1990, the group recorded with Snooks Eaglin.

● ALBUMS: *Talk To You By Hand* (Black Top 1984)★★★, *She Knocks Me Out* (Black Top 1985)★★★, with Sam Myers *My Love Is Here To Stay* (Black Top 1986)★★★, with Sam Myers *Sins* (Black Top 1987)★★★, *She Knocks Me Out* (Black Top 1988)★★★, *Rack 'Em Up* (Black Top 1989)★★★, *Tell Me What I Wanna Hear* (Black Top 1991)★★★, *Live At The Grand Emporium* (Black Top 1995)★★★, with Sam Myers *What's What They Want* (Black Top 1997)★★★.

● COMPILATIONS: *Through The Years* (Black Top 1992)★★★.

GADDY, BOB

b. 4 February 1924, Vivian, West Virginia, USA. Gaddy took a childhood interest in the piano from watching his minister, Clayton Jones, playing in church. Gospel music remained his musical focus until he was drafted into the army in 1943. Transferred to the San Francisco area, he frequented the local clubs and bars, encouraged by his friends to play the latest boogie hits. Demobbed in 1946, he made his way to New York, where he met Brownie McGhee and sat in with his band, the Three B's. Soon afterwards, he and McGhee formed the Mighty Houserockers and played a four-year residency at Billy's Tavern, a New Jersey nightclub. Through McGhee, Gaddy made records for Jackson, Jax, Dot and Harlem, before signing with Old Town in 1955. Over the next five years, records such as 'Operator', 'Paper Lady' and 'Woe, Woe Is Me' achieved success principally in the New York area, but were popular enough for him to tour the Midwest and the south. Other tracks from his nine singles tended to be minimally disguised rewrites of more popular songs by artists such as Chuck Willis and Ray Charles. As the 50s ended, Gaddy formed a new partnership with guitarist Larry Dale which lasted until the 70s. When rediscovered in 1986, he was working as a cook in a Madison Avenue restaurant.

● ALBUMS: *Rip'n'Run* (Ace 1986)★★★, *Bob Gaddy And Friends* (Moonshine 1986), *Harlem Hit Parade* (Ace 1987)★★★, *Harlem Blues Operator* (Ace 1993)★★★, *Old Town Blues Vol. 1 Downtown Sides* (Ace 1993)★★★.

GAINES, GRADY

b. 14 May 1934, Waskom, Texas, USA. By the time his family moved to Houston, the 12-year-old Gaines was already intent upon following Louis Jordan's example and becoming a saxophonist. He took lessons and at the E.L. Smith Junior High School, he met Calvin Owens, a student music teacher at the time. While in senior high school, he met Little Richard at the Club Matinee and played with his band, the Tempo Toppers. Gaines worked on studio sessions for Duke/Peacock until 1955, when Little Richard asked him to join his touring band. The association lasted for three years, during which time they recorded 'Keep A Knockin'' and appeared in *Don't Knock The Rock*, *The Girl Can't Help It* and *Mister Rock And Roll*. When Little Richard renounced rock 'n' roll in favour of religion in 1958, Gaines and the band named themselves the Upsetters and hired Dee Clark to be their singer. They also worked and recorded with Little Willie John and Sam Cooke, appearing on the latter's 'Twisting The Night Away'. During the 70s, Gaines worked with Joe Tex, Little Johnny Taylor, Curtis Mayfield and Millie Jackson. He left the music business in 1980 but made a comeback five years later that resulted in a contract with Black Top. His records call on the services of veterans such as Carol Fran and Clarence Hollimon, Teddy Reynolds and Lloyd Lambert, as well as featuring his regular vocalist, Big Robert Smith.

● ALBUMS: *Full Gain* (Black Top 1987)★★★, *Gulf Coast Blues Vol. 1* (Black Top 1990)★★★, *Black Top Blues-A-Rama Vol. 4* (Black Top 1990)★★★, *Horn Of Plenty* (Black Top 1992)★★★.

GAINES, ROY

b. 12 August 1934, Houston, Texas, USA. The brother of Grady Gaines, Roy became interested in the electric guitar at an early age and began fraternizing with other local young blues guitarists such as Clarence Hollimon and Johnny Copeland. Gaines made his debut with an obscure release on the Miami-based Chart label before coming to the attention of local Houston bandleader and head of Duke Records' house band, Bill Harvey. Gaines was featured with Harvey's band on various releases by Big Mama Thornton and Bobby Bland in 1955 for the Duke and Peacock labels, before being enticed away by an impressed Chuck Willis. After moving to New York City, Gaines recorded with Willis for Atlantic as well as signing to RCA Victor's Groove subsidiary under his own name. This resulted in two releases in 1956. The following year he signed to DeLuxe, returned to Victor in 1958 and experienced a lean decade in the 60s with only two releases on the small Del-Fi and Uni labels. In the 70s, Gaines was again in demand, both for public appearances and as guitarist with the celebrated Crusaders. In 1981, Red Lightnin Records interrupted his busy touring schedule and recorded a fine album, *Gainelining*, which underlined Gaines' four decades of musical influence.

● ALBUMS: *Gainelining* (Red Lightnin 1981)★★★★.

GAITHER, BILL

Gaither's first issued recordings were made in 1935. This session included an unissued tribute to Leroy Carr, who had died the same year, and Gaither, billed on many of his records as 'Leroy's Buddy', recorded a 'Life Of Leroy Carr' as late as 1940. Gaither's guitar playing was, not surprisingly, much in the manner of Carr's partner Scrapper Blackwell, while his regular pianist Honey Hill imitated Carr. Gaither's light, wistful voice continues the imitative process, as do his bittersweet lyrics, which sometimes contain interesting topical material. Evidently popular with contemporary black record buyers, and more of an original than his avowed indebtedness to his inspirations might suggest, Gaither nevertheless lacks both the musical variety and the poetic depth of Carr and Blackwell.

● COMPILATIONS: *Leroy's Buddy 1935-1941* (Magpie 1987)★★★, *Leroy's Buddy 1936-1939* (Neovox 1990)★★★.

GALLAGHER, RORY

b. 2 March 1949, Ballyshannon, Co. Donegal, Eire, d. 15 June 1995. Having served his musical apprenticeship in the Fontana and Impact Showbands, Gallagher put together the original Taste in 1965. This exciting blues-based rock trio rose from regional obscurity to the verge of international fame, but broke up acrimoniously five years later. Gallagher was by then a guitar hero and embarked on a solo voyage supported by Gerry McAvoy (bass) and Wilgar Campbell (drums). He introduced an unpretentious approach, which marked a career that deftly retained all the purpose of the blues without erring on the side of excessive reverence. Gallagher's early influences were Lonnie Donegan, Woody Guthrie, Chuck Berry and Muddy Waters and he strayed very little from those paths. The artist's refreshing blues guitar work, which featured his confident bottleneck playing, was always of interest and by 1972 Gallagher was a major live attraction. Campbell was replaced by Rod De'ath following the release of Live In Europe, while Lou Martin was added on keyboards. This line-up remained constant for the next six years and was responsible for Gallagher's major commercial triumphs, Blueprint and Irish Tour '74. De'ath and Martin left the group in 1978. Former Sensational Alex Harvey Band drummer Ted McKenna joined the ever-present McAvoy but was in turn replaced by Brendan O'Neill. Former Nine Below Zero member and blues harmonica virtuoso Mark Feltham became a full-time 'guest', as Gallagher quietly continued with his career. Shunning the glitzy aspect of the music business, he toured America over 30 times in addition to touring the globe twice. His record sales reached several millions and he retained a fiercely loyal following. He had several opportunities to record with his heroes, such as Donegan, Waters, Jerry Lee Lewis and Albert King, and his love for his homeland resulted in contributions to the work of the Fureys, Davy Spillane and Joe O'Donnell. Gallagher retained his perennial love for the blues, his original Stratocaster guitar (now badly battered) and the respect of many for his uncompromising approach. He died following complications after a liver transplant in 1995.

● ALBUMS: Rory Gallagher (Polydor 1971)★★★, Deuce (Polydor 1971)★★★, Live! In Europe (Polydor 1972)★★★, Blueprint (Polydor 1973)★★★★, Tattoo (Polydor 1973)★★★★, Irish Tour '74 (Polydor 1974), Saint ... And Sinner (Polydor 1975)★★★, Against The Grain (Chrysalis 1975)★★★, Calling Card (Chrysalis 1976)★★★, Photo Finish (Chrysalis 1978)★★★, Top Priority (Chrysalis 1979)★★★, Stage Struck (Chrysalis 1980)★★★, Jinx (Chrysalis 1982)★★★, Defender (Demon 1987)★★, Fresh Evidence (Castle 1990)★★.

● COMPILATIONS: In The Beginning (Emerald 1974)★★★, The Story So Far (Polydor 1976)★★★, The Best Years (1976)★★★, Best Of Rory Gallagher And Taste (Razor 1988)★★★★, Edged In Blue (Demon 1992)★★★, Rory Gallagher Boxed 4-CD set (1992)★★★.

● VIDEOS: Live In Cork (Castle Hendring Video 1989).

GANT, CECIL

b. 4 April 1913, Nashville, Tennessee, USA, d. 4 February 1951, Nashville, Tennessee, USA. Usually regarded as a blues singer and pianist, Gant's crooning style had a significantly wider appeal, somewhat in the manner of Nat 'King' Cole and Billy Eckstine. After playing clubs in the Nashville area in the late 30s, he joined the US Army and sang at a major War Bond Rally in Los Angeles. Signed to the Gilt-Edge label he had an enormous hit in 1945 with 'I Wonder', which he wrote with Raymond Leveen; the label credit read 'Private Cecil Gant'. Dressed in Army khaki, and billed as 'The GI Sing-sation', he toured extensively, playing to large, enthusiastic black and white audiences. After the war he appeared at clubs in Los Angeles and elsewhere, and recorded for several labels, including King, Bullet, Four Star, Downbeat/Swingtime and Imperial. For Decca (1950-51), he cut several precursors to Bill Haley, such as 'Rock Little Baby' and 'We're Gonna Rock', but was never able achieve anything to match the engaging 'I Wonder'. He died of pneumonia at the comparatively early age of 37.

● COMPILATIONS: Cecil Boogie (Flyright 1976)★★★, Rock Little Baby (Flyright 1976)★★★, Killer Diller Boogie (Magpie 1979)★★★, Rock This Boogie (Krazy Kat 1983)★★★, Cecil Gant (Krazy Kat 1990)★★★.

GARLAND, TERRY

b. 1953, Johnson City, Tennessee, USA. Although interested in blues, Garland spent the first 20 years of his professional career playing guitar in a variety of bar and show bands, performing popular chart-based rock 'n' roll and latterly, R&B. Tiring of this rigorous life, he took to playing acoustic blues in clubs around the southern states. The 90s rehabilitation of the dobro in the blues idiom saw Terry Garland become the latest in a long line of solo artists, including John Hammond and Keb' Mo', to employ the instrument. As a Tennessee child of the 50s Garland naturally picked out the blues of Howlin' Wolf and Lightnin' Hopkins as his inspiration. By the 60s he had begun to play in a series of local R&B groups, but a major turning point came when he opened a show for Leon Russell - his first solo performance. He subsequently began to write his own songs, adding them to his existing canon of traditional country and delta blues numbers. Encouraged by friends, he prepared an album that was subsequently rejected by every blues-orientated American label. Instead, interest came from the New York-based First Warning and *Trouble In Mind* was recorded with the assistance of Nighthawks harmonica player Mark Wenner. Garland performed songs by Mississippi Fred McDowell, Bukka White, Skip James and others with confidence, with only an occasional penchant for excess. The album featured two of his own songs alongside a selection of 'one-take' versions of blues classics from Willie Dixon, Jimmy Reed and the more contemporaneous Johnny Winter. Q magazine afforded it a four-star review, writer Martin Longley judging it 'one of the year's best blues albums'. *Edge Of The Valley* relied on a more polished production and sophisticated instrumentation but was also well received. Garland signed to Demon Records in 1996 to record his third collection, *The One To Blame*. Including Robert Johnson's 'Phonograph Blues', the gospel standard 'A Closer Walk With Thee' and Jerry Lee Lewis's 'It'll Be Me', it displayed the same powerful conviction as its predecessors, but showed the artist's smoky, curdled vocals in their best light to date.

● ALBUMS: *Trouble In Mind* (First Warning 1991)★★★, *Edge Of The Valley* (First Warning 1992)★★★, *The One To Blame* (Demon 1996)★★★★.

GARLOW, CLARENCE

b. 27 February 1911, Welsh, Louisiana, USA, d. 24 July 1986, Beaumont, Texas, USA. Brought up in the black community in south Louisiana and east Texas, Garlow, aka Bon Ton, became proficient on both guitar and accordion. On the former, his principal influence was T-Bone Walker, and the smooth, jazzy Walker sound can be heard on many of his records, particularly those of the late 40s and early 50s, which appeared on locally distributed record labels such as Macy's, Lyric and Feature. Other records show a more rocking R&B tendency, in particular the classic pairing of 'Route 90' and 'Crawfishin'' on a single for Flair Records. Later, there was a fine zydeco pairing on Folk Star Records, but while recording for Jay Miller he moved towards the swamp blues sound. Garlow retired from playing in the early 60s, but worked for some years as a postman and a disc jockey in Beaumont, Texas.

● COMPILATIONS: *Bon Ton Roola* (Flyright 1986)★★★.

GARNER, LARRY

b. 1952, New Orleans, Louisiana, USA. Unlike many of his contemporaries, Garner draws upon a natural talent for storytelling and music making that differentiates him from those who attempt to find a personal synthesis of prevailing styles and influences. Raised in the Baton Rouge area, Garner learned guitar from his uncle, George Lathers. By the age of 11, he was playing with a gospel group, the Stars Of Joy, broadcasting on WXOK in Zachary, Louisiana. Four years later, he joined his cousin in the Twisters, an R&B band that played in various Baton Rouge clubs, including the Black Cat Lounge and the Jackson Club. Garner served with the army in Korea, playing at every base to which he was sent. On his return, he abandoned music for 10 years to raise a family and work at a local chemical plant. In 1983, he began to sit in on open nights at Tabby's Blues Box, owned by self-styled 'King of Swamp Blues', Tabby Thomas. Two years later Garner formed his own band and rapidly gained a reputation for performing his own songs. One, 'Dog House Blues', gained him a B.B. King Lucille Award in 1988. Two years later, he released his own cassette of original material which led to the recording of

his first album, *Double Dues*. By the time *Too Blues* was released in 1993, he had become a regular at festivals throughout the UK and Europe. A move to Verve/Gitanes and the opportunity to utilize a larger budget and guest musicians has not changed his pragmatic approach to music-making.
● ALBUMS: *Catch The Feeling* cassette (1990)★★, *Chemical City Shakedown* (Sidetrack 1991)★★★, *Double Dues* (JSP 1991)★★★, *Louisiana Swamp Blues Vol. 3* (1992)★★★, *Too Blues* (JSP 1993)★★★★, *You Need To Live A Little* (Verve/Gitanes 1995)★★★, *Baton Rouge* (Verve 1996)★★★.

GARRETT, ROBERT 'BUD'

b. 1916, Free Hill, Tennessee, USA. A jack of all trades when not playing music, Garrett has resided for most of his life in Free Hill, an isolated community founded by freed slaves around 1830. He recorded a splendid electric blues single for Excello in 1962, and played occasional festivals from the 80s, by which time he was the only performer in Free Hill of the live music that had been otherwise supplanted by disco and cable television. His music included a few originals, which often employed a talking blues structure, but consisted largely of blues standards by the likes of Little Milton and T-Bone Walker, and country music by artists such as Don Williams and Merle Haggard, adapted to blues formats.
● ALBUMS: *The Excello Story* (1972)★★★, *Free Hill* (1985)★★★.

GATTON, DANNY

b. 4 September 1945, Washington DC, USA, d. 4 October 1994, USA. Guitarist and songwriter Danny Gatton first picked up a guitar at the age of nine. Inspired by guitarist Charlie Christian and Bob Wills' Texas Playboys, Gatton soon developed a unique individual style. Much of this was due to his customization of a standard Les Paul guitar into what he termed the 'Les Paulveriser'. He enhanced this sound by making home recordings using two reel-to-reel tapes that produced an echo effect when one machine was played slightly out of synchronization with the other. Through his thirties and forties he played regularly in Washington to an audience who appreciated his unique take on jazz, blue-

grass and rockabilly, issuing a series of exclusively mail-order albums that gradually expanded his audience. Eventually, one of these, *Unfinished Business*, provoked enough critical feedback to prompt Elektra Records into offering him a contract. However, despite further strong reviews, neither *88 Elmira Street* nor *Cruisin' Deuces* succeeded commercially. Gatton collaborated with jazz musician Joey DeFrancesco on his *Relentless* project but, depressed by the loss of his contract with Elektra, he committed suicide in October 1994.
● ALBUMS: *88 Elmira Street* (Elektra 1991)★★★, *Cruisin' Deuces* (Elektra 1993)★★★.

GEDDINS, BOB

b. 1913, Marlin, Texas, USA, d. 16 February 1991, Oakland, California, USA. A black entrepreneur, Geddins operated a series of labels from the late 40s, recording blues and gospel in the Bay Area. Lacking capital and distribution, he had to lease his recordings to larger labels; if a hit resulted, the artists were lured away. In this way, Geddins lost Lowell Fulson, Jimmy McCracklin, Roy Hawkins, Ray Agee and Koko Taylor. Among other hits, Geddins composed Johnny Ace's 'Last Letter' and 'Haunted House' for Johnny Fuller (the latter was also a hit for Gene Simmons and the Compton Brothers.) Geddins also wrote the classic 'My Time After Awhile', and reworked a pre-war Curtis Jones song into 'Tin Pan Alley'. Geddins was a prime mover behind the Oakland blues scene of the 40s and 50s, but his business abilities were not the equal of his composing and producing talents.

GEORGIA TOM

(see Dorsey, Thomas A.)

GEREMIA, PAUL

b. 21 April 1944, Providence, Rhode Island, USA. Like his contemporary Roy Bookbinder, Geremia has spent a long and fruitful career out of the spotlight, playing the college circuit, small clubs and folk festivals. He was initially influenced by folk artists and took up the harmonica before learning the guitar. Attending the 1964 Newport Folk Festival, he saw bluesmen such as Sleepy John Estes, Mississippi John Hurt, Skip James and Robert Pete Williams, and as a result took up blues-playing as a full-time career. While being particularly known for the authenticity of his Piedmont guitar techniques, Geremia has a comprehensive knowledge of most regional styles. His albums, mostly for smaller specialist labels, have appeared infrequently since 1968 and serve to illustrate his skill.

● ALBUMS: *Just Enough* (Folkways 1968)★★★, *Paul Geremia* (Sire 1971)★★★, *Hard Life Rockin' Chair* (Adelphi 1973)★★★, *I Really Don't Mind Livin'* (Flying Fish 1983)★★★, *My Kinda Place* (Flying Fish 1987)★★★, *Gamblin' Woman Blues* (Red House 1993)★★★, *Self-Portrait In Blues* (Shamrock 1995)★★★, *Live From Uncle Sam's Backyard* (Red House 1997)★★★★.

GIBSON, CLIFFORD

b. 17 April 1901, Louisville, Kentucky, USA, d. 21 December 1963, St. Louis, Missouri, USA. The bulk of Gibson's recordings (20 titles) were made in 1929, by which time he was one of the most respected blues guitarists in St. Louis. Influenced by Lonnie Johnson, Gibson had a similar clear diction and a penchant for original, moralizing lyrics. His guitarwork, characterized by extended treble runs, was outstanding: clean, precise, inventive, and at times astonishingly fast. Away from the studios, he worked as a street musician, assisted by a performing dog. He recorded (in a small band format) as Grandpappy Gibson for Bobbin in 1960.

● COMPILATIONS: *Beat You Doing It* (Yazoo 1988)★★★.

GIBSON, LACY

b. 1 May 1936, Salisbury, North Carolina, USA. Gibson's family settled in Chicago in 1949 and he quickly became involved in the city's blues scene, receiving tips on blues guitar playing from musicians such as Muddy Waters and T-Bone Walker. Besides working with innumerable blues artists, he was also involved in the jazz scene. He recorded with Buddy Guy in 1963 and worked on many sessions. Gibson had two singles of his own on the Repeto label, and had material released on albums by the Alligator, Red Lightnin', El Saturn, and Black Magic labels. He is a strong vocalist and very talented blues guitarist who seems to be equally at home in small west-side Chicago bars or European concert halls.

● ALBUMS: four tracks only *Living Chicago Blues Volume Five* (1980)★★★★, *Switchy Titchy* (Black Magic 1983)★★★, *Crying For My Baby* (Delmark 1996)★★.

GILLESPIE, DANA

b. 30 March 1949, Woking, Surrey, England. A former British water-skiing champion at the age of 15, Gillespie embarked on a singing career during the folk boom of the mid-60s. She befriended Donovan, who played guitar on her 1965 single, 'Donna Donna', but was later drawn towards acting with roles in the Hammer film *The Lost Continent* and the stage musical *Liz*. Dick Rowe, the Decca A&R man who turned down the Beatles, allegedly said to her, 'It doesn't really matter if you can sing or not, you've got a great pair of tits'. However, Gillespie subsequently proved her worth throughout her incredibly varied career. Gillespie's 1969 album, *Box Of Surprises*, presaged spells in *Catch My Soul* and *Jesus Christ Superstar*, and she was then signed to Tony DeFries's Mainman management stable, which also included David Bowie. She was saddled with an overtly sexual image, dressed as a scantily clad, basque-wearing vamp on *Weren't Born A Man*, and as a male sailor scanning soft-core pornography (of herself) on *Ain't Gonna Play No Second Fiddle*, but this approach detracted from any musical content the sets had to offer. In later years Gillespie has continued to perform throughout Europe and the USA with the Dana Gillespie Blues Band, comprising Dave Rowberry (piano, ex-Animals), Ed Deane (guitar), Charlie Hart (bass) replaced by Adrian Stout, Chris Hunt (drums) and Mike Paice (saxophone, harmonica). By the mid-90s Gillespie had won numerous blues magazine polls as best female vocalist, making a nonsense of Dick Rowe's original judgement.

● ALBUMS: *Foolish Seasons* (1967)★★, *Box Of Surprises* (Decca 1969)★★, *Catch My Soul* stageshow soundtrack (1970)★★, *Jesus Christ Superstar* stageshow soundtrack (1973)★★, *Weren't Born A Man* (RCA 1973)★★★, *Ain't Gonna Play No Second Fiddle* (RCA 1974)★★, *Mardi Gras* stageshow soundtrack (1976)★★, with the Mojo Blues Band *The Boogie Woogie Flu* (1981)★★★, *Dana Gillespie's Blue Job* (Ace 1982)★★★, *Solid Romance* (1984)★★★, *Below The Belt* (Ace 1985)★★★, *It Belongs To Me*

(Bellaphon 1986)★★★, *Hot News* (1987)★★★, *Sweet Meat* (Blue Horizon 1989)★★★, *Amor* (1990)★★★, *Blues It Up* (Ace 1990)★★★, *Where Blue Begins* (1991)★★★, with Joachim Palden *Boogie Woogie Nights* (1991)★★★, *Blues One ...* (Wolf 1995)★★★, *Have I Got Blues For You* (Wolf 1996)★★★★.

GILLUM, WILLIAM McKINLEY 'JAZZ'

b. 11 September 1904, Indianola, Mississippi, USA, d. 29 March 1966, Chicago, Illinois, USA. Gillum had a difficult childhood, starting with the deaths of his parents during his infancy. He was made to live with his uncle, a deacon and apparently also a bully. This harrowing period was rendered bearable only by the boy's interest in music, and he quickly learned to play the organ and the harmonica. Gillum ran away at the age of seven and found work in fields and stores, augmenting his income by playing harmonica on street corners until 1923, when he travelled north to Chicago to attempt a career in the music business. He formed a long association with Big Bill Broonzy and started his recording career with him in 1934. The blues harmonica came into its own in 1937 when John Lee 'Sonny Boy' Williamson began his immensely successful career. Although second only to Williamson in popularity, Gillum was nowhere near as inventive a musician or as exciting a singer. His strength lay in his ability as a songwriter. Nevertheless, his work as a performer and sideman was much in demand throughout the 30s and 40s when he was a stalwart of the Bluebird/Victor labels. In 1961 he recorded an album for Folkways Records but participated only marginally in the 'blues boom' before he was shot dead during an argument in 1966. Despite his limitations, at his best Gillum recorded some very satisfactory performances and was popular both with his black audience and white collectors.
● ALBUMS: *You Got To Reap What You Sow* (1970)★★★.
● COMPILATIONS: *Jazz Gillum* (Travellin' Man 1986)★★★, *Best Of Blues 1935-46* (Best Of Blues 1988)★★★.

GILMORE, BOYD

b. 12 June 1910, Belzoni, Mississippi, USA, d. 23 December 1976, Fresno, California, USA. A guitarist, although seemingly not recorded as such, and an exuberant singer, Gilmore recorded for Modern in 1952 with Ike Turner on piano and James Scott Jnr. on guitar; Scott was an early victim of recording technology when an introduction and guitar break by Elmore James were spliced into 'Ramblin' On My Mind' The following year, Gilmore recorded for Sun Records, backed by Earl Hooker's band, but the results were not issued until later. Gilmore performed in delta juke joints for a while, also playing in St. Louis and Pine Bluff, Arkansas, before settling in California for the remainder of his life.
● COMPILATIONS: *Memphis & The Delta* (1969)★★★, *Mississippi Blues* (1972)★★★, *Sun Records The Blues Years* (1985)★★★.

GLENN, LLOYD

b. 21 November 1909, San Antonio, Texas, USA, d. 23 May 1985, Los Angeles, California, USA. Glenn's economic, propulsive technique helped to establish the west coast blues piano style. Having been taught ragtime by his father and uncle, he worked with a number of territory bands, including the Royal Aces and Boots And His Buddies, while in his teens. He first recorded as a member of Don Albert's band for Vocalion Records in 1936. Five years later, he moved to Los Angeles, where he worked the club circuit and became a session musician, most notably on T-Bone Walker's 'Call It Stormy Monday'. He made his first records for Imperial in December 1947 and the following year for RPM. He worked with Edgar Hayes' Stardusters and when the band's Exclusive recordings were bought by Swing Time in 1949, he was taken on as the label's A&R man. There, he formed a long-term relationship with Lowell Fulson and had hits of his own with 'Old Time Shuffle' and 'Chica Boo'. He stayed with Fulson when the latter moved to Checker and secured his own contract with Aladdin, having a minor hit with 'Southbound Special'. A 1960 Chess session remained unissued until individual titles appeared on two compilation albums. Glenn rarely travelled far from Los Angeles, but did visit Europe in 1982 and recorded in Stockholm and in Paris with Clarence 'Gatemouth' Brown. *Blue Ivories* also contained a number of his Swing Time and Aladdin recordings.

● ALBUMS: with Clarence 'Gatemouth' Brown *Heat Wave* (Black & Blue 1982)★★★, *Blue Ivories* (Stockholm 1985)★★★, *After Hours* (Pathe Marconi 1986)★★★, *Honky Tonk* (Night Train 1991)★★★, *Chica Boo* (Night Train 1995)★★★.

● COMPILATIONS: *Wrinkles* (Chess 1989)★★★, *Chess Blues* (Chess 1992)★★★.

GLINN, LILLIAN

b. *c*.1902, near Dallas, Texas, USA. Glinn's career as a blues-singing recording artist and vaudeville performer was brief but successful. She was the protégée of Hattie Burleson, a Texas blues singer who first heard Glinn sing in a Dallas church. Although religious, Glinn allowed herself to pursue the worldly course that led to R.T. Ashford securing her a recording contract with Columbia Records in 1927. During the following two years she recorded 22 titles for that label. Her blues were notable for their apposite lyrics sung in a warm, mature manner. She was still young when she gave up her career to return to the 'other world' of the church, and when interviewed by Paul Oliver in 1970 she was reluctant to recall her long-gone temporal fame.

● COMPILATIONS: *Lillian Glinn: Columbia Blues Issues* (VJM 1987)★★★.

GOOD ROCKIN' CHARLES

b. Charles Edwards, 4 March 1933, Pratt City, Alabama, USA, d. 18 May 1989, Chicago, Illinois. One of the journeyman musicians of the Chicago blues scene, Charles Edwards was engaged to play harmonica on a Jimmy Rogers session in the 50s, but failed to appear; an attempt by Eli Toscano to record him failed for similar reasons, and it was not until 1975 that he recorded an album. This, and a trip to Europe, revealed him to be, if not a innovative performer, then an outgoing and entertaining one, and a harmonica player of considerable authority, influenced by both Sonny Boy 'Rice Miller' and John Lee 'Sonny Boy' Williamson.

● ALBUMS: *Good Rockin' Charles* (Rooster 1976)★★★.

GORDON, JIMMIE

Blues artist Gordon was based in St. Louis, USA, and was billed on one record as 'Peetie Wheatstraw's brother'; on another, 'Black Gal', he appeared as 'Joe Bullum', an attempt by Decca to pass him off as Joe Pullum. Like 'Black Gal', many of his recordings were covers of then-popular blues. Gordon was a slightly anonymous figure, and has excited little attention from researchers. Nevertheless, his records are often worthwhile, for he combines the ingratiating approach of Bumble Bee Slim with some of Wheatstraw's forcefulness, and was often backed by enjoyable small jazz bands. He was also a more than competent pianist, although he seldom played on his own records.

● COMPILATIONS: *Mississippi Murder* (Document 1987)★★★, *Jimmie Gordon* (Blues Document 1989)★★★.

GORDON, ROSCO

b. 23 December 1933, Memphis, Tennessee, USA. A self-taught pianist with no acknowledged influences other than a presumed awareness of the work of Amos Milburn and Little Willie Littlefield. Gordon was part of the Beale Streeters group in the late 40s, alongside Johnny Ace, B.B. King and later, Bobby Bland. Ike Turner, then a freelance producer and talent scout, recognized the potential of Gordon's powerful singing and recorded him for Modern. He was still a teenager when he first recorded at Sam Phillips' Memphis Recording Service in January 1951. Phillips sold masters to both Chess Records in Chicago and RPM in Los Angeles, and thus, Gordon's 'Booted' appeared on both labels, a possible factor in its becoming the number 1 R&B hit in the spring of 1952. The follow-up, 'No More Doggin'', was another Top 10 R&B hit and typified what became known as 'Rosco's Rhythm', a loping boogie shuffle rhythm that predated and perhaps influenced Jamaican ska and blue-heat music. Gordon signed to Phillips' own Sun label in 1955, recording a regional hit, 'The Chicken', which led to his appearance in the film *Rock Baby, Rock It* two years later. Moving to New York, he formed the duo Rosco and Barbara, making singles for Old Town. Many tracks recorded during this time remained unissued until the 70s and 80s. His most well-known song reached number 2 in the R&B charts and was recorded in 1960 for the Chicago-based label Vee Jay. With its catchy sax-driven riff, 'Just A Little Bit' captured the imaginations of British R&B groups as well as black record buyers. A version by Merseybeat band the Undertakers was a minor hit in 1964. Further records for ABC, Old Town, Jomada, Rae-Cox and Calla made little impression and in 1970, Gordon created his own label, Bab-Roc, issuing records by himself and his wife Barbara. An album of new compositions plus remakes of his hits was recorded for Organic Productions in 1971 but never released. A brief visit to England in 1982 brought an onstage reunion with B.B. King at London's 100 Club. At that time he was financing recordings from his own cleaning business.

● ALBUMS: *The Legendary Sun Performers: Rosco Gordon* (Charly 1977)★★★, *Best Of Rosco Gordon Vol. 1* (Ace 1980)★★★, *Rosco Gordon Vol. 2* (Ace 1982)★★★, *Keep On Diggin'* (Mr R&B 1981)★★★, *The Memphis Masters* (Ace 1982)★★★, *Rosco Rocks Again* (JSP 1983)★★★, *Bootin' Boogie* (1990)★★★, *Lets Get High* (Charly 1990)★★★.

GRAND, OTIS
b. Fred Bishti, 14 February 1950, Beirut, Lebanon. Grand has spent most of his life in the USA, with a few years in France. He began playing guitar at the age of 13, citing his influences as B.B. King, T-Bone Walker, Otis Rush and Johnny Otis, and he has played with many San Francisco Bay area blues artists. Otis Grand And The Dance Kings created a sensation when they burst onto the British blues scene in the late 80s, enhanced on the first album (a W.C. Handy award nomination) by the presence of Joe Louis Walker. The second album includes guests Jimmy Nelson, Pee Wee Ellis, and Walker again. A great live attraction, Grand was voted UK Blues Guitarist Of The Year in 1990 and still appears in annual polls throughout the 90s due to his constant touring schedule. He currently resides in Croydon, gateway to the blues!

● ALBUMS: *Always Hot* (Special Delivery 1988)★★★, *He Knows The Blues* (1991)★★★, with Philip Walker *Big Blues From Texas* (1992)★★★, with Joe Houston *The Return Of Honk* (JSP 1994)★★, *Nothing Else Matters* (Sequel 1994)★★★, *Perfume And Grime* (Sequel 1996)★★★.

GRANDERSON, JOHN LEE
b. 11 April 1913, Ellendale, Tennessee, USA, d. 22 August 1979, Chicago, Illinois, USA. Granderson left home when he was in his teens, moving to Chicago, Illinois, in 1928. Although not a professional musician, he did work with John Lee 'Sonny Boy' Williamson, among others. He turned to music full-time in the 60s and was featured as sideman and leader on many anthologies, although he never made a full album in his own right. Granderson sang and played guitar close to the style of the Memphis musicians of his youth. He stopped performing in public in 1975 and died of cancer in 1979.

● COMPILATIONS: with Johnny Young, Carl Martin, John Wrencher *The Chicago String Band* (Testament 1994)★★★.

GRANT, LEOLA B. 'COOT'
b. Leola B. Pettigrew, 17 June 1893, Birmingham, Alabama, USA. Aka Patsy Hunter and Leola B. Wilson. The daughter of a black tavern owner and Indian mother, the attractive Leola B. was directed to a life as an entertainer at a very early age. Between the ages of eight and 17 she was part of Mayme Remington's Pickaninnies and toured Europe and South Africa. Around 1912 she met, and later married, 'Kid' Wesley Wilson with whom she formed a vaudeville duo. Both their act and their marriage were lasting and successful; their career on record began in 1925 and continued until 1946. Grant gave up performing in 1955 and Wilson died in 1958. Their recordings together reflected their stage personae of squabbling husband and wife, but Grant also recorded serious blues numbers under her own name, some in the company of the celebrated guitarist Blind Blake (1926) and others with the Sidney Bechet/Mezz Mezzrow quintet (1946)

● COMPILATIONS: *The Complete Blind Blake* (1991)★★★.

GRAVENITES, NICK
b. Chicago, Illinois, USA. Gravenites grew up on Chicago's south side. He entered university in 1956 and was immediately drawn to its bohemian circle. Having discovered several blues nightclubs, including Frader's Jukebox Lounge, Gravenites joined a loosely knit group

of white aficionados, which included Charlie Musselwhite, Mike Bloomfield and Paul Butterfield. The last-named recorded a Gravenites composition, 'Born In Chicago', on his band's debut album, but it was with Bloomfield that the artist forged a fruitful partnership. In 1967 they formed the short-lived Electric Flag and, having settled in San Francisco, the duo became an integral part of the Bay Area live circuit. *Live At Bill Graham's Fillmore West* captured part of one informal appearance while other tracks, recorded at the same show, formed the basis for Gravenites' solo debut, *My Labors*. The set also featured several studio masters on which Nick was supported by Quicksilver Messenger Service, whose first album he had co-produced. The group later recorded several of his compositions, notably 'Joseph's Coat', which Gravenites later took to Big Brother And The Holding Company during his tenure in the band. Janis Joplin, their former lead singer, meanwhile, completed an impassioned reading of his 'Work Me Lord' on *Kozmic Blues*. The artist wrote and performed part of the soundtrack of *Steelyard Blues* (1973), and remained an active figure during the 70s and 80s, fronting Nick Gravenites Blues, Monday Night Live (with Huey Lewis), as well as several projects with former Quicksilver guitarist John Cipollina. Gravenites remains a highly respected figure, particularly in Europe, where he has toured extensively.

● ALBUMS: with various artists *Live At Bill Graham's Fillmore West* (1969), *My Labors* (1969)★★★, *Steelyard Blues* film soundtrack (1973)★★, *Blue Star* (1980)★★★, *Funkyard In Malibu* (1981)★★★, with John Cipollina *Monkey Medicine* (1982)★★★.

GRAY, ARVELLA

b. Walter Dixon, 28 January 1906, Somerville, Texas, USA, d. 7 September 1980, Chicago, Illinois, USA. Brought up in farm work, Gray left home early and travelled, eventually moving north. In 1930, he lost his sight and two fingers of his left hand in a fight, and took to making music for a living. He played blues, with a rudimentary bottleneck guitar style, on the streets of Chicago for many years, and became well known for his regular appearances at the Maxwell Street outdoor market and other loca-

tions around the city. He attracted the attention of younger blues fans and, in the 60s and 70s, appeared in concerts, festivals and even a couple of short films. His repertoire was limited, but he made a number of records, including some singles, which he sold on the streets.

● ALBUMS: *The Singing Drifter* (1972)★★★.

GRAY, HENRY

b. 19 January 1925, Kenner, Louisiana, USA. Having grown up in rural Louisiana, where he taught himself piano at an early age, Gray moved to Chicago in the 40s. He soon built a solid reputation as a band pianist in the city's blues clubs, and as accompanist on records by artists such as Junior Wells and Billy Boy Arnold. His own recordings in the early 50s featured strong, rocking blues, but they remained unissued for many years. Following a long period with the Howlin' Wolf band, he moved back to Louisiana in 1969. He has continued to work in music, including stints at Tabby Thomas's Blues Box club, and has made several fine records, most notably singles on Jay Miller's Blues Unlimited label and Sunland, and an album recorded during a European tour in 1977. His recorded work in the 90s has been patchy.

● ALBUMS: *They Call Me Little Henry* (1977)★★★★, *Lucky Man* (Blind Pig 1988)★★★, with Clarence Edwards and Short Fuse *Thibodeaux's Cafe* (Sidetrack 1995)★★, *Don't Start That Stuff* (Sidetrack 1996)★★★.

GREEN, CLARENCE

b. 15 March 1929, Galveston, Texas, USA. A self-taught blues piano player, Clarence 'Candy' Green performed on radio and in the numerous clubs of Galveston, a naval town known as the 'Playground Of the South'. His first record was 'Green's Bounce', made in Houston for Eddie's in 1948. His brother Cal Green was a guitarist who also recorded. Clarence recorded 'Hard Headed Woman' (Peacock) before starting army service in 1951. Returning to Texas two years later, he remained a familiar figure in local clubs throughout the 50s, sometimes recording as Galveston Green and working with Clarence 'Gatemouth' Brown. In 1966 he recorded the soulful 'I Saw You Last Night' for Duke Records.

● ALBUMS: *Lady in Red* (1982)★★★.

GREEN, L.C.

b. 23 October 1921, Minter City, Mississippi, USA, d. 24 August 1985, Pontiac, Michigan, USA. Vocally and for his repertoire, L.C. Greene, whose records were issued without the final 'e' to his name, was indebted to John Lee 'Sonny Boy' Williamson. His amplified guitar playing is clearly Mississippi Delta-derived, but probably owes something to the popularity of fellow Detroit blues singer John Lee Hooker. Greene recorded in the early 50s (often with his cousin Walter Mitchell on harmonica) for Joe Von Battle's shoestring operation, which leased a few sides to Dot Records, but he never equalled the fortunes of Hooker, whom he equalled for guitar talent and power, although not for songwriting ability.

● COMPILATIONS: *Detroit Blues Guitar Killers!* (1977)★★★.

GREEN, LEOTHUS 'PORK CHOPS'

Biographical detail is scanty for this remarkable blues pianist and is largely based on the memories of Roosevelt Sykes and Little Brother Montgomery. It is likely that Green originated from Mississippi, but he made his name working in St. Louis, Missouri. He is believed to have died around 1944. His recordings spanned the years 1929-37 and show him to have been a distinctive and versatile performer who deserves greater recognition than he has received to date. His most significant role was in influencing Sykes, for whom he acted as a blues catalyst to some degree. Green also taught Sykes to play Montgomery's most famous and difficult composition, known as 'The Forty-fours'.

● COMPILATIONS: *The Piano Blues, Volume 18* (1983).

GREEN, LIL

b. 22 December 1919, Mississippi, USA, d. 14 April 1954. Growing up in Chicago, Green began to sing in clubs in the mid-30s. By the end of the decade she was appearing regularly at some of the city's best-known nightspots, and was recording with artists such as Big Bill Broonzy, who wrote several songs for her, including 'Country Boy Blues' and 'My Mellow Man'. Green composed some well-known songs herself, among them 'Romance In The Dark', later covered by Mary Ann McCall, Jeri Southern and Billie Holiday. In the early 40s she toured with Tiny Bradshaw and Luis Russell but never really broke away from the black theatre circuit and those areas of the record business that catered specifically for black audiences. The limitations this placed upon her career were severe, even in the case of one of Green's most popular recordings, Joe McCoy's 'Why Don't You Do Right'. The record was heard by Peggy Lee, who was then with Benny Goodman And His Orchestra. Their cover version was an enormous hit, thus further shading Green's fortunes. Although signed by Atlantic Records in 1951, she was in poor health and died in 1954.

● COMPILATIONS: *Romance In The Dark* 1940-46 recordings (RCA 1971)★★★.

GREEN, PETER

b. Peter Greenbaum, 29 October 1946, Bethnal Green, London, England. Having served an apprenticeship in various semi-professional groups, including the Muskrats and the Tridents, Peter Green became one of several guitarists who joined John Mayall's Bluesbreakers as a temporary substitute for Eric Clapton during the latter's late 1965 sabbatical. When Mayall's preferred choice returned to the fold, Green joined Peter Bardens (organ), Dave Ambrose (bass) and Mick Fleetwood (drums) in a short-lived club band, the Peter B's. The quartet completed one single for Columbia Records: 'If You Wanna Be Happy'/'Jodrell Blues' in February 1966. The b-side, an instrumental, showcased Green's already distinctive style. The entire unit subsequently formed the instrumental core to the Shotgun Express, backing singers Rod Stewart and Beryl Marsden, but the guitarist found this role too restrictive and left after a matter of weeks. Green rejoined Mayall in July 1966 when Clapton left to form Cream. Over the next 12 months Green made several telling contributions to the Bluesbreakers' recordings, most notably on the group's third album, *A Hard Road*. This powerful release featured two of the guitarist's compositions, of which 'The Supernatural', a riveting instrumental, anticipated the style he would forge later in the decade. The seeds of Green's own group were sown during several sessions without Mayall and a Bluesbreakers 'solo' single, 'Curly', was released in March 1967. Two months later Green left to form his own group with drummer Mick Fleetwood. The two musicians added a second guitarist, Jeremy Spencer, to form Fleetwood Mac, whose line-up was eventually completed by another former Mayall sideman, John McVie. Fleetwood Mac became one of the most popular groups of the era, developing blues-based origins into an exciting, experimental unit. Green's personality, however, grew increasingly unstable and he became estranged from his colleagues. 'Pete should never have taken acid,' Fleetwood later recalled. 'He was charming, amusing, just a wonderful person (but) off he went and never came back.'

Green has followed an erratic course since leaving the group in May 1970. His solo debut, *The End Of The Game*, was a perplexing collection, consisting of six instrumentals, all of which were little more than jams. An atmospheric single, 'Heavy Heart', followed in June 1971, while a collaboration with one Nigel Watson, 'Beasts Of Burden', was issued the following year. Green also made sporadic session appearances but following a cameo role on Fleetwood Mac's *Penguin* album, the guitarist dropped out of music altogether. The mid-70s proved particularly harrowing; this tormented individual was committed to two mental institutions in the wake of his unsettled behaviour. Green returned to active recording in 1979 with *In The Skies*, a light but optimistic collection that showed traces of his erstwhile fire and included a version of 'A Fool No More', first recorded by Fleetwood Mac. A second album, *Little Dreamer*, offered a more blues-based perspective while two further releases attempted to consolidate the artist's position. In 1982 Green, now calling himself Greenbaum, began touring with a group named Kolors, but the results were unsatisfactory. A hastily concocted album consisting of out-takes and unfinished demos was issued, the last to bear the guitarist's name as leader. A collaboration with former Mungo Jerry singer Ray Dorset aside, this once-skilful musician again abandoned music. Nicknamed the 'Wizard' by local children, Green lived a hermit-like existence, shunning any links with his past. Rumours frequently circulated about his return to the music business, but most were instigated by tabloid journalists pining for his reappearance. In 1995 Gary Moore recorded an album of Peter Green

tracks, *Blues For Greeny*. In 1996 rumours were confirmed that Green was becoming active again. He had purchased a guitar, was keen to play some old blues material, showed up onstage at a Gary Moore gig and best of all played live in May 1996. In August he played with the Splinter Group, Cozy Powell (drums), Nigel Watson (guitar) and Neil Murray (bass) at the Guildford Blues Festival. Although shaky on some numbers, he excelled on two familiar Freddie King songs, 'The Stumble' and 'Going Down'. His new manager Stuart Taylor stated about Green's future, back in music; 'I am cautiously optimistic'. An album from the Splinter group was released in June 1997, and although flawed, it demonstrates Green's commitment to regaining the crown he never sought in the first place - as the UK's finest ever white blues guitarist.

● ALBUMS: *The End Of The Game* (Reprise 1970)★★, *In The Skies* (PVK 1979)★★★, *Little Dreamer* (PVK 1980)★★★, *Whatcha Gonna Do* (PVK 1981)★★, *Blue Guitar* (Creole 1981)★★, *White Sky* (Headline 1982)★★, *Kolors* (Headline 1983)★★, *Legend* (Creole 1988)★★, tribute album *Rattlesnake Guitar: The Music Of Peter Green* (Coast To Coast 1995)★★★, *The Peter Green Splinter Group* (Snapper 1997)★★.

● COMPILATIONS: *Backtrackin'* (Backtrackin' 1990)★★★.

● FURTHER READING: *Peter Green: The Biography*, Martin Celmins.

GREY GHOST

b. Roosevelt Thomas Williams, 7 December 1903, Bastrop, Texas, USA, d. 17 July 1996. For blues researchers, Williams lived up to his nickname for most of his life, known only as a reported influence on Mercy Dee. Williams hoboed around the south-west performing from the 20s to the late 40s, until he settled in Austin. He was recorded by a folklorist in 1940 ('Hitler Blues') and was also recorded after his retirement in 1965. None of these recordings were issued until 1987. Despite an out-of-tune piano, he was clearly a major player in the tradition of the 'Santa Fe' group that included Robert Shaw, Buster Pickens and Pinetop Burks. Grey also had a working pianist's repertoire of ballads and pop songs. Recorded again in 1988, he played a remarkably strident version of 'Somebody Stole

My Gal', which, though slower, was still very impressive.

● ALBUMS: *Grey Ghost* (1987)★★★, *Texas Piano Professors* (1989)★★★.

GRIFFIN BROTHERS

Based in Washington DC around Jimmy and Ernest 'Buddy' Griffin from Norfolk, Virginia, the Griffin Brothers Orchestra comprised Jimmy on trombone, Buddy on piano, Wilbur Dyer and Virgil Wilson on saxophone, with Jimmy Reeves and Emmett 'Nab' Shields on bass and drums. Introduced to Randy Wood in 1950, the band began recording for his label Dot Records; their biggest hits were the songs of their vocalists Margie Day - 'Street Walkin' Daddy' and 'Little Red Rooster', among others - and Tommy Brown - 'Tra-La-La' and 'Weepin' And Cryin''. During a tour in the south in April 1950, Jimmy and Buddy were asked to participate in the Roy Brown session for DeLuxe that resulted in his biggest hit, 'Hard Luck Blues'. However, they returned to their own band, which now included Noble 'Thin Man' Watts on tenor saxophone, and recorded with Dot Records until they split up in 1954. The brothers each made their own solo recordings for Dot after the split, and subsequently, Jimmy went to Atco Records in New York, while Buddy had some success in Chicago on the Chess label with vocalist Claudia Swann.

● COMPILATIONS: *Riffin' With The Griffin Brothers Orchestra* (Ace 1985)★★★, with Margie Day *I'll Get A Deal* (1986)★★★.

GRIFFIN, R.L.

b. 1943, Kilgore, Texas, USA. In 1967, Griffin arrived in Dallas en route to Los Angeles, where he had an uncle. He was already an established musician in his home-town, having played drums in his high school music director's jazz band, and led his own group, the Carvettes. While in Dallas, he sat in on drums with Big Bo & The Arrows, a popular local group with a number of records on Duchess and Gay-Shel. Griffin stayed on, joined the Arrows and became part of the Dallas music scene. He made his first record, 'I'll Follow You', on Gay-Shel with the band. After leaving the Arrows to pursue a singing career, he often worked with Freddie King, who also came from east Texas. He took

Bobby Bland as an early model and later became friendly with Z.Z. Hill. In 1979, he recorded extensively with Al 'TNT' Braggs as his producer, with Braggs' brother James, Andrew 'Junior Boy' Jones and Smokin' Joe Kubek playing guitar on various tracks. A number of singles were released on the Classic label, including 'There Is Something On Your Mind', 'It Don't Have To Be This Way' and 'I Don't Think I'm Going To Make It'. Griffin opened his first club, the Blues Alley, in 1985, later changing its name to the Blues Palace. In 1991, he made a well-received appearance at the Utrecht Blues Estafette.

● ALBUMS: *I Wanna Be Rich* (Galexc 1992)★★★, *It Don't Have To Be This Way* (Black Grape 1994)★★★.

GRIFFITH, SHIRLEY

b. 26 April 1908, Brandon, Mississippi, USA, d. 18 June 1974, Indianapolis, Indiana, USA. Griffith (a male blues singer despite his given name) learned guitar at the age of 10, and gained further instruction from Tommy Johnson, his greatest influence, in the mid-20s. By the end of the decade he had settled in Indianapolis, his home for the rest of his life. He worked with Scrapper Blackwell, but his closest associate was J.T. Adams, with whom he recorded in the early 60s. Griffith was little heard of thereafter, although he recorded a capable solo album in the 70s.

● ALBUMS: *Indiana Avenue Blues* (1963)★★★, *Saturday Blues* (1963)★★★, *Mississippi Blues* (1973)★★★, *Indianapolis Jump* (1976)★★★.

GROSSMAN, STEFAN

b. 16 April 1945, Brooklyn, New York, USA. Grossman discovered traditional music during his forays into Manhattan's Greenwich Village. He studied under Rev. Gary Davis and absorbed the country-blues technique of Son House, Mississippi John Hurt and Skip James before forming the influential Even Dozen Jug Band in 1963. Three years later, Grossman recorded and annotated the instruction record *How To Play Blues Guitar*, and worked with the Fugs, a radical East Side poet/bohemian group. He also played with the Chicago Loop, which featured pianist Barry Goldberg, prior to leaving for Europe in 1967. He remained in Italy and Britain for many years, recording a succession of impressive, if clinical, country blues albums. A superb guitarist, his work is best heard on *Yazoo Basin Boogie* and *Hot Dogs*, while further tuition albums provided valuable insights into the rudiments of different techniques. In the late 70s Grossman helped establish the Kicking Mule label, which acted as a channel for his own releases and those working in a similar vein.

● ALBUMS: *How To Play Blues Guitar* (1966)★★, *Aunt Molly's Murray Farm* (Fontana 1969)★★★, *Grammercy Park Sheik* (Fontana 1969)★★★★, with Danny Kalb *Crosscurrents* (1969)★★★, *Yazoo Basin Boogie* (Transatlantic 1970)★★★★, *Ragtime Cowboy Jew* (Transatlantic 1970)★★★★, *Those Pleasant Days* (Transatlantic 1971)★★★, *Hot Dogs* (Transatlantic 1972)★★★, *Stefan Grossman Live* (Transatlantic 1973)★★★, *Guitar Instrumentals* (Transatlantic 1973)★★★, *Memphis Jellyroll* (1974)★★★, *Bottleneck Seranade* (Transatlantic 1975)★★★, *How To Play Ragtime Guitar* (Xtra 1975)★★, *My Creole Belle* (1976)★★★, *Country Blues Guitar* (Kicking Mule 1977)★★★★, *Fingerpicking Guitar Techniques* (Kicking Mule 1977)★★, *How To Play Blues Guitar, Volume 2* (Kicking Mule 1978)★★, *Stefan Grossman And John Renbourn* (Kicking Mule 1978)★★★, with John Renbourn *Under The Volcano* (Kicking Mule 1980)★★★★, *Thunder On The Run* (Kicking Mule 1980)★★★, *Shining Shadows* (Shanachie 1988)★★★.

● VIDEOS: *Legends Of Traditional Finger Style Guitar* (Music Sales 1995).

● FURTHER READING: *Ragtime Blues Guitarists*, Stefan Grossman. *The Country Blues Song Book*, Stefan Grossman and Steven Calt.

GROUNDHOGS

The original Groundhogs emerged in 1963 when struggling UK beat group the Dollarbills opted for a more stylish name; Tony 'T.S.' McPhee (b. 22 March 1944, Humberstone, Lincolnshire, England; guitar), John Cruickshank (vocals/harp), Bob Hall (piano), Pete Cruickshank (b. 2 July 1945, Calcutta, India; bass) and Dave Boorman (drums) also adopted a 'John Lee' prefix in honour of mentor John Lee Hooker, whom the quintet subsequently backed in concert and on record. John Lee's Groundhogs recorded two singles before

breaking up in 1966. McPhee completed several solo tracks with producer Mike Vernon before rejoining Pete Cruickshank in Herbal Mixture, a short-lived pseudo-psychedelic group. In 1968 the two musicians formed the core of a re-formed Groundhogs alongside Steve Rye (vocals/harmonica) and Ken Pustelnik (drums). The new unit made its debut with the rudimentary *Scratching The Surface*, but were then reduced to a trio by Rye's departure. A second set, *Blues Obituary*, contained two tracks, 'Mistreated' and 'Express Man', which became in-concert favourites as the group embarked on a more progressive direction. This was confirmed with *Thank Christ For The Bomb*, the Groundhogs' powerful 1970 release which cemented a growing popularity. McPhee composed the entire set and his enthusiasm for concept albums was maintained with its successor, *Split*, which examined schizophrenia. Arguably the group's definitive work, this uncompromising selection included the stage classic, 'Cherry Red'. Pustelnik left the group following the release of *Who Will Save The World?* in 1972. Former Egg drummer Clive Brooks (b. 28 December 1949, London, England) was an able replacement, but although the Groundhogs continued to enjoy fervent popularity, their subsequent recordings lacked the fire of those early releases. The trio was also beset by managerial problems and broke up in 1975, although McPhee maintained the name for two disappointing releases, *Crosscut Saw* and *Black Diamond*. The guitarist resurrected the Groundhogs sobriquet in 1984 in the wake of interest in an archive release, *Hoggin' The Stage*. Although Pustelnik was one of several musicians McPhee used for touring purposes, the most effective line-up was completed by Dave Anderson on bass, formerly of Hawkwind, and drummer Mike Jones. McPhee has in recent years appeared as a solo performer and as part of a 70s nostalgia tour, together with various incarnations of his respected band. The Groundhogs' name endures mainly through a live reputation second to none.

● ALBUMS: *Scratching The Surface* (Liberty 1968)★★, *Blues Obituary* (Liberty 1969)★★★, *Thank Christ For The Bomb* (Liberty 1970)★★★, *Split* (Liberty 1971)★★★★, *Who Will Save The World?* (United Artists 1972)★★★, *Hogwash*

(United Artists 1972)★★★, *Solid* (WWA 1974)★★, *Crosscut Saw* (United Artists 1976)★★, *Black Diamond* (United Artists 1976)★★, *Razor's Edge* (Conquest 1985)★★, *Back Against The Wall* (Demi-Monde 1987)★★, *Hogs On The Road* (Demi-Monde 1988)★★, as Tony McPhee's Groundhogs *Who Said Cherry Red?* (Indigo 1996)★★.
● COMPILATIONS: *Groundhogs Best 1969-1972* (United Artists 1974)★★★, *Hoggin' The Stage* double album (Psycho 1984)★★★, *Moving Fast, Standing Still*, comprises McPhee solo album *2 Sides Of* plus *Razor's Edge* (Raw Power 1986)★★, *No Surrender* (Total 1990)★★, *Classic Album Cuts 1968 - 1976* (1992)★★★, *The Best Of ...* (EMI Gold 1997)★★★.

GUESNON, CREOLE GEORGE

b. 25 May 1907, New Orleans, Louisiana, USA, d. 5 May 1968, New Orleans, Louisiana, USA. A jazz banjoist and guitarist, Guesnon worked in many 'Crescent City' bands from 1927 to 1965, often recording as a sideman from 1951. He also toured with Little Brother Montgomery's Jackson-based Southland Troubadours in the mid-30s, and it may have been this experience that prompted 'Mississippi Town', a blues tribute to Jackson recorded in 1940. ('Iberville And Franklin' did the same for New Orleans.) Guesnon did not play on these recordings, which show him to have been a clear-voiced singer, as adept at ballads as with the blues.
● COMPILATIONS: *Blues Bands* (1990)★★★.

GUITAR GABLE

b. Gabriel Perrodin, 17 August 1937, Bellvue, Louisiana, USA. Learning guitar in his teens Gable was influenced by the ringing, melodic style of Guitar Slim. He recorded for Jay Miller with his band the Musical Kings in 1956-57, and several successful singles were issued on Excello Records. The music was very much in the south Louisiana R&B mould, with a touch of New Orleans rock 'n' roll; Gable's distinctive guitar effectively complements the lead vocals of King Karl. Guitar Gable's band retained its popularity in local clubs throughout the rest of the 50s, but it appears that he retired from performing when he joined the army around 1959.
● ALBUMS: *Cool, Calm, Collected* (Flyright 1984)★★★.

GUITAR GABRIEL
(see Jones, Nyles)

GUITAR NUBBIT

b. Alvin Hankerson, 1923, Fort Lauderdale, Florida, USA. Nicknamed 'Nubbit' following the loss of the tip of his right thumb at the age of three in a hurricane, Hankerson grew up in Georgia, relocating to Boston, Massachusetts, in 1945. Taking up guitar in 1948, he was unable to teach himself and abandoned the instrument after a year, only resuming in 1954 when he took some lessons. In the early 60s, he recorded for the local Bluestown label and, being a young, original blues singer, caused some excitement among the attentive white audiences. His isolation from the mainstream of blues led to some remarkable lyrics ('I whistled to my shotgun, and it crawled down off the wall'), but heard at length, his music lacks variety. After a brief exposure on the local folk scene, Nubbit returned to obscurity. In 1990 he released a 12-inch single, 'Reliving The Legend'.
● ALBUMS: *Reliving The Legend* (Matchbox 1990)★★.

GUITAR SHORTY

b. David William Kearney, 8 September 1939, Houston, Texas, USA. A penchant for acrobatics disguises Shorty's real talent as a blues guitarist. He grew up in Kissimmee, Florida, where his uncle Willie Quarterman introduced him to the guitar. At 17 he was playing in the house band at Tampa's Club Royal, where he first acquired his stage name. A year later, he went to Chicago with singer Clarence Jolly and recorded a single, 'You Don't Treat Me Right', for Cobra Records. After returning to Florida, he toured with Ray Charles and Guitar Slim, whose own onstage antics led him to incorporate flips into his act. By 1959, he was in Los Angeles, where he recorded three singles for the Pull label. He then spent the next five years touring through Canada, before settling in Seattle and marrying Jimi Hendrix's step-sister, Marsha. While continuing to work up and down the west coast, it was not until 1985 that he had another record release, 'They Call Me Guitar Shorty', on Olive Branch. Another single, 'On The Rampage', followed, which in 1989 became the title track of his first album. Two years later, he made his

British debut at the Langbaurgh International Blues Festival and also recorded *My Way On The Highway* with the Otis Grand Blues Band. *Topsy Turvy* was recorded in New Orleans and Austin, Texas, in April 1993, with second guitarist Clarence Hollimon and his wife, Carol Fran, duetting on the opening track, 'I'm So Glad I Met You'. *Get Wise To Yourself* was further proof of the 'late developer syndrome'.

● ALBUMS: *Jericho Alley Blues Flash! Vol. 2* (Diving Duck 1988)★★★, *On The Rampage* (Olive Branch 1989)★★★, with Otis Grand Blues Band *My Way On The Highway* (JSP 1992)★★★, *Topsy Turvy* (Black Top 1993)★★★, *Alone In His Field* (Trix 1995)★★★, *Get Wise To Yourself* (Black Top 1996)★★★.

GUNTER, ARTHUR

b. 23 May 1926, Nashville, Tennessee, USA, d. 16 March 1976, Port Huron, Michigan, USA. Gunter wrote and recorded 'Baby Let's Play House' for Excello in the summer of 1954. That December, the Thunderbirds vocal group recorded their version, issued on DeLuxe, in Miami. Three months later, it was one side of Elvis Presley's fourth Sun single. This marked the point at which Gunter realized that he had no ambition to write another hit. His father was a preacher; he and his brothers, Jimmy and Junior, and cousin Julian, sang spirituals as the Gunter Brothers Quartet. He learned guitar from another brother, Larry, and absorbed blues old and new - Blind Boy Fuller and Big Boy Crudup, Jimmy Reed and Blind Lemon Jefferson. He frequented the record store run by Ernie Young, founder of Excello and Nashboro. There he met pianist Skippy Brooks, and played with Brooks' band, the Kid King Combo. Most of the time he performed just with cousin Julian on drums. 'Baby Let's Play House' was his first record, and a hit locally. None of his succeeding 11 singles did as well, and Excello dropped him in 1961. His brother Little Al also made two singles for the company. Gunter moved to Port Huron in 1966 and completely abandoned music. In 1973 he won $50,000 in the Michigan State Lottery, and played as part of the Ann Arbor Blues Festival's 'Music Of Detroit' afternoon.

● COMPILATIONS: *Black And Blues* (Excello 1987)★★★, *Baby Let's Play House: The Best Of Arthur Gunter* (Excello 1995)★★★.

GUY, BUDDY

b. George Guy, 30 July 1936, Lettsworth, Louisiana, USA. An impassioned and influential guitarist, Buddy Guy learned to play the blues on a rudimentary, home-made instrument, copying records he heard on the radio. By the mid-50s he was sitting in with several of the region's leading performers, including Slim Harpo and Lightnin' Slim. In 1957 Guy moved north to Chicago. He initially joined the Rufus Foreman Band but was quickly established as an artist in his own right. The guitarist's first single was released the following year, but his career prospered on meeting Willie Dixon. This renowned composer/bassist brought the young musician to Chess Records where, as part of the company's house band, he appeared on sessions by Muddy Waters and Howlin' Wolf. Guy also made several recordings in his own right, of which the frenzied 'First Time I Met The Blues' and the gutsy 'Stone Crazy' are particularly memorable. As well as pursuing his own direction, Guy also established a fruitful partnership with Junior Wells. Having completed telling contributions to the harpist's early releases, *Hoodoo Man Blues* and *It's My Life Baby*, the guitarist recorded a series of excellent albums for the Vanguard label that combined classic 'Chicago' blues with contemporary soul styles. His fiery playing was rarely better and Guy won attention from the rock audience through appearances at the Fillmore auditorium and his support slot on the Rolling Stones' 1970 tour. The artist's career lost momentum during the 70s as the passion that marked his early work receded. Guy has nonetheless retained a considerable following on the international circuit. In 1990 he was one of the guests during Eric Clapton's memorable blues night at London's Royal Albert Hall. The following year he released the magnificent *Damn Right I Got The Blues* which was recorded with the assistance of Clapton, Jeff Beck and Mark Knopfler. The critical acclaim put Guy firmly back into the higher echelon of outstanding blues guitarists currently performing. This standing was further enhanced by the excellent *Feels Like Rain*. The trilogy of recent albums was completed with *Slippin' In* in 1994, although for many this was an anti-climactic and disappointing record. *Live! The Real Deal* was an excellent live album recorded with

G.E. Smith and the Saturday Night Live Band.
● ALBUMS: *Blues From Big Bill's Copa Cobana* (1963), *A Man And The Blues* (Vanguard 1968)★★★★, *Coming At You* (Vanguard 1968)★★★, *This Is Buddy Guy* (Vanguard 1968)★★★★, *Blues Today* (Vanguard 1968)★★★, *This Is Buddy Guy* (Vanguard 1969)★★★★, *Hot And Cool* (Vanguard 1969)★★★, *First Time I Met The Blues* (Python 1969)★★★, with Junior Wells *Buddy And The Juniors* (Harvest 1970)★★★★, *Hold That Plane!* (Vanguard 1972)★★★, *Buddy Guy And Junior Wells Play The Blues* (Atlantic 1972)★★★★, *Got To Use Your House* (Blues Ball 1979)★★★, *Dollar Done Fell* (JSP 1982)★★★, *DJ Play My Blues* (JSP 1982)★★★, with Wells *Drinking' TNT And Smokin' Dynamite* (Red Lightnin' 1982)★★★, *The Original Blues Brothers - Live* (Blue Moon 1983)★★★, *Ten Blue Fingers* (JSP 1985)★★★, *Live At The Checkerboard, Chicago, 1979* (JSP 1988)★★★, *Breaking Out* (JSP 1988)★★★, with Wells *Alone & Acoustic* (Hightone 1991)★★★★, *Damn Right I Got The Blues* (Silvertone 1991)★★★★, with Wells *Alive In Montreux* (1992)★★★, *My Time After Awhile* (1992)★★★, *Feels Like Rain* (Silvertone 1993)★★★★, *American Bandstand Vol. 2* (1993)★★★, *Slippin' In* (Silvertone 1994)★★★, *Live! The Real Deal* (Silvertone 1996)★★★.
● COMPILATIONS: *I Left My Blues In San Francisco* (Chess 1967)★★★, *In The Beginning* (Red Lightnin' 1971)★★, *I Was Walking Through The Woods* (Chess 1974)★★★, *Chess Masters* (Charly 1987)★★★★, *Stone Crazy* (Alligator 1988)★★★, *I Ain't Got No Money* (Flyright 1989)★★★, *The Best Of Buddy Guy* (Rhino 1992)★★★, *The Complete Chess Studio Sessions* (Chess 1992)★★★★.
● VIDEOS: *Messin' With The Blues* (BMG Video 1991), *Buddy Guy Live: The Real Deal* (Wienerworld 1996).
● FURTHER READING: *Damn Right I Got The Blues: Blues Roots Of Rock N Roll*, Donald E. Wilcock and Buddy Guy.

GUY, PHIL

b. 28 April 1940, Lettsworth, Louisiana, USA. Phil, the younger brother of Buddy Guy, learned to play guitar as a child. He followed in Buddy's footsteps, playing after him with local artists Big Poppa and Raful Neal. He recorded as accompa-nist for his brother in 1957, for Neal around 1958, and for Slim Harpo (James Moore) in the mid-60s. He joined his brother's band in Chicago in 1969, and has been based there ever since. He has worked and recorded with many of the city's leading artists, such as his brother, Junior Wells, Byther Smith, and Jimmy Dawkins. Phil spent most of the 80s consolidating his own musical career, showing himself to be a tough electric Chicago bluesman, with a raw guitar style influenced by artists including Guitar Slim. He has recorded several fine sets for JSP; albums have also appeared on Isabel and Red Lightning.
● ALBUMS: *The Red Hot Blues Of Phil Guy* (JSP 1982)★★★, *Bad Luck Boy* (JSP 1983)★★★, *It's A Real Mutha Fucka* (JSP 1985)★★★, *I Was Once A Gambler* (JSP 1987)★★★, *Tina Nu* (JSP 1989)★★★, *Tough Guy* (Red Lightnin' 1989)★★★.
● COMPILATIONS: *Breaking Out On Top - The Best Of The JSP Sessions* (JSP 1995)★★★★.

HALL, BOB

b. *c.*1943, London, England. At the time of the release of his debut solo album in 1993, Hall had established a significant reputation as a blues pianist and keyboard player. Howlin' Wolf, John Lee Hooker, Chuck Berry, Mississippi Fred McDowell, Little Walter, Homesick James, Savoy Brown, Snooky Pryor, Lightnin' Slim, Alexis Korner, Jack Bruce, Muddy Waters, Jo Ann Kelly and the Groundhogs are among the many artists he has accompanied. Moreover, despite appearing on nearly 100 separate blues albums, Hall never gave up his day job as a solicitor in Swindon, Wiltshire, and Sheffield,

Yorkshire. He first heard blues via Winifred Atwell's boogie-woogie in the early 50s, when he started playing as an 11-year-old in Bermondsey, London. However, it was his first exposure to Howling Wolf's 'Smokestack Lightning' that really initiated his lifelong obsession with the blues. He was trained by Brighton teacher Mr Heckman, a former collaborator with Stéphane Grappelli, and his father, also a pianist. By the time he enrolled at Durham University he was enraptured by the British blues boom pioneered by the Yardbirds, and applied continually for piano positions through *Melody Maker*'s situations vacant column. Eventually he gained an audition for the Dollar Bills, led by Tony McPhee, which proved successful. The group soon changed its name to the Groundhogs, and Hall's first live experience came backing John Lee Hooker on his UK tour in 1964. From that point onwards he began an odyssey of support appearances for blues greats such as Fred McDowell, Little Walter, Howlin' Wolf and Muddy Waters, both on stage and on record. He also wrote much of the material for a band called Tramp, which included Mick Fleetwood, Dave Kelly and Jo Ann Kelly. Sadly, after one album for Spark Records, the group fell apart. Together with Rolling Stones pianist Ian Stewart, drummer Charlie Watts and another pianist, George Green, Hall then recorded *Jamming The Boogie* for Black Lion Records, another record that achieved significant acclaim. Between such projects he continued to meet and play with visiting American blues artists. To commemorate the 50th anniversary of the release of the first boogie-woogie record, his next project was Rocket 88 (1981), which also involved Alexis Korner, Jack Bruce, Watts and Stewart. Two years were then lost to illness in the early 80s. It was only in the 90s that Hall began to think of himself as a songwriter rather than accompanist, leading to the release of *At The Window* in 1993, although he continued to tour and record in a group format with the Blues Band.

● ALBUMS: with Dave Kelly *Survivors* (Appaloosa 1979)★★★, *At The Window* (Lake 1993)★★★, *Alone With The Blues* (Lake 1995)★★★.

HALL, JIMMY

Co-founder of 70s R&B-influenced boogie band Wet Willie, Hall recorded his solo debut following the group's break-up in 1980. With backing from former bandmates, including brother Jack Hall, the album featured the hit single 'I'm Happy That Love Has Found You'. The follow-up was a musically diverse album, blending rockabilly, swing and bebop, but was to be Hall's last for Epic Records. He worked with Dickey Betts (Allman Brothers Band) and Chuck Leavell in BHLT, but it was for his featured vocals on Jeff Beck's *Flash* that Hall received greatest praise, gaining a Grammy nomination for Best Male Vocalist. During the 90s Hall has toured with his band the Prisoners Of Love, and worked as band leader and vocalist, saxophonist and harmonica player for Hank Williams Jr. In 1996 he released a new solo album which, featuring material by blues greats including Muddy Waters and Elmore James, proved to be his most blues-oriented record to date. It was also noticeable how Hall's voice had matured into a distinctive blues instrument.

● ALBUMS: *Touch You* (Epic 1980)★★★, *Cadillac Tracks* (Epic 1982)★★★, *Rendezvous With The Blues* (Capricorn 1996)★★★.

HALL, VERA

b. *c.*1906, Livingstone, Alabama, USA, d. 29 January 1964, Tuscaloosa, Alabama, USA. Primarily a gospel singer whose speciality was the unaccompanied spiritual, Vera Hall was discovered by author Ruby Tarrt, who introduced her to John and Alan Lomax. Between 1937 and 1940 the Lomaxes recorded in excess of 50 a cappella spirituals, blues and children's songs by Hall, together with a further 60 duetting with her cousin, Dock Reed. She resurfaced in the late 40s when folklorist Harold Courlander found her working as a housekeeper in Tuscaloosa and recorded her as part of his 'Negro Folk Music Of Alabama' project for Folkways Records. Alan Lomax returned to Alabama in 1959 and included her in his 'Southern Folk Heritage' series for Atlantic Records, the most memorable of which was her haunting field holler, 'Wild Ox Moan'.

HAMMOND, JOHN

b. John Paul Hammond III, 13 November 1943, he is the son of jazz and rock producer John Hammond Jnr. The younger Hammond took up blues guitar and harmonica while at college and joined the New York coffee-house scene in 1963. In the same year he recorded the first of five albums for Vanguard Records. On *So Many Roads*, he was backed by the Hawks, the group who later became the Band. Even after the folk/blues boom had subsided, Hammond continued with his Chicago-blues based music, playing at small clubs and campuses. He continued to record frequently, for Atlantic Records (1968-70), where Robbie Robertson and Bill Wyman were among the accompanists, and Columbia Records (1971-73), where he took part in a so-called 'supersession' in 1973 with Dr. John and Mike Bloomfield. Hammond's work was also heard on the soundtrack of the film *Little Big Man* in 1970. Oblivious to musical fashion, Hammond maintains his commitment to blues. He has released albums on a range of labels including Capricorn, Sonet, Rounder, Demon and Point Blank, the Virgin subsidiary. It is as a tireless live performer that Hammond shines; his acoustic blues is heard all over the world at blues and folk festivals. His dedication to his art is inspiring.

● ALBUMS: *John Hammond* (Vanguard 1963)★★★, *Big City Blues* (Vanguard 1964)★★★, *Country Blues* (Vanguard 1965)★★★, *So Many Roads* (Vanguard 1965)★★★, *Mirrors* (Vanguard 1967)★★★, *I Can Tell* (Atlantic 1968)★★★, *Sooner Or Later* (Atlantic 1968)★★★, *Southern Fried* (Atlantic 1970)★★★, *Source Point* (Columbia 1971)★★★, *Little Big Man* film soundtrack (1971)★★★, *I'm Satisfied* (Columbia 1972)★★★, *When I Need* (Columbia 1973)★★, *Triumvirate* (Columbia 1973)★★★, *Spirituals To Swing* (Vanguard 1973)★★, *Can't Beat The Kid* (Capricorn 1975)★★★, *My Spanish Album* (1975)★★★, *John Hammond: Solo* (Vanguard 1976)★★★, *Footwork* (Vanguard 1978)★★★, *Hot Tracks* (Vanguard 1978)★★★, *Mileage* (Sonet 1980)★★★, *Frogs For Snakes* (Rounder 1982)★★★, *John Hammond Live* (Rounder 1984)★★★, *Nobody But You* (Rounder 1987)★★★, *Prophet And Higher Ground* (1988)★★★, *Got Love If You Want It* (Point Blank 1992)★★★, *Source Point* (1993)★★★, *Trouble No More* (Point Blank 1993)★★★, *Frogs For Snakes* (Rounder 1994)★★★, *Found True Love* (Pointblank 1995)★★★.

● COMPILATIONS: *The Best Of John Hammond* (Vanguard 1970)★★★★.
● VIDEOS: *From Bessie Smith To Bruce Springsteen* (Columbia 1991).
● FURTHER READING: *Hammond On Record*, John Hammond.

HAMMOND, JOHN, JNR.

b. John Henry Hammond II, 15 December 1910, New York City, USA, d. July 1987. Hammond became a jazz fan as a child and in the early 30s was a record reviewer for *Melody Maker*. Hammond also used his inherited wealth to finance recordings at a time when economic depression had made record companies unwilling to invest in jazz. He produced Billie Holiday's first session as well as tracks by Teddy Wilson, Bessie Smith, Mildred Bailey and Artie Shaw. In 1936 a chance hearing of a broadcast by Count Basie from Kansas City (Hammond was listening on his car radio outside a Chicago hotel where Benny Goodman was appearing) led him to actively promote Basie's career. In 1938/9, Hammond devised and organized the *Spirituals To Swing* concerts at New York's Carnegie Hall. These were designed to show the full breadth of black American music and featured gospel (Rosetta Tharpe), blues (Big Bill Broonzy), New Orleans jazz (Sidney Bechet) and contemporary dance music (Benny Goodman, who married Hammond's sister, Alice). In the early 40s, he worked for Columbia Records and after army service moved to Keynote, Mercury and Vanguard as a staff producer. Hammond returned to Columbia in 1958 and was chiefly responsible for signing such folk revival artists as Pete Seeger and Bob Dylan, who was known at the company as 'Hammond's folly' in the early years of his contract. Hammond was the producer of Dylan's first two albums. While chiefly involved with jazz and blues - he supervised reissues of Bessie Smith and Robert Johnson, and was a founder of the Newport Jazz Festival - Hammond continued to bring new artists to Columbia during the 60s and 70s, most notably Leonard Cohen, George Benson and Bruce Springsteen. His son, John Hammond III (often confusingly titled John Hammond Jnr. himself, which leads to his father being mistakenly identified as Hammond Snr.) is a noted white blues singer whose recording career began in the mid-60s.

HAMSTERS

Based in Southend, Essex, this blues-rock trio was formed at a rehearsal on 1 April 1987 by ex-Dr Feelgood member 'Snail's Pace Slim'. Named after an alias used by the Sex Pistols, the band began playing locally, their powerful live performances belying the inoffensiveness of their name. Setting up their own mailing list to promote records and gigs, they currently hold an astonishing 18,000 names on database, justifying their strong belief in self-promotion. Perennial regulars on the club/pub circuit in the south of England, the enthusiasm of the band's loyal live following easily outweighs the harsh criticism meted out to them by members of the press. They have also released several albums to date, including their debut *Electric Hamsterland*, which consisted entirely of Hendrix cover versions.

● ALBUMS: *Electric Hamsterland* (On The Beach 1990)★★, *Hamsterjam* (1992)★★★, *Route 666* (1994)★★★.

HANDY, W.C.

b. William Christopher Handy, 16 November 1873, Muscle Shoals, Alabama, USA, d. 28 March 1958. Handy began his musical career as a cornetist with a brass band and also led a vocal quartet that appeared at the 1893 Chicago Exposition. For the next few years he worked with minstrel shows, taught, and listened extensively to the richly varied music he heard on his travels around the south. Among this music were early examples of the blues. Fascinated, Handy began noting down many of the songs, which he then adapted for his own performances. In this way he popularized the emergent form, but also made it impossible to discover just how much of the music attributed to him he actually wrote and how much originated with itinerant singers. In 1917 Handy took his Memphis Orchestra to New York, where he recorded, but by the 20s he was playing only sporadically, his career interrupted by an eye disease that soon resulted in blindness.

Although he made subsequent appearances in bands and on recording sessions with noted jazzmen such as Jelly Roll Morton and Red Allen, Handy spent most of the 20s and 30s engaged in his music publishing company which handled all the marvellous and highly popular tunes credited to him. Among these were 'Memphis Blues', 'Beale Street Blues', 'Yellow Dog Blues', 'Ole Miss' and the tune with which his name is most readily linked, 'St Louis Blues'. In 1941 he published his autobiography. Late in life Handy was much celebrated; a tribute concert was held at Carnegie Hall in 1938 and in 1956 Louis Armstrong and his All Stars played 'St Louis Blues' in company with the New York Philharmonic Orchestra, conducted by Leonard Bernstein, at the Lewisohn Stadium in New York. The film *St. Louis Blues* (1958), starring Nat 'King' Cole as Handy, failed accurately to represent his story. A statue to Handy stands in Memphis and he is one of only two people from the world of jazz and blues to be depicted on US postage stamps (the other is Duke Ellington). Handy, justifiably, if inaccurately, termed 'The Father of the Blues', died in March 1958.

● COMPILATIONS: *Father Of The Blue Tune* (1923-62)★★★.

HARE, AUBURN 'PAT'

b. 20 December 1930, Parkin, Arkansas, USA, d. 26 September 1980, St. Paul, Minnesota, USA. Pat Hare is best known for his excellent work as an accompanying guitarist with Little Junior Parker's Blue Flames, and then with the Muddy Waters band in Chicago, Illinois. He appeared on several records by both, during the 50s and early 60s. Prior to that he had played with Howlin' Wolf and done session work in Memphis at the Sam Phillips studio, where he accompanied James Cotton on his earliest recordings. While there, he recorded several tracks under his own name (not issued until many years later), including one titled 'I'm Gonna Murder My Baby'. This title proved to be prophetic, as he was convicted in 1964 for murdering his girlfriend and a policeman; he died of cancer while still serving his sentence in prison.

● ALBUMS: *The Sun Box* (1985)★★★.

HARLEM HAMFATS

Despite their name, the Hamfats were based in Chicago, Illinois, and were perhaps the first group created (by J. Mayo Williams) solely to make records. With some variation, the personnel consisted of New Orleans trumpeter Herb Morand, the brothers Joe and Charlie McCoy on guitar and mandolin, clarinettist Odell Rand, pianist Horace Malcolm, John Lindsay or Ransom Knowling on bass, and Pearlis Williams or Fred Flynn on drums. Morand and Joe McCoy (as 'Hamfoot Ham') handled the vocals. The Hamfats blended New Orleans jazz with blues, the primary aim being to provide entertaining, danceable music. Their first release, 'Oh! Red', was a considerable hit in 1936, and was frequently reworked, both by the Hamfats themselves and by others. They recorded extensively, and were also used as studio accompanists until 1939, by which time Morand had returned to New Orleans, and changing fashions had made their sound no longer commercially attractive.
● ALBUMS: *Hot Chicago Jazz, Blues & Jive* (Folklyric 1986)★★★, *Harlem Hamfats 1936-1939* (Document 1989)★★★, *Harlem Hamfats 1936/37* (Neovox 1989)★★, with Rosetta Howard *Harlem Hamfats* (Earl Archives 1990)★★★.
● COMPILATIONS: *Complete Recorded Works In Chronological Order, Vols. 1-4* (Document 1995)★★★.

HARMAN, JAMES

b. 8 June 1946, Anniston, Alabama, USA. One of the leading white harmonica players on America's west coast, Harman's love of the instrument was instilled in him by his father. As a youngster in Alabama, James played with a local blues musician called Radio Johnson, and bought R&B records. By the age of 16 he was leading his own band. In 1970 he moved to California and had to abandon music for some years due to health problems. However, he did not refrain from playing music for long, and in the 80s he made acclaimed recordings for the Rivera and Rhino labels. Harman is a fine singer and harmonica player whose approach to the blues is one of fun and enjoyment.
● ALBUMS: *Those Dangerous Gentlemens* (Rhino 1987)★★★, *Extra Napkins* (Rivera

1988)★★★, *Strictly Live ... In '85 Volume One* (Rivera 1990)★★★, *Two Sides To Every Story* (Black Top 1993)★★★, *Cards On The Table* (Black Top 1994)★★★, *Black And White* (Black Top 1995)★★★, *Extra Napkins* (Cannonball 1997)★★.
● COMPILATIONS: *Icepick's Story* (Me And My Blues 1997)★★★★.

HARMONICA FATS

b. Harvey Blackston, 8 September 1927, McDade, Louisiana, USA. Fats taught himself to play harmonica while growing up on his grandfather's farm. He subsequently moved to Los Angeles during World War II and became a professional musician in 1956. In the early 60s his debut recording, a raunchy cover of Hank Ballard's 'Tore Up', was a hit and remains a popular item. For some years Fats worked on tours with major artists, but in the 70s he returned to club work, and has recorded for many labels. His gruff vocals and down-home harmonica are often backed by soul bands. In 1986 Fats teamed up with local disc jockey and bandleader Bernie Pearl, whose music is much more in sympathy with Fats' straightforward, rocking blues approach.
● ALBUMS: with Bernie Pearl *Live At Café Lido* (1990)★★★, with Pearl *I Had To Get Nasty* (1991)★★★, with Pearl *Two Heads Are Better* (Bee Bump 1994)★★★, with Bernie Pearl *Blow Fat Daddy Blow* (Bee Bump 1996)★★.

HARRIS, ALFRED

b. possibly Mississippi, USA. An obscure harmonica player and singer, Alfred Harris (aka Blues King Harris or Johnny Harris) recorded on three separate occasions in the 50s, each time under a different name. The first, in 1950 or 1951, was during a field trip by the Bihari brothers, in Mississippi, Arkansas or Tennessee, and featured Harris with a second guitarist, playing acoustic, in a very down-home style. A few years later there was a session in Chicago, with James Bannister and Earl Dranes, in a more electric, urban style. Neither of these two sessions was issued until many years later. Finally, there was a single, also recorded in Chicago, in 1956.
● ALBUMS: *Harmonica Blues Kings* (1986)★★★.

HARRIS, COREY

b. 21 February 1969, Denver, Colorado, USA. One of the new breed of young, acoustic country bluesmen currently reinventing the Delta Blues, Harris is a talented multi-instrumentalist who draws inspiration from a wide range of musical influences. After gaining a degree in anthropology, he visited Cameroon several times in the early 90s, studying the local patois Pidgin before returning to America to teach for a year in Louisiana. While he was teaching, Harris began performing on the streets of New Orleans (playing guitar, trumpet and kazoo), and he has stated in interviews how his experience as a street musician 'helped [me] to project, and [know] what songs to play to get people's attention.' Like fellow modern-day bluesmen Alvin Youngblood Hart and Eric Bibb, Harris only covers old blues songs that are still relevant, and the songs on his albums draw more lyrical inspiration from rap than from the blues. Musically he blends acoustic blues with African rhythms (including playing the jun-jun, a drum indigenous to West Africa), building upon the influence of country blues legend Taj Mahal. His last album, *Fish Ain't Bitin'*, was acclaimed as one of the finest blues releases of the year.
● ALBUMS: *Between Midnight And Day* (Alligator 1995)★★★, *Fish Ain't Bitin'* (Alligator 1997)★★★★.

HARRIS, EDWARD P.

b. 22 August 1923, Leasburg, North Carolina, USA, d. 22 October 1953, Newark, New Jersey, USA. Harris learned guitar from his father, and is said to have been an itinerant musician before settling in Newark, but his background is otherwise obscure. None of the records he made between 1950 and 1952 were ever released under Harris's real name; he was variously known as Carolina Slim, Lazy Slim Jim, Jammin' Jim, Paul Howard and Country Paul. His music is a blend, probably acquired mainly from records, of the contemporary Texas styles of Lightnin' Hopkins and the 30s North Carolina/Georgia music of Buddy Moss and Blind Boy Fuller.
● ALBUMS: *Faded Picture Blues* (1970)★★★, *Carolina Blues & Boogie* (1985)★★★.

HARRIS, HI TIDE

b. 26 March 1946, San Francisco, California, USA, d. 1990, Japan. His real name was reportedly Willie Boyd or Willie Gitry. He was brought up in Richmond, California, and sang in vocal groups as a youngster; he also learned to play guitar in the early 60s, going on to play with Big Mama Thornton, Jimmy McCracklin, and others (he also recorded with McCracklin). Following a spell in Los Angeles (1969-71), he formed his own band around 1972. In 1973 he joined Charlie Musselwhite's band, and the following year he toured and recorded with John Mayall. Harris was also involved in film work: he wrote the theme song for *Mandingo* (sung by Muddy Waters) and sang on the soundtrack of *Leadbelly*. Harris was 'an excellent guitarist in both the slide and regular fingerstyles' (*Blues Unlimited*).
● ALBUMS: *Celebrating With Hi-Tide Harris* (1980)★★, *Nice & High!* (P-Vine 1995)★★★.

HARRIS, PEPPERMINT

b. Harrison D. Nelson Jnr., 17 July 1925, Texarkana, Texas, USA. This blues singer acquired his moniker in the 40s when Bob Shad, proprietor of Sittin' In With Records, simply could not remember his new signing's real name. Harris chose to hold onto the name as a means of keeping his religious family from knowing that he engaged in the practice of singing that form of music. Harris's major recordings were recorded for Aladdin Records in the early 50s, the best known being his 1951 number 1 R&B waxing 'I Get Loaded' (more recently covered by Elvis Costello and Los Lobos). Harris later recorded for many different labels including Modern Records, X, Cash & Money, Combo, Checker Records, Duke Records, Jewel Records and others. He continued to record into the 70s.
● ALBUMS: *Sittin' In With Historical Recordings* (1979)★★★, *I Get Loaded* (Route 66 1987)★★★ *Shout And Rock* (Sundown 1988)★★★, *Texas On My Mind* (Collectables 1996)★★.
● COMPILATIONS: *Houston Can't Be Heaven* (1989)★★★.

HARRIS, WILLIAM

Born around the turn of the 20th century, Harris was a blues singer and guitarist from the Mississippi Delta who made recordings in 1927 and 1928 (although not all of them have survived). This makes him one of the very earliest musicians from that hugely influential area to make a record, and he is also of considerable interest in his own right. His vocals had a plaintive, crying effect that lent great emotional power to his songs, which varied from rocking dance tunes to intense slow blues, punctuated by flashing single string runs, and wedded to lyrics notable for their memorable if rather bizarre imagery (e.g., 'Have you ever woke up with bullfrogs on your mind?'). This all adds up to a very distinctive and compelling musical legacy.

● ALBUMS: *William Harris And Buddy Boy Hawkins* (1978)★★★.

HARRIS, WYNONIE

b. 24 August 1915, Omaha, Nebraska, USA, d. 14 June 1969. As a youth Harris played drums in and around his home-town before moving to Los Angeles in the early 40s. There he played, danced, sang and worked in several non-musical capacities in various clubs and theatres, also appearing in a film, *Hit Parade Of 1943*. Along with many other singers of the time, Harris was heavily influenced by Louis Jordan and, after a spell with the Lucky Millinder big band, he went solo as an R&B singer. He had already had a minor hit with Millinder, 'Who Threw The Whiskey In The Well?', and followed this up with 'Bloodshot Eyes' and 'Good Rocking Tonight'. Unfortunately for his career prospects, audiences were turning towards the emerging and very much younger rock 'n' roll singers. Harris regularly worked with jazz-orientated groups, including those led by Illinois Jacquet, Lionel Hampton and Charles Mingus. Essentially a contemporary urban blues singer with an extrovert, jumping style, Harris had the misfortune to appear at a time when the music scene did not embrace his particular style of blues. In the early 50s he was forced to retire, but attempted a comeback in the early 60s and again in 1967. The times were a little more receptive to Harris's undoubted talent, but by that time he had developed lung cancer, from which he died on 14 June 1969. His son, Wesley Devereaux, is a good popular singer who has inherited his father's feeling for the blues.

● COMPILATIONS: with Roy Brown *Battle Of The Blues* (King 1958)★★★, *Mr Blues Meets The Master Saxes* (1945-46 recordings)★★★★, *Good Rockin' Blues* rec. 1947-52 (King 1970)★★★★.

● FURTHER READING: *Rock Mr. Blues: The Life And Music Of Wynonie Harris*, Tony Collins.

HARRISON, VERNON 'BOOGIE WOOGIE RED'

b. 18 October 1925, Rayville, Louisiana, USA, d. 2 July 1992, Detroit, Michigan, USA. Though born in Louisiana, pianist Vernon Harrison was taken to Detroit when he was two years old and, like his contemporaries Eddie Burns and Eddie Kirkland, he became a stalwart of the Detroit blues scene, using the billing of 'Boogie Woogie Red'. He was best known for his session work with John Lee Hooker and, although a very active club performer for three decades, the first album in his own right did not materialize until the early 70s. In 1973 he toured Europe as part of the American Blues Legends package, but suffered the misfortune of breaking his wrist during the tour, somewhat marring his European debut. His overall recorded output was small and he preferred to work as an accompanist.

HART, ALVIN YOUNGBLOOD

b. 2 March 1963, Oakland, California, USA. Born and raised in Oakland, modern-day country bluesman Hart draws inspiration from his ancestral home in Carrollton, Mississippi (the run-down shacks pictured on his *Big Mama's Door* album are actually the homes of his grandmother and great-grandfather). Although he briefly played in high school rock bands, Hart was naturally drawn to the blues and tried to break into the local scene in Los Angeles. Dismayed with the commercialization of the blues, he decided to become a solely acoustic player in the mid-80s. Although he gave up playing for a period and worked at a variety of day jobs, Hart returned to music and quickly established himself as a distinctive and passionate acoustic blues player. A support slot for Taj Mahal in February 1995 brought Hart's name to a wider audience, and his debut release for the Sony-licensed OKeh label was a vital collection of songs by artists as diverse as Lead Belly ('Gallows Pole'), Charlie Patton ('Pony Blues') and Blind Willie McTell ('Hillbilly Willie's Blues'). Still living in Mississippi where he runs a guitar repair shop with his wife, Hart is now signed to Hannibal following a disagreement with Sony over the promotion of his album. His reputation as a live performer was further enhanced by US support slots for Buddy Guy, Los Lobos and Richard Thompson.

● ALBUMS: *Big Mama's Door* (OKeh 1996)★★★★.

HART, HATTIE

b. *c*.1900, USA. One of the finest of the female blues singers in Memphis, Hart was a strong-voiced, darkly sensuous singer, whose lyrics celebrated sex and drugs. She made a largely unissued session with the guitarists Allen Shaw and Willie Borum in 1934, and previous to this had recorded with the Memphis Jug Band. It is thought that she recorded in Chicago in 1938 as Hattie Bolten, which may have been her married or her maiden name. She had left Memphis by 1946, and her subsequent whereabouts are unknown.

● ALBUMS: *Memphis Girls* (1988)★★★, *Blue Ladies Vol. 2* (1989)★★★, *Memphis Jug Band Associates And Alternate Takes* (1991)★★★.

HAWKINS, 'SCREAMIN' JAY'

b. Jalacy Hawkins, 18 July 1929, Cleveland, Ohio, USA. Reportedly raised in Cleveland by a tribe of Blackfoot Indians, young Jalacy became interested in music at an early age, teaching himself piano at the age of six and, having mastered the keyboard, he then learned to play saxophone in his early teens. Hawkins was also an adept young boxer, winning an amateur *Golden Gloves* contest at the age of 14 and becoming Middleweight Champion of Alaska in 1949. He judged music to be the easier option, and became a professional musician, playing piano with artists such as Gene Ammons, Arnett Cobb, Illinois Jacquet, James Moody, Lynn Hope, and on one occasion, Count Basie. In 1950, Hawkins began developing an act based more on his almost operatic bass-baritone voice, and the following year he joined Tiny Grimes' Rocking Highlanders as pianist and occasional vocalist, making his recording debut with the band for Gotham Records in 1952 (the record was withdrawn after three weeks) and for Atlantic

Records in 1953 (the results remain unissued). Leaving Grimes, Hawkins was befriended by blues shouter Wynonie Harris, who brought the young musician to New York City as his protégé. At this point, Hawkins' fortunes began to take an upswing, first with his debut records under his own name for the Timely label, followed by superior efforts for Mercury/Wing and Grand Records. In 1956, Screamin' Jay (as he was now known) signed with Columbia's reactivated OKeh subsidiary and enjoyed enormous success with his manic - and apparently drunken - rendition of his own 'I Put A Spell On You', which he had recorded earlier as a ballad for Grand Records. Released in October 1956, the original version was quickly withdrawn as a result of the public outrage caused by the 'suggestive and cannibalistic' sound effects provided by Hawkins. A suitably truncated substitution was soon made. Despite these efforts, an airplay ban remained in force, but the record sold over a million copies regardless, becoming a classic of rock music and invoking hundreds of cover versions from Nina Simone to the Alan Price Set and Creedence Clearwater Revival. Remaining with OKeh until 1958, Hawkins ran the gamut of his weird-but-wonderful repertoire with recordings of straight R&B songs such as 'Little Demon' and 'Person To Person', tongue-in-cheek, semi-operatic standards such as 'I Love Paris' and 'Temptation', and the unclassifiable and uniquely strange 'Hong Kong', 'Alligator Wine' and 'There's Something Wrong With You'. To enhance this ghoulish strangeness, on his tours with rock 'n' roll package shows, Hawkins was encouraged by Alan Freed to use macabre props such as skulls, snakes and shrunken heads and to begin his act from the inside of a coffin. Again uproar followed, resulting in a largely unrepresentative album release and, worse still, Hawkins' only 50s film appearance in *Mister Rock 'N' Roll* being cut out in case parents boycotted the film's release. Shunned by the mass media, Hawkins spent most of the 60s playing one-nighters and tired rock 'n' roll revival gigs, making the occasional one-off recording agreement with tiny independent labels. *The Night And Day Of Screaming Jay Hawkins*, recorded in London for producer Shel Talmy's Planet label, was more conservative in tone. A brace of late 60s albums extended his idiosyncratic reputation and it was during these sessions that Hawkins recorded the original 'Constipation Blues', a lavatorial performance destined to become an intrinsic part of his stage act. He enjoyed a cameo role in the much-praised film *American Hot Wax*, and later won a starring role as the laconic hotel desk clerk in Jim Jarmusch's *Mystery Train*. Hawkins later collaborated with modern garage band the Fleshtones. A 1991 release, *Black Music For White People*, which included readings of two Tom Waits compositions, 'Ice Cream Man' and 'Heart Attack And Vine', as well as a rap interpretation of 'I Put A Spell On You', revealed a largely undiminished power. His influence on other performers, notably Screaming Lord Sutch, Arthur Brown and Alice Cooper, should not be underestimated. Having toured and recorded steadily through the 70s and 80s, Hawkins recently formed a new band, the Fuzztones, and made successful tours of Europe and America.

● ALBUMS: *At Home With Screamin' Jay Hawkins* (Epic 1958)★★★, *I Put A Spell On You* (Epic 1959)★★★★, *The Night & Day Of Screamin' Jay Hawkins* (Planet 1965)★★★, *What That Is* (Philips 1969)★★, *Screamin' Jay Hawkins* (Philips 1970)★★★, *A Portrait Of A Man & His Woman* (1972)★★★, *I Put A Spell On You* (1977)★★★, *Frenzy* (Edsel 1982)★★, *Real Life* (Charly 1983)★★, *Midnight* (1985)★★, *Live And Crazy* (Midnight Music 1986)★★★, *Feast Of The Mau Mau* (Edsel 1988)★★, *Real Life* (Charly 1989)★★★, *I Is* (1989)★★★, *I Want To Do It In A Cave!* (1990)★★★, *Voodoo Jive* (1990)★★★, *Black Music For White People* (Demon 1991)★★★, *Stone Crazy* (Demon 1993)★★★, *Somethin' Funny Goin' On* (Demon 1994)★★★.

● COMPILATIONS: *I Put A Spell On You* (Direction 1969)★★★, *Screamin' The Blues* (Red Lightin' 1982)★★★, *Frenzy* (Edsel 1986)★★★, *I Put A Spell On You* (Charly 1989)★★★, *Spellbound 1955-1974* (Bear Family 1990)★★★, *Voodoo Jive: The Best Of Screamin' Jay Hawkins* (Rhino 1990)★★★, *Cow Fingers And Mosquito Pie* (Epic 1991)★★★, *Screamin' Jay Hawkins - 1952-1955* (Magpie 1991)★★★, *From Gotham And Grand* (SJH 1992)★★★, *Portrait Of A Man* (Edsel 1995)★★★.

● FILMS: *American Hot Wax* (1976), *Mystery Train* (1989).

HAWKINS, ROY

Based in Richmond, California, Hawkins was an early discovery of label-owner Bob Geddins who found him playing piano and singing in an Oakland club in 1946. With a band that included William Staples on tenor saxophone and Ulysses James on guitar, Hawkins had his first recordings released on Geddins' Cavatone and Down Town labels in 1948. Some of the tracks raised sufficient interest for Modern Records to purchase Hawkins' contract and some of the Down Town masters. This new label began recording him seriously over the next three years with some of Los Angeles' finest musicians, including Maxwell Davis, T-Bone Walker and Johnny Moore. Hawkins' biggest hits were the visionary 'Why Do Everything Happen To Me', reaching number 3 in the US charts in 1950, and the ironic 'The Thrill Is Gone', which reached number 6 in the USA in 1951. Subsequent Modern/RPM sessions and those for Rhythm (1958) and Kent (1961) featured Hawkins only singing, backed by a guest pianist (a car accident had left him paralyzed in one arm). Latterly becoming a shadowy figure, known only to west coast blues fans, Hawkins and his recordings were nevertheless very influential in their day and have been covered by the likes of Ray Charles, B.B. King and James Brown. It is believed that Hawkins died in poverty in 1973.

● ALBUMS: *Why Do Everything Happen To Me* (Route 66 1979)★★★, *Highway 59* (Ace 1984)★★★.

HAWKINS, TED

b. Theodore Hawkins Jnr., 28 October 1937, Biloxi, Mississippi, USA, d. 1 January 1995, Los Angeles, California, USA. Hawkins was more of a modern-day 'songster' than a bluesman, his repertoire encompassing pop hits, country and folk standards, soul numbers and originals. He grew up with gospel music, and learned to play guitar at the age of 12, taught in the bluesy 'Vestapol' (or open C) style by local musicians. He played with such force that he protected his left hand with a glove. As a boy, he was sent to a reformatory, and spent several terms in prison. He left home in the 50s, hoboing first to Chicago, Illinois, then to New York, Pennsylvania and New Jersey, eventually settling in California. He recorded 'Baby'/'Whole

Lot Of Women' for the Hollywood-based Money label in 1966; in 1971 he was spotted busking by producer Bruce Bromberg with whom he made an album in 1972. He continued to perform on street corners and California's Ocean Front Walk; this aspect of Hawkins' career was documented on the *Venice Beach Tapes*, recorded, ironically, in Tennessee in 1985. *Happy Hour* consolidated his reputation, particularly in Britain where he had a sizeable following. Despite retaining an undoubtedly 'rural' feel in performance, Hawkins owed much vocally to his hero Sam Cooke and to the great soul stylists of the 60s. Above all, he was one of the finest contemporary interpreters of melancholic material.

● ALBUMS: *Watch Your Step* (Rounder 1982)★★★, *Happy Hour* (Rounder 1986)★★★, *On The Boardwalk: The Venice Beach Tapes* (no label 1986)★★★, *Dock Of The Bay: The Venice Beach Tapes II* (Unamerican Activities 1987)★★, *I Love You Too* (P.T. Music 1989)★★, *The Next Hundred Years* (Geffen 1994)★★★, *Songs From Venice Beach* (Evidence 1995)★★★.
● COMPILATIONS: *The Best Of Venice Beach Tapes* (Unamerican Activities 1989)★★★, *The Kershaw Sessions* (Strange Fruit 1995)★★★.
● VIDEOS: *Ted Hawkins: Amazing Grace* (Geffen Home Video 1995).

HAWKINS, WALTER 'BUDDY BOY'

Hawkins represents one of the most fascinating lacunae in the history of the blues. It is rumoured that he was raised around Blythville, Mississippi, but what minimal research has been undertaken has never produced anything conclusive. What is certain is that he was a unique performer who used a guitar style and vocal delivery that have defied categorization. He recorded 12 tracks for Paramount between 1927 (Chicago) and 1929 (Richmond, Indiana), much prized by collectors, that featured his oddly constructed blues, rag tunes and the peculiar 'Voice Throwing Blues' which gave rise to speculation that he may have been a medicine show ventriloquist. Evidence from his songs certainly seems to indicate that he was a rambler or hobo.

● ALBUMS: *Complete Recordings* (Matchbox 1983)★★★.

HEALEY, JEFF

b. 25 March 1966, Toronto, Ontario, Canada. Blind since developing eye cancer at the age of twelve months, Healey is a white blues-rock guitarist and singer who plays in an unusual, instinctive lap-held style. He received his first guitar at the age of three and has been a proficient multi-instrumentalist since childhood. At 15, he formed Blue Directon and gigged regularly in the Toronto area. In 1985, Healey was invited to play alongside Texas bluesman Albert Collins who, much impressed, in turn introduced him to Stevie Ray Vaughan. The Jeff Healey Band - Joe Rockman (b. 1 January 1957, Toronto, Canada; bass/vocals) and Tom Stephen (b. 2 February 1955, St. John, New Brunswick, Canada; drums) - was formed the same year and began playing across Canada. They released singles on their own Forte label - and produced accompanying videos - before signing to Arista Records in 1988. *See the Light* was released in 1989 and came wrapped in a sash bearing tributes from guitar giants such as Vaughan and B.B. King. It sold nearly two million copies; a world tour followed later in the year. A film, *Roadhouse* (1989), starring Patrick Swayze and Ben Gazzara, featured Healey in an acting/singing role as a blind blues guitarist. *Hell To Pay* tended more towards hard rock and featured Mark Knopfler, George Harrison, Jeff Lynne and Bobby Whitlock in addition to Healey's regular band. It went on to sell over 2 million copies worldwide. *Feel This* was a strong and energetic rock/blues album, and the back-to-his-roots *Cover To Cover* was a collection of favourite songs by some of Healey's mentors. He wanted this record to be fun and to recall the times when he made little money from his music.

● ALBUMS: *See The Light* (Arista 1989)★★★★, *Hell To Pay* (Arista 1990)★★, *Feel This* (Arista 1992)★★★, *Cover To Cover* (Arista 1995)★★★.
● FILMS: *Roadhouse* (1989).

HEARTSMAN, JOHNNY

b. 9 February 1937, San Fernando, California, USA, d. 27 December 1996. Heartsman grew up in Oakland and became renowned as 'one of the blues' most accomplished instrumentalists' (Dick Shurman). As a youngster he was inspired to play guitar by the music of T-Bone Walker, Pee Wee Crayton, and Lafayette Thomas. He quickly developed into a sought-after bandleader and studio musician. He recorded on guitar, bass, organ, and flute (he made his own first recordings in 1957 for the Music City label) and has played with a long list of west coast blues, R&B, and soul artists including Jimmy McCracklin, Joe Simon, Johnny Fuller, Jimmy Wilson, and Tiny Powell. Buddy Guy borrowed much of Heartsman's playing on his version of 'My Time After Awhile'. In 1976 Heartsman settled in Sacramento, California, and has recorded only infrequently since then. He died following a heart attack in December 1996.

● ALBUMS: *Sacramento* (Crosscut 1987)★★★, *The Touch* (Alligator 1991)★★★, with The Blues Company *Made In Germany* (1994)★★★, *Still Shinin'* (Have Mercy 1994)★★★.

HEGAMIN, LUCILLE

b. 29 November 1894, Macon, Georgia, USA, d. 1 March 1970, New York City, New York, USA. Hegamin was recorded from 1920 onwards, in the wake of Mamie Smith's breakthrough for black singers. Her background was in vaudeville, which required versatility and the ability to respond to popular taste. Her repertoire on record is more blues-inflected black pop than pure blues, but the songs often have great charm, and Hegamin's delivery, forceful but melodious and flexible with precise, clear diction, is very appealing. She stopped recording in 1926, excluding one 1932 record, but continued stage and club work (she gained stardom with the touring company of *Shuffle Along* in the role played on Broadway by Florence Mills) until 1934, when she became a nurse. Coaxed out of retirement, she made some fine recordings in 1961 and 1962 before returning to the church work that occupied her final years.

● ALBUMS: *Songs We Taught Your Mother* (1962)★★★, *Blue Flame* (VJM 1979)★★★.

HEMPHILL, JESSIE MAE

b. 18 October 1937, Mississippi, USA. A member of a family whose musical activities can be traced back a number of generations (her grandfather Sid Hemphill and aunt Rosa Lee Hill both made recordings), from the 50s onwards, Hemphill spent many years playing and singing. She sang blues, most of which she wrote herself, based on her own experiences, and played guitar in a local style, using droning chords and beating time on a tambourine with her foot. She also played drums in a fife and drum band, one of the last active examples of an old Mississippi tradition. She has made a number of recordings, including a couple of singles issued by a venture owned by Memphis State University, and has frequently played at concerts and festivals as far afield as Europe. In 1995 her career effectively ended when she had a stroke. Since then she has been confined to a wheelchair.

● ALBUMS: *She Wolf* (Vogue 1988)★★★, *Feelin' Good* (High Water 1991)★★★★.

HEMPHILL, SID

b. 1876, Como, Mississippi, USA, d. *c.*1963, Senatobia, Mississippi, USA. Hemphill played guitar, drums, mandolin, banjo and harmonica besides the fife, panpipes and fiddle that appear on the recordings his band made in 1942 for the Library of Congress. These stand as vital documentation of two black traditions: string band music, and the fife and drum bands of northwest Mississippi. The repertoire played by Hemphill and his musicians seemed to have remained largely unchanged since around 1900, and included blues-ballads, religious music, popular songs and dance tunes. The latter owed much to white music and so, more generally, did their fife and drum music, which displayed little improvisation or syncopation, in contrast to more recent recordings. Hemphill, who was the father of Rosa Lee Hill, was recorded for the last time in 1959.

● ALBUMS: *Sounds Of The South* (1960)★★★, *Traveling Through The Jungle* (1974)★★★, *Afro-American Folk Music From Tate And Panola Counties, Mississippi* (1978)★★★.

HENDERSON, BUGS

b. 1944, Palm Springs, California, USA. A guitarist who has enjoyed cult status for more than a decade, Henderson grew up in Tyler, Texas, close to the Louisiana border. By the early 60s, he was recording sessions at the town's Robin Hood Studios, where later, ZZ Top recorded their early albums. In 1964, he was in a local garage band, the Sensors, when he met Ronnie Weiss with whom he formed Mouse And The Traps, a folk rock band that eventually relocated to

Dallas and had a minor hit with 'Public Execution'. In 1971, he returned to Tyler and played in a country band until he was contacted by John Nitzinger, who was recording for Capitol Records and needed a guitarist. Despite touring with Leon Russell, B.B. King and the Allman Brothers, Henderson left in 1974 to form his own trio with Bobby Chitwood and Ron Thompson. With the Shuffle Kings, he has kept the trio formula for most of the succeeding 20 years, occasionally augmenting the line-up with a rhythm guitarist or a keyboard player. Unwilling to be classified, he refers to what he produces as 'American music', running the gamut from Link Wray and the Ventures to B.B. King. That diversity is celebrated in the album of the same name, which features contributions from, among others, Johnny Winter, Jimmie Vaughn, Bill Hamm and Joe Ely.

● ALBUMS: *At Last* (Armadillo/Taxim 1978/1992)★★★, *Still Flyin'* (Flying High 1981)★★★, *American Music* (Bingo Pajama/Flat Canyon 1988/1994)★★★★, *Texan Eagles* (Aulica 1992)★★★, *Gitarbazndrumz* (Poor David's 1992)★★★, *Years In The Jungle* (Trigger 1993)★★★, *Daredevils Of The Red Guitar* (Flat Canyon 1994)★★★.

HENDERSON, DUKE

d. 1972, Los Angeles, California, USA. While T-Bone Walker was conducting his master class in blues guitar playing, Wynonie Harris was teaching aspiring singers their lessons in blues shouting. From the three Apollo sessions anthologized on *Get Your Kicks*, it seems that Duke Henderson was one of his earliest and most able pupils, although it is also possible to hear some Joe Turner mannerisms. Nothing is known of how he came to be recording three months after Harris with some of the same musicians, the élite of Los Angeles jazz artists, including Jack McVea, Lucky Thompson, Jewell Grant, Marshal Royal, Teddy Buckner and Rabon Tarrant. Henderson went on to record for Globe, Excelsior, Downbeat, Modern, London and Imperial before cutting 'Country Girl' for Specialty, his only other title to be reissued. One further session for Flair as Big Duke yielded the topical 'Hey Dr. Kinsey'. In the early 50s, he worked as a disc jockey for KPOP, doing back-to-back R&B and gospel shows, the latter as Brother Henderson. He later became a minister at the Bethany Apostle Community Church. In the 60s, he had gospel shows on KGFJ and XERB.

● ALBUMS: *Get Your Kicks* (Delmark 1994)★★★, *Specialty Legends Of Jump Blues Vol. 1* (Specialty/Ace 1994)★★★, *Get Your Kicks* (Delmark 1995)★★★.

HENDERSON, ROSA

b. Rosa Deschamps, 24 November 1896, Henderson, Kentucky, USA, d. 6 April 1968, New York City, New York, USA. Henderson was a person of many aliases; her most well-known stage name was the one she took from her husband and vaudeville partner Douglas 'Slim' Henderson, but others were more arbitrarily chosen. She had records issued under the titles Flora Dale, Rosa Green Mae/Mamie Harris, Sara Johnsson, Sally Ritz, Josephine Thomas, Gladys White and Bessie Williams. Her large record output and continuing success on the stage indicate the popularity of her big voice and engaging persona. Her blues was largely divorced from any country influence but sometimes showed considerable awareness of contemporary musical trends. Her career appears to have ended in the early 30s.

● ALBUMS: *Mean Mothers* (1980)★★★, *Big Mamas* (1982)★★★.
● COMPILATIONS: *Complete Recorded Works 1923-31 Vols. 1-4* (Document 1995)★★★.

HENDRIX, JIMI

b. Johnny Allen Hendrix, 27 November 1942, Seattle, Washington, USA, d. 18 September 1970, London, England. (His father subsequently changed his son's name to James Marshall Hendrix.) More superlatives have been bestowed upon Hendrix than any other rock guitarist. Unquestionably one of music's most influential figures, he brought an unparalleled vision to the art of playing electric guitar. Self-taught (and with the burden of being left-handed with a right-handed guitar) he spent hours absorbing the recorded legacy of southern-blues practitioners, from Robert Johnson to B.B. King. The aspiring musician joined several local R&B bands while still at school, before enlisting as a paratrooper in the 101st Airborne Division. It was during this period that Hendrix met Billy

Cox, a bass player upon whom he called at several stages in his career. Together they formed the King Kasuals, an in-service attraction later resurrected when both men returned to civilian life. Hendrix was discharged in July 1962 after breaking his right ankle. He began working with various touring revues backing, among others, the Impressions, Sam Cooke and the Valentinos. He enjoyed lengthier spells with the Isley Brothers, Little Richard and King Curtis, recording with each of these acts, but was unable to adapt to the discipline their performances required. The experience and stagecraft gained during this formative period proved essential to the artist's subsequent development. By 1965 Hendrix was living in New York. In October he joined struggling soul singer Curtis Knight, signing a punitive contract with the latter's manager, Ed Chaplin. This ill-advised decision returned to haunt the guitarist. In June the following year, Hendrix, now calling himself Jimmy James, formed a group initially dubbed the Rainflowers, then Jimmy James And The Blue Flames. The quartet, which also featured future Spirit member Randy California, was appearing at the Cafe Wha? in Greenwich Village when Chas Chandler was advised to see them. The Animals' bassist immediately recognized the guitarist's extraordinary talent and persuaded him to go to London in search of a more receptive audience. Hendrix arrived in England in September 1966. Chandler became his co-manager in partnership with Mike Jeffries (aka Jeffreys), and immediately began auditions for a suitable backing group. Noel Redding (b. 25 December 1945, Folkestone, Kent, England) was selected on bass, having recently failed to join the New Animals, while John 'Mitch' Mitchell (b. 9 July 1947, Ealing, Middlesex, England), a veteran of the Riot Squad and Georgie Fame's Blue Flames, became the trio's drummer. The new group, dubbed the Jimi Hendrix Experience, made its debut the following month at Evereux in France. On returning to England they began a string of club engagements that attracted pop's aristocracy, including Pete Townshend and Eric Clapton. In December the trio released their first single, the understated, resonant 'Hey Joe'. Its UK Top 10 placing encouraged a truly dynamic follow-up in 'Purple Haze'. The latter was memorable for Hendrix's guitar pyrotechnics and a lyric that incorporated the artist's classic line: ''Scuse me while I kiss the sky'. On tour his trademark Fender Stratocaster and Marshall Amplifier were punished night after night, as the group enhanced its reputation with exceptional live appearances. Here Hendrix drew on black culture and his own heritage to produce a startling visual and aural bombardment. Framed by a halo of long, wiry hair, his slight figure was clad in a bright, rainbow-mocking costume. Although never a demonstrative vocalist, his delivery was curiously effective. Hendrix's playing technique, meanwhile, although still drawing its roots from the blues, encompassed an emotional range far greater than any contemporary guitarist. Rapier-like runs vied with measured solos, matching energy with ingenuity, while a wealth of technical possibilities - distortion, feedback and even sheer volume - brought texture to his overall approach. This assault was enhanced by a flamboyant stage persona in which Hendrix used the guitar as a physical appendage. He played his instrument behind his back, between his legs or, in simulated sexual ecstasy, on the floor. Such practices brought criticism from radical quarters, who claimed the artist had become an 'Uncle Tom', employing tricks to curry favour with a white audience - accusations that neglected similar showmanship from generations of black performers, from Charley Patton to 'T-Bone' Walker. Redding's clean, uncluttered bass lines provided the backbone to Hendrix's improvisations, while Mitchell's drumming, as instinctive as his leader's guitar work, was a perfect foil. Their concessions to the pop world now receding, the Experience completed an astonishing debut album that ranged from the apocalyptic vision of 'I Don't Live Today', to the blues of 'Red House' and the funk of 'Fire' and 'Foxy Lady'. Hendrix returned to America in June 1967 to appear, sensationally, at the Monterey Pop Festival. During one number (Dylan's 'Like A Rolling Stone') he paused to inform the crowd that he was retuning his guitar, and later in the same song admitted that he had forgotten the words. Such unparalleled confidence only served to endear him to the crowd. His performance was a musical and visual feast, topped off by a sequence that saw him playing the guitar with his teeth, and then burning the instrument with lighter fuel. He was now fêted in his homeland, and following an ill-advised tour supporting the Monkees, the Experience enjoyed reverential audiences on the country's nascent concert circuit. *Axis: Bold As Love* revealed a new lyrical capability, notably in the title track and the jazz-influenced 'Up From The Skies'. 'Little Wing', a delicate love song bathed in unhurried guitar splashes, offered a gentle perspective, closer to that of the artist's shy, offstage demeanour. Released in December 1967, the collection completed a triumphant year, artistically and commercially, but within months the fragile peace began to collapse. In January 1968 the Experience embarked on a gruelling American tour encompassing 54 concerts in 47 days. Hendrix was now tiring of the wild man image that had brought him initial attention, but he was perceived as diffident by spectators anticipating gimmickry. An impulsive artist, he was unable to disguise below-par performances, while his relationship with Redding grew increasingly fraught as the bassist rebelled against the set patterns he was expected to play. *Electric Ladyland*, the last official Experience album, was released in October. This extravagant double set was initially deemed 'self-indulgent', but is now recognized as a major work. It revealed the guitarist's desire to expand the increasingly limiting trio format, and contributions from members of Traffic (Chris Wood and Steve Winwood) and Jefferson Airplane (Jack Casady) embellished several selections. The collection featured a succession of virtuoso performances - 'Gypsy Eyes', 'Crosstown Traffic' - while the astonishing 'Voodoo Chile (Slight Return)', a posthumous number 1 single, showed how Hendrix had brought rhythm, purpose and mastery to the recently invented wah-wah pedal. *Electric Ladyland* included two UK hits, 'The Burning Of The Midnight Lamp' and 'All Along The Watchtower'. The latter, an urgent restatement of the Bob Dylan song, was particularly impressive, and received the ultimate accolade when the composer adopted Hendrix's interpretation when performing it live on his 1974 tour. Despite such creativity, the guitarist's private and professional life was becoming problematic. He was arrested in Toronto for possessing

heroin, but although the charges were later dismissed, the proceedings clouded much of 1969. Chas Chandler had, meanwhile, withdrawn from the managerial partnership and although Redding sought solace with a concurrent group, Fat Mattress, his differences with Hendrix were now irreconcilable. The Experience played its final concert on June 29 1969; Hendrix subsequently formed Gypsies Sons And Rainbows with Mitchell, Billy Cox (bass), Larry Lee (rhythm guitar), Juma Sultan and Jerry Velez (both percussion). This short-lived unit closed the Woodstock Festival, during which Hendrix performed his famed rendition of the 'Star Spangled Banner'. Perceived by some critics as a political statement, it came as the guitarist was being increasingly subjected to pressures from different causes. In October he formed an all-black group, Band Of Gypsies, with Cox and drummer Buddy Miles, intending to accentuate the African-American dimension in his music. The trio made its debut on 31 December 1969, but its potential was marred by Miles' comparatively flat, pedestrian drumming and unimaginative compositions. Part of the set was issued as *Band Of Gypsies*, but despite the inclusion of the exceptional 'Machine Gun', this inconsistent album was only released to appease former manager Chaplin, who acquired the rights in part-settlement of a miserly early contract. The Band Of Gypsies broke up after a mere three concerts and initially Hendrix confined his efforts to completing his Electric Ladyland recording studio. He then started work on another double set, *First Rays Of The New Rising Sun* (finally released in 1997), and later resumed performing with Cox and Mitchell. His final concerts were largely frustrating, as the aims of the artist and the expectations of his audience grew increasingly separate. His final UK appearance, at the Isle Of Wight festival, encapsulated this dilemma, yet still drew an enthralling performance.

The guitarist returned to London following a short European tour. On 18 September 1970, his girlfriend, Monika Danneman, became alarmed when she was unable to rouse him from sleep. An ambulance was called, but Hendrix was pronounced dead on arrival at a nearby hospital. The inquest recorded an open verdict, with death caused by suffocation due to inhalation of vomit. Eric Burdon claimed at the time to possess a suicide note, but this has never been confirmed. Two posthumous releases, *Cry Of Love* and *Rainbow Bridge*, mixed portions of the artist's final recordings with masters from earlier sources. These were fitting tributes, but many others were tawdry cash-ins, recorded in dubious circumstances, mispackaged and mistitled. This imbalance has been redressed of late with the release of fitting archive recordings, but the Hendrix legacy also rests in his prevailing influence on fellow musicians. Many guitarists have imitated his technique; few have mastered it, while none at all have matched him as an inspirational player. In November 1993 a tribute album, *Stone Free*, was released, containing a formidable list of performers including the Pretenders, Eric Clapton, Cure, Jeff Beck, Pat Metheny and Nigel Kennedy, a small testament to the huge influence Hendrix has wielded and will continue to wield as the most inventive rock guitarist of all time. The litigation regarding ownership of his recordings that had been running for many years was resolved in January 1997, when the Hendrix family finally won back the rights from Alan Douglas. This was made possible by the financial weight of Microsoft co-founder Paul Allen, who in addition to helping with legal expenses has financed the Jimi Hendrix Museum, which will be located in Seattle. A major reissuing programme started in 1997 including out-takes from the recording of *Electric Ladyland*. The reissued catalogue on Experience/MCA records is now the definitive and final word. The quality is as good as 25 year-old tapes will allow.

● ALBUMS: *Are You Experienced?* (Track 1967)★★★★★, *Axis: Bold As Love* (Track 1967)★★★★★, *Electric Ladyland* (Track 1968)★★★★, *Band Of Gypsies* (Track 1970)★★★, *Cry Of Love* (Polydor 1971)★★★, *Experience* (Ember 1971)★, *Isle Of Wight* (Polydor 1971)★★, *Rainbow Bridge* (Reprise 1971)★★, *Hendrix In The West* (Polydor 1971)★★★, *More Experience* (Ember 1972)★, *War Heroes* (Polydor 1972)★★, *Loose Ends* (Polydor 1974)★★, *Crash Landing* (Polydor 1975)★★, *Midnight Lightnin'* (Polydor 1975)★★, *Nine To The Universe* (Polydor 1980)★★, *The Jimi Hendrix Concerts* (Columbia 1982)★★★, *Jimi Plays Monterey* (Polydor 1986)★★★, *Live At Winterland* (Polydor 1987)★★★, *Radio One* (Castle 1988)★★★★, *Live And Unreleased* (Castle 1989)★★★, *First Rays Of The New Rising Sun* (Experience/MCA 1997)★★★, *South Saturn Delta* (Experience/MCA 1997)★★★.

● COMPILATIONS: *Smash Hits* (Track 1968)★★★★, *The Essential Jimi Hendrix* (Polydor 1978)★★★★, *The Essential Jimi Hendrix Volume Two* (Polydor 1979)★★★, *The Singles Album* (Polydor 1983)★★★★, *Kiss The Sky* (Polydor 1984)★★★, *Cornerstones* (Polydor 1990)★★★, *Blues* (Polydor 1994)★★★, *Exp Over Sweden* (Univibes 1993)★★, *Jimi In Denmark* (Univibes 1995)★★.

● VIDEOS: *Jimi Hendrix Plays Berkeley* (Palace Video 1986), *Jimi Plays Monterey* (Virgin Vision 1986), *Jimi Hendrix* (Warner Home Video 1986), *Experience* (Palace Video 1987), *Rainbow Bridge* (Hendring 1988), *Live At The Isle Of Wight 1970* (Rhino 1990), *Jimi Hendrix Live At Monterey* (1994), *Jimi At Woodstock* (BMG 1995), *Jimi At The Atlanta Pop Festival* (BMG 1995), *Jimi Hendrix Experience* (BMG 1995), *Jimi Hendrix Plays The Great Pop Festivals* (BMG 1995).

● FURTHER READING: *Jimi: An Intimate Biography Of Jimi Hendrix*, Curtis Knight. *Jimi Hendrix*, Alain Dister. *Jimi Hendrix: Voodoo Child Of The Aquarian Age*, David Henderson. *Scuze Me While I Kiss The Sky: The Life Of Jimi Hendrix*, David Henderson. *Hendrix: A Biography*, Chris Welch. *Hendrix: An Illustrated Biography*, Victor Sampson. *The Jimi Hendrix Story*, Jerry Hopkins. *Crosstown Traffic: Jimi Hendrix And Post-War Pop*, Charles Shaar Murray. *Jimi Hendrix: Electric Gypsy*, Harry Shapiro and Caesar Glebbeek. *Are You Experienced?*, Noel Redding and Carole Appleby. *Hendrix Experience*, Mitch Mitchell and John Platt. *And The Man With The Guitar*, Jon Price and Gary Geldeart. *The Jimi Hendrix Experience In 1967 (Limited Edition)*, Gerad Mankowitz and Robert Whitaker (Photographers). *Jimi Hendrix: A Visual Documentary, His Life, Loves And Music*, Tony Brown. *The Hendrix Experience*, Mitch Mitchell with John Platt. *Jimi Hendrix: Starchild*, Curtis Knight. *Hendrix: Setting The Record Straight*, John McDermott with Eddie Kramer. *The Illustrated Jimi Hendrix*, Geoffrey Guiliano. *Cherokee Mist - The Lost Writings Of Jimi Hendrix*, Bill Nitopi (compiler). *Voodoo Child:*

The Illustrated Legend Of Jimi Hendrix, Martin L. Green and Bill Sienkiewicz. *The Ultimate Experience*, Adrian Boot and Chris Salewicz. *The Lost Writings Of Jimi Hendrix*, Jimi Hendrix. *The Complete Studio Recording Sessions 1963-1970*, John McDermott. *Complete Guide To The Music Of*, John Robertson. *The Inner World Of Jimi Hendrix*, Monika Dannemann. *Jimi Hendrix Experience*, Jerry Hopkins. *Jimi Hendrix: Voices From Home*, Mary Willix. *The Man, The Music, The Memorabilia*, Caesar Glebbeek and Douglas Noble.

HENLEY, JOHN LEE

b. 13 February 1919, Canton, Mississippi, USA. Henley learned harmonica as a child and played for country dances. Moving to Chicago in 1943, he spent some time with John Lee 'Sonny Boy' Williamson and picked up a good deal of technique, although his only record, recorded in 1958, owes more to the other Sonny Boy 'Rice Miller' Williamson, whom Henley had heard in Mississippi. He claimed to have accompanied Big Boy Spires, his regular partner at the time, on a 1953 recording session, but never regarded himself as a professional musician. Mid-60s recordings for Testament explored his early repertoire, with titles such as 'Slidin' Devil,' 'Old Mule' and 'Two Step', but nothing was issued.
● ALBUMS: *World Of Trouble* (1982)★★★.

HENRY, BIG BOY

b. Richard Henry, 21 May 1921, Beaufort, North Carolina, USA. More enterprising than the majority of his contemporaries, Henry has been recording himself since 1947. He was born on the Atlantic seaboard; his parents separated in his childhood, and in 1933 his mother took him north to New Bern. He was drawn to the community's musicians, particularly Guitar Shorty and Fred Miller, who played at The Honey Hole on A Street. Having learned guitar from Miller, in 1938 Henry became his partner, playing songs by Blind Boy Fuller and Buddy Moss. In 1947, he took a job at Hawks Radio in New Bern, who sponsored a broadcast with the pianist Julius Lane. The pair used the Hawks Webcor tape recorder to prepare programmes and some of these titles appear on Henry's first album. In 1950 and 1953, he had opportunities to record for King (abandoned when he became hoarse)

and for Bob Shad, then working for Mercury Records. A four-title session with Sonny Terry and Brownie McGhee was never issued, Shad claiming that the tapes had been stolen. In despair, Henry gave up music except for church services and became a minister in the Missionary Baptist Church. Having gone back to Beaufort, he returned to music in 1980. Three years later, he made two singles for Audio Arts and began to record and release material on his own Home Town label. Between 1986 and 1993, he issued nine cassettes via his own four-track recorder, mixer and shrink-wrapping machine. His 1993 album also features Dave Peabody, Chicago Bob Nelson and Gary Erwin.
● ALBUMS: *I'm Not Lying This Time* (Swingmaster 1988)★★★, *Strut His Stuff* (Swingmaster 1989)★★★, *Carolina Blues Jam* (Erwin Music 1993)★★★, *Poor Man's Blues* (New Moon 1995)★★★.

HICKS, EDNA

b. 14 October 1895, New Orleans, Louisiana, USA, d. 16 August 1925, Chicago, Illinois, USA. Sister of Herb Morand, and step-sister of Lizzie Miles, Hicks was a light-voiced singer reminiscent of Esther Bigeou. In musical comedy from 1916, she recorded vaudeville blues for no fewer than eight companies in 1923-24. Her death, the result of burns after a domestic accident with gasoline, robbed the blues of a promising artist.

HILL, BERTHA 'CHIPPIE'

b. 15 March 1905, Charleston, South Carolina, USA, d. 7 May 1950, New York City, New York, USA. Bertha Hill was in showbusiness as a singer and dancer aged 14, when she claimed to have stolen the show from Ethel Waters. Nicknamed for her youth and small stature, she settled in Chicago in the 20s. Her dark, hard voice was especially suited to blues, and good trumpeters seemed to inspire her; her finest recordings are those with Joe 'King' Oliver and Louis Armstrong. She retired in the late 20s after marrying, but was persuaded to return to singing and recording for the growing white jazz audience in the mid-40s. Still a fine singer, she was a success at the 1948 Paris Jazz Festival, but a promising second career was ended by a hit-and-run driver.
● ALBUMS: *Sounds Of The Twenties Vol. 4*

(*c*.1965)★★★, *The Great Blues Singers*
(*c*.1965)★★★, *Ida Cox/Chippie Hill*
(*c*.1975)★★★, *When Women Sang The Blues*
(1976)★★★, *Montana Taylor* (1991)★★★.

HILL, JESSIE

b. 9 December 1932, New Orleans, Louisiana,
USA, d. 17 September 1996. Jessie Hill's primary
claim to fame was the classic New Orleans R&B
hit 'Ooh Poo Pah Doo - Part II' in 1960. His first
musical experience was as a drummer at the age
of seven. At 15 he played in a Dixieland band
and at 20 formed an R&B group called the
House Rockers. He briefly worked with
Professor Longhair and Huey Smith in the mid-
50s before re-forming the House Rockers in
1958, abandoning the drums to sing. After Hill
performed 'Ooh Poo Pah Doo' as a joke at his
gigs, Joe Banashak of Minit Records heard the
song and agreed to record it. Arranged by Allen
Toussaint, it eventually reached number 3 on
the R&B charts and number 28 on the national
pop charts. Hill had only one other minor chart
single before moving to Los Angeles, where he
wrote songs performed by Sonny And Cher, Ike
And Tina Turner and Iron Butterfly. He
recorded one album later in his career and there
is a collection of his Minit sides on Charly
Records.
● ALBUMS: *Naturally* (1972)★★.
● COMPILATIONS: *Y'all Ready Now?* (Charly
1980)★★★, *Golden Classics* (Collectables)★★★.

HILL, MICHAEL

b. 1952, South Bronx, New York, USA. Very
much a modern bluesman, Hill took Jimi
Hendrix and Eric Clapton as his early models,
and through them, encountered the music of
B.B. King, Albert King and T-Bone Walker. He
also saw Buddy Guy opening for the Mothers Of
Invention in Central Park. In the early 70s, he
formed Brown Sugar, which included his brother
Kevin on bass and sisters Kathy and Wynette
singing backing vocals. Hill went on to play in
Dadahdoodahda with Vernon Reid, who later
formed Living Color, and became part of Black
Rock Coalition, which Reid helped to form in
1985. In 1987, he started another band, the
Blues Mob, with Kevin, Tony Lewis and Doug
Booth, while also performing with Bluesland, a
larger version of Brown Sugar. The latter

recorded 'Bluestime In America' for *The History
Of Our Future*. At the same time a demo of Blues
Mob, with Fred McFarlane replacing Booth on
keyboards, was sent to Alligator boss Bruce
Iglauer, who signed them to the label in 1994.
Bloodlines contained original songs, with the
exception of Reid's 'Soldier's Blues', in which
Hill commented perceptively, and not without
humour, on the quality of black life in his
country, its dangers and shortcomings. Though
couched in a rock format, his music is very
much the blues of today.
● ALBUMS: *Bloodlines* (Alligator 1994)★★★,
Have Mercy! (Alligator 1996)★★★.

HILL, ROSA LEE

b. 25 September 1910, Como, Mississippi, USA,
d. 22 October 1968, Senatobia, Mississippi, USA.
The daughter of Sid Hemphill, Rosa Lee Hill
grew up in a musical family, playing a broad
repertoire for both whites and blacks. Her
recordings are confined to blues, which she sang
'from my mouth, and not from the heart',
feeling them to be incompatible with her religious faith. Her blues are typical of Panola
County, where she spent her whole life: accompanied by a droning guitar, her songs have an
inward-looking, brooding feel, comparable to
those of Fred McDowell. Hill and her husband
were sharecroppers and lived in dire poverty,
particularly towards the end of their lives, when
their house burned down and they had to move
into a tumbledown shack.
● ALBUMS: *Blues Roll On* (1961)★★★,
Mississippi Delta Blues Vol. 2 (*c*.1970)★★★, *Roots
Of The Blues* (1977)★★★.

HILL, Z.Z.

b. Arzel Hill, 30 September 1935, Naples, Texas,
USA, d. 27 April 1984. A singer in the mould of
Bobby 'Blue' Bland, Hill served his musical
apprenticeship in Dallas lounge bars. He
recorded for his brother Matt's MH label before
signing to Kent Records in 1964. A string of
mature, sophisticated singles followed,
including 'Hey Little Girl' (1965) and 'I Found
Love' (1966). More 'adult' than contemporaries
at Stax, such records struggled for acceptance
outside the south and failed to reach the R&B
chart. Although Hill left Kent in 1968, the label
continued to release his material and three

years later secured a Top 30 R&B hit with his 1964 recording, 'I Need Someone (To Love Me)'. The artist enjoyed similar success with the engaging 'Don't Make Me Pay For His Mistakes', which peaked at number 17 (US R&B). Other releases were less fortunate, but the singer's work with Jerry 'Swamp Dogg' Williams improved the situation. Later spells with Hill/United Artists and Columbia were marred by corporate indecision. In 1981, Hill signed with Malaco, a company devoted to classic southern soul. His albums there, including *Down Home*, *The Rhythm And The Blues* and *I'm A Blues Man*, proved his most artistically satisfying. Hill died of a heart attack in April 1984.

● ALBUMS: *A Whole Lot Of Soul* (Kent 1969)★★★, *The Brand New Z.Z. Hill* (1971)★★★, *Dues Paid In Full* (Kent 1972)★★★, *The Best Thing That's Ever Happened To Me* (Mankind 1972)★★★★, *Keep On Loving You* (1975)★★★, *Let's Make A Deal* (Columbia 1978)★★★, *Mark Of Z.Z.* (1979)★★★, *Z.Z. Hill* (Malaco 1981)★★★, *Down Home* (Malaco 1982)★★★★, *The Rhythm And The Blues* (Malaco 1982)★★★★, *I'm A Blues Man* (Malaco 1983)★★★, *Bluesmaster* (Malaco 1984)★★★.

● COMPILATIONS: *Dues Paid In Full* (Kent 1984)★★★, *In Memorium 1935-1984* (Malaco 1985)★★★, *Whoever's Thrilling You (Is Killing Me)* (Stateside 1986)★★★, *Greatest Hits* (Malaco 1986)★★★★, *The Best Of Z.Z. Hill* (Malaco 1986)★★★, *The Down Home Soul Of Z.Z. Hill* rec. 1964-68 (1992)★★★.

HOAX

Comprising Hugh Coltman (vocals/harmonica), Jon Amor and Jess Davey (guitars), Robin Davey (bass guitar), and Dave Raeburn (drums), and already earmarked as the 'Great White Hope', the Hoax create original blues-based music with the brash arrogance of the innately talented. With the exception of drummer Raeburn, the band's members all grew up in Great Cheverell, Wiltshire, England. The Davey brothers investigated their parents' extensive blues album collection and teamed up with schoolfriends Coltman and Amor with the intention of forming a band. Enlisting the services of Raeburn, they rehearsed for three weeks and set off for their first gig, using the name suggested by a newspaper report on the recent appear-

ances of crop circles in their area. Over the next two years, they built up a strong fanbase in Britain and Europe before determining to turn professional. They were spotted by Code Blue boss Mike Vernon while opening for the Texas bar band led by Smokin' Joe Kubek. *Sound Like This* was well received when issued in October 1994 and the band increased its work schedule, opening for the likes of Robert Cray and Walter Trout. Their first American tour began in July 1995, including six gigs with Buddy Guy and others with Joe Ely and Chris Duarte. Although their twin-guitar work is sometimes reminiscent of Wishbone Ash, their determination to avoid the clichés of their chosen musical genre makes the Hoax an intriguing prospect. Their second album gained them many new fans in the rock world, and lost them a number of blues purists. *Unpossible* was hard to fault as a heavy blues rock album but they are currently treading a fine line of two musical styles. The band left their label Code Blue in late 1997 and at the same time parted company with their drummer Dave Raeburn.

● ALBUMS: *Sound Like This* (Code Blue 1994)★★★, *Unpossible* (Code Blue 1997)★★★.

HOGAN, SILAS

b. 15 September 1911, Westover, Louisiana, USA, d. 9 January 1994. Hogan learned guitar from his uncles, but also from records by artists such as Kokomo Arnold and Blind Lemon Jefferson. He moved to Baton Rouge during his late 20s and over the years established himself on the city's blues scene. His band first recorded in 1959, with a record issued under the name of drummer Jimmy Dotson. From 1962-65 Hogan made a series of fine blues singles with producer Jay Miller, issued on Excello Records. These included upbeat R&B as well as gloomy downhome blues, but their quality is consistently high - the band always tight, and Hogan singing with power and conviction. The influence of Jimmy Reed and Lightnin' Slim is occasionally evident, but Hogan always retains his own distinctive sound. During the blues revival of the late 60s and early 70s, a few recordings were made by Hogan in Baton Rouge and released on Arhoolie and Blue Horizon. Later, in the 80s, he became one of the resident artists at Tabby Thomas's Blues Box, and recorded an album

issued by Blues South West in the UK.
● ALBUMS: *Free Hearted Man* (1961-65)★★★, *Trouble At Home* (1962-65)★★★, *The Godfather* (1989)★★★, *So Long Blues* (Ace 1994)★★★.

HOGG, JOHN

b. 1912, Westconnie, Texas, USA. John Hogg was the impetus behind Smokey Hogg's (his cousin) decision to pursue a music career in Los Angeles in 1947. John had been there since 1942, after several years of roaming which took him as far from his Texas home of Greenville as Denver, Colorado and Oklahoma - where he worked as a rodeo performer. He was never a committed bluesman but did have the advantage of being taught some guitar by the Los Angeles-based Pee Wee Crayton. Hogg played occasional gigs, retaining his day job. He recorded for Mercury and Octive in 1951, probably on the strength of his relationship with Smokey, and proved himself a performer of some ability. His practice of treating music as a sideline continued, although he did record again for Advent Records in 1974, appearing that year at the San Diego Blues Festival.
● COMPILATIONS: *Texas Blues* (1965)★★★.

HOGG, SMOKEY

b. Andrew Hogg, 27 January 1914, Westconnie, Texas, USA, d. 1 May 1960, McKinney, Texas. USA. Born in north-east Texas, Smokey came from a clan that included blues singers Lightnin' Hopkins and John Hogg. He learned to play the guitar and piano early in life under the instruction of his father, Frank. One of seven children, he looked upon music as a means of escape from labour in the fields. He sang around Dallas and Greenville and was popular enough to be known as Little Peetie Wheatstraw after his idol. He played in clubs with men such as B.K. Turner (Black Aces) and D.C. Bender. In 1937 he recorded two tracks for Decca Records, which, although much valued by collectors, made no impression on the blues-buying public of the time. During World War II he was drafted and served in the US Army, but by 1947 he was in Los Angeles, where he recorded for the Exclusive label, again without much success. His breakthrough came after he had moved back to Texas where he recorded 'Too Many Drivers', released under the Modern label in 1947. Back

in Los Angeles, but still for Modern, he recorded his biggest hit, 'Little School Girl'. Now established, he began, like many of his contemporaries, to hop from label to label, recording for Specialty, Imperial, SIW, Mercury and many smaller concerns. He enjoyed a good deal of popularity, especially with older fans, and this allowed him to survive the initial impact of rock 'n' roll. Hogg's work seems to be something of an acquired taste and collectors are divided quite violently when judging its worth. He had no such problems with his black audience when his rural blues were sung to a small (often saxophone-led) band accompaniment and were appearing on labels from Texas to the coast.
● ALBUMS: including *Smokey Hogg* (1962)★★★, *I'm So Lonely* (1964)★★★, *Original Folk Blues* (1967)★★★, *Sings The Blues* (1971)★★★, with Earl Hooker, Lightnin' Hopkins *Hooker, Hopkins And Hogg* (Specialty 1973)★★★, *U Better Watch That Jive* (1974)★★, *Going Back Home* (Krazy Kat 1984)★★, *Everybody Needs Help* (1986)★★.
● COMPILATIONS: *Angels In Harlem* rec. 1949-58 (Ace 1992)★★★.

HOGG, WILLIE 'SMOKEY'

b. 19 November 1908, Centerville, Texas, USA. Poor recording, and the record company's half-hearted attempt to pass him off as the real (and long dead) Smokey Hogg, obscured the genuine abilities of this New York-based blues singer, who played good electric guitar in duet with Benny Jefferson, and sang traditionally based blues in a high voice. Stylistically, he was in the south-western mainstream, his music more reminiscent of Lowell Fulson than of the man he claimed to be, although, as might be expected, there are echoes of the real Smokey Hogg.
● COMPILATIONS: *The All Star Blues World Of Spivey Records* (1970)★★★.

HOKUM BOYS

'Hokum', with its connotations of verbal cleverness, was first applied to black music on record in the billing of 'Tampa Red's Hokum Jug Band' (performing 'It's Tight Like That', hokum's archetypal song). Tampa and his partner Georgia Tom were prominent in the hokum craze of the late 20s and early 30s. The Hokum

Boys were varied in personnel, and appeared on various labels; besides Tampa and Tom, participants included Big Bill Broonzy, Ikey Robinson, Jimmy Blythe, Blind Blake, Teddy Edwards, Casey Bill Weldon, Black Bob, Washboard Sam and 'hokum girl' Jane Lucas. Also celebrating the spirit of hokum were Frankie Jaxon (vocalist with the Hokum Jug Band) and Kansas City Kitty. Hokum groups favoured danceable rhythms and skilful musicianship, but the 'hokum' part of the billing seems chiefly to refer to the verbal content, heavily reliant on *double entendres* that are often ingenious and sometimes witty, and which probably seemed less tedious in the pre-album era. It has been plausibly suggested that the appeal of the Hokum Boys, apart from their obvious entertainment value, was to a black audience newly migrated from the south, and keen to confirm its newly urbanized sophistication.

● ALBUMS: *You Can't Get Enough Of That Stuff* (1976)★★★, *The Remaining Titles* (1988)★★★, *The Famous Hokum Boys* (Matchbox 1989)★★★.
● COMPILATIONS: *Complete Recordings 1935-1937* (Document 1987)★★★.

HOLE, DAVE

b. 30 March 1948, Heswall, Cheshire, England. Dave Hole's family moved to Perth, Western Australia, when Dave was four years old. The music of the Rolling Stones inspired him to pick up the guitar, and through them he discovered Muddy Waters and Howlin' Wolf. He had been playing for some 10 years before he took up slide guitar. A broken little finger caused him to play over the fretboard with the slide on his index finger, an unconventional method also adopted by Stan Webb. With various musicians, Hole led bands for some 20 years, playing the 'booze barns' around the Western Territory. A self-produced cassette that he sold at gigs found its way to Europe and America, where a *Guitar Player* article resulted in a contract with Alligator. The same album, *Short Fuse Blues*, prompted Gary Moore to add Hole to his 1992 European tour. Like many of his American counterparts, Hole is happy to play rousing, bar-band blues rock that is best heard live, but which remains entertaining on the albums that have followed.

● ALBUMS: *Short Fuse Blues* (Provogue 1992)★★★, *The Plumber* (Provogue 1993)★★★, *Working Overtime* (Provogue 1993)★★, *Steel On Steel* (Provogue 1995)★★★.
● COMPILATIONS: *Whole Lotta Blues* (Provogue 1996)★★★.

HOLLEY, 'LYIN'' JOE

b. c.1915, USA. Holley was recorded in April 1977 by George Paulus of Barrelhouse Records, who estimated his age as 'early sixties'. Holley had travelled throughout the southern USA and played in St. Louis and Detroit before settling in Chicago. He reputedly played blues piano at house parties and at the Provident Barber Shop on Saturdays for many years, and his recordings reveal a traditionally based pianist with a large repertoire and an ability to improvise memorable lyrics over a tough piano accompaniment. Holley is important as 'one of the last of the house party entertainers' but remains a very obscure figure, although he is reportedly still living in the Chicago area.

● ALBUMS: *So Cold In The USA* rec. 1977 (JSP 1982)★★★, *Piano Blues Legends* four tracks only (1983).

HOLLOWAY, RED

b. James W. Holloway, 31 May 1927, Helena, Arkansas, USA. Holloway grew up in a musical family - his father and mother were both musicians - and he initially played piano. He grew up in Chicago where he attended DuSable High School and the Conservatory of Music. While still at school, where his classmates included Von Freeman and Johnny Griffin, he took up the baritone saxophone, later switching to tenor. He played in and around Chicago, working with Gene Wright's big band for three years before entering the US Army. After his discharge he returned to Chicago, where he became deeply involved in the local jazz scene, playing with such artists as Yusef Lateef and Dexter Gordon. In 1948 he joined Roosevelt Sykes for a US tour. He remained based in Chicago throughout the 50s and early 60s, playing with many leading blues artists. In the early 60s he was resident in New York, then went back to Chicago for some time. In the mid-60s Holloway toured with Lionel Hampton and 'Brother' Jack McDuff and also led his own small groups. Towards the end of the decade he settled on the west coast. At first he worked in the studios, but eventually secured a lengthy club engagement in Los Angeles. In the early part of his career Holloway worked with many bluesmen, including Willie Dixon, Junior Parker, Bobby Bland, Lloyd Price, John Mayall, Muddy Waters, Chuck Berry and B.B. King. His jazz affiliations over the years include leading artists such as Billie Holiday, Ben Webster, Jimmy Rushing, Sonny Rollins, Red Rodney, Lester Young and Wardell Gray. He has worked with big bands, including Juggernaut, but became best known internationally after he teamed up with Sonny Stitt in 1977. During this partnership, Holloway began playing alto saxophone (at Stitt's insistence). After Stitt's death, Holloway resumed touring on his own, but occasionally worked with jazzmen such as Jay McShann and Clark Terry and jazz singer Carmen McRae. A driving player with a rich and bluesy sound, Holloway's late emergence on the international stage has attracted well-deserved attention to a solid and dependable musician.

● ALBUMS: *The Burner* (Prestige 1963)★★★, *Cookin' Together* (Prestige 1964)★★★, *Sax, Strings & Soul* (Prestige 1964)★★★, *Red Soul* (Prestige 1966)★★★, with Sonny Stitt *Just Friends* (1977)★★★, *Red Holloway And Company* (Concord 1986)★★★, with Carmen McRae *Fine And Mellow* (1987)★★★★, with Clark Terry *Locksmith Blues* (Concord 1988)★★, with Knut Riisnaes *The Gemini Twins* (1992)★★★.

HOLLYWOOD FATS

b. Michael Mann, 17 March 1954, d. December 1986, Los Angeles, California, USA. Hollywood Fats must be considered the father of the modern west-coast blues guitar. Having dropped out of school, he spent years on the road where he played with artists including J.B. Hutto, John Lee Hooker, Albert King and Muddy Waters. When Fats returned to Los Angeles he formed the Hollywood Fats Band in the mid-70s. In 1979 the group, which included Larry Taylor (ex-Canned Heat), Al Blake, Fred Kaplan and Richard Innes, recorded *Hollywood Fats*. Two years later Fats joined the band of his friend James Harman and recorded several albums, and later recorded with Smokey Wilson (*88th Street Blues* 1983), Rod Piazza (*Harpburn* 1986),

and William Clarke (*Tip Of The Top* 1987). In 1986 Hollywood Fats was drafted into the Blasters, with whom he spent his final months before suffering a fatal heart attack at the age of 32.

● ALBUMS: *Hollywood Fats* (Stomp 1979)★★★, with James Harman Band *Those Dangerous Gentlemens* (Rhino 1987)★★★, with Harman *Extra Napkins* (Rivera 1988)★★★, with Harman *Strictly Live...In '85 Volume One* (Rivera 1990)★★★, *Rock This House* (Black Top 1993)★★★.

HOLMES BROTHERS

Comprising Sherman Holmes (b. 29 September 1939, Plainfield, New Jersey, USA), Wendell Holmes (b. 19 December 1943, Plainfield, New Jersey, USA), Popsy Dixon (b. 26 July 1942, Virginia Beach, Virginia, USA) and Gib Wharton (b. 15 September 1955, Mineral Wells, Texas, USA), the Holmes Brothers took almost three decades to become an overnight sensation. Both men sang in the church choir in Christchurch (now Salud), Virginia, where they grew up. Sherman studied clarinet and piano before taking up the bass, while Wendell learned trumpet, organ and guitar. In 1959, Sherman took a break from studying music theory and composition at Virginia State University to visit New York, and never returned south. When Wendell graduated from high school in 1963, his brother brought him to New York. After working with Jimmy Jones and Charlie And Inez Foxx, they formed their own band, the Sevilles, which lasted from 1963 to 1966, after which they worked in a variety of Top 40 bands. The Holmes Brothers band finally came together in 1980, when they were joined by drummer Dixon, who proved to possess a strong tenor voice. Steel guitarist Wharton played in Texas country groups until he decided to move to New York in 1988. Each of the band's albums reveals the breadth of their repertoire, which they have claimed contains some 250 songs. Their long experience of playing all forms of popular music has enabled them to fuse elements of gospel, C&W, R&B and soul, and present them in an easily assimilable form.

● ALBUMS: *In The Spirit* (Rounder 1989)★★★★, *Where It's At* (Rounder 1991)★★★★, *Soul Street* (Rounder 1993)★★★,

Lotto Land: Original Soundtrack Recording (Stony Plain 1996)★★★, *Promised Land* (Rounder 1997)★★★.

HOLMES, WINSTON, AND CHARLIE TURNER

Turner played rack harmonica and guitar, and was an accomplished player of blues and rag-time (and, on unissued titles, of Sousa marches); Holmes sang, but played no instrument, although he appears to play clarinet in a photograph promoting a record by Lottie Kimbrough on his Merritt label. Neither the clarinettist nor Kimbrough, who was sick, arrived for the session, so Holmes and Kimbrough's sister Estella sat in. As might be inferred, Holmes was an energetic and resourceful music promoter in Kansas City, arranging concerts and recording sessions on his own and other labels; he was responsible for the debut (on Merritt) of Rev. J.C. Burnett. Holmes's own recordings, both with Turner and with Kimbrough, reveal a surreal sense of humour, and possibly a medicine-show background; along with the blues, he parodied sentimental ballads and black church services, throwing in yodelling, whistling and bird calls.
● ALBUMS: *Lottie Kimbrough And Winston Holmes* (*c*.1988)★★★.

HOLMES, WRIGHT

b. 4 July 1905, Hightower, Texas, USA. Apart from a spell of wartime defence work in the north, Holmes was based in Houston from 1930, by which time he was already a blues singer and guitarist, working in clubs on Dowling Street. His first recordings in 1947 were not issued because the producer felt he sounded too much like Lightnin' Hopkins, a judgment belied by three titles recorded the same year, and issued by Miltone and Gotham. Some of Holmes's lyrics come from Texas Alexander ('Alley Special' is based on two Alexander recordings), but both words and music (including vocal melodies) sound improvised; his guitar playing determinedly obscures its basic pulse with syncopations, changes of tempo, and explosive, random-sounding runs. Holmes gave up blues by 1950, and was last seen in 1967, by which time he had lost a leg and turned to religion.
● ALBUMS: *Alley Special* (1988)★★★.

HOLTS, ROOSEVELT

b. 15 January 1905, Tylertown, Mississippi, USA. Although he had been singing and playing blues guitar since his 20s, Holts was over 60 before he became known outside of his home area of southern Mississippi and Louisiana. A friend and companion of Tommy Johnson during the 30s, Holts learned to play many of that artist's pieces. In the 50s, he settled in Louisiana, and it was there he was discovered in the 60s. The Johnson connection seems to have rather preoccupied those who produced his records, but his repertoire was much wider and more substantial, and both his instrumental and vocal skills were remarkable for a performer of his age. For a short time around the end of the 60s, he issued some singles on his own label, Bluesman.
● ALBUMS: *Presenting The Country Blues* (Bluesman 1968)★★★.

HOMESICK JAMES

b. James Williamson, 3 May 1914, Somerville, Tennessee, USA. Williamson's father was a drummer and by the age of 14, he was playing guitar at local dances and taverns. Williamson developed a 'bottleneck' style by sliding a pocket-knife up and down the strings. In 1932 he moved north to Chicago and by the end of the decade had formed a small band which toured the southern states during the 40s. Among its members were Snooky Pryor and Baby Face Leroy Foster. His first recording was 'Lonesome Ole Train' (Chance 1952). From the mid-50s, Williamson worked regularly with his cousin Elmore James, playing second guitar on many of the latter's most famous records. Now known as Homesick James, he recorded his own most famous track for USA in 1962. An updated version of Robert Johnson's 'Crossroads', its pounding rhythms and heavily amplified bottleneck made it a landmark in city blues. After the death of Elmore James in 1963, Homesick James saw himself as the standard-bearer of his cousin's powerful guitar style. He recorded for Prestige and toured Europe in 1973, where he made an album with Pryor for Jim Simpson's Birmingham, England-based label, Big Bear.
● ALBUMS: *Blues From The Southside* (1964)★★★, *Homesick James & Snooky Pryor* (Big Bear 1973)★★★★, *Ain't Sick No More*

(1973)★★, *Home Sweet Homesick* (Big Bear 1976)★★★, *Goin' Back In The Times* (Earwig 1994)★★, *Juanita* (Appaloosa 1994)★★★, *Got To Move* (Trix 1994)★★, *Words Of Wisdom* (Icehouse 1997)★★★.

HOOKER, EARL

b. Earl Zebedee Hooker, 15 January 1930, Clarksdale, Mississippi, USA, d. 21 April 1970. Hooker's interest in music was kindled at an early age. A self-taught guitarist, he began his itinerant career as a teenager, and having toured America's southern states in the company of Robert Nighthawk, Ike Turner and many others, Earl made his first, rudimentary recordings in 1952. The artist followed a sporadic release schedule throughout the 50s, but by the end of the decade Hooker had settled in Chicago where he began a more consistent output. However, his early work was spread over several of the city's independent outlets, and although undeniably talented, the difficult search for success saw Hooker aping the styles of contemporaries rather than forging one of his own. The guitarist asserted his gifts more fully in the wake of the blues revival and became one of the city's most highly regarded talents. He made a rare UK television appearance on the pioneering music programme *Ready Steady Go*, performed in-concert at London's Royal Albert Hall and toured Europe with the American Folk-Blues festival. Hooker also completed albums for several specialist labels, and led his own band, Electric Dust, but the tuberculosis against which he had battled throughout his life finally took its toll. Earl Hooker died in a Chicago sanitarium in April 1970.

● ALBUMS: *Don't Have To Worry* (1969)★★★, *Sweet Black Angel* (1970)★★★, with Lightnin' Hopkins, Smokey Hogg *Hooker, Hopkins And Hogg* (Specialty 1973)★★★, *Do You Remember* (1973)★★★, with Steve Miller *Hooker And Steve* (Arhoolie 1975)★★★, *First And Last Recordings* (Arhoolie 1975)★★★, *Two Bugs And A Roach* (Arhoolie 1976)★★★, *Play Your Guitar, Mr. Hooker* (Black Magic 1985)★★★.

● COMPILATIONS: *There's A Fungus Amung Us* (1972)★★★, *The Leading Brand* (Red Lightnin' 1978)★★★, with Magic Sam *Calling All Blues* (Charly 1986)★★★.

HOOKER, JOHN LEE

b. 22 August 1917, Clarksdale, Mississippi, USA. Born into a large family of agricultural workers, Hooker's first musical experiences, like those of so many other blues singers, were in church. A contrivance made from an inner tube attached to a barn door represented his first makeshift attempts at playing an instrument, but he subsequently learned some guitar from his stepfather William Moore, and they played together at local dances. At the age of 14, he ran away to Memphis, Tennessee, where he met and played with Robert Lockwood. A couple of years later he moved to Cincinnatti, where he stayed for about 10 years and sang with a number of gospel quartets. In 1943, he moved to Detroit, which was to be his home for many years, and began playing in the blues clubs and bars around Hastings Street, at the heart of that city's black section. Over the years he had developed the unique guitar style that was to make his music so distinctive and compelling. In 1948 he was finally given the chance to record. Accompanied only by his own electric guitar and constantly tapping foot, 'Boogie Chillen', with its driving rhythm and hypnotic drone of an accompaniment, was a surprise commercial success for Modern Records. Over the next few years, they leased a large amount of his material first from Bernie Besman and later from legendary Detroit entrepreneur Joe Von Battle (both of whom also tried a few Hooker issues on their own Sensation and JVB labels, respectively). Most of these early recordings feature Hooker performing entirely solo; only a few are duets with Eddie Kirkland or another guitarist, and there are one or two with a band. It seems that this solo setting was not typical of his live work at the time, which would have used a small band, probably including piano, second guitar and drums, but his idiosyncratic sense of timing has always made him a difficult musician to accompany, and it may be that recording him solo was the most reliable way of ensuring a clean take. Nevertheless, his solo sound on these early records was remarkably self-sufficient. His unique open-tuned guitar enabled him to combine a steady rhythm with inspired lead picking, thereby making full use of his rich, very bluesy baritone vocals. Although this one-man-band format might suggest a throwback to a more down-home ambience, there is a certain hipness and urbane sophistication about these performances that represent a significant departure from the rural background of Hooker's music and contribute very strongly to his characteristic sound. While a solo blues singer was something of an anachronism by this time, there is no doubt that the records sold consistently.

From the late 40s to the early 50s, Hooker recorded prolifically and enjoyed an enormously successful run with Modern, producing such classic records as 'Crawling King Snake', 'In The Mood', 'Rock House Boogie' and 'Shake Holler & Run'. As well as these successes under his own name, he saw records released on a wide variety of labels, under a deliberately bewildering array of different pseudonyms: Johnny Williams on Gotham, Birmingham Sam And His Magic Guitar on Savoy, John Lee Booker on Chess, Delta John on Regent, The Boogie Man on Acorn, Johnny Lee on DeLuxe and Texas Slim or John Lee Cooker on King. Most of these were also leased from Joe Von Battle. His recording success led to tours. He played the R&B circuit across the country and this further developed his popularity with the black American public. In 1955, he severed his connection with Modern and began a long association with Vee Jay Records of Chicago.

By this time, the solo format was finally deemed too old-fashioned for the contemporary R&B market and all of these recordings used a tight little band, often including Eddie Taylor on guitar, as well as piano and various combinations of horns. The association with Vee Jay proved very satisfactory, both artistically and commercially, producing a string of hits such as 'Dimples', 'Maudie' and 'Boom Boom' and promoting further extensive tours. In the late 50s, as the market for R&B was beginning to contract, a new direction opened up for Hooker and he began to appear regularly at folk clubs and folk festivals. He found himself lionized by a new audience consisting mainly of young, white listeners. The folk connection also resulted in new recordings, issued on album by Riverside. These reverted to the solo format, with an acoustic guitar. While these recordings lacked the hard edge of the best of his earlier commercial sides, they were fascinating for the fact that the producers encouraged him to dig back into his older repertoire. Several songs reflecting his rural Mississippi background, such as 'Bundle Up And Go' and 'Pea Vine Special' were given his distinctive treatment. These records spread his name more widely when they were released overseas. In the early 60s his reputation grew as he was often cited by younger pop and rock musicians, in particular the Rolling Stones, as a major influence. As a result international tours soon followed. Throughout this period, he continued to release singles and albums on Vee Jay, but records also appeared on other labels. Later in the 60s, he made a number of records for Bluesway, aimed at this younger market. The connection with a new generation of musicians led to various 'super sessions', predictably of varying quality, but it perhaps bore fruit most successfully in the early 70s with the release of *Hooker 'N' Heat*, in which he played with the American rock blues band Canned Heat. Their famous long improvised boogies clearly owed a great deal to the influence of the older man. Although the popular enthusiasm for blues waned for a while in the late 70s and early 80s, Hooker's standing has rarely faltered and he has continued to tour, latterly with the Coast To Coast Blues Band. His early recordings have been repackaged and re-released over and over again, with those companies who used him pseudonymously in the early days now proudly taking the opportunity to capitalize on his real name. He has also made many new records but few of these have been of outstanding quality. A remarkable transformation came in 1989 when he recorded *The Healer*. This superb album featured guests on most tracks including Bonnie Raitt, Los Lobos and, arguably the finest track, a duet with Carlos Santana on the title track. If such a thing as 'Latin blues' existed, this was it. This album has since become one of the biggest-selling blues albums of all time and has helped fuel a blues revival in prompting older statesmen to record again. *Mr Lucky* reached number 3 in the UK album charts, setting a record for Hooker, at 74, as the oldest artist to achieve that position. On this second guest album he was paired with Ry Cooder, Van Morrison, Albert Collins, and a gamut of other superstars. In his old age, Hooker has begun to fulfil the role of elder statesman of the blues, even appearing in an advertisement for a multinational chemical corporation, but this has not prevented him from touring and he continues to perform widely and often. Hooker is genuinely loved by fellow musicians; Bonnie Raitt stated in 1992 that his guitar sound was one of the most erotic things she had ever heard. The Hooker boom continued right through 1992 with the use of a new version of 'Boom Boom' for a Lee Jeans television advertisement. Both the single and the subsequent album were considerable hits. Following a hernia operation in 1994 the great man decided to slow down and enjoy his cars and houses. Another fine release, *Chill Out*, came in 1995, again produced by Roy Rogers. Shortly after its release it was announced that Hooker had retired from performing and was prepared to rest until they 'lowered his bones into the earth'. However, he was back on stage performing in 1996 and released a new album in 1997. *Don't Look Back* was a Van Morrison production and bore clear signs of his influence; Morrison's 'The Healing Game' and Jimi Hendrix's 'Red House' were the highlights, and 'Don't Look Back' was beautifully understated, with some fine noodling organ and guitar from Charles Brown and Danny Caron respectively. This formidable man is the last surviving giant of the blues, and therefore, represents our final touchstone with a body of music that is both rich in history and unmatched in its importance.

● ALBUMS: *The Folk Blues Of John Lee Hooker* (Riverside 1959)★★★★, *I'm John Lee Hooker* (Vee Jay 1959)★★★★, *Travelin'* (Vee Jay 1960)★★★★, *Sings The Blues* (King 1960)★★★★, *Thats My Story* (Riverside 1960)★★★★, *House Of The Blues* (Chess 1960)★★★★, *The Blues* (Crown 1960)★★★, *The Folk Lore Of John Lee Hooker* (Vee Jay 1961)★★★★, *Burnin'* (Vee Jay 1962)★★★, *John Lee Hooker On Campus* (1963)★★★, *The Big Soul Of John Lee Hooker* (Vee Jay 1963)★★★, *Don't Turn Me From Your Door* (Atco 1963)★★★, *John Lee Hooker At Newport* (Vee Jay 1964)★★★★, *I Want To Shout The Blues* (Stateside 1964)★★★, *And Seven Nights* (Verve/Folkways 1965)★★★, *Real Folk Blues* (Chess 1966)★★★★, *It Serves You Right To Suffer* (Impulse 1966)★★★, *Live At The Cafe Au Go Go* (Bluesway 1966)★★★, *Urban Blues* (Bluesway 1967)★★★, *Simply The Truth* (Bluesway 1968)★★★, *You're Leaving Me Baby* (1969)★★★, *If You Miss 'Im* (Bluesway 1969)★★★, *Tupelo Blues* (1969)★★★, *Alone* (1970)★★★, *Hooker 'N' Heat* (Specialty 1971)★★★★, *Endless Boogie* (ABC 1971)★★★, *Never Get Out Of These Blues Alive* (Crescendo 1972)★★★, *John Lee Hooker's Detroit* (1973)★★★, *Live At Kabuki Wuki* (Bluesway 1973)★★, *Mad Man's Blues* (Chess 1973)★★★, *Free Beer And Chicken* (1974)★★, *Blues Before Sunrise* (1976)★★★, *No Friend Around* (1979)★★, *This Is Hip* (1980)★★★, *Black Snake Blues* (1980)★★★, *Moanin' The Blues* (1982)★★★, *Lonesome Mood* (1983)★★★, *Solid Sender* (1984)★★, *Jealous* (Pointblank 1986)★★★, *The Healer* (Chameleon 1989)★★★★★, *The Detroit Lion* (1990)★★, *Boogie Awhile* (1990)★★, *More Real Folk Blues: The Missing Album* (1991)★★★, *Mr. Lucky* (Charisma 1991)★★★★, *Boom Boom* (Point Blank 1992)★★★, *Chill Out* (Point Blank 1995)★★★★, with the Groundhogs *Hooker & The Hogs* rec. 1965 (Indigo 1996)★★, *The First Concert - Alone* 1976 recording (Blues Alliance 1996)★★★, *Don't Look Back* (Silvertone 1997)★★★.

● COMPILATIONS: *The Best Of John Lee Hooker* (Vee Jay 1962)★★★, *Collection: John Lee Hooker - 20 Blues Greats* (Déjà Vu 1985)★★★, *The Ultimate Collection 1948-1990* (1992)★★★★, *The Best Of John Lee Hooker 1965-1974* (1992)★★★★, *Blues Brother* (1992)★★★, *The Vee Jay Years 1955 - 1964* (1992)★★★★, *Gold Collection* (1993)★★★, *The Legendary Modern Recordings 1948-54* (1993)★★★★, *Helpless Blues* (Realisation 1994)★★★, *Original Folk Blues ... Plus* (Ace 1994)★★★★, *The Rising Sun Collection* (Just A Memory 1994)★★★, *Whiskey & Wimmen* (Charly 1994)★★★, *The EP Collection Plus* (See For Miles 1995)★★★★, *The Early Years* (Tomato 1995)★★★, *I Feel Good* (Jewel 1995)★★★, *Alternative Boogie: Early Studio Recordings 1948-1952* (Capitol 1996)★★★.

● VIDEOS: *Survivors - The Blues Today* (Hendring Video 1989), *John Lee Hooker/Lowell Fulson/Percy Mayfield* (1992), *John Lee Hooker And Friends 1984-1992* (Vestapol 1996), *Rare Performances 1960-1984* (Vestapol 1996).

● FURTHER READING: *Boogie Chillen: A Guide To John Lee Hooker On Disc*, Les Fancourt.

● FILMS: *The Blues Brothers* (1980).

HOPKINS, JOEL

b. 3 January 1904, Centreville, Texas, USA, d. 15 February 1975, Galveston, Texas, USA. An elder brother of Lightnin' Hopkins, guitarist Joe learned his trade from Blind Lemon Jefferson when they travelled together during the 20s. Joel Hopkins spent most of his life working outside of music, but in 1947 he accompanied his brother Lightin' on his famous Gold Star recording of 'Short Haired Woman'. He resurfaced in 1959 to record a handful of archaic Texas blues for historian and folklorist Mack McCormick. The latter part of his life was spent in ill health, and he died from a heart attack in 1975.

● ALBUMS: including with Lightnin' Hopkins *Joel & Lightnin' Hopkins 1959* (1990)★★★.

HOPKINS, LIGHTNIN'

b. Sam Hopkins, 15 March 1912, Centreville, Texas, USA, d. 30 January 1982. One of the last great country blues singers, Hopkins' lengthy career began in the Texas bars and juke joints of the 20s. Towards the end of the decade he formed a duo with a cousin, Texas Alexander, while his Lightnin' epithet was derived from a subsequent partnership with barrelhouse pianist Thunder Smith, with whom he made his first recordings. Hopkins' early work unveiled a masterly performer. His work first came to prominence when, after being discovered by Sam Charters at the age of 47, *The Roots Of Lightnin' Hopkins* was released in 1959 and numerous sessions followed. His sparse acoustic guitar and narrated prose quickly made him an important discovery, appealing to the audience of the American folk boom of the early 60s. His harsh, emotive voice and compulsive, if irregular, guitarwork, conveyed an intensity enhanced by the often personal nature of his lyrics. He became one of post-war blues most prolific talents, completing hundreds of sessions for scores of major and independent labels. This inevitably diluted his initial power, but although Hopkins' popularity slumped in the face of Chicago's electric combos, by the early 60s he was re-established as a major force on the college and concert-hall circuit. In 1967 the artist was the subject of an autobiographical film, *The Blues Of Lightnin' Hopkins*, which subsequently won the Gold Hugo award at the Chicago Film Festival. Like many other bluesmen finding great success in the 60s (for example, Muddy Waters and John Lee Hooker), he too recorded a 'progressive' electric album: *The Great Electric Show And Dance*. He maintained a compulsive work-rate during the 70s, touring the USA, Canada and, in 1977, Europe, until ill health forced him to reduce such commitments. Hopkins was a true folk poet, embracing social comments with pure blues. He died in 1982, his status as one of the major voices of the blues assured.

● ALBUMS: *Strums The Blues* (Score 1958)★★★, *Lightnin' And The Blues* (Herald 1959)★★★, *The Roots Of Lightnin' Hopkins* (Folkways 1959)★★★, *Down South Summit Meeting* (1960)★★★★, *Mojo Hand* (Fire 1960)★★★★, *Country Blues* (Tradition 1960)★★★, *Lightnin' In New York* (Candid 1961)★★★, *Autobiography In Blues* (Tradition 1961)★★★, *Lightnin'* (Bluesville 1961)★★★, *Last Night Blues* (Bluesville 1961)★★★, *Blues In My Bottle* (Bluesville 1962)★★★★, *Lightnin' Strikes Again* (Dart 1962)★★★, *Sings The Blues* (Crown 1962)★★★, *Lightnin' Hopkins* (Folkways 1962)★★★★, *Fast Life Woman* (Verve 1962)★★★, *On Stage* (Imperial 1962)★★, *Walkin' This Street* (Bluesville 1962)★★★★, *Lightnin' And Co* (Bluesville 1963)★★★, *Smokes Like Lightnin'* (Bluesville 1963)★★★, *First Meetin'* (World Pacific 1963)★★★, *Lightnin' Hopkins And The Blues* (Imperial 1963)★★★, *Goin' Away* (Bluesville 1963)★★★, *Hootin' The Blues* (Folklore 1964)★★★, *Down Home Blues* (Bluesville 1964)★★★★, *The Roots Of Lightnin' Hopkins* (Verve/Folkways 1965)★★★★, *Soul Blues* (Prestige 1966)★★★, *Something Blue* (Verve/Folkways 1967)★★★, *The Great Electric Show And Dance* (1968)★★★, *Free Form Patterns* (International Artists 1968)★★★, *King Of Dowling Street* (1969)★★★, *California Mudslide* (Vault/Rhino 1969)★★★.

● COMPILATIONS: *Legacy Of The Blues Volume Twelve* (Sonet 1974)★★★★, *The Best Of Lightnin' Hopkins* (Tradition 1964)★★★, *The Gold Star Sessions - Volumes 1&2* (Arhoolie 1990)★★★★, *The Complete Prestige/Bluesville Recordings* 7CD set(Prestige/Bluesville 1992)★★★★, *The Complete Aladdin Recordings* (EMI 1992)★★★★, *Sittin' In With Lightnin' Hopkins* (Mainstream 1992)★★★, *Blues Is My*

Business rec. 1971 (1993)★★★, *You're Gonna Miss Me* (1993)★★★, *Mojo Hand: The Lightnin' Hopkins Anthology* (Rhino 1993)★★★★, *It's A Sin To Be Rich* rec. 1973 (1993)★★★, *Coffee House Blues* rec. 1960-62 (1993)★★★★, *Po' Lightnin'* (Arhoolie 1995)★★★★, *Blue Lightnin'* (Jewel 1995)★★★, *Hootin' The Blues* (Prestige 1995)★★★★, *The Rising Sun Collection* (Just A Memory 1995)★★★★, *Autobiography In Blues* (Tradition 1996)★★★★, *Country Blues* (Tradition 1996)★★★★.
● VIDEOS: *Rare Performances 1960-1979* (Vestapol 1995).
● FURTHER READING: *Lightnin' Hopkins: Blues'*, M. McCormick.

HORTON, WALTER 'SHAKEY'

b. 6 April 1918, Horn Lake, Mississippi, USA, d. 8 December 1981, Chicago, Illinois, USA. Horton, also aka 'Mumbles' and 'Big Walter', claimed to have taught himself harmonica by the time he was five years old, and certainly the extraordinary skill he achieved speaks of a very special affinity with the instrument. By his teens, he was in Memphis and beginning to make a living from music. He later claimed to have been on recordings by the Memphis Jug Band in 1927, but as he would have been only nine years old, this seems unlikely. More plausibly, he may have been the harmonica accompanist on Buddy Doyle's 1939 records. Throughout the 40s, he continued to develop his skills on the instrument, but it was not until 1951 that he recorded in his own right, back in Memphis. Over the next two years he made a series of recordings, many of which were not issued until many years later, but which demonstrate Horton's remarkable talent, singing and playing his harmonica with great skill and imagination. One of the finest recordings was 'Easy', a slow instrumental solo, accompanied only by Jimmy DeBerry's guitar, issued on Sun in 1953. Later that year, he was again in Chicago and issued two sides under Johnny Shines' name. With Horton's brilliant, soaring and swooping harmonica work and Shines' uniquely powerful, impassioned vocals, 'Evening Sun', with its flip-side 'Brutal Hearted Woman', was widely regarded as one of the finest blues records from post-war Chicago. Throughout the decade, he was playing regularly in Chicago, sometimes with Shines, or with Muddy Waters. He appeared on some of the latter's recordings, as well as others by Jimmy Rogers, Arbee Stidham and Sunnyland Slim. In the 60s, he reached a new audience, travelling widely in the USA and touring Europe with blues packages. As time went on, he demonstrated his versatility by adding pop and jazz themes to his repertoire, as well as showing a fondness for Latin tunes such as 'La Cucaracha' and 'La Paloma'. He was always primarily a blues player and the tough, electric sounds of Memphis and Chicago remained the essence of his music through many fine recordings in the 60s and 70s.
● ALBUMS: *Walter Horton And Carey Bell* (Alligator 1972)★★★, *Fine Cuts* (Blind Pig 1978)★★★★, *Little Boy Blue* (JSP 1980)★★★★, *Mouth Harp Maestro* (Ace 1988)★★★, with Joe Hill Louis, Mose Vinson *The Be-Bop Boy* (1993)★★★.

HOUSTON, CISCO

b. Gilbert Vandine Houston, 18 August 1918, Wilmington, Delaware, USA, d. 25 April 1961, San Bernadino, California, USA. Houston's family moved to California in 1919. Having spent his early years in a variety of simple jobs, he found himself, like many others in the 30s, unemployed. He wanted to become a comedian, but obtained only secondary roles in a few Hollywood movies. Houston subsequently became involved in theatre work and a number of folk festivals, as well as union meetings and political gatherings. He then travelled with Woody Guthrie and Will Geer. In 1940 Houston joined the US merchant marines with Guthrie and performed for the benefit of fellow seamen. It was after the war that the two returned to New York and Houston began touring, performing at concerts and recording. In 1959, the US State Department sent him, together with Sonny Terry and Brownie McGhee, to India on a cultural exchange. By this time Houston knew that cancer of the stomach was threatening his life. Despite this fact, he still performed at the 1960 Newport Folk Festival and continued to record for Vanguard. He made his last appearance in Pasadena at a folk concert, in spite of his illness, and died in 1961. Tom Paxton commemorated his memory in the song 'Fare Thee Well Cisco'.
● ALBUMS: *900 Miles And Other Railroad*

Ballads (Folkways 1952)★★★, *Sings Cowboy Ballads* (Folkways 1952)★★★, *Hard Travelin'* (Folkways 1954)★★★, *Sings Folk Songs* (Folkways 1955)★★★, *The Cisco Special* (Vanguard 1961)★★★, *I Aint Got No Home* (Vanguard 1962)★★★, *Sings The Songs Of Woody Guthrie* (Vanguard 1963)★★★★, *Songs Of The Open Road* (Folkways 1964)★★★★, *Passing Through* (Verve/Folkways 1965)★★★.
● COMPILATIONS: *The Folkways Years 1944-1961* (Smithsonian/Folkways 1994)★★★★.
● FURTHER READING: *900 Miles - The Ballads, Blues And Folksongs Of Cisco Houston.*

HOUSTON, EDWARD 'BEE'
b. 19 April 1938, San Antonio, Texas, USA, d. 19 March 1991, Los Angeles, California, USA. Houston ran a band in San Antonio and did back-up work for visiting artists such as Brook Benton, Little Willie John, Junior Parker and Bobby Bland. In 1961 he moved to the west coast, and played with McKinley Mitchell, Little Johnny Taylor and (his most enduring association) Big Mama Thornton. His playing was influenced by Clarence 'Gatemouth' Brown and B.B. King, but his album was both lacking in individuality and was too soul-influenced for the white blues audience at whom it was aimed. As a result he failed to become a name artist. Little was heard of Houston thereafter until it was reported that he had died from alcoholism in 1991.
● ALBUMS: *Bee Houston* (1970)★★.

HOUSTON, JOE
b. 1927, Austin, Texas, USA. Joe Houston was inspired to take up the saxophone after seeing Count Hastings playing with Tiny Bradshaw's Orchestra, and lists Joe Thomas, Charlie Parker and Arnett Cobb among his other influences. By 1949 he became associated with Big Joe Turner, and made his recording debut on Turner's sole release on the Rouge label and probably played on Turner's first Freedom session. Houston's own recording career began in 1949 with Freedom Records, although his biggest successes were with 'Worry-Worry-Worry' (recorded by Bob Shad for his Sittin In With label, but actually issued on Mercury in 1951), 'Cornbread And Cabbage Greens' and 'Blow, Joe, Blow' (both for Macy's Records, also in 1951), and with 'All Night

Long' (recorded for both the Money and Caddy labels, after Houston relocated to Los Angeles in 1955). Other recordings were issued on a gamut of labels: Modern, RPM, Crown, Imperial, Bay'ou, Combo, Lucky, Recorded In Hollywood, Cas, Dooto and other independent Los Angeles labels. In recent years, Houston has made a comeback with numerous personal appearances.
● ALBUMS: *Kicking Back* (c.1983)★★★, *Rockin' At The Drive In* (Ace 1984)★★★, *Earthquake* (Pathe Marconi 1985)★★★, *Rockin' 'N' Boppin'* (Saxophonograph 1989)★★★, *Cornbread And Cabbage Greens* (Ace 1992)★★★, with Otis Grand *The Return Of Honk* (JSP 1994)★★★.

HOVINGTON, FRANK
b. 9 January 1919, Reading, Pennsylvania, USA, d. 21 June 1982, Felton, Delaware, USA. Raised in Frederica, Delaware, Hovington was playing banjo and guitar by 1934, learning from Adam Greenfield and William Walker. From 1939-71, he played intermittently with Gene Young. Hovington's music and repertoire were influenced by the omnipresent Blind Boy Fuller, but he played with a firm thumb beat, and sometimes took considerable rhythmic liberties. Moving to Washington DC in 1948, Hovington occasionally went to Philadelphia, where he worked with Doug Quattlebaum and Washboard Slim (Robert Young); in Philadelphia. He also played with Blind Connie Williams, and this, together with his occasional work in jazz and gospel groups, probably accounts for the relative sophistication of his harmonies.
● ALBUMS: *Lonesome Road Blues* (1975)★★★, *Lonesome Home Blues* (1982)★★★.

HOWARD, CAMILLE
b. 29 March 1914, Galveston, Texas, USA. Howard took over the stool from Betty Hall Jones as pianist with Roy Milton's Solid Senders in the early 40s. She recorded with Milton on all his prime recordings for Specialty Records and his own Roy Milton/Miltone labels of the 40s and early 50s, and was occasionally featured singing her 'Groovy Blues', 'Mr Fine', 'Thrill Me' and 'Pack Your Sack, Jack', among others. Remaining with Milton, Howard simultaneously pursued her own recording career from 1946 when she recorded for the small Pan American

label with James Clifford's band and, more notably, with her own sessions for Specialty which resulted in her successful instrumental boogies (including her biggest hit 'X-temperaneous Boogie') and small band R&B vocals (like the similarly successful 'Money Blues'). In 1953 Howard was signed to Federal for two west coast sessions and she went to Chicago and Vee Jay for her final single in 1956. Camille Howard still lives in Los Angeles, where her voice and keyboard skills are reserved only for spiritual performances. Her reissued material on Ace Records covers her most interesting work.
● ALBUMS: with Edith Mackey, Priscilla Bowman, Christine Kittrell *Rock 'N' Roll Mamas* (1985)★★★, with Lil Armstrong And Dorothy Donegan *Brown Gal 1946-1950* (Krazy Kat 1987)★★★, *X-Temperaneous Boogie* (1989)★★★, *Rock Me Daddy: Camille Howard Vol 1*(Ace 1993)★★★★, *X-Temporaneous Boogie: Camille Howard Vol 2* (Ace 1996)★★★★.

HOWARD, ROSETTA
b. *c.*1914, Chicago, Illinois, USA, d. 1974, Chicago, Illinois, USA. Initially a dancer, Rosetta Howard moved into singing by joining in with juke-box selections at the club where she worked, graduating to live work in Chicago with Jimmie Noone, Eddie Smith and Sonny Thompson. Her warm tones can be heard on a distinguished series of light-hearted, jazz-tinged blues recordings made with the Harlem Hamfats between 1937 and 1939, and she also recorded with Henry 'Red' Allen. In 1947 Howard recorded with Willie Dixon's Big Three Trio, including a fine version of 'Ebony Rhapsody', but from the early 50s she devoted her time to church work at Thomas A. Dorsey's Pilgrim Baptist Church.
● ALBUMS: *Rosetta Howard* (1989)★★★, *Harlem Hamfats (With Rosetta Howard)* (Earl Archives 1990)★★★.

HOWELL, PEG LEG
b. Joshua Barnes Howel, 5 March 1888, Eatonton, Georgia, USA, d. 11 August 1966, Atlanta, Georgia, USA. Howell's music is a complex mixture of blues, street vendors' cries, gamblers' argot, fragments of narrative ballads and, in the company of his 'Gang' (usually guitarist Henry Williams and fiddler Eddie

Anthony), white fiddle pieces, ragtime, and other dance music. As a soloist, he sang introspective pieces, with a plaintive delivery, accompanied by short melodic fragments on guitar. His work with his group was very different, the lyrics delivered in a low growl as part of perhaps the liveliest, and rowdiest, party music on record. Also a bootlegger (for which he served time in jail), Howell abandoned music in 1934 when Anthony died, and was very ill when found in 1963. An album was released that year, primarily to generate royalties, but it is hard listening.
● ALBUMS: *The Legendary Peg Leg Howell* (1963)★★, *Peg Leg Howell Volume 1, 1926-1927* (Matchbox 1983)★★★, *Peg Leg Howell Volume 2, 1928-1929* (Matchbox 1983)★★★, *Complete Recorded Works Vols. 1 & 2* (Matchbox 1994)★★★.

HOWLIN' WILF
(see Hunter, James)

HOWLIN' WOLF
b. Chester Arthur Burnett, 10 June 1910, West Point, Mississippi, USA, d. 10 January 1976, Hines, Illinois, USA. Howlin' Wolf was one of the most important of the southern expatriates who created the post-war blues out of their rural past and moulded it into the tough 'Chicago sound' of the 50s. He was one of six children born to farmer Dock Burnett and his wife Gertrude, and spent his earliest years around Aberdeen, Mississippi, where he sang in the local baptist church. In 1923 he relocated to Ruleville, Mississippi, and 10 years later moved again to work on Nat Phillips' plantation at Twist, Arkansas. By this time he was working in music, appearing at local parties and juke joints. He had been inspired by performers like Charley Patton and Tommy Johnson, both of whom he had met, and he took much of the showmanship of his act from them, although his hoarse, powerful voice and eerie 'howling' were peculiarly his own. Other seminal Mississippi figures, Robert Johnson and Son House, also proved influential. During this period he enjoyed many nicknames such as 'Big Foot' and 'Bull Cow' but it was as Howlin' Wolf that his fame grew. He was a huge man with a commanding presence and threatening aspect, whom contemporary

Johnny Shines once likened to a wild animal, saying that he (Shines) was scared to lay his hand on him.

Throughout the 30s Wolf combined farming with working in music, sometimes travelling in the company of people such as Shines, Robert Johnson, and Sonny Boy 'Rice Miller' Williamson. Williamson, who courted and married Wolf's half-sister Mary, taught his new brother-in-law to play some harmonica and Wolf also experimented with the guitar. Wolf's first marriage had been to a sister of singer Willie Brown and it was during this time that he married his second wife, Lillie Handley. It was a union that lasted until his death. During 1941-44 Wolf was drafted into the army but once he had left, he formed his own group and gained sufficient fame to be approached by KWEM, a west Memphis radio station that was competing for local black listeners and recognized Wolf's potential. For KWEM, Wolf worked as a disc jockey as well as performing himself, and this brought him to the attention of Sam Phillips, who was recording material in Memphis and leasing it to others for sale in the black communities of the northern and western areas of the USA. Phillips, who considered Wolf to be one of the greatest talents he knew, originally made separate agreements with the Bihari Brothers in California and the Chess Brothers of Chicago to issue Wolf's recordings. The success of the early recordings led to something of a war between these two camps, with each trying to attract him under their own aegis. On the evidence of some of the songs that he recorded at the time, it seems that Wolf was tempted to take a 'stroll out west', but in the event he went to Chicago, 'the onliest one who drove out of the south like a gentleman'.

In Memphis, Wolf, whose recording sessions were often under the direction of Ike Turner, had been lucky to employ the talents of guitarist Willie Johnson, who refused to move north, and in Chicago that good fortune continued as he worked first with Jody Williams and then the unique Hubert Sumlin. The raw delta sound of Wolf's earlier records assured him of a ready-made audience once he reached Chicago, and he quickly built a powerful reputation on the club circuit, extending it with such classic records as 'Smokestack Lightning' and 'Killing Floor'. Like his great rival Muddy Waters, he maintained his audience, and a Chess recording contract, through the lean times of rock 'n' roll and into the blues boom of the 60s. He came to Europe with the AFBF in 1964 and continued to return over the next ten years. The Rolling Stones and the Yardbirds did much to publicize Wolf's (and Waters') music, both in Europe and white America, and as the 60s progressed, the newer artists at Chess saw their target audience as the emerging white 'love and peace' culture and tried to influence their material to suit it. Wolf's music was a significant influence on rock and many of his best-known songs - 'Sitting On Top Of The World', 'I Ain't Superstitious', 'Killin' Floor', 'Back Door Man' and 'Little Red Rooster' - were recorded by acts as diverse as the Doors, Cream, the Rolling Stones, the Yardbirds and Manfred Mann. Few, however, rivalled the power or sexual bravura displayed on the originals and only Don Van Vliet (Captain Beefheart) came close to recapturing his aggressive, raucous voice. A compelling appearance on the teen-oriented *Shindig* television show (at the behest of the Rolling Stones) was a rare concession to commerciality. His label's desire for success, akin to the white acts he influenced, resulted in the lamentable *The Howlin' Wolf Album*, which the artist described as 'dog shit'. This ill-conceived attempt to update earlier songs was outshone by *The London Howlin' Wolf Sessions*, on which Wolf and long-serving guitarist Hubert Sumlin were joined by an array of guests, including Eric Clapton, Steve Winwood, and Rolling Stones members Bill Wyman and Charlie Watts. Wolf, along with others like Muddy Waters, resisted this move but were powerless to control it. They were, of course, men in their 50s, set in their ways but needing to maintain an audience outside the dwindling Chicago clubs. Fortunately, Wolf outlived this trend, along with that for piling well-known artists together into 'super bands'. Wolf continued to tour but his health was declining. After a protracted period of illness Howlin' Wolf died of cancer in the Veterans Administration Hospital in 1976. His influence has survived the excesses of the 'swinging 60s' and is to be seen today in the work of many of the emerging black bluesmen such as Roosevelt 'Booba' Barnes.

● ALBUMS: *Moaning In The Moonlight* (Chess

1959)★★★, *Howlin' Wolf* aka *The Rocking Chair Album* (Chess 1962)★★★★, *Howlin' Wolf Sings The Blues* (Crown 1962)★★★, *The Real Folk Blues* (Chess 1966)★★★★, *Big City Blues* (1966)★★★, *The Super Blues Band* (1967)★★★, *Evil* (Chess 1967)★★★, *More Real Folk Blues* (Chess 1967)★★★★, *This Is Howlin' Wolf's New Album* aka *The Dog Shit Album* (Cadet 1969)★★, *Message To The Young* (Chess 1971)★★, *The London Sessions* (Chess 1971)★★★, *Live And Cookin' At Alice's Revisited* (Chess 1972)★★, *AKA Chester Burnett* (Chess 1972)★★★, *The Back Door Wolf* (Chess 1973)★★★★, *Change My Way* (Chess 1975)★★★, *Ridin' In The Moonlight* (Ace 1982)★★★, *Live In Europe 1964* (Sundown 1988)★★★, *Memphis Days Vol. 1* (Bear Family 1989)★★★, *Memphis Days Vol. 2* (Bear Family 1990)★★★, *Howlin' Wolf Rides Again* (Ace 1991)★★★.

● COMPILATIONS: *Going Back Home* (1970)★★★, *Chess Blues Masters* (Chess 1976)★★★★, *The Legendary Sun Performers* (Charly 1977)★★★, *Chess Masters* (Chess 1981)★★★★, *Chess Masters 2* (Chess 1982)★★★★, *Chess Masters 3* (Chess 1983)★★★, *The Wolf* (Blue Moon 1984)★★★, *Golden Classics* (Astan 1984)★★★, *The Howlin' Wolf Collection* (Déjà Vu 1985)★★★★, *His Greatest Hits* (Chess 1986)★★★, *Cadillac Daddy: Memphis Recordings, 1952* (Rounder 1987)★★★, *Howlin' For My Baby* (Sun 1987)★★★, *Shake For Me - The Red Rooster* (Vogue 1988)★★★, *Smokestack Lightnin'* (Vogue 1988)★★★, *Red Rooster* (Joker 1988)★★★, *Moanin' And Howlin'* (Charly 1988)★★★, *Howlin' Wolf* 5-LP box set (Chess 1991)★★★★, *Going Down Slow* 5-CD box set (Roots 1992)★★★★, *Gold Collection* (1993)★★★, *The Wolf Is At Your Door* (Fan 1994)★★★, *The Complete Recordings 1951-1969* 7-CD box set (Charly 1994)★★★★, *The Genuine Article - The Best Of* (MCA 1994)★★★★, *The Very Best Of Howlin' Wolf* 3-CD set (Charly 1995)★★★★, *His Best* (Chess 1997)★★★★.

HUFF, LUTHER

b. 5 December 1910, Fannin, Mississippi, USA, d. 18 November 1973, Detroit, Michigan, USA. Luther and younger brother Percy made only two records in 1951, but they cleaved so startlingly and entertainingly to the old traditions that they have been prized ever since. They learned guitar from older brother Willie and cousin Donnee Howard and, like them, played at fish fries and country picnics. One picnic, held at a plantation in Belzoni, lasted 13 days. Luther bought a mandolin in 1936 and taught himself to play. Drafted into the army in 1942, Luther saw service in England, France and Belgium, where, in 1944, he recorded two acetates, now lost. In 1947, he moved to Detroit and started what would be a large family of 12 children. Percy stayed in Jackson, Mississippi, driving a taxicab. On a visit in 1950, Luther bumped into Sonny Boy Williamson (Rice Miller), who suggested that he and Percy record for Trumpet. Needing train fare home to Detroit, Huff contacted Lillian McMurry and, in January and February 1951, the pair recorded 'Dirty Disposition', '1951 Blues', 'Bull Dog Blues' and 'Rosalee', the latter pair featuring Luther's mandolin. Luther returned north to work at the Chrysler factory, and later, for Plymouth, making little effort to continue as a musician. In 1968, along with brothers Willie and Percy, he was recorded by Adelphi Records, but the results were never issued.

● ALBUMS: *Delta Blues - 1951* (1990)★★★.

HUGHES, JOE 'GUITAR'

b. 29 September 1937, Houston, Texas, USA. A product of Houston's third ward, Joe 'Guitar' Hughes turned to music at an early age under the influence of the work of T-Bone Walker. He claims to have used money earned washing dishes to buy his first electric guitar at the age of 14 and to have been appearing professionally by the time he was 16. His first band was the Dukes Of Rhythm, which included in its line-up Hughes' neighbour and friend Johnny Copeland. When this group disbanded in 1964 Hughes joined Grady Gaines working for Little Richard's old group the Upsetters. His next job was working as a member of Bobby Bland's band, which he left in the wake of Bland's supporting star Al 'TNT' Braggs. After three years with Braggs, Hughes moved on to playing lead with Julius Jones and the Rivieras and from there to various groups operating around the Houston area. An upsurge of interest in the post-war Texas blues brought Hughes to some prominence during the early 80s, since which

time he has toured in Europe and recorded for Double Trouble Records of Holland. *Texas Guitar Slinger* was co-produced by Jerry Jenkins.
● ALBUMS: *Craftsman* (Double Trouble 1988)★★★, *Down & Depressed: Dangerous* (Munich 1993)★★★, *Live At Vrendenburg* (Double Trouble 1993)★★★, *Texas Guitar Slinger* (Bullseye 1996)★★★.

HULL, PAPA HARVEY, AND LONG CLEVE REED

Probably from northern Mississippi, Hull and Reed, together with guitarist Sunny Wilson, formed a small group of black songsters. Reed and Wilson's two-guitar accompaniment was a blend of parlour guitar and ragtime. They sang blues, but much of their repertoire was from the turn of the century, when blues was not yet the dominant black music, and included ballads, medicine show material, and coon songs; their harmony singing, too, was of an earlier age. Long Cleve Reed may also have been Big Boy Cleveland, who recorded shortly after Hull and Reed, playing a slide guitar blues and 'Quill Blues', a fife solo unparalleled on commercial race records.
● ALBUMS: *The Songster Tradition* (1991)★★★.

HUMES, HELEN

b. 23 June 1913, Louisville, Kentucky, USA, d. 13 September 1981. Coming from a happy, close-knit, musical family, Humes learned to play trumpet and piano. As a child she sang with the local Sunday school band, which boasted future jazz stars such as Dicky Wells and Jonah Jones. In 1927 she made her first records for the OKeh label in St. Louis. Humes then went to New York where she recorded again, this time accompanied by James P. Johnson, and worked for several years with the orchestra led by Vernon Andrade, star of Harlem's Renaissance Ballroom. She also recorded with Harry James. In 1937 she was offered a job by Count Basie but turned it down because the pay was too meagre. The following year she changed her mind and signed up, replacing Billie Holiday. Her recordings with Basie mixed attractive performances of poor-quality songs and marvellous versions of the better material she was given. She left Basie in 1941 to freelance, and by 1944 was working on the west coast; she had moved into the then popular R&B field. Humes had a big hit with 'Be-Baba-Leba', recorded with Bill Doggett. On a 1947 session in New York, supervised by John Hammond Jnr., she made some excellent mainstream jazz records with Buck Clayton and Teddy Wilson. By the 50s, despite another big hit with 'Million Dollar Secret', her career was in the doldrums as the R&B tag she had acquired proved somewhat limiting. This hiatus continued into the late 60s, at which time she retired to care for ailing members of her family. In 1973 the writer and record producer Stanley Dance persuaded her out of retirement and into an appearance with Basie at the Newport Jazz Festival. This date was a great success and Humes returned to full-time singing. Equally at home with ballads, to which she brought faultless jazz phrasing, blues shouting and R&B rockers, Humes was one of the outstanding singers of her day. Her light, clear voice retained its youthful sound even into her 60s, and late-period recordings were among the best she ever made.
● ALBUMS: including *T'ain't Nobody's Biz-ness If I Do* (Contemporary 1959)★★★, *Helen Humes* (1959)★★★, *Songs I Like To Sing* (1960)★★★, *Swingin' With Humes* (1961)★★★, *Helen Comes Back* (1973)★★★, *Helen Humes* (1974)★★★, *On The Sunny Side Of The Street* (Black Lion 1974)★★★, *Sneaking Around* (Black And Blue 1974)★★★, *The Incomparable Helen Humes* (1974)★★★, *Talk Of The Town* (1975)★★★, *Helen Humes And The Muse All Stars* (Muse 1979)★★★, *Helen* (Muse 1980)★★★, *The New Years Eve* (Le Chant Du Monde 1980)★★★, *Live At The Aurex Jazz Festival, Tokyo, '81* (1980)★★★, *Let The Good Times Roll* (Black And Blue 1983)★★★, *Swing With Helen Humes And Wynton Kelly* (Contemporary 1983)★★★, *Helen Humes With The Connie Berry Trio* (Audiophile 1988)★★★, *New Million Dollar Secret* (Whiskey Women And Song 1988)★★★, *Deed I Do* (Contemporary 1995)★★★.
● COMPILATIONS: *Be-Baba-Leba* rec. 1944-52 (Whiskey Women And Song 1991)★★★.

HUNTER, 'LONG JOHN'

b. John Thurman Hunter, 13 July 1931, Ringold, Louisiana, USA. The son of a sharecropper, Hunter was raised on a farm in Magnolia, Arkansas. Until his mid-20s, he heard little else but country music, only hearing blues after moving to Beaumont, Texas, to work in a box factory. Attending a B.B. King gig, he was inspired to attempt to play the guitar after witnessing its effect on women. From 1955, he spent three years in Houston, having one record, 'Crazy Girl', released on the Duke label. On 7 August 1957, he moved with his band, The Hollywood Bearcats, to El Paso. Soon after his arrival, he was engaged to play the Lobby Club, a residence he held for more than a decade. Between 1961 and 1971, he made four rock-oriented singles, including 'El Paso Rock' and 'The Scratch', for Yucca Records in Alamogordo, New Mexico. In 1986, he recorded his first album for the Boss label. His second, *Ride With Me*, was recorded in Austin in 1992 with Texas veterans T.D. Bell and Erbie Bowser, and the Antones' rhythm section. Hunter's lean guitar style and characterful voice are evidence that there is more to Texas blues than Albert Collins.

● ALBUMS: *Texas Border Town Blues* (Boss 1986)★★★, *Ride With Me* (Antones 1992)★★★, *Border Town Legend* (Alligator 1996)★★★★, *Swinging From The Rafters* (Alligator 1997)★★★.

HUNTER, ALBERTA

b. 1 April 1895, Memphis, Tennessee, USA, d. 17 October 1984. Growing up in Chicago, Hunter began her remarkable career singing at Dago Frank's, one of the city's least salubrious whorehouses. There she sang for the girls, the pimps and the customers, earning both their admiration and good money from tips. Later, she moved on and marginally upwards to a job singing in Hugh Hoskins' saloon. She continued to move through Chicago's saloons and bars, gradually developing a following. She entered the big time with an engagement at the Dreamland Cafe, where she sang with Joe 'King' Oliver's band. Among the songs she sang was 'Down Hearted Blues', which she composed in collaboration with Lovie Austin and which was recorded in 1923 by Bessie Smith. Early in her career she sometimes performed and occasionally recorded under different names, including May Alix and Josephine Beaty. During the 20s and early 30s Hunter often worked in New York, singing and recording with many leading jazzmen of the day, among them Louis

Armstrong, Sidney Bechet, Eubie Blake, Fletcher Henderson and Fats Waller. She also appeared in various shows on and off Broadway. A visit to London prompted so much interest that she was offered the role of Queenie in *Show Boat* at the Drury Lane Theatre, playing opposite Paul Robeson in the 1928/9 season. During the 30s she frequently returned to London to appear at hotels and restaurants, including an engagement at the Dorchester Hotel with Jack Jackson's popular band. She also appeared in the UK musical film *Radio Parade Of 1935*. The 30s saw her in Paris and Copenhagen too, consistently meeting with enormous success. In the 40s she continued to appear at New York clubs and to make records, notably with Eddie Heywood. These recordings include two of her own compositions, 'My Castle's Rockin'' and 'The Love I Have For You'. In the war years she toured extensively to perform for US troops. In the early 50s she visited the UK with Snub Mosley and again toured with the USO, this time to Korea. She played a number of club dates, but, due to increasingly hard times, in 1954 she retired from showbusiness. At that time, aged 60, she began a new career as a nurse. In 1961 writer and record producer Chris Alberston persuaded her to record two albums, but she continued to concentrate on her new profession. Then, in 1977, her employers belatedly realized that diminutive Nurse Hunter was 82 and insisted that she should retire. Having already lived a remarkably full life she could have been forgiven for calling it a day, but she was a tough and spirited lady. She supplied the score for the film *Remember My Name* (1978) and, invited to sing at Barney Josephson's club, The Cookery in Greenwich Village, New York, she was a smash hit and began her singing career anew. She made numerous club and concert appearances, made more records and appeared on several television shows. Hunter sang with power and conviction, her contralto voice having a distinct but attractive vibrato. Inimitably interpreting every nuance of the lyrics, especially when they were her own, she made many fine recordings. Even late in her career, she ably controlled her audiences with a delicate but firm hand, all the time displaying a sparkling wit and a subtle way with a risqué lyric. It is hard to think of any singer who has improved upon her performances of certain songs, notably 'The Love I Have For You' and 'Someday, Sweetheart'.

● COMPILATIONS: including *Alberta Hunter With Lovie Austin And Her Blues Serenaders* (1961)★★★, *Amtrak Blues* (c.1980)★★★, *Classic Alberta Hunter: The Thirties* rec. 1935-40 (Stash 1981)★★★★, *The Legendary* (DRG 1983)★★★, *The Glory Of* (Columbia 1986)★★★.

● VIDEOS: *My Castle's Rockin'* (Virgin Vision 1992).

HUNTER, JAMES

b. 1962. As a youngster in Essex, England, Hunter was interested in 50s rock 'n' roll, leading to a later appreciation of Chicago blues, particularly the music of Little Walter. He received his first electric guitar in 1977 when he was around 15 years of age, while his first band, the DMFs, played at Colchester Labour Club in 1983. He initially recorded with a rockabilly band for a compilation issued by Lost Moment Records in 1984. Two years later he moved to London, and began performing as Howling Wilf. With his band the Vee-Jays he quickly established himself as one of the mainstays of the capital's blues scene, and was touted as one of England's best young blues singers. In 1989 he disbanded the Vee-Jays and took his music in more of an R&B direction, assembling a band that at present includes Jonathan Lee (drums), Dave Lagnado (double bass), Nick Lunt (baritone saxophone) and Damian Hand (tenor saxophone). His biggest break came when he was invited to play guitar with Van Morrison's Rhythm & Blues Revue, and he featured prominently on the Morrison albums *A Night In San Francisco* and *Days Like This*. Hunter has also worked with a diverse group of artists, including Solomon Burke, Mary Love and Captain Sensible, and briefly appeared in the West End musical *Buddy*. His debut album featured a winning mix of Hunter originals and choice cover versions, including duets with Van Morrison (on 'Turn On Your Lovelight' and 'Ain't Nothing You Can Do') and Doris Troy (on 'Hear Me Calling'). Central to the album's success were Hunter's vocals, with his powerful and expressive voice belying his comparatively young age.

● ALBUMS: *Believe What I Say* (Ace 1996)★★★★.

HURT, MISSISSIPPI JOHN

b. John Smith Hurt, 3 July 1893, Teoc, Mississippi, USA, d. 2 November 1966. One of the major 'rediscoveries' during the 60s folk blues revival, Mississippi John Hurt began playing at informal gatherings and parties at the turn of the century, when guitars were still relatively uncommon. Although he worked within the idiom, Hurt did not regard himself as a blues singer and his relaxed, almost sweet, intonation contrasted with the aggressive approaches of many contemporaries. In 1928 he recorded two sessions for the OKeh label. These early masters included 'Candy Man Blues', 'Louis Collins' and 'Ain't No Tellin' (aka 'A Pallet On The Floor'), songs that were equally redolent of the ragtime tradition. For the ensuing three decades, Hurt worked as a farm-hand, reserving music for social occasions. His seclusion ended in 1963. Armed with those seminal OKeh recordings, a blues aficionado, Tom Hoskins, followed the autobiographical lyric of 'Avalon Blues' and travelled to the singer's home-town. He persuaded Hurt to undertake a series of concerts, which in turn resulted in several new recordings. Appearances at the Newport Folk Festival ensued, before the artist completed several sessions for the Vanguard label, supervised by folk-singer Patrick Sky. These included masterly reinterpretations of early compositions, as well as new, equally compelling pieces. Hurt's re-emergence was sadly brief. He died at Grenada County Hospital on 2 November 1966 following a heart attack, having inspired a new generation of country-blues performers.

● ALBUMS: *Mississippi John Hurt - Folk Songs And Blues* (Piedmont 1963)★★★, *Live* (Piedmont 1964)★★★, *Worried Blues* (Piedmont 1964)★★★, *Blues At Newport* (Vanguard 1965)★★★, *Last Sessions* (Vanguard 1966)★★, *Mississippi John Hurt - Today* (Vanguard 1967)★★★.

● COMPILATIONS: *The Immortal Mississippi John Hurt* (Vanguard 1967)★★★, *Avalon Blues* (Heritage 1982)★★★, *Shake That Thing* (Blue Moon 1986)★★★, *Monday Morning Blues* (Flyright 1987)★★★, *Mississippi John Hurt, Sacred And Secular 1963* (Heritage 1988)★★★, *Memorial Anthology* (Edsel 1994)★★★, *Legend* (Rounder 1997)★★★.

HUTCHISON, FRANK

b. 20 March 1897, Raleigh County, West Virginia, USA, d. 9 November 1945, Dayton, Ohio, USA. Hutchison grew up in Logan County, in an area where many black workers were constructing the railroad to serve the mines. He listened to their music and was taught to play the harmonica and guitar as a child. His main teachers were guitarists Henry Vaughan and Billy Hunt, from whom he learned to play country-blues in the bottleneck style; however, it seems that he used a penknife, rather than a bottleneck, to fret the strings. Hutchison worked in the mines as a teenager, but during the 20s he mostly made his living entertaining around the mining camps. His repertoire included blues numbers, which was highly unusual for a white musician in that area at the time. Between 1926 and 1929, he recorded 32 sides for OKeh Records and all but three were issued. Some were old ballads, and some, such as 'K.C. Blues', effectively displayed his harmonica and guitar playing talents. Among the songs associated with him is 'Coney Isle' which, with a few small variations and renamed 'Alabam', became a major hit for Cowboy Copas in 1961. The best remembered is 'The Train That Carried My Girl From Town', which Doc Watson later recorded. In the face of the Depression, Hutchison moved to Chesapeake, Ohio, where he worked on steamboats, before he returned to Lake, West Virginia, to open a shop and post office. In April 1942, he lost everything in a fire and he returned to Ohio, where he died of liver cancer in 1945. Once known affectionately as the Pride Of West Virginia, he was, by then, almost forgotten. In 1974, Rounder Records released an album of his work, while some of his recordings appear on compilation albums by CBS, County, Old Homestead, Vetco and Folkways Records.

● COMPILATIONS: *The Train That Carries My Girl From Town* covers 20s (Rounder 1974)★★★.

HUTTO, J.B

b. Joseph Benjamin Hutto, 26 April 1926, Elko, near Blackville, South Carolina, USA, d. 12 June 1983, Chicago, Illinois, USA. Hutto's family moved to Augusta, Georgia when he was three years old, and he later sang in the Golden Crowns Gospel Singers, before moving to Chicago in 1949. While in Chicago he began to play drums and sing blues with Johnny Ferguson's Twisters, and during the intervals he taught himself to play Ferguson's guitar. In 1954 he recorded for the Chance label and these tracks are now considered to be classics of postwar blues. Hutto's slide guitar demonstrated that he was influenced by Elmore James but had utilized his style to create a unique, personal sound; however, at the time of release, the records met with little success. In 1965 J.B. and his unit the Hawks were the resident band at Turner's Blue Lounge (he worked there for over 10 years), when they recorded for the influential Vanguard series *Chicago/The Blues/Today*. Following this, Hutto recorded for many collector labels including Testament, Delmark, JSP, Amigo, Wolf, Baron, Black And Blue, and Varrick, with much of the later material, in particular, being licensed to different companies, and appearing on numerous anthologies. Hutto's music was raunchy, electric slide guitar blues that found great favour among young white blues enthusiasts. During live sets he would walk out into the audience and climb over tables in clubs, while continuing to play; 'party blues' was how one critic so aptly described it. Hutto died of cancer in June 1983. He was a major influence on his nephew Lil' Ed Williams who continued to perform some of Hutto's songs.

● ALBUMS: *Masters Of Modern Blues* (Testament 1966)★★★, *Hawk Squat* (Delmark 1967)★★★, *Sidewinder* (Delmark 1972)★★★, *Slideslinger* (1982)★★★, *Slippin' And Slidin'* (1983)★★★, *High & Lonesome* (1993)★★★, with Sunnyland Slim *Hawk Squat* 1966-68 recordings (Delmark 1994)★★★.

INMATES

The Inmates - Bill Hurley (vocals), Peter Gunn (b. Peter Staines; guitar), Tony Oliver (guitar), Ben Donnelly (bass) and Jim Russell (drums) - emerged in the late 70s as a UK R&B group in the style of Dr. Feelgood. Their adaptation of 'Dirty Water', a garage-band classic originally recorded by the Standells, led to the Inmates' debut album. In common with several similarly styled groups, the quintet was unable to transfer their live excitement onto record, and despite other promising collections, the band was restricted to a narrow, pub rock-influenced ghetto. Singer Bill Hurley recorded the solo *Double Agent* in 1985, but its gritty mixture of soul and R&B classics fared no better than those of the parent group. *Meet The Beatles, Live In Paris* is a set of Beatles songs performed in a hard R&B and Chicago blues vein.
● ALBUMS: *First Offence* (Polydor 1979)★★★, *Shot In The Dark* (Radar 1980)★★★, *Heatwave In Alaska* (1982)★★★, *True Live Stories* (1984)★★★, *Five* (Lolita 1984)★★★, *Meet The Beatles, Live In Paris* (1988)★★★, *Fast Forward* (Sonet 1989)★★★, *Inside Out* (New Rose 1991)★★★, *Wanted* (1993)★★★.

IRONING BOARD SAM

b. Sammie Moore, 1939, Rockfield, South Carolina, USA. Sam learned to play the organ as a youngster, concentrating on boogie-woogie and gospel music before turning to blues while playing in Miami, Florida. He formed his first band in 1959 and acquired his stage name while based in Memphis, when he mounted his keyboard on an ironing board. Initially he loathed the name but turned it to his advantage by giving away ironing boards at his shows! *Blues Unlimited* described Sam as having 'a really great voice and his songs have strong lyrics'. His music has appeared on several labels including Holiday Inn, Atlantic, Styletone and Board, and his live sets feature 'very fine, intense blues and

jazz' (*Living Blues*). His onstage antics include playing in a tank of water! He is now based in New Orleans.
● COMPILATIONS: two tracks only *Blues Is Here To Stay* (1973), *The Human Touch* (Orleans 1995)★★★.

JACKSON, 'NEW ORLEANS' WILLIE

Jackson sang comic renditions of opera tunes in blackface at a New Orleans ice cream parlour. His mid-20s recordings are versatile and vaudevillian, with strong dance numbers, *double entendres*, and humorous vignettes of Darktown life, ranging from the church to politics and the judiciary. He also sang a number of traditionally based blues, covered contemporary hits such as 'Kansas City Blues', and made the first recording of 'T.B. Blues', generally associated with Victoria Spivey.
● ALBUMS: *New Orleans Willie Jackson* (1989)★★★.

JACKSON, ARMAND 'JUMP'

b. 25 March 1917, New Orleans, Louisiana, USA, d. 31 January 1985, Chicago, Illinois, USA. Jackson's forceful 'sock' rhythm was heard on many of the blues records made in Chicago in the late 40s and 50s. In 1946-47, he appeared as bandleader on sessions for Columbia, Specialty and Aristocrat; vocalists included St. Louis Jimmy, Roosevelt Sykes, Sunnyland Slim and Baby Doo Caston. As well as performing, Jackson was active as a booking agent, and in 1959 founded La Salle Records, recording himself, Eddie Boyd, Eddy Clearwater, Little Mack Simmons and Sunnyland Slim, among others. In

1962 he was the drummer for the inaugural American Folk Blues Festival tour of Europe, although by this date his swing era sound had largely been supplanted in Chicago blues by the 'back beat' of Fred Below.

● ALBUMS: *Chicago Rock With Jump Jackson And Friends* (Redita 1988)★★★, *Nothing Like The Rest* (Cold Wind 1995)★★★.

JACKSON, BO WEAVIL

Bo Weavil Jackson presents another of those conundrums that are sent to frustrate researchers of early blues recordings. Virtually nothing is known of his life apart from the fact that he was discovered playing for tips on the streets of Birmingham, Alabama, USA, and on two occasions in 1926, he made recordings in Chicago. The first of these was for Paramount under the name Jackson and the second for Vocalion as Sam Butler. His real identity remains a mystery, as does his place of origin. Paramount publicity referred to his being from the Carolinas, although all references in his songs seem to point to a long familiarity with Alabama. Whoever he was, he was an outstanding performer whose high-pitched, expressive voice and chilling slide guitar can be enjoyed as much today as when first recorded. There are 13 known tracks attributed to Jackson; four are religious numbers and the remainder are early blues made up from individual traditional verses subjected to the singer's personal interpretation.

● ALBUMS: *Complete Recordings* (1982)★★★, *1926* (Matchbox 1983)★★★.

JACKSON, BULLMOOSE

b. Benjamin Clarence Jackson, 1919, Cleveland, Ohio, USA, d. 31 July 1989, Cleveland, Ohio, USA. Jackson become interested in music at an early age, and received singing and violin lessons by the age of four. In high school he learned to play the saxophone, and upon his graduation in the late 30s he was hired by legendary trumpeter Freddie Webster to play alto and tenor with his Harlem Hotshots. Living briefly in Buffalo, New York, in the early 40s, Jackson returned to Cleveland to a job at the Cedar Gardens, where in 1944, he was discovered by bandleader Lucky Millinder who needed a musician to replace tenor saxophonist Lucky Thompson. Initially recording simply as a talented accompanist with Millinder's orchestra on Decca and as a guest musician with Big Sid Catlett's band on Capitol, Jackson astounded his colleagues by substituting for blues shouter Wynonie Harris one night in Lubbock, Texas. He remained a part of the Millinder aggregation until June 1948 with the huge success of his R&B hit 'I Love You, Yes I Do'. He began making records under his own name from 1945 with King/Queen and Superdisc as well as appearing on Millinder's Decca tracks. He also made an appearance in the 1948 musical film *Boarding House Blues*. Jackson enjoyed great success on King Records between 1947 and 1954 with ballads such as 'I Love You, Yes I Do' (which spawned innumerable cover versions for every conceivable market), 'All My Love Belongs To You' and 'Little Girl Don't Cry'. Bullmoose was also responsible for some of the hottest, most suggestive R&B ever recorded, and it is these titles - 'Big Ten-Inch (Record)', 'I Want A Bow-Legged Woman', 'Nosey Joe' and 'Oh John' - that have found favour with the current crop of jump and R&B revival bands. Jackson moved to Chess's short-lived Marterry subsidiary in 1955, switched to the tiny Encino label in 1956, and was reduced to making re-recordings of his old hits in the early 60s for Warwick and 7 Arts. By that time he had taken a job with a catering firm during the week and only played the occasional weekend gig. In 1974 he made a cameo appearance in the dramatic film *Sincerely The Blues*, led a jazz band at the Smithsonian Institute in 1976, and went on to tour France and North Africa with Buck Clayton's Quartet. In 1983 Jackson was tracked down by the Pittsburgh-based band the Flashcats, who had been covering his risqué R&B songs, and after 35 years he was big news again with a sell-out tour, a new recording contract with Bogus Records, a celebrated show at Carnegie Hall and a European tour with the Johnny Otis Show in 1985.

● ALBUMS: *Big Fat Mamas Are Back In Style Again* (1980)★★★, *Moosemania!* (Bogus 1985)★★★, *Moose On The Loose* (Bogus 1985)★★★.

JACKSON, JIM

b. c.1890, Hernando, Mississippi, USA, d. 1937, Hernando, Mississippi, USA. Emerging from the minstrel and medicine show circuit, Jackson was a well-known figure around the Memphis area where he worked with artists such as Robert Wilkins, Furry Lewis and Gus Cannon. His first record, 'Jim Jackson's Kansas City Blues, Parts 1 & 2', recorded for Vocalion in October 1927, became one of the first, and biggest, 'race' hits. He later recorded 'Parts 3 & 4' and many variations on its basic theme. He continued to record for various labels up until 1930, and some 40 tracks of his work are extant. Jackson was never an outstanding guitarist and his success was based on his humour; although it has not dated well, occasional numbers such as 'I Heard The Voice Of A Pork Chop' can still raise a smile.

● ALBUMS: *Best Of Jim Jackson 1928-1930* (Earl Archives 1987)★★, *Kansas City Blues* (Agram 1988)★★, *Jim Jackson 1927-1929* (Blues Document 1989)★★.

JACKSON, JOHN

b. 25 February 1924, Woodville, Virginia, USA. Born into a musical family, Jackson began to play guitar at around five years old, learning from a convict who worked on a chain gang. Jackson's music, at least some of which was learned from records, covers a wide range of traditional southern material, including blues, rags, country dance tunes and ballads (which have earned him the description of songster rather than blues singer), and he plays in a style related to other black guitarists from the eastern states, such as Blind Blake and Blind Boy Fuller. Since the 60s Jackson has made many records, including one where he played second guitar to Buddy Moss, as well as concert and festival appearances, both in the USA and overseas.

● ALBUMS: *Blues And Country Dance Tunes from Virginia* (Arhoolie 1965)★★★, *In Europe* (Arhoolie 1969)★★★.

● VIDEOS: *John Jackson* (Kay Jazz 1988).

JACKSON, LI'L SON

b. Melvin Jackson, 16 (or 17) August 1915, Barry, Texas, USA, d. 30 May 1976, Dallas, Texas, USA. Having been raised in a sharecropping environment and taught to play guitar by his father, Johnny, Lil' Son ran away from home during the 30s. He has been described as a sincere man and religion seems to have played an important part in his life. He worked with the Blue Eagle Four Spiritual group before being drafted into the army. He served in the UK, France and Germany before returning to take up a career as a blues singer. Friends persuaded Melvin Jackson to send in a fairground recording to Bill Quinn, the owner of Gold Star Records, in the hope that it might lead to a recording contract. It did, and between 1948 and 1954 Jackson, who had moved on to the more prestigious Imperial label, made records in a style that combined his rural roots with currently acceptable R&B sounds. These sold well, particularly in his home state, Texas, and on the west coast, where many black Texans had settled. He toured extensively, but after a road accident retired from music to work in an automobile scrap yard; he was also employed by his local church. Fortunately Chris Strachwitz of Arhoolie Records traced and recorded him in 1960, in a more simple setting. Jackson died of cancer in 1976.

● ALBUMS: *Lil Son Jackson* (Arhoolie 1960)★★★, *Blues Come To Texas* (Arhoolie 1981)★★★, *Rockin' An' Rollin'* (Pathe Marconi 1984)★★★.

● COMPILATIONS: *Mississippi Delta Blues Vols. 1 & 2* (Arhoolie 1994)★★★, *Complete Imperial Recordings* 2-CD set (Capitol 1995)★★★.

JACKSON, PAPA CHARLIE

b. c.1885, New Orleans, Louisiana, USA, d. 1938, Chicago, Illinois, USA. Papa Charlie Jackson belonged to the first generation of rural black singers to record. He was a banjo player who had toured the South in medicine shows and worked anywhere else where he thought he might make money. He became popular after his first records were issued by Paramount in 1924, by which time he seems to have already moved to Chicago, where he often performed for tips in the Maxwell Street market. Like numerous banjoists from the minstrel tradition, Jackson was something of a humorist and many of his 70 or more recordings were sanitized versions of bawdy songs. He recorded with Freddie Keppard's Jazz Cardinals in 1926, taking the vocal on 'Salty Dog', a number he had already recorded under his own name with marked success. Despite providing support for artists such as Ma Rainey, Lucille Bogan and Ida Cox, Jackson's recording activities suffered a hiatus between 1930 and 1934 owing to the onset of the Depression and the demise of Paramount. He recorded for Vocalion in 1934 and recorded an unreleased session with Big Bill Broonzy in 1935. He scuffled on Chicago's west side until his death in 1938.

● ALBUMS: *Fat Mouth 1924 - 1927* (Yazoo 1988)★★★.

JACKSON, PEG LEG SAM

b. Arthur Jackson, 18 December 1911, Jonesville, South Carolina, USA, d. 27 October 1977, Jonesville, South Carolina, USA. Also known as Peg Pete, Jackson learned to play the harmonica when he was 10 years old by listening to local men, Butler Jennings and Biggar Mapps, who played in an older style known as 'accordion'. He had already learned many secular and spiritual songs from his mother, Emily. He left home about this time, spending much of his adult life travelling, and learned his blues style in the late 20s from Elmon 'Keg Shorty' Bell. He lost the lower part of his right leg under a freight train in Durham, North Carolina, in 1930. Seven years later, he teamed up with Pink Anderson on the medicine show circuit, which he worked for the next 30 years, mostly in partnership with Chief Thundercloud. He also played regularly in Rocky Mount, North Carolina, at Fenner's Warehouse, a focal point for musicians such as Tarheel Slim, Willie Trice and Brownie McGhee. In later years, the right side of his face was scarred while trying to break up a domestic argument. He was first recorded by Pete Lowry in August 1970, in the company of Baby Tate and Pink Anderson. Jackson became a favourite at folk festivals and also recorded in New York with Louisiana Red. He died on the family homestead he had left as a child.

● ALBUMS: *Medicine Show Man* (1973)★★★, *Joshua* (1975)★★★.

JACOBS, 'BOOGIE JAKE'

b. Matthew Jacobs, *c.*1929, Marksville, Louisiana, USA. Like many blues artists with a small discography, Jacobs was a reluctant performer, even at the height of his (limited) popularity. Learning guitar from a neighbour, Ernest Barrow, Jacobs' first public performance was with his second cousin, Little Walter Jacobs, at the Golden Lantern Club in Marksville. Soon afterwards, he moved to Baton Rouge, met drummer Joe Hudson, and played clubs such as the Apex & Rhythm. He came to the notice of Jay Miller and was invited to play on a Slim Harpo session, supposedly playing the distinctive guitar riff on 'King Bee'. Miller recorded Jacobs some time later, in company with Lazy Lester and Katie Webster; of several titles, only 'Early Morning Blues' and 'I Don't Know Why' were issued decades later on Flyright. In 1959, he was approached by New Orleans record distributor Joe Banashak, who proposed that Jacobs launch his Minit label. 'Early Morning Blues' and 'Bad Luck And Trouble' ('I Don't Know Why' in disguise) were recorded in June of that year. About a month later, a second single was recorded, 'Loaded Down', and the swamp-pop 'Chance For Your Love'. Jacobs' music had the flavour of the juke joint and his first single was picked up for national distribution by Chess Records. For a time, he toured with other Minit artists and alongside Lightnin' Slim, but disillusionment caused him to take his family west to California, remaining outside music throughout the 60s. His appearance at the 1974 San Francisco Blues Festival led to more regular work and a session for the Blues Connoisseur label in 1977. At this time, he had formed a partnership with another Louisiana migrant, 'Schoolboy' Cleve White.

● ALBUMS: *Loaded Down With The Blues* (1987)★★★.

JAMES, COLIN, AND THE LITTLE BIG BAND

b. Colin James Munn, 1964, Regina, Saskatchewan, Canada to Quaker parents. James' first muscial love was folk inspired but by his early teens he had developed a keen interest in the blues. His school work suffered as he proceeded to master blues guitar and upon leaving school at 16 he moved to Winnipeg and formed the HooDoo Men. In 1983 James befriended the late Stevie Ray Vaughan and he became a mentor to the young Canadian. Having impressed a Virgin Records executive by literally dancing on his table at a gig, he was signed and released *Colin James* in 1988. His band at this time comprised; John Ferreira (saxophone), Dennis Marenko (bass), Rick Hopkins (keyboards), Darrel Mayes (drums). The debut, although competent, did not demonstrate the excitement of his live gigs. Much more satisfying and gutsy was *Sudden Stop*, aided no doubt by Z. Z. Top's producer Joe Hardy. 'Just Came Back' from the album became a major hit in Canada and he duetted with Bonnie Raitt on another track.

James gigged solidly for eighteen months promoting a successful album and it was not until the end of 1993 that he found enough time to put out a new release. *The Little Big Band* was an powerful and tasteful jump blues and R&B excursion showcasing great brass and James' fluid guitar style. The line-up included Chuck Leavell on piano and utilised the Roomful Of Blues horn section in addition to the continuing presence of Ferreira on sax. In 1994 he signed to Elektra Records and the following year a much more mainstream rock album *Bad Habits* was released.

● ALBUMS: *Colin James* (Virgin 1988), *Sudden Stop* (1990), *Colin James And The Little Big Band* (Pointblank 1993), *Bad Habits* (Elektra 1995).

JAMES, ELMORE

b. 27 January 1918, Richland, Mississippi, USA, d. 23 May 1963. Although his recording career spanned 10 years, Elmore James is chiefly recalled for his debut release, 'Dust My Broom'. This impassioned, exciting performance, based on a virulent composition by country blues singer Robert Johnson, was marked by the artist's unfettered vocals and his searing electric slide guitar. James's formative years were spent in Mississippi juke joints where he befriended Rice Miller (Sonny Boy Williamson), a regular performer on the US radio station KFFA's *King Biscuit Time* show. Elmore accompanied Miller for several years, and through his influence secured his initial recording contract in 1951. James then moved to Chicago where he formed the first of several groups bearing the name 'the Broomdusters'. Subsequent recordings included different variations on that initial success - 'I Believe', 'Dust My Blues' - as well as a series of compositions that proved equally influential.

'Bleeding Heart' and 'Shake Your Moneymaker' were later adopted, respectively, by Jimi Hendrix and Fleetwood Mac, while the guitarist's distinctive 'bottleneck' style resurfaced in countless British blues bands. James's style was accurately copied by Jeremy Spencer of Fleetwood Mac - the band often had 'Elmore James' segments in their act during the late 60s. Another James devotee was Brian Jones of the Rolling Stones, whose early stage name of Elmo Lewis, and bottleneck guitar work paid tribute to James. John Mayall's 'Mr. James' was a thoughtful tribute to this significant performer who sadly did not live to enjoy such acclaim. In May 1963, James suffered a fatal heart attack at the home of his cousin, Homesick James, who, along with J.B. Hutto, then assumed the late musician's mantle.

● COMPILATIONS: *Blues After Hours* (Crown 1961)★★★★, *Original Folk Blues* (Kent 1964)★★★★, *The Sky Is Crying* (Sphere Sound 1965)★★★, *The Best Of Elmore James* (Sue 1965)★★★★, *I Need You* (Sphere Sound 1966)★★★, *The Elmore James Memorial Album* (Sue 1966)★★★★, *Something Inside Of Me* (Bell 1968)★★★, *The Late Fantastically Great Elmore James* (Ember 1968)★★★, *To Know A Man* (Blue Horizon 1969)★★★, *Whose Muddy Shoes* (Chess 1969)★★★, *Elmore James* (Bell 1969)★★★, *Blues In My Heart, Rhythm In My Soul* (1969)★★★, *The Legend Of Elmore James* (United Artists 1970)★★★, *Tough* (Blue Horizon 1970)★★★, *Cotton Patch Hotfoots* (Polydor 1974)★★★, *All Them Blues* (DJM 1976)★★★, with Robert Nighthawk *Blues In D'Natural* (1979)★★★★, *The Best Of Elmore James* (Ace 1981)★★★, *Got To Move* (Charly 1981)★★★, *King Of The Slide Guitar* (Ace 1983)★★★★, *Red Hot Blues* (Blue Moon 1983)★★★, *The Original Meteor And Flair Sides* (Ace 1984)★★★★, *Come Go With Me* (Charly 1984)★★★, *One Way Out* (Charly 1985)★★★, *The Elmore James Collection* (Déjà Vu 1985)★★★★, *Let's Cut It* (Ace 1986)★★★, *King Of The Bottleneck Blues* (Crown 1986)★★★★, *Shake Your Moneymaker* (Charly 1986)★★★★, *Pickin' The Blues* (Castle 1986)★★★, *Greatest Hits* (Blue City 1988)★★★, *Chicago Golden Years* (Vogue 1988)★★★, *Dust My Broom* (Instant 1990)★★★★, *Rollin' And Tumblin' - The Best Of* (Relic 1992)★★★★, *Elmore James Box*

Set (Charly 1992)★★★★, *The Classic Early Recordings 1951-56* 3-CD box set (Flair/Ace 1993)★★★★, *The Best Of Elmore James: The Early Years* (Ace 1995)★★★★.

JAMES, ETTA

b. Jamesetta Hawkins, 25 January 1938, Los Angeles, California, USA. James's introduction to performing followed an impromptu audition for Johnny Otis backstage at San Francisco's Fillmore Auditorium. 'Roll With Me Henry', her 'answer' to the Hank Ballard hit 'Work With Me Annie', was retitled 'The Wallflower' in an effort to disguise its risqué lyric and became an R&B number 1. 'Good Rockin' Daddy' provided another hit, but the singer's later releases failed to chart. Having secured a contract with the Chess group of labels, James, also known as Miss Peaches, unleashed a series of powerful songs, including 'All I Could Do Was Cry' (1960), 'At Last' (1961), 'Trust In Me' (1961), 'Don't Cry Baby' (1961), 'Something's Got A Hold On Me' (1962), 'Stop The Wedding' (1962) and 'Pushover' (1963). She also recorded several duets with Harvey Fuqua. Heroin addiction sadly blighted both her personal and professional life, but in 1967 Chess took her to the Fame studios. The resultant *Tell Mama* was a triumph, and pitted James's abrasive voice with the exemplary Muscle Shoals house band. Its highlights included the proclamatory title track, a pounding version of Otis Redding's 'Security' (both of which reached the R&B Top 20) and the despairing 'I'd Rather Go Blind', which was later a UK Top 20 hit for Chicken Shack. The 1973 album *Etta James* earned her a US Grammy nomination, despite her continued drug problems, which she did not overcome until the mid-80s. A 1977 album, *Etta Is Betta Than Evah*, completed her Chess contract, and she moved to Warner Brothers. A renewed public profile followed her appearance at the opening ceremony of the Los Angeles Olympics in 1984. *Deep In The Night* was a critics' favourite. A live album, *Late Show*, released in 1986, featured Shuggie Otis and Eddie 'Cleanhead' Vinson, and was followed by *Seven Year Itch*, her first album for Island Records in 1989. This, and the subsequent release, *Stickin' To My Guns*, found her back on form, aided and abetted once more by the Muscle Shoals team. Her ability to take and

shape a song demonstrates the depth of her great ability to 'feel' the essence of the lyric and melody. All her cover versions, from 'Need Your Love So Bad' to 'The Night Time Is The Right Time', are given her indelible stamp. Following the use in a television advertisement of her version of Muddy Waters' 'I Just Want To Make Love To You' she must have been surprised to find herself near the top of the UK charts in 1996. She is both emotional and 'foxy', yet still remains painfully underexposed; perhaps this hit will open the door to her extraordinary voice.

● ALBUMS: *Miss Etta James* (Crown 1961)★★★★, *At Last!* (Argo 1961)★★★★, *Second Time Around* (Argo 1961)★★★★, *Twist With Etta James* (Crown 1962)★★★★, *Etta James* (Argo 1962)★★★★, *Etta James Sings For Lovers* (Argo 1962)★★★★, *Etta James Top Ten* (Argo 1963)★★★, *Etta James Rocks The House* (Argo 1964)★★★, *The Queen Of Soul* (Argo 1965)★★★★, *Call My Name* (Cadet 1967)★★★, *Tell Mama* (Cadet 1968)★★★★★, *Etta James Sings Funk* (Cadet 1970)★★★, *Losers Weepers* (Cadet 1971)★★★, *Etta James* (Chess 1973)★★★, *Come A Little Closer* (Chess 1974)★★★, *Etta Is Betta Than Evah!* (Chess 1977)★★★, *Deep In The Night* (Warners 1978)★★★★, *Changes* (MCA 1980)★★★, *Red, Hot And Live* (1982)★★★, *The Heart And Soul Of* (1982)★★★, with Eddie 'Cleanhead' Vinson *Blues In The Night: The Early Show* (Fantasy 1986)★★★, *Blues In The Night: The Late Show* (Fantasy 1986)★★★, *Seven Year Itch* (Island 1989)★★★, *Stickin' To My Guns* (Island 1990)★★★★, *Something's Gotta Hold On Me (Etta James Vol. 2)* (Roots 1992)★★★, *The Right Time* (Elektra 1992)★★★, *Mystery Lady: Songs Of Billie Holiday* (Private Music 1994)★★★, *Love's Been Rough On Me* (Private 1997)★★★.

● COMPILATIONS: *The Best Of ...* (Crown 1962)★★★★, *Etta James Top Ten* (1963)★★★, *The Soul Of Etta James* (Ember 1968)★★★★, *Golden Decade* (Chess 1972)★★★★, *Peaches* (Chess 1973)★★★★, *Good Rockin' Mama* (Ace 1981)★★★★, *Chess Masters* (Chess 1981)★★★, *Tuff Lover* (Ace 1983)★★★★, *Juicy Peaches* (Chess 1985)★★★, *R&B Queen* (Crown 1986)★★★, *Her Greatest Sides, Volume One* (Charly 1987)★★★★, *R&B Dynamite* (Ace 1987)★★★★, *Rocks The House* (Charly 1987)★★★, *Tell Mama* (1988)★★★★,

Chicago Golden Years (Vogue 1988)★★★, *Come A Little Closer* (Charly 1988)★★★, *Chicago Golden Years* (Vogue 1988)★★★, *Juicy Peaches* (Charly 1989)★★★★, *Etta James Volume 1* and *2* (1990)★★★★, *Legendary Hits* (Jazz Archives 1992)★★★, *Back In The Blues* (Zillion 1992)★★★, *The Soulful Miss Peaches* (Charly 1993)★★★★, *Something's Got A Hold* (Charly 1994)★★★, *I'd Rather Go Blind - The World Of Etta James* (Trace 1993)★★★, *The Gospel Soul Of Etta James* (Disky 1993)★★★, *Blues In The Night, The Early Show* (Fantasy 1994)★★★, *Blues In The Night, The Late Show* (Fanatsy 1994)★★★, *Miss Peaches Sings The Soul* (That's Soul 1994)★★★, *Live From San Francisco '81* (Private Music 1994)★★★, *The Genuine Article: The Best Of* (MCA/Chess 1996)★★★★.
● VIDEOS: *Live At Montreux* (Island Visual Arts 1990), *Live At Montreux: Etta James* (Polygram Music Video 1992).
● FURTHER READING: *Rage To Survive*, Etta James with David Ritz.

JAMES, FRANK 'SPRINGBACK'

James recorded his piano blues between 1934 and 1937. The first tracks, released in the depths of the Depression, sold in miserable quantities; they show a strong affinity with the styles of St. Louis. Later recordings mostly included Willie Bee James on guitar, and are influenced by the popular recording team of Leroy Carr and Scrapper Blackwell. James wrote strong, original lyrics, but was often a monotonous performer. Sometimes, however, he struck a more compelling stance, as on the erotic 'Snake Hip Blues' and the seemingly autobiographical 'Poor Coal Loader' and 'Will My Bad Luck Ever Change?'.
● ALBUMS: *Frank 'Springback' James* (Document 1988)★★★.

JAMES, JESSE

It was once believed that James was a convict, brought to the studio under guard to make his four recordings in 1936, and that he broke down before they were completed. This romantic extrapolation from the lyrics of 'Lonesome Day Blues' - 'I'm goin' to the Big House, an' I don't even care . . . I might get four or five years, lord, an' I might get the chair' - seems to be untrue; James was probably Cincinnati-based, as he

accompanied titles by Walter Coleman. James was a rough, two-fisted barrelhouse pianist, with a hoarse, declamatory vocal delivery, equally suited to the anguished 'Lonesome Day Blues', a robust version of 'Casey Jones' and the earthily obscene 'Sweet Patuni', which was issued much later on a bootleg 'party' single.
● ALBUMS: *Piano Blues Vol. 2 - The Thirties* (1987)★★.

JAMES, JOHN

This guitarist from Wales is very well regarded, but lacks the high profile afforded to other, less talented, guitar players. His style defies categorization, as he plays through jazz, folk and blues forms with equal ease. His first release, *Morning Brings the Light*, for Transatlantic Records, highlighted his exceptional ability. Despite much television work, and tours with Eddie Walker as the duo Carolina Shout, James remains largely unknown to the British public. He has also recorded soundtrack music for television. *Carolina Shout* included such variations as Bob Wills' 'San Antone Rose', and Sam Cooke's 'Another Saturday Night'.
● ALBUMS: *Morning Brings The Light* (Transatlantic 1970)★★★, *John James* (1971)★★★, with Pete Berryman *Sky In My Pie* (1971)★★★, *Guitar Jump* (Kicking Mule 1977)★★★, with Sam Mitchell *I Got Rhythm* (Kicking Mule 1978)★★★, *Acoustica Eclectica* (Stoptime 1984)★★★, *Guitar Music* (Stoptime 1988)★★★, with Eddie Walker *Carolina Shout* (1989)★★★.

JAMES, SKIP

b. Nehemiah Curtis James, 9 June 1902, Bentonia, Mississippi, USA, d. 3 October 1969, Philadelphia, Pennsylvania, USA. A solitary figure, James was an emotional, lyrical performer whose talent as a guitar player and arranger enhanced an already impressive body of work. His early career included employment as a pianist in a Memphis whorehouse, as well as the customary appearances at local gatherings and roadhouses. In 1931 he successfully auditioned for the Paramount recording company, for whom he completed an estimated 26 masters. These exceptional performances included 'Devil Got My Woman', written when his brief marriage broke down, as well as 'Hard

Time Killin' Floor Blues' and 'I'm So Glad', which was subsequently recorded by Cream. James abandoned music during the late 30s in favour of the church and was ordained as a Baptist minister in 1942. He briefly resumed more secular pursuits during the 50s, and was brought back to public attention by guitarists John Fahey, Bill Barth and Canned Heat's Henry Vestine, who discovered the dispirited singer in a Mississippi hospital. James remained a reserved individual, but his accomplished talents were welcomed on the thriving folk and college circuit where he joined contemporaries such as Mississippi John Hurt and Sleepy John Estes. Two superb collections for the Vanguard label, *Skip James Today* and *Devil Got My Woman*, showcased James's remarkable skills. His high, poignant voice brought an air of vulnerability to an often declamatory genre and his albums remain among the finest of the country-blues canon. Recurring illness sadly forced James to retire and he died in 1969 following a prolonged battle with cancer.

● ALBUMS: *The Greatest Of The Delta Blues Singers* (Melodeon 1964)★★★, *Skip James Today!* (Vanguard 1965)★★★★, *Devil Got My Woman* (Vanguard 1968)★★★★, *Live At The 2nd Fret, Philadelphia, 1966* (Document 1988)★★.

● COMPILATIONS: *I'm So Glad* (Vanguard 1978)★★★★, *The Complete 1931 Session* (Yazoo 1986)★★★★, *The Complete 1931 Recordings* (Document 1992)★★★★, *The Complete Early Recordings* (Yazoo 1994)★★★★, *She Lyin'* (Edsel 1994)★★★★, *Skip's Piano Blues* (Edsel 1996)★★★.

● FURTHER READING: *I'd Rather Be The Devil*, Stephen Calt.

JAMES, STEVE

b. 15 July 1950, New York City, New York, USA. James took up his father's guitar when he was 12 and a few years later was playing bass in a rock 'n' roll band. When the blues boom brought Muddy Waters and Mississippi John Hurt to town, he moved from Manhattan to the East Village, worked in a guitar factory and played for coins on the Bowery. He moved to Bristol, Tennessee, in 1973, where he played old-time music and wrote *Old Time Country Guitar*. Travelling through the south, he learned first-

hand from Bukka White, Walter 'Furry' Lewis and R.L. Burnside. While living in Memphis he formed a band with Lum Guffin called the White Hots. In the late 70s, he moved to San Antonio, Texas, working in a museum, doing solo gigs and supporting saxophonist Clifford Scott. *Two Track Mind* was an enhanced reissue of a self-produced cassette, consisting of material by Big Bill Broonzy, Sylvester Weaver, Mance Lipscomb and others. *American Primitive* contained more original songs, at times featuring a small group that included harmonica player Gary Primich.

● ALBUMS: *Two Track Mind* (Antone's 1993)★★★, *American Primitive* (Antone's 1994)★★★, *Art And Grit* (Antone's 1996)★★★.

JAMES, WILLIE BEE

Chicago-based James could sing blues to good effect - he issued a fine 78 on Vocalion Records - but the bulk of his recording was done as a studio guitarist for Bluebird Records during the 30s. James's light, swinging guitar was reminiscent of Big Bill Broonzy, but he was equally at home backing relatively unemotional northern singers such as Bumble Bee Slim, Merline Johnson and Curtis Jones, as well as duetting with Tennessee guitarist John Henry Barbee or the pianist Frank James, and as a member of Tampa Red's pop-inflected Chicago Five.

● ALBUMS: including *Chicago Blues* (1985), *Mississippi Country Blues Vol. 2* (1987), *The Yas Yas Girl* (1989).

JANSCH, BERT

b. 3 November 1943, Glasgow, Scotland. This highly gifted acoustic guitarist and influential performer learned his craft in Edinburgh's folk circle before being absorbed into London's burgeoning circuit, where he established a formidable reputation as an inventive guitar player. His debut, *Bert Jansch*, is a landmark in British folk music and includes 'Do You Hear Me Now', a Jansch original later covered by Donovan, the harrowing 'Needle Of Death', and an impressive version of Davey Graham's 'Angie'. The artist befriended John Renbourn, who played supplementary guitar on Jansch's second selection, *It Don't Bother Me*. The two musicians then recorded the exemplary *Bert And John*, which was released alongside *Jack Orion*, Jansch's third solo album. This adventurous collection featured a nine-minute title track and a haunting version of 'Nottamun Town', the blueprint for a subsequent reading by Fairport Convention. Jansch continued to make exceptional records, but his own career was overshadowed by his participation in the Pentangle alongside Renbourn, Jacqui McShee (vocals), Danny Thompson (bass) and Terry Cox (drums). Between 1968 and 1973 this accomplished, if occasionally sterile, quintet was one of folk music's leading attractions, although the individual members continued to pursue their own direction during this time. The Danny Thompson-produced *Moonshine* marked the beginning of his creative renaissance with delightful sleeve notes from the artist: 'I hope that whoever listens to this record gets as much enjoyment as I did from helping me to make it'. *LA Turnaround*, released following the Pentangle's dissolution, was a promising collection and featured assistance from several American musicians including former member of the Monkees, Michael Nesmith. Although Jansch rightly remains a respected figure, his later work lacks the invention of those early releases. It came to light that much of this lethargy was due to alcoholism, and by his own admission, it took six years to regain a stable condition. In the late 80s he took time out from solo folk club dates to join Jacqui McShee in a regenerated Pentangle line-up, with whom he continues to tour. In the mid-90s he was performing regularly once again with confidence and fresh application. This remarkable reversal after a number of years of indifference was welcomed by his loyal core of fans. *When The Circus Comes To Town* was an album that easily matched his early pivotal work. Not only does Jansch sing and play well but he brilliantly evokes the atmosphere and spirit of the decade in which he first came to prominence. *Live At The 12 Bar* is an excellent example of his sound in the mid-90s, following a successful residency at London's 12 Bar Club.

● ALBUMS: *Bert Jansch* (Transatlantic 1965)★★★★, *It Don't Bother Me* (Transatlantic 1965)★★★★, *Jack Orion* (Transatlantic 1966)★★★★, with John Renbourn *Bert And John* (1966)★★★★, *Nicola* (Transatlantic 1967)★★★, *Birthday Blues* (Transatlantic 1968)★★★, *Lucky Thirteen* (1969)★★★, with

Renbourn *Stepping Stones* (Vanguard 1969)★★★, *Rosemary Lane* (Transatlantic 1971)★★★, *Moonshine* (Reprise 1973)★★★, *LA Turnaround* (Charisma 1974)★★, *Santa Barbara Honeymoon* (Charisma 1975)★★, *A Rare Conundrum* (Charisma 1978)★★, *Avocet* (Charisma 1979)★★, *Thirteen Down* (Sonet 1980)★★, *Heartbreak* (Logo 1982)★★, *From The Outside* (Konexion 1985)★★, *Leather Launderette* (Black Crow 1988)★★, *The Ornament Tree* (Run River 1990)★★, *When The Circus Comes To Town* (Cooking Vinyl 1995)★★★★, *Live At The 12 Bar* (Jansch 1996)★★★

● COMPILATIONS: *The Bert Jansch Sampler* (Transatlantic 1969)★★★★, *Box Of Love* (Transatlantic 1972)★★★, *The Essential Collection Vol. 1 (Strolling Down The Highway)* (Transatlantic 1987)★★★★, *The Essential Collection Vol. 2 (Black Water Side)* (Transatlantic 1987)★★★, *The Gardener: Essential Bert Jansch 1965-71* (1992)★★★★, *The Collection* (Castle 1995)★★★★.

JARRETT, PIGMEAT

b. James Jarrett Jnr., 8 December 1899, Cordele, Georgia, USA, d. 5 September 1995. Barrelhouse blues pianist Pigmeat Jarrett moved to Kentucky as a child where his Geechee father worked as a coalminer, his mother being half-Geechee, half-Cherokee. Some years later the family settled in Cincinnati, the city with which he would become synonymous. Jarrett attended the local Beecher Stowe School: 'I got my nickname there from the teacher', he told *Living Blues* magazine, 'because every time she seen me I had a piece of hog.' His mother sang at church, but would have nothing to do with the nascent blues movement, considering it to be the 'devil's music'. Her son did not share her opinion, picking up the basics from local 'open house' gatherings. Later he helped run whiskey from Newport during prohibition. He also began to play alongside local musicians and visiting stars such as Bessie Smith. His first ventures out of town came courtesy of covert train rides in cattle trucks - a method of transport he shared with bluesmen such as Blind Lemon Jefferson and Leroy Carr. In the 30s he found employment on steam paddlers, operating on the Ohio and Illinois Rivers. The Depression and the subsequent introduction of juke-boxes curtailed his employment somewhat, and for a time he joined a 16-piece house band, moving progressively into jazz as opportunities for blues artists dwindled. Later he started a small electrical shop. Despite his long career, Jarrett was recorded only once, when blues scholar Steve Tracy produced his 1980 album *Look At The People*. He was later honoured at the Cincinnati Public Library with a Pigmeat Jarrett Day in 1992 and also performed at the Chicago Blues Festival that year.

● ALBUMS: *Look At The People* (June Appal 1980)★★★.

JAXON, FRANKIE

b. 3 February 1895, Montgomery, Alabama, USA. Nicknamed for his short stature, Frankie 'Half Pint' Jaxon entered showbusiness at the age of 15 as a singer, dancer, comedian and female impersonator, and was also active as a producer of revues. After singing and dancing in amateur shows and in the streets outside theatres and saloons, Jaxon became an actor with a tent show. By 1912 he had formed a double act with Gallie DeGaston, with which they toured the deep south. From then until the mid-40s Jaxon worked almost non-stop, singing, dancing, acting, sometimes straight, sometimes in blackface, and occasionally in drag. He appeared on radio and recorded in a variety of genres, and was at his most outrageous doing a lascivious drag vocal for Tampa Red's Hokum Jug Band, changing the subject of 'How Long How Long' from passing time to penis size. Contrastingly, he also recorded gospel with the Cotton Top Mountain Sanctified Singers. More typical were his many titles recorded with small jazz groups, several of which were reworkings of his signature tune, 'Fan It'. He also worked in theatre administration on the black theatre circuit, was a frequent broadcaster and made numerous records with blues artists including Cow Cow Davenport and Thomas A. Dorsey. Jaxon also appeared on club and theatre dates with several noted jazzmen, Bennie Moten and King Oliver, and recorded with the Harlem Hamfats, Lillian Armstrong, Red Allen, and Barney Bigard. Jaxon's singing style was unusual in that he frequently used a shrill, high-pitched voice that matched his female imper-

sonation act. Nothing is known of Jaxon after 1944, but he is believed to have entered government service, and by now it must be presumed that he is dead.

● COMPILATIONS: *Frankie Jaxon And Tampa Red's Hokum Jug Band* (1928), *Red Allen And The Blues Singers Vol. 1* and 2 (1940), *Can't You Wait Till You Get Home* (Collectors Items 1986)★★★, *Frankie Half Pint Jaxon, 1927-1940* (Blues Document 1989)★★★, *Frankie Half Pint Jaxon, 1937-1939* (Document 1989)★★★.

JEFFERSON, BLIND LEMON

b. July 1897, Wortham (Couchman), Texas, USA, d. December 1929, Chicago, Illinois, USA. Jefferson was one of the earliest and most influential rural blues singers to record. He was one of seven children born to Alex Jefferson and Classie Banks (or Bates) and was either blind or partially blind from early childhood. As his handicap precluded his employment as a farmhand he turned to music and sang at rural parties, on the streets of small towns, in cafes, juke joints and brothels. This mode of life turned him into a wanderer and he travelled far, although he always maintained his links with Texas. Like many 'blind' singers, stories are told of his ability to find his way around and read situations. He was usually armed and was even said to have been involved in shooting incidents. In late 1925 or early 1926, he was taken to Chicago by a Dallas record retailer to record for Paramount Records. His first offerings were two religious tracks that were issued under the pseudonym 'Reverend L.J. Bates'. Soon after this, he was to begin the long series of blues recordings that made him famous throughout black America and even affected the work of rural white musicians. Between 1926 and 1929 he had more than 90 tracks issued, all bar two appearing on Paramount. His only known photograph, taken from a Paramount publicity shot, shows a portly man of indeterminate age wearing clear glasses over closed eyes set in a 'baby' face. He was accorded the distinction (shared with Ma Rainey) of having a record issued with his picture on the label and described as 'Blind Lemon Jefferson's Birthday Record'. He had a good vocal range, honed by use in widely different venues, and a complicated, dense, free-form guitar style that became

a nightmare for future analysts and copyists due to its disregard for time and bar structure; however, it suited his music perfectly and spoke directly to his black audience, both in the city and in the country. His success can be measured by the fact that he once owned two cars and could afford to hire a chauffeur to drive them. He is also said to have employed boys to lead him. Lead Belly and T-Bone Walker both claimed to have worked for him in this capacity during their youth. His later recordings seemed to lose some of the originality and impact of his earlier work but he remained popular until his sudden and somewhat mysterious death. Legend has it that he froze to death on the streets of Chicago, although a more likely story is that he died of a heart attack while in his car, possibly during a snowstorm, and was abandoned by his driver. At this late date it is unlikely that the truth will ever be established. His records continue to be issued after his death and some recorded tributes have been made. His body was transported back to Texas for burial.
● COMPILATIONS: *The Folk Blues Of Blind Lemon Jefferson* (Riverside 1953)★★★, *Penitentiary Blues* (Riverside 1955)★★★, *Classic Folk Blues* (Riverside 1957)★★★, *Blind Lemon Jefferson* (Riverside 1957)★★★, *Blind Lemon Jefferson Volume 2* (Riverside 1958)★★★, *The Immortal Blind Lemon Jefferson* (Milestone 1968)★★★, *The Immortal Blind Lemon Jefferson* (Milestone 1969)★★★, *Black Snake Moan* (Milestone 1970)★★★, *Collection* (Déjà Vu 1986)★★★, *King Of The Country Blues* (Yazoo 1988)★★★, *The Complete* (1991)★★★, *The Best Of Blind Lemon Jefferson* (Wolf 1994)★★★.

JEFFERY, ROBERT

b. 14 January 1915, Tulsa, Oklahoma, USA, d. 20 July 1976, San Diego, California, USA. A blues guitarist, influenced by Blind Lemon Jefferson, as well as a pianist, Jeffery worked with a carnival as a young man, snake-charming and boxing against allcomers. He moved to California 'with the rest of the Okies' in the Depression, working as a car mechanic and playing piano on weekends, often at a club owned by Thomas Shaw. After his retirement, he made some festival appearances and recordings on piano in the 70s, and was still a good gui-

tarist, although he insisted he had given it up.
● ALBUMS: *San Diego Blues Jam* (1974)★★★, *Off Yonder Wall* (Fat Possum 1997)★★★.

JENKINS, BOBO

b. John Pickens Jenkins, 7 January 1916, Forkland, Alabama, USA, d. 14 August 1984, Detroit, Michigan, USA. After hoboing from 1928, and wartime army service, Jenkins settled in Detroit from 1944. In 1954, he recorded for Chess Records, singing and playing guitar on a classic record, with both sides notable for the swooping, amplified harmonica of Robert Richard; 'Democrat Blues' was unusual in being politically explicit. In the 50s Jenkins also recorded for Boxer and Fortune (the latter session again featuring Richard on excellent versions of 'Baby Don't You Want To Go' and '10 Below Zero'). At this time, Jenkins worked as a photographer in the ghetto bars, and his pictures are a valuable and fascinating record of the musicians and their audience. In the 70s, he founded the Big Star label, and issued three albums.
● ALBUMS: *Detroit Blues - The Early 1950s* (1966)★★★, *The Life Of Bobo Jenkins* (Big Star 1972)★★★, *Here I Am A Fool In Love Again* (Big Star 1975)★★★, *Detroit All Purpose Blues* (Big Star 1978)★★★, *Blues For Big Town* (1989)★★★.

JENKINS, GUS

b. 24 March 1931, Birmingham, Alabama, USA, d. December 1985, Los Angeles, USA. Like many of his generation, Jenkins drew his influences from 40s blues and spent much of his mature career adapting to the demands of rock 'n' roll and R&B. As his earliest recordings for Chess and Specialty show, Jenkins, like Jimmy McCracklin, modelled himself on St. Louis pianist Walter Davis. Both largely unissued sessions took place in 1953 and featured 'Cold Love' and 'Mean And Evil', which along with 'Eight Ball' and 'I Ate The Wrong Part', were based on Davis originals. Thereafter, Jenkins recorded extensively for Combo and Flash, before he started his own Pioneer label in 1959. Most of these recordings were piano or organ instrumentals with his own or Mamie Perry's vocals. He continued this policy through the early 60s with a series of singles on General Artists. Late in the decade, he converted to Islam and assumed the name Jaarone Pharoah.

● ALBUMS: *Cold Love* (Diving Duck 1987)★★★, *Jericho Alley Blues Flash* (Diving Duck 1988)★★★, *Chess Blues* (MCA/Chess 1992)★★★, *Bloodstains On The Wall/Country Blues From Specialty* (Specialty/Ace 1994)★★★, *The Specialty Story* (Specialty/Ace 1994)★★★.

JOHNSON, 'BIG' JACK

b. 30 July 1940, Lambert, Mississippi, USA. Johnson's father led a local band and at the age of 13 Jack was sitting in on acoustic guitar. He was inspired by B.B. King's records to switch to electric guitar five years later, and in 1962 he sat in with Frank Frost and Sam Carr, with whom he continues to work sporadically. This group recorded an album for Sam Phillips in 1963 (credited to Frank Frost And The Nighthawks) and another for Jewel in 1966, again under Frost's name. In 1979 they made an album as 'The Jelly Roll Kings', featuring Johnson's first vocals on record, and his first album under his own name, released in 1987, confirmed that he had very strong traditional Mississippi blues roots. His follow-up album in 1989 was more experimental and musically less successful, but a single for Rooster in 1990 found him back on form. *We Got To Stop This Killin'* was an excellent album.

● ALBUMS: *The Oil Man* (1987)★★★, with the Oilers *We Got To Stop This Killin'* (MC Records 1997)★★★★.

JOHNSON, 'BLIND' WILLIE

b. *c*.1902, Marlin, Texas, USA, d. *c*.1949, Beaumont, Texas, USA. Blind Willie Johnson was arguably the greatest and most popular 'sanctified' singer to record in the pre-World War II era. His forceful singing and stunning guitar work ensured that he continued to sell records even into the Depression. His blindness has been attributed to many causes, the most likely being that his stepmother threw lye-water in his face during a jealous fit when he was about seven. That he should turn to music after this is a recurring motif in the stories of many blind black singers, but even earlier, Johnson had admitted to a desire to preach. Now he combined the two talents to produce outstandingly powerful religious music as he played for tips on the streets. Despite this commitment to the church there seems to have been a secular side to his music, and it remains probable that he recorded two unissued blues under the pseudonym of Blind Texas Marlin at his second session for Columbia Records. Johnson began recording for the label in December 1927, by which time he had moved to Dallas; his first release became an instant success, selling in excess of 15,000 copies. Between then and April 1930 he recorded a total of 30 issued tracks (all for the same company), maintaining a level of quality that is amazing even by today's standards. Early research on Johnson's life was done by Sam Charters when he interviewed Johnson's wife Angeline in the late 50s. The picture was fleshed out, 20 years later, by the work of Dan Williams who reported on Johnson's travelling habits, including a spell in the company of Blind Willie McTell. Charters also noted the influence exerted on his singing style by an obscure, older singer named Madkin Butler, and his early commitment to the Church Of God In Christ. Many of Johnson's recordings feature a second, female vocalist, and it was long assumed that this was Angeline. Now it seems more likely that this is an early girlfriend (possibly wife) of Johnson's, called Willie B. Harris, whose affiliations were with the 'Sanctified' church. Willie Johnson had returned to the Baptist fold by the time he married Angeline in June 1930. When using a second vocalist Johnson favoured a ragged, antiphonal approach to his singing, in which he usually employed a marked false bass, and when performing alone he used his guitar as the second voice, often leaving it to complete his own vocal lines. He could finger-pick, but is most famous for his outstanding slide technique. Possibly his most well-known piece today is the free-form guitar impersonation of a congregation moaning 'Dark Was The Night And Cold The Ground', which was used in its original form in Pasolini's film *The Gospel According To Saint Mark* and adapted by Ry Cooder as the theme music to *Paris, Texas*. Johnson lived his later years in Beaumont, Texas, and it was there that his house caught fire some time in the 40s. Johnson survived the fire but returned to the house and slept on a wet mattress covered by newspapers. This resulted in the pneumonia that killed him.

● COMPILATIONS: *Blind Willie Johnson 1927-1930* (RBF 1965)★★★, *Praise God I'm Satisfied* (Yazoo 1976)★★★, *Sweeter As The Years Go By* (Yazoo 1990)★★★, *Dark Was The Night: The Essential Recordings* (Indigo 1995)★★★.

JOHNSON, ALFRED 'SNUFF'

b. 10 August 1913, Cedar Creek, Texas, USA. Recorded for the first time at the age of 75, Johnson's repertoire contains examples from several eras of Texas blues. Unlike Mance Lipscomb (also discovered late in life), whom he remembers seeing in the late 20s, Johnson is not a guitar virtuoso, having spent his working life on farms, playing music for recreation and amusement. One of 14 children in a musical family, he learned to play by watching his uncle, Will Tims. After World War II, he joined up with local musicians Teodar Jackson, Edgar Davis and harmonica player Ammie Deaver, who, like him, played for country suppers and house parties and also in church. Johnson never considered making music to be a real profession and thus escaped the notice of succeeding generations of musicologists. While performing songs learned from records such as John Lee Hooker's 'Hobo Blues' and Muddy Waters' 'Two Trains Running', he also essays versions of such Texas stalwarts as 'Black Gal', 'Blues In The Bottle' and 'Spend My Money' (learned from his uncle), as well as songs by Lil' Son Jackson and Frankie Lee Sims. There is a charm to his performances but they reflect the passing of a strong musical tradition rather than its personification.
● ALBUMS: *Will The Circle Be Unbroken* (Black Magic 1994)★★.

JOHNSON, BESSIE

A gospel singer from one of the Sanctified sects, Johnson was from Columbus, Mississippi, and was last heard of in Arkansas in 1964. Remembered by Lonnie McIntorsh as 'the singingest woman I've ever known', Johnson possessed a huge contralto voice, with a rasping vibrato as wide as a church door. She was at her best when accompanied by McIntorsh's metronomic guitar, or that of Will Shade; her own Sanctified Singers were endearingly ragged, and she had to order them to 'Come on' or 'Get the beat'. The fact that recordings including such *ad libs* were released speaks for their raw authen-

ticity. Two tracks by the Memphis Sanctified Singers (on which Shade played guitar) beautifully contrast her rough style with Melinda Taylor's sweeter voice.
● ALBUMS: *Bessie Johnson* (c.1965)★★★.
● COMPILATIONS: *It Ain't Easy Being Blue* (Marvista 1995)★★★.

JOHNSON, EDITH

b. Edith North, 2 January 1903, St. Louis, Missouri, USA, d. 28 February 1988, St. Louis, Missouri, USA. In 1925, Edith married Jesse Johnson, who was OKeh Records' 'race' talent scout in St. Louis, and went to work in his record shop. In 1929, she recorded 18 splendid blues tracks, playing good piano on 'Nickel's Worth Of Liver Blues', and having a hit with 'Honey Dripper Blues'. Her voice was light but tough, sometimes hinting at violence, and making the threat explicit on 'Good Chib Blues'. Her husband's disapproval ended her singing career until 1961, when she made a few recordings that showed her still to be an expressive vocalist, with some interesting compositions. By this time, she had been for many years a successful operator of small businesses, and her elegant appearance belied the toughness of her repertoire.
● ALBUMS: *The Blues In St. Louis* (1984)★★★. *Honey Dripper Blues* (1991)★★★.

JOHNSON, ELLA

b. 22 June 1923, Darlington, North Carolina, USA. Johnson moved to New York City at the age of 17 to be with her brother, bandleader Buddy Johnson, who began featuring her unique voice on the most successful of his many fine songs on Decca Records. Beginning with 'Please, Mr Johnson' in 1940, she continued with blues and jazz standards-to-be, 'That's The Stuff You Gotta Watch', 'Since I Fell For You' and 'I Still Love You', among dozens of others. She had a solitary release on the small Harlem label in 1946, and moved to Mercury Records with Buddy's band in 1953, where she recorded her first album, *Swing Me*. She continued to have strong sellers such as 'I Don't Want Nobody (To Have My Love But You)', and moved on to Roulette in 1958; her final few releases in the early 60s were on Old Town and Mercury. By the mid-60s, Buddy Johnson had disbanded and

Ella, still a relatively young woman, retired to be with him in his last few years until his death in 1977. She still lives in New York, but has not resumed her musical career.
● ALBUMS: *Swing Me* (Mercury 1956, reissued Official 1988)★★★, *Say Ella* (Juxebox 1987)★★★.

JOHNSON, HENRY
b. 8 December 1908, Union, South Carolina, USA, d. February 1974, Union, South Carolina, USA. Johnson was an elderly man before he became known as a blues singer outside his immediate home area, but he had learned guitar in childhood from his brother, and later taught himself piano. Johnson sang religious material in church in his younger days, and later in quartets, appearing on radio with the West Spring Friendly Four and the Silver Star Quartet in the 30s. His musical career was only ever part-time, but on his retirement, he was discovered by blues enthusiasts and made a number of recordings, as well as personal appearances in South Carolina. He appeared on two albums, exhibiting a strong, distinctive singing voice and a powerful guitar style, especially when playing bottleneck. Oddly, a single was issued in the UK, featuring two fine solo performances.
● ALBUMS: including *Union County Flash* (1973)★★★, *New Beginnings* (1993)★★★.

JOHNSON, JAMES 'STUMP'
b. 17 January 1902, Clarksville, Tennessee, USA, d. 5 December 1969, St. Louis, Missouri, USA. Called 'Stump' on account of his short stature, Johnson was the brother of Jesse Johnson, and was raised in St. Louis from 1909. He learned piano in pool rooms, his brother's record shop, and Boots' club on the levee. In 1928, he made his first records and enjoyed a success with 'The Duck's Yas-Yas-Yas'. Johnson continued to record until 1933, although gambling seems to have been more important to him than music. He employed a typical St. Louis four-to-the-bar chordal bass, with economical right-hand decoration, and sang in a wistful voice, sometimes delivering remarkably forthright sexual material. He recorded again in 1964, but was, sadly, clearly in decline.
● ALBUMS: *The Duck's Yas-Yas-Yas* (Agram 1988)★★★.

JOHNSON, JIMMY
b. James Thompson, 25 November 1928, Holly Springs, Mississippi, USA. Johnson came from a musical family and was a singer and guitarist with several gospel groups until 1959, nine years after he moved to Chicago. At that time he sat in with Magic Sam and Freddie King, following the lead of his blues-playing brothers Syl Johnson and Mac Thompson (aka Mac Johnson), but in the 60s Jimmy was much more involved in the soul scene. He returned to the blues in the 70s and played second guitar with Jimmy Dawkins and Otis Rush, but after recording for MCM in 1975, he has enjoyed a moderately successful solo career. His beautiful, gospel-tinged songs and performances put him in the premier rank of modern blues artists.
● ALBUMS: including *Johnson's Whacks* (1979)★★★, *Bar Room Preacher* (1983)★★★, *Heap See* (Blue Phoenix 1985)★★★, *I'm A Jockey* (Verve 1994)★★★.

JOHNSON, JOHNNIE
b. 1924, Fairmont, West Virginia, USA. Johnson's name may not be well-known but his sound has been heard by millions: he was the piano player on most of Chuck Berry's classic Chess Records tracks. Johnson began learning to play piano at the age of seven without the benefit of lessons, influenced by jazz and boogie-woogie musicians such as Earl Hines, Meade 'Lux' Lewis and Clarence 'Pinetop' Smith. After a spell in the US Army Johnson began performing professionally in 1946, and in 1952, leading the Sir John Trio, he hired the young Berry as his guitarist. Berry soon began writing the group's songs and became its leader. Chess artist Muddy Waters suggested the group audition for that label and Berry was signed in 1955. Johnson played on Berry hits such as 'Maybellene', 'Roll Over Beethoven' and 'Johnny B. Goode', which Berry has stated he wrote for Johnson. Johnson also played in Berry's road band but in the 60s left, working with blues guitarist Albert King, among others. Johnson led his own band in the 70s but still worked with Berry on occasion. He was featured in the 1986 Berry concert film *Hail! Hail! Rock And Roll* and later appeared as a guest on Keith Richards' debut solo album, *Talk Is Cheap*. Johnson has recorded sparingly under his own name, releasing his first solo album in 1987.

● ALBUMS: *Blue Hand Johnnie* (1987)★★★, *Rockin' Eighty-Eights* (1991)★★★, *Johnnie B. Bad* (Elektra 1992)★★★, with the Kentucky Headhunters *That'll Work* (1993)★★★, *Johnnie Be Back* (Music Masters 1995)★★★.
● COMPILATIONS: *Complete Recorded Works Vols. 1-3* (Document 1995)★★★.

JOHNSON, LONNIE

b. Alonzo Johnson, 8 February 1889, New Orleans, Louisiana, USA, d. 16 June 1970. A hugely influential and original blues musicians, in the early 1900s Johnson played guitar and violin in saloons in his home-town, performing mainly around the red-light district of Storyville. Shortly before the outbreak of war he visited Europe, returning to New Orleans in 1919. During his absence most of his closest relatives died in an influenza epidemic and upon his return, Johnson soon took to the road. He played guitar and banjo in bands in St. Louis and then Chicago, where he established his reputation as one of the USA's most popular blues singers. For two years the OKeh Record Company issued one of his records every six weeks. During this period he became a member of the house band at OKeh, recording with many leading jazz and blues artists, sometimes as accompanist, and at other times as duettist. Among the blues singers with whom he recorded were Texas Alexander and Victoria Spivey. The jazz musicians with whom he played on 20s sessions included Duke Ellington, Eddie Lang, McKinney's Cotton Pickers, King Oliver and, most notably, Louis Armstrong. During the 30s Johnson divided his time between record sessions, club dates and radio shows. This was not all; like many of his New Orleans compatriots, he seems to have had a deep suspicion that the bubble would one day burst, and consequently he worked regularly outside music, usually at menial and physically demanding jobs. In the 40s Johnson began to gain popularity, adopting the amplified guitar and singing programmes of blues intermingled with many of his own compositions, one of which, 'Tomorrow Night', was a successful record. In the 50s he played in the UK but performed mostly in the USA, living and playing in Chicago and, later, Cincinnati, before settling in Philadelphia. In the 60s he again visited Europe and also appeared in New York and in Canada, where he became resident, eventually owning his own club in Toronto in the last few years before his death in 1970. Johnson's ability to cross over from blues to jazz and back again was unusual among bluesmen of his generation. He brought to his blues guitar playing a level of sophistication that contrasted vividly with the often bitter directness of the lyrics he sang. His mellow singing voice, allied to his excellent diction, helped to make him one of the first rhythm balladeers. He strongly influenced numerous blues and jazz guitarists, among them T-Bone Walker, Lowell Fulson, B.B. King, Teddy Bunn, Eddie Durham and Charlie Christian.
● COMPILATIONS: *Lonesome Road* (King 1958)★★★★, *Blues By Lonnie* (Bluesville 1960)★★★★, *Blues And Ballads* (Bluesville 1960)★★★★, *Losing Game* (Bluesville 1961)★★★★, *Another Night To Cry* (Bluesville 1963)★★★★, *24 Twelve Bar Blues* (King 1966)★★★★, *Tomorrow Night* (King 1970). *The Complete Folkways Recordings* (1993)★★★★, *Stompin' At The Penny* (Columbia Legacy 1994)★★★★, *Playing With The Strings* rec. 1925-1932 (JSP 1995)★★★.

JOHNSON, LUTHER 'GEORGIA SNAKE BOY'

b. Lucius Brinson Johnson, 30 August 1934, Davidsboro, Georgia, USA, d. 18 March 1976. Johnson was a guitarist, bassist and vocalist who formed his first band in Chicago at the age of 19. His boyhood ambition was to play with Muddy Waters; he achieved this in the 60s. Johnson played in the raw, urban style of Waters, and was also proficient at older country blues styles. His first recording (as 'Little Luther') was for Chess Records and he also recorded with Waters' sideman for the Spivey and Douglas labels. In the 70s he made two albums for the Black And Blue company while touring Europe. Johnson lived in Boston, Massachusetts, from 1970 until his death from cancer in 1976.
● ALBUMS: *Born In Georgia* (Black And Blue 1972)★★★, *On The Road Again* rec. 1972 (1991)★★★.
● COMPILATIONS: *Chicken Shack* (1967/8)★★, *They Call Me The Snake* (1993)★★★.

JOHNSON, LUTHER 'GUITAR JUNIOR'

b. 11 April 1939, Itta Bena, Mississippi, USA. Johnson's early musical experience was in gospel and he taught himself guitar around 1954, switching to blues before he moved with his family to Chicago's west side in 1955, where he played local clubs and teamed up with Magic Sam in the early 60s. Johnson is now regarded as one of the foremost exponents of the guitar-based west side blues style. He spent most of the 70s as a member of Muddy Waters' band, with whom he recorded, and also had his own recordings issued on the Big Beat, MCM, Black And Blue, Alligator, Blue Phoenix (the latter also available on Rooster Blues) and Bullseye Blues labels; he was also featured on three albums by the Nighthawks. He has come into his own in the 90s with a series of solo albums which are solid rather than spectacular.
● ALBUMS: *Luther's Blues* (1976)★★★, *I Changed* (1979)★★★, *Doin' The Sugar Too* (1984)★★★, *I Want To Groove With You* (Bullseye Blues 1990)★★★, *It's Good To Me* (1992)★★, *Country Sugar Papa* (Bullseye Blues 1994)★★★, *Slammin' On The West Side* (Telarc 1996)★★, *Live Downstairs At The Rynborn* (Rynborn Blues 1997)★★.

JOHNSON, LUTHER 'HOUSEROCKER'

Johnson was a blues singer and guitarist based in Atlanta, Georgia, USA, who learned a few rudiments of music from his father but was largely self-taught. His career began around the mid-60s when he worked as a backing musician for major blues artists appearing in Altanta's clubs, and in the early 80s he began establishing a reputation with his band, the Houserockers. He works regularly at Blind Willie's, Atlanta's best-known blues club, both as a bandleader (his group is now known as the Shadows) in his own right and as backing guitarist for bigger names. He achieved a measure of international prominence in 1990 with the release of a well-received album on Ichiban; the mixture of blues standards and original material revealed a talented modern blues musician with his roots deep in the tradition.
● ALBUMS: *Takin' A Bite Outta The Blues* (Ichiban 1990)★★★.

JOHNSON, MARY

b. c.1900, Eden Station, Mississippi, USA. Johnson had six children by Lonnie Johnson during their marriage (1925-32). She began her own recording career in 1929 in the company of Henry Brown's piano and Ike Rodgers' trombone. Mary continued to appear on the St. Louis music scene at least up until her last recordings as a blues singer in 1936, working with stalwarts such as Roosevelt Sykes, Peetie Wheatstraw, Tampa Red and Thomas A. Dorsey. By the 40s she was doing church work and in 1948 she recorded for the Coleman Label with the Mary Johnson Davis Gospel Singers. By the name she employed for these recordings it appears likely that she had remarried. Johnson had been employed as a hospital worker in St. Louis for years before she retired in 1959.
● ALBUMS: *Ike Rodgers' Gut Bucket Trombone* (1968)★★★, *Piano Blues Vol. 19* (1984)★★★, *I Just Can't Take It* (Agram 1989)★★★.

JOHNSON, MERLINE

b. c.1912, Mississippi, USA. Information on Johnson's early years is sketchy. She began recording in 1937, and enjoyed a successful recording career for several years, making a large number of records before 1941, accompanied by some of the major blues musicians in Chicago at that time, including Big Bill Broonzy, Lonnie Johnson and Blind John Davis (sometimes credited as Her Rhythm Rascals). Her vocals were tough and confident, occasionally reminiscent of Memphis Minnie, with an inclination to the sensual as well as the witty. Her nickname, 'The Yas Yas Girl' (a rare American instance of rhyming slang) bears out this image. Some of her records, however, had a jazzier orientation. She recorded again at a single session after the war in 1947, but nothing further is known of her.
● COMPILATIONS: *The Yas Yas Girl* (Best Of Blues 1988)★★★, *The Yas Yas Girl 1937-40 Vols. 1-3* (Document 1995)★★★.

JOHNSON, ROBERT

b. Robert Leroy Johnson, 8 May 1911 (sources for this date vary), Hazlehurst, Mississippi, USA, d. 13 August 1938, Greenwood, Mississippi, USA. For a subject upon which it is dangerous to generalize, it hardly strains credulity to suggest that

Johnson was the fulcrum upon which post-war Chicago blues turned. The techniques that he had distilled from others' examples, including Charley Patton, Son House and the unrecorded Ike Zinnerman, in turn became the template for influential musicians such as Muddy Waters, Elmore James and those that followed them. Credited by some writers with more originality than was in fact the case, it was as an interpreter that Johnson excelled, raising a simple music form to the level of performance art at a time when others were content to iterate the conventions. He was one of the first of his generation to make creative use of others' recorded efforts, adapting and augmenting their ideas to such extent as to impart originality to the compositions they inspired. Tempering hindsight with perspective, it should be noted that only his first record, 'Terraplane Blues', sold in any quantity; even close friends and family remained unaware of his recorded work until decades later, when researchers such as Gayle Dean Wardlow and Mack McCormick contacted them. In all, Johnson recorded 29 compositions at five sessions held between 23 November 1936 and 20 June 1937; a further 'bawdy' song recorded at the engineers' request is as yet unlocated. It has never been established which, if any, of his recordings were specifically created for the studio and what proportion were regularly performed, although associate Johnny Shines attested to the effect that 'Come On In My Kitchen' had upon audiences. Similarly, the image of shy, retiring genius has been fabricated out of his habit of turning away from the engineers and singing into the corners of the room, which Ry Cooder identifies as 'corner loading', a means of enhancing vocal power. That power and the precision of his guitar playing are evident from the first take of 'Kind-hearted Women Blues', which, like 'I Believe I'll Dust My Broom' and 'Sweet Home Chicago', is performed without bottleneck embellishment. All eight titles from the first session in San Antonio, Texas, exhibit the attenuated rhythm patterns, adapted from a boogie pianist's left-hand 'walking basses', that became synonymous with post-war Chicago blues and Jimmy Reed in particular. Several alternate takes survive and reveal how refined Johnson's performances were, only 'Come On In My Kitchen' being

played at two contrasting tempos. Eight more titles were recorded over two days, including 'Walkin Blues', learned from Son House, and 'Cross Road Blues', the song an echo of the legend that Johnson had sold his soul to the Devil to achieve his musical skill. 'Preachin' Blues' and 'If I Had Possession Over Judgement Day' were both impassioned performances that show his ability was consummate. The balance of his repertoire was recorded over a weekend some seven months later in Dallas. These 11 songs run the gamut of emotions, self-pity, tenderness and frank sexual innuendo giving way to representations of demonic possession, paranoia and despair. Fanciful commentators have taken 'Hellhound On My Trail' and 'Me And The Devil' to be literal statements rather than the dramatic enactment of feeling expressed in the lyrics. Johnson's ability to project emotion, when combined with the considered way in which he lifted melodies and mannerisms from his contemporaries, gainsay a romantic view of his achievements. Nevertheless, the drama in his music surely reflected the drama in his lifestyle, that of an itinerant with a ready facility to impress his female audience. One such dalliance brought about his end a year after his last session, poisoned by a jealous husband while performing in a jook joint at Three Forks, outside Greenwood, Mississippi. At about that time, Columbia A&R man John Hammond was seeking out Johnson to represent country blues at a concert, entitled 'From Spirituals To Swing', that took place at New York's Carnegie Hall on 23 December 1938. Big Bill Broonzy took Johnson's place. Robert Johnson possessed unique abilities, unparalleled among his contemporaries and those that followed him. The importance of his effect on subsequent musical developments cannot be diminished but neither should it be seen in isolation. His name was kept alive in the 80s by a comprehensive reissue project, while in the 90s he was included as part of the US stamp series celebrating the classic blues artists. Even in his absence he managed to provide controversy - when a cigarette was removed from the original painting, the decision was described by tobacco baron Philip Morris as 'an insult to America's 50 million smokers'.

● COMPILATIONS: *King Of The Delta Blues Singers* (Columbia 1961)★★★★★, *King Of The*

Delta Blues Singers, Volume 2 (Columbia 1970)★★★★, *Robert Johnson Delta Blues Legend* (Charly 1992)★★★★★, *Hellhound On My Trail: The Essential Recordings* (Indigo 1995)★★★★★, *The Complete Recordings* (Columbia Legacy 1996)★★★★★.
● VIDEOS: *The Search For Robert Johnson* (1992).
● FURTHER READING: *Searching For Robert Johnson*, Peter Guralnick. *The Devil's Son-in-Law*, P. Garon. *Love In Vain: Visions Of Robert Johnson*, Alan Greenberg.

JOHNSON, TOMMY

b. *c*.1896, Mississippi, USA, d. 1 November 1956. Although his recorded output was contained within a mere four sessions, undertaken in February and August 1928, Johnson remains one of the pivotal figures of delta blues. His work includes 'Cool Drink Of Water Blues', which featured the memorable lyric 'I asked her for water and she brought me gasoline', later adopted by Howlin' Wolf, while a 60s group comprised of enthusiasts took their name from 'Canned Heat Blues'. Johnson's haunting falsetto wrought emotion from his excellent compositions which influenced several artists including the Mississippi Sheiks and Robert Nighthawk. Although Johnson ceased recording prematurely, he remained an active performer until his death from a heart attack in 1956.
● COMPILATIONS: *The Famous 1928 Tommy Johnson/Ishman Bracey Session* (1970)★★★, *The Complete Recordings 1928-1930* (Wolf 1988)★★★★, *Tommy Johnson (1928-29)* (Document 1991)★★★★.
● FURTHER READING: *Tommy Johnson*, David Evans.

JOHNSON, WILLIE

b. Willis Lee Johnson, 4 March 1923, Memphis, Tennessee, USA, d. 26 February 1995, Chicago, Illinois, USA. Johnson was the musical linchpin behind one of the most enduring artists of the twentieth century - Howlin' Wolf. He began playing with Wolf as a teenager. He was there at the Memphis Recording Service studios when the former Chester Arthur Burnett cut his first record, 'Moanin' At Midnight', in the spring of 1951. However, when that record became a huge hit and Wolf moved to Chicago, Johnson initially remained in Memphis, where he accompanied other stellar blues artists including Bobby Bland, Elmore James and Sonny Boy Williamson. He cut his own records alongside harmonica player Little Sammy Lewis for Sun Records as well as sessions with Willie Nix for RPM and Checker Records. Johnson's side of the Lewis single, 'So Long Baby Goodbye', remains his only issued vocal. Within three years, however, Wolf returned to Memphis to bring his erstwhile guitarist back with him to Chicago. Johnson remained with Wolf throughout his residencies at clubs such as the 708 Club, the Zanzibar and Silvio's, and also made memorable studio appearances on singles such as 'Who's Been Talkin'?' (1957) and 'Smokestack Lightning' (1956). His performance on the latter was particularly stunning, his easy, evocative style matching tempos beautifully with Wolf's emphatic delivery. However, his relationship with Wolf was precarious, given that Wolf insisted on an alcohol ban for members of his band and Johnson's capacity for drinking was already reaching legendary proportions. There were many disputes, but Johnson finally left Wolf's company for good in 1959 after a show at Theresa's Lounge. That was effectively the end of his creative musical career as alcohol gained increasing control over his life, although he did continue his long service at the 'Mag Wheel' factory. He did, however, continue to make sporadic appearances at local clubs, relying on his versatility and adapting to whatever artist he was supporting. Various blues aficionados tempted him out of semi-retirement during the 80s and 90s, though he would often fail to arrive or be too drunk to play. However, he played one acclaimed set at the Earwig Music's 15th Anniversary Party at Buddy Guy's Legends venue on 2 June 1994, appearing alongside old friends Sunnyland Slim and Homesick James. Plans to record for Earwig were aborted when he died at home in February 1995. Ironically, his death came at the exact moment that his classic guitar-playing on 'Smokestack Lightning' was being aired daily on a television advert.

JONES, ALBENNIE

b. 29 November 1914, Gulfport, Mississippi, USA, d. 24 June 1989, Bronx, New York, USA. Jones arrived in New York in 1932, her only

singing experience at the Mt. Holy Baptists Church in Gulfport. Her first professional engagement was at the Elk's Rendezvous Club, which proved so successful that she was retained for nine months. Other nightclubs she sang in included the Club Harlem, the Village Vanguard and Murrains Cafe. Her first recordings for National in 1944/5 featured jazz musicians Dizzy Gillespie, Don Byas, Edmond Hall, Sammy Price and Cliff Jackson. She toured the south and Midwest with Blanche Calloway and Eddie 'Cleanhead' Vinson, and worked alongside Gillespie and Tiny Bradshaw with the Erskine Hawkins Orchestra. After the war, she recorded three sessions for Decca, backed by Price's group. In the early 50s she fell over on stage, suffering an injury that forced her to use a crutch at club dates. Because of this, she retired from music shortly afterwards and eventually succumbed to leukemia.
● ALBUMS: *Ladies Sing The Blues* (Savoy 1980)★★★.

JONES, BESSIE

b. 8 February 1902, Smithville, Georgia, USA, d. October 1984, USA. Jones became the greatest exponent of the music of the black communities of the Georgia Sea Islands. The islanders' isolation led to the retention of many African cultural elements, and there are also cultural affinities with the Bahamas, where many Royalist slaveholders fled from the Sea Islands during the American Revolution. Jones was the possessor of a deep, rich, but very flexible voice, whether singing spirituals, children's songs, slave songs or (very rarely) blues. She was a moving spirit behind the formation of the Sea Islands Singers in the 60s, and continued to tour after the group disbanded owing to the deaths of several members.
● ALBUMS: including *So Glad I'm Here* (Rounder 1975)★★★ *Georgia Sea Island Song* (1977)★★★, *Step It Down* (Rounder 1979)★★★, *Been In The Storm So Long* (1990)★★★.

JONES, BIRMINGHAM

b. Wright Birmingham, 9 January 1937, Saginaw, Michigan, USA. Moving to Chicago around 1950, Jones was a saxophonist and guitarist with various blues bands throughout the 50s. By the middle of the decade, when he recorded for

Ebony, he was a talented Little Walter imitator on harmonica. A 1965 session for Vivid was unissued for many years, and did not live up to the promise of the Ebony 78. Jones returned to club work, but had largely retired from the music business by the mid-70s.
● ALBUMS: *Chills And Fever* (1985)★★★.

JONES, CURTIS

b. 18 August 1906, Naples, Texas, USA, d. 11 September 1971, Munich, Germany. One of a coterie of bluesmen who were to make Europe their home, pianist Jones began his recording career in 1947 and his first release, 'Lonesome Bedroom Blues', was a major hit. The song remained in Columbia's catalogue until the demise of the 78 rpm record, eventually becoming a blues standard in the repertoire of others. On the strength of that success, Jones enjoyed a prolific recording career until 1941 whereupon he worked outside of music. In 1958 blues enthusiasts located him living in rundown conditions in Chicago. In the 60s Jones recorded albums for Bluesville, Delmark, Decca and Blue Horizon. He died in penury, his grave in Germany being sold in 1979 because no-one had paid for its upkeep.
● ALBUMS: *Lonesome Bedroom Blues* (1962)★★★.
● COMPILATIONS: *Blues And Trouble 1937-40* (1983)★★★, *In London 1963* (See For Miles 1985)★★, *Curtis Jones (1937-1941)* (Blues Document 1990)★★★, *Complete Recorded Works 1937-53 Vols. 1-4* (Document 1995)★★★★.

JONES, EDDIE 'GUITAR SLIM'

b. 10 December 1926, Greenwood, Mississippi, USA, d. 7 February 1959, New York City, New York, USA. Jones took the stage styles of his heroes T-Bone Walker and Gatemouth Brown and added his own particular flamboyance to become the first truly outrageous blues performer of the modern era. Along the way he wrote and recorded some blues that remain standards to this day. Raised in Mississippi he combined the intensity associated with singers from that area with the flair of his Texan models. He sang in church choirs in his home state before forming a trio with pianist Huey Smith working around New Orleans. A lean six footer, he took on the persona of 'Guitar Slim', building

a reputation for his extravagant stage antics and offstage drinking problem. One of the first performers to turn to the solid-bodied electric guitar, he began the experimentation with feedback control that reached its apogee with Jimi Hendrix in the late 60s. He combined this with garish stage-wear in fantastic colours (including matching dyed hair) and a gymnastic act that would see him leave the stage and prowl the audience - and even the street outside - with the aid of a guitar cable that could extend to 350 feet, and which connected to a PA system rather than to an amplifier, thereby reaching high volume levels. The reputation that he built up in the clubs led Imperial Records to record him, as Eddie Jones, in 1951; although not successful at the time, Imperial later fared better when they recredited the recordings to Guitar Slim. Slim's break came when he recorded in 1952 for the Bullet label in Nashville. The hit 'Feelin' Sad' aroused the interest of Specialty Records and sparked off Slim's most productive period. His first release for the new label was to become his anthem, 'The Things That I Used To Do', arranged by his pianist Ray Charles and featuring a distinctive guitar signature that has been reproduced almost as often as the Elmore James 'Dust My Broom' riff. The record made Slim a blues force across the nation. In 1956 he left Specialty for Atco which hoped to sell him to the teenage public as Chess had done with Chuck Berry. This approach was not a success and before Slim could make a comeback, he died from the combined effects of drinking, fast living and pneumonia.
● COMPILATIONS: *The Things That I Used To Do* (Specialty 1970)★★★, *The Atco Sessions* (Atlantic 1987)★★★, *Sufferin' Mind* (Specialty 1991)★★★★, *The Slaves Eat First* (Mysoundworks 1995)★★★.

JONES, FLOYD

b. 21 July 1917, Marianna, Arkansas, USA, d. 19 December 1989, Chicago, Illinois, USA. Brought up in the Mississippi Delta, Jones had been playing guitar for some years by the time he settled in Chicago around 1945. He soon became part of a seminal group of musicians that had come up from the south and who were in the process of developing the new electric Chicago blues sound. He played with his guitarist cousin

Moody Jones and harmonica player Snooky Pryor and their first record together, 'Stockyard Blues' and 'Keep What You Got', is a classic of its time and place. Under his own name, he made a number of records for JOB, Chess and Vee Jay in the early 50s, including 'Dark Road' which owed much to the work of Tommy Johnson. Rediscovered in the 60s' blues boom, he made records again for Testament and Advent.
● ALBUMS: *Baby Face Leroy & Floyd Jones* (1984)★★★, with Eddie Taylor *Masters Of Modern Blues* (Testament 1994)★★★.

JONES, JOE

b. 12 August 1926, New Orleans, Louisiana, USA. Jones was a pianist and vocalist who made his mark in 1960 with the R&B/novelty single 'You Talk Too Much'. His career began in the mid-40s as a valet and bandleader for B.B. King. Jones recorded under his own name as early as 1954 and went on the road as a pianist for Shirley And Lee. Jones's big hit was co-written with pianist Reginald Hall, and recorded for the small local label Ric Records. However, as the record began to take off, it was discovered that Jones had recorded the song already for Roulette Records. They lodged an injunction and the Ric version was withdrawn. Jones was unable to follow that hit and went into publishing, production and management, his greatest success in that area being with the Dixie Cups and, to a lesser degree, Alvin Robinson.
● ALBUMS: *You Talk Too Much* (1961)★★★.

JONES, LITTLE HAT

b. Dennis Jones. Jones was a taut-voiced street singer from San Antonio, Texas, where he recorded 10 blues for ARC Records in 1929 and 1930, also accompanying Texas Alexander on one session. His trademark was a fast, rolling guitar introduction, followed by a marked rallentando as he or Alexander began singing. Only on 'Hurry Blues' did he maintain the pace of his introduction throughout, making the record label mistitle (for 'Worried Blues') inadvertently appropriate. An eclectic guitarist, Jones blended fingerpicking, strumming and boogie basses into a style that, while recognizably within the Texas mainstream, was distinctively his own.
● ALBUMS: *Texas Blues Guitar* (Earl Archives 1987)★★★.

JONES, LITTLE JOHNNY

b. 1 November 1924, Jackson, Mississippi, USA, d. 19 November 1964, Chicago, Illinois, USA. Jones was a key figure in the development of post-war blues piano in Chicago. In the late 40s, he succeeded Big Maceo (a major influence on his own playing) as Tampa Red's partner, and helped move Tampa's music towards the amplified ensemble sound. Besides playing on many sessions, Jones made a few splendid recordings under his own name, two with Muddy Waters and six with the Elmore James band, which he adorned from 1952-60. His extrovert personality is apparent on the rocking 'Sweet Little Woman', but he was also capable of sensitive blues like 'Doin' The Best I Can'. Late in life, he was taped live, both solo and with Billy Boy Arnold on harmonica, on titles that admirably display both his ebullient and introspective sides.
● ALBUMS: *Chicago Piano Plus* (1972)★★★, *Johnny Jones With Billy Boy Arnold* (Alligator 1979)★★★, with Tampa Red *Tampa Red* (Krazy Kat 1982)★★★, *King Of The Slide Guitar* (1983)★★★, *Midnight Blues* (Cream 1987)★★★, *Knights Of The Keyboard* (1988)★★★, *Trouble Monkey* (Audioquest 1995)★★★.

JONES, MAGGIE

b. Fae Barnes, *c*.1900, Hillsboro, Texas, USA. Jones worked in black revue from around 1922, first in New York and later in the Dallas/Fort Worth area until her retirement from showbusiness in about 1934. Her history thereafter is unknown. Her Columbia recordings, made between 1924 and 1926, besides including some of the most sensitive recorded playing by Louis Armstrong and Charlie Green, are the work of one of the finest of the female vaudeville blues singers, demonstrating her resonant voice and outstanding technique, powered by a remarkable ability to sustain a note. Never as highly rated as Bessie Smith or Clara Smith, she easily bears comparison with either.
● COMPILATIONS: *Volume 1* (*c*.1985)★★★, *Volume 2* (*c*.1985)★★★.

JONES, MOODY

b. 8 April 1908, Earle, Arkansas, USA. From a rural farming background, Jones moved to East St. Louis in the late 20s, by which time he was already making music on home-made instru-

ments. Later, he learned guitar and in 1938, moved to Chicago and joined the blues circuit there. Along with his cousin Floyd Jones and harmonica player Snooky Pryor, he made some records in the late 40s. Their sound combined a powerful down-home Mississippi/Arkansas style with influences from records by artists such as Sonny Boy Williamson - the classic ingredients of post-war Chicago blues. Jones recorded a few tracks under his own name in the early 50s, but these were not issued at the time, despite the emotional quality of his vocals. In later years, he abandoned the blues and became a Christian minister.
● ALBUMS: *Snooky Pryor* (Flyright 1988)★★★.

JONES, NYLES

b. Robert L. Jones, aka Guitar Gabriel, 12 October 1924, Atlanta, Georgia, USA, d. 2 April 1996. At the age of five he moved to Winston-Salem, North Carolina, with his bluesman father and began playing guitar when eight years old, meeting many of the area's leading blues artists, including Rev. Gary Davis and Blind Boy Fuller, both of whom had a great influence on his own music. He left home at the age of 16 and travelled throughout the country, meeting Lightnin' Hopkins, who also left his mark on Jones's music. In 1970 he recorded in Pittsburgh for Gemini, and the resulting album and single were acclaimed for their raw blues passion. However, Jones became disillusioned at the lack of financial reward and returned to Winston-Salem in the mid-70s, assuming the name Guitar Gabriel. He was rediscovered and recorded again in 1991, under the supervision of Tim Duffy.
● ALBUMS: *My South/MyBlues* (1970)★★★, as Guitar Gabriel *Toot Blues* (1991)★★★, as Guitar Gabriel *Guitar Gabriel Volume 1* (Music Maker 1995)★★★.

JONES, PAUL

b. 24 February 1942, Portsmouth, Hampshire, England. Jones began his singing career while studying at Oxford University. One of several aspirants 'sitting in' with the trailblazing Blues Incorporated, he subsequently joined the Mann Hugg Blues Brothers, which evolved into Manfred Mann in 1963. This superior R&B act enjoyed several notable hits, including '5-4-3-2-

1', 'Do Wah Diddy Diddy' and 'Pretty Flamingo'. The dissatisfied vocalist left the line-up in July 1966, enjoying two UK Top 5 hits with the decidedly poppy 'High Time' (1966) and 'I've Been A Bad, Bad Boy' (1967). The latter was drawn from the soundtrack to *Privilege*, a socio-political film set in the near future in which Jones starred with the fashion model Jean Shrimpton. Subsequent singles, including 'Thinking Ain't For Me', 'It's Getting Better' and 'Aquarius', were minor successes as the artist increased his thespian commitments. Numerous appearances on stage and on celluloid followed, although he maintained a singing career through occasional solo recordings. Jones also contributed to the original recording of the Tim Rice/Andrew Lloyd Webber musical *Evita*, but in 1979 he rekindled his first musical love with the formation of the Blues Band. He has continued to lead this popular unit whenever acting commitments allow and Jones hosts two weekly blues/gospel radio programmes, demonstrating that his enthusiasm is backed up by a sound knowledge of both genres. In the early 90, Jones suprised a great many people with his polished performances, co-starring with Elaine Delmar, in the UK tours of the nostalgia shows *Hooray for Hollywood* and *Let's Do It*.

● ALBUMS: *My Way* (HMV 1966)★★★, *Privilege* film soundtrack (HMV 1967)★★★, *Love Me Love My Friends* (HMV 1968)★★, *Come Into My Music Box* (Columbia 1969)★★, *Crucifix On A Horse* (Vertigo 1971)★★, *Drake's Dream* film soundtrack (President 1974)★★, with Jack Bruce *Alexis Korner Memorial Concert Vol. 1* (Indigo 1995)★★★, *Mule* (Fat Possum 1995)★★★.

● COMPILATIONS: *Hits And Blues* (One-Up 1980)★★, *The Paul Jones Collection: Volume One: My Way* (RPM 1996)★★, *The Paul Jones Collection: Volume Two: Love Me, Love My Friend* (RPM 1996)★★.

JONES, TUTU

b. Johnny Jones Jnr., 9 September 1967, Dallas, Texas, USA. Given his nickname while still a baby by his guitar-playing father, Jones began his musical career at the age of six, playing drums for his uncle's band, L.C. Clark And The Four Deuces. Entering his teenage years, Jones hooked up with local bluesman and club owner R.L. Griffin, which gave him the opportunity to work behind Barbara Lynn, Little Milton, Little Joe Blue and Z.Z. Hill. Through his work with Blue, he took an interest in playing the guitar, which led to him playing drums with one band and guitar with another. In 1989, he formed Tutu Jones And The Right Time Showband, supporting Clarence Carter and Denise LaSalle, among others. His first album consisted of original material that nevertheless revealed the acknowledged influences of Freddie King, Little Milton and Stevie Ray Vaughan. His guitar playing is clean and fluent, making up in bravura what it lacks in originality. His songwriting is similarly derivative but confident, flirting with blues and soul clichés without entirely succumbing to their temptation. His occasional indulgence in hyperbole, best exemplified in the titles of two proficient instrumentals, 'Too Blues To Be True' and 'Outstanding', may indicate a requisite sense of humour.

● ALBUMS: *I'm For Real* (JSP 1994)★★★, *Blue Texas Soul* (Bullseye Blues 1996)★★★.

JOPLIN, JANIS

b. 19 January 1943, Port Arthur, Texas, USA, d. 4 October 1970, Los Angeles, California, USA. Having made her performing debut in December 1961, this expressive singer subsequently enjoyed a tenure at Houston's Purple Onion club. Drawing inspiration from Bessie Smith and Odetta, Joplin developed a brash, uncompromising vocal style quite unlike accustomed folk madonnas Joan Baez and Judy Collins. The following year she joined the Waller Creek Boys, an Austin-based act that also featured Powell St. John, later of Mother Earth. In 1963 Janis moved to San Francisco where she became a regular attraction at the North Beach Coffee Gallery. This initial spell was blighted by her addiction to amphetamines and in 1965 Joplin returned to Texas in an effort to dry out. She resumed her university studies, but on recovery turned again to singing. The following year Janis was invited back to the Bay Area to front Big Brother And The Holding Company. This exceptional improvisational blues act was the ideal foil to her full-throated technique and although marred by poor production, their debut album captures an early optimism. Joplin's reputation blossomed following the

Monterey Pop Festival, of which she was one of the star attractions. The attendant publicity exacerbated growing tensions within the line-up as critics openly declared that the group was holding the singer's potential in check. *Cheap Thrills*, a joyous celebration of true psychedelic soul, contained two Joplin 'standards', 'Piece Of My Heart' and 'Ball And Chain', but the sessions were fraught with difficulties and Joplin left the group in November 1968. Electric Flag members Mike Bloomfield, Harvey Brooks and Nick Gravenites helped assemble a new act, initially known as Janis And The Joplinaires, but later as the Kozmic Blues Band. Former Big Brother Sam Andrew (guitar, vocals), plus Terry Clements (saxophone), Marcus Doubleday (trumpet), Bill King (organ), Brad Campbell (bass) and Roy Markowitz (drums) made up the band's initial line-up which was then bedevilled by defections. A disastrous debut concert at the Stax/Volt convention in December 1968 was a portent of future problems, but although *I Got Dem Ol' Kozmic Blues Again Mama* was coolly received, the set nonetheless contained several excellent Joplin vocals, notably 'Try', 'Maybe' and 'Little Girl Blue'. However, live shows grew increasingly erratic as her addiction to drugs and alcohol deepened. When a restructured Kozmic Blues Band, also referred to as the Main Squeeze, proved equally uncomfortable, the singer dissolved the band altogether, and undertook medical advice. A slimmed-down group, the Full Tilt Boogie Band, was unveiled in May 1970. Brad Campbell and latecomer John Till (guitar) were retained from the previous group, while the induction of Richard Bell (piano), Ken Pearson (organ) and Clark Pierson (drums) created a tighter, more intimate sound. In July they toured Canada with the Grateful Dead, before commencing work on a 'debut' album. The sessions were all but complete when Joplin died of a heroin overdose at her Hollywood hotel.

The posthumous *Pearl* was thus charged with poignancy, yet it remains her most consistent work. Her love of 'uptown soul' is confirmed by the inclusion of three Jerry Ragovoy compositions - 'My Baby', 'Cry Baby' and 'Get It While You Can' - while 'Trust Me' and 'A Woman Left Lonely' show an empathy with its southern counterpart. The highlight, however, is Kris Kristofferson's 'Me And Bobby McGee', which allowed Joplin to be both vulnerable and assertive. The song deservedly topped the US chart when issued as a single. Although a star at the time of her passing, Janis Joplin has not been accorded the retrospective acclaim afforded other deceased contemporaries. She was latterly regarded as one-dimensional, lacking in subtlety or nuance. Yet her impassioned approach was precisely her attraction and her sadly brief catalogue is marked by bare-nerved honesty.

● ALBUMS: *I Got Dem Ol' Kozmic Blues Again Mama!* (Columbia 1969)★★★, *Pearl* (Columbia 1971)★★★, *Janis Joplin In Concert* (Columbia 1972)★★★.

● COMPILATIONS: *Greatest Hits* (Columbia 1973)★★★★, *Janis* film soundtrack including live and rare recordings (1975)★★★, *Anthology* (Columbia 1980)★★★, *Farewell Song* (Columbia 1982)★★★, *Janis* 3-CD box-set (Legacy 1995)★★★★, *18 Essential Songs* (Columbia 1995)★★★.

● FURTHER READING: *Janis Joplin: Her Life And Times*, Deborah Landau. *Going Down With Janis*, Peggy Caserta as told to Dan Knapp. *Janis Joplin: Buried Alive*, Myra Friedman. *Janis Joplin: Piece Of My Heart*, David Dalton. *Love, Janis*, Laura Joplin. *Pearl: The Obsessions And Passions Of Janis Joplin*, Ellis Amburn.

● FILMS: *American Pop* (1981).

JORDAN, CHARLEY

b. *c.*1890, Mabelvale, Arkansas, USA, d. 15 November 1954, St. Louis, Missouri, USA. Jordan arrived in St. Louis in 1925, and became a major figure on the city's blues scene, being closely associated with Peetie Wheatstraw, and acting as a talent scout for record companies. In 1928, he was crippled by a shooting incident connected with his bootlegging activities. Jordan recorded extensively from 1930-37, playing light, clean, but often very complex, rag-time-influenced guitar, and singing his wittily original lyrics in a high, taut voice. He accompanied many of his St. Louis contemporaries on disc, notably 'Hi' Henry Brown, for whom his second guitar work is a dazzling display of improvising skills.

● COMPILATIONS: *It Ain't Clean* (Agram 1980)★★★, *Charley Jordan 1932-1937* (Document 1987)★★★.

JORDAN, LUKE

b. *c*.1890, possibly either Appomattox or Campbell county, Virginia, USA, d. *c*.1945, Lynchburg, Virginia, USA. The blues scene in pre-war Virginia was poorly documented at the time and few of its members managed to record. Post-war research by Bruce Bastin reveals that Luke Jordan was a prime mover in the blues enclave centred around Lynchburg. It seems that he did not work outside music but relied on his talent and local fame. Victor Records discovered him in 1927 and he recorded for them in Charlotte, North Carolina, in August of that year. Jordan's records sold well enough to justify transporting him to New York for a further two sessions in November 1929. Of the total of 10 tracks that he recorded, eight saw release, although only six have been located. The extant sides present a high-pitched singer, given to a fast delivery, backed by a niftily picked Gibson guitar. From the evidence of his records it would seem that a large part of his repertoire was made up from vaudeville songs, although the gambling song 'Pick Poor Robin Clean' may have its roots in the folk tradition. His masterpiece was 'Church Bell Blues', a bravura performance forever associated with him in local tradition, while 'Cocaine Blues' became an early 'crossover' when it was recorded by white bluesman Dick Justice in 1929.
● COMPILATIONS: *The Songster Tradition* (1990)★★★.

JUMPIN' THE GUNN

This blues trio were formed in Inverness, Scotland, but it was in Memphis, Tennessee, USA, in the summer of 1992, that the three members, Andy Gunn (guitar), Steve Skelton (keyboards) and Vikki Kitson (vocals), began jamming together in a neighbourhood bar on Beale Street. Their name was taken from an album title of 70s US rock band Jo Jo Gunne. They were initially spotted by John Wooler of the Pointblank Records label at a folk festival there, and he recognized in them the talent and potential that merged their own resolute songwriting with US and native blues influences. Highlighted by Kitson's rock-edged delivery (natural comparisons to Janis Joplin followed), the group's debut album, *Shades Of Blue*, was recorded in Memphis in 1992. Songs such as

'More And More', 'Green All Over' and 'Crossed Wires' confirmed the promise, with Gunn's songwriting providing Kitson with ample ammunition to produce a range of moods from screaming defiance to emotive resignation.
● ALBUMS: *Shades Of Blue* (Pointblank 1993)★★★.

KANSAS CITY RED

b. 7 May 1926, Drew, Mississippi, USA, d. 6 June 1991, Chicago, Illinois, USA. A drummer and blues singer, in the 40s Red worked for Robert Nighthawk (who recorded Red's song, 'The Moon Is Rising'), and in the 50s for Earl Hooker. He became a club owner in Chicago, and a fixture on the city's blues scene, playing with Johnny Shines, Walter Horton and Sunnyland Slim, and leading his own bands, one of which provided early professional experience for Jimmy Reed. Red claimed to have recorded demos for Chess, JOB and Vee Jay Records, but his debut as a name artist came on a 1975 anthology. Thereafter, he continued to do occasional session drumming for several of his Chicago colleagues, and to combine bar management with live gigs.
● ALBUMS: *Bring Another Half Pint* (1975)★★★.

KATON, MICHAEL

This acclaimed blues rock guitarist/vocalist grew up in Ipsilanti, Michigan, USA, and his musical family background soon inspired him to take up the guitar. Katon began playing with local bands in clubs and roadhouse bars around Detroit from the age of 15, and spent 20 years paying his dues in classic blues fashion, working

with a succession of blues and jazz bands. Subsequently based in Hell, Michigan, he released his solo debut, *Boogie All Over Your Head*, on his own Wild Ass label, with Swedish label Garageland picking up Katon in Europe. The straightforward R&B boogie style, gravelly vocals and stylish blues guitar of *Proud To Be Loud* endeared Katon to both the blues and heavy metal crowds, and live shows with Ed Phelps (guitar, harmonica), Johnny Arizona (bass) and Gary Rasmussen (drums) proved to be wild affairs, particularly due to the guitarist's penchant for four- and five-hour sets. Blues label Provogue were suitably impressed, offering Katon a European contract. Katon gave up drinking to concentrate on his guitar playing, resulting in the harder, more focused *Get On The Boogie Train*, and while his lyrics retained their customary humour, he also produced a fine slice of urban blues in 'Cadillac Assembly Line', a lament for Detroit's declining motor industry. *Rip It Hard* continued in the traditional blues-boogie vein, and while, like many bluesmen, major commercial success evades Katon, he remains a respected guitarist in the field.
● ALBUMS: *Boogie All Over Your Head* (Wild Ass 1985)★★★, *Proud To Be Loud* (Wild Ass 1988)★★★, *Get On The Boogie Train* (Wild Ass 1992)★★★★, *Rip It Hard* (Wild Ass 1994)★★★, *Rub* (Provogue 1996)★★★.

KEB' MO'

b. Kevin Moore, Los Angeles, California, USA. Although he was born on the west coast of America, Kevin Moore's parents came from Texas and Louisiana and so instilled in him an appreciation of blues and gospel. At 21, he and his band were hired by violinist Papa John Creach as his backing band. Three years later, he was employed by A&M's Almo Music as contractor and arranger of the company's demo sessions. In 1980, he made an album for Chocolate City, a subsidiary of Casablanca Records, just before the label's collapse. He met veteran bandleader Monk Higgins in 1983, joining the saxophonist's Whodunit Band on guitar and playing a residency at Marla's Memory Lane. In 1990, he was contacted by the Los Angeles Theater Center to play a blues guitarist in a play called *Rabbit Foot*, and he continued this line of work by becoming understudy to Chick Streetman in

Spunk, adapted from the writings of Zora Neale Hurston. The nickname for his blues persona was given to him by drummer Quentin Dennard when Moore sat in with his jazz band. Dennard also backs him on *Keb' Mo'*, an album that tempers its blues bias. It includes Robert Johnson's 'Come On In My Kitchen' and 'Kind Hearted Woman', with elements of folk and soul music. Moore is adept at electric and acoustic guitar styles, with a tasteful approach to the use of slide. These skills stood him in good stead when he portrayed Robert Johnson in *Can't You Hear The Wind Howl?*, a documentary-drama narrated by Danny Glover and including interviews with musicians and acquaintances who knew or were influenced by Johnson. On *Just Like You* the material is even more varied, from the beautiful, feel-good pop/soul of 'More Than One Way Home' to the raw acoustic blues of 'Momma, Where's My Daddy', and some singer-songwriter pop thrown in, featuring Bonnie Raitt and Jackson Browne ('Just Like You'). Keb is an exciting new talent with a voice that can melt hearts and make you shiver.
● ALBUMS: *Rainmaker* (Chocolate City 1981)★★, *Keb' Mo'* (OKeh 1994)★★★, *Just Like You* (OKeh 1996)★★★★.

KEENE, STEVEN

b. Brooklyn, New York, USA. Contemporary folk/blues artist Steven Keene began his travels under the guidance of his uncle Tex as part of a circus troupe operating in the southern regions of the USA. Learning to play guitar and harmonica, he eventually left the circus to take up more regular employment at a lumber mill in Austin, Texas. Spending his evenings playing on the local blues scene, he subsequently moved to Memphis to form his own band. After touring throughout the region, he left for New York's Greenwich Village and solo performances in small folk clubs. Returning to a band format, he secured more lucrative gigs at venues such as the Lonestar Roadhouse and CBGB's. The New York independent label Moo Records invited him to record a debut album at this time. *No Alternative*, released in 1996, consisted of songs whittled down from an original tally of 50 compositions. The musicians involved included Bob Dylan collaborators John Jackson, Tony Garrier and Bucky Baxter, as well as guitarist Danny

Kalb from the Blues Project. It featured a mélange of folk, blues and rock songs, with declamatory titles such as 'Far Better Friend Than Lover' and Before You Save The World, Save Yourself. Three obscure Dylan songs, 'Never Say Goodbye', 'Walkin' Down The Line' and 'Sign On The Window', were also included.
● ALBUMS: *No Alternative* (Moo 1996).★★★

KELLY, ARTHUR LEE 'GUITAR'

b. 14 November 1924, Clinton, Louisiana, USA. Like many blues singers, Kelly learned to play religious songs first, but his main interest was in the blues. In the 40s, he was living near Baton Rouge and beginning to develop his own guitar style, under the influence of local artist Lightning Slim, as well as copying records by artists such as Muddy Waters and Lightnin' Hopkins. Although active on the blues scene through the boom in Baton Rouge blues in the 50s, he never made any records during this time. In the 60s, he formed a small group along with Silas Hogan and at last in 1970, he appeared on a couple of albums of Louisiana blues artists, as well as a single on Excello. He continued his partnership with Hogan for many years, but he has also toured widely, including visits to Europe.
● COMPILATIONS: *Louisiana Blues* (1970).

KELLY, DAVE

b. 1948, London, England. Kelly's first instrument was trombone, but he became a bottleneck slide guitar specialist, sitting in with John Lee Hooker and Muddy Waters during a 1966 visit to the USA. On his return, Kelly joined his first R&B band which evolved into the John Dummer Blues Band, with whom he recorded in 1968-69. Leaving the group, he performed as a solo artist on the folk club circuit, and played on numerous recording sessions involving a loose-knit circle of London blues musicians that included his sister Jo Ann Kelly (guitar/vocals), Bob Hall (piano) and Bob Brunning (bass). They recorded together as Tramp and as Firefall, while Kelly also played on albums by visiting US blues singers Son House and Arthur Crudup (*Roebuck Man*, 1974). Around this time Kelly made his first two solo albums for Mercury with accompaniment from Peter Green, Jo Ann, Brunning and Steve Rye (harmonica). Kelly also

led an early 70s group called Rocksalt and in 1974 rejoined John Dummer in the Ooblee Dooblee Band. In the late 70s he became a founder-member of the Blues Band and when the group temporarily split up, he formed his own band with fellow Blues Band members Rob Townshend (drums) and Gary Fletcher (bass), plus Mick Rogers (guitar), Lou Stonebridge (keyboards) and John 'Irish' Earle (saxophone). With numerous personnel changes (including the addition of Peter Filleul on keyboards and Tex Comer on bass), the group continued for several years, touring Europe and recording occasionally for the German label Metronome and Apoloosa, owned by Italian blues fan Franco Ratti. During the 80s, Kelly developed a parallel career in writing jingles and film and television soundtrack music. He rejoined the Blues Band when it re-formed in 1989.
● ALBUMS: *Keep It In The Family* (Mercury 1969)★★★, *Dave Kelly* (Mercury 1971)★★★, with Bob Hall *Survivors* (Appaloosa 1979)★★★, *Willin'* (Appaloosa 1979)★★★, *Feels Right* (Cool King 1981)★★★, *Dave Kelly Band Live* (Appaloosa 1983)★★, *Heart Of The City* (Line 1987)★★★, *...When The Blues Come To Call ...* (Hypertension 1994)★★★.
● COMPILATIONS: *Making Whoopee 1979/1982* (RPM 1993)★★★.

KELLY, JACK

b. c.1905, Mississippi, USA, d. c.1960, Memphis, Tennessee, USA. Kelly's first jug band, formed in 1925, included Frank Stokes, Dan Sane and Will Batts. Kelly, Batts, Sane and juggist D.M. Higgs recorded as the South Memphis Jug Band in 1933. (Kelly, Batts and a guitarist, possibly Ernest Lawlars, recorded again in 1939.) Their sound was characterized by Kelly's vibrant singing, the broad, bluesy tones of Batts' fiddle and the complex interplay of twin guitars. Kelly's penchant for re-recording the tune of 'Highway No. 61 Blues' is offset by a talent for striking lyrics. After the band broke up in 1934, Kelly worked either solo, with Stokes, or in *ad hoc* bands. In 1953, he recorded for Sun, playing piano with Walter 'Shakey' Horton and Joe Hill Louis. A 78 rpm record was scheduled, but never released; part of one side was issued many years later.
● COMPILATIONS: *Sun Records The Blues Years*

(1985)★★★, *Jack Kelly & His South Memphis Jug Band 1933-1939* (Blues Document 1991)★★★.

KELLY, JO ANN

b. 5 January 1944, Streatham, London, England, d. 21 October 1990. This expressive blues singer, sister of Blues Band guitarist Dave Kelly, was renowned as one of the finest of the genre. She made her recording debut in 1964 on a privately pressed EP and appeared on several specialist labels before contributing a series of excellent performances to guitarist Tony McPhee's Groundhogs recordings, issued under the aegis of United Artists. Her self-titled solo album displayed a hard, gritty vocal delivery evocative of Memphis Minnie and confirmed the arrival of a major talent. In 1969, the singer appeared live with Mississippi Fred McDowell and later made several tours of the USA. Kelly became a constituent part of the British blues circuit, recording with the John Dummer Blues Band, Chilli Willi And The Red Hot Peppers and Stefan Grossman. In 1972, she completed an album with Woody Mann, John Miller and acoustic guitarist John Fahey, before forming a group, Spare Rib, which performed extensively throughout the UK. Kelly recorded a second solo album, *Do It*, in 1976 and maintained her popularity throughout the 70s and 80s with appearances at European blues festivals and judicious live work in Britain. Her last performance was at a festival in Lancashire in August 1990, when she was given the award for Female Singer of the Year by the British Blues Federation. Having apparently recovered from an operation in 1989 to remove a malignant brain tumour, she died in October 1990.

● ALBUMS: *Jo Ann Kelly* (Columbia 1969)★★★, *Jo Ann Kelly, With Fahey, Mann And Miller* (1972)★★★, with Pete Emery *Do It* (Red Rag 1976)★★★, *It's Whoopie* (1978)★★, with Mississippi Fred McDowell *Standing At The Burying Ground* (Red Lightnin' 1984)★★, *Just Restless* (Appaloosa 1984)★★★, *Women In (E)Motion* rec. 1988 (Indigo/Traditon & Moderne 1995)★★★.

● COMPILATIONS: with Tony McPhee *Same Thing On Our Minds* (Sunset 1969)★★, *Retrospect 1964-1972* (Connoisseur 1990)★★★.

KELLY, VANCE

b. 24 January 1954, Chicago, Illinois, USA. Kelly's urban soul-blues came to prominence in 1995 when his debut album, *Call Me*, won a *Living Blues* magazine award in 1995. Rooted in the music of the Windy City from birth, Kelly was born on Maxwell Street, where musicians played impromptu open-air sets every Sunday. His father was a gospel musician, while his uncle was an occasional blues player. By the age of seven Kelly was already playing guitar, and began sitting in at blues clubs in his early teens, backing the West-Side singer Mary Lane. His musical education was broadened in the late seventies by work in the disco field, but it was an invitation to join saxman A.C.Reed's band in 1987 that provided Kelly with an opportunity to gain valuable experience on the road. After playing with Reed for three years Kelly moved on to develop his own sound, which not only reflected his diversity by mixing blues, R&B, funk and disco, but also catered to the demands of the club audiences: 'If the older folks come in, I want to take them back to the Delta blues. When the middle-aged folks come in, they just want to hear regular-type blues. If a younger crowd comes in, they want to hear up-to-date type blues.' Though hardly known outside Chicago before the release of *Call Me*, that album's critical reception saw Kelly reaping the rewards of his long apprenticeship. The follow-up, *Joyriding In The Subway*, featured John Primer repeating his co-guitar and production duties from the debut album, and was another fine mix of cover versions and originals (co-written by Kelly and his daughter, Vivian), covering a variety of styles from traditional blues to contemporary R&B. An excellent guitarist and singer, Kelly has established himself as one of the leading exponents of modern Chicago blues.

● ALBUMS: *Call Me* (Wolf 1994)★★★★, *Joyriding In The Subway* (Wolf 1995)★★★.

KENNEDY, JESSE 'TINY'

b. 20 December 1925, probably Chattanooga, Tennessee, USA. Blues shouter Kennedy first came to prominence in Kansas City in November 1949, where he recorded a session for Capitol Records with Jay McShann's Quintet. In 1951, he joined Tiny Bradshaw's Orchestra as vocalist, recording two unusual tracks with

Bradshaw's band for King Records; the tracks were curious in that the two risqué blues feature Kennedy duetting with himself as both deep-voiced macho male and shrill female! While touring with the orchestra in the south in 1951-52, Kennedy made some recordings under his own name with local musicians for Trumpet Records at Sam Phillips' Sun studio in Memphis, including the successful 'Strange Kind Of Feelin'', which was later covered by Elmore James. Gotham Records' 20th Century subsidiary leased the hit for the northern market, and Trumpet Records tried unsuccessfully to record another hit by Kennedy in New York City in 1953. Nevertheless, he recorded a fine session for RCA-Victor's Groove subsidiary in April 1955 as the contradictory 'Big Tiny Kennedy'; the recordings included a remake of his Trumpet hit, after which he seems to have drifted into obscurity.

● ALBUMS: with Clayton Love, Jerry 'Boogie' McCain *Strange Kind Of Feelin'* (1990)★★★.

KENT, WILLIE

b. 24 February 1936, Sunflower, Mississippi, USA. Kent was brought up in Shelby, Mississippi, and was influenced by the blues he heard on the radio. He settled in Chicago in 1952 and was soon able to hear the top blues artists live in the clubs, although he was under-age. Kent began working as a singer in 1957 and started to play guitar the following year. He quickly switched to bass and formed his own group around 1959. As a bass player, Kent worked in the 60s with Hip Linkchain, Jimmy Dawkins, and Luther 'Guitar Junior' Johnson. In 1975, he shared a live album with Willie James Lyons for the MCM label, and he has subsequently had his intense, powerful vocals and bass playing issued on various labels.

● ALBUMS: with Willie James Lyons *Ghetto* (MCM 1975)★★★, *I'm What You Need* (Big Boy 1989)★★★, *Ain't It Nice* (1991)★★★.

KEY, TROYCE

b. 1937, Jordon Plantation (70m from Monroe), Louisiana, USA, d. 9 November 1992, Oakland, California, USA. In the early 50s Key became interested in blues after hearing a record by Lightnin' Hopkins and he began playing guitar following a serious illness that resulted in hospi-

talization. During this time he was greatly influenced by the records of Fats Domino, Johnny Otis, Muddy Waters, and others. He was signed by Warner Brothers Records in 1958 and had three singles released. Key teamed up with J.J. Malone in 1961 and they recorded together around three years later; they also had two albums released by Red Lightnin' and enjoyed a near-hit in Britain in 1980 with the single 'I Gotta New Car (I Was Framed)'. He continued, until his death from leukaemia, to present his good-natured, rocking blues in Oakland, California, at his own club called Eli Mile High, which was also the name of his blues record label.

● ALBUMS: with J.J. Malone *I've Gotta New Car* (Red Lightnin' 1980)★★★, with Malone *Younger Than Yesterday* (Red Lightnin' 1982)★★★.

KIDD, KENNETH

b. 1935, Newton, Mississippi, USA, d. June 1995. Aka Prez Kenneth, as a youngster Kidd sang in the church choir but was also attracted to the blues. He settled in Chicago in 1956 and soon tried to learn guitar, switching to bass because he found it easier. In the 60s, Kidd recorded in a Jimmy Reed vein for the Biscayne label. His track 'Devil Dealing' was the prototype for G.L. Crockett's hit 'It's A Man Down There', but he received no credit. Towards the end of the decade he formed his own label, Kenneth Records, and although he recorded on a Hip Linkchain session in 1976, little was heard of him in the subsequent years. He continued to work occasionally in west side Chicago clubs until his death in 1995.

KIMBROUGH, JUNIOR

b. David Kimbrough, 28 July 1930, Hudsonville, Mississippi, USA. Kimbrough describes his music as 'cottonpatch blues' but commentators prefer to see it as the resurgence of the 'juke joint' style, once synonymous with Frank Frost, of which Kimbrough and R.L. Burnside are currently the finest exponents. His synthesis of the North Mississippi hill country musical tradition relies upon minimal instrumentation, mesmeric repetition and the seemingly random but instinctive orchestration of basic blues disciplines. Picking up his brother's guitar at the age of eight, Kimbrough absorbed the music of neighbours Mississippi Fred McDowell and Eli Green, became part of their circle and has played for parties and jukes ever since. Cited by rockabilly artist Charlie Feathers and others as a major influence and thus, by inference, vital to the creation of the 'Sun sound', Kimbrough has organized his own parties in and around Holly Springs since the mid-60s, backed by the Soul Blues Boys, a band that usually consists of members of his and Burnside's families. He was filmed at the Chewalla Rib Shack for the film *Deep Blues* and 'Jr. Blues' was featured on the soundtrack album. Both subsequent albums predominantly feature his own songs, which rely heavily upon the recognizable 'floating' verses associated with the area.

● ALBUMS: *Deep Blues* (Atlantic/Anxious 1992)★★★, *All Night Long* (Fat Possum/Demon 1993)★★★, *Sad Days, Lonely Nights* (Fat Possum/Capricorn 1994)★★★.

KING SOLOMON HILL

b. Joe Holmes, 1897, McComb, Mississippi, USA, d. 1949, Sibley, Louisiana, USA. Controversy long surrounded the identity of this itinerant blues singer. He fused the styles of his friends Sam Collins and Ramblin' Thomas (respectively, south Mississippi and east Texas/Louisiana musicians), and elements from Blind Lemon Jefferson, into the eerie bottleneck guitar sound that accompanied his chilling falsetto on his 1932 recordings. His stage-name was derived from his address in Louisiana King Solomon Hill Baptist Church, having given its name to the community of Yellow Pines. Holmes's masterpieces are 'The Gone Dead Train' and 'Whoopee Blues', the former a hobo's lament that is made all the more impressive by his near impenetrable diction. 'Whoopee Blues' transforms an anodyne Lonnie Johnson song, imbuing it with the brimstone reek of hell with which the singer threatens his wayward girlfriend.

● COMPILATIONS: *Backwoods Blues* (1991)★★★.

KING, AL

b. Alvin Smith, 8 August 1926, Monroe, Louisiana, USA. Anything other than church music was forbidden in the Smith household, so it was not until Alvin Smith sang with USO bands while serving in the World War II that he discovered his taste for the musical life. Moving to San Francisco and then Los Angeles, he made his recording debut, 'Homesick Blues', for Recorded In Hollywood in 1951. Two years later he led the Savoys, who recorded 'Chop Chop Boom' with saxophonist Jack McVea for Combo. Returning north to Oakland, he recorded 'On My Way' for Music City, on which he was accompanied by the guitarist Johnny Heartsman, and then joined Jimmy McCracklin's touring band, which led to two singles on which he was teamed with a female singer (their records were released under the collective name of Al And Nettie). One of the singles, 'Now You Know', was an answer record to McCracklin's 'Just Got To Know'. In 1964, now calling himself Al King, he made 'Reconsider Baby', the record most closely associated with his name. Recorded for Triad and later leased to the Atlantic subsidiary Shirley, it remains one of the best versions of Lowell Fulson's composition, not least for Heartsman's contribution. King made further records for Flag, Sahara, Modern and Kent during the 60s and a final session for Ronn in 1970, but failed to repeat the successful formula.

● COMPILATIONS: *West Coast Winners* (Moonshine 1985)★★★, *On My Way* (Diving Duck 1986)★★★, *More West Coast Winners* (Moonshine 1989)★★, *Cruisin' And Bluesin'* (Ace 1990)★★★.

KING, ALBERT

b. Albert Nelson, 23 April 1923 (although three other dates have also been published), Indianola, Mississippi, USA, d. 21 December 1992, Memphis, Tennessee, USA. Despite the fact that his work has been overshadowed by that of his regal namesake B.B. King, this exceptional performer was one of the finest in the entire blues/soul canon. King's first solo recording, 'Bad Luck Blues', was released in 1953, but it was not until the end of the decade that he embarked on a full-time career. His early work fused his already distinctive fretwork to big band-influenced arrangements and included his first successful single, 'Don't Throw Your Love On Me Too Strong'. However, his style was not fully defined until 1966 when, signed to the Stax label, he began working with Booker T. And

The MGs. This tightly knit quartet supplied the perfect rhythmic punch, a facet enhanced by a judicious use of horns. 'Cold Feet', which included wry references to several Stax stablemates, and 'I Love Lucy', a homage to King's distinctive 'Flying V' guitar, stand among his finest recordings. However, this period is best remembered for 'Born Under A Bad Sign' (1967) and 'The Hunter' (1968), two performances that became an essential part of many repertoires including those of Free and Cream. King became a central part of the late 60s 'blues boom', touring the college and concert circuit. His classic album, *Live Wire/Blues Power*, recorded at San Francisco's Fillmore Auditorium in 1968, introduced his music to the white rock audience. More excellent albums followed in its wake, including *King Does The King's Thing*, a tribute collection of Elvis Presley material, and *Years Gone By*. His work during the 70s was largely unaffected by prevailing trends. 'That's What The Blues Is All About' borrowed just enough from contemporary styles to provide King with a Top 20 R&B single, but the bankruptcy of two outlets dealt a blow to King's career. A five-year recording famine ended in 1983, and an astute programme of new material and careful reissues kept the master's catalogue alive. King remained a commanding live performer and an influential figure. A new generation of musicians, including Robert Cray and the late Stevie Ray Vaughan continued to acknowledge his timeless appeal, a factor reinforced in 1990 when King guested on guitarist Gary Moore's 'back-to-the-roots' collection, *Still Got The Blues*. King died late in 1992.

● ALBUMS: *The Big Blues* (King 1962)★★★, *Born Under A Bad Sign* (Atlantic 1967)★★★★, *King Of The Blues Guitar* (Atlantic 1968)★★★★, *Live Wire/Blues Power* (King 1968)★★★★, with Steve Cropper, 'Pops' Staples *Jammed Together* (Stax 1969)★★★, *Years Gone By* (Stax 1969)★★★★, *King, Does The King's Thing* (Stax 1970)★★★, *Lovejoy* (Stax 1971)★★★, *The Lost Session* (1971)★★★, *I'll Play The Blues For You* (Stax 1972)★★★, *Live At Montreux/Blues At Sunrise* (Stax 1973)★★★, *I Wanna Get Funky* (Stax 1974)★★, *The Pinch* (Stax 1976)★★, *Albert* (Utopia 1976)★★★, *Truckload Of Lovin'* (Utopia 1976)★★, *Albert Live* (Utopia 1977)★★★, *King Albert* (1977)★★★, *New Orleans Heat* (Tomato 1978)★★★, *San Francisco '83* (Stax 1983)★★★, *I'm In A 'Phone Booth, Baby* (Stax 1984)★★★, with John Mayall *The Lost Session* rec. 1971 (Stax 1986)★★, *Red House* (Essential 1991)★★★, *Blues At Sunset* (Stax 1996)★★★.

● COMPILATIONS: *Laundromat Blues* (Edsel 1984)★★★, *The Best Of Albert King* (Stax 1986)★★★, *I'll Play The Blues For You: The Best Of Albert King* (Stax 1988)★★★, *Let's Have A Natural Ball* rec. 1959-63 (Modern Blues Recordings 1989)★★★, *Wednesday Night In San Francisco (Live At The Fillmore)* and *Thursday Night In San Francisco (Live At The Fillmore)* (Stax 1990)★★, *Live On Memory Lane* (Monad 1995)★★★, *Hard Bargain* (Stax 1996)★★★★.

KING, B.B.

b. Riley B. King, 16 September 1925, Indianola, Mississippi, USA. The son of a sharecropper, King went to work on the plantation like any other young black in Mississippi, but he had sung in amateur gospel groups from childhood. By the age of 16, he was also playing blues guitar and singing on street corners. When he was 20 years old, he temporarily quit sharecropping and went to Memphis, where he busked, and shared a room for almost a year with his second cousin, Bukka White. However, it was not until 1948 that he managed to pay off his debts to his former plantation boss. After leaving farming, he returned to Memphis, determined to become a star. He secured work with radio station KWEM, and then with WDIA, fronting a show sponsored by the health-tonic Pepticon, which led to disc jockeying on the *Sepia Swing Show*. Here he was billed as 'The Beale Street Blues Boy', later amended to 'Blues Boy King', and then to 'B.B. King'. Radio exposure promoted King's live career, and he performed with a band whose personnel varied according to availability. At this stage, he was still musically untutored, and liable to play against his backing musicians, but it was evident from his first recordings made for Bullet Records in 1949, that his talent was striking.

The Bullet recordings brought King to the attention of Modern Records, with whom he recorded for the next 10 years. As he began to tour beyond the area around Memphis, his first marriage, already under strain, ended in divorce in 1952.

By that time, he was a national figure, having held the number 1 spot in the *Billboard* R&B chart for 15 weeks with 'Three O'Clock Blues'. He had embarked on the gruelling trail of one-nighters that has continued ever since. Through the 50s, King toured with a 13-piece band, adopting a patriarchal attitude to his musicians that has been compared to that of a kindly plantation boss. Briefly, he operated his own Blues Boy's Kingdom label, but had no success. Modern, however, were steadily producing hits for him, although their approach to copyright-standard practice in its day was less ethical, with the label owners taking fictitious credit on many titles. B.B. King's blues singing was heavily melifluent, influenced by Peter J. 'Doctor' Clayton and gospel singer Sam McCrary of the Fairfield Four. However, his true revolutionary importance was as an electric guitarist. He admired Charlie Christian and Django Reinhardt as well as Lonnie Johnson, Blind Lemon Jefferson, and also saxophonist Lester Young. He derived ideas about phrasing and harmony from all these musicians. His extensive use of sixths clearly derived from jazz. His sound, however, consisted chiefly of a synthesis of the bottleneck styles of the delta blues (including that of Bukka White) with the jazzy electric guitar of 'T-Bone' Walker. To Walker's flowing, crackling music, King added finger vibrato, his own substitute for the slide, which he had never managed to master. The result was a fluid guitar sound, in which almost every note was bent and/or sustained. This, together with King's penchant for playing off the beat, gave his solos the pattern of speech, and the personification of his beautiful black, gold plated, pearl inlaid Gibson 335 (or 355) guitar as 'Lucille' seemed highly appropriate.

In 1960, King switched labels, moving to ABC in the hope of emulating Ray Charles's success. The times were against him, however, for black tastes were moving towards soul music and spectacular stage presentation. King had always felt a need to make the blues respectable, removing sexual boasting and references to violence and drugs. As a result of these endeavours his lyrics were, ironically, closer to those of soul, with their emphasis on love, respect and security in relationships. He remained popular, as his interplay with the audience on a live album recorded in Chicago in 1964 illustrates, but by the mid-60s, his career seemed in decline, with the hits coming from Modern's back catalogue rather than his new company. Revitalization came with the discovery of the blues by young whites - initially musicians, and then the wider audience. In 1968, King played the Fillmore West with Johnny Winter and Mike Bloomfield, who introduced him as 'the greatest living blues guitarist', provoking a standing ovation before he had even played a note. His revival of Roy Hawkins' 'The Thrill Is Gone', which made innovatory use of strings, provided the crucial pop crossover. Consequently, in 1969, King paid his first visit to Europe, where the way had been prepared by Eric Clapton (and where an ignorant reviewer called him an 'up-and-coming guitarist of the Clapton-Peter Green school'). In 1970, he recorded his first collaboration with rock musicians, produced by Leon Russell, who played on and composed some numbers, as did Carole King. King's career has been smooth sailing ever since, and he has been in demand for commercials, movie soundtracks, television show theme tunes, and guest appearances (e.g., with U2 on 1989's 'When Love Comes To Town'). His workaholic schedule probably results, in part, from a need to finance his compulsive gambling, but he has also worked unobtrusively to provide entertainment for prisoners (co-founding the Foundation for the Advancement of Inmate Rehabilitation and Recreation in 1972).

His professional life is marked by a sense of mission, coupled with a desire to give the blues status and acceptability. This he has achieved, bringing the blues into the mainstream of entertainment, although he has done so by removing much of the sense of otherness that first brought many whites to it. Sometimes his live performances can be disappointingly bland, with sing-along segments and misplaced attempts to ingratiate, as when he proudly told a Scottish audience of his meeting with Sheena Easton. His recordings since the 70s have been of inconsistent quality. King has deliberately kept in touch with his roots, returning to Mississippi each year to play, but the adulation of rock musicians has been a mixed blessing. Recordings made in London with, among others, Alexis Korner, Steve Winwood and Ringo Starr proved particularly disappointing. Equally, his collaboration with jazz-funk band the Crusaders, who produced and played on two albums, stifled his invention, and it has often seemed that King's creativity has run into the sands of MOR pop in a 12-bar format. These are the times when he is most likely to return with a brilliant, vital album that goes back to his roots in jazz, jump and the Delta. At the end of 1995 King announced that, as he had turned 70 years of age, he would be drastically reducing his performing schedule which he had maintained for many decades. Instead of a regular 300 or more gigs a year, he would be winding down in his old age, to a modest 200!

B.B. King has achieved the blues singer's dream - to live in Las Vegas and to have full access to the material benefits that the American way of life still withholds from so many black Americans. Without a doubt, though, things have changed for him; the teenager playing in the 40s streets became a man with whom the chairman of the Republican Party in the 80s considered it an honour to play guitar. B.B. King was a great influence on the sound of the blues, the sincerity of his singing and the fluency of his guitar spawning a flock of imitators as well as having a more general effect on the music's development, as reflected in the playing of Buddy Guy, his namesakes Freddie and Albert King, 'Little' Joe Blue and innumerable others. Arguably, his most far-reaching effect has been on rock music. King's limitations include an inability to play guitar behind his own singing. This has led him to make a strict demarcation between the two, and has encouraged rock guitarists to regard extended solos as the mark of authentic blues playing. In lesser hands, this has all too easily become bloated excess or meaningless note-spinning. B.B. King has always aspired to elegance, logic and purpose in his guitar playing; it is ironic that his success has spawned so many imitators possessing so little of those very qualities. B.B. King's career, like that of other black musicians in America, has been circumscribed by the dictates of the industry. Like Louis Armstrong, he has nevertheless achieved great art through a combination of prodigious technical gifts and the placing of his instinctive improvisatory skills at the service of emotional expression. Also like Armstrong, he stayed firmly within the compass of showbusiness, attempting to give the public what he perceives it to want. His greatest music, however, testifies to his standing as a titanic figure in popular music.

● ALBUMS: *Singin' The Blues* (Crown 1957)★★★, *The Blues* (Crown 1958)★★★, *B.B. King Wails* (Crown 1959)★★★, *B.B. King Sings Spirituals* (Crown 1960)★★, *The Great B.B. King* (Crown 1961)★★★, *King Of The Blues* (Crown 1961)★★★, *My Kind Of Blues* (Crown 1961)★★★, *More B.B. King* (Crown 1962)★★★, *Twist With B.B. King* (Crown 1962)★★, *Easy Listening Blues* (Crown 1962)★★★, *Blues In My Heart* (Crown 1962)★★★, *B.B. King* (Crown 1963)★★★, *Mr. Blues* (ABC 1963)★★★, *Rock Me Baby* (1964)★★★★, *Live At The Regal* (ABC 1965)★★★★★, *Confessin' The Blues* (ABC 1965)★★★, *Let Me Love You* (1965)★★★, *B.B. King Live On Stage* (1965)★★★, *The Soul Of B.B. King* (1966)★★★, *The Jungle* (1967)★★★, *Blues Is King* (Bluesway 1967)★★★★, *Blues On Top Of Blues* (Bluesway 1968)★★★, *Lucille* (Bluesway 1968)★★★★, *Live And Well* (1969)★★★★, *Completely Well* (MCA 1969)★★★, *Back In The Alley* (MCA 1970)★★★, *Indianola Mississippi Seeds* (MCA 1970)★★★★, *Live In Cook County Jail* (MCA 1971)★★★★, *In London* (MCA 1971)★★★, *L.A. Midnight* (ABC 1972)★★★, *Guess Who* (ABC 1972)★★★, *To Know You Is To Love You* (ABC 1973)★★★, with Bobby Bland *Together For The First Time ... Live* (MCA 1974)★★★★, *Friends* (ABC 1974)★★★, *Lucille Talks Back* (MCA 1975)★★★★, with Bland *Together Again ... Live* (MCA 1976)★★★, *King Size* (MCA 1977)★★★, *Midnight Believer* (MCA 1978)★★★, *Take It Home* (MCA 1979)★★★, *Now Appearing At Ole Miss* (MCA 1980)★★, *There Must Be A Better World Somewhere* (MCA 1981)★★★★, *Love Me Tender* (MCA 1982)★★, *Blues 'N' Jazz* (MCA 1983)★★, *Six Silver Strings* (MCA 1985)★★, *Do The Boogie* (Ace 1988)★★★, *Lucille Had A Baby* (Ace 1989)★★, *Live At San Quentin* (MCA 1990)★★★★, *Live At The Apollo* (GRP 1991)★★★, *Singin' The Blues & The Blues* (Ace 1991)★★★, *There's Always One More Time* (MCA 1992)★★★★, *Blues Summit* (MCA 1993)★★★★, with Diane Schuur *Heart To Heart* (GRP 1994)★★, *Lucille And Friends* (MCA 1995)★★★, *Deuces Wild* (MCA 1997)★★★.

● CD ROM: *On The Road With B.B. King* (MCA 1996)★★★★.

● COMPILATIONS: *The Best Of B.B. King* (Galaxy 1962)★★, *His Best - The Electric B.B. King* (Kent 1968)★★★, *The Incredible Soul Of B.B. King* (Kent 1970)★★★, *The Best Of B.B. King* (MCA 1973)★★★★, *The Rarest King* (Blues Boy 1980)★★★, *The Memphis Master* (Ace 1982)★★★, *B.B. King - 20 Blues Greats* (Déjà Vu 1985)★★★, *Introducing (1969-85)* (MCA 1987)★★★, *Across The Tracks* (Ace 1988)★★★, *My Sweet Little Angel* (Ace 1992)★★★, *King Of The Blues* 4-CD box set (MCA 1993)★★★★, *Gold Collection* (1993)★★★, *King Of The Blues* (Pickwick 1994)★★★, *Heart & Soul: A Collection Of Blues Ballads* (Pointblank Classic 1995)★★★, *The Collection: 20 Master Recordings* (Castle 1995)★★★, *How Blue Can You GetClassic Live Performances 1964-1994* (MCA 1996)★★★★.

● VIDEOS: *Live At Nick's* (Hendring 1987), *A Blues Session* (Video Collection 1988), *Live In Africa* (BMG Video 1991), *Blues Master, Highlights* (Warner Music 1995), *The Blues Summit Concert* (MCA 1995).

● FURTHER READING: *The Arrival Of BB King; The Authorized Biography*, Charles Sawyer. *B.B. King*, Sebastian Danchin. *Blues All Around Me, The Autobiography Of B.B. King*, B.B. King and David Ritz.

KING, EARL

b. Earl Silas Johnson IV, 7 February 1934, New Orleans, Louisiana, USA. The son of a blues pianist, King became an accomplished guitarist and singer with local bands before making his first recordings in 1953 for Savoy ('Have You Gone Crazy') and Specialty ('A Mother's Love'). Strongly influenced by Guitar Slim (Eddie Jones), during the mid-50s he worked with Huey Smith's band and made his biggest hit, 'Those Lonely Lonely Nights' with Smith on piano. This was on Johnny Vincent's Ace label, for whom King was house guitarist. In 1958, he made a version of 'Everyone Has To Cry Sometime' as Handsome Earl. He went on to record for Rex and Imperial where he made 'Come On' and the R&B hit 'Trick Bag' (1962) which featured King's influential guitar figures. He was also starting to enjoy success as a song-writer, composing the Lee Dorsey hit 'Do Re Mi', 'He's Mine' for Bernadine Washington, 'Big

Chief' recorded by Professor Longhair and 'Teasin' You', Willie Tee's 1965 R&B hit. Jimmy Clanton, Dr. John and Fats Domino were others who recorded King compositions. During the 60s and early 70s, King himself made recordings for Amy, Wand, Atlantic and Motown, although the Allen Toussaint-produced Atlantic session was not released until 1981 and the Motown tracks remain unissued. King remained active into the 80s, recording with *Room Full Of Blues* for Black Top. His Imperial tracks were reissued by EMI in 1987.

● ALBUMS: *New Orleans Rock 'N' Roll* (Sonet 1977)★★★, *Street Parade* (Charly 1981)★★★, *Room Full Of Blues* (Black Top 1988)★★★, *Glazed* (Black Top 1988)★★★, *Sexual Telepathy* (Black Top 1990)★★★, *Hard River To Cross* (1993)★★★.

● COMPILATIONS: *Soul Bag* (Stateside 1987)★★★.

KING, EDDIE

b. 21 April 1938, Talledega, Alabama, USA. King was orphaned in 1950 and eventually settled in Chicago, where he played in various blues clubs. He worked as a guitarist with Muddy Waters, Howlin' Wolf, and Willie Dixon in the 50s before he began a long association with 'Little' Mack Simmons at the end of the decade. He recorded with Simmons and Detroit Junior and also released singles under his own name in the early 60s. He worked briefly with Willie Cobbs and he recorded further singles (sometimes in the company of his sister Mae Bee May) and in 1987 he and his sister released an album on Double Trouble. In the early 90s he was to be found working as lead guitarist for Koko Taylor. Eddie Taylor was a member of the Burning Chicago Blues Machine that recorded *Boogie Blues* on GBW label in 1992. He sang four songs. His second solo album was on drummer Joe Roesch's record label and received excellent reviews.

● ALBUMS: *The Blues Has Got Me* (Double Trouble 1987)★★★, *Another Cow's Dead* (Roesch 1997)★★★★.

KING, FREDDIE

b. Billy Myles, 30 September 1934, Gilmer, Texas, USA, d. 28 December 1976, Dallas, Texas. Freddie (aka Freddy) was one of the triumvirate of Kings (the others being B.B. and Albert) who ruled the blues throughout the 60s. He was the possessor of a light, laid-back, but not unemotional voice and a facile fast-fingered guitar technique that made him the hero of many young disciples. He learned to play guitar at an early age, being influenced by his mother, Ella Mae King, and her brother Leon. Although forever associated with Texas and admitting a debt to such artists as T-Bone Walker he moved north to Chicago in his mid-teens. In 1950, he became influenced by local blues guitarists Eddie 'Playboy' Taylor and Robert Lockwood. King absorbed elements from each of their styles, before encompassing the more strident approaches of Magic Sam and Otis Rush. Here, he began to sit in with various groups and slowly built up the reputation that was to make him a star. After teaming up with 'Lonesome' Jimmy Lee Robinson to form the Every Hour Blues Boys he worked and recorded with Little Sonny Cooper's band, Earlee Payton's Blues Cats and Smokey Smothers. These last recordings were made in Cincinnati, Ohio, in August 1960 for Sydney Nathan's King/Federal organization, and on the same day, King recorded six titles under his own name, including the influential instrumental hit 'Hideaway'. He formed his own band and began touring, bolstering his success with further hits, many of them guitar showpieces, some trivialized by titles such as 'The Bossa Nova Watusi Twist', but others showing off his 'crying' vocal delivery. Many, such as '(I'm) Tore Down', 'Have You Ever Loved A Woman' and particularly 'The Welfare (Turns Its Back On You)', became classics of the (then) modern blues. He continued to record for King Federal up until 1966, his career on record being masterminded by pianist Sonny Thompson. He left King Federal in 1966 and took up a short tenure (1968-69) on the Atlantic subsidiary label Cotillion. Ironically, the subsequent white blues-boom provided a new-found impetus. Eric Clapton was a declared King aficionado, while Chicken Shack's Stan Webb indicated his debt by including three of his mentor's compositions on his group's debut album. The albums that followed failed to capture the artist at his best. This was not a particularly successful move, although the work he did on that label has increased in value with the passage of time. The same could be said for his next musical liaison, which saw him working with Leon Russell on his Shelter label. Much of his work for Russell was over-produced, but King made many outstanding recordings during this period and a re-evaluation of that work is overdue. There was no denying the excitement it generated, particularly on *Getting Ready*, which was recorded at the famous Chess studio. This excellent set included the original version of the much-covered 'Going Down'. Live recordings made during his last few years indicate that King was still a force to be reckoned with as he continued his good-natured guitar battles with allcomers, and usually left them far behind. *Burglar* featured a duet with Eric Clapton on 'Sugar Sweet', but the potential of this new relationship was tragically cut short in December 1976 when King died of heart failure at the early age of 43. His last stage appearance had taken place three days earlier in his hometown of Dallas.

● ALBUMS: *Freddie King Sings The Blues* (King 1961)★★★, *Let's Hideaway And Dance Away* (King 1961)★★★★, *Boy-Girl-Boy* (King 1962)★★★, *Bossa Nova And Blues* (King 1962)★★, *Freddie King Goes Surfing* (King 1963)★★, *Freddie King Gives You A Bonanza Of Instrumentals* (King 1965)★★★, *24 Vocals And Instrumentals* (King 1966)★★★, *Hide Away* (King 1969)★★★★, *Freddie King Is A Blues Master* (Atlantic 1969)★★★, *My Feeling For The Blues* (Atlantic 1970)★★★, *Getting Ready* (Shelter 1971)★★★★, *Texas Cannonball* (Shelter 1972)★★★, *Woman Across The Water* (Shelter 1973)★★★, *Burglar* (RSO 1974)★★★, *Larger Than Life* (RSO 1975)★★★.

● COMPILATIONS: *King Of R&B Volume 2* (1969)★★★, *The Best Of Freddie King* (Shelter 1974)★★★★, *Original Hits* (1977)★★★, *Rockin' The Blues - Live* (Crosscut 1983)★★★, *Takin' Care Of Business* (Charly 1985)★★★, *Live In Antibes, 1974* (Concert 1988)★★★, *Live In Nancy, 1975 Volume 1* (Concert 1989)★★★, *Blues Guitar Hero: The Influential Early Sessions* (1993)★★★, *King Of The Blues* (EMI/Shelter 1996)★★★★, *Key To The Highway* (Wolf 1995)★★★.

● VIDEOS: *Freddie King Jan 20 1973* (Vestapol 1995), *Freddie King In Concert* (Vestapol 1995), *Freddie King: The Beat 1966* (Vestapol 1995).

KING, LITTLE JIMMY

b. Manuel Gales, 4 December 1964, Memphis, Tennessee, USA. Citing Albert King and Jimi Hendrix as influences, King's guitar style exhibits an uneasy amalgam of both disparate elements, which as yet, he has been unable to mould into a recognizably individual sound. He and twin brother Daniel received acoustic guitars for Christmas when they were six. Being left-handed like his mentors, he learned to play 'upside-down-and-backwards' and graduated to an electric model soon afterwards. As a teenager, he played in whichever Beale Street clubs would let him in. In 1984 he was seen by Albert King and worked with his band for four years, at the end of which he changed his name legally to King and was 'adopted' as a grandson by his bandleader. After King's death, he took over the band and renamed it the Memphis Soul Survivors, with whom his first album was made. For his second, King recruited the Hi Rhythm Section, calling them the King James Version Band, and also cut several tracks with Double Trouble, the late Stevie Ray Vaughan's band. More noticeably than his debut album, this was caught between traditional blues and its rock equivalent, a problem that artists like King have not yet resolved.

● ALBUMS: *Little Jimmy King And The Memphis Soul Survivors* (Bullseye Blues 1991)★★★, *Something Inside Of Me* (Bullseye Blues 1994)★★, *Soldier For The Blues* (Bullseye Blues 1997)★★.

KING, SAUNDERS

b. 13 March 1909, Staple, Louisiana, USA. Starting out as a singer, and obtaining a job with the NBC network, King took up the electric guitar in 1938 after hearing Charlie Christian. King formed his own band in 1942, and became popular around the San Francisco area; he then began recording for the small Rhythm Records and the first session produced his biggest hit, 'Saunders Blues'. The song achieved more fame under the title 'S.K. Blues' and became a staple in the repertoires of many blues shouters, such as Jimmy Witherspoon and Big Joe Turner. Later recordings for Modern/RPM/Flair (who bought the Rhythm masters and cheekily reissued 'S.K. Blues' as 'New S.K. Blues'!), Cavatone and Aladdin failed to emulate the success of 'S.K. Blues', and his final recordings were made in 1961 for Galaxy, after which he retired from professional music, although he was brought back in 1979 when asked to guest on Carlos Devadip Santana's *Oneness* album. Over the years, Saunders King has taken a back seat to the mighty 'T-Bone' Walker, but it is often overlooked that he, in fact, was recorded playing electrified blues guitar before Walker made his recording debut on that instrument.

● COMPILATIONS: *What's Your Story, Morning Glory* (Blues Boy 1987)★★★, *The First King Of The Blues* (Ace 1988)★★★.

KINSEY, BIG DADDY

b. Lester Kinsey, 18 March 1927, Pleasant Grove, Mississippi, USA. An acknowledged disciple of Muddy Waters, Kinsey owned his first guitar at the age of six. Before travelling north in 1944, he had seen both Waters (then still McKinley Morganfield) and pianist Pinetop Perkins play at local parties and juke houses. Moving to Gary, Indiana, he played harmonica in a local band, the Soul Brothers. As his own family grew, he trained each of his sons, Ralph, Donald and Kenneth, to play an instrument and eventually to perform as a family unit. By the late 60s, the band was working the Ramada Inn circuit, the first black unit to do so. For much of the 70s, Daddy Kinsey worked local clubs with non-family musicians while his sons worked with Albert King and Bob Marley. In 1984, they were reunited as the Kinsey Report and the following year made their debut album, which inevitably included a 'Tribute To Muddy'. The following year, the sons signed to Alligator and their father toured with them as their opening act. They also backed him on 'Can't Let Go', assisted by Lucky Peterson on keyboards. Kinsey's albums on Verve/Gitanes benefit from superlative accompaniment from musicians such as Buddy Guy, John Primer, James Cotton, Pinetop Perkins, Johnnie Johnson and Willie Smith. *I Am The Blues* is dedicated to Muddy Waters and Kinsey is plainly content to continue in his shadow.

● ALBUMS: as the Kinsey Report *Bad Situation* (Rooster Blues 1985)★★★, *Can't Let Go* (Blind Pig 1989)★★★, *I Am The Blues* (Verve/Gitanes 1993)★★, *Ramblin' Man* (Verve/Gitanes 1994)★★★.

KIRKLAND, EDDIE

b. 16 August 1928, Kingston, Jamaica, West Indies. The career of guitarist Eddie Kirkland spans 40 years and a variety of musical styles. Soon after his birth the family relocated to the southern states of America and at the age of 15 he took a day job at the Ford Motor Company in Detroit. He met John Lee Hooker and became his regular accompanist both on the club circuit and on record, proving to be one of the few who could follow Hooker's erratic style. Kirkland's first recordings were made in 1952 and throughout the decade he recorded for RPM, King, Cobra, Fortune and Lupine. In 1961 he made his first deviation from 'down-home' blues when he recorded with King Curtis and Oliver Nelson for Prestige. In the mid-60s he moved to Macon, Georgia, where he turned to soul music, eventually signing to Otis Redding's enterprise Volt, in 1965. Redding used Kirkland in his touring band, but Kirkland's role as a soul artist was never more than minor. In the 70s, he returned to his blues roots, recording for Pete Lowery's Trix label, both solo and with small bands, and has since maintained a heavy touring schedule at home and in Europe.
● ALBUMS: *The Devil And Other Blues Demons* (Trix 1972)★★★, *Pickin' Up The Pieces* (GRP 1981)★★★, *The Way It Was* (Red Lightnin' 1983)★★★, *Have Mercy* (Pulsar 1993)★★★, *All Around The World* (Deluge 1993)★★★, *Some Like It Raw* (Deluge 1994)★★★, *Where You Get Your Sugar?* (Deluge 1995)★★★, *Front And Center* (Trix 1995)★★★.

KNOWLING, RANSOM

b. 24 June 1912. Knowling played bass, and was best known for his extensive work as a session player, used by producer Lester Melrose on hundreds of blues records in Chicago in the 30s and 40s, by artists such as Big Bill Broonzy, Tampa Red and Sonny Boy 'Rice Miller' Williamson. His rock-solid bass work was also used to add a more urban sound to the work of country blues singers such as Tommy McClennan. In later years he claimed never to have liked the blues, preferring more sophisticated sounds, but he owes virtually all his fame to that idiom. Although known to have died, details of Ransom's death are scant.

KOERNER, 'SPIDER' JOHN

b. 31 August 1938, Rochester, New York, USA. Koerner, who earned his nickname due to his previous employment at an automobile shop where he climbed shelves to reach parts, studied aeronautical engineering at the University of Minnesota. He was into his second year as a student before he picked up a guitar for the first time. Bitten by the folk bug, he left college and drove aimlessly around America - he even enlisted in the US Marine Corps at one point. When he eventually returned to Minneapolis he met Bob Dylan and, more importantly, Dave Ray. As he later told *Folk Roots* magazine, 'I kind of fell into that bunch'. On a visit to Rochester he also met Tony Glover - and with him and Ray formed an acoustic blues trio, Koerner, Ray And Glover. They played the coffee-house circuit together before eventually securing a recording contract with Audiophile Records through contacts at the influential *Little Sandy Review* magazine. However, the liaison with Ray and Glover was never intended to be a permanent one, and after the success of his debut *Spider's Blues* set he concentrated on a solo career. In 1969 he recorded a more pop-orientated album with pianist Willie Murphy, *Running, Jumping, Standing Still*. This included 'I Ain't Blue', a song later covered by Bonnie Raitt. *Music Is Just A Bunch Of Notes* was recorded for Ray's new Sweet Jane imprint in 1972, but afterwards Koerner left the USA for Denmark. There his interest in blues faded in favour of folk; he formed another trio in Denmark, accompanied by washboard and harmonica, but issued only one further recording, *Some American Folk Songs Like They Used To Be*. He returned to the USA in 1977 and spent a long period with no musical involvement. He did tour the UK, however, appearing at the Cambridge Folk Festival alongside a series of club dates. He has continued recording into the 90s, often linking up with old friends Ray and Glover in a resurrected version of the trio that first established him as one of the most talented songwriters of his generation.
● ALBUMS: *Spider's Blues* (Elektra 1965)★★★, with Willie Murphy *Running, Jumping, Standing Still* (1968)★★★, *Music Is Just A Bunch Of Notes* (Sweet Jane 1972)★★★, *Some American Folk Songs Like They Used To Be* (Sweet Jane 1974)★★★, *Nobody Knows The Trouble I've Been*

(Red House 1986)★★★, *Raised By Humans* (Red House 1992)★★★, *Star Geezer* (Red House 1996)★★★.

KOERNER, RAY AND GLOVER

This US trio, who were a pivotal influence on the Beatles, among many others, were among the first to authenticate the notion that 'white men *can* play the blues'. Tony 'Little Sun' Glover, Dave Ray and John 'Spider' Koerner first began to play together in the early 60s. Koerner had previously been a contemporary of Bob Dylan at the University of Minnesota. By the time he linked up with Ray and Glover, he had perfected a unique take on country blues, employing a customized seven-string guitar and rack harmonica while writing new blues songs rather than relying on standards. The trio released their first album for Audiophile Records in 1963, which eventually brought them to the attention of Elektra Records. They reissued the album (minus four tracks on the original to ensure a better pressing quality), and also hosted the follow-up collection. Koerner was still clearly the artistic force behind each of these sets - a situation exemplified by the fact that Ray (guitar) and Glover (harmonica) rarely appeared on the same track. Unlike Koerner, who launched his solo career in 1965 with *Spider Blues*, they never toured Europe. Although they reunited sporadically, each member of the trio subsequently took a solo path, primarily because the basis of their collaboration had never been formalized. As Dave Ray told *Folk Roots* in 1996: 'It was travel arrangements primarily. We were often in the same town, so we all showed up in the same place at the same time. We didn't really do that many turns together.' However, there were further reunions over ensuing years, the most notable being a support to the Who at the Guthrie Theater in 1968 and a performance at the Winnipeg Festival in 1995. In the early 70s Ray also founded Sweet Jane Records, a label that issued recordings by Koerner as well as Bonnie Raitt and Junior Wells. Ray And Glover also released three albums in the late 80s and early 90s, which were issued on the punk labels Treehouse and Tim Kerr Records.

● ALBUMS: *Blues, Rags & Hollers* (Audiophile/Elektra 1963)★★★, *Lots More Blues, Rags & Hollers* (Elektra 1964)★★★, *The Return Of Koerner, Ray & Glover* (Elektra 1965)★★★, *Live At St. Olaf Festival* (Elektra 1968)★★★, *One Foot In The Groove* (Tim Kerr 1996)★★★.

● VIDEOS: *Blues, Rags & Hollers: The Koerner, Ray & Glover Story* (Latch Lake 1986).

KORNER, ALEXIS

b. 19 April 1928, Paris, France, d. 1 January 1984. An inspirational figure in British music circles, Korner was already versed in black music when he met Cyril Davies at the London Skiffle Club. Both musicians were frustrated by the limitations of the genre and transformed the venue into the London Blues And Barrelhouse Club, where they not only performed together but also showcased visiting US bluesmen. When jazz trombonist Chris Barber introduced an R&B segment into his live repertoire, he employed Korner (guitar) and Davies (harmonica) to back singer Ottilie Patterson. Inspired, the pair formed Blues Incorporated in 1961 and the following year established the Ealing Rhythm And Blues Club in a basement beneath a local cinema. The group's early personnel included Charlie Watts (drums), Art Wood (vocals) and Keith Scott (piano), but later featured Long John Baldry, Jack Bruce, Graham Bond and Ginger Baker in its ever-changing line-up. Mick Jagger and Paul Jones were also briefly associated with Korner, whose continued advice and encouragement proved crucial to a generation of aspiring musicians. However, disagreements over direction led to Davies' defection following the release of *R&B From The Marquee*, leaving Korner free to pursue a jazz-based path. While former colleagues later found success with the Rolling Stones, Manfred Mann and Cream, Korner's excellent group went largely unnoticed by the general public, although he did enjoy a residency on a children's television show backed by his rhythm section of Danny Thompson (bass) and Terry Cox (drums). The name 'Blues Incorporated' was dropped when Korner embarked on a solo career, punctuated by the formation of several temporary groups, including Free At Last (1967), New Church (1969) and Snape (1972). While the supporting cast on such ventures remained fluid, including for a short time singer Robert Plant, the last two units featured Peter Thorup who also collaborated with Korner on CCS, a pop-based big band that scored notable hits with 'Whole Lotta Love' (1970), 'Walkin'' and 'Tap Turns On The Water' (both 1971). Korner also derived success from his BBC Radio 1 show that offered a highly individual choice of material. He also broadcast on a long-running programme for the BBC World Service. Korner continued to perform live, often accompanied by former Back Door virtuoso bassist Colin Hodgkinson, and remained a highly respected figure in the music fraternity. He joined Charlie Watts, Ian Stewart, Jack Bruce and Dick Heckstall-Smith in the informal Rocket 88, and Korner's 50th birthday party, which featured appearances by Eric Clapton, Chris Farlowe and Zoot Money, was both filmed and recorded. In 1981, Korner began an ambitious 13-part television documentary on the history of rock, but his premature death from cancer in January 1984 left this and many other projects unfulfilled. However, Korner's stature as a vital catalyst in British R&B was already assured.

● ALBUMS: by Alexis Korner's Blues Incorporated *R&B From The Marquee* (Ace Of Clubs 1962)★★★★, *Alexis Korner's Blues Incorporated* (Ace Of Clubs 1964)★★★, *Red Hot From Alex* aka *Alexis Korner's All Star Blues Incorporated* (Transatlantic 1964)★★★★, *At The Cavern* (Oriole 1964)★★★, *Sky High* (Spot 1966)★★, *Blues Incorporated (Wednesday Night Prayer Meeting)* (Polydor 1967)★★★; by Alexis Korner *I Wonder Who* (Fontana 1967)★★★, *A New Generation Of Blues* aka *What's That Sound I Hear* (Transatlantic 1968)★★★, *Both Sides Of Alexis Korner* (Metronome 1969)★★★, *Alexis* (Rak 1971)★★★, *Mr. Blues* (Toadstool 1974)★★★, *Alexis Korner* (Polydor 1974)★★★, *Get Off My Cloud* (Columbia 1975)★★★, *Just Easy* (Intercord 1978)★★★, *Me* (Jeton 1979)★★★, *The Party Album* (Intercord 1980)★★★, *Juvenile Delinquent* (1984)★★, *Live In Paris: Alexis Korner* (Magnum 1988)★★★; by New Church *The New Church* (Metronome 1970); by Snape *Accidentally Born In New Orleans* (Transatlantic 1973)★★★, *Snape Live On Tour* (Brain 1974)★★★.

● COMPILATIONS: *Bootleg Him* (Rak 1972)★★★, *Profile* (Teldec 1981)★★★, with Cyril Davies *Alexis 1957* (Krazy Kat 1984)★★★, with Colin Hodgkinson *Testament* (Thunderbolt 1985)★★★, *Alexis Korner 1961-1972* (Castle 1986)★★★, *Hammer And Nails* (Thunderbolt 1987)★★★, *The Alexis Korner Collection* (Castle 1988)★★★, *And ....* (Castle 1994)★★, *On The Move* (Castle 1996)★★.

● VIDEOS: *Eat A Little Rhythm And Blues* (BBC Video 1988).

● FURTHER READING: *Alexis Korner: The Biography*, Harry Shapiro.

KOTTKE, LEO

b. 11 September 1945, Athens, Georgia, USA. This inventive guitarist drew inspiration from the country-blues style of Mississippi John Hurt, and having taken up the instrument as an adolescent, joined several aspiring mid-60s groups. Induction into the US Navy interrupted his progress, but the artist was discharged following an accident that permanently damaged his hearing. Kottke subsequently ventured to Minneapolis where a spell performing in the city's folk clubs led to a recording contract. *Circle Round The Sun* received limited exposure via two independent outlets, but his career did not fully flourish until 1971 when John Fahey invited Kottke to record for his company, Takoma. *Six And Twelve String Guitar* established the artist as an exciting new talent, with a style blending dazzling dexterity with moments of introspection. Kottke's desire to expand his repertoire led to a break with Fahey and a major contract with Capitol Records. *Mudlark* included instrumental and vocal tracks, notably a version of the Byrds' 'Eight Miles High', and while purists bore misgivings about Kottke's languid, sonorous voice, his talent as a guitarist remained unchallenged. Several excellent albums in a similar vein ensued, including *Greenhouse*, which boasted an interpretation of Fahey's 'Last Steam Engine Train', and the in-concert *My Feet Are Smiling*. Prodigious touring enhanced Kottke's reputation as one of America's finest acoustic 12-string guitarists, although he was unable to convert this standing into commercial success. He later switched labels to Chrysalis, but by the 80s had returned to independent outlets. His crafted approach continues to flourish, especially on 1997's excellent *Standing In My Shoes*.

● ALBUMS: *12-String Blues: Live At The Scholar Coffee House* (Oblivion 1968)★★★, *Six And Twelve String Guitar* (Takoma/Sonet 1971)★★★, *Circle Round The Sun* (Symposium 1970)★★★,

Mudlark (Capitol 1971)★★★, *Greenhouse* (Capitol 1972)★★★★, *My Feet Are Smiling* (Capitol 1973)★★★★, *Ice Water* (Capitol 1974)★★★★, *Dreams And All That Stuff* (Capitol 1975)★★, *Chewing Pine* (Capitol 1975)★★★, *Leo Kottke* (Chrysalis 1976)★★★★, *Burnt Lips* (Chrysalis 1979)★★★, *Balance* (Chrysalis 1979)★★, *Leo Kottke Live In Europe* (Chrysalis 1980), *Guitar Music* (Chrysalis 1981)★★★, *Time Step* (Chrysalis 1983)★★★★, *A Shout Towards Noon* (Private Music 1986)★★★, *Regards From Chuck Pink* (Private Music 1988)★★★★, *My Father's Face* (Private Music 1989)★★★, *That's What* (Private Music 1990)★★★, *Great Big Boy* (Private Music 1991)★★★, *Peculiaroso* (Private Music 1994)★★★, *Live* (Private Music 1995)★★★, *Standing In My Shoes* (Private Music 1997)★★★★.
● COMPILATIONS: *Leo Kottke 1971-1976 - Did You Hear Me?* (Capitol 1976)★★★, *The Best Of Leo Kottke* (Capitol 1977)★★★, *The Best Of Leo Kottke* (EMI 1979)★★★, *Essential Leo Kottke* (Chrysalis 1991)★★★★.

KUBEK, SMOKIN' JOE

b. 30 November 1956, Grove City, Pennsylvania, USA. Having grown up in Irving, Texas, Kubek was playing in Dallas clubs at the age of 14. Three years later, he took a deeper interest in blues, prompted by Eric Clapton and Peter Green, and formed his first band. Shortly afterwards, he played rhythm guitar behind Freddie King until King's death in December 1976. After a short spell with Robert Whitfield's Last Combo, he joined Al Braggs' band. Examples of his work can be heard on Braggs' 1979 production of tracks by R.L. Griffin. He also recorded with Charlie Robinson, Big Ray Anderson and Ernie Johnson, and on Little Joe Blue's album, *It's My Turn Now*. In 1989, he teamed up with singer/guitarist B'Nois King, from Monroe, Louisiana, whose soul-tinged vocals and jazz-orientated style contrasted well with Kubek's more strident finger and slide techniques. *The Axe Man* is an album of covers recorded before their Bullseye Blues debut. Subsequent releases have consolidated their reputation as a solid, entertaining band.
● ALBUMS: *The Axe Man* (Double Trouble 1991)★★★, *Steppin' Out Texas Style* (Bullseye Blues 1991)★★★, *Chain Smokin' Texas Style* (Bullseye Blues 1992)★★★, *Texas Cadillac* (Bullseye Blues 1994)★★★, *Cryin' For The Moon* (Bullseye Blues 1995)★★★, *Got My Mind Back* (Bullseye Blues 1996)★★★.

LACEY, RUBIN, REV.

b. 2 January 1901, Pelahatchie, Mississippi, USA, d. c.1972, Bakersfield, California, USA. Learning guitar and mandolin from the unrecorded George Hendrix as a young man, Lacey moved to Jackson, where he contributed to the musical ideas of Tommy Johnson and Ishman Bracey. In 1927, he recorded a solitary, but outstanding 78 rpm record. Lacey's secular career ended when he became a preacher in 1932, but when rediscovered in 1966 he was a mine of information about both his blues and his preaching careers, and became the chief subject of Alfred Rosenberg's book *The Art Of The American Folk Preacher*.
● COMPILATIONS: *Sorrow Come Pass Me Around* (1975), *Son House And The Great Delta Blues Singers* (1990), *Best Kept Secret* (Lady Bianca 1995).

LAMB, PAUL, AND THE KINGSNAKES

b. 9 July 1955, Blyth, Northumberland, England. Lamb's initial interest in blues came from listening to John Mayall's records; he then discovered the music of Sonny Terry, in whose style he thoroughly immersed himself for 12 years. He played in folk clubs and in 1975 was successful in a harmonica championship held in Germany. Around 1980, he began playing

amplified harmonica, initially in Walter 'Shakey' Horton's style, and as a member of the Blues Burglars he recorded for Red Lightnin' in 1986. Shortly afterwards, Lamb moved to London and formed his own band. In 1990, 1991 and 1992 Paul Lamb And The Kingsnakes were voted UK Blues Band of the Year, and Lamb himself received the Instrumentalist of the Year award which he won for a further five years, well into the 90s. The present line-up of the King Snakes is Martin Deegan (drums), Chad Strentz (vocals), Jim Mercer (bass), and the weathered-looking but highly accomplished guitarist John Whitehill (b. 11 February 1952, Newcastle-upon-Tyne, England). Lamb and his band may never receive mass acceptance, but those who follow the genre know that they are currently one of the most exciting bands playing white-boy Chicago blues to have appeared for many years. Lamb's playing has been heard in the stage musical *Tommy*, in television advertisements for Nissan cars, and in television drama, *Spender* and *Crocodile Shoes*. He recorded a top 40 single 'Harmonica Man' for PWL (Pete Waterman) in 1995 under the name Bravado (UK number 37). The many awards in magazines such as *Blueprint* represent a worthy recognition of Lamb's unrivalled position as a brilliant harmonica player at the forefront of British blues. *Blues & Rhythm* described the band as 'lazily cocksure and coolly aggressive'.
● ALBUMS: *Paul Lamb And The Kingsnakes* (Ace 1991)★★, *Shifting Into Gear* (Tight & Juicy 1993)★★★, *Fine Condition* (Indigo 1995)★★★★, *She's A Killer* (Indigo 1996)★★★.

LANDRETH, SONNY

Being born in Canton, Mississippi, USA, birthplace or thereabouts of Elmore James, did not mean that Sonny Landreth had to play slide guitar, but it certainly makes good copy. In fact, after five years in Jackson, Mississippi, the family moved to Lafayette, Louisiana, and Landreth grew up surrounded by Cajun music and its lifestyle. At the age of 10, he began studying trumpet in school, and three years later took up the guitar. At 20, he left college and, with his band Brer Rabbit, moved to Colorado. There he met Robben Ford, and worked in Michael Murphy's band. He also developed his unique slide technique, chording

behind the steel at the 12th fret. Returning to Louisiana, he became involved with several Cajun bands, including Zachary Richard, Beausoleil, Red Beans & Rice, and in 1979 became the first white musician in Clifton Chenier's band. His first recordings were made for Huey Meaux in 1973. Then, in 1981, he made *Blues Attack*, the first of two albums for Jay Miller's Blues Unlimited label. *Way Down In Louisiana* was issued in 1985. When not playing sessions, Landreth toured with his band, Bayou Rhythm. In 1988, he and the band backed John Hiatt on his *Slow Turning* album, touring America and Europe as 'The Goners'. Landreth spent the next two years preparing his *Outward Bound* album, eventually released in 1992. Landreth has been compared to Ry Cooder and David Lindley but his distinctive blend of rock, blues and Cajun music gives him prominence in the hierarchy of slide guitarists.
● ALBUMS: *Blues Attack* (Blues Unlimited 1981)★★★, *Way Down In Louisiana* (Blues Unlimited 1985)★★★, with John Hiatt *Slow Turning* (A&M 1988)★★★, with John Mayall *A Sense Of Place* (Island 1990)★★★★, *Outward Bound* (1992)★★★, *South Of I-10* (Zoo Entertainment 1995)★★★.

LANG, EDDIE

b. Edward Langlois, 15 January 1936, New Orleans, Louisiana, USA, d. 10 May 1985, New Orleans, Louisiana, USA. Lang grew up liking country and hillbilly music, so much so that when he became a member of Jessie Hill's House Rockers, he would often regale audiences with a Hank Williams song. In 1952 he joined Guitar Slim's band and his diminutive stature earned him the nickname Little Eddie. It was the artist credit used when both artists recorded for Nashville's Bullet label, although Eddie's 'My Baby Left Me' did less well than Slim's 'Feelin' Sad'. Apart from a solitary title for Savoy that was not released for 27 years, Lang next recorded for RPM in 1956, and 'Come On Home' became a regional hit. 'Troubles, Troubles' and three other titles, although recorded by Johnny Vincent for Ace with a band that included Mac Rebennack on guitar, were released on the new Ron label. In 1966 he signed with Seven-B Records and again, two singles were released, although a second session, including 'I'm Gonna

Make You Eat Those Words' and 'The Fooler', remained unissued until 1987. Lang's greatest success came in 1973, when his SuperDome single, 'Food Stamp Blues', sold some 80,000 copies. His career was ended in 1979 by a stroke and he died from a second seizure in 1985.

● ALBUMS: *Southern Blues* (Savoy 1981)★★★, *Rough Dried Blues* (Charly 1987)★★★, *Loaded Down With The Blues* (Charly 1987)★★★, *Troubles, Troubles* (Rounder 1988)★★★, *Good To The Last Drop* (Charly 1989)★★★.

LANG, JONNY

b. 29 January 1981, Fargo, North Dakota, USA. Blues guitarist/singer Jonny Lang was signed to A&M Records as a child prodigy before his six-teenth birthday - having only received his first guitar at the age of 13. By this time he had already earned a strong regional reputation as an interpreter of the blues, eventually moving from Fargo to Minneapolis to become leader of Kid Jonny Lang And The Big Bang. That group's independently released *Smokin'* album under-scored Lang's growing reputation, selling an impressive 25,000 copies without the aid of national distribution. By the time A&M stepped in for his signature, he had also played alongside such blues greats as Luther Allison, Lonnie Brooks and Buddy Guy. *Lie To Me*, produced by David Z (Janet Jackson, Collective Soul, Fine Young Cannibals), was an impressive major label debut. Although more mainstream in its combination of blues and soul textures than the raw *Smokin'*, it confirmed Lang as a guitarist of impressive range and astonishing maturity. It included songs written by David Z, Lang's key-board player, Bruce McCabe, Dennis Morgan and Lang himself, alongside cover versions of material by Sonny Boy Williamson ('Good Morning Little School Girl') and Ike Turner ('Matchbox').

● ALBUMS: *Smokin'* (Own Label 1996)★★, *Lie To Me* (A&M 1997)★★★.

LATIMORE

b. Benjamin Latimore, 7 September 1939, Charleston, Tennessee, USA. This singer, who performed under his surname only, brought a blues feeling to 70s soul music. His passionate vocal delivery and keyboard-dominated style was particularly popular with his female audi-ence. Latimore sang gospel music as a child in his family's Baptist church but did not sing pro-fessionally until his first year of college, where he worked with a group called the Hi-Toppers. The group had already recorded for Excello Records when Latimore took over the piano position; he never recorded with the group but remained with them until 1962. At that time he joined Joe Henderson's revue as pianist, and with that group backed artists such as Ben E. King, Slim Harpo and Jimmy Reed in concert. Latimore left Henderson in 1964 and worked as an opening act for teen-idol Steve Alaimo. He also recorded some unsuccessful singles for the Dade label at this time, but finally achieved a hit in 1973 for the related Glades label, with a remake of 'T-Bone' Walker's 'Stormy Monday'. The following year Latimore reached his com-mercial height with a number 1 R&B single, 'Let's Straighten It Out'. He charted with 13 sin-gles for Glades altogether in the 70s, reaching the R&B Top 10 twice more. In 1982, he switched to Malaco Records, for whom he con-tinues to record.

● ALBUMS: *Latimore* (Glades 1973)★★★, *More, More, More* (Glades 1974)★★★, *Latimore III* (Glades 1975)★★★★, *It Ain't Where You Been . . . .* (Glades 1977)★★★, *Dig A Little Deeper* (Glades 1978)★★★, *Singing In The Key Of Love* (Malaco 1982)★★★, *Good Time Man* (Malaco 1985)★★★, *Every Way But Wrong* (Malaco 1988)★★★, *I'll Do Anything For You* (Malaco 1988)★★★, *Slow Down* (Malaco 1989)★★★, *The Only Way Is Up* (1992)★★★, *Catchin' Up* (1994)★★★.

● COMPILATIONS: *Sweet Vibrations - The Best Of ...* (Sequel 1991)★★★★.

LAURY, LAWRENCE 'BOOKER T'

b. 1914, USA, d. 23 September 1995, Memphis, Tennessee, USA. One of the true originals in the field of boogie-woogie and barrelhouse blues piano, Laury's period of greatest activity stretched from the 20s to the 50s. Laury, a Memphis blues pianist active in the 20s, went unrecorded until the late 70s, but even in 1990 was still a vigorous survivor from the barrel-house tradition. He was dismissed from playing during the intermission spot at the tourist-ori-entated Blues Alley club because he was 'too old-fashioned'. He learned piano from Mose

Vinson and Memphis Slim, whom he claimed to be a cousin; however, Laury's rough, energetic playing and powerful vocals were much less polished than Slim's. Following the death of his wife in the mid-50s he retired from the music business, but was persuaded by Slim to make his return to performing in the 70s. Laury supported Slim on his European tour, and also accompanied him on treks through Africa and Asia in the 70s and 80s. In 1989 he featured in the Jerry Lee Lewis biopic *Great Balls Of Fire*, and his version of the sexually explicit 'Big Leg Woman' is based on Lewis's adaptation of the original recording by Johnny Temple. Heralded as one of the last great authentic blues pianists, he recorded his debut album in 1994 at the age of 80. Sadly he died of cancer within a year of its release, just as his contribution to the development of blues piano was being widely acknowledged.
● ALBUMS: *Nothing But The Blues* (1980)★★★, *Memphis Piano Blues Today* (1991)★★★, *Blues On The Prowl* (Wolf 1994)★★★.

LAWHORN, SAMMY
b. Samuel David Lawhorn, 12 July 1935, Little Rock, Arkansas, USA, d. 29 April 1990, Chicago, Illinois, USA. Soon after Sammy Lawhorn's birth, his mother and stepfather moved to Chicago, leaving him to be brought up by his grandparents. By the time he was 12, his mother had bought him a Stella and soon after that a Supro electric guitar. Three years later, he was gigging around Helena with Elmon (Drifting Slim) Mickle. He also became a King Biscuit Boy, backing Sonny Boy Williamson (Rice Miller) and Houston Stackhouse, who taught him to play slide. From 1953, Lawhorn spent five years in the navy and was wounded while serving in Korea as an aerial photographer. On his return, he linked up with harmonica player Willie Cobbs and played on the original recording of 'You Don't Love Me'. After appearing in Chicago with Cobbs, he decided to remain in the city and backed Junior Wells at Theresa's Club. After jamming with Muddy Waters at Pepper's Lounge, he joined Muddy's band in 1964, touring and recording with him for some 10 years until his excessive drinking habits made him an unreliable character.

Thereafter, alcohol and the onset of arthritis sent him into a decline from which he never recovered. His only album suffered from a lack of rehearsal and commitment, a less than fitting memorial to a once-strong musician.
● ALBUMS: *After Hours* (Isabel 1986)★★, with the Teardrops and Little Mac Simmons *My Little Girl* (Wolf 1995)★★★.

LAY, SAM
b. 20 March 1935, Birmingham, Alabama, USA. The drummer Fred Below put the backbeat into the blues and elevated the records of Muddy Waters and Little Walter, among a host of others, into defining statements. Close behind him is Sam Lay, the inventor of the 'double shuffle'. Lay began playing drums at 14 and joined his first band, the Moon Dog Combo, in 1956. The following year he joined the Thunderbirds, before spending 1959 in Little Walter's band. He then became the backbone of Howlin' Wolf's band, where he stayed from 1960 to 1966. He was the driving force behind 'Down In The Bottom', 'The Red Rooster', 'Goin' Down Slow', 'Built For Comfort' and 'Killing Floor'. He then joined the Paul Butterfield Blues Band, played on the group's first two influential albums and also backed Bob Dylan on his controversial electric debut at the 1965 Newport Folk Festival. In the ensuing years, he worked with most of the best-known names in the blues world, having a particular regard for his work on Muddy Waters' *Fathers And Sons* album. Lay leads his own band, which features former Commander Cody harmonica player Billy C. Farlowe and guitarist Chris James, as well as freelancing when the opportunity arises. *Shuffle Master* combines original material with a number of cover versions, while *Live*, recorded at Nashville's Boardwalk Cafe, relies upon more traditional material.
● ALBUMS: *The Paul Butterfield Blues Band* (Elektra 1966)★★★★, with Muddy Waters *Fathers And Sons* (Chess 1969)★★★, *Shuffle Master* (Appaloosa 1993)★★★, *Live* (Appaloosa 1995)★★★, *Stone Blues* (Evidence 1996)★★★.

LAZY LESTER
b. Leslie Johnson, 20 June 1933 (or 1923), Torras, Louisiana, USA. Blues harmonica player and vocalist Lazy Lester recorded numerous singles for Excello Records in the late 50s and early

60s. Forming his first band in 1952, the musician's first significant job was as a sideman for bluesman Lightnin' Slim. Owing to his slow-moving, laid-back approach, Johnson received his performing name during this period from record producer J.D. Miller, who was known for his 'swamp pop' sound. Miller recorded Lester and placed him with the Nashville-based Excello in 1958. Lester's first solo single was 'Go Ahead' (1956), and his first local hit was 'Sugar Coated Love'/'I'm A Lover Not A Fighter'. The latter was covered in the UK by the Kinks. Lester continued to record as a leader until 1965. He also played harmonica for such artists as the blues-rock guitarist Johnny Winter (an early recording in 1961) and Lonesome Sundown. At the end of the 60s, Lester moved around the country and did not record again until 1987, for the UK Blues 'N' Trouble label. The following year he recorded *Harp & Soul* for Alligator Records, and was back touring the USA in the late 80s and early 90s, enjoying new-found acclaim.

● ALBUMS: *True Blues* (Excello 1966)★★★★, *Lazy Lester Rides Again* (Blue Horizon 1987)★★★, *Harp & Soul* (Alligator 1988)★★★, *I'm A Lover Not A Fighter* (Ace 1994)★★★.

● COMPILATIONS: *They Call Me Lazy* (Flyright 1977)★★★★, *Poor Boy Blues - Jay Miller Sessions* (Flyright 1987)★★★★.

LEAD BELLY

b. Huddie William Ledbetter, 20 January 1889, Jeder Plantation, Mooringsport, Louisiana, USA, d. 6 December 1949, New York City, New York, USA. Lead Belly's music offers an incredible vista of American traditions, white as well as black, through his enormous repertoire of songs and tunes. He learned many of them in his youth when he lived and worked in western Louisiana and eastern Texas, but to them he added material from many different sources, including his own compositions, throughout the rest of his life. He played several instruments, including mandolin, accordion, piano and harmonica, but was best known for his mastery of the 12-string guitar. In his early 20s, he met and played with Blind Lemon Jefferson, but the encounter was to leave little if any lasting impression on his music. His sound remained distinctive and individual, with his powerful, yet deeply expressive, vocals and his 12-string guitar

lines, which could be booming and blindingly fast or slow and delicate as appropriate. His style and approach to music developed as he played the red-light districts of towns such as Shreveport and Dallas - a tough, often violent background that was reflected in songs like 'Fannin Street' and 'Mr Tom Hughes Town'.

Although he built up a substantial local reputation for his music as a young man, he served a number of prison sentences, including two stretches of hard labour for murder and attempted murder, respectively. While serving the last of these sentences at the Louisiana State Penitentiary at Angola, he was discovered by the folklorist John A. Lomax, then travelling throughout the south with his son Alan, recording traditional songs and music - frequently in prisons - for the Folk Song Archive of the Library of Congress. On his release (which he claimed was due to his having composed a song pleading with the governor to set him free), Lead Belly worked for Lomax as a chauffeur, assistant and guide, also recording prolifically for the Archive. His complete Library of Congress recordings, made over a period of several years, were issued in 1990 on 12 albums. Through Lomax, he was given the opportunity of a new life, as he moved to New York to continue to work for the folklorist. He also embarked on a reborn musical career with a new and very different audience, playing university concerts, clubs and political events, appearing on radio and even on film. He also made many records, mainly aimed at folk music enthusiasts. However, he did have the chance to make some 'race' recordings which were marketed to the black listener, but these enjoyed little commercial success, probably because Lead Belly's music would have seemed somewhat old-fashioned and rural to the increasingly sophisticated black record buyer of the 30s; although 50 songs were recorded, only six were issued.

The New York folk scene, however, kept him active to some extent, and he played and recorded with artists such as Josh White, Woody Guthrie, Sonny Terry and Brownie McGhee. There was also a series of recordings in which he was accompanied by the voices of the Golden Gate Quartet, although this was an odd pairing and seemed rather contrived. Some newly composed songs, such as 'New York City' and in particular, the pointed 'Bourgeois Blues', which described the racial prejudice he encountered in Washington DC, show how his perspectives were being altered by his new circumstances. It was his apparently inexhaustible collection of older songs and tunes, however, that most fascinated the northern audience, embracing as it did everything from versions of old European ballads ('Gallis Pole'), through Cajun-influenced dance tunes ('Sukey Jump') and sentimental pop ('Daddy, I'm Coming Home'), to dozens of black work songs and field hollers ('Whoa Back Buck'), southern ballads ('John Hardy'), gospel ('Mary Don't You Weep'), prison songs ('Shorty George'), many tough blues ('Pigmeat Papa') and even cowboy songs ('Out On The Western Plains'). His best-known and most frequently covered songs, however, are probably the gentle C&W-influenced 'Goodnight Irene', later to be a hit record for the Weavers (one of whose members was Pete Seeger, who was also to write an instruction book on Lead Belly's unique 12-string guitar style) and 'Rock Island Line', which was a hit for Lonnie Donegan in the UK a few years later. His classic 'Cottonfields' was a major success for the Beach Boys. In 1949, he travelled to Europe, appearing at jazz events in Paris, but the promise of wider appreciation of the man and his music was sadly curtailed when he died later that same year.

Note: In keeping with the Lead Belly Society in the USA we have adopted the correct spelling, and not the more commonly used Leadbelly.

● COMPILATIONS: *Take This Hammer* (Folkways 1950)★★★, *Rock Island Line* (Folkways 1950)★★★, *Lead Belly's Legacy Vol 3* (Folkways 1951)★★★, *Easy Rider: Lead Belly's Legacy Volume 4* (Folkways 1951)★★★, *Lead Belly Memorial Vol 1 and 2* (Stinson 1951)★★★, *Play-Party Songs* (Stinson 1951)★★★, *More Play-Party Songs* (Stinson 1951)★★★, *Lead Belly Memorial Vols 3 & 4* (Stinson 1951)★★★, *Sinful Songs* (Allegro 1952)★★★, *Last Sessions Vols 1 and 2* (Folkways 1958)★★★, *Sings Folk Songs* (Folkways 1959)★★★, *Lead Belly: Huddie Leadbetter's Best* (Capitol 1962)★★★, *Midnight Special* (RCA Victor 1964)★★★, *Keep Your Hands Off Her* (Verve/Folkways 1965)★★★, *The Library Of Congress Recordings* (Elektra 1966)★★★, *From The Last Sessions* (Verve/Folkways 1967)★★★, *Bourgeois Blues* (Collectables 1989)★★★, *Alabama Bound* (RCA Bluebird 1989)★★★, *Lead Belly Sings Folk Songs* (Smithsonian/Folkways 1990)★★★, *Complete Library Of Congress Sessions* (1990)★★★, *King Of The 12 String Guitar* (Columbia/Legacy 1991)★★★, *Midnight Special* (Rounder 1991)★★★★, *Gwine Dig A Hole To Put The Devil In* (Rounder 1991)★★★★, *Let It Shine On Me* (Rounder 1991)★★★★, *The Very Best Of* (1993)★★★, *Storyteller Blues* (Drive Archive 1995)★★★, *Lead Belly In Concert* (Magnum 1996)★★★, *In The Shadow Of Gallows Pole* (Tradition 1996)★★★.

● FURTHER READING: *The Midnight Special: The Legend Of Lead Belly*, Richard M. Garvin and Edmond G. Addeo. *The Life And Legend Of Lead Belly*, Charles Wolfe and Kip Lornell. *Negro Folk Songs As Sung By Lead Belly*, John Lomax.

LEAKE, LAFAYETTE

b. 1 June 1920, Wynomie, Mississippi, USA, d. 14 August 1990, Chicago, Illinois, USA. Lafayette Leake was a blues pianist whose prime contribution was his collaboration with Chess Records producer Willie Dixon. After moving to Chicago, Leake first worked with Dixon in 1951, replacing Leonard 'Baby Doo' Caston in Dixon's group the Big Three Trio. Leake performed on many Chess sessions during the 50s and 60s, playing on recordings by Howlin' Wolf, Chuck Berry, Sonny Boy 'Rice Miller' Williamson, Bo Diddley, Junior Wells and Otis Rush. Leake joined Dixon's Chicago Blues All Stars, appearing on the 1969 *I Am The Blues*. He also recorded for the Cobra, Ovation and Spivey labels. Leake died after suffering a diabetic coma.

LEAVY, CALVIN

b. 1942, Scott, Arkansas, USA. Leavy began his musical career in the gospel field at the age of 16, but in 1969 he recorded, singing and playing rhythm guitar, a strong southern blues entitled 'Cummins Prison Farm'. The song featured an excellent guitar break from Robert Tanner. The recording was released by Calvin C. Brown, owner of Soul Beat Records and became a surprise hit about a year after it was made; it was subsequently picked up by Shelby Singleton Enterprises. Leavy made several more records for Soul Beat (and associate label Acquarian), often in the company of his bass-playing brother Hosea. Soon afterwards, however, he dropped into obscurity and little has been heard of him, although his hit has become a blues standard. Last reports seem to indicate he was playing bass guitar with a gospel group.

● ALBUMS: *Cummins Prison Farm* (1977)★★★.

LEE, 'LITTLE' FRANKIE

b. 29 April 1941, Mart, Texas, USA. Lee began singing as a child, encouraged by his grandmother and, after leaving school, he sang blues around the clubs in Houston, Texas, turning professional at the age of 22. He began recording in 1963 and had singles released on the Houston labels Great Scott and Peacock. After settling in the San Francisco bay area in 1973, he made singles for Elka and California Gold. Lee had tracks issued on several anthologies but had to wait until 1984 for the first complete album under his own name, recorded for the Hightone label. Lee admits to varied influences, including Reverend Claude Jeter, Sam Cooke, Roy Acuff and the Everly Brothers, although he has infused these elements into a strong southern soul/blues style.

● ALBUMS: *Face It!* (Hightone 1984)★★★.

LEE, ALVIN

b. 19 December 1944, Nottingham, England. Guitarist Lee began his professional career in the Jaybirds, a beat trio popular both locally and in Hamburg, Germany. In 1966, an expanded line-up took a new name, Ten Years After, and in turn became one of Britain's leading blues/rock attractions with Lee's virtuoso solos its main attraction. His outside aspirations surfaced in 1973 with *On The Road To Freedom*, a collaboration with American Mylon Lefevre, which included support from George Harrison, Steve Winwood and Mick Fleetwood. When Ten Years After disbanded the following year, the guitarist formed Alvin Lee & Co. with Neil Hubbard (guitar), Tim Hinkley (keyboards), Mel Collins (saxophone), Alan Spenner (bass) and Ian Wallace (drums). Having recorded the live *In Flight*, Lee made the first of several changes in personnel, but although he and Hinkley were joined by Andy Pyle (bass, ex-Blodwyn Pig) and Bryson Graham (drums) for *Pump Iron!*, the

group struggled to find its niche with the advent of punk. Lee toured Europe fronting Ten Years Later (1978-80) and the Alvin Lee Band (1980-81), before founding a new quartet, known simply as Alvin Lee, with Mick Taylor (guitar, ex-John Mayall; Rolling Stones), Fuzzy Samuels (bass, ex-Crosby, Stills, Nash And Young) and Tom Compton (drums). This promising combination promoted *RX-5*, but later disbanded. In 1989, Lee reconvened the original line-up of Ten Years After to record *About Time*. Lee released *Zoom* in 1992 with Sequel Records, after finding the major companies were not interested. Although offering nothing new, it was a fresh and well-produced record, and featured George Harrison on backing vocals.

● ALBUMS: with Mylon Lefevre *On The Road To Freedom* (Columbia 1973)★★★, *In Flight* (Columbia 1975)★★★, *Pump Iron!* (Columbia 1975)★★, *Rocket Fuel* (Polydor 1978)★★, *Ride On* (Polydor 1979)★★★, *Free Fall* (Avatar 1980)★★, *RX-5* (Avatar 1981)★★★, *Detroit Diesel* (21 Records 1986)★★★, *Zoom* (Sequel 1992)★★, *Nineteen Ninety Four* (Magnum Music 1994)★★, *I Hear You Rockin'* (Viceroy 1994)★★★, *Going Back Home* (Blind Pig 1994)★★★, *Pure Blues* (Chrysalis 1995)★★★, *Sweetheart Of The Blues* (Delmark 1995)★★★, *Braille Blues Daddy* (Justin Time 1995)★★★.

LEE, JOE, AND JIMMY STROTHERS

Lee was 71 years old when he and Strothers recorded for the Library of Congress in 1936; both men were inmates of the Virginia State Farm at Lynn. Lee sang 11 unaccompanied spirituals with great intensity, and duetted with Strothers on 'Do Lord Remember Me', on which he also played the fingerboard of Strothers' guitar with two straws, while the latter played in the orthodox fashion. Strothers, who also played banjo, was a street and medicine show entertainer who had been blinded in an explosion (and was serving time for killing his wife with an axe). His repertoire of blues, work songs, dance tunes, gospel, humorous songs (including obscenity) and a protest song about the contract labour system, forms a most important body of black music.

● ALBUMS: *Negro Religious Songs and Services* (c.1960), *Red River Runs* (1979).

LEE, JOHN

b. John Arthur Lee, 24 May 1915, Mt. Willing, Alabama, USA. Few post-war country blues tracks merit the description 'masterpiece', but John Lee's July 1951 recording of 'Down At The Depot' deserves the accolade. In essence a standard train blues, it is elevated by his propulsive slide guitar playing and keening vocal. Lee came from a musical family, in which all seven brothers, a sister and both parents played guitar. However, the significant influence on his playing was Uncle Ellie Lee, renowned in Evergreen, Alabama, as its finest exponent of slide technique, using a knife rather than a bottleneck. Both 'Down At The Depot' and the equally impressive 'Blind Blues' bear witness to his tutelage. Lee was also influenced by Brewton musician Levi Kelley. He supplemented practical instruction with the records of Blind Blake, Blind Lemon Jefferson and Leroy Carr. Moving to Montgomery in 1945, he soon had, by his own estimation, 'the town sewed up' when it came to playing at house parties and suppers. In 1951 he heard talent scout Ralph Bass advertise for talent on WMGY radio; four of the six songs he recorded were released on two Federal singles, representing some of the last instances of country blues being issued on a major label. Lee retired from active performance in 1960. He was rediscovered in 1973 after a three-year search and recorded sessions in Montgomery and Cambridge, Massachusetts, at which he revealed an equally individual piano style.
● ALBUMS: *Down At The Depot* (Rounder 1974)★★★.

LEE, LOVIE

b. Edward Lee Watson, 17 March 1924, Chattanooga, Tennessee, USA. A nickname bestowed in infancy has its drawbacks in later life, especially if you're a member of Muddy Waters' band. With his seven brothers and sisters, Lee moved to Meridian, Mississippi, when he was 12 years old. There he learned to play the piano in his grandfather Henry Austin's restaurant, coming under the influence of Cap King, the area's principal barrelhouse musician. From 1940-57, Lee worked at a woodworking factory and led Lovie's Swinging Cats, playing at fairs and clubs around Meridian. In 1951, he took in Carey Bell, then a 14-year-old runaway, whom he coached in his harmonica playing. In 1957 Lee brought Bell to Chicago, where they discovered that work was not as plentiful as they had expected. Lee took a job at the Brody Seating Company and formed a band called the Sensationals, using guitarists Lee Jackson and Byther Smith at different times. They played west and south side clubs, including Cinderella's, Florence's and Porter's Lounge. He had retired from his day job when he received a phone call from Muddy Waters asking him to join what would prove to be his last band, along with 'Mojo' George Buford, John Primer, Earnest Johnson and Jesse Clay. In the late 70s, he began to release cassettes of his own music, and had a session released in Alligator's 'Living Chicago Blues' series. Tracks from his own releases formed part of *Good Candy*, along with a 1992 session featuring Carey and Lurrie Bell, and offered an engaging portrait of a minor talent.
● ALBUMS: *Lovie's Music* cassette (Blues On Blues 1978)★★★, *Living Chicago Blues Vol. 3* (Alligator 1978/1991)★★★, *Lovie's Music 2* cassette (Blues On Blues 1979)★★★, *Lovie Lee* cassette (Blues On Blues 1992)★★★, *Good Candy* (Earwig 1994)★★★.

LEECAN, BOBBY, AND ROBERT COOKSEY

Both b. USA. Bobby Leecan was a fine and fluent single string guitarist, banjoist and an occasional kazooist and vocalist. He made most of his recordings in the company of Robert Cooksey, whose rather sweet, warbling harmonica favoured clear tone production rather than the slurs and bends of most blues players. Their output lies in the borderland between blues, vaudeville and jazz, ranging from 'Dirty Guitar Blues' to 'Ain't She Sweet', and blending easily with the jazz cornet of Tom Morris. Some sources suggest that they were based in Philadelphia.
● ALBUMS: *The Remaining Titles* (Matchbox 1986)★★★, *The Blues Of Bobbie Leecan & Robert Cooksey* (Collector's Classics 1988)★★★.

LEFT HAND FRANK

b. Frank Craig, 5 October 1935, Greenville, Mississippi, USA. Frank had a rocking good-time approach to the traditional sound of 50s Chicago blues, although his distinctive guitar and vocals were only captured on record for the first time in 1978. At the end of the 70s he enjoyed some international acclaim, but remains one of the blues' lesser-known figures. He received his first guitar for his fourth birthday and quickly learned to play blues and country. He moved to Chicago at the age of 14 and was inspired to play blues by listening to the sounds he could hear emanating from the doors of the clubs. He played behind many of the city's blues musicians, including Junior Wells, Theodore 'Hound Dog' Taylor and Willie Cobbs, and recorded on several occasions as a bass player. He is now based in California.

● ALBUMS: *Living Chicago Blues Volume One* four tracks only (1978), with Jimmy Rogers *The Dirty Dozens* (JSP 1985)★★★.

LEFTY DIZZ

b. Walter Williams, 29 April 1937, Osceola, Arkansas, USA, d. 7 September 1993. Dizz was taught the rudiments of music by his father, after the family had moved north to Kankakee, Illinois, and he has been a stalwart of the Chicago blues scene since the late 50s, having accompanied numerous blues artists as rhythm or lead guitarist. He reportedly made his first record (credited to the 'Wallets') for the King label in 1960, and he recorded with Junior Wells in the mid-60s. For many years he was based at the Checkerboard Lounge in Chicago. Records under his own name have appeared on the CJ, JSP, Black And Blue, and Isabel labels. He can also be heard on a bootleg of the Rolling Stones. His stage name referred to his left-handed playing and his youthful habit of imitating Dizzy Gillespie. Lefty's forte was tough, gritty guitar blues.

● ALBUMS: *Ain't It Nice To Be Loved* (1989)★★★.
● COMPILATIONS: *Chicago Blues At Burnley* (JSP 1991)★★★.

LEGENDARY BLUES BAND

Formed in June 1980, the Legendary Blues Band emerged from the Muddy Waters band of the mid to late 70s. The original line-up consisted of Jerry Portnoy (harmonica), Louis Myers (guitar, harmonica), Pinetop Perkins (piano), Calvin Jones (bass) and Willie Smith (drums), with the vocals shared among all the members. There were numerous personnel changes over the subsequent years and Smith and Jones are the only remaining original members. The sound remains solidly in the Chicago blues vein. They recorded two albums for the Rounder label in the early 80s and signed with Ichiban in 1989.

● ALBUMS: *Life Of Ease* (Rounder 1981)★★★, *Red Hot 'N' Blue* (Rounder 1983)★★★, *Woke Up With The Blues* (Ichiban 1989)★★★, *Keeping The Blues Alive* (Ichiban 1990)★★★, *U B Da Judge* (Ichiban 1991)★★★, *Blue Devil Blues* (Amazing 1991)★★★, *No Beginner* (Amazing 1993)★★★.

LENOIR, J.B.

b. 5 March 1929, Monticello, Mississippi, USA, d. 29 April 1967, Champaign, Illinois, USA. Christened with initials, Lenoir was taught to play the guitar by his father, Dewitt. Other acknowledged influences were Blind Lemon Jefferson, Arthur 'Big Boy' Crudup and Lightnin' Hopkins, with the latter's single-string runs and verse tags becoming an integral part of the mature Lenoir style. He relocated to Chicago in 1949, and was befriended by Big Bill Broonzy and Memphis Minnie. Having leased his first recordings to Chess in 1952, label owner Joe Brown issued Lenoir's first success, 'The Mojo Boogie', on JOB Records in 1953. A propulsive dance piece sung in a high, keening tenor, it typified an important element of Lenoir's repertoire. The second main element was exhibited the following year with the release on Parrot of 'Eisenhower Blues', an uncompromising comment upon economic hardship, which the singer laid at the President's door. Also released that year, 'Mama Talk To Your Daughter' was another light-hearted boogie that became his signature tune. Subsequent records for Chess neglected the serious side of his writing, attempts at emulating previous successes taking preference over more sober themes such as 'We Can't Go On This Way' and 'Laid Off Blues'. Lenoir revealed that seriousness in an interview with Paul Oliver in 1960; this mood was in turn reflected in a series of recordings initiated by Willie Dixon and released to coincide with his appearance at the 1965 American Folk Blues Festival tour of Europe. *Alabama Blues* perfectly reconciled the two extremes of his style, remakes of 'The Mojo Boogie' and 'Talk To Your

Daughter' tempering the stark reality of the title song, 'Born Dead' and 'Down In Mississippi', in which Lenoir, with both passion and dignity, evoked America's civil rights struggle of the time. The great benefit that might have accrued from what, in hindsight, was the master work of his career, was prevented by his tragic death in a car crash.

● ALBUMS: *Alabama Blues* (Chess 1965)★★★★, *Natural Man* (Chess 1968)★★★, *Chess Blues Masters* (Chess 1976)★★★★, *The Parrot Sessions 1954-55* (Relic 1989)★★★★, *His J.O.B. Recordings 1951-1954* (Flyright 1989)★★★★, *Mama Watch Your Daughter* (1993)★★★, *Vietnam Blues: The Complete L + R Recordings* (Evidence 1995)★★★★, with Geoffrey Richardson *Follow Your Heart* (Mouse 1995).

LEVY, RON

b. Reuvain Zev ben Yehoshua Ha Levi, 29 May 1951, Cambridge, Massachusetts, USA. Ron Levy played clarinet during his childhood and, inspired by a Ray Charles concert, started playing piano at the age of 13. He soon took up organ too, and, influenced by Booker T, Billy Preston and Jimmy Smith, was a quick learner. Two years later he was backing up blues artists performing in the Boston area. At 17 the young musician was discovered and hired by blues legend Albert King. Still in high school, Levy worked with King, who had become his legal guardian, for 18 months. From December 1969 to February 1976 he played piano and organ in B.B. King's band. The period from that time until 1980 saw him work with the Rhythm Rockers, led by 'Guitar' Johnny Nicholas and featuring the young Ronnie Earl on lead guitar. As the house band of the Speakeasy in Cambridge they honed their skills backing up great blues musicians, among them Walter Horton, Johnny Shines and Roosevelt Sykes. After working with Luther 'Guitar Jnr' Johnson for three years, Levy played with Roomful Of Blues from 1983 to 1987. In addition to recording with his own band, Ron Levy's Wild Kingdom, he has played on numerous recordings by other artists, and since 1985, has produced a steady stream of albums for labels such as Black Top, Rounder and Bullseye.

● ALBUMS: *Ron Levy's Wild Kingdom* (Black Top 1986)★★★, *Safari To New Orleans* (Black Top 1988)★★★, *B-3 Blues & Grooves* (1992)★★★, *It's Getting Harder* (Miss Butch 1995)★★★, *Zim Zam Zoom* (Bullseye 1996)★★★.

LEWIS, NOAH

b. 3 September 1895, Henning, Tennessee, USA, d. 7 February 1961, Ripley, Tennessee, USA. Lewis's ability to play two harmonicas at once, one with his nose, secured him work on the travelling medicine shows, but his recorded music is notable more for its melancholy expressiveness than showmanship - a descriptive train imitation ('Chickasaw Special') apart. He combined technical accomplishment with exceptional breath control and a very subtle, sensitive handling of emotional nuance, whether on his 1927 solos, leading his own jug band in 1930, or as a member of Cannon's Jug Stompers, with whom he recorded from 1928-30. His singing had the same emotional depth as his harmonica playing, most notably on 'Viola Lee Blues' (recorded by the Grateful Dead in the 60s). Lewis lived in poverty, and died of gangrene as a consequence of frostbite.

● ALBUMS: *Gus Cannon & Noah Lewis* (1991)★★★.

LEWIS, SMILEY

b. Overton Amos Lemons, 5 July 1913, DeQuincy, Louisiana, USA, d. 7 October 1966. While failing to gain the commercial plaudits his work deserved, this New Orleans-based artist was responsible for some of that city's finest music. He made his recording debut, as Smiling Lewis, in 1947, but his strongest work appeared during the 50s. 'The Bells Are Ringing' (1952) took him into the US R&B chart, and his biggest hit came three years later with 'I Hear You Knocking'. This seminal slice of Crescent City blues featured pianist Huey 'Piano' Smith and bandleader Dave Bartholomew, and was revived successfully in 1970 by Dave Edmunds. Smiley's career was dogged by ill luck. His original version of 'Blue Monday' was a hit in the hands of Fats Domino, while Elvis Presley took another song, 'One Night', and by altering its risqué lyric, secured a massive pop hit in the process. A further powerful Lewis performance, 'Shame, Shame, Shame', has subsequently become an

R&B standard and it was even covered by the Merseybeats on their EP *On Stage* in 1964. This underrated artist continued recording into the 60s, but died of cancer in 1966.

● ALBUMS: *I Hear You Knocking* (Imperial 1961)★★★.

● COMPILATIONS: *Shame Shame Shame* (1970)★★★, *The Bells Are Ringing* (1978)★★★, *Caledonia's Party* (KC 1986)★★★, *New Orleans Bounce - 30 Of His Best* (Sequel 1991)★★★.

LEWIS, WALTER 'FURRY'

b. 6 March 1893, Greenwood, Mississippi, USA, d. 14 September 1981, Memphis, Tennessee, USA. Furry Lewis was a songster, a blues musician, a humorist and an all-round entertainer. Raised in the country, he picked up the guitar at an early age and moved into Memphis around 1900 where he busked on the streets. After he ran away from home, he had experience working on travelling medicine shows under the influence of Jim Jackson. He worked with W.C. Handy and claimed that Handy presented him with his first good guitar. Hoboing across country in 1916, he had an accident while hopping a train and consequently lost a leg. After this he moved to Memphis and, while performing and recording, he supplemented his income by sweeping the streets. Apart from periods working on riverboats and with medicine shows in the 20s, this remained the style of his life for approximately the next 40 or more years. He recorded 11 titles for Vocalion in 1927, eight for Victor in 1928 and four more for Vocalion in 1929. He had a guitar style that incorporated aspects of both the Mississippi county style and the lighter, more ragged Memphis sound, supplemented by some impressive slide work. His voice was clear and his approach to lyrics often self-mockingly humorous. Several of his recordings were ballads and his treatment of these was equally original. Well known around the city, he sometimes appeared as part of the Memphis Jug Band. He was one of the first pre-war blues artists to be 'rediscovered', and from 1959 he pursued a second successful career on the college circuit and played in several movies, including an unlikely appearance with Burt Reynolds in *W.W. And The Dixie Dance Kings*. Still an able performer he made many recordings during this period and was confirmed an Honorary Colonel of the State of Tennessee in 1973. Highly regarded by many performers, he received a touching tribute from Joni Mitchell on 'Furry Sings The Blues', which was featured on her 1976 album *Heijera*.

● ALBUMS: *Furry Lewis Blues* (Folkways 1959)★★★, *Back On My Feet Again* (Prestige 1961)★★★, *Done Changed My Mind* (1962★★, *Presenting The Country Blues* (1969)★★★, *In Memphis* (1970)★★, *On The Road Again* (1970)★★, *When I Lay My Burden Down* (1970)★★★, *Live At The Gaslight* (1971)★★★.

● COMPILATIONS: *Furry Lewis In His Prime 1927-29* (Yazoo 1988)★★★, *Shake 'Em On Down* (Ace/Fantasy 1994)★★★.

LIGGINS, JIMMY

b. 14 October 1922, Newby, Oklahoma, USA, d. 18 July 1983, Durham, North Carolina, USA. Starting out as a disc jockey and boxer before becoming the driver for his brother Joe's band, the Honeydrippers, Jimmy Liggins taught himself guitar and formed his own band in 1947. Signing for Art Rupe's Specialty label, he immediately had major hits with 'I Can't Stop It', 'Cadillac Boogie' and, notably, 'Teardrop Blues'. Following a serious accident in 1948 when he was shot in the mouth, he continued with big sellers for Specialty Records, including his most successful release, 1953's 'Drunk'. Like Joe, he left Specialty in 1954, and recorded for Aladdin, before becoming a record distributor and forming his own Duplex Records which survived on few releases from 1958-78, financed from a diverse musical business, ranging from teach-yourself-piano charts to artist management.

● ALBUMS: including with Joe Liggins *Saturday Night Boogie Woogie Man* (1974)★★★, *I Can't Stop It* (1981)★★★, *Jimmy Liggins & His Drops Of Joy* (Ace 1989)★★★, *Vol. 2: Rough Weather Blues* (1993)★★★.

LIGHTFOOT, ALEXANDER 'PAPA GEORGE'

b. 2 March 1924, Natchez, Mississippi, USA, d. 28 November 1971, Natchez, Mississippi, USA. A self-taught harmonica player, Papa Lightfoot first recorded in 1949 for Peacock Records as part of the Gondoliers vocal group. He had a sporadic recording career in New Orleans in the early 50s (and accompanied Champion Jack Dupree on the King label). The majority of his 50s recordings remained unreleased until Bob Hite, famed blues collector and lead singer with Canned Heat, persuaded Liberty Records to issue them in their 1968 *Legendary Masters* series. This resulted in Lightfoot being rediscovered in 1969 and recording for the Los Angeles-based Vault Records. He was unable to capitalize on this new-found fame: the following year he fell ill and in 1971 died from a heart attack in his home-town.

● ALBUMS: *Natchez Trace* (Vault 1969)★★★.
● COMPILATIONS: *Goin' Back To The Natchez Trace* (Ace 1995)★★★.

LIGHTNIN' SLIM

b. Otis Hicks, 13 March 1913, St. Louis, Missouri, USA, d. 27 July 1974, Detroit, Michigan, USA. It is as a Louisiana blues stylist that Hicks is best known, having settled in that state in his early teens. He learned guitar from his father and his brother, and made a name for himself on the Baton Rouge blues circuit during the 40s. In 1954, he recorded for J.D. 'Jay' Miller's Feature label, and began that producer's long and fruitful relationship with the blues. These early recordings had a tough, spare sound that helps to place them alongside the very finest down-home blues of the 50s, and the quality was largely maintained over much of the next decade, with many singles leased to Excello Records. His partnership with harmonica player Lazy Lester was particularly effective and releases such as 'Mean Old Lonesome Train', 'Hoodoo Blues' and, especially, 'Rooster Blues', provided him with commercial success and kept him in demand for tours both locally and further afield. Many of his releases demonstrate his particular facility for taking raw material from the work of other popular bluesmen, such as Muddy Waters and Lightnin' Hopkins, and turning it into something entirely his own. The relationship with Miller finally came to an end in 1965, but within a few years, Slim found a wider forum for his music when he became a regular visitor to Europe.

● ALBUMS: *Rooster Blues* (Excello 1960)★★★★, *Lightnin' Slim's Bell Ringer* (Excello 1965)★★★★, *High And Lowdown* (Excello 1971)★★★, *Over Easy* (Excello 1971)★★, *The*

Early Years (1976)★★★, *London Gumbo* (Sonet 1978)★★, *The Feature Sides* (Flyright 1981)★★★, *We Gotta Rock Tonight* (Flyright 1986)★★★, *Blue Lightnin'* (Indigo 1992)★★★, *King Of The Swamp Blues* rec. 1954 (Flyright 1992)★★★, *It's Mighty Crazy* 1954-58 recordings (Ace 1995)★★★★, *Nothing But The Devil* (Ace 1996)★★★★.

LIL' ED AND THE BLUES IMPERIALS

b. Ed Williams, Lil' Ed learned slide guitar from his uncle J.B. Hutto. Singing his own compositions, he formed the Blues Imperials in 1975 and built up a reputation on the Chicago club scene. In 1986 Lil' Ed recorded for Alligator with Dave Weld (guitar), James Young (bass) and Louis Henderson (drums). In 1989 Mike Garrett and Kelly Littleton replaced Weld and Henderson.

● ALBUMS: *Roughhousin'* (Alligator 1986)★★★, *Chicken, Gravy & Biscuits* (Alligator 1989)★★★, *What You See Is What You Get* (1993)★★★.

LINCOLN, CHARLEY

b. Charley Hicks, 11 March 1900, Lithonia, Georgia, USA, d. 28 September 1963, Cairo, Georgia, USA. Like his younger brother, Robert 'Barbecue Bob' Hicks, Lincoln learned guitar from Curley Weaver's mother, but was less accomplished than Bob. He recorded from 1927-30, probably thanks to his brother's hit-making status, and his blues are a mix of the sad and the mildly risqué, backed by a simple 12-string guitar. Despite being billed as 'Laughing Charley' on a duet with Bob, Lincoln was prone to extreme mood swings under the influence of drink, from introverted to choleric; this trait was exacerbated by the alcoholism that followed various family tragedies, notably the premature death of his brother in 1929. On Christmas Day 1955, he senselessly murdered a man, and spent the rest of his life in prison, repentant and performing only religious songs.

● COMPILATIONS: *Charley Lincoln* (Matchbox 1983)★★★, *Complete Recordings 1927-1930* (1984)★★★.

LINKCHAIN, HIP

b. Willie Richard, 10 November 1936, near Jackson, Mississippi, USA, d. 13 February 1989, Chicago, Illinois, USA. As a baby, Linkchain was known as Long Linkchain. He heard the blues at home and learned to play acoustic guitar, switching to electric after settling in Chicago in the early 50s. He formed his first band in 1959 and recorded singles in the 60s for the Lola and Sann labels under the name 'Hip Lanchan'. In the 70s he had a single issued by Blues King, and on the JSP label, an album featuring further titles from this session plus earlier tracks. Albums also appeared on MCM, Rumble (with Jimmy Dawkins), Teardrop (including a collaboration with Jimmy Rogers) and a highly acclaimed set for Black Magic. He died of cancer in 1989. Linkchain's guitar style was unique in the west side Chicago tradition, and he was a talented songwriter and singer.

● ALBUMS: *Airbuster* (Black Magic 1987)★★★★.

LINN COUNTY

Formed in Chicago, Illinois, USA, this powerful, blues-based quintet - Stephen Miller (organ, vocals), Fred Walk (guitar, sitar), Larry Easter (saxophones, flute), Dino Long (bass) and Jerome 'Snake' McAndrew (drums) - subsequently moved to San Francisco. Their impressive debut, *Proud Flesh Soothsayer*, included the lengthy 'Protect And Serve/Bad Things' which showcased the exhilarating interplay between the unit's instrumental protagonists. A more orthodox collection, *Fever Shot*, nonetheless featured several hard-edged, disciplined performances, while a final release, *Till The Break Of Dawn*, offered a vibrant reading of John Lee Hooker's 'Boogie Chillun' as its highlight. By this point McAndrew had been replaced by Clark Pierson, but the group was unable to capitalize upon their cult status and broke up soon afterwards. Miller completed a solo album, which featured the entire Linn County line-up, before joining the Elvin Bishop group. Pierson subsequently drummed in Janis Joplin's Full Tilt Boogie Band.

● ALBUMS: *Proud Flesh Soothsayer* (1968)★★★, *Fever Shot* (1969)★★★, *Till The Break Of Dawn* (1970)★★★.

LIPSCOMB, MANCE

b. 9 April 1895, Navasota, Texas, USA, d. 30 January 1976, Navasota, Texas, USA. The son of a former slave and professional fiddle player,

Lipscomb initially learned that instrument and later the guitar. For many years he played on a solely local basis, while working as a farmer, and only made his first recordings at the age of 65, in 1960. Over the following 15 years, he made a series of highly regarded albums, mainly for Chris Strachwitz's Arhoolie label. On the strength of these and his frequent live performances, he built up a very strong reputation for his skills as a singer of a wide range of material. His remarkably extensive repertoire encompassed gospel, rags, ballads and other traditional songs, as well as Texas-style blues. He also appeared in several films, including one biopic, *A Well Spent Life*.

● ALBUMS: *Texas Songster, Volumes 1 - 6* (1960, 1964, 1964, 1967, 1970, 1974)★★★, *You'll Never Find Another Man Like Mance* (Arhoolie 1964), *Texas Songster In A Live Performance* (Arhoolie 1966)★★★.

● COMPILATIONS: *Texas Songster* CD compilation of the *Texas Songster* series (Arhoolie 1989)★★★★, *You Got To Reap What You Sow* (Arhoolie 1993)★★★, *Right On Time* (Bullseye 1995)★★★.

● FURTHER READING: *I Say Me For A Parable: The Oral Autobiography*, Mance Lipscomb with Glen Alyn.

● FILMS: *A Well Spent Life*.

LITTLE CHARLIE AND THE NIGHTCATS

The line-up comprises Rick Estrin (b. 5 October 1950, San Francisco, California, USA; vocal, harmonica), Charlie Baty (b. 10 July 1953, Birmingham, Alabama, USA; guitar), Brad Lee Sexton (b. 11 November 1948, South Carolina, USA; bass) and Dobie Strange (b. 15 November 1948, Red Bluff, California, USA; drums). One of the most popular bands performing in the west coast Chicago blues style, the Nightcats grew out of a 1973 meeting between Estrin and Baty, at that time a harmonica player himself. Estrin had been professional since 1968, when a jam with Lowell Fulson turned into a three-week booking. By 1975, he had turned down the opportunity to join Muddy Waters' band, and meanwhile, Baty was in Sacramento, where he had started a band. When Estrin tired of San Francisco a year later, he contacted Baty with the idea of putting together a group. In 1982, the band pressed a single which they then sold at gigs, and began to put together a tape, which in 1986 they submitted to Bruce Iglauer at Alligator. A year later, *All The Way Crazy* was released. With their succeeding albums, the band established a reputation for hard driving music with a humorous edge to the lyrics. Estrin is their principal composer; Robert Cray recorded his 'I'm Just Lucky That Way', while 'My Next Ex-Wife' won the 1993 W.C. Handy award for Best Blues Song Of The Year.

● ALBUMS: *All The Way Crazy* (Alligator 1987)★★★, *Disturbing The Peace* (Alligator 1988)★★★, *The Big Break* (Alligator 1989)★★★, *Captured Live* (Alligator 1991)★★★, *Night Vision* (Alligator 1993)★★★, *Straight Up!* (Alligator 1995)★★★.
● COMPILATIONS: *Deluxe Edition* (Alligator 1997)★★★.

LITTLE FEAT

The compact rock 'n' roll funk displayed by Little Feat put them out of step with other Californian rock bands of the early 70s. By combining elements of country, folk, blues, soul and boogie they unwittingly created a sound that became their own, and has to date never been replicated or bettered. The band comprised Lowell George (b. 13 April 1945, Hollywood, California, USA, d. 29 June 1979), who had already had experience with the earthy garage band the Standells and with the Mothers Of Invention, plus, Roy Estrada (b. Santa Ana, California, USA; bass), Bill Payne (b. 12 March 1949, Waco, Texas, USA; keyboards) and Richie Haywood (drums). Although they signed to the mighty Warner Brothers Records in 1970, no promotional push was given to the band until their second album in 1972. The public later latched on to the debut, *Little Feat*. It remains a mystery as to why the band were given such a low profile. George had already been noticed as a potentially major songwriter; two of his songs, 'Truck Stop Girl' and 'Willin'', were taken by the Byrds. The debut sold poorly and, quite inexplicably, so did their second and third albums. The band were understandably depressed and began to fragment. Lowell began writing songs with John Sebastian amid rumours of a planned supergroup featuring Phil Everly. Fortunately, their record company made a further advance to finance *Feats Don't Fail Me Now*; with the revised band now comprising Paul Barrere (b. 3 July 1948, Burbank, California, USA; guitar), Kenny Gradney (b. New Orleans, Louisiana, USA; bass) and Sam Clayton (b. New Orleans, Louisiana, USA; percussion). Deservedly, they made the album charts in the USA, although the excellent material was no better than their three previous albums. *Feats Don't Fail Me Now* marked the development of other members as credible songwriters and George's role began to diminish. The European critics were unanimous in praising the band in 1975 on the 'Warner Brothers Music Show'. This impressive package tour featured Graham Central Station, Bonaroo, Tower Of Power, Montrose, Little Feat and the headliners, the Doobie Brothers, who were then enjoying unprecedented acclaim and success. Without exaggeration, Little Feat blew everyone off the stage with a series of outstanding concerts, and, from that moment onwards, they could do no wrong. *The Last Record Album* in 1975 contained George's finest (albeit short) winsome love song, 'Long Distance Love'; the sparseness of the guitar playing and the superb change of tempo with drum and bass, created a song that evoked melancholy and tenderness. The opening question and answer line: 'Ah Hello, give me missing persons, tell me what is it that you need, I said oh, I need her so, you've got to stop your teasing' - is full of emotional pleading. George, meanwhile, was overindulging with drugs, and his contribution to *Time Loves A Hero* was minimal. Once again they delivered a great album, featuring the by now familiar and distinctive cover artwork by Neon Park. Following the double live *Waiting For Columbus*, the band disintegrated and George started work on his solo album, *Thanks, I'll Eat It Here* (which sounded like a Little Feat album); two notable tracks were 'Missing You', and '20 Million Things To Do'. During a solo concert tour George had a heart attack and died, the years of abuse having taken their toll. The remaining band re-formed for a benefit concert for his widow and at the end of a turbulent year, the barrel was scraped to release *Down On The Farm*. The record became a considerable success, as did the compilation *Hoy-Hoy*.
In 1988, almost a decade after they broke up, the band re-formed and *Let It Roll* became their most

successful album to date. The band had ex-Pure Prairie League Craig Fuller taking Lowell's place, and the musical direction was guided by the faultless keyboard playing of Bill Payne. A second set from the re-formed band came in 1990, and although it disappointed many, it added fuel to the theory that this time they intended to stay together. *Shake Me Up* finally buried the ghost of George, as the critics accepted that the band was a credible force once again and could claim rightful ownership of both its name and history, without forgetting Lowell George's gigantic contribution. Fuller was not present on *Ain't Had Enough Fun*; the band recruiting a female lead singer, Shaun Murphy, instead.

● ALBUMS: *Little Feat* (Warners 1971)★★★, *Sailin' Shoes* (Warners 1972)★★★★, *Dixie Chicken* (Warners 1973)★★★★, *Feats Don't Fail Me Now* (Warners 1974)★★★★, *The Last Record Album* (Warners 1975)★★★★, *Time Loves A Hero* (Warners 1977)★★★★, *Waiting For Columbus* (Warners 1978)★★★, *Down On The Farm* (Warners 1979)★★★, *Let It Roll* (Warners 1988)★★, *Representing The Mambo* (Warnera 1990)★★, *Shake Me Up* (Polydor 1991)★★, *Ain't Had Enough Fun* (Zoo 1995)★★.

Solo: Lowell George *Thanks I'll Eat It Here* (Warners 1979)★★★. Paul Barrere *On My Own Two Feet* (Warners/Mirage 1983)★★.

● COMPILATIONS: *Hoy Hoy* (Warners 1981)★★★★, *As Time Goes By - The Best Of Little Feat* (Warners 1986)★★★★.

LITTLE HATCH

b. Provine Hatch Jnr., 25 October 1921, Sledge, Mississippi, USA. Though some 10 years older than Little Walter Jacobs, Hatch was one of many harmonica players to be tagged 'Little Walter Jnr.' The seventh of nine sons who all played harmonica, he was seven when he owned his first harp. The family moved to Helena, Arkansas, in the mid-30s, where Hatch first encountered Howlin' Wolf, Johnny Shines, Robert Lockwood and Sonny Boy 'Rice Miller' Williamson. After serving in the Navy during the war, on his return he moved to Kansas City, where he has since remained. While running his own business and then working for the Hallmark Company by day, he played in KC clubs such as Cotton-Eyed Joe's and

Nightingales'. In 1962 he played with guitarist George Jackson before forming his own band, the Houserockers. His first album, as *The Little Hatchet Band*, was recorded live by a German student during June and July 1970 with a band that included Troy Banks, Bill Wells and Lewis Patties. At the end of the decade, he retired from music for nearly 10 years before resuming in 1987. *Well, All Right!* was also recorded live, at The Grand Emporium in Kansas City, with guitarist Bill Dye, Joe Whitfeld on bass and drummer C. Jaisson H. Taylor. All the material is claimed to be original, but songs by Albert King and Little Walter are little more than barely disguised.

● ALBUMS: *The Little Hatchet Band* (M&M 1974)★★, *Well, All Right!* (Modern Blues 1993)★★★.

● COMPILATIONS: *Texas Harmonica Rumble, Vol. 2* (Fan Club 1992)★★★.

LITTLE MILTON

b. James Milton Campbell Jnr., 7 September 1934, Inverness, Mississippi, USA. Having played guitar from the age of 12, Little Milton (he legally dropped the James when he discovered that he had a brother of the same name on his father's side) made his first public appearances as a teenager in the blues bars and cafés on Greenville's celebrated Nelson Street. He first appeared on record accompanying pianist Willie Love in the early 50s, then appeared under his own name on three singles issued on Sam Phillips' Sun label under the guidance of Ike Turner. Although their working relationship continued throughout the decade, it was on signing to Chicago's Chess/Checker outlet that Milton's career flourished. An R&B-styled vocalist in the mould of Bobby Bland and 'T-Bone' Walker, his work incorporated sufficient soul themes to maintain a success denied to less flexible contemporaries. Propelled by an imaginative production, Milton had a substantial hit in 1965 with the optimistic 'We're Gonna Make It', and followed with other expressive performances, including 'Who's Cheating Who?' (1965), plus the wry 'Grits Ain't Groceries' (1968). Campbell remained with Chess until 1971, whereupon he switched to Stax. 'That's What Love Will Do' returned the singer to the R&B chart after a two-year absence, but despite his appearance in the pivotal *Wattstax* film, Little Milton was unable to maintain a consistent recording career. A series of ill-fitting funk releases from the late 70s reinforced the perception that the artist was at his peak with blues-edged material, something proved by his excellent contemporary work for Malaco Records. In the 90s he was with Delmark Records and experienced something of a resurgence during the most recent blues boom.

● ALBUMS: *We're Gonna Make It* (Checker 1965)★★★, *Little Milton Sings Big Blues* (Checker 1966)★★★, *Grits Ain't Groceries* (Chess 1969)★★★, *If Walls Could Talk* (Chess 1970)★★★, *Waiting For Little Milton* (Stax 1973)★★★, *Blues 'N' Soul* (Stax 1974)★★★, *Montreux Festival* (Stax 1974)★★★, *Friend Of Mine* (1976)★★★, *Me For You, You For Me* (1976)★★★, *In Perspective* (1981)★★★, *I Need Your Love So Bad* (1982)★★★, *Age Ain't Nothing But A Number* (1983)★★★, *Playin' For Keeps* (Malaco 1984)★★★, *Annie Mae's Cafe* (Malaco 1987)★★★, *Movin' To The Country* (Malaco 1987)★★★, *I Will Survive* (Malaco 1988)★★★, *Too Much Pain* (1990)★★★, *Reality* (1992)★★★, *I'm A Gambler* (Malaco 1994)★★★, *Live At Westville Prison* (Delmark 1995)★★★, *Cheatin' Habit* (Malaco 1996)★★★.

● COMPILATIONS: *Little Milton's Greatest Hits* (1972)★★★★, *Little Milton* (1976)★★★, *Sam's Blues* (1976)★★★, *Walkin' The Back Streets* (1981)★★★, *Raise A Little Sand* (Red Lightnin' 1982)★★★, *His Greatest Hits* (Chess 1987)★★★, *Chicago Golden Years* (Vogue 1988)★★★, *Hittin' The Boogie (Memphis Days 1953-1954)* (Zu Zazz 1988)★★★, *The Sun Masters* (Rounder 1990)★★★, *Welcome To The Club: The Essential Chess Recordings* (MCA 1994)★★★★, *Little Milton's Greatest Hits* (Malaco 1995)★★★★, *The Complete Stax Singles* (Ace 1995)★★★★.

LITTLE SON JOE

b. Ernest Lawlars, 18 May 1900, Hughes, Arkansas, USA, d. 14 November 1961, Memphis, Tennessee, USA. Lawlars is best known for his musical partnership with his wife, Memphis Minnie, but he had been playing guitar and singing blues for some years around Memphis before they collaborated, including a period with Rev. Robert Wilkins, whom he accompanied on record in 1935. He teamed up with Minnie in the late 30s, replacing her previous husband and partner, Joe McCoy. Like McCoy, Lawlars also made records under his own name, including the well-known 'Black Rat Swing', but he mainly appeared in the supporting role, on a large number of sides covering most of the 40s and the early years of the following decade. As their popularity in Chicago waned, they settled back in Memphis and retired from music in the 50s.

● ALBUMS: *Memphis Minnie* (1964)★★★, *Chicago Blues* (1982), *World Of Trouble* (1982)★★★.

LITTLE SONNY

b. Aaron Willis, 6 October 1932, Greensboro, Alabama, USA. Despite the claims of his first album, its evidence shows that Little Sonny Willis is an adequate harmonica player and reluctant singer whose music career has been, at best, intermittent. With little experience in music apart from singing in church choirs, Willis moved to Detroit in 1954. Working as a photographer in the bars of the Hastings Street area, he also picked up the rudiments of the harmonica. His first gig was in the Good Time Bar with Washboard Willie's band. Willis gained some harmonica tuition from Sonny Boy 'Rice Miller' Williamson, from whom he adopted his nickname. In March 1956, he formed his own band with pianist Chuck Smith, guitarist Louis (Big Bo) Collins and drummer Jim Due Crawford. Two years later Smith, Crawford and Eddie Burns backed Willis on his debut record, 'I Gotta Find My Baby', for Duke Records. Another record, 'Love Shock', recorded by Joe Von Battle, was leased to Excello. An unissued 1961 session for Chess Records presaged a five-year recording silence, followed by singles for Speedway, Revilot (including the instrumental 'The Creeper') and Wheel City at the end of the decade. In 1969 he recorded his first album for the Stax subsidiary Enterprise. *New King Of The Blues Harmonica*, an album of mostly uninventive instrumentals, evoked Hans Christian Andersen fairy tales. A second album, *Hard Goin' Up*, released in 1973, was a more honest, balanced exercise. Albert King recorded Willis's 'Love Shock' and 'Love Mechanic' for Tomato in 1978. *King Albert* was recorded in Detroit and used Willis's sons, Aaron Jnr., Anthony and

Eddie, in the back-up band. Perhaps their father had read *King Lear*.

● ALBUMS: *New King Of The Blues Harmonica* (Stax 1969)★★, *Hard Goin' Up* (Stax 1973)★★★, *New Orleans Rhythm And Blues* (Black Magic 1994)★★★, *Sonny Side Up* (Sequel 1995)★★★, *Blues With A Feeling* (Sequel 1996)★★★★.

LITTLE WALTER

b. Marion Walter Jacobs, 1 May 1930, Marksville, Louisiana, USA, d. 15 February 1968. A major figure of post-war blues, Little Walter is credited for bringing the harmonica, or 'French harp', out from its rural setting and into an urban context. His career began at the age of 12 when he left home for New Orleans, but by 1946 Jacobs was working in Chicago's famed Maxwell Street. Early recordings for the Ora Nelle label were the prelude to his joining the Muddy Waters band, where he helped forge what became the definitive electric Chicago blues group. The harmonica player emerged as a performer in his own right in 1952 when 'Juke', an instrumental recorded at the end of a Waters session, topped the R&B chart, where it remained for eight consecutive weeks. Little Walter And The Night Caps - David Myers (guitar), Louis Myers (guitar) and Fred Below (drums) - enjoyed further success when 'Sad Hours' and 'Mean Old World' reached the Top 10 in the same chart. The group then became known as Little Walter And The Jukes and, although obliged to fulfil recording agreements with Waters, Jacobs actively pursued his own career. He enjoyed further R&B hits with 'Blues With A Feeling' (1953), 'Last Night' (1954) and the infectious 'My Babe' (1955). The last song, patterned on a spiritual tune, 'This Train', was a second number 1 single and became much covered during later years. Other notable releases included 'Mellow Down Easy' and 'Boom Boom (Out Go The Lights)' which were later recorded, respectively, by Paul Butterfield and the Blues Band. A haunting version of 'Key To The Highway' (1958), previously recorded by Big Bill Broonzy, gave Walter his final Top 10 entry. He nonetheless remained a pivotal figure, undertaking several tours, including one of Britain in 1964. His career, however, was undermined by personal problems. A pugnacious man with a quick temper and a reputation for heavy drinking, he died on

15 February 1968 as a result of injuries sustained in a street brawl. This ignominious end should not detract from Little Walter's status as an innovative figure. The first musician to amplify the harmonica, his heavy, swooping style became the lynchpin for all who followed him, including Norton Buffalo, Butterfield and Charlie Musselwhite.

● ALBUMS: *The Best Of Little Walter* (Checker 1958)★★★★, *Little Walter* (Pye International 1964)★★★★, *Hate To See You Go* (Chess 1969)★★★, *Thunderbird* (Syndicate Chapter 1971)★★★, *On The Road Again* (Xtra 1979)★★★, *Quarter To Twelve* (Red Lightnin' 1982)★★★.

● COMPILATIONS: *Chess Masters* (Charly 1983)★★★★, *Boss Blues Harmonica* (Vogue 1986)★★★★, *Confessin' The Blues* (Chess 1986)★★★★, *Windy City Blues* (Blue Moon 1986)★★★, *Collection: Little Walter 20 Blues Greats* (Déjà Vu 1987)★★★, *The Blues World Of Little Walter* (Delmark 1988)★★★★, *The Best Of Little Walter Volume 2* (Chess 1989)★★★, *The Chess Years 1952 - '63* 4-CD box set (Chess 1993)★★★★, *Blues With A Feeling* (MCA/Chess 1995)★★★★.

LITTLE WHITT AND BIG BO

Based in Tuscaloosa, Alabama, USA, the blues talents of 'Little Whitt' Wells (b. 19 February 1931, Ralph, Alabama, USA) and 'Big Bo' McGhee (b. 1928, Alabama, USA) remained largely undiscovered until the mid-90s, despite the fact that Wells had previously turned down offers to play guitar with Freddie King, Howlin' Wolf and 'Little' Junior Parker. Harmonica player McGhee boasts a similarly intriguing past - having previously worked as a long-distance lorry driver shipping explosives and at one time having died on an operating table. He was revived several hours later after morgue technicians noticed a heartbeat. Wells was first turned on to the blues by the records of Blind Boy Fuller and Blind Lemon Jefferson, his father buying him his first guitar when he was 11. He originally met McGhee prior to forming his own band, Little Whitt And The Downbeats. For his part, McGhee started playing harmonica at the age of six. He continued to practise the instrument while hauling chemicals and dynamite as a 'suicide jockey' lorry driver in the 30s. They began playing together full-time at the turn of the 80s, forming the Kokomo Blues Band. In 1995 the duo travelled to the UK, helped by sponsorship from Debbie Bond and Mike McCracken of the Alabama Blues Project, who also helped out by playing on stage.

● ALBUMS: various *Moody Swamp Blues* (Alabama Blues Project 1995)★★★.

LITTLEFIELD, 'LITTLE' WILLIE

b. 16 September 1931, El Campo, Texas, USA. By the age of 16, Littlefield was emulating his hero Amos Milburn, shouting the blues and hammering the pianos of nearby Houston's Dowling Street clubs. He made his recording debut the following year for the local Eddie's Records and for the Freedom label. In August 1949, Littlefield was discovered by the Bihari brothers, who had flown to Houston to find their own version of Aladdin's Amos Milburn, and signed him to their Los Angeles-based Modern label. Littlefield's first Modern session, recorded in Houston, resulted in the huge hit 'It's Midnight', which featured his schoolfriend, Don Wilkerson, on tenor saxophone. From October 1949, Littlefield was recording in Los Angeles, but subsequent releases did not match the promise of the debut single, in spite of bands that included Jimmy 'Maxwell Street' Davis, Chuck Norris and Johnny Moore. In 1952, Littlefield signed with Federal Records and continued to make fine records in his own right and in duets with Lil Greenwood and Little Esther Phillips. His first Federal session resulted in his best-known recording, 'K.C. Lovin'' which was later altered slightly by Leiber And Stoller and recorded by Wilbert Harrison as 'Kansas City'. By 1957, Littlefield had moved to northern California, where he recorded for the Rhythm label. He stayed in San José throughout the 60s and 70s, making occasional club appearances, but in the early 80s he moved with his family to the Netherlands, and has since experienced a minor comeback with new material on various European labels and frequent appearances at jazz and blues festivals.

● ALBUMS: *K.C. Loving* (1977)★★★, *It's Midnight* (Route 66 1980)★★★, *Little Willie Littlefield - Volume One* (1980)★★★, *Little Willie Littlefield - Volume Two* (1981)★★★, *I'm In The Mood* (Oldie Blues 1984)★★★, *Jump With Little Willie Littlefield* (Ace 1984)★★★, *Happy Pay Day* (Ace 1985)★★★, *House Party* (Oldie Blues 1988)★★★, *Plays Boogie Woogie* (Schubert 1988)★★★.

● COMPILATIONS: *Yellow Boogie & Blues* (Oldie Blues 1995)★★★, *Going Back To Kay Cee* (Ace 1995)★★★.

LITTLEJOHN, JOHNNY

b. John Wesley Funchess, 16 April 1931, Learned, Mississippi, USA, d. 1 February 1994, Chicago, Illinois, USA. Littlejohn taught himself to play guitar and was inspired by Henry Martin, a blues guitarist friend of his father. In 1946, he left home and was an itinerant worker before settling in Gary, Indiana, in 1951 and taking up the guitar seriously. He quickly became a popular attraction and later relocated to Chicago. A chronically underrated slide guitarist and singer, Littlejohn recorded for numerous labels, including Ace, Margaret, Bluesway, and Wolf, but his best work is to be found on Arhoolie and Rooster. Although often categorized as an Elmore James-influenced player, he could also recall the smooth approach of B.B. King with his picking and singing.

● ALBUMS: *John Littlejohn's Chicago Blues Stars* (Arhoolie 1968)★★★, *So-Called Friends* (Rooster 1985)★★★.

LOCKWOOD, ROBERT, JNR.

b. 27 March 1915, Marvell, Arkansas, USA. In his youth, Lockwood learned some guitar from Robert Johnson, who was evidently a major influence. Lockwood's earliest recordings emphasize that debt. He worked the Mississippi Delta area throughout the 30s, playing with musicians such as Sonny Boy 'Rice Miller' Williamson and Howlin' Wolf. In 1941, he was in Chicago, Illinois, making his first records as a solo artist, as well as some accompaniments to Peter J. 'Doctor' Clayton. Lockwood spent some time as one of the resident musicians on the famous *King Biscuit Time* radio programme, broadcast from Helena, Arkansas. In the early 50s he settled in Chicago where he recorded with Sunnyland Slim. Johnson's influence was detectable, but the style was becoming distinctly urban in orientation. Throughout that decade Lockwood played the blues clubs, and often accompanied Little Walter on record. As his status as one of Chicago's master guitarists grew, he also contributed to material from Muddy Waters, Eddie Boyd and others. In 1960, he made some classic recordings with Otis Spann, his delicate runs and big, chunky chords betraying a more sophisticated, jazzy direction. Indeed, these sessions are considered by many to be among the greatest piano/guitar duo recordings of all time. He has continued to be very active in music through the ensuing years, working with Willie Mabon, among others. In the late 70s he formed a touring and recording partnership with John Ed 'Johnny' Shines, and into the 90s he was still producing high-calibre work, notably on an album with Ronnie Earl. In 1995 he received a National Heritage Award at the White House. His 12-string guitar album is particularly noteworthy, recorded in 1975 and reissued in 1996.

● ALBUMS: *Steady Rolling Man* (Delmark 1973)★★★, *Contrasts* (Trix 1973)★★★★, *Windy City Blues* (1976)★★★, *Does 12* (Trix 1977)★★★, *Johnny Shines & Robert Lockwood - Dust My Broom* rec. 50s (Flyright 1980)★★★, *Hangin' On* (Rounder 1980)★★★, *Johnny Shines & Robert Lockwood: Mr Blues Is Back To Stay* (Rounder 1981)★★★, *Robert & Robert* (Black & Blue 1982)★★★, *What's The Score* (1990)★★★, *Plays Robert Johnson & Robert Lockwood Jr.* (1992)★★★, *Contrasts* (Trix 1995)★★★, *Got To Find Me A Woman* (Verve 1997)★★★.

LOFTON, CRIPPLE CLARENCE

b. 28 March 1887, Kingsport, Tennessee, USA, d. 9 January 1957. Living and playing in Chicago from the age of 20, pianist and vocalist Lofton became a popular accompanist to visiting blues singers, in many instances appearing in this role on record. He worked steadily through the 30s, proving very popular in the Windy City, and enjoyed the fleeting benefits of the boogie-woogie craze. Influenced by Charles 'Cow Cow' Davenport and Jimmy Yancey, he in turn influenced a number of other pianists, notably Meade 'Lux' Lewis.

● COMPILATIONS: *Clarence's Blues (1930s)* (Oldie Blues 1988)★★★.

LOMAX, ALAN AND JOHN A.

A well-known and well-read folklorist, Alan Lomax (b. 15 January 1915, Austin, Texas, USA) travelled with his father, John A. Lomax (b. John Avery Lomax, 23 September 1875, Goodman, Mississippi, USA, d. 26 January 1948, Greenville, Mississippi, USA), on field recording trips during the 30s, collecting folk songs and tunes from various states in the USA. They collected songs for the Library of Congress Archive, for which Woody Guthrie was later recorded. Until that time, John Lomax had been an administrator at a college, and had collected cowboy songs, including 'Home On The Range', as a hobby. As a result of the Depression and economic crash of the 30s, John Lomax became jobless, and started collecting folk songs and related material on a full-time basis. By the time Alan was 23 years old he was assistant director of the Archive of Folk Song at the Library of Congress. The Lomaxes met a number of singers who later became almost household names, including Lead Belly and Muddy Waters. Lead Belly was discovered in a Louisiana prison, but John Lomax managed to secure his release, employing him as a chauffeur. Lomax later took him to New York where he performed to college audiences. In 1934, John Lomax became honorary consultant and head of the Library of Congress archive of folk song. Alan Lomax travelled to Britain during the 50s and collaborated with Ewan MacColl on the radio series *Ballads And Blues*. He later returned to the USA to conduct field recordings in the southern states. The results were subsequently released on Atlantic Records as part of a series called 'Southern Folk Heritage'. John and Alan Lomax were also responsible for collecting a number of the songs of the Ritchie family of Kentucky. In addition to his many other activities, Alan Lomax was a fine performer in his own right, as can be heard on *Texas Folk Songs*, which contains the standards 'Ain't No More Cane On The Brazo's' and 'Billy Barlow'. *Alan Lomax Sings Great American Ballads*, on HMV, included Guy Carawan (banjo) and Nick Wheatstraw (guitar). It featured such classics as 'Frankie', 'Darlin' Corey' and 'Git Along Little Doggies'. The latter song had been recorded by John Lomax in 1908, and originates from an Irish ballad, converted and adapted by cowboys. After World War II, Alan was the Director of Folk Music for Decca, subsequently working for the Office of War Information from 1943-44, and then for the army's Special Services Section until 1945. As a singer, Alan performed both in the USA and Britain. Twelve years of research culminated in *Cantometrics*, a set of seven cassettes with a book.

● ALBUMS: John A. Lomax *The Ballad Hunter, Lectures On American Folk Music* 10-LP box set (Folkways 50s)★★★, Alan Lomax *Alan Lomax Sings Great American Ballads* (HMV 1958)★★★, *Texas Folk Songs* (1958)★★★, *Folk Song Saturday Night* (60s)★★★, *Murderer Is Home* (1976)★★★, various artists *The Alan Lomax Collection Sampler* (Rounder 1997)★★★★.

● FURTHER READING: Alan Lomax *American Folk Song And Folk Lore*, with Sidney Robertson Cowell. *Mister Jelly Roll - The Fortunes Of Jelly Roll Morton, New Orleans, Creole And Inventor Of Jazz, The Folksongs Of North America, The Land Where The Blues Began*. Editor of *Folk Songs Of North America In The English Language, Folk Song Style And Culture, Cantometrics - An Approach To The Anthropology Of Music*. John A. Lomax *Cowboy Songs, Adventures Of A Ballad Hunter, Cowboy Songs And Other Frontier Ballads, Songs Of The Cattle Trail And Cow Camp*. John And Alan Lomax *American Ballads And Folk Songs, Cowboy Songs And Other Frontier Ballads, Negro Folk Songs As Sung By Lead Belly, Folksong USA, Our Singing Country, The Penguin Book Of American Folk Songs*

LONESOME SUNDOWN

b. Cornelious Green, 12 December 1928, Donaldsonville, Louisiana, USA, d. 23 April 1995, Gonzales, Louisiana. Green taught himself piano while growing up, then took guitar lessons in his early 20s. He joined Clifton Chenier's band in 1955, and can be heard on several of that artist's recordings on the Specialty label. The following year he recorded for the first time in his own right and 16 singles were issued over the next nine years under the name given to him by producer Jay Miller - Lonesome Sundown. Many of these, such as 'My Home Is A Prison' and 'Lonesome Lonely Blues', were classic examples of the unique Louisiana sound - swamp blues - with a resonant production, featuring a strong, booming rhythm section, rippling piano and support from Lazy Lester or John Gradnigo on harmonica and Lionel Prevost on tenor saxophone. Green's vocals and biting lead guitar invariably provided just the right

gritty edge. A religious conversion towards the end of this period led to his withdrawal from the music scene, but he returned, if only briefly, to record an excellent album for the Joliet label in the late 70s. He was severely debilitated in later years following two strokes, and died in 1995.

● ALBUMS: *Been Gone Too Long* (Alligator 1980)★★★, *Lonesome Whistler* (Flyright 1986)★★★,

● COMPILATIONS: *If Anybody Asks You (My Home Ain' t Here* (Flyright 1988)★★★, *I'm A Mojo Man: The Best Of The Excello Singles* (Ace 1995)★★★★.

LOUIS, BIG JOE

b. Jamaica. Moving to England when he was 12, Jamaican-born Louis did not start playing guitar until he was over 20, having learnt to play music on the clarinet. Living in Kent, Louis played in a duo with guitarist David Purdy while avidly building up his collection of obscure blues records, before moving to London in 1984. After initially performing with harmonica player Shakey Vick, Louis played low-key sets around the capital with various personnel who gradually became known as 'Big' Joe Louis And His Band (the 'Big' was there simply 'to get further up the listings'). With a strong live reputation built up over ten years of touring, and some well-received studio sets, Louis and his band (now known as Big Joe Louis And His Blues Kings) are an important force in modern British blues. The current line-up, comprising George Sueref (guitar, harmonica, piano), Brian Nevill (drums) and Matt Radford (bass), recorded 1996's *Big Sixteen*, which was nominated for a British Blues Connection award. Louis's encyclopedic knowledge of blues is also put to good use as a researcher for the Mechanical Copyright Protection Society.

● ALBUMS: *Big Joe Louis And His Blues Kings* (Blue Horizon 1988)★★★, *Big Sixteen* (1996).

LOUIS, JOE HILL

b. Lester Hill, 23 September 1921, Whitehaven Tennessee, USA, d. 5 August 1957. Hill learned blues harmonica from Will Shade as a teenager and was given the name Joe Hill Louis after victory in a boxing match. He performed in Memphis in the late 40s, where he became known as 'The Be-Bop Boy', and developed a one-man band act with guitar, foot-drum and harmonica. Louis's first recordings were made for Columbia in 1949 before he took over B.B. King's radio spot as the Pepticon Boy on WDIA in Memphis. This led to 'Boogie in the Park', a single produced by Sam Phillips for his short-lived Phillips label in 1950. Next, Phillips signed Louis to the Bihari Brothers' Modern label, for which 'I Feel Like A Million' was a local hit. By 1952, Phillips was recording him with a backing group on tracks such as 'We All Gotta Go Sometime', and also used Louis to accompany such artists as the Prisonaires and Rufus Thomas, for whose 'Tiger Man' (1953) he supplied a scintillating guitar solo. There were other tracks for Checker, Meteor and Ace. His final records were made for House Of Sound shortly before his death from tetanus in Memphis in August 1957.

● COMPILATIONS: *Blues In The Morning* reissue (1972)★★★, *The One Man Band 1949-56* reissue (Muskadine 1979)★★★.

LOUISIANA RED

b. Iverson Minter, 23 March 1936, Vicksburg, Mississippi, USA. Although beginning as a sincere imitator of his various heroes, including Muddy Waters, Lightnin' Hopkins and John Lee Hooker, Louisiana Red has gained stature of his own as an instinctive and creative blues singer and guitarist. Red spent his earliest years in a variety of orphanages, his mother having died a week after his birth, and his estranged father a victim of Ku Klux Klan violence. Raised in Pittsburg by an aunt, Corrine Driver, he owned his first guitar at the age of 11 and had instruction from the veteran Crit Walters. At the age of 16, he joined the army and served in Korea. On his return, although claiming to have recorded with Waters and Little Walter, his first known record, 'Gonna Play My Guitar', was released under the name of Playboy Fuller on his own Fuller label. Another session for Checker as Rocky Fuller yielded a single, 'Soon One Morning'; further titles were reissued during the 80s. Working alongside Hooker and Eddie Kirkland, he gained a reputation as 'a guitar fiend'. Much of the 50s was spent travelling throughout the south. In 1960 he moved to New Jersey and made his first record as Louisiana Red for Atlas; 'I Done Woke Up' was backed by James Wayne & The Nighthawks. After recording an unissued session for Bobby Robinson's Fury label, Red was signed to Roulette in 1962 by veteran producer Henry Glover, and the subsequent album, *The Lowdown Backporch Blues*, brought him much critical praise. During 1965 he was comprehensively recorded for Festival Records by Herb Abramson, from which the Atco album *Louisiana Red Sings The Blues* was assembled. Further titles appeared on the Red Lightnin' *Hot Sauce* album. Other sessions took place in 1967, 1971 and 1973. He recorded a number of sessions in 1975 for Blue Labor, from which two volumes of *The Blues Purity Of Louisiana Red* were issued; he also participated on albums by Peg Leg Sam, Johnny Shines, Roosevelt Sykes and Brownie McGhee. In 1976 he moved to Germany, where he has remained, touring Europe extensively and recording for several labels including Black Panther, JSP, L + R, Orchid, MMG and Blues Beacon. He is a dependable if mercurial performer, his spontaneity sometimes a brick wall but often a springboard.

● ALBUMS: *The Lowdown Backporch Blues* (Vogue 1984)★★★, *Midnight Rambler* (Tomato 1988)★★★, *Live At 55* (1991)★★★, *Sings The Blues ...* (Blue Sting 1994)★★★, *Sittin' Here Wonderin'* early 50s recording (Earwig 1995)★★★★.

● COMPILATIONS: *The Best Of Louisiana Red* (Evidence 1995)★★★★, *Midnight Rambler* (Charly 1996)★★★.

LOVE, CLAYTON

b. 15 November 1927, Mattson, Mississippi, USA. While studying as a medical student at Alcorn, Love formed the Shufflers with some of his fellow students, including Jesse Flowers and Henry Reed, to play clubs and colleges around Vicksburg. His cousin, Earl Reed, had a big band which had recorded for Trumpet Records in Jackson. With his encouragement, Love contacted Lillian McMurray and a session was arranged. 'Shufflin' With Love', released in 1951, was a ragged imitation of bands led by Louis Jordan and Roy Milton that toured the south. Other records, for Aladdin, Modern and Groove, followed over the next years. By then, he had met up with Ike Turner, a childhood friend from his Clarksdale days. Turner's band, the Kings Of

Rhythm, was based in St. Louis and in 1957, with Love as their lead vocalist, the band recorded three singles for Federal, including the regional hit 'The Big Question'. He then joined pianist Roosevelt Marks' group and sang on two singles for Bobbin. Love became a full-time teacher in the 60s and only resumed a musical career on his retirement. In 1990, along with fellow pianists Johnnie Johnson and Jimmy Vaughn, he recorded four titles for *Rockin' Eighty-Eights*, including a remake of 'The Big Question' and Fats Domino's 'Goin' Home'.

● ALBUMS: *Strange Kind Of Feelin'* (Acoustic Archives/Alligator 1990/1993)★★★, with Johnnie Johnson, Jimmy Vaughn *Rockin' Eighty-Eights* (Modern Blues Recordings 1991)★★★, with Ike Turner *Trailblazer* (Charly 1991)★★★, with Little Milton *The Bobbin Blues Masters Parts 1 & 2* (Collectables 1995)★★★.

LOVE, WILLIE

b. 4 November 1906, Duncan, Mississippi, USA, d. 19 August 1953, Jackson, Mississippi, USA. A musician from an early age, Love's career was spent almost entirely in and around the Mississippi Delta country. In the 40s and 50s, he was a regular performer on the famous radio show *King Biscuit Time*, but his music is known now only because of a handful of records issued on the Trumpet label in the mid-50s. These are tough, down-home blues, on which he demonstrated considerable proficiency on the piano, as well as an effective singing voice. 'Nelson Street Blues', in which he describes the street of that name in Greenville, Mississippi, is particularly notable for its strong and fascinating evocation of time and place. Among his accompanists were Elmore James, Little Milton and Joe Willie Wilkins.

● COMPILATIONS: *Clownin' With The World* (1990)★★★, *Delta Blues 1951* (1990)★★★, *A Good Man Is Hard To Find* (Orleans 1995)★★★.

LUCAS, ROBERT

b. 1962, Long Beach, California, USA. A 13-year-old Lucas watched Jimi Hendrix play 'Hear My Train A-Comin'' in the documentary about his life and asked his local record store for more acoustic blues. He was sold Robert Johnson's *King Of The Delta Blues Singers* and a compilation of Leroy Carr/Scrapper Blackwell record-ings. His hands were too small to properly learn the guitar, so he took up the harmonica instead. By the age of 20, he was playing harmonica and guitar with the Bernie Pearl Blues Band behind such bluesmen as Big Joe Turner, George Smith, Lowell Fulson, Pee Wee Crayton and Percy Mayfield. In 1983 he joined the Confessors, an R&B band with whom he stayed for three years. He then formed his own band, Luke And The Locomotives, but also performed solo gigs at which he demonstrated a comprehensive slide guitar technique. His first solo release in 1989 was a self-produced cassette on Delta Man Music, *Across The River*, which was followed a year later by the first of a series of albums on Audioquest which combined solo and small group recordings. *Luke And The Locomotives* cut out the acoustic playing and featured amplified blues. Having dispensed with the band, Lucas has returned to playing solo. On *Layaway* he further expanded his musical horizons by featuring keyboards and a horn section.

● ALBUMS: *Across The River* (Delta Man Music 1989)★★★, *Usin' Man Blues* (Audioquest 1990)★★★, *Luke And The Locomotives* (Audioquest 1991)★★, *Built For Comfort* (Audioquest 1992)★★★, *Dodgin' The Dirt* (Roadrunner 1993)★★★, *Layaway* (Audioquest 1994)★★★, *Completely Blue* (Audioquest 1997)★★.

LUCAS, WILLIAM 'LAZY BILL'

b. 29 May 1918, Wynne, Arkansas, USA. Bill Lucas's first instrument was a guitar, financed by selling a pig, but he really wanted a piano. Living on a farm with five siblings it seemed like a dream when his father actually bought him one in 1932. However, when the family moved to Cape Girardeau, Missouri, the piano was left behind. Lazy Bill had no real contact with the blues until he met Big Joe Williams in St. Louis in 1940. Converted, he moved to Chicago in 1941 and turned back to the piano after playing guitar in support of many of the famous artists of the day. He was one of Little Hudson's Red Devils and recorded with his own Blue Rhythms for the Chance label in 1954. Experiencing difficulties due, in part, to the nervous condition that had rendered him virtually blind since childhood, he moved to Minneapolis, Minnesota, in 1964 where he continued to play, appearing at festivals and recording for his own Lazy label in 1970 and later for the Philo label.

● ALBUMS: *The News About The Blues* (Wild 1970)★★★, *Lazy Bill And His Friends* (Lazy 1971)★★★, *Lazy Bill Lucas* (Philo 1974)★★★.

LUSK, PROFESSOR EDDIE

b. 21 September 1948, Chicago, Illinois, USA, d. 26 August 1992, Chicago, Illinois, USA. Lusk's parents were both ministers in the Pentecostal Church and ran The Lusk Bible Way Center on Chicago's South Side. When he was old enough, his mother delegated the piano-playing duties to her son. Lusk was also tempted by the blues sounds emanating from Pepper's Lounge nearby and spent his teenage years struggling against their influence. He was ordained in the Pentecostal faith in 1968 but found the temptation of the blues too strong. He became music director at the Shiloh Academy, thus inspiring the nickname given to him by Professor Longhair. He worked with Luther Allison for three years and throughout the 80s recorded with artists such as Fenton Robinson, Syl Johnson, Koko Taylor, Buddy Guy and Michael Coleman, and toured with Jimmy Dawkins, Phil Guy and Otis Rush. He formed his own band, the Professor's Blues Review with vocalist Gloria Hardiman, and recorded 'Meet Me With Your Black Drawers On' for the 1987 anthology *The New Bluebloods*. On his only solo album, *Professor Strut*, Hardiman was replaced by Karen Carroll. He continued to be in demand for sessions, some of which remain unissued. He and his band appeared in the 1991 film *V. I. Warshawski*, and later in the year toured Europe with Coleman and Kenny Neal. In the summer of 1992, Lusk was diagnosed with colon cancer, brought on by AIDS. In desperation, he took his own life by jumping into the Chicago River.

● ALBUMS: *The New Bluebloods* (Alligator/Sonet 1987)★★★, *Professor Strut* (Delmark 1988)★★★.

LUTCHER, JOE

Brother of Nellie Lutcher, Joe moved from Lake Charles, Louisiana, to California where he played his alto saxophone with the Nat 'King' Cole Trio, the Will Mastin Trio and the Mills Brothers. He then signed for Capitol Records in the summer of 1947 (at the same time as Nellie) and had strong sellers with his 'Strato Cruiser', 'No Name Boogie' and the US Top 10 hit 'Shuffle Boogie'. Leaving Capitol in 1948, Lutcher's Jump Band went on to record for Specialty Records, Modern (resulting in a moderate hit with 'Mardi Gras' in 1949, which uncovered his Louisiana connections), London, Peacock, and several small obscure independent labels. Meanwhile, Lutcher undertook some session work, before giving up the 'devil's music' and becoming an evangelist in the mid-50s; he is said to be responsible for converting Little Richard from secular to spiritual music in the late 50s.

● ALBUMS: *Joe Joe Jump* (Charly 1982)★★★.

LYONS, WILLIE JAMES

b. 5 December 1938, Alabama, USA, d. 26 December 1980, Chicago, Illinois, USA. A west side Chicago blues guitarist in the 50s, Lyons worked as an accompanist with many artists, including Luther Allison, Jimmy Dawkins and Bobby Rush. Unaccountably ignored by Chicago record companies, he was taken up by French blues enthusiasts in the 70s. He recorded as an accompanist, made a disappointing half album, and in 1979 visited Europe, where he recorded his only full album. This proved to be the work of a fine singer and guitarist, influenced by B.B. King and Freddie King, 'T-Bone' Walker and Lowell Fulson.

● ALBUMS: *Ghetto* (1976)★★, *Chicago Woman* (1980)★★★.

MABON, WILLIE

b. 24 October 1925, Hollywood, Tennessee, USA, d. 19 April 1986, Paris, France. Accompanying himself on piano and secondly on harmonica, Mabon sang an urbane blues style similar to Charles Brown. He moved from Memphis, Tennessee, to Chicago in 1942 and was first recorded in 1949 as a member of the Blues Rockers group. After military service he became a popular entertainer in Chicago's Black Belt, and by the early 50s, was well established as an R&B singer with a number of successful records to his credit. Signed as a solo artist to Chess Records in 1951, Mabon immediately hit with a novelty blues, 'I Don't Know' (R&B number 1, 1952), a remake of a Cripple Clarence Lofton record from 1938. Mabon had other hits with 'I'm Mad' (R&B number 1, 1953), 'Poison Ivy' (R&B Top 10, 1954) and 'Seventh Son' (1955). After leaving Chess in 1956, he continued to record on various small labels, getting his best success on Formal in 1962 with 'Got To Have Some'. During the 70s and 80s, Mabon would flit back and forth between Chicago and Europe, making occasional albums for German and French labels, most of which were poorly received. He found a wider audience in Europe, playing the Montreux Jazz Festival and festivals in Berlin and Holland. A polished performer, with a measure of glossy sophistication to his singing, Mabon retained a strong affinity with the earthier aspects of the blues and was an influence upon Mose Allison.

● ALBUMS: *Funky* (1972)★★, *Cold Chilly Woman* (1973)★★★, *Come Back* (1973)★★★, *Live And Well* (1974)★★★, *Shake That Thing* (1975)★★, *Sings 'I Don't Know' And Other Chicago Blues Hits* (1977)★★★, *Chicago Blues Session* (Evidence 1980)★★★.

● COMPILATIONS: *Chicago 1963* (1974)★★★, *I'm The Fixer: Original USA Recordings 1963-64* (Flyright 1986)★★★, *The Seventh Son* (Crown Prince 1987)★★★, *Blues Roots Volume 16* (Chess 1988)★★★, *I Don't Know* (Wolf 1995)★★★.

MACK, BOBBY

b. 19 June 1954, Fort Worth, Texas, USA. Dismissed early in his career as a second-rate Stevie Ray Vaughan, Texan guitarist Mack has begun to develop his own identity with two well-received studio sets, and some tough live appearances with his band Night Train. During the 70s, Mack was playing a mix of blues and rock in a covers band, Thrills, before forming his own Austin-based blues outfit. Austin was at this time the centre of an underground blues movement that included Stevie Ray Vaughan and his brother Jimmy (who went on to form the Fabulous Thunderbirds with Kim Wilson), and the informal atmosphere of impromptu jamming sessions and joint bills provided invaluable experience for a young bluesman. After briefly giving up music, Mack went on to put together Night Train with bass player Danny Turansky, and Thrills drummer Steve Fulton. With various personnel passing through the band, Mack changed the name to Bobby Mack & The Night Train to establish a firmer identity, recording a six-track mini-album under this name in 1985. Following a piecemeal New Zealand-only release, *Say What?*, which included demo sessions with the Neville Brothers, Mack put out the *Red Hot And Humid* live album. Recorded for a live radio show in Austin, its success led to a contract with the Dutch label Provogue. Following his Provogue debut, *Honey Trap*, Mack set up the Palindrome label to release the album in America, and has since worked on several of the label's releases, including production duties for harp player Willie Foster. His latest release, *Sugar All Night*, was notable for featuring predominantly original material.

● ALBUMS: *Bobby Mack & Night Train* mini-album (1985)★★★, *Say What?* (Metro 1989)★★, *Red Hot And Humid* (1990)★★★, *Honey Trap* (Provogue 1990)★★★, *Sugar All Night* (Provogue 1996)★★★.

MACK, LONNIE

b. 1941, Harrison, Indiana, USA. Lonnie Mack began playing guitar while still a child, drawing early influence from a local blues musician, Ralph Trotts, as well as established figures Merle

Travis and Les Paul. He later led a C&W act, Lonnie And The Twilighters, and by 1961 was working regularly with the Troy Seals Band. The following year, Mack recorded his exhilarating instrumental version of Chuck Berry's 'Memphis'. By playing his Gibson 'Flying V' guitar through a Leslie cabinet, the revolving device that gives the Hammond organ its distinctive sound, Mack created a striking, exciting style. 'Memphis' eventually reached the US Top 5, while an equally urgent original, 'Wham', subsequently broached the Top 30. *The Wham Of That Memphis Man* confirmed the artist's vibrant skill, which drew on blues, gospel and country traditions. Several tracks, notably 'I'll Keep You Happy', 'Where There's A Will' and 'Why', also showed Mack's prowess as a soulful vocalist, and later recordings included a rousing rendition of Wilson Pickett's 'I Found A Love'. The guitarist also contributed to several sessions by Freddy King and appeared on James Brown's 'Kansas City' (1967). Mack was signed to Elektra in 1968 following a lengthy appraisal by Al Kooper in *Rolling Stone* magazine. *Glad I'm In The Band* and *Whatever's Right* updated the style of early recordings and included several notable remakes, although the highlight of the latter set was the extended 'Mt. Healthy Blues'. Mack also added bass to the Doors' *Morrison Hotel* (1970) and undertook a national tour prior to recording *The Hills Of Indiana*. This low-key, primarily country album was the prelude to a six-year period of seclusion which ended in 1977 with *Home At Last*. Mack then guested on Michael Nesmith's *From A Radio Engine To The Photon Wing*, before completing *Lonnie Mack And Pismo*, but this regeneration was followed by another sabbatical. He re-emerged in 1985 under the aegis of Texan guitarist Stevie Ray Vaughan, who co-produced the exciting *Strike Like Lightning*. Released on the Alligator label, a specialist in modern blues, the album rekindled this talented artist's career, a rebirth that was maintained on the fiery *Second Sight*.

● ALBUMS: *The Wham Of That Memphis Man* (Fraternity 1963)★★★★, *Glad I'm In The Band* (Elektra 1969)★★★, *Whatever's Right* (Elektra 1969)★★★, *The Hills Of Indiana* (Elektra 1971)★★★, *Home At Last* (Capitol 1977)★★, *Lonnie Mack With Pismo* (Capitol 1977)★★, *Strike Like Lightning* (Alligator 1985)★★★,

Second Sight (Alligator 1987)★★★, *Live! Attack Of The Killer V* (Alligator 1990)★★.

● COMPILATIONS: *For Collectors Only* (Elektra 1970)★★★, *The Memphis Sound Of Lonnie Mack* (1974)★★★, *Roadhouses And Dance Halls* (Epic 1988)★★★.

MACON, JOHN WESLEY 'SHORTSTUFF'

b. 1933, Crawford, Mississippi, USA, d. 28 December 1973, Macon, Mississippi, USA. In the mid-60s, Macon was brought briefly to public attention by his cousin Big Joe Williams. Although 30 years younger than Williams, he performed a remarkably archaic style of blues, featuring simple, insistently rhythmic guitar, often without chord changes, and mode packed vocals that often recalled the field holler. After the trip north with Williams that resulted in his too few recordings, Macon returned home to undeserved obscurity until his death.

● ALBUMS: *Mr. Shortstuff & Big Joe Williams* (1965)★★★, *Hell Bound & Heaven Sent* (1967)★★★.

MAGIC SAM

b. Samuel Gene Maghett, 14 February 1937, Grenada County, Mississippi, USA, d. 1 December 1969. Although Sam's immediate family were not musical, he received encouragement from his uncle, 'Shakey Jake' Harris, a popular blues singer on Chicago's west side. Maghett arrived in the city in 1950 and by the age of 20 had secured a recording contract with Cobra Records, an emergent independent label. His debut single, 'All Your Love', a compulsive, assured performance that highlighted Sam's crisp guitar figures, set the pattern for several subsequent releases, but progress faltered upon his induction into the army in 1959. Not a natural soldier, Sam deserted after a couple of weeks' service and was subsequently caught and sentenced to six months' imprisonment. He was given a dishonourable discharge on release, but the experience had undermined Sam's confidence and his immediate recordings lacked the purpose of their predecessors. However, his debut album, *West Side Soul*, encapsulated an era when Maghett not only re-established his reputation in Chicago clubs, but had become an attraction on the rock circuit with appearances at the Fillmore and Winterland venues in San Francisco. This vibrant record included 'Sweet Home Chicago', later revived by the Blues Brothers. A second collection, *Black Magic*, confirmed his new-found status but its release was overshadowed by Sam's premature death from a heart attack in December 1969. Only days before, Maghett had agreed to sign with the renowned Stax label. His passing robbed the blues genre of a potentially influential figure.

● ALBUMS: *West Side Soul* (Delmark 1968)★★★★, *Black Magic* (Delmark 1969)★★★★.

● COMPILATIONS: *Sweet Home Chicago* (1968)★★★, *Magic Sam (1937-1969)* (1969)★★★, *Magic Sam Live* rec. 1964 (Delmark 1981)★★★★, *West Side Soul* (Delmark 1984)★★★, with Earl Hooker *Calling All Blues* (Charly 1986)★★★, *The Magic Sam Legacy* (Delmark 1989)★★★, *Give Me Time* (Delmark 1992)★★★, *The Late Great Magic Sam* (Evidence 1995)★★★.

MAGIC SLIM

b. Morris Holt, 7 August 1937, Torrence, Grenada, Mississippi, USA. Blues guitarist and vocalist Magic Slim became interested in music during childhood. He moved first to nearby Grenada, Mississippi, and then to Chicago in 1955, where he worked as bassist for Magic Sam, who gave Holt his name. He obtained a false identity card so that he was able to play bass with Sam in the bars and clubs. After completing that stay, he switched back to guitar and performed with a Chicago band called Mr. Pitiful And The Teardrops. When that band broke up, he moved back to Mississippi before returning to Chicago once again in 1965, where he re-formed the Teardrops with his two brothers (Nick, the bassist, became a permanent member). The band recorded its first single for the local Wes label in 1966, and another for the equally small Mean Mistreater label in 1970. It was not until 1978 that Magic Slim And The Teardrops began recording in earnest, contributing four tracks to an Alligator Records anthology. That was followed by a live album for the small Candy Apple label as well as recordings made in France, which were released in the USA on Alligator as *Raw Magic* in 1982. That same year he recorded the highly praised *Grand Slam* for Rooster Blues

Records. A live album recorded in Austria, *Chicago Blues Session*, followed in 1987. *Gravel Road*, released on the small Blind Pig label in the USA, was issued in 1990. His sound is perhaps the tightest of any Chicago blues band working at the present time. This consistently satisfying blues musician has recorded singles for numerous labels but, recently, has recorded mainly for the Wolf Record label in Austria.

● ALBUMS: *Live 'N Blue* (Candy Apple 1980)★★★, *Raw Magic* (Alligator 1982)★★★, *Grand Slam* (Rooster 1982)★★★★, *Chicago Blues Session Volume Three* (1986)★★★, with the Teardrops *Son Of A Gun* (Rooster 1988)★★★, *Gravel Road* (Blind Pig 1990)★★★, with the Teardrops *Teardrop* (Wolf 1995)★★★, *Alone And Unplugged* (Wolf 1995)★★★, *Magic Blues* (Wolf 1995)★★★, with the Teardrops *The Zoo Bar Collection Vol 4: Spider In My Stew* (Wolf 1996)★★★, with Eddie Shaw and W. Williams *A Tribute To Magic Sam* (Evidence 1997)★★★, *Scufflin'* (Blind Pig 1997)★★★.

MAIDEN, SIDNEY

b. 1923, Mansfield, Louisiana, USA. A shadowy figure about whom little has been written, Maiden was evidently influenced by John Lee (Sonny Boy) Williamson when learning the harmonica. At some point during the forties, he made the journey west to work in the shipyards around Richmond, California. There he met K.C. Douglas and the pair began to work clubs in the area. In 1948 he and Douglas recorded for Bob Geddins' Down Town, with his 'Eclipse Of The Sun' becoming a notable performance for collectors. He next recorded in April 1952 for Imperial, an eight-track session with The Blues Blowers, possibly including Douglas and Otis Cherry on drums, from which just one single was released. Moving to Los Angeles the following year, he joined up with drummer B. Brown and guitarist Haskell Sadler to inaugurate the Flash label, each man recording one single. 'Hurry Hurry Baby' was an unsteady boogie piece distantly akin to Jimmy Reed's 'You Don't Have To Go'. In 1957, he recorded 'Hand Me Down Baby' with guitarist Slim Green for the Dig label. Four years later, he was recruited by Arhoolie boss Chris Strachwitz to participate in sessions with Douglas and Mercy Dee, during which he also recorded an album leased to

Bluesville. During the 60s, he formed his own group and worked the Fresno area, since when his whereabouts and fate are unknown.

● ALBUMS: *Jericho Alley Blues Flash* (1988)★★★.

MALACO RECORDS

An independent soul, blues and gospel label based in Jackson, Mississippi, USA, Malaco Records was founded in 1962 by Tommy Couch from Tucombia, Alabama, and by Gerald 'Wolf' Stephenson from Columbia, Mississippi, as a booking agency for local and touring acts visiting Mississippi. It started recording relatively obscure talent and leasing recordings to more established labels, as well as allowing other labels and artists to use their recording studios. Its first release was 'Misty Blue' by Dorothy Moore in 1975. Dave Clark joined the label in 1980, after which Malaco built a formidable roster of soul and blues artists, including Denise Latimore, Johnnie La Salle, Dorothy Taylor, Shirley Moore, Bobby Brown 'Blue Band', Little Milton, Artie 'Blues Boy' White and Poonanny. It has become one of the major labels catering for the audience interested in this form of music. Malaco's biggest hit came with Z.Z. Hill's 'Down Home Blues' in 1982 which sold more than 500,000 copies. Malaco bought the Muscle Shoals Studio in 1985 and so became associated with the Muscle Shoals Sound that spawned musicians such as Jimmy Johnson, David Hood, Roger Hawkins and Harrison Calloway. It has recently established a subsidiary, Waldoxy. The gospel division of Malaco started in 1976 and within a few years it had become the third largest gospel label in the USA. Its subsidiaries also include Savoy and Blackberry records. The Malaco gospel label features 165 artists and 500 releases in its catalogue headed by Jerry Mannery. Its artists include Mississippi Mass Choir, Rev. James Cleveland, Rev. James Moore, Williams Brothers, Dorothy Norwood, Albertina Walker, Florida Mass Choir, Rev. Clay Evans, Sensational Nightingales, Jackson Southernairs, and the Philadelphia Mass Choir.

MALONE, J.J.

b. 20 August 1935, Pete's Corner, Alabama, USA. Malone was playing guitar and harmonica before his 13th birthday, and he began performing at dances and parties when he was 17. In the mid-50s he spent a year in the Air Force and formed his first band the Rockers, later called Tops In Blues. Once out of the armed services in 1957, he formed the Rhythm Rockers in Spokane, Washington, and they worked all over the west coast. In 1966, he settled in Oakland, California, and recorded for the Galaxy label, enjoying a hit with 'Its A Shame' in 1972, and he subsequently had records issued by the Red Lightnin', Cherrie, Paris Album and Eli Mile High labels. Malone is a soulful vocalist, adept on both piano and guitar and equally convincing at straight blues, rocking R&B, or funk-influenced material.

● ALBUMS: with Troyce Key *I've Gotta New Car* (Red Lightnin' 1980)★★★, *Bottom Line Blues* (1991)★★★.

MARGOLIN, BOB

b. 9 May 1949, Brookline, Massachusetts, USA. Margolin's right of passage to the blues came through Chuck Berry, who sparked his interest in the guitar and introduced him to the music of the classic Muddy Waters band. After working in local blues groups, Margolin worked alongside Luther 'Georgia Boy' Johnson, who had been in Waters' band during the 60s. In 1973, he received the call to join Muddy Waters and played with the band until the early 80s, appearing on seven albums for Chess and Blue Sky and backing Waters on his appearance in *The Last Waltz*, the Band's farewell concert film. He had begun to front his own band by that time, and when Waters died in 1983 he took up a full-time solo career. Now calling himself Steady Rollin' Bob Margolin, his first two albums pay more than ample tribute to his former boss and to post-war Chicago blues, and feature men such as Jimmy Rogers, Pinetop Perkins and Willie Smith. *Down In The Alley*, with guest vocalists Nappy Brown and John Brim, broadened its perspective, but in his live performances Margolin remains a sincere recreator of his primary influences.

● ALBUMS: *The Old School* (Powerhouse 1989)★★, *Chicago Blues* (Powerhouse 1991)★★, *Down In The Alley* (Alligator 1994)★★★, *My Blues And My Guitar* (Alligator 1995)★★★★, *Up And In* (Alligator 1997)★★★.

MARKHAM, PIGMEAT

b. Dewey Markham, 1904, Durham, North Carolina, USA, d. 13 December 1981. Best known as a comedian, Markham began his long career in 1917, dancing in travelling shows. He travelled the southern 'race' circuit with blues singer Bessie Smith and later appeared on burlesque bills with Milton Berle, Red Buttons and Eddie Cantor. By the 50s, Markham was one of black America's most popular entertainers through his shows at the Regal in Chicago, the Howard in Washington and, in particular, New York's famed Apollo. Despite being black, he applied burnt cork make-up to his face, a device that caused many of his fans to believe he was actually white. He later made several successful appearances on the influential *Ed Sullivan* television show and was signed by Chess during the 60s. The Chicago-based label issued several in-concert albums and his 1968 novelty hit, 'Here Comes The Judge'. This tongue-in-cheek recording was inspired by the artist's catch-phrase, which was used extensively on the American television comedy series *Rowan And Martin's Laugh-In*. Although hampered by a competitive version by Shorty Long, Markham enjoyed a Top 20 hit in the USA and UK. Although this was a one-off achievement, Pigmeat Markham remained a well-known figure until his death in December 1981.

MARS, JOHNNY

b. 7 December 1942, Laurens, South Carolina, USA. During his youth, his family moved around the south-east, and Mars began playing harmonica before he was in his teens, influenced by older local players and his sister's collection of blues records. He moved to New Paltz, New York, in 1958 and joined a high school band. In 1961, he was in the Train Riders and a few years later in Burning Bush (as bass guitarist and occasional harmonica player). In 1967, Mars settled in San Francisco, where he led his own band, then moved to England in 1972, working as a singer and harmonica player. He has subsequently recorded for the Big Bear, JSP, Ace, Sundance, President, and Lamborghini labels, sometimes with guitarist Ray Fenwick. Mars is a fine vocalist and a modern, adventurous, blues harmonica player.
● ALBUMS: *Oakland Boogie* (Big Bear 1976)★★★, *King Of The Blues Harp* (JSP 1980)★★★, *Life On Mars* (Lamborghini 1984)★★★, *Stateside* (MM&K 1995)★★★.

MARTIN, CARL

b. 15 April 1906, Big Stone Gap, Virginia, USA, d. 1978. Like his father, the multi-instrumentalist Martin played in a string band, although he is also known for his work in the blues field. In his teens he met Howard Armstrong and, in 1930, the two musicians, along with Martin's brother Roland, recorded under the name of the Tennessee Chocolate Drops. It gives some indication of their sound that the record was also issued in the company's country music series (under a different credit). A couple of years later, Martin moved to Chicago and joined the blues circuit, recording under his own name and accompanying artists as diverse as Tampa Red and Freddie Spruell. In the 60s, Martin and Armstrong, with guitarist Ted Bogan, brought the old string band sound to a new audience.
● ALBUMS: including *Martin, Bogan And Armstrong* (1973)★★★, *Carolina Blues* (1992)★★★, with Johnny Young, John Lee Granderson, John Wrencher *The Chicago String Band* (Testament 1994)★★★.

MARTIN, FIDDLIN' JOE

b. 8 January 1900, Edwards, Mississippi, USA, d. 21 November 1975, Walls, Mississippi, USA. Martin learned guitar and trombone as a boy, later adding mandolin and bass fiddle (hence his nickname). He switched to washboard and drums in the 40s after damaging his hands in a fire. He worked with many Delta blues singers, including Charley Patton, Willie Newbern, Johnnie Temple, Memphis Minnie, Willie Brown and Son House, recording with the last two for the Library of Congress in 1940. Martin played drums for Howlin' Wolf until Wolf moved north, but his most enduring association was with Woodrow Adams; he appeared on all Adams' recordings, and they worked Mississippi juke joints together until Martin's death.
● COMPILATIONS: *Walking Blues* (1979)★★★.

MARTIN, SARA

b. 18 June 1884, Louisville, Kentucky, USA, d. 24 May 1955, Louisville, Kentucky, USA. A melodious but rather inflexible singer, Martin appears nevertheless to have been a popular success, recording over 120 tracks for OKeh between 1923 and 1928. These include the first recorded blues with guitar accompaniment (by Sylvester Weaver), and the first with a jug band (that of Clifford Hayes, billed as 'Sara Martin's Jug Band'). Although Chicago-based, Martin maintained close connections with Louisville, from where Hayes and Weaver also originated. She worked in vaudeville from 1915-31, there-after devoting herself to the church and to running a nursing home in Louisville from the 40s until her death.

● COMPILATIONS: *Clifford Hayes Vol. 2* (1987), with Sylvester Weaver *The Accompanist* (1988), *Sara Martin* (1990).

MAYALL, JOHN

b. 29 November 1933, Macclesfield, Cheshire, England. The career of England's premier white blues exponent and father of British blues has now spanned five decades and much of that time has been unintentionally spent acting as a musical catalyst. Mayall formed his first band in 1955 while at college, and as the Powerhouse Four the group worked mostly locally. Soon afterwards, Mayall enlisted for National Service. He then became a commercial artist and finally moved to London to form his Blues Syndicate, the forerunner to his legendary Bluesbreakers. Along with Alexis Korner, Cyril Davies and Graham Bond, Mayall pioneered British R&B. The astonishing number of musicians who have passed through his bands reads like a who's who. Even more remarkable is the number of names who have gone on to eclipse Mayall with either their own bands or as members of highly successful groups. Pete Frame, author of *Rock Family Trees*, has produced a detailed Mayall specimen, which is recommended. His roster of musicians included John McVie, Hughie Flint, Mick Fleetwood, Roger Dean, Davey Graham, Eric Clapton, Jack Bruce, Aynsley Dunbar, Peter Green, Dick Heckstall-Smith, Keef Hartley, Mick Taylor, Henry Lowther, Tony Reeves, Chris Mercer, Jon Hiseman, Steve Thompson, Colin Allen, Jon Mark, Johnny Almond, Harvey Mandel, Larry Taylor, and Don 'Sugercane' Harris.

His 1965 debut, *John Mayall Plays John Mayall*, was a live album which, although badly recorded, captured the tremendous atmosphere of an R&B club. His first single, 'Crawling Up A Hill', is contained on this set and it features Mayall's thin voice attempting to compete with an exciting, distorted harmonica and Hammond organ. *Bluesbreakers With Eric Clapton* is now a classic, and is highly recommended to all students of white blues. Clapton enabled his boss to reach a wider audience, as the crowds filled the clubs to catch a glimpse of the guitar hero. *A Hard Road* featured some clean and sparing guitar from Peter Green, while *Crusade* offers a brassier, fuller sound. *The Blues Alone* showed a more relaxed style, and allowed Mayall to demonstrate his musical dexterity. *Diary Of A Band Vol. 1* and *Vol. 2* were released during 1968 and capture their live sound from the previous year; both feature excellent drumming from Keef Hartley, in addition to Mick Taylor on guitar. *Bare Wires*, arguably Mayall's finest work, shows a strong jazz leaning, with the addition of Jon Hiseman on drums and the experienced brass section of Lowther, Mercer and Heckstall-Smith. The album was an introspective journey and contained Mayall's most competent lyrics, notably the beautifully hymn-like 'I Know Now'. The similarly packaged *Blues From Laurel Canyon* (Mayall often produced his own art-work) was another strong album which was recorded in Los Angeles, where Mayall lived. This marked the end of the Bluesbreakers name and, following the departure of Mick Taylor to the Rolling Stones, Mayall pioneered a drumless acoustic band featuring Jon Mark on acoustic guitar, Johnny Almond on tenor saxophone and flute, and Stephen Thompson on string bass. The subsequent live album, *The Turning Point*, proved to be his biggest-selling album and almost reached the UK Top 10. Notable tracks are the furious 'Room To Move', with Mayall's finest harmonica solo, and 'Thoughts About Roxanne' with some exquisite saxophone from Almond. The same line-up plus Larry Taylor produced *Empty Rooms*, which was more refined and less exciting. The band that recorded *USA Union* consisted of Americans Harvey Mandel, 'Sugercane' Harris and Larry Taylor. It gave Mayall yet another success, although he struggled lyrically. Following the double reunion *Back To The Roots*, Mayall's work lost its bite, and over the next few years his output was of poor quality. The halcyon days of name stars in his band had passed and Mayall suffered record company apathy. His last album to chart was the desultory *New Year, New Band, New Company* in 1975, featuring for the first time a female vocalist, Dee McKinnie, and future Fleetwood Mac guitarist Rick Vito. Following a run of albums that had little or no exposure, Mayall stopped recording, playing only infrequently close to his base in California. He toured Europe in 1988 to small but wildly enthusiastic audiences. That same year he signed to Island Records and released *Chicago Line*. Renewed activity and interest occurred in 1990 following the release of his finest album in many years, *A Sense Of Place*. Mayall was interviewed during a short visit to Britain in 1992 and sounded positive, happy and unaffected by years in the commercial doldrums. *Wake Up Call* changed everything once more. Released in 1993, the album is one of his finest ever, and became his biggest-selling disc for over two decades. The 90s have so far been kind to Mayall; the birth of another child in 1995, and a solid new release, *Spinning Coin*, the same year. The replacement for the departing Coco Montoya is yet another highly talented guitarist (a fortune with which Mayall is clearly blessed) - Buddy Whittington is the latest, continuing a tradition that started with Clapton and Green. As the sole survivor from the four 60s UK R&B/blues catalysts, Mayall has played the blues for so long without any deviation that it is hard to think of any other white artist to compare. He has outlived his contemporaries from the early days (Korner, Bond and Davis), and recent reappraisal has put him back at the top of a genre that he can justifiably claim to have furthered more than any other Englishman.

● ALBUMS: *John Mayall Plays John Mayall* (Decca 1965)★★★★, *Bluesbreakers With Eric Clapton* (Decca 1966)★★★★★, *A Hard Road* (Decca 1967)★★★★, *Crusade* (Decca 1967)★★★, *The Blues Alone* (Ace Of Clubs 1967)★★★★, *Diary Of A Band Vol. 1* (Decca 1968)★★★, *Diary Of A Band Vol. 2* (Decca 1968)★★★, *Bare Wires* (Decca 1968)★★★★★, *Blues From Laurel Canyon* (Decca 1968)★★★★, *Turning Point* (Polydor 1969)★★★★, *Empty Rooms* (Polydor 1970)★★★★, *USA Union* (Polydor 1970)★★★, *Back To The Roots* (Polydor 1971)★★★, *Beyond The Turning Point* (Polydor 1971)★★★, *Thru The Years* (Decca 1971)★★★, *Memories* (Polydor 1971)★★★, *Jazz Blues Fusion* (Polydor 1972)★★★, *Moving On* (Polydor 1973)★★, *Ten Years Are Gone* (Polydor 1973)★★, *Down The Line* (London US 1973)★★, *The Latest Edition* (Polydor 1975)★★, *New Year, New Band, New Company* (ABC 1975)★★, *Time Expired, Notice To Appear* (ABC 1975)★★, *John Mayall* (Polydor 1976)★★, *A Banquet Of Blues* (ABC 1976)★★, *Lots Of People* (ABC 1977)★★, *A Hard Core Package* (ABC 1977)★★, *Primal Solos* (London 1977)★★★, *Blues Roots* (Decca 1978)★★, *Last Of The British Blues* (MCA 1978)★★, *Bottom Line* (DJM 1979)★★, *No More Interviews* (DJM 1979)★★, *Roadshow Blues* (DJM 1980)★★, *Last Edition* (Polydor 1983)★★, *Behind The Iron Curtain* (PRT 1986)★★, *Chicago Line* (Island 1988)★★, *Archives To Eighties* (Polydor 1989)★★★, *A Sense Of Place* (Island 1990)★★★★, *Wake Up Call* (Silvertone 1993)★★★★, *The 1982 Reunion Concert* (Repertoire 1994)★★, *Spinning Coin* (Silvertone 1995)★★, *Blues For The Lost Days* (Silvertone 1997)★★★★.

● COMPILATIONS: *Looking Back* (Decca 1969)★★★★, *World Of John Mayall* (Decca 1970)★★★★, *World Of John Mayall Vol. 2* (Decca 1971)★★★★, *The John Mayall Story Vol. 1* (Decca 1983)★★★, *The John Mayall Story Vol. 2* (Decca 1983)★★★, *London Blues 1964-1969* (Polygram 1992)★★★★, *Room To Move 1969-1974* (Polygram 1992)★★★★.

● VIDEOS: *John Mayall's Bluesbreakers: Blues Alive* (PVE 1995).

● FURTHER READING: *John Mayall: Blues Breaker*, Richard Newman.

MAYES, PETE

b. 1938, Houston, Texas, USA. Mayes was given his first guitar by an uncle after experimenting with string and wire. According to his own story, by the age of 14 he had already worked with Lester Williams, although he did not meet T-Bone Walker, the doyen of all Texas guitarists, until 1954. During the next 20 years, he often worked with Walker and made the acquaintance of many other bluesmen who would later come to fame, most prominently Joe Hughes. Mayes' first recordings were made in support of Junior Parker and, in 1978, he entered a studio again while in Paris on tour with Bill Doggett. In the meantime, he had three singles issued under his own name on the Ovide label. In 1984, he appeared in the film *Battle Of The Guitars*, the soundtrack of which was issued on album. His own debut album was recorded in Houston during 1984-85 for the Dutch company Double Trouble.

● ALBUMS: *I'm Ready* (Double Trouble 1986)★★★.

MAYS, CURLEY

b. 26 November 1938, Maxie, Louisiana, USA. A nephew of Gatemouth Brown and a cousin of Phillip Walker, Mays was raised in Beaumont, Texas, where he taught himself to play guitar when he was in his early teens. He worked on the streets and in the clubs around Beaumont until his break came in 1959 when he began a three-year stint with the Etta James Revue. Over the years, he also worked with the Five Royales, James Brown and Tina Turner. After a period spent working in hotel bands in Las Vegas, Mays formed his own band in the mid-60s and returned to Texas, where he appeared regularly in clubs from San Antonio to Houston. Veteran Texas bluesman Zuzu Bollin remembered him as a consummate showman blessed with the ability to play the guitar with his bare feet!

MAYWEATHER, EARRING GEORGE

b. 27 September 1928, Montgomery, Alabama, USA, d. 12 February 1995, Boston, Massachusetts, USA. Like Little Sonny Willis, young George received his first harmonica as a Christmas present when he was six, along with an apple and an orange. Although he heard John Lee 'Sonny Boy' Williamson's records, he was largely a self-taught musician until he arrived in Chicago in September 1949. There he befriended Little Walter, who helped him with harp selection and how to find keys in different positions. In 1951 he linked up with his next-door neighbour, J.B. Hutto, and with Eddie 'Porkchop' Hines on percussion, the group played at weekends on Maxwell Street market. However, work was scarce, so Mayweather joined Bo Diddley and for a time alternated between both groups. He then formed a group with Eddie Taylor, refusing Walter's offer to replace him in Muddy Waters' band. He

recorded with J.B. Hutto on the Chance session that produced 'Combination Boogie' and 'Pet Cream Man', and with Eddie Taylor on 'You'll Always Have A Home' and 'Don't Knock At My Door'. In the late 80s Mayweather moved to Boston where he established himself at the 1369 Jazz Club. *Whup It!*, recorded with the nucleus of Luther Johnson's Magic Rockers, consists almost entirely of Chicago blues standards by Howlin' Wolf, Muddy Waters, Jimmy Rogers and Little Walter, and just one original, 'Cheatin' On Me'. It represents an accurate and fitting memorial. He died of liver cancer in 1995.

● ALBUMS: *Whup It! Whup It!* (Tone-Cool 1992)★★★.

MCCAIN, JERRY

b. 19 June 1930, Gadsden, Alabama, USA. From a musical family, McCain learned harmonica as a child, and played with local group the Upstarts in the early 50s. He first recorded in Jackson, Mississippi, for Lillian McMurry's Trumpet label in 1954 ('Wine-O-Wine', 'Stay Out Of Automobiles', 'East Of The Sun'). A competent singer and fiery harmonica player, McCain next signed to Excello where he recorded a number of songs from 1956-59. After other tracks for Cosimo Mattasa's Rex label and for OKeh, McCain left music in the early 60s. He returned to the studio in 1965, recording '728 Texas' for Stan Lewis's Jewel label. In the 70s and 80s he worked as a private investigator while continuing to make occasional records and perform at blues festivals. The Atlanta Rhythm Section provided the backing for McCain's cover versions of Slim Harpo's hits, while *Love Desperado* contained some of his best work including the anti-drug piece, 'Burn The Crackhouse Down'.

● ALBUMS: *Sings Slim Harpo* (1973)★★★, *Blues 'N' Stuff* (Ichiban 1989)★★★, *Love Desperado* (Ichiban 1992)★★★★.

● COMPILATIONS: *That's What They Want* (Excello 1995)★★★.

MCCALL, CASH

b. Maurice Dollison, 28 January 1941, New Madrid, Missouri, USA. McCall was a songwriter, session musician and vocalist in the R&B and gospel fields. Best known for his 1966 R&B hit 'When You Wake Up', McCall began singing with the gospel Belmont Singers at the age of 12.

Moving to Chicago in the 60s, he played guitar for the Five Blind Boys of Mississippi, Pilgrim Jubilee Singers and Gospel Songbirds. His secular recording career began in 1963 for Onederful Records. He next signed to the small Thomas label, for which he recorded his only R&B chart hit. Subsequent releases for labels such as Checker, Ronn, Paula, and Columbia Records did not fare as successfully. In 1967, McCall wrote 'That's How Love Is', a hit for Otis Clay, and also penned songs for artists including Etta James and Tyrone Davis.

● ALBUMS: *Omega Man* (1973)★★★, *No More Doggin'* (L&R 1983)★★★.

McCauley, Jackie

Having left the legendary Irish R&B band Them during the recording of their debut album, Irish singer-songwriter McCauley went on to form the Belfast Gypsies with Mike Scott and Ken McCleod. Their sole album was a bizarre psychedelic oddity produced by the legendary Kim Fowley. Following the break-up of the Gypsies, McCauley moved to Dublin and formed Cult with Paul Brady, but this potentially interesting band did not release any records. Relocating to London, McCauley formed Trader Horne with ex-Fairport Convention singer Judy Dyble, releasing the acclaimed acoustic album *Morning Way*. Dyble then left to get married, and after briefly continuing with Saffron Summerfield, McCauley dissolved the band. In 1971 he released his solo debut, with backing from British jazz musicians Henry Lowther and Roy Babbington, but a reluctance to undertake live promotional work doomed the album to failure. McCauley then played with the bands Wand and Mackerel Sky, and the Christian rocker Bryan Haworth, before becoming Lonnie Donegan's guitarist and MD. In addition to extensive session work, he co-wrote Status Quo's 1982 hit 'Dear John'. During the 80s he performed as part of Poor Mouth, with Clive Bunker (ex-Jethro Tull), Philip Rynhart (ex-Taj Mahal) and Tommy Lundy (ex-Katmandu), releasing the *Gael Force* album. In 1994 he recorded his second solo album, *Headspin*, which included a cover version of Bob Dylan's 'Just Like Tom Thumb Blues'.

● ALBUMS: *Jackie McCauley* (Dawn 1971)★★, *Headspin* (Breaking 1994)★★★.

McClennan, Tommy

b. 8 April 1908, Yazoo City, Mississippi, USA, d. c.1960, Chicago, Illinois, USA. McClennan's biography is fairly typical of many blues singers of his time and place. He was raised on the J.F. Sligh farm in rural Mississippi and learned to play the guitar at an early age. Working for tips on the streets and at private parties, he became acquainted with other performers such as Honeyboy Edwards and Robert Petway. Petway and McClennan shared a style so close that, later on record, it became difficult to tell them apart, a confusion they sometimes compounded by recording together. McClennan had a limited but effective percussive guitar style, often played by working on a single string. His voice was rough but full of humour, and also capable of expressing poignancy and subtle emotions. Around 1939, he moved to Chicago (as did Petway) and made a name for himself playing at clubs where expatriate southerners gathered to hear the 'down-home' sounds of their younger days. McClennan was an uncompromising character who, according to a famous story told by Big Bill Broonzy, found himself in trouble by refusing to adapt his songs to conform with northern sensibilities. His refusal to be impressed by the big city found expression in his often used, self-addressed, facetious aside: 'Play it right, you're in Chicago'. Although his 40-track career on record ended in 1942, he continued to play in the clubs into the post-war boom typified by Muddy Waters and Howlin' Wolf. One of his two known photographs shows him in the company of Sonny Boy Williamson (Rice Miller), Little Walter and Elmore James. His death is unconfirmed, but word of mouth suggests that he died, in poverty, around 1960.

● COMPILATIONS: *Travelin' Highway Man 1939-1942* (Travellin' Man 1990)★★★, *I'm A Guitar King* (1990)★★, *The Bluebird Recordings 1939-1942* (RCA 1997)★★★★.

McCoy, Charlie

b. 28 March 1941, Oak Hill, West Virginia, USA. When McCoy was eight years old, he ordered a harmonica for 50 cents and a box-top, but he was more interested in the guitar. He played in rock 'n' roll bands in Miami, where Mel Tillis heard him and suggested that he visit Nashville to work as a singer. Although his singing career did not take off, he played drums for US hitmakers Johnny Ferguson and Stonewall Jackson. In 1961, McCoy recorded as a singer for US Cadence Records and entered the charts with 'Cherry Berry Wine'. He then formed a rock 'n' roll band, Charlie McCoy And The Escorts, which played in Nashville clubs for several years. McCoy played harmonica on Ann-Margret's 'I Just Don't Understand' and Roy Orbison's 'Candy Man', and the success of the two records led to offers of session work. McCoy became the top harmonica player in Nashville, playing up to 400 sessions a year. He worked with Bob Dylan, playing harmonica on 'Obviously Five Believers', trumpet on 'Rainy Day Women, Nos. 12 And 35', and bass on several other tracks. The success of Dylan and other rock musicians in Nashville prompted McCoy and other sessionmen to form Area Code 615. McCoy had a US chart hit in 1972 with a revival of 'Today I Started Loving You Again', but, considering his love of blues harmonica player Little Walter, his records are comparatively unadventurous and middle-of-the-road. Nevertheless, he often reached the US country charts with instrumental interpretations of over-worn country songs. McCoy joined Barefoot Jerry and was featured on the group's 1974 US country hit, 'Boogie Woogie'. He now limits his session appearances, largely because he is musical director of the television series *Hee-Haw*. McCoy frequently visits the UK and has played the Wembley Country Festival with other Nashville musicians.

● ALBUMS: *The Real McCoy* (Monument 1969)★★, *Charlie McCoy* (Monument 1972)★★, *Good Time Charlie* (Monument 1973)★★, *The Fastest Harp In The South* (Monument 1973)★★, *Nashville Hit Man* (Monument 1974)★★, *Christmas Album* (Monument 1974)★★, *Harpin' The Blues* (Monument 1975)★★, *Charlie My Boy* (Monument 1975)★★, *Play It Again, Charlie* (Monument 1976)★★, *Country Cookin'* (Monument 1977)★★, *Appalachian Fever* (Monument 1979)★★, *One For The Road* (1986)★★, *Charlie McCoy's 13th* (1988)★★, *Beam Me Up, Charlie* (1989)★★.

● COMPILATIONS: *Greatest Hits: Charlie McCoy* (Monument 1990)★★★.

McCoy, Joe

b. 11 May 1905, Raymond, Mississippi, USA, d. 28 January 1950, Chicago, Illinois, USA. An early start learning guitar prepared McCoy for a diverse recording career. At first, he partnered his wife, Memphis Minnie, and they made many blues records together in the late 20s and early 30s. McCoy (under the pseudonym Kansas Joe) played beautifully tight, two-guitar arrangements, alternating between them on lead vocals, and occasionally playing as a duet. When the couple split up, McCoy was well-established in Chicago and continued to record as accompanist to other artists, under his own name or a variety of pseudonyms (including religious records as Hallelujah Joe). He adopted a more urbane blues style as time went on and, in 1936, he began a long and successful series of recordings with the jazz-orientated group the Harlem Hamfats.

● COMPILATIONS: *Kansas Joe McCoy 1934-1944* (Best Of Blues 1987)★★★, *Memphis Minnie And Kansas Joe, Complete Recordings* 4 vols. (1991)★★★.

McCoy, Robert

b. 31 March 1912, Aliceville, Alabama, USA, d. 1978, Birmingham, Alabama, USA. Jabbo Williams was a family friend, and Cow Cow Davenport and Pinetop Smith were visitors to the McCoy home. McCoy claimed to have played piano on record behind Jaybird Coleman in 1930 and, in 1937, he accompanied a number of Birmingham artists at a session organized by Lucille Bogan, of whose band he was a member. After war service, McCoy largely retired (although he claimed to have recorded with Jerry McCain). In the early 60s he was extensively recorded by a local enthusiast; attempts to commercialize his sound with R&B musicians and songs failed, but his exploration of the older repertoire resulted in some valuable performances. Heavily indebted to Race Records for material, and stylistically influenced by Leroy Carr, McCoy nevertheless preserved the rough, percussive piano styles of Birmingham. He had become a church deacon by 1975.

● COMPILATIONS: *Blues And Boogie Woogie Classics* (Oldie Blues 1979)★★★, *Birmingham Sessions* (1988)★★★, *Complete Recorded Works In Chronological Order 1937-40* (Wolf 1991)★★★.

McCRACKLIN, JIMMY

b. James David Walker, 13 August 1921, St. Louis, Missouri, USA. A former professional boxer, McCracklin began his singing career in 1945. Four years later he formed his own band, the Blues Blasters, in San Francisco, but almost a decade passed before the artist secured minor fame for his single 'The Walk'. This gritty slice of R&B crossed over into the pop charts via Dick Clark's *American Bandstand* show where it was favoured by the resident dancers. In the wake of this success, McCracklin continued to enjoy intermittent chart success. 'Just Got To Know' (1961) and 'Think' (1965) reached the US R&B Top 10, but later blues/soul-styled releases fared less well and confined this underrated performer's appeal to a more specialist audience.

● ALBUMS: *Jimmy McCracklin Sings* (Crown 1961)★★★, *I Just Gotta Know* (Imperial 1961)★★★, *Twist With Jimmy McCracklin* (Crown 1962)★★★, *Every Night, Every Day* (Imperial 1965)★★★, *Think* (Imperial 1965)★★★, *My Answer* (Imperial 1966)★★★, *New Soul Of Jimmy McCracklin* (Imperial 1966)★★★, *A Piece Of Jimmy McCracklin* (Minit 1968)★★★, *Let's Get Together* (Minit 1968)★★★, *Stinger Man* (Minit 1969)★★★, *High On The Blues* (Stax 1971)★★, *Yesterday Is Gone* (Stax 1972)★★, *Same Lovin'* (Evejim 1989)★★, *A Taste Of The Blues* (Bullseye Blues 1994)★★★.

● COMPILATIONS: *The Best Of* (Imperial 1966)★★★★, *Jimmy McCracklin And His Blues Blasters* (Pinnacle 1981)★★★, *Blues And Soul* (Stateside 1986)★★★, *I'm Gonna Have My Fun* (Route 66 1986)★★★, *You Deceived Me* (Crown Prince 1986)★★★, *Blast 'Em Dead* (Ace 1988)★★★, *Everybody Rock!* (Charly 1989)★★★, *The Mercury Recordings* rec. 1958-60 (Bear Family 1992)★★★★, *The Walk: Jimmy McCracklin At His Best* (Razor & Tie 1997)★★★★.

McCRAY, LARRY

b. 5 April 1960, Magnolia, Arkansas, USA. McCray was given his first guitar by his sister Clara when he was 12 years old. Soon afterwards the pair moved to Saginaw, Michigan, to be followed over several months by the rest of the family. He played saxophone in high school, but at home he persevered with the guitar, with his brothers Carl and Steve on bass and drums. Like most of his generation, he listened to funk music as well as blues and liked Eric Clapton and Jeff Beck as much as Albert King, B.B. King and Albert Collins. While working a day job, he gigged with Lazy Lester and jammed with his brothers. A basement tape from those sessions brought about his contract with PointBlank. *Ambition* was the label's initial release and to promote it, McCray toured Europe with Gary Moore. While that album was heavily rock-orientated, *Delta Hurricane*, recorded in Memphis with production assistance by Mike Vernon, reverted to a more traditional blues stance, with McCray paying homage to the guitarists that had influenced him.

● ALBUMS: *Ambition* (PointBlank 1990)★★★, *Delta Hurricane* (PointBlank 1993)★★★, *Meet Me At The Lake* (Atomic Theory 1997)★★★.

McDOWELL, MISSISSIPPI FRED

b. 12 January 1904, Rossville, Tennessee, USA, d. 3 July 1972, Memphis, Tennessee, USA. A self-taught guitarist, McDowell garnered his early reputation in the Memphis area with appearances at private parties, picnics and dances. He later moved to Como, Mississippi, and was employed as a farmer until discovered by field researcher Alan Lomax in 1959. Sessions for Atlantic and Prestige confirmed the artist as one of the last great exponents of the traditional bottleneck style and McDowell became a leading light of the 60s blues renaissance. He undertook several recordings with his wife, Annie Mae and, in 1964, appeared at the *Newport Folk Festival* alongside other major 'rediscoveries' Mississippi John Hurt and Sleepy John Estes; part of his performance was captured on the attendant film. The following year he completed the first of several releases for the California-based Arhoolie label. These recordings introduced a consistency to his work which deftly combined blues and spiritual material. McDowell also became a frequent visitor to Europe, touring with the American Folk Blues Festival and later appearing in concert in London, where he was supported by Jo Ann Kelly. He appeared on several Dutch television programmes and in two documentary films, *The Blues Maker* (1968) and *Fred McDowell* (1969). The artist was then signed to the Capitol label, for which he recorded *I Don't Play No Rock 'N' Roll*. Arguably one of the finest releases of its genre, its intimate charm belied the intensity the performer still brought to his work. Despite ailing health McDowell continued to follow a punishing schedule with performances at festivals throughout the USA, but by the end of 1971, such work had lessened dramatically. He died of cancer in July 1972. Although his compositions were not widely covered, the Rolling Stones recorded a haunting version of 'You've Got To Move' on *Sticky Fingers* (1971). McDowell's influence is also apparent in the approach of several artists, notably that of Bonnie Raitt.

● ALBUMS: *Mississippi Delta Blues* (Arhoolie 1964)★★★★, *My Home Is In The Delta* (Bounty 1964)★★★, *Amazing Grace* (1964)★★★, *Mississippi Delta Blues Volume 2* (Arhoolie 1966)★★★★, *I Do Not Play No Rock 'N' Roll* (Capitol 1969)★★★★, *Mississippi Fred McDowell And His Blues Boys* (Arhoolie 1969)★★★, *Mississippi Fred McDowell In London 1* (Sire/Transatlantic 1970)★★★, *Mississippi Fred McDowell In London 2* (Transatlantic 1970)★★★, *Going Down South* (Polydor 1970)★★★, *Mississippi Fred McDowell* (Arhoolie 1971)★★★, *The First Recordings* (Rounder 1997)★★★★.

● COMPILATIONS: *1904-1972* (Xtra 1974)★★★, with Johnny Woods *Eight Years Ramblin'* (Revival 1977)★★★, *Keep Your Lamp Trimmed And Burning* (Arhoolie 1981)★★★, with Jo Ann Kelly *Standing At The Burying Ground* (Red Lightnin' 1984)★★★★, with Phil Guy *A Double Dose Of Dynamite* (Red Lightnin' 1986)★★★, *Fred McDowell 1959* (KC 1988)★★★, *When I Lay My Burden Down* (Blue Moon 1988)★★★, *1962* (Heritage 1988)★★★, *The Train I Ride* (1993)★★★, *Good Morning Little Schoolgirl* (Arhoolie 1994)★★★, *Ain't Gonna Worry* (Drive Archives 1995)★★★, *Mississippi Fred McDowell* (Bullseye 1995)★★★, *I Do Not Play No Rock 'n' Roll* (Capitol 1996)★★★, *Standing At The Burying Ground* 1969 live recording (Sequel 1996)★★★★.

McGhee, Brownie

b. Walter Brown McGhee, 30 November 1915, Knoxville, Tennessee, USA, d. 16 February 1996, Oakland, California, USA. McGhee learned guitar from his father, and started a musical career early on, playing in church before he was 10 years old, and on the road with medicine shows, carnivals and minstrel troupes in his early teens. His travels took him into the Carolinas, and his time there proved very influential in moulding his musical style. His younger brother was Granville 'Sticks' McGhee, also a singer and blues guitarist. He met Sonny Terry in 1939, and their partnership was to become one of the most enduring in blues. The following year, he made his first records, reminiscent of those of Blind Boy Fuller; indeed some of them bore the credit 'Blind Boy Fuller No.2'. Also around this time, he settled in New York, where his career took a rather different turn, as he took up with a group of black musicians - including Terry, Lead Belly and Josh White - favoured by the then small white audience for the blues. They also became part of the Folkways Records cognoscenti with Pete Seeger and Woody Guthrie. For a number of years, he catered very successfully both for this audience, playing acoustic blues in an older style, and for an entirely separate one. Throughout the late 40s and early 50s, he recorded electric blues and R&B aimed at black record buyers. In retrospect, it is this second type that stands up best, and indeed, some of his records from this period rank among the finest blues to come out of New York in the post-war years. He was also very prolific as an accompanist, playing superb lead guitar on records by other artists such as Champion Jack Dupree, Big Chief Ellis and Alonzo Scales, as well as his brother 'Sticks'. His partnership with Terry became more firmly established during this period, and, as the original market for blues and R&B faded, they carved a very strong niche for themselves, playing concerts, festivals and clubs, and making albums aimed at the growing audience for folk music. For many years, they travelled the world and made record after record, establishing their names among the best-known of all blues artists. However, critical opinion seems agreed that their music suffered to a large degree during this period, as it was diluted for such a wide international audience and successive recordings trod similar ground. After making many of their successful recordings for Vanguard Records, the duo then appeared widely in musical theatre productions, including *Cat On A Hot Tin Roof*, *Finian's Rainbow* and

Simply Heaven. They also contributed to the soundtracks of films including *Book Of Numbers*, *Lead Belly*, *Buck And The Preacher* and *A Face In The Crowd*. McGhee's partnership with Terry eventually ended in the mid-70s after a build-up of internal tensions. While Terry continued to work until his death in 1986 McGhee retired to Oakland, California. He was in the process of making a live comeback when he was struck by cancer which resulted in his death early in 1996.
● COMPILATIONS: *Let's Have A Ball* (Magpie 1978)★★★, *Brownie McGhee 1944-1955* (Travellin' Man 1990)★★★, *The 1958 London Sessions* (1990)★★★, *Carolina Blues* (1992)★★★, *Rainy Day* (Charly 1996)★★★.
● VIDEOS: *Born With The Blues 1966-1992* (Vetsapol 1997).

McGHEE, GRANVILLE 'STICKS'

b. 23 March 1918, Knoxville, Tennessee, USA, d. 15 August 1961, New York City, New York, USA. Like his more famous brother, Brownie McGhee, Granville learned guitar from his father. After seeing action in World War II, he moved to New York in 1946. The following year, he made his first record, 'Drinkin' Wine Spo-Dee-O-Dee', under his own name. However, it was a later cut of the same song, made for Atlantic in 1949, with a group that included Big Chief Ellis as well as Brownie, that gave him his biggest success. Over the next few years, he made several more records, and appeared as accompanist on others, most notably to Sonny Terry. However, he did not manage to make the move to the new, young, white audience into which his brother tapped so successfully in the late 50s and onwards.
● COMPILATIONS: *Drinkin' Wine Spo-Dee-O-Dee* (1982)★★★, *Sticks McGhee & His Spo-Dee-O-Dee Buddies* (Ace 1995)★★★.

McKINLEY, L.C.

b. between 1914 and 1920, Winona, Mississippi, USA, d. 19 January 1970. McKinley is one of the mystery figures of the post-war Chicago blues. He had a much smoother style than most of his contemporaries and was obviously influenced by T-Bone Walker. McKinley was playing in Chicago in the 40s, and recorded as an accompanist to Tampa Red in 1953 and then, under his own name, for States the following year, for Vee

Jay Records in 1955, and finally for Bea And Baby in 1959, before he dropped out of the music scene. Willie Dixon reputedly attempted to revive his musical career in the 60s, but to little avail.
● COMPILATIONS: *Chicago Bluesmasters Volume Four* (1985), two Bea And Baby tracks *Meat And Gravy From Cadillac Baby Volume Three: Trying To Make A Living* (1978).

McMAHON, ANDREW 'BLUEBLOOD'

b. 12 April 1926, Delhi, Louisiana, USA, d. 17 February 1984, Monroe, Louisiana, USA. McMahon played blues and hillbilly music in Mississippi and worked with Bukka White in Memphis, Tennessee, before moving to Chicago in 1949. During the 50s he worked with J.B. Hutto and Jimmy Dawkins, and played bass guitar for Howlin' Wolf and recorded during 1960-73. McMahon recorded under his own name for the Bea And Baby label in 1971, and as 'Blueblood' for Dharma Records in 1973. After leaving Wolf, he led a band around the Chicago clubs and recorded a live album for MCM in 1976, following which he returned to his home state and left music. Although he was a limited singer, McMahon always seemed to attract all-star line-ups for his recording sessions.
● ALBUMS: *Blueblood* (Dharma 1973)★★★, *Go Get My Baby* (MCM 1976)★★.

McMULLEN, FRED

A shadowy figure, McMullen recorded for ARC in New York in January 1933, playing immaculate bottleneck blues guitar, whether behind his own vocals or with one or other of the Atlanta guitarists Curley Weaver and Buddy Moss. They also recorded as a trio, with Moss on harmonica. McMullen was listed only once in the 1932 Atlanta City Directory, and Moss maintained that he had returned to his home-town of Macon, Georgia, after the session. The intensity of 'De Kalb Chain Gang' ('They whipped me and they slashed me, forty-five all in my side') suggests that it was autobiographical, and that he may have been on his way home following release from prison when he encountered the Atlanta musicians.
● COMPILATIONS: *Georgia Blues Guitars* (1988), *Buddy Moss* (Travellin' Man 1990).

McSHANN, JAY 'HOOTIE'

b. 12 January 1909, Muskogee, Oklahoma, USA. After playing in many territory bands in the southwest and midwest, pianist McShann settled in Kansas City in the mid-30s, playing in Buster Smith's band, which also included Charlie Parker, in 1937. The following year, McShann formed his own unit which included Gene Ramey and Gus Johnson as well as Parker. By 1941, with the departure from Kansas City of Harlan Leonard, McShann's became the city's top band, Count Basie having moved on to greater things a few years earlier. The most popular member of the band was singer Walter Brown, who was featured on a handful of hit records, although McShann was himself an above-average blues shouter. In retrospect, the 1941 band is regarded as the most interesting of those McShann led because the saxophone section included the fast-developing and revolutionary talent of Parker. In fact, all McShann's bands had the virtues common to most Kansas City bands, those of lithely swinging, blues-based, exciting jazz. In 1944, McShann folded the band to enter the armed forces, reforming in 1945 on the west coast. Once again he showed himself to have a good ear for singers by hiring Jimmy Witherspoon. During the 50s and 60s, McShann was active, sometimes leading small groups, sometimes working as a solo act, but the jazz world was largely indifferent. By the 70s, however, he had become a popular figure on the international festival circuit, playing piano and singing the blues with flair and vigour. His recording career was also revitalized, and the 70s and 80s saw a steady stream of fine recordings, many of which were in the authentic tradition of the blues. The remarkable McShann was still performing at Blues Festivals in the mid-90s.

● ALBUMS: *McShann's Piano* (1966), *Confessin' The Blues* (1969), *Live In France* (1969), *Roll 'Em* (1969-77), *With Kansas City In Mind* (Swaggie 1969-72 recordings), *Jumpin' The Blues* (1970), *The Man From Muskogee* (1972), *Going To Kansas City* (1972), *Kansas City Memories* (Black And Blue 1973), *Vine Street Boogie* (1974), *Kansas City Joys* (1976), *Crazy Legs And Friday Strut* (1976), *Live At Istres* (1977), *Kansas City On My Mind* (1977), *After Hours* (1977), *The Last Of The Blue Devils* (1977), *Blues And Boogie* (1978), *Kansas City Hustle* (1978), *A Tribute To Fats Waller* (1978), *The Big Apple Bash* (1978), *Tuxedo Junction* (1980), with Al Casey *Best Of Friends* (JSP 1982), *Swingmatism* (Sackville 1982), *Just A Lucky So And So* (1983), *At The Cafe Des Copains* (Sackville 1983-89), *Magical Jazz* (1984), *Airmail Special* (Sackville 1985), *A Tribute To Charlie Parker* (S&R 1991), *Some Blues* (Chiaroscuro 1993), *The Missouri Connection* (Reervoir 1993), *Some Blues* (Chiaroscuro 1994).

● COMPILATIONS: *Hootie's KC Blues* (1941-42), *Blues From Kansas City* (MCA 1941-1943 recordings), *The Band That Jumps The Blues* (1947-49).

● VIDEOS: *Roosevelt Sykes/Jay 'Hootie' McShann* (1992).

McTELL, 'BLIND' WILLIE

b. 5 May 1901, McDuffie County, Georgia, USA, d. 19 August 1959, Almon, Georgia, USA. Blind from birth, McTell began to learn guitar in his early years, under the influence of relatives and neighbours in Statesboro, Georgia, where he grew up. In his late teens, he attended a school for the blind. By 1927, when he made his first records, he was already a very accomplished guitarist, with a warm and beautiful vocal style, and his early sessions produced classics such as 'Statesboro Blues', 'Mama Tain't Long Fo Day' and 'Georgia Rag'. During the 20s and 30s, he travelled extensively from a base in Atlanta, making his living from music and recording, on a regular basis, for three different record companies, sometimes using pseudonyms which included Blind Sammie and Georgia Bill. Most of his records feature a 12-string guitar, popular among Atlanta musicians, but particularly useful to McTell for the extra volume it provided for singing on the streets. Few, if any, blues guitarists could equal his mastery of the 12-string. He exploited its resonance and percussive qualities on his dance tunes, yet managed a remarkable delicacy of touch on his slow blues. In 1934, he married, and the following year recorded some duets with his wife, Kate, covering sacred as well as secular material. In 1940, John Lomax recorded McTell for the Folk Song Archive of the Library of Congress, and the sessions, which have since been issued in full, feature him discussing his life and his music, as well as playing a variety of material. These offer an invaluable insight into the art of one of the true blues greats. In the 40s, he moved more in the direction of religious music, and when he recorded again in 1949 and 1950, a significant proportion of his songs were spiritual. Only a few tracks from these sessions were issued at the time, but most have appeared in later years. They reveal McTell to be as commanding as ever, and indeed, some of the recordings rank among his best work. In 1956, he recorded for the last time at a session arranged by a record shop manager, unissued until the 60s. Soon after this, he turned away from the blues to perform exclusively religious material. His importance was eloquently summed up in Bob Dylan's strikingly moving elegy, 'Blind Willie McTell'.

● COMPILATIONS: *Blind Willie McTell 1940* (Melodeon 1956)★★★★, *Last Session* (Bluesville 1960)★★★★, *Complete Library Of Congress Recordings* (1969)★★★★, *Complete Recorded Works 1927-1935* (Yazoo 1990)★★★★, *Pig 'N Whistle Red* (1993)★★★, *The Definitive Blind Willie McTell* (Columbia Roots 'N' Blues 1994)★★★★, *Statesboro Blues: The Essential Recordings Of Blind Willie McTell* (Indigo 1995)★★★★.

MEMPHIS JUG BAND

Perhaps the most important and certainly the most popular of the jug bands, the Memphis Jug Band flourished on record between 1927 and 1934, during which time they recorded some 80 tracks - first for Victor then later for Columbia/OKeh Records. On one occasion they moonlighted for Champion using the name the Picaninny Jug Band. Their repertoire covered just about every kind of music that anybody could wish to hear, and their personal appearances ran from fish-frys to bar mitzvahs. Recording for their own people, they restricted themselves to ballads, dance tunes (including waltzes), novelty numbers and blues. Usually a knockabout conglomeration, they could produce blues of feeling and beauty when required. The group had an ever-changing personnel that revolved around the nucleus of Charlie Burse and Will Shade. Other members included some of the stars of the Memphis blues scene such as Memphis Minnie, Casey Bill Weldon, Jab Jones, Milton Robey, Vol Stevens, Ben Ramey, Charlie Polk and Hattie Hart. Basically a string band

augmented by such 'semi-legitimate' instruments as harmonicas, kazoos, washboards and jugs blown to supply a bass, the MJB had a constantly shifting line-up featuring violins, pianos, mandolins, banjos and guitars in different combinations. This, coupled with ever-changing vocalists, lent their music a freshness, vitality and variety that enables it to charm, entertain or move the listener as much today as it did during the great days of Beale Street. Although they ceased to record in 1934, this loose aggregation of musicians continued to work around Memphis until well into the 40s; some of its members were recorded again by researchers in the 60s.

● COMPILATIONS: *The Memphis Jug Band 1927-1934* (Matchbox 1986)★★★, *The Memphis Jug Band: Vol 1 (1927-28)* (Roots 1988)★★★, *Vol 2 (1928-29)* (Roots 1988)★★★, *Vol 3 (1930)* (Roots 1988)★★★, *Vol 5 (1932-34)* (Roots 1988)★★★, *The Memphis Jug Band - Alternate Takes And Associates* (1991)★★★.

MEMPHIS MINNIE

b. Lizzie Douglas, 3 June 1897, Algiers, Louisiana, USA, d. 6 August 1973, Memphis, Tennessee, USA. Raised in Walls, Mississippi, Memphis Minnie learned banjo and guitar as a child, and ran away from home at the age of 13 to play music in Memphis; she worked for a time with Ringling Brothers Circus. When in Mississippi, she played guitar with Willie Brown, and in the 20s made a common-law marriage with Casey Bill Weldon. However, she was with Kansas Joe McCoy by the time of their joint recording debut in 1929. Her guitar playing had a strong rhythm, coupled with the ragtime influence common among the Memphis musicians, and her singing was tough and swaggering. 'Bumble Bee' was a hit, and Joe and Minnie recorded extensively, both together and separately; their guitar duets were among the finest in blues. Apart from songs about sex and relationships, Minnie sang about her meningitis (calling it, with gallows humour, 'Memphis Minnie-jitis'), about her father's mule, 'Frankie Jean', and about the guitarist 'Mister Tango'. The McCoys moved to Chicago in the early 30s, but split up in 1935, apparently as a result of Joe's jealousy of his wife's success. By this time, Minnie's music was reflecting changing tastes, usually featuring a piano and string bass, and sometimes trumpet or clarinet and a drummer. She was a star of the Chicago club scene, as she continued to present herself on disc as the tough, independent woman she was in reality. In 1939, she began recording with her third husband, Little Son Joe (Ernest Lawlars) on second guitar. They were early users of amplification, and made swinging music, although it lacked the rich complexity of her early recordings. Her lyrics were of considerable originality, as on a graceful tribute to Ma Rainey, recorded in 1940, six months after Rainey's death. 'Me And My Chauffeur Blues', with its boogieing guitar, also became widely known. In the late 40s, Memphis Minnie ran a touring vaudeville company, and she continued to record after the war, playing tough electric guitar. Her efforts to keep up with trends were proving less successful, however, and in the mid-50s, she and Joe retired to Memphis. Joe was already unwell, and died in 1961, while Minnie was incapacitated from the late 50s, and lived out her life in nursing homes.

● COMPILATIONS: *Hoodoo Lady 1933-1937* (Columbia 1991)★★★, *Memphis Minnie & Kansas Joe Complete Recordings Vols. 1-4* (Paltram 1991)★★★, *Memphis Minnie 1935-41 Vols. 1-5* (1992)★★★, *The Postwar Recordings Vols. 1-3* (1992)★★★, *Blues Classics* (1993)★★★, *Bumble Bee* (Indigo 1994)★★★.

● FURTHER READING: *Woman With Guitar: Memphis Minnie's Blues*, Paul and Beth Garon.

MEMPHIS SLIM

b. Peter Chatman, 3 September 1915, Memphis, Tennessee, USA, d. 24 February 1988. One of the most popular performers of the blues idiom, Memphis Slim combined the barrelhouse/boogie-woogie piano style of the pre-war era with a sophisticated vocal intonation. A prolific songwriter, his best-known composition, 'Every Day I Have The Blues', has been the subject of numerous interpretations, and versions by Count Basie and B.B. King helped establish the song as a standard of its genre. Although Slim began his career in 1934, deputizing for pianist Roosevelt Sykes, his reputation did not prosper until he moved to Chicago at the end of the decade. He supported many of the city's best-known acts, including John Lee 'Sonny Boy' Williamson, and, in 1940, became the regular accompanist to Big Bill Broonzy. The artist made his recording debut for the Bluebird label that year but remained with Broonzy until 1944, when he formed his own group, the House Rockers. In 1949 Slim enjoyed an R&B number 1 with 'Messin' Around', the first in a series of successful singles, including 'Blue And Lonesome' (1949), 'Mother Earth' (1951) and 'The Come Back' (1953). He remained a popular attraction in Chicago throughout the ensuing decade, but following prestigious appearances at New York's Carnegie Hall and the Newport Jazz Festival, the artist moved to Paris, where he was domiciled from 1961 onwards. Slim toured and recorded extensively throughout Europe, an availability that, perversely, has irritated blues purists who view his work as overtly commercial. His later work certainly lacked the purpose of the young musician, but by the time of his death from kidney failure in 1988, Memphis Slim's role in the development of blues was assured.

● ALBUMS: *Memphis Slim At The Gate Of The Horn* (Vee Jay 1959)★★★, *'Frisco Bay Blues* (1960)★★★, *The Real Boogie Woogie* (Folkways 1960)★★★★, *Memphis Slim* (Chess 1961)★★★★, *Chicago Blues* (Folkways 1961)★★★★, *Broken Soul Blues* (United Artists 1961)★★★, *Just Blues* (Bluesville 1961)★★★★, *Tribute To Big Bill Broonzy* (Candid 1961)★★★★, *Memphis Slim USA* (Candid 1962)★★★, *No Strain* (Bluesville 1962)★★★★, *All Kinds Of Blues* (Bluesville 1963)★★★★, *Alone With My Friends* (Battle 1963)★★★, *Baby Please Come Home* (Battle 1963)★★★, *Steady Rolling Blues* (Bluesville 1964)★★★, *Memphis Slim* (King 1964)★★★, *If The Rabbit Had A Gun* (Disc 1964)★★★, *The Real Folk Blues* (Chess 1966)★★★, *Self Portrait* (Scepter 1966)★★★, *Legend Of The Blues* (1967)★★★, *Mother Earth* (1969)★★★, *Legend Of The Blues Vol 2* (Beacon 1969)★★, *Messin' Around With The Blues* (1970)★★★, *Born With The Blues* (1971)★★★, *Bad Luck And Trouble* (1971)★★, with Peter Green *Blue Memphis* (Barclay 1971)★★, *South Side Reunion* (1972)★★★, *Old Times New Times* (Barclay 1972)★★★, *Soul Blues* (Ember 1973)★★, *Rock Me Baby* (Polydor 1973)★★★, *Classic American Music* (Barclay 1973)★★★, *Memphis Slim At Lausanne* (1974)★★★, *Memphis Slim Live* (1974)★★, *Memphis Slim*

(1974)★★★, *With Matthew Murphy* (1974)★★, *Blues Man* (1975)★★, *Going Back To Tennessee* (Barclay 1975)★★★, *Rock Me Baby* (1975)★★★, *All Them Blues* (1976)★★★, *Chicago Boogie* (Black Lion 1976)★★, *Fattening Frogs For Snakes* (1976)★★, *Chicago Blues* (1978)★★★, *The Blues Every Which Way* (Verve 1981)★★★, *Blues And Women* (1981)★★★, *Boogie Woogie Piano* (Columbia 1984)★★★, with Matt Murphy *Together Again For The First Time (Live In 1985)* (Antone's 1988)★★★.
● COMPILATIONS: *Legacy Of The Blues Volume Seven* (Sonet 1973)★★★, *Memphis Slim (20 Blues Greats)* (Déjà Vu 1986)★★★, *The Memphis Slim Story* (Déjà Vu 1989)★★★.
● VIDEOS: *Memphis Slim And Paul Jones At Ronnie Scotts* (Hendring Video 1988), *Live In Nice* (MMG Video 1991).

MERCY DEE

b. Mercy Dee Walton, 30 August 1915, Waco, Texas, USA, d. 2 December 1962, Murphy's, California, USA. From an early interest in the piano, stimulated by the many local players of the instrument, Mercy Dee developed an instantly recognizable blues style, with much use of trills and crashing treble chords, complemented by lyrics packed with powerful, memorable imagery. After moving to California in his 20s, he recorded in a variety of settings between 1949 and 1955, even including rock 'n' roll and pop, but it was in slow blues, such as the much-covered 'One Room Country Shack', and humorous numbers such as 'GI Fever' that he could be heard at his best. An album for Arhoolie recorded in the early 60s is particularly worthwhile, as it concentrated on those aspects of his music.
● ALBUMS: *Mercy Dee* (Arhoolie 1961)★★★, *GI Fever* (1985)★★★, *Mercy's Troubles (Troublesome Mind)* (Arhoolie 1992)★★★.

MERRYWEATHER, NEIL

Having made his recording debut with John Richardson and Robin Boers, bassist Merryweather achieved minor fame in 1969 with the release of *Word Of Mouth*. Although ostensibly a vehicle for his group, the set is better recalled for stellar contributions made by Steve Miller, Barry Goldberg and Charlie Musselwhite, each of whom shared the artist's apprenticeship on Chicago's thriving R&B and blues circuit. The latter two musicians also contributed to *Ivar Avenue Reunion*, before Merryweather formed a more permanent group around Lynn Carey (vocals), J.J. Velker (keyboards), Ed Roth (keyboards) and Coffi Hall (drums). Having completed *Vacuum Cleaner*, credited to 'Merryweather And Carey', the bassist and vocalist formed Mama Lion in 1972. The itinerant Merryweather also established two subsequent units, the Spacerangers and Eyes, but despite such meritorious perseverance, has been unable to secure commercial success.
● ALBUMS: *Neil Merryweather, John Richardson and Robin Boers* (1968)★★★, *Word Of Mouth* (1969)★★★, *Ivar Avenue Reunion* (1970)★★★, *Vacuum Cleaner* (1971)★★★, *Spacerangers* (Mercury 1974)★★★, *Kryptonite* (1975)★★★, *Differences* (1978)★★★.

MESSER, MIKE

b. Michael Messer, England. Alongside Bob Greenwood and Steve Phillips, Messer is the pre-eminent UK guitarist to incorporate the national steel guitar, as well as slide guitar, into his acoustic performances. He won the UK Acoustic Blues Artist of the Year award in 1991, sponsored by *British Blues Connection*, though this was as much an endorsement for his capacity for incorporating styles other than the blues into his playing. Musical ideas borrowed from Hawaiian slide guitar, reggae, jazz and King Sunny Ade's worldbeat sound all illuminate his playing. The latter style was particularly evident on the breakthrough album that won him his initial strong notices, *Slidedance*: 'If you look at what was happening in this country, and also what I was doing at that time, there's a big world music influence, which we were all very into - I was also, at that time, producing tracks with S.E. Rogie and with Ted Hawkins . . . I intentionally made the album so it wasn't a blues album.' The same description could equally apply to his 1993 collaboration with Terry Clarke and the Lubbock, Texas, guitarist Jesse Taylor, entitled *Rhythm Oil*. The tour that accompanied its release saw Messer experiment further with elements including house and reggae, with a version of Fred McDowell's 'Worried Life' offering an outstanding distillation of blues and contemporary music. He also tours regularly with his own band, featuring Ed Genis (rhythm guitar) and Andy Crowdy (stand up bass). Further evidence of his standing came when Newtone Strings launched a new brand of strings with Messer's name attached, specifically aimed at the national guitar.

● ALBUMS: *Slidedance* (Minidoka 1990)★★★★, with Terry Clarke, Jesse Taylor *Rhythm Oil* (Minidoka 1993)★★★★, *Moonbeat* (Appaloosa 1995)★★★.

MIDDLETON, VELMA

b. 1 September 1917, St. Louis, Missouri, USA, d. 10 February 1961, Sierra Leone. During the 30s, Middleton sang and danced in various clubs, sometimes as a solo, often in the chorus line. In 1942, she was hired to sing with the Louis Armstrong big band and remained when the All Stars were formed, touring the world and, as a result, becoming far more famous than many other, better singers. She was still touring with Armstrong when she collapsed and died in Sierra Leone in February 1961. Although her singing style was uninspired, Middleton had an earthily infectious sense of humour that blended with Armstrong's, and their performances together were always hugely entertaining.

● ALBUMS: with Louis Armstrong *Satchmo At Symphony Hall* (1947), *Louis Armstrong Plays W. C. Handy* (1954).

MIGHTY SAM

b. Sam McClain, 15 April 1943, Monroe, Louisiana, USA. Introduced to gospel as a child, McClain served his apprenticeship in a schoolfriend's R&B group. In 1963, he joined the Dothan Sextet and remained their lead singer for the next three years. Disc jockey 'Papa' Don Schroeder 'discovered' Sam and signed him to the Bell subsidiary Amy, where the artist recorded eight singles. The Fame studio house band provided the perfect accompaniment to McClain's rasping interpretations, which evoked those of Bobby Bland and Little Milton. Ballads such as 'In The Same Old Way' (1967) and 'When She Touches Me' (1967), and the deep country soul of 'Sweet Dreams' (1968) stand among his finest offerings. In 1970, following Schroeder's retirement, Mighty Sam joined Atlantic Records

for two excellent singles before switching to Malaco Records for a solitary release. After years of neglect, during which the singer was almost penniless, he re-emerged on the Orleans label. A *Live In Japan* set followed. Sam's distinctive growl can also be heard on *Hubert Sumlin's Blues Party*, one of the finest blues collections of the late 80s. *Give it Up To Love* demonstrated his voice reaching a glorious peak and it is probably his finest album. A great pity however that this man has not received wider success and recognition.

● ALBUMS: *Mighty Soul* (Amy 1969)★★★, *Your Perfect Companion* (1986)★★★, *Live In Japan* (Orleans 1987)★★★, *Give It Up To Love* (Audioquest 1996)★★★★, *Sledgehammer Soul And Down Home Blues* (Audioquest 1997)★★★.

● COMPILATIONS: *Nothing But The Truth* (Charly 1988)★★★.

MILBURN, AMOS

b. 1 April 1927, Houston, Texas, USA, d. 3 January 1980, Houston, Texas, USA. After service in the US Navy in World War II, Milburn formed his own blues and R&B band in Houston in which he played piano and sang, and in 1946 he was offered a contract by the Aladdin label. Between November 1948 and February 1954 he and his band, the Aladdin Chicken Shackers, had an extraordinary run of 19 consecutive Top 10 hits on the *Billboard* R&B chart, including four number 1s ('Chicken Shack Boogie', 'A&M Blues', 'Roomin' House Boogie' and 'Bad, Bad Whiskey'). His romping boogies about drinking and partying were hugely popular and for two years (1949 and 1950) he was voted Top R&B Artist by *Billboard*. Following the break-up of his band in 1954 he never achieved the same level of success, and he left Aladdin in 1956. He then recorded as part of a duo with Charles Brown for the Ace label, and in 1963 recorded an album for Motown Records. In the 60s he played clubs around Cincinnati and Cleveland, Ohio, drawing heavily on his catalogue of old hits, but did not have any more hit records. In 1970 he suffered the first of a series of strokes. In 1972 he retired and returned to his home-town of Houston where he died eight years later.

● ALBUMS: with Wynonie Harris *Party After Hours* (Aladdin 1955)★★★, *Rockin' The Boogie* (Aladdin 1955)★★★, *Let's Have A Party* (Score

1957)★★★, *Amos Milburn Sings The Blues* (Score 1958)★★★, *The Blues Boss* (Motown 1963)★★★, *13 Unreleased Masters* (Pathé-Marconi 1984)★★.

● COMPILATIONS: *Million Sellers* (Imperial 1962)★★★★, *Greatest Hits* Aladdin recordings (Official Records 1988)★★★★, *Blues & Boogie: His Greatest Hits* (Sequel 1991)★★★★, *Down The Road Apiece: The Best Of ...* (EMI 1994)★★★★, *The Complete Aladdin Recordings Of Amos Milburn* (Mosaic 1995)★★★★.

MILES, LIZZIE

b. Elizabeth Mary Pajaud, née Landreaux, 31 March 1895, New Orleans, Louisiana, USA, d. 17 March 1963. As a teenager, Miles sang with outstanding early jazzmen from the age of 16, including Joe 'King' Oliver, Freddie Keppard, Kid Ory and Bunk Johnson. By the early 20s, she had established a reputation in Chicago and New York and toured Europe in the middle of the decade. The late 20s found her resident in New York, singing in clubs and recording with Oliver and Jelly Roll Morton. Illness kept her out of the business for a few years, but she returned to work in New York and Chicago in the late 30s and early 40s. Miles then abandoned her career, but she returned to nightclub work in the 50s, made records and re-established her reputation in the wake of the Dixieland revival, singing with Bob Scobey, Sharkey Bonano and George Lewis. She retired in 1959, turning her back on music to embrace religion. Often singing in Louisiana Creole patois, Miles had a robust and earthy style that made her a distinctive performer, despite a rather narrow vocal range. Miles was an all-round entertainer, applying her powerful delivery impartially to blues, pop songs, ballads, Creole songs, and improbable Creolized (French language) versions of 'Bill Bailey' and 'A Good Man Is Hard To Find'.

● ALBUMS: *George Lewis Live At The Hangover Club* (1953-54), *Moans And Blues* (1954), with Red Camp *Torch Lullabies My Mother Sang Me* (1955).

MILES, LUKE

b. 8 May 1925, Lachute, Louisiana, USA, d. 23 November 1987, Los Angeles, California, USA. Another of Lightnin' Hopkins' protégés, Miles had a fitful recording career. His initial inspiration was John Lee 'Sonny Boy' Williamson, although he was not interested in the harmonica. He moved to Houston, Texas, in 1952, where he met and became a friend of Lightnin' Hopkins. Since Miles was 6 feet 5 inches tall, Hopkins bestowed upon him the nickname 'Long Gone'. He accompanied Hopkins during a series of sessions recorded by Mack McCormick. Miles sang harmony and talked on two tracks, 'Baby' and 'Prison Blues Come Down On Me'; two further songs remained unissued. He moved to Los Angeles in May 1961, where he met arranger/producer Robert 'Bumps' Blackwell, who arranged a contract with Mercury, from which a single was released. Material from the two sessions, with contributions from Sonny Terry and Brownie McGhee, was released on Sundown 20 years later. In 1964, Miles recorded an album for World Pacific with guitarist Willie Chambers and bassist Leroy Vinnegar and the following year cut two singles with Bruce Bromberg for Two Kings. A final single, 'Hello Josephine', was recorded for Kent in 1969. Miles made occasional appearances in clubs and at festivals, but drug problems kept him inactive musically. After surviving a 1985 operation for lung cancer, he briefly returned to performing before succumbing to brain cancer in 1987. An album session with the William Clarke Band for Satch Records remains unissued.

● ALBUMS: *Long Gone* (World Pacific 1964)★★★, *Country Boy* (Sundown 1982)★★★, with Lightnin' Hopkins *Prison Blues* (Collectables 1989)★★★.

● COMPILATIONS: *Suckin' And Blowin'* (Sundown 1982)★★★, *Pick Your Choice* (Shoe 1984)★★★.

MILLER, BIG

b. Clarence Horatio Miller, 18 December 1922, Sioux City, Iowa, USA, d. 9 June 1992. Miller's parents were Henry Miller, a Sioux, who was a preacher, and Nora Epperson, a descendant of slaves. His first influence in music came from his father's church but he also heard the blues sung by men working on the railroad. In the 30s, while still a student, he formed a band, but with the outbreak of World War II he joined the army. After serving in the Pacific and in Europe, he

began entertaining his fellow soldiers. In 1949 he joined Lionel Hampton's band, then had a five-year spell with Jay McShann. Miller's abiding interest in the blues was such that writer-poet Langston Hughes wrote a series of songs especially for him and he also performed at Carnegie Hall in *The Evolution Of The Blues Song* with Jon Hendricks and Miriam Makeba, the recording of which won the Grand Prix Du Disque. In 1963 Miller moved to Australia, then to Hawaii. In 1967 he toured with The Evolution Of The Blues Song and was stranded in Vancouver. Taking a liking for Canada, he settled in Alberta and became a respected performer and educator, teaching at the Banff School of Fine Arts and the Grant MacEwan Community College. He was also the recipient of an Honorary Doctorate from Athabasca University. In 1981 the Canadian National Film Board produced a biographical film, *Big And The Blues*. Miller had a commanding style and his rich voice lent itself especially well to the material he favoured. His influences in the blues were Joe Turner, Jimmy Rushing, 'T-Bone' Walker and Jimmy Witherspoon, whom he followed into the McShann band. He also admired the ballad style of Billy Eckstine. Miller's chosen lifestyle was such that he has left behind considerably fewer recordings than his undoubted talent deserves.
● COMPILATIONS: *The Last Of The Blues Shouters* (Southland 1990)★★★.

MILLER, CLARENCE 'BIG'

b. 18 December 1922, Sioux City, Iowa, USA, d. 9 June 1992, Edmonton, Alberta, Canada. Miller moved to Kansas City as a child and his style is in that city's tradition of big-voiced, sophisticated blues singing. In the late 40s and early 50s, he worked with the big bands of Jay Mcshann, Lionel Hampton, Duke Ellington and others. Miller began recording in 1957 for the Savoy label, and continued to record and tour internationally, primarily in a jazz context, until his death in 1992.

MILLER, J.D. 'JAY'

b. 1923, El Campo, Texas, USA, d. 23 March 1996, Lafayette, Louisiana, USA. One of the best-known and most successful record producers from Louisiana, Miller started out as a musician, playing with country and Cajun bands around

Lake Charles from the late 30s. After a spell in the services, he started to make records aimed at a small localized market for Cajun music in south-west Louisiana; these, by obscure artists such as Lee Sonnier and Amidie Breaux, were among the first records in the idiom to appear after the war, and established his position as a pioneer in the field. He continued to record Cajun music and C&W on his Feature and Fais Do-Do labels, including the earliest records by Jimmie C. Newman and Doug Kershaw, and later on Kajun and Cajun Classics, which featured important figures such as Nathan Abshire and Aldus Roger. However, it was when he turned his attention in the mid-50s to black music that Miller began to develop his best-known and most enduring legacy. Between 1954, when he first recorded Lightnin' Slim and the early 60s, he established an extraordinary list of blues and country artists, including Slim, Lonesome Sundown, Slim Harpo, Lazy Lester, Lefty Frizzell, Kitty Wells, Silas Hogan and many others, whose work he leased to the Nashville label, Excello. He also continued to release records on labels of his own, Zynn and Rocko, including rockabilly and local pop by artists such as Johnny Jano and Warren Storm, and in the 70s, on Blues Unlimited. His list of artists is enormous, but just as important was the characteristic sound he achieved in his studio in Crowley, which has become inextricably linked with the indigenous sounds of Louisiana. He died following complications from quadruple bypass surgery in 1996.

MILTON, ROY

b. 31 July 1907, Wynnewood, Oklahoma, USA, d. 18 September 1983, Los Angeles, California, USA. Growing up on his Chickasaw grandmother's reservation, Milton encountered blues music when his family moved to Tulsa. In the late 20s, he was a vocalist with the Ernie Fields Orchestra; while on tour in Texas, he replaced the band's drummer after the latter was arrested. He left the Fields band in 1933 and moved to Los Angeles. After a couple of years he formed Roy Milton And The Solid Senders with pianist Camille Howard, Buddy Floyd and Hosea Sapp. In December 1945 they recorded 'R.M. Blues', which became an immediate hit, establishing both Roy Milton and Specialty

Records and spearheading the wave of small R&B units that tolled the death knell of the big bands. Milton remained with Specialty for 10 years, recording ballads and pop tunes alongside more popular blues and boogie material such as 'Milton's Boogie', 'Hop, Skip And Jump', 'T-Town Twist' and 'Best Wishes'. After Specialty, he recorded for Dootone, King and Warwick, but by the end of the 60s his style of music had become outdated. He appeared with Johnny Otis at the 1970 Monterey Jazz Festival and resumed a solo career that also brought him to Europe. He fell ill in 1982 and was confined to his home until his death a year later.

● COMPILATIONS: *Big Fat Mama* (Jukebox Lil 1985)★★★, *Grandfather Of R&B* (Jukebox Lil 1987)★★★, *Roy Milton And His Solid Senders* (Specialty/Ace 1990)★★★, *Groovy Blues* (Specialty/Ace 1992)★★★, *Blowin' With Roy* (Specialty/Ace 1994)★★★.

MINTER, IVERSON
(see Louisiana Red)

MISSISSIPPI SHEIKS
This musical combination flourished between 1930 and 1935, during which time they recorded more than 80 tracks for various 'race' labels. The Sheiks was a string band made up of members and friends of the Chatman family, and included Lonnie Chatman (guitar, violin), Sam Chatman (guitar), Walter Vincson (guitar, violin), Bo (Carter) Chatman (guitar), and Charlie McCoy (banjo, mandolin). Vocal chores were handled by all the members. Most of these individuals pursued independent musical careers either at this time or later. The instrumental abilities of all members were extremely high and their repertoire covered all ground between popular waltzes to salacious party songs, with a fair quantity of high-quality blues thrown in. Their work also appeared under the names the Mississippi Mud Steppers, the Down South Boys and the Carter Brothers.

● COMPILATIONS: *Sitting On Top Of The World* (1972)★★★, *Stop And Listen Blues* (1973)★★★, *The Mississippi Sheiks* (1984)★★★.

MITCHELL, WALTER
b. 19 March 1919, Pickens, Arkansas, USA, d. 10 January 1990, Toledo, Ohio, USA. Although his first years were spent in Louisiana, Mitchell was brought up in Detroit after his mother died around 1926, by which time he had already taken up the harmonica. Hoboing back in the south, he spent many years travelling through Louisiana, Arkansas and east Texas. Due to his diminutive stature, he earned the nickname Little Walter some time before Walter Jacobs appropriated it. Inducted into the army, he claims to have fought in both the European and Far Eastern campaigns before a foot injury brought about his discharge. Returning to Detroit, he put together the Boogie Blues Boys, which also featured his cousin, guitarist L.C. Green. In 1948, Mitchell recorded for Joe Von Battle with a band that included Robert Richard on second harmonica and pianist Boogie Woogie Red. Four years later, he accompanied Green on a session in Gallatin, Tennessee, for Dot Records. The pair remained together throughout the 50s, after which Mitchell worked with a number of Detroit musicians, including Baby Boy Warren, Eddie Burns and the Griswold brothers. Though sparsely recorded, Mitchell's records remain sought-after collector's items.

● COMPILATIONS: *Detroit Ghetto Blues* (Nighthawk 1974)★★★, *Harp Suckers!* (St. George 1983)★★★.

MODERN RECORDS
Modern Records was founded Los Angeles, California, USA, in 1945 by brothers Jules, Saul And Joe Bihari. They secured early success with Hadda Brooks and Johnny Moore's Three Blazers, and within two years Modern had become one of the leading post-war R&B labels on the west coast, alongside Imperial Records and Aladdin Records. The Biharis manufactured their own records, building one of the largest pressing plants in the region, and an agreement with a network of independent distributors ensured Modern's releases enjoyed national distribution. Etta James's 'Wallflower', Jessie Belvin's 'Goodnight My Love' and the Cadets' 'Stranded In The Jungle' were some of the label's most successful recordings during the early 50s. John Lee Hooker, Lightnin' Hopkins and Willie 'Smokey' Hogg also recorded for Modern but its eminent position was undermined by its practice of 'covering' other R&B hits. Nevertheless, the Biharis were able to

establish several subsidiary companies, including RPM, founded in 1950, and Flair, founded in 1953. B.B. King was RPM's most important signing as this seminal blues singer/guitarist remained with the company until the 60s. Rosco Gordon ('No More Doggin') and Johnny 'Guitar' Watson ('Those Lonely, Lonely Nights') were among the other artists enjoying success on this outlet. Meanwhile, Richard Berry's influential 'Louie Louie' was first issued on Flair. In 1951, armed with a Magnechord tape recorder, Joe Bihari undertook the first of several field trips to the Mississippi. He made several important juke-joint blues recordings on location, notably with impassioned slide guitarist Elmore James. In 1952 Modern set up the Meteor label in Memphis, Tennessee, USA. It was managed by a fourth Bihari brother, Lester. By the end of the 50s the Modern group was being eclipsed by newer independent companies, notably Atlantic Records. The Biharis opted to concentrate on a newly founded budget line, Crown Records, which, following bankruptcy, was succeeded by Kent Records. These outlets revived recordings from Modern's halcyon era, but the entire operation ceased trading during the 80s following the death of Jules Bihari. The best of its catalogue has since been repacked for compact disc by UK licensees Ace Records.

MOLTON, FLORA

b. 1908, Virginia, USA, d. 31 May 1990, Washington DC, USA. Molton began preaching at the age of 17, not taking up guitar until 1943, when she moved to Washington DC. Virtually blind, she supported herself by playing in the streets. From 1963, she made appearances on the folk circuit, and was later signed by a European record company when she visited Europe in 1987. Her slide guitar playing in 'Vastopol' (open D) was basic but intense, owing much to the blues whose verbal content she fiercely rejected. Her delivery was generally reminiscent of an unsophisticated Sister Rosetta Tharpe, particularly when Molton was assisted by more skilful musicians.
● ALBUMS: *Flora Molton And The Truth Band* (1982)★★★, *Gospel Songs* (1988)★★.

MONTGOMERY, LITTLE BROTHER

b. Eurreal Wilford Montgomery, 18 April 1906, Kentwood, Louisiana, USA, d. 6 September 1985, Chicago, Illinois, USA. Impressed by the piano players who visited his parents' house, including Jelly Roll Morton and Cooney Vaughan, Little Brother began playing at the age of five. At the age of 11 he ran away, and worked as a musician for the rest of his life. He played the southern jukes and lumber camps as a solo blues pianist, singing in his unmistakable voice, nasal and with a strong vibrato, yet somehow pleading and wistful. With Friday Ford and Dehlco Robert he developed 'The Forty-Fours' into one of the most complex themes in the repertoire, calling his own version 'Vicksburg Blues'. In the 20s Montgomery played jazz in New Orleans with Clarence Desdune and toured Mississippi with Danny Barker; he also worked briefly with Buddy Petit, and on the blues side toured with Big Joe Williams. In 1928 Brother headed for Chicago, playing blues at rent parties with Blind Blake among others, and recording as an accompanist in 1930, under his own name in 1931. During the 30s he returned south to Jackson, Mississippi, from where he travelled as leader of the jazz-playing Southland Troubadours until 1939. He continued to play blues, and on a single day in 1935 recorded no fewer than 18 titles and five accompaniments to other singers for Bluebird, including his instrumental masterpieces 'Shreveport Farewell' and 'Farish Street Jive', the latter a technically daunting blend of boogie and stride. In 1941 Montgomery settled in Chicago. He worked with Kid Ory at Carnegie Hall in 1949, and was for a long time a member of the Franz Jackson Band; he also continued to work solo (including a residency at an Irish tavern in the 60s) and to record, and was on the first releases by Otis Rush and Magic Sam. In 1960 he visited Europe for the first time, and began recording for a white audience. As well as promoting young protegées such as Elaine McFarland (later 'Spanky' of Spanky And Our Gang) and Jeanne Carroll, Montgomery recorded himself at home, issuing material on his FM label, named from the initials of himself and his devoted wife Janet Floberg, whom he married in 1967. With her encouragement and support, he was active in music until not long before his death. Montgomery was a consummate musician, with a huge repertoire and an excellent memory, but his recordings mostly reflect the preferences, first of record companies in the 30s, then of the white audience of the 60s and after; he was a giant of the blues, but it should not be forgotten that he was also a capable pop singer, and an excellent jazz pianist.

● ALBUMS: *Little Brother Montgomery* (Windin' Ball 1954)★★★, *Tasty Blues* (Bluesville 1961)★★★, *Blues* (1961)★★★, *Little Brother Montgomery* (1961)★★★, *Farro Street Jive* (1961)★★★, *Church Songs* (1962)★★★, *Chicago: The Living Legends* (1962)★★★, *After Hour Blues* (1969)★★★, *1930-1969* (1971)★★★, *Little Brother Montgomery* (1972)★★★, *Bajes Copper Station* (1973)★★★, *Crescent City Blues* (1977)★★★, *Tishomingo Blues* (1980)★★★, *Unissued Recordings Vol. 1* (Magpie 1987)★★★, *Unissued Recordings Vol. 2* (Magpie 1988)★★★, *Little Brother Montgomery At Home* (1990)★★★.

● FURTHER READING: *Deep South Piano, The Story Of Little Brother Montgomery*, Karl Gert Zur Heide.

MOONEY, JOHN

b. 3 April 1955, East Orange, New Jersey, USA. His combination of Delta guitar patterns with New Orleans second-line rhythms gives Mooney the edge when slide guitarists are under consideration. He was 12, living in Rochester and playing guitar to Ernest Tubb songs on the radio when he first heard Son House's records; four years later he was playing alongside House. After spending time in Arizona and California, he moved to New Orleans in 1976 and learned the city's complex rhythmic style from Professor Longhair and the Meters. He formed his band, Bluesiana, in 1983, which has since featured bass guitarists George Porter Jnr. and Glenn Fukunaga, and drummers John Vidacovich and Kerry Brown, among others. *Sideways In Paradise* consisted of a series of acoustic duets with Jimmy Thackery recorded in Jamaica in 1984. *Testimony* enlisted the help of Dr. John, Jon Cleary and Ivan Neville, while *Travelin' On* was recorded live in Germany at the 1991 Breminale Festival. His debut for the House Of Blues label in 1996 was particularly noteworthy.

● ALBUMS: *Comin' Your Way* (Blind Pig 1977)★★★, with Jimmy Thackery *Sideways In Paradise* (Seymour/Blind Pig 1985)★★★, *Late Night* (Bullseye Blues 1990)★★★, *Telephone King* (Powerhouse 1991)★★★, *Testimony* (Domino 1992)★★, *Travelin' On* (CrossCut 1993)★★★, *Against The Wall* (House Of Blues 1996★★★★.

MOORE, 'WHISTLIN'' ALEX

b. 11 November 1899, Dallas, Texas, USA, d. 20 January 1989, Dallas, Texas, USA. A lifelong individualist and eccentric, Moore came in later life to be regarded as a patriarch of Texas piano blues, although his inspirational technique wilfully avoided categorization. He grew up in Freedman's Town, a section of Dallas where the children of slaves congregated. He became interested in piano while working as a delivery boy for a grocery store, and developed his style in the dives and whorehouses of north Dallas. He recorded six titles for Columbia in December 1929, including the first version of 'Blue Bloomer Blues', and recorded this blues again for Decca in February 1937. With typical initiative, he financed his own session, recording eight titles, of which only two were later issued on album. A session for RPM in 1951 yielded five titles, two issued on a single, a third on album. In July 1960, Chris Strachwitz and Paul Oliver recorded him extensively for Arhoolie and Oliver's 'Conversations With The Blues' project. He was a member of the 1969 American Folk Blues Festival tour of Europe and recorded another album in Stuttgart, Germany. Throughout the 70s he was a feature of the festival circuit. In 1987 he received a Lifetime Achievement Award from the National Endowment for the Arts. Two years later, he recorded his last album for Rounder. Idiosyncratic to the end, he was returning home from a domino game at the Martin Luther King Centre in south Dallas and died on the bus, riding at the front, no doubt.

● ALBUMS: *Alex Moore* (Arhoolie 1960)★★★, *In Europe* (Arhoolie 1981)★★★, *Wiggle Tail* (Rounder 1988)★★★, *From North Dallas To The East Side* (Arhoolie 1994)★★★.

● COMPILATIONS: *Complete Recorded Works 1929-37* (Document 1994)★★★.

MOORE, ARNOLD DWIGHT 'GATEMOUTH'

b. 8 November 1913, Topeka, Kansas, USA. At the age of 16, Moore went to Kansas City, where he sang with the bands of Bennie Moten, Tommy Douglas and Walter Barnes. Moore was one of the few survivors of the infamous 'Natchez Rhythm Club Fire' tragedy that wiped out most of Barnes' orchestra. His first recordings were made for the small K.C. labels Chez Paree and Damon, and they caused enough of a stir to interest National Records. They brought Moore to Chicago and New York for four sessions in 1945-46 and were successful with Moore's 'I Ain't Mad At You, Pretty Baby', 'Did You Ever Love A Woman?' and 'Christmas Blues'. In 1947, Moore joined King Records and re-recorded his National hits along with some new material. By the end of that year he had introduced Wynonie Harris to King and had abandoned blues for a new career as the Reverend Moore. He became a gospel disc jockey and recorded gospel music in the early 50s for Chess/Aristocrat, Artists and Coral, and albums for Audio Fidelity (1960) and Bluesway (1973). However, Johnny Otis did manage to persuade Moore to recreate some of his blues for a Blues Spectrum album in 1977.

● ALBUMS: *Gatemouth Moore* (1950)★★★, *Rev. Dwight 'Gatemouth' Moore & his Gospel Singers* (Audio Fidelity 1960)★★★, *After Twenty-One Years* (Bluesway 1973)★★★, *Great R&B Oldies* (Blues Spectrum 1977)★★★.

MOORE, GARY

b. 4 April 1952, Belfast, Northern Ireland. This talented, blues-influenced singer and guitarist formed his first major band, Skid Row, when he was 16 years old - initially with Phil Lynott, who left after a few months to form Thin Lizzy. Skid Row continued as a three-piece, with Brendan Shields (bass) and Noel Bridgeman (drums). They relocated from Belfast to London in 1970 and signed a contract with CBS Records. After just two albums they disbanded, leaving Moore to form the Gary Moore Band. Their debut, *Grinding Stone*, appeared in 1973, but progress was halted the following year while Moore assisted Thin Lizzy after guitarist Eric Bell had left the band. This liaison lasted just four months before Moore was replaced by Scott Gorham and Brian Robertson. Moore subsequently moved into session work before joining Colosseum II in 1976. He made three albums with them, and also rejoined Thin Lizzy for a 10-week American tour in 1977 after guitarist Brian Robertson suffered a severed artery in his hand. Moore finally became a full-time member of Thin Lizzy, but he subsequently left midway through a US tour and formed a new band called G-Force, though this outfit soon floundered. Moore then resumed his solo career, cutting a series of commercially ignored albums until he scored hit singles in 1985 with 'Empty Rooms' and another collaboration with Phil Lynott, 'Out In The Fields'. His 1989 album *After The War* revealed a strong celtic influence, and also featured guest artists such as Ozzy Osbourne and Andrew Eldritch (Sisters Of Mercy). However, his breakthrough to mainstream commercial acceptance came in 1990 with the superb, confident guitarwork and vocals of *Still Got The Blues*. Mixing blues standards and originals, Moore was acclaimed as one of the UK's foremost artists, a stature which the subsequent release of *After Hours* - featuring cameo appearances from B.B. King and Albert Collins - only confirmed. In 1994 with Jack Bruce and Ginger Baker, in BBM, he released an accomplished and satisfying album, but personality conflicts made the future impossible. In 1995 he released the excellent *Blues For Greeny*, an album of songs written by Peter Green and played on Green's Gibson Les Paul guitar which had been a gift from Green to Moore many years earlier. *Dark Days In Paradise* had little blues on offer; instead Moore attempted rock, AOR and pop. Just as his followers were becoming used to his style of the most recent years, he switched, and the album's tepid success no doubt reflected their rejection of his new approach.

● ALBUMS: with Skid Row *Skid Row* (Columbia 1970)★★★, with Skid Row *34 Hours* (Columbia 1971)★★★, as Gary Moore Band *Grinding Stone* (Columbia 1973)★★, with Skid Row *Alive And Kicking* (Columbia 1978)★★, *Back On The Streets* (MCA 1979)★★★★, with Greg Lake Band *Greg Lake* (Chrysalis 1981)★★, *Corridors Of Power* (Virgin 1982)★★★, with Greg Lake Band *Manoeuvers* (Chrysalis 1983)★★, *Rockin' Every Night - Live In Japan* (Virgin 1983)★★★, *Live* (Jet 1984)★★★, *Run For Cover* (Ten

1985)★★★, *Wild Frontier* (Ten Ten 1988)★★★, *After The War* (Virgin 1989)★★★, *Still Got The Blues* (Virgin 1990)★★★★, *After Hours* (Virgin 1992)★★★, *Blues Alive* (Virgin 1993)★★★★, *Blues For Greeny* (Virgin 1995)★★★★, *Dark Days In Paradise* (Virgin 1997)★★.
● COMPILATIONS: *Anthology* (Raw Power 1986)★★★, *The Collection* double album (Castle 1990)★★★, *CD Box Set* (Virgin 1991)★★★, *Ballads + Blues 1982 - 1994* (Virgin 1994)★★★★.
● VIDEOS: *Emerald Aisles* (Virgin Vision 1986), *Video Singles: Gary Moore* (Virgin Vision 1988), *Gary Moore: Live In Sweden* (Virgin Vision 1988), *Evening Of The Blues* (Virgin Vision 1991), *Live Blues* (1993), *Ballads And Blues 1982-1994* (1995), *Blues For Greeny Live* (Warner Musicvision 1996).

MOORE, JAMES

(see Slim Harpo)

MOORE, JOHNNY B.

b. 24 January 1950, Clarksdale, Mississippi, USA. Moore was first taught to play the guitar at the age of seven by his Baptist minister father. Four years later he was already playing in early evening sessions at local juke-joints. In 1964 he moved north to Chicago to join his father who had moved there six years earlier. He learned to read music at school and after leaving to work in a lamp factory, played evenings and weekends around the city. In 1975, Koko Taylor asked him to join her band, the Blues Machine. Two years later, he took part in the New Generation of Chicago Blues, a Berlin concert hosted by Willie Dixon. He subsequently toured Europe three times with Taylor and twice with Dixon, working with the latter until his death in 1992. His records show him to be a worthy performer, adept with a bottleneck and an adequate soloist in the post-B.B. King manner, who nevertheless conducts himself with undue restraint.
● ALBUMS: *Hard Times* (B.L.U.E.S. R&B 1987)★★★, *Lonesome Blues* (Wolf 1992)★★★, *911 Blues* (Wolf 1994)★★, *Live At Blue Chicago* (Delmark 1996)★★, *Troubled World* (Delmark 1997)★★.
● COMPILATIONS: *From West Helena To Chicago* (Wolf 1988)★★★.

MOORE, MONETTE

b. 19 May 1902, Gainesville, Texas, USA, d. 21 October 1962, Garden Grove, California, USA. Moore was also known as Ethel Mayes, Nettie Potter, Susie Smith and Grace White. Interested in music from an early age, Moore taught herself piano in her early teens and became a fan of Mamie Smith. Among the first wave of classic blues singers, from 1923 onwards she was recording in New York City for Paramount, Vocalion, Columbia and RCA Victor. She also worked with the orchestras of Charlie 'Fess' Johnson, Walter Page and Lucky Millinder in myriad shows and revues. She was briefly married to singer/pianist/songwriter John Erby in the late 20s and in 1933 she opened her own nightclub, Monette's Place, but continued performing and recording. In the early 40s, she moved out to the west coast to record for various specialist labels with Teddy Bunn, Hilton 'Nappy' Lamare and George Lewis, then started a new career in television and films. In 1960 she secured a singing job on the Mark Twain Riverboat at Disneyland theme park in Anaheim, California, where she suffered a critical emphysema attack and died before reaching hospital. Although she did not enjoy an extensive recording career, Moore was a very effective jazz and blues stylist who easily coped with the various styles she encountered during her 40-year career.

MOORE, WILLIE C.

b. 22 April 1913, Kinston, North Carolina, USA, d. 2 May 1971, Albany, New York, USA. Moore began playing guitar about 1930, and in 1934 won a talent contest organized by J.B. Long. It has been speculated that Moore recorded as Boll Weenie Bill for ARC, but this now seems unlikely. When located in 1970, he still possessed a wide repertoire, but died after preliminary recordings had been made.
● COMPILATIONS: *Another Man Done Gone* (1978)★★★.

MORGAN, MIKE

b. 30 November 1959, Dallas, Texas, USA. Morgan was a motorcycle racer before applying himself seriously to playing blues guitar. He wears an eyepatch over his right eye as the result of a racing crash, making his appearance rather piratical. His band, the Crawl, was formed in the mid-80s with harmonica player Lee McBee. The band's repertoire placed them alongside Anson Funderburgh And The Rockets and Ronnie Earl's Broadcasters and successive albums have not seen any concerted stylistic change. In line with the James Harman and William Clarke bands, they have experimented with an acoustic approach without much success. Morgan stopped touring with the band in the early 90s. His 1994 collaboration with Jim Suhler of Monkey Beat pitted his more traditional stance against Suhler's post-SRV thrash without complete success.

● ALBUMS: *Raw & Ready* (Black Top 1990)★★★, *Mighty Fine Dancin'* (Black Top 1991)★★, *Full Moon Over Dallas* (Black Top 1992)★★★, *Ain't Worried No More* (Black Top 1994)★★★, with Jim Suhler *Let The Dogs Run* (Black Top 1994)★★, *Looky Here* (Black Top 1996)★★★★.

● COMPILATIONS: *Lowdown And Evil* (Black Top 1996)★★★.

MORSE, ELLA MAE

b. 12 September, 1924, Mansfield, Texas, USA. A singer with an appealing jazz/blues style, Morse first sang with a band organized by her pianist mother and her father who was a drummer. At the age of 12 she was heard at a Houston Jam session by Jimmy Dorsey, who hired her as replacement for June Richmond. Her stay with Dorsey was a brief one, and she returned to Texas and sang with local bands. Subsequently she was heard singing in a San Diego club by Freddie Slack, who had been the pianist when she was with the Dorsey band. He signed her as the vocalist on his first Capitol recording session in 1942, which resulted in 'Cow Cow Boogie'. The record became a million-seller, and Morse had further hits in the 40s with 'Mr. Five By Five', 'Shoo Shoo Baby', 'Tess's Torch Song (If I Had A Man)', 'Milkman, Keep Those Bottles Quiet', 'The Patty Cake Man', 'Captain Kidd', 'Buzz Me', and 'House Of Blue Lights' (1946). She also appeared in a few minor films such as *Reveille With Beverly*, *Ghost Catchers*, *South Of Dixie*, and *How Do You Do It?* Morse retired for a time, but made a spectacular comeback in 1952 with another enormous hit, 'Blacksmith Blues', on which she was accompanied by Nelson

Riddle and his orchestra. She continued to perform over the years, and was spotted in 1987 at Michael's Pub in New York, sharing the billing with another 40s survivor, Nellie Lutcher.

● COMPILATIONS: *The Morse Code* (1957)★★★, *Sensational* 1951-57 recordings (Capitol 1986)★★★, *Barrel House, Boogie And The Blues* (Pathé Marconi 1984)★★★, *The Hits Of* (Pathé Marconi 1984)★★★, *Capitol Collectors* (Capitol 1992)★★★.

MOSS, EUGENE 'BUDDY'

b. 26 January 1914, Hancock County, Georgia, USA, d. October 1984, Atlanta, Georgia, USA. It was as a harmonica player that Moss first appeared on record, in 1930, as one of the Georgia Cotton Pickers with Barbecue Bob and Curley Weaver. Although he apparently learned guitar from Bob, his playing was distinctly in the ragtime-inflected Eastern blues tradition of artists such as Blind Blake. Moss had his own style, however, a carefully crafted blues sound that later established his name as one of the most popular Atlanta-based singers of the 30s. He recorded prolifically between 1933 and 1935, sometimes backed by Weaver and occasionally Blind Willie McTell. On later dates he teamed up with Josh White and the two musicians accompanied each other on their respective recordings. Altogether, Moss made over 60 tracks in these three years, but there followed a long hiatus when he was sentenced to a prison term soon after the 1935 session. He was released in 1941 and recorded again, this time with Sonny Terry and Brownie McGhee. The outbreak of war cut short his prospects and he earned his living working outside music until he was rediscovered in the 60s, although this led to only a few new recordings and live appearances.

● COMPILATIONS: *Georgia Blues 1930-1935* (Travellin' Man 1983)★★★, *Red River Blues* (Travellin' Man 1988)★★★, *Buddy Moss 1930-1941* (Travellin' Man 1990)★★★.

MR. BO

b. Louis Collins, 7 April 1932, Indianola, Mississippi, USA, d. 19 September 1995. Collins moved to Chicago in 1946 and by the early 50s had settled in Detroit. His musical apprenticeship began in the time-honoured tradition with appearances at blues house parties, where he was often to be found in the company of Washboard Willie, John Lee Hooker, Vernon Harrison 'Boogie Woogie Red', Little Sonny and others. By the late 50s he had adopted the sobriquet Mr. Bo, at which time he released his first recordings. He issued singles on labels including Northern, Big D, Reel and Diamond Jim. His fluent guitar playing and steady, understated vocals impressed many, particularly on the original version of 'If Trouble Was Money', a song he co-wrote with his brother. Both Charlie Musselwhite and Albert Collins have subsequently covered the song. Though still playing regularly on the club scene, his profile diminished in the 70s and 80s. In 1993 a resurgence of interest in his original singles led to an appearance at the Blues Estafette in Holland, his first European appearance. He returned to the studio in 1995 for the first time in 20 years, as well as appearing in a local television advertisement. He died from pneumonia later that year before being able to reap the rewards of the new interest surrounding him.

MUDDY WATERS

b. McKinley Morganfield, 4 April 1915, Rolling Fork, Mississippi, USA, d. 30 April 1983, Chicago, Illinois, USA. One of the dominant figures of post-war blues, Muddy Waters was raised in the rural Mississippi town of Clarksdale, in whose juke-joints he came into contact with the legendary Son House. Having already mastered the rudiments of the guitar, Waters began performing and this early, country blues period was later documented by Alan Lomax. Touring the south making field recordings for the Library Of Congress, this renowned archivist taped Waters on three occasions between 1941-42. The following year Waters moved to Chicago where he befriended Big Bill Broonzy, whose influence and help proved vital to the younger performer. Waters soon began using amplified, electric instruments and by 1948 had signed a recording contract with the newly founded Aristocrat label, the name of which was later changed to Chess Records. Waters' second release, 'I Feel Like Goin' Home'/'I Can't Be Satisfied', was a minor R&B hit and its understated accompaniment from bassist Big Crawford set a pattern for several further singles, including 'Rollin' And Tumblin'', 'Rollin' Stone' and 'Walking Blues'. By 1951 the guitarist was using a full backing band and among the musicians who passed through its ranks were Otis Spann (piano), Jimmy Rogers (guitar), Little Walter, Walter 'Shakey' Horton and James Cotton (all harmonica). This pool of talent ensured that the Muddy Waters Band was Chicago's most influential unit and a score of seminal recordings, including 'Hoochie Coochie Man', 'I've Got My Mojo Working', 'Mannish Boy', 'You Need Love' and 'I'm Ready', established the leader's abrasive guitar style and impassioned singing. Waters' international stature was secured in 1958 when he toured Britain at the behest of jazz trombonist Chris Barber. Although criticized in some quarters for his use of amplification, Waters' effect on a new generation of white enthusiasts was incalculable. Cyril Davies and Alexis Korner abandoned skiffle in his wake and their subsequent combo, Blues Incorporated, was the catalyst for the Rolling Stones, the Graham Bond Organisation, Long John Baldry and indeed British R&B itself. Paradoxically, while such groups enjoyed commercial success, Waters struggled against indifference. Deemed 'old-fashioned' in the wake of soul music, he was obliged to update his sound and repertoire, resulting in such misjudged releases as *Electric Mud*, which featured a reading of the Rolling Stones' 'Let's Spend The Night Together', the ultimate artistic *volte-face*. The artist did complete a more sympathetic project in *Fathers And Sons* on which he was joined by Paul Butterfield and Mike Bloomfield, but his work during the 60s was generally disappointing. *The London Sessions* kept Waters in the public eye, as did his appearance in the Band's *The Last Waltz*, but it was an inspired series of collaborations with guitarist Johnny Winter that signalled a dramatic rebirth. This pupil produced and arranged four excellent albums that recaptured the fire and purpose of Muddy's early releases and bestowed a sense of dignity to this musical giant's legacy. Waters died of heart failure in 1983, his status as one of the world's most influential musicians secured.

● ALBUMS: *Muddy Waters Sings Big Bill Broonzy* (Chess 1960)★★★, *Muddy Waters At Newport, 1960* (Chess 1963)★★★★, *Muddy Waters, Folk Singer* (Chess 1964)★★★★, *Muddy, Brass And The Blues* (Chess 1965)★★, *Down On Stovall's Plantation* (Testament 1966)★★★, *Blues From

Big Bill's Copacabana (Chess 1968)★★★, *Electric Mud* (Cadet 1968)★★, *Fathers And Sons* (Chess 1969)★★★, *After The Rain* (Cadet 1969)★★, *Sail On* (Chess 1969)★★★, *The London Sessions* (MCA 1971)★★★, *Live At Mister Kelly's* (1971)★★★, *Experiment In Blues* (1972)★★★, *Can't Get No Grindin'* (MCA 1973)★★★, *Mud In Your Ear* (Musicor 1973)★★★, *London Revisited* (1974)★★, *The Muddy Waters Woodstock Album* (Chess 1975)★★, *Unk In Funk* (Chess 1977)★★, *Hard Again* (Blue Sky 1977)★★, *I'm Ready* (Blue Sky 1978)★★, *Muddy Waters Live* (Blue Sky 1979)★★★, *King Bee* (Blue Sky 1981)★★, *Muddy Waters In Concert 1958* (1982)★★★, *Paris 1972* (Pablo 1997)★★★.
● COMPILATIONS: *The Best Of Muddy Waters* (Chess 1957)★★★★★, *The Real Folk Blues* (Chess 1966)★★★★, *More Real Folk Blues* (Chess 1967)★★★★, *They Call Me Muddy Waters* (Chess 1970)★★★, *Vintage Mud* (1970)★★★, *McKinley Morganfield* aka *Muddy Waters* (Chess 1971)★★★★, *Back In The Early Days* (Red Lightnin' 1982)★★★, *Chess Masters* 3 Volumes (Chess 1981/1982/1983)★★★★, *Rare And Unissued* (Chess 1982)★★★, *Rolling Stone* (Chess 1982)★★★, *Trouble No More (Singles, 1955-1959)* (Chess/MCA 1989)★★★, *Muddy Waters* 6-LP box set (Chess 1989)★★★★★, *The Chess Box 1947-67* 9-CD set (Charly 1990)★★★★★, *Funky Butt* rec. early 70s (1993)★★★, *Gold Collection* (1993)★★★★, *The King Of Chicago Blues* (Charly 1995)★★★★.
● VIDEOS: *Messin' With The Blues* (BMG 1991), *Live* (BMG 1993).
● FURTHER READING: *The Complete Muddy Waters Discography*, Phil Wight and Fred Rothwell.

MURPHY, MATT

b. 27 December 1929, Sunflower, Mississippi, USA. Murphy moved to Memphis as a child and learned guitar in the 40s. He joined Tuff Green's band before becoming lead guitarist with Junior Parker's Blue Flames, playing on recording sessions with Parker and Bobby Bland. Murphy's brother Floyd replaced him with Parker's band when Matt moved to Chicago in 1952. There he spent seven years in Memphis Slim's band, also recording as the Sparks with Sam Chatman (bass, vocals) and John Calvin (saxophone). He toured Europe in 1963 with the Folk Blues package, recording with Sonny Boy 'Rice Miller' Williamson in Denmark. Murphy found a wider audience through his role in the film *The Blues Brothers* as Aretha Franklin's husband and his subsequent tours with the Blues Brothers package. Floyd Murphy joined him for his first solo album, recorded for Antone's in 1990.
● ALBUMS: *Way Down South* (Antone's 1990)★★★, *The Blues Don't Bother Me* (Roesch 1996).
● FILM: *The Blues Brothers* (1980).

MUSSELWHITE, CHARLIE

b. 31 January 1944, Mississippi, USA. Musselwhite grew up in Memphis where he was inspired to learn harmonica by hearing Sonny Terry on the radio. In 1962, Musselwhite moved to Chicago, performing with Johnny Young, Big Joe Williams and J.B. Hutto. He also linked up with another white blues musician, Mike Bloomfield, before the latter went on to join Paul Butterfield's group. Musselwhite then emigrated to California, making his first solo recordings for Vanguard. From 1974-75 he made two albums for Chris Strachwitz's Arhoolie label and later cut an instructional record for Stefan Grossman's Kickin' Mule. A growing reputation made Musselwhite a favourite on the festival circuits in the USA and Europe. *Mellow Dee* was recorded during a German tour while *Cambridge Blues* was recorded live at Britain's leading folk festival for Mike Vernon's Blue Horizon label. In 1990, Musselwhite joined Alligator, where John Lee Hooker guested on his 1991 album. Although heavily influenced by Little Walter, Louis Myers and Junior Wells, Musselwhite has made his own niche and is probably today's most popular white blues harmonica player.
● ALBUMS: *Stand Back, Here Comes Charlie Musselwhite* (Vanguard 1967)★★★, *Charlie Musselwhite* (Vanguard 1968)★★★★, *Stone Blues* (Vanguard 1968)★★★, *Tennessee Woman* (Vanguard 1969)★★★, *Memphis, Tennessee* (Vanguard 1969)★★★, *Taking My Time* (Arhoolie 1974)★★★, *Going Back Down South* (Arhoolie 1975)★★★, *The Harmonica According To Charlie Musselwhite* (Kickin' Mule 1979)★★★, *Curtain Call* (Red Lightnin' 1982)★★★, *Memphis, Tennessee* (Crosscut 1984)★★★, *Mellow Dee* (Crosscut 1986)★★, *Cambridge Blues* (Blue Horizon 1988)★★, *Tell*

Me Where Have All The Good Times Gone (Blue Rock-It 1988)★★★, *Ace Of Harps* (Alligator 1990)★★★★, *Signature* (Alligator 1991)★★★, *Memphis Charlie* (Alligator 1993)★★★★, *In My Time ...* (Alligator 1994)★★★, *Rough News* (1997)★★.
● COMPILATIONS: *The Blues Never Die* (Vanguard 1994)★★★.

MYERS, DAVE

b. 30 October 1926, Byhalia, Mississippi, USA. The older brother of Louis Myers, Dave bought a guitar after the family moved to Chicago in 1941. During 1951 he became a member of the Aces, leaving in 1955, a year after Louis. In the late 50s and early 60s he was part of a rock 'n' roll band with Louis, and when the Aces re-formed at the end of the 60s, he had the opportunity to record with them and as accompanist to artists including Carey Bell, Howlin' Wolf, Robert Lockwood, Jimmy Rogers, Homesick, James Williamson and Hubert Sumlin.

MYERS, LOUIS

b. 18 September 1929, Byhalis, Mississippi, USA, d. 18 September 1994. Growing up in a musical family, Myers began playing harmonica at the age of eight, and guitar about two years later. He moved to Chicago in 1941 and played with Big Boy Spires for three years. With his brother Dave Myers, Junior Wells and later, drummer Fred Below, he formed the Aces and in the 50s became known for his light, jazzy and swinging guitar blues artists (including some years with the re-formed Aces); his own material appeared on the Abco, Advent, and JSP labels. Although he was primarily known for his fluent guitar work, he was also an impressive harmonica player in the modern amplified style.
● ALBUMS: *I'm A Southern Man* (Testament 1978)★★★, *Wailin' The Blues* (JSP 1983)★★★.

MYERS, SAMMY

b. 19 February 1936, Laurel, Mississippi, USA. Originally one of Elmore James' Broomdusters working the Chicago circuit, Sammy Myers' early fame rests on a song he recorded for Johnny Vincent's Jackson, Mississippi-based Ace label. 'Sleeping In The Ground', with its Jimmy Reed-like lope supplied by The King Mose Royal Rockers, is one of the classic post-war harmonica blues. It was recorded in Jackson in 1957 and the partially blind singer/harmonica player, who also plays drums, went on to produce further singles for the Fury and Soft labels (the latter credited to Little John Myers) before moving back to make his livelihood in the clubs. He recorded for Vincent again, seeing the results issued as part of an album in 1981. Later he formed an unlikely partnership with the much younger, Texan guitarist Anson Funderburgh, performing with much success as featured artist with Funderburgh's group the Rockets. This partnership celebrated ten years together with an extended UK tour in 1997.
● ALBUMS: *Kings Of The Blues, Vol. 2* (1979)★★★, *Genuine Mississippi Blues* (1981)★★★. With Anson Funderburgh *My Love Is Here To Stay* (Black Top 1986)★★★, *Sins* (Black Top 1987)★★★, *Rack 'Em Up* (Black Top 1989)★★★, *What's What They Want* (Black Top 1997)★★★.

NEAL, KENNY

b. 14 October 1957, New Orleans, Louisiana, USA. The oldest son in Baton Rouge's most famous musical family, six of whom are professional musicians, Neal has been groomed throughout the 90s for blues stardom, but in a time of transition it remains an aim rather than an achievement. He accompanied his father to gigs from an early age, was given his first harmonica by Slim Harpo at the age of three, played piano onstage three years later, and at 13 stepped into the breach when Raful Neal needed a bass player. In 1976, he played bass in Buddy

Guy's band. Four years later, he moved to Toronto and brought his brothers north to work as the Neal Brothers Blues Band. Later, he joined the Downchild Blues Band, then Canada's top blues band. In 1984, he moved back to Baton Rouge to assemble another band. When he accompanied his father on the *Louisiana Legend* album, King Snake owner Bob Greenlee signed him to a solo contract. *Bio On The Bayou* created a stir on its release in 1987; Alligator boss Bruce Iglauer leased the album, remixed it and changed its title, and acquired Neal's contract. In 1991, he took a role in the Broadway production of *Mule Bone*, a musical version of a play written by poet Langston Hughes and folklorist Zora Neale Hurston. He won that year's Theatre World Award for the most outstanding new talent appearing in a Broadway play. *Walking On Fire* features two songs, 'Morning After' and 'Bad Luck Card', on which he set Hughes' poems to music. *Bayou Blood* dispensed with the horn sections normally present on his records, updating the 60s Excello sound. *Hoodoo Moon* reflected the increasing maturity of his several talents and the promise of his eventual success.

● ALBUMS: *Bio On The Bayou* aka *Big News From Baton Rouge* (King Snake/Alligator 1987/8)★★★★, *Devil Child* (Alligator 1989)★★★, *Walking On Fire* (Alligator 1991)★★★, *Bayou Blood* (Alligator 1993)★★★, *Hoodoo Moon* (Alligator 1994)★★★★.
● COMPILATIONS: *Deluxe Edition* (Alligator 1997)★★★★.

NEAL, RAFUL

b. 6 June 1936, Baton Rouge, Louisiana, USA. That rare thing in the blues, a late developer, Neal was not interested in music until seeing Little Walter play at the Temple Room in Baton Rouge in 1958. Buying a harmonica the next day, he was helped by a friend, Ike Brown, to learn its rudiments. Some time later, he was engaged to join the road band of guitarist Little Eddie Lang. His own first group was called the Clouds, and featured Buddy Guy and drummer Murdock Stillwood. When Guy left, Lazy Lester was one of his replacements. The band toured Louisiana and east Texas, finding its first residency at the Streamline Club in Port Allen, where Neal took up residence. He recorded 'Sunny Side Of Love' for Peacock in 1968 with

little success, and was then refused by Crowley producer Jay Miller. 'Change My Way Of Living', recorded for La Louisianna in 1969, fared better, and was followed by two records on Whit. During the 70s, he brought his teenage son, Kenny Neal, into his band and, as time went by, other sons, Noel, Raful Jnr., Larry and Darnell, were also recruited. With Kenny now a star in his own right, Raful continues to play in the Baton Rouge area, with forays further afield to play festivals and to record.

● ALBUMS: *Lousiana Legend* (Blue Horizon 1987)★★★, *I Been Mistreated* (Ichiban 1991)★★★.

NELSON BROTHERS

English roots rock band the Nelson Brothers comprise Steve Nelson (lead vocals, acoustic guitar), Simon Nelson (acoustic and electric guitars, dulcimer, keyboards and sitar), Ben Nicholls (bass) and Andrew Tween (drums, marimba). Their music combines the ethnic traditions of New Orleans Cajun, Celtic folk and Afro-Caribbean rhythms, accompanied by the brothers' lucid songwriting. The Nelsons grew up in Stafford, West Midlands, England, where they were members of various local bands as teenagers. Culling influences from the albums of Johnny Cash, Paul Simon, Hank Williams, Woody Guthrie and Bob Dylan, as well as jazz and rock, they began to write their own songs together while still teenagers. Their first group was entitled Alias, whose live repertoire included songs drawn from the songbooks of the Byrds and Rolling Stones as well as originals. Alias won both the 'new talent' and 'songwriting' categories of a national competition sponsored by Pye Records, but split due to musical differences before recording. The brothers then journeyed to Amsterdam, Netherlands, together as the first stage in a round-the-world trek, taking in Europe, North Africa, America and finally Bermuda (becoming residents at the Bermuda Folk Club). Upon returning to England they took up college courses (Steve reaching gold medal standard at the London Academy Of Music and Dramatic Art while Simon studied jazz guitar and composition). In 1983 Simon spent a year in Australia, working with acts such as the Arizona Smoke Revue, before he returned to England in the following year to team up with Steve again, fresh from another stint in Bermuda. The late 80s saw them back at college, both achieving Bachelor and Masters degrees, and in 1990 they built their own demo/jingle studio. They also set about forging a proper band together, with the aforementioned line-up the eventual result. Their debut album arrived in November 1993, with studio guests including Abdul Tee Jay (from Sierra Leone), Geraint Watkins (accordion) and Sugar Hajischacalli (bouzouki). The title track, 'Hometown', was written in collaboration with Steve Booker.

● ALBUMS: *Hometown* (Round Tower 1993)★★★.

NELSON, JIMMY 'T-99'

b. 7 April 1928, Philadelphia, Pennsylvania, USA. Nelson joined his brother (who later became famous as a singer with the Johnny Otis Orchestra under the stage-name Redd Lyte) on the west coast in the mid-40s, and began shouting the blues after seeing Big Joe Turner. While singing with the Peter Rabbit Trio in 1951, Nelson was signed to Modern's RPM subsidiary, with whom he had big R&B hits with 'T-99 Blues' and 'Meet Me With Your Black Dress On'. In 1955 Nelson moved to Houston, Texas, where he recorded for Chess and a host of small Texas and California independent labels. From the mid-60s he worked outside the music business until he was recorded with Arnett Cobb's band by Roy Ames in 1971 for Home Cooking Records. In recent years he has resumed performing and has toured Europe.

● ALBUMS: *Jimmy 'Mr T-99' Nelson* (Ace 1981)★★★, *Watch That Action!* (Ace 1987)★★★, with Arnett Cobb And His Mobb *Sweet Sugar Daddy* (1990)★★★.

NELSON, ROMEO

b. Iromeio Nelson, 12 March 1902, Springfield, Tennessee, USA, d. 17 May 1974, Chicago, Illinois, USA. A Chicago resident from the age of six (apart from a 1915-19 interlude in East St. Louis, where he learned piano), Nelson played rent parties and clubs until the early 40s, otherwise supporting himself by gambling. In 1929 he recorded four titles for Vocalion, among them 'Head Rag Hop' and 'Gettin' Dirty Just Shakin' That Thing', which are two of the finest rent party showpieces on record. Both are complex,

endlessly inventive and full of puckish humour, the former track (based on Pinetop Perkins' 'Pinetop's Boogie Woogie') being taken at breakneck speed. When interviewed in the 60s, Nelson had retired from music altogether.

● COMPILATIONS: *The Piano Blues Vol. 3 Vocalion* (1977)★★★.

NELSON, TRACY

b. 27 December 1944, Madison, Wisconsin, USA. Tutored on both piano and guitar as a child, Nelson began a singing career while studying at Wisconsin University. She was a member of two bands, including the Imitations, prior to recording her solo debut, *Deep Are The Roots*, in 1965. Charlie Musselwhite (harmonica) and Peter Wolfe (guitar) added support to a set drawing much of its inspiration from blues singers Ma Rainey and Bessie Smith. In 1966 Nelson became a founder member of Mother Earth, an excellent country/blues attraction which she later came to dominate as the original members pursued other projects. By 1973, when they were recording regularly in Nashville, the group had become known as Tracy Nelson/Mother Earth, and that year's *Poor Man's Paradise* was, effectively, a solo album. The singer's independent career was officially launched the following year with *Tracy Nelson*, which included a powerful version of Bob Dylan's 'It Takes A Lot To Laugh, It Takes A Train To Cry'. Ensuing recordings revealed a mature, self-confident vocalist working in an eclectic style redolent of Bonnie Raitt. Recording opportunities decreased during the 80s, although Nelson continues to perform live; in 1990 she completed several live dates in the UK.

● ALBUMS: *Deep Are The Roots* (Prestige 1965)★★★, *Tracy Nelson* (1974)★★★, *Poor Man's Paradise* (Columbia 1975)★★★★, *Sweet Soul Music* (MCA 1975)★★★★, *Time Is On My Side* (MCA 1976)★★★, *Home Made Songs* (Flying Fish 1978)★★★, *Come See About Me* (1980)★★★, *Doin' It My Way* (Adelphi 1981)★★★, *In The Here And Now* (Rounder 1993)★★★, *I Feel So Good* (Rounder 1995)★★★, *Move On* (Rounder 1996)★★★.

NEVILLE BROTHERS

The Nevilles represented the essence of 40 years of New Orleans music distilled within one family unit. The Nevilles comprised Art (b. Arthur Lanon Neville, 17 December 1937, New Orleans, Louisiana, USA; keyboards, vocals), Charles (b. 28 December 1938, New Orleans, Louisiana, USA; saxophone, flute), Aaron (b. 24 January 1941, New Orleans, Louisiana, USA; vocals, keyboards) and Cyril (b. 10 January 1948, New Orleans, Louisiana, USA; vocals). Each member was also a capable percussionist. They have, individually and collectively, been making an impression on R&B, rock 'n' roll, soul, funk and jazz since the early 50s. Art was the leader of the Hawkettes, whose 1954 Chess Records hit 'Mardi Gras Mambo' has become a New Orleans standard, reissued every year at Mardi Gras time. From 1957 he released solo singles on Specialty Records, and in the early 60s, both he and Aaron worked (separately) for the legendary producer Allen Toussaint. Aaron had emerged from vocal group the Avalons, and although he had a minor R&B hit in 1960 with Toussaint's 'Over You', it was not until 1967 that he achieved fame with the soul ballad 'Tell It Like It Is', a million-seller which reached number 2 in the charts. Charles Neville, meanwhile, had been working - on the road, or back home as part of the Dew Drop Inn's house band - with many legendary names: B.B. King, Bobby Bland and Ray Charles, among them. In 1968 Art formed the Meters, one of the Crescent City's most innovative and respected outfits. Featuring Leo Nocentelli (guitar), George Potter Jnr. (bass), Joseph Modeliste (drums) and, later, Cyril Neville (percussion), they were New Orleans' answer to Booker T. And The MGs, and besides their own albums, they could be heard on early 70s releases by Paul McCartney, Robert Palmer, LaBelle and Dr. John. *The Wild Tchoupitoulas* was a transitional album, featuring the Meters' rhythm section and all four Neville Brothers; by 1978 they were officially a group. Despite a considerable 'cult' following, particularly among fellow musicians, it took them until 1989 and the release of the Daniel Lanois-produced *Yellow Moon*, to find a wider audience. A single, 'With God On Our Side', was extracted and became a minor hit; Aaron, duetting with Linda Ronstadt, achieved his greatest chart success since 'Tell It Like It Is', when 'Don't Know Much' reached US and UK number 2 and won them the first of two Grammy awards. In 1990, as a band, they released *Brother's Keeper* and appeared on the soundtrack of the movie *Bird On A Wire*.

● ALBUMS: as the Wild Tchoupitoulas *The Wild Tchoupitoulas* (Antilles 1976)★★★, *The Neville Brothers* (Capitol 1978)★★★, *Fiyo On The Bayou* (A&M 1981)★★★★, *Neville-ization* (Black Top 1984)★★★★, *Live At Tipitina's* (Spindletop 1985)★★★, *Neville-ization II* (1987)★★★, *Uptown* (EMI America 1987)★★, *Live At Tipitina's Volume 2* (Demon 1988)★★★, *Yellow Moon* (A&M 1989)★★★★, *Brother's Keeper* (A&M 1990)★★★★, *Family Groove* (A&M 1992)★★★, *Live On Planet Earth* (A&M 1994)★★★, *Mitakuye Oyasin Oyasin/All My Relations* (A&M 1996)★★★.

● COMPILATIONS: *Treacherous: A History Of The Neville Brothers 1955-1985* (Rhino 1986)★★★★, *Legacy: A History Of The Nevilles* (Charly 1990)★★★★, *Treacherous Too!* (Rhino 1991)★★★, *With God On Our Side* 2-CD (A&M 1997)★★★.

● VIDEOS: *Tell It Like It Is* (BMG Video 1990).

NEWBERN, 'HAMBONE' WILLIE

b. c.1899, USA, d. c.1947, USA. Sleepy John Estes, who was taught guitar by Newbern, met him while working on medicine shows in Mississippi. Songs such as 'She Could Toodle-Oo' and 'Way Down In Arkansas', made at his sole recording session in 1929, come from his medicine-show repertoire, but Newbern was also a master of the personal blues, composing a remarkable account of his arrest at Marked Tree, Arkansas. His surest claim to fame, however, rests in being the first to record 'Roll And Tumble Blues'. Estes later reported the rumour that Newbern's death was the result of an assault in prison.

● COMPILATIONS: *The Greatest Songsters* (1990)★★★.

NICHOLSON, J.D.

b. James David Nicholson, 12 April 1917, Monroe, Louisiana, USA, d. 27 July 1991, Los Angeles, California, USA. Nicholson learned to play the piano in church from the age of five. He later emigrated to the west coast where, influenced by the popular black recording artists of the day, he built up a solo act and travelled and performed all over California. In the mid-40s he teamed up with Jimmy McCracklin and they made their first recordings together; Nicholson played, McCracklin sang and both their styles were very much in the mould of Walter Davis. Over the next decade, Nicholson accompanied a number of well-known artists, such as Lowell Fulson and Ray Agee, and also made some records under his own name. Later in the 50s, he joined Jimmy Reed's band, and also played with Little Walter. He made a few more records in the 60s.

● COMPILATIONS: *Mr. Fullbright's Blues Vol. 2* (1990)★★★.

NIGHTHAWK, ROBERT

b. Robert McCollum, 30 November 1909, Helena, Arkansas, USA, d. 5 November 1967. Having left home in his early teens, McCollum initially supported himself financially by playing harmonica, but by the 30s had switched to guitar under the tutelage of Houston Stackhouse. The two musicians, together with Robert's brother Percy, formed a string band that was a popular attraction at local parties and gatherings. Robert left the south during the middle of the decade, allegedly after a shooting incident, and settled in St. Louis. He took the name Robert McCoy, after his mother's maiden name, and made contact with several Mississippi-born bluesmen, including Big Joe Williams and John Lee 'Sonny Boy' Williamson. McCoy accompanied both on sessions for the Bluebird label, who then recorded the skilled guitarist in his own right. His releases included 'Tough Luck' and the evocative 'Prowlin' Nighthawk', which in turn engendered the artist's best-known professional surname. Nighthawk then discovered the electric guitar which, when combined with his already dexterous slide technique, created a sound that allegedly influenced Earl Hooker, Elmore James and Muddy Waters. The latter musician was instrumental in introducing Nighthawk to the Aristocrat (later Chess) label. It was here the artist completed his most accomplished work, in particular two 1949 masters, 'Sweet Black Angel' and 'Anna Lee Blues'. Both songs were procured from Tampa Red, whose dazzling, clear tone bore an affinity to jazz and was an inspiration for Nighthawk's approach. However, his disciple was unable or unwilling to consolidate the success these recordings secured, and although he continued to record in Chicago, Nighthawk often returned to Helena where he performed with his son, Sam Carr. The guitarist's last substantial session was in 1964 when he completed two tracks, 'Sorry My Angel' and 'Someday', with a backing band that included Buddy Guy and Walter 'Shakey' Horton. Robert Nighthawk died in his home-town on 5 November 1967, leaving behind a small but pivotal body of work.

● COMPILATIONS: *Bricks In My Pillow* (1977)★★★, with Elmore James *Blues In D Natural* (1979)★★★★, *Complete Recordings, Vol. 1 1937* (1985)★★★★, *Complete Recordings, Vol. 2 1938-40* (1985)★★★★, *Live On Maxwell Street* (Rounder 1988)★★★, *Black Angel Blues* (Chess 1989)★★★, *Houston Stackhouse* (Testament 1995)★★★, with the Wampus Cats *Toastin' The Blues* (Inside Memphis 1996)★★★.

NINE BELOW ZERO

A powerful and exciting UK R&B band of the late 70s, the group took its name from a song by Sonny Boy 'Rice Miller' Williamson and was led by guitarist/singer Dennis Greaves and virtuoso harmonica player Mark Feltham. With Peter Clark (bass, vocals) and Kenny Bradley (drums), Feltham recorded the EP *Packed Fair And Square* (1979). This led to a recording contract with A&M Records and a live recording at London's Marquee Club where Nine Below Zero had a residency. The producer was Glyn Johns. With Stix Burkey replacing Bradley, the second album included some original songs while *Third Degree* was a minor UK hit. The band dissolved in the mid-80s as Feltham concentrated on session work and Greaves went on to a solo career and became a member of the Truth. However, Feltham revived Nine Below Zero at the end of the decade, signing a new recording contract with the China label. By the mid-90s they were recording with the mighty A&M when roots blues was experiencing a small rebirth.

● ALBUMS: *Live At The Marquee* (A&M 1980)★★★★, *Don't Point Your Finger* (A&M 1981)★★★, *Third Degree* (A&M 1982)★★★★, *Live At The Venue* (China 1990)★★★, *Off The Hook* (China 1992)★★★, *Live In London* (Indigo

1995)★★★, *Ice Station Zebro* (A&M 1996)★★, *Covers* (Zed 1997)★★.

NIX, DON

b. 27 September 1941, Memphis, Tennessee, USA. Saxophonist Nix was one of several aspiring high school musicians forming the basis of the Mar-Keys. This renowned instrumental group enjoyed several R&B-styled bestsellers and became the house band for the Stax record company during the mid-60s, performing on sessions for Otis Redding, Rufus Thomas, Wilson Pickett and Sam And Dave. Nix moved to California in 1965 where he became acquainted with several 'southern' expatriates, notably Leon Russell and Delaney And Bonnie. Nix produced the latter's *Home*, then subsequently worked with Albert King and John Mayall, and completed several uneven, yet endearing albums. In 1972 he toured with the ambitious Alabama State Troupers, an *ad hoc* musical carnival that also included Lonnie Mack, Jeannie Greene, Marlin Greene and Furry Lewis. Although never a well-known figure, Nix retained the respect of his contemporaries.
● ALBUMS: *In God We Trust* (Shelter 1971)★★★, *Living By The Days* (Elektra 1971)★★★, *Hobos, Heroes And Street Corner Clowns* (Stax 1974)★★★, *Gone Too Long* (1976)★★★, *Skyrider* (1979)★★★.
● FURTHER READING: *Road Stories And Recipes*, Don Nix.

NIX, WILLIE

b. 6 August 1922, Memphis, Tennessee, USA, d. 8 July 1991, Leland, Mississippi, USA. Starting as a dancer and comedian, Nix switched to drums, and worked in Mississippi, Arkansas and Tennessee from his Memphis base in the 40s and 50s. Recorded in 1951 by Sam Phillips as a blues-singing drummer, Nix appeared on albums for Sun, RPM and Checker. Nix moved to Chicago in 1953 where he played the clubs, and recorded four tracks for Chance/Sabre. His recordings were intense and exuberant, always powered by his propulsive, swinging drumming. Returning to Memphis he supported himself by migrant labour and some guitar playing. He had largely retired by the end of the 60s, and spent the rest of his life notoriously telling tall tales and behaving eccentrically.

● ALBUMS: *Chicago Slickers Vol. 2* (1981)★★★, *Sun Records The Blues Years* (1985)★★★.

NIXON, ELMORE

b. 17 November 1933, Crowley, Louisiana, USA, d. June 1975, Houston, Texas, USA. Little is known of Nixon, although his piano is to be heard on many more records than he made under his own name. His family moved to Houston in 1939, where he would remain until his death. At some stage he trained to join the church, which is presumed to be where he learned to play piano. By his early teens, he was already backing Peppermint Harris on his Gold Star debut. Thereafter he recorded with many Texas artists as a member of alto saxophonist Henry Hayes' Four Kings, including Carl Campbell, Milton Willis, L.C. Williams, Hubert Robinson, Ivory Lee and Hop Wilson. His debut record, 'Foolish Love', was made in 1949 for Sittin In With with the Hayes band. His own music reflected the jump music of the time, having affinities with Little Willie Littlefield. Other sessions followed for Peacock, Mercury, Savoy and Imperial, the latter in 1955. During the mid-60s, he worked with Clifton Chenier, recording on Chenier's sessions for Arhoolie and with Lightnin' Hopkins for Jewel. At other times he led his own band, working around Texas and Louisiana. He underwent serious surgery in 1970 and was largely inactive until his death.
● ALBUMS: *Shout And Rock* (1986)★★.

NIXON, HAMMIE

b. 22 January 1908, Brownsville, Tennessee, USA, d. 17 August 1984, Brownsville, Tennessee, USA. Nixon was the leading blues harmonica player in Brownsville, and a frequent visitor to Memphis, playing in street bands on jug, kazoo and harmonica. In Brownsville he was an associate of Sleepy John Estes and James 'Yank' Rachell, contributing beautiful, mournful playing to both men's 20s and 30s recordings. He was a major early influence on John Lee 'Sonny Boy' Williamson, and later on Little Walter. When Estes was located in 1962, Nixon was also found (proving to be a cheery extrovert, despite his sorrowful harmonica sound), and came out of musical retirement to tour and record with Estes until the latter's death. Thereafter, Nixon continued to play concerts and festivals, and made occasional recordings, though these were often disappointing, as they often overemphasized his kazoo and his rudimentary guitar.

● ALBUMS: *Hammie Nixon* (1976)★★, *Tappin' That Thing* (1984)★★.

NOLEN, JIMMY

b. 3 April 1934, Oklahoma City, Oklahoma, USA, d. 18 December 1983, Atlanta, Georgia, USA. The inventor of the 'Chicken Scratch' and thus the father of funk guitar, Nolen was the archetypal sideman who also had a fitful solo recording career. After learning the violin, he took up the guitar at 14, inspired by T-Bone Walker. Singer Jimmy Wilson saw him in a Tulsa club and brought him back to Los Angeles, where Nolen began his recording career backing trumpeter Monte Easter and Chuck Higgins, and under his own name for John Fullbright's Elko label. In the autumn of 1956, he recorded three sessions for Federal, from which six singles were released to little effect. During this time, he also worked with Johnny Otis, playing on many sessions for Otis's Dig label and recording some sides of his own. He remained with Otis for a couple of years and played on 'Ma, He's Making Eyes At Me' and 'Willie And The Hand Jive'. In 1959, Nolen signed with Specialty subsidiary Fidelity, from which just one single emerged. Much of the early 60s was spent backing harmonica player George Smith before joining James Brown's band, where in February 1965 his guitar licks became the defining element of 'Papa's Got A Brand New Bag'. Apart from a two-year break between 1970 and 1972, Nolen remained with Brown for the rest of his career, which ended suddenly with a fatal heart attack while the band was in Atlanta, Georgia.

● ALBUMS: with Pete 'Guitar' Lewis, Cal Green *Scratchin'* (Charly 1991)★★★.

● COMPILATIONS: *Mr Fullbright's Blues* (P-Vine 1977)★★★, *Blues Guitar Blasters* (Ace 1988)★★★, *Dapper Cats, Groovy Tunes & Hot Guitars* (Ace 1992)★★★, *Elko Blues Vol. 1* (Wolf 1995)★★★.

ODEN, JAMES BURKE

b. 26 June 1903, Nashville, Tennessee, USA, d. 30 December 1977, Chicago, Illinois, USA. He was also known as St. Louis Jimmy, Big Bloke, Poor Boy and Old Man Oden. Although he was a moderately capable pianist, Oden's fame rests mainly on his prowess as a blues singer and composer. His most famous song, 'Going Down Slow', has been recorded by many famous blues artists, including an outstanding version by Howlin' Wolf aided by Willie Dixon, and was something of an anthem among white groups during the 60s. He was born, according to some sources, to Henry Oden, a dancer, and Leana West. Both parents died before he was eight years old and his early life remains a blank, largely because he wished it so, until he emerged in St. Louis, Missouri, at the age of 14, working in a barber's shop. St. Louis had a thriving blues community during the 20s and Jimmy Oden found himself a niche within it. He taught himself piano during this period but did not play professionally, believing that there were many better players than himself who would be able to accompany him. His main influence would appear to be Walter Davis, although his most constant companions were Big Joe Williams and Roosevelt Sykes. It was in the company of Sykes and violinist Curtis Mosby that he made his first foray into a recording studio in 1932. He moved north to Chicago in 1933 and was active in the blues scene of that city from that time until the 50s, performing, writing, and sometimes managing a band for Eddie Boyd, as well as being involved in the founding of the JOB record label. On one of his later sessions he was backed by the then emerging Muddy Waters and, after his activities were restricted by a serious car accident, he took up lodgings in the basement of Waters' house, paying his rent by supplying the occasional song. He benefited briefly from the resurgence of interest in the blues during the 60s, recording albums for such labels as Delmark, Bluesville and Spivey. His death was the result of bronchopneumonia.

ODETTA

b. Odetta Holmes Felious Gorden, 31 December 1930, Birmingham, Alabama, USA. A classically-trained vocalist, Odetta sang in the chorus of the 1947 Broadway production of *Finian's Rainbow*, before opting for a career in folk music. Successful residencies in San Francisco clubs, the Hungry i and Tin Angel, inspired interest in New York circles although her early releases revealed a still maturing talent. Odetta had been brought up in the blues tradition, but moved increasingly towards folk during the late 50s. Odetta had sung jazz and blues for the RCA and Riverside labels, and, only occasionally, folk for the Tradition label. Her blues was sung in the Bessie Smith tradition, but without the same emotion. Nevertheless, she recorded standards including 'House Of The Rising Sun' and 'Make Me A Pallet On Your Floor'. In 1960 she took to the solo acoustic guitar and moved to Vanguard. Possessed of a powerful voice, her style embraced gospel, jazz and blues, but eventually Odetta fell foul of the changing trends and fashions in music, and much was forgotten of her earlier work from the 50s and 60s. The singer was championed by Pete Seeger and Harry Belafonte, the latter of whom Odetta accompanied on a 1961 UK hit, 'Hole In The Bucket', while her solo career flourished with a succession of albums for the Vanguard label. The artist's emotional mixture of spiritual, ethnic and jazz styles is best captured in person and thus *Odetta At Town Hall* and *Odetta At Carnegie Hall* remain her most representative sets by revealing the full extent of her varied repertoire.
● ALBUMS: *Odetta And Larry* (Fantasy 1955)★★★, *Odetta Sings Ballads And Blues* (Tradition 1956)★★★, *Odetta At The Gate Of Horn* (Tradition 1957)★★★, *My Eyes Have Seen* (Vanguard 1959)★★★, *Christmas Spirituals* (Vanguard 1960)★★★, *Ballads For Americans* (Vanguard 1960)★★★, *Odetta At Carnegie Hall* (Vanguard 1961)★★★★, *Odetta And The Blues* (Riverside 1962)★★★, *Sometimes I Feel Like Crying* (RCA Victor 1962)★★★, *Odetta At Town Hall* (Vanguard 1962)★★★★, *Odetta* (1963)★★★, *Odetta Sings Folk Songs* (1963)★★★, *One Grain Of Sand* (Vanguard 1963)★★★, *It's A Mighty World* (1964)★★★, *Odetta Sings Of Many Things* (1964)★★★, *Odetta Sings Dylan* (1965)★★★, *Odetta In Japan* (1965)★★★★, *Odetta* (1967)★★★, *Odetta Sings The Blues* (1968)★★★, *Odetta Sings* (1971)★★★, *It's Impossible* (1978)★★★.
● COMPILATIONS: *Best Of Odetta* (1967)★★★, *The Essential Odetta* (1989)★★★.

ODOM, ANDREW

b. 15 December 1936, Denham Springs, Louisiana, USA, d. 23 December 1991. Odom occasionally worked under the name of 'BV' or 'Big Voice'. He sang in a church choir as a child; his family moved north in the mid-50s, settling in St. Louis, Missouri. While there Odom sometimes worked with Albert King and reputedly recorded in the late 50s. He moved to Chicago in 1960 where he had long associations with Earl Hooker and Jimmy Dawkins. Singles under Odom's name have appeared on several local labels, and he made his debut album for Bluesway in 1969. He also recorded for Wasp Music and French labels MCM and Isabel. Odom was an intense, powerful blues singer, influenced by B.B. King and Bobby Bland.
● ALBUMS: *Farther On Down The Road* (1969)★★★, *Feel So Good* (1982)★★★.

OFFITT, LILLIAN

b. 4 November 1938, Nashville, Tennessee, USA. On the evidence of her half dozen releases, Lillian Offit was a plain but lusty blues shouter, of small stature and commensurate talent. She was still attending college when she visited the offices of Nashboro Records in the hope of making a gospel record. Owner Ernie Young suggested that she try secular music, and 'Miss You So' was issued on Excello in 1957. It was successful enough for her to turn professional, and two further singles were issued, with diminishing success. In 1958 she moved to Chicago to become featured singer with the Earl Hooker band at Robert's Show Lounge. Through Hooker, she met Me London, owner of Chief Records, and cut her first record for the label in February 1960. 'Will My Man Be Home Tonight', heavily featuring Hooker's slide guitar, became a hit in the Chicago area. 'My Man I A Lover', recorded in May 1960, and 'Troubles' from a year later, repeated the downward curve of Excello releases. She left music to start a family, preventing her from joining the 1964 American Folk Blues Festival tour, her place taken by Sugar Pie DeSanto. She was last sighted in 1974 as part of the Streakers Rated—X Revue in St. Joseph, Michigan.

● ALBUMS: including *Chicago Calling* (1986)★★★.

OKEY DOKEY STOMPERS

British blues band the Okey Dokey Stompers were formed in Dagenham, Essex, England, in September 1992 from the ashes of the Corn Beef City Blues Band and the Impossibles. Comprising Stevie 'Young Blood' Cook (lead guitar), 'Automatic' Nick Nichols (vocals, harp), Gary 'Reverend Coco' Choules (bass), Johnny 'Boy' (keyboards) and 'Marky' Mark Ward (drums), members had also taken part in gigging bands such as Big Joe Louis, the Hoods and Night Prowler. Of these former incarnations, the Impossibles earned the greatest notoriety, as finalists in the Best Of British Blues competition sponsored by Banks Brewery in 1990/1. As the Okey Dokey Stompers the band played a shattering 400 gigs in their first two years, with a sound located somewhere between Texas and west coast rhythm and blues. A strong following for their energetic live shows led to the recording of a debut CD, *Dangerman Blues*, which was distributed by Hot Shot Records.

● ALBUMS: *Dangerman Blues* (Dyna-might 1994)★★★, *I Told You So* (Dixiefrog 1994)★★★, *World Wide Open* (Provogue 1995)★★★, *Hurry On Home* (Philo 1995)★★★.

OTIS, JOHNNY

b. 28 December 1921, Vallejo, California, USA. Born into a family of Greek immigrants, Otis was raised in a largely black neighbourhood where he thoroughly absorbed the prevailing culture and lifestyle. He began playing drums in his mid-teens and worked for a time with some of the locally based jazz bands, including, in 1941, Lloyd Hunter's orchestra. In 1943 he gained his first name-band experience when he joined Harlan Leonard for a short spell. Some sources suggest that, during the difficult days when the draft was pulling musicians out of bands all across the USA, Otis then replaced

another ex-Leonard drummer, Jesse Price, in the Stan Kenton band. In the mid-40s Otis also recorded with several jazz groups, including Illinois Jacquet's all-star band and a septet led by Lester Young, which also featured Howard McGhee and Willie Smith. In 1945 Otis formed his own big band in Los Angeles. In an early edition assembled for a recording session, he leaned strongly towards a blues-based jazz repertoire and hired such musicians as Eli Robinson, Paul Quinichette, Teddy Buckner, Bill Doggett, Curtis Counce and singer Jimmy Rushing. This particular date produced a major success in 'Harlem Nocturne'. He also led a small band, including McGhee and Teddy Edwards, on a record date backing Wynonie Harris. However, Otis was aware of audience interest in R&B and began to angle his repertoire accordingly. Alert to the possibilities of the music and with a keen ear for new talent, he quickly became one of the leading figures in the R&B boom of the late 40s and early 50s. Otis also enjoyed credit for writing several songs, although, in some cases, this was an area fraught with confusion and litigation. Amongst his songs was 'Every Beat Of My Heart', which was a minor hit for Jackie Wilson in 1951 and a massive hit a decade later for Gladys Knight. Otis was instrumental in the discovery of Etta James and Willie Mae 'Big Mama' Thornton. A highly complex case of song co-authorship came to light with 'Hound Dog', which was recorded by Thornton. Otis, who had set up the date, was listed first as composer, then as co-composer with its originators, Leiber And Stoller. After the song was turned into a multi-million dollar hit by Elvis Presley other names appeared on the credits and the lawyers stepped in. Otis had a hit record in the UK with an updated version of 'Ma, He's Making Eyes At Me' in 1957. During the 50s Otis broadcast daily in the USA as a radio disc jockey, and had a weekly television show with his band and also formed several recording companies, all of which helped to make him a widely recognized force in west coast R&B. During the 60s and 70s, Otis continued to appear on radio and television, touring with his well-packaged R&B-based show. His son, Johnny 'Shuggie' Otis Jnr., appeared with the show and at the age of 13 had a hit with 'Country Girl'. In addition to his busy musical career, Otis also found time to write a book, *Listen To The Lambs*, written in the aftermath of the Watts riots of the late 60s.

● ALBUMS: *Mel Williams And Johnny Otis* (1955)★★★, *Rock 'N' Roll Parade, Volume 1* (Dig 1957)★★★, *The Johnny Otis Show* (Capitol 1958)★★★★, *Cold Shot* (Kent 1968)★★★★, *Cuttin' Up* (Epic 1970)★★, *Live At Monterey* (Epic 1971)★★, *The New Johnny Otis Show* (Alligator 1981)★★, *Spirit Of The Black Territory Bands* (1993)★★.

● COMPILATIONS: *The Original Johnny Otis Show* (Savoy1985)★★★★, *The Capitol Years* (Capitol 1989)★★★★.

● FURTHER READING: *Upside Your head! Rhythm And Blues On Central Avenue*, Johnny Otis.

OTIS, SHUGGIE

b. John Otis Jnr., 30 November 1953, Los Angeles, California, USA. A precociously talented guitarist, Otis was encouraged by his bandleader father, Johnny Otis, who had him playing bass and lead guitar onstage in his early teens. Johnny Otis featured him on his 1969 Kent album, *Cold Shot*, and through that Al Kooper espoused his cause and recorded his debut album for Columbia. Father and son then both signed to Epic, and Shuggie appeared on his father's albums, *Cuttin' Up* and *The Johnny Otis Show Live At Monterey!*, as well as doing session work for Sugarcane Harris and playing bass on one track on Frank Zappa's *Hot Rats*. Three further solo albums of indifferent quality were issued before Otis retired at the grand old age of 22. In the years that followed, he continued to do session work for his father but drug problems hampered his efforts at reviving his own career. An album recorded for Big Bear in 1991, *At The Blues Summit*, remains unissued.

● ALBUMS: *Kooper Session: Al Kooper Introduces Shuggie Otis* (Columbia 1969)★★★, *Here Comes Shuggie Otis* (Epic 1970)★★, *Freedom Flight* (Epic 1971)★★, *Inspiration Information* (Epic 1975)★★, *Omaha Bar-B-Q* (Epic 1976)★★, *Shuggie's Boogie: Shuggie Otis Plays The Blues* (Epic/Legacy 1994)★★★.

OWENS, CALVIN

b. 1929, Houston, Texas, USA. His Creole mother told her son stories about Louis Armstrong, so

that by the age of 13 Owens was keen to play the trumpet. A year later, he joined up with the Leonard Dunkins Revue, a vaudeville band that played various musical styles and at the time featured Willie Mae Thornton as one of its singers. After that, Owens led a series of bands of his own, as well as touring Texas, Oklahoma and Louisiana with various territory bands. During the 40s, his band backed men such as Big Joe Turner and T-Bone Walker when they were in town. Owens also worked with the young Amos Milburn, and also Leroy Ervin and Lightnin' Hopkins. In 1949, he toured briefly with the Brownskin Models before joining I.H. Smalley's band, who regularly backed guitarist Lester Williams. Owens also worked in the house band at the Eldorado Ballroom until 1953, when B.B. King asked him to join his touring group. He remained with the band for four years and became King's music director. Owens returned to Houston in 1957 and became an A&R director for Don Robey, appearing on many Duke and Peacock recordings. In 1979, he returned to work for B.B. King for another five years, appearing on *Live At Ole Miss* and *Live In London*, for which he also wrote the arrangements. During this time he married and settled in Belgium, his wife's home country. *True Blue* was recorded there, with guest appearances by King and Johnny Copeland. The album and its successor, *That's Your Booty*, brilliantly recreate the heyday of big band blues, with lavish brass arrangements and driving rhythm.

● ALBUMS: *True Blue* (Sequel 1993)★★★★, *That's Your Booty* (Coast To Coast 1995)★★★★.

OWENS, JACK

b. 17 November 1904, Bentonia, Mississippi, USA, d. 9 February 1997. Along with Skip James and the unrecorded Henry Stuckey, Owens was one of the originators of the distinctive blues style developed in Bentonia after World War I, featuring 'deep' lyrics much concerned with death and loneliness, given a high and melismatic delivery. The complex three-finger guitar accompaniment, often in an eerie E minor tuning, blends inextricably with the equally affecting vocal line. Owens was not recorded until 1966, but proved to be a major musician, playing very extended songs with long guitar breaks. He was proud of his guitar prowess and, although fondest of E minor, he could play in seven tunings. He lived in Bentonia all his life, farming and at one time operating a juke-joint. His wife's death in 1985 allowed him to play a few concerts further afield; in 1989 he played in Chicago, still a master musician at 84. In later years he received a US government grant.

● ALBUMS: *It Must Have Been The Devil* (1971)★★★, *Bentonia Country Blues* (1979)★★★, *50 Years - Mississippi Blues In Bentonia* (1991)★★★, with Bud Spires *It Must Have Been The Devil* (Testament 1995)★★★.

OWENS, JAY

b. Jerome Owens, 1947, Lake City, Florida, USA. Blind singer and guitarist Owens purveys music that is accurately described by the title of his first album. His first musical inspiration was his uncle Clarence Jenkins, a popular local blues musician, whom Owens quickly learned to accompany on the bass strings of his first guitar. Further tuition in chords and tunings came from Ink Spots guitarist Jimmy McLin, who lived nearby. In high school he joined Albert Wright And The Houserockers, a revue band that also featured shake dancers. Although both parents were ministers in the Pentecostal Church, they encouraged their son's musical education. He joined Chuck Mills' band, the Barons, and travelled throughout America, working with Al Green, O.V. Wright, Donny Hathaway, Little Milton and Bobby Womack. He also worked with Faith Hope And Charity, a vocal group whose lead singer, Zulema Cusseaux, left to pursue a solo career in New York, taking Owens with her. After several years, he left to form a series of his own bands, including Soundtrack And The Pocket, a blues trio that gigged at New York venues such as Manny's Car Wash and the Lone Star Cafe. He was introduced to Mike Vernon through Lazy Lester; Vernon heard his songs and invited him to England, where he was a hit at the 1992 Burnley Blues Festival. *Blues Soul*, consisting entirely of original material which skilfully blended blues, soul and gospel influences, was well received. Now with Code Blue, *Movin' On* repeated the same feat, proving the emergence of a serious songwriting talent.

● ALBUMS: *The Blues Soul Of...* (Indigo/Code Blue 1992/1994)★★★, *Movin' On* (Code Blue 1995)★★★★.

PAGE, CLEO

Very much one of the mystery men of the blues, this singer/guitarist caused a minor stir in the 70s with his powerful, raw blues records which were issued on small Los Angeles labels including Goodie Train and Las Vegas. In 1979 JSP Records released enough material for an album which was described by Jim DeKoster in *Living Blues* as 'one of the most striking blues albums of the past year', but Page remains elusive. His music is tough, no-nonsense, mostly original blues, with sometimes startling lyrics; although JSP also issued a more contemporary-sounding risqué single entitled 'Hamburger-I Love To Eat It', which was not on the album.

● ALBUMS: *Leaving Mississippi* (JSP 1979)★★★.

PALADINS

This blues-based trio are based in San Diego, California, USA, emerging from the same roots-rock movement that produced the Blasters and Los Lobos. Otis Rush-influenced guitar player and vocalist Dave Gonzalez is backed by Tom Yearsley (bass) and Jeff Donavan (drums); together they produce music that mixes rock 'n' roll, rockabilly, jive and blues in a genre-defying mix, honed to perfection by their endless touring schedule. The band were signed to hardcore blues label Alligator in 1988, releasing two albums before parting company two years later. Paradoxically they are now signed to the 4AD label (home of determinedly 'indie' acts such as Cocteau Twins, Birthday Party and the Pixies), which was looking to expand its roster with acts from widely differing genres. A live CD, *Million Mile Club*, was released in 1997, and captured the manic energy of the band in concert (the title refers to the band having clocked up a million road miles while touring, at an average of two to three thousand miles a week). The one new song on the album, '15 Days (Under The Hood)', was a joint celebration of cars and the band's commitment to the road.

● ALBUMS: *Years Since Yesterday* (Alligator 1988)★★★, *Let's Buzz* (Alligator 1990)★★★, *Million Mile Club* (4AD 1997)★★★.

PARKER, 'LITTLE' JUNIOR

b. Herman Parker Jnr., 3 March 1927, West Memphis, Arkansas, USA, d. 18 November 1971, Blue Island, Illinois, USA. Despite his later fame some confusion still exists regarding the parentage and birth details of Little Junior Parker (Clarksdale, Mississippi, and 1932 are sometimes quoted, and his parents' names have variously been cited as Herman Snr., Willie, Jeanetta or Jeremeter). It is certain that they were a farming family situated near enough to West Memphis for Little Junior (who had started singing in church) to involve himself in the local music scene at an early age. His biggest influence in those early days was Sonny Boy 'Rice Miller' Williamson, in whose band Parker worked for some time before moving on to work for Howlin' Wolf, later assuming the leadership of the latter's backing band. He was a member of the *ad hoc* group the Beale Streeters, with Bobby Bland and B.B. King, prior to forming his own band, the Blue Flames, in 1951, which included the well-regarded guitarist Auburn 'Pat' Hare. His first, fairly primitive, recordings were made for Joe Bihari and Ike Turner in 1952 for the Modern label. This brought him to the attention of Sam Phillips and Sun Records where Parker enjoyed some success with his recordings of 'Feeling Good', although the period is better recalled for the downbeat 'Mystery Train', which was later taken up by the young Elvis Presley. His greatest fame on record stemmed from his work on Don Robey's Duke label operating out of Houston, Texas, and it was along with fellow Duke artist Bobby 'Blue' Bland that Little Junior headed the highly successful Blues Consolidated Revue, which quickly became a staple part of the southern blues circuit. His tenure with Robey lasted until the mid-60s with his work moving progressively away from his hard blues base. In his later days, Parker appeared on such labels as Mercury, United Artists and Capitol, enjoying intermittent chart success with 'Driving Wheel' (1961), 'Annie Get Your Yo-Yo' (1962) and 'Man Or Mouse' (1966). His premature death in 1971 occurred while he was undergoing surgery for a brain tumour and robbed R&B of one of its most influential figures.

● ALBUMS: with Bobby Bland *Blues Consolidated* (Duke 1958)★★★, with Bland *Barefoot Rock And You Got Me* (1960)★★★, *Driving Wheel* (Duke 1962)★★★★, *Like It Is* (Mercury 1967)★★★, *Honey-Drippin' Blues* (1969)★★★, *Blues Man* (1969)★★★, *The Outside Man* (1970)★★★, *Dudes Doing Business* (1971)★★, *Blue Shadows Falling* (Groove Merchant 1972)★★, *Good Things Don't Happen Every Day* (Groove Merchant 1973)★★, *I Tell Stories, Sad And True ...* (1973)★★, *You Don't Have To Be Black To Love The Blues* (People 1974)★★, *Love Ain't Nothin' But A Business Goin' On* (1974)★★★.

● COMPILATIONS: *The Best Of Junior Parker* (Duke 1966)★★★★, *Sometime Tomorrow My Broken Heart Will Die* (1973)★★★, *Memorial* (Vogue 1973)★★★, *The ABC Collection* (1976)★★★★, *The Legendary Sun Performers - Junior Parker And Billy 'Red' Love* (Charly 1977)★★★, *I Wanna Ramble* (Ace 1982)★★★, *Junior's Blues: The Duke Recordings Vol. 1* (1993)★★★★.

PARKER, BOBBY

b. 31 August 1937, Lafayette, Louisiana, USA. With a reputation based upon one record from 1961, guitarist Parker spent 30 years in obscurity before recording his first album. His family moved to east Los Angeles in 1943 and Parker acquired his first guitar three years later. While still in high school he formed a band with future rockers Don Harris and Dewey Terry. After winning a talent contest at Johnny Otis's Barrelhouse club, he was offered the guitar spot with Otis Williams & The Charms. From there, he worked in Bo Diddley's touring band for three years and then joined Paul 'Hucklebuck' Williams' orchestra. While with them he made his first single, 'Blues Get Off My Shoulder', for Vee Jay in Chicago. The b-side, 'You Got What It Takes', became a hit for Marv Johnson but featured composer credits for Berry Gordy and Billy Davis. In 1961 Parker settled in Washington DC and released his first and only hit, 'Watch Your Step' on V-Tone, basing the tune on Dizzy Gillespie's 'Manteca'. The Spencer Davis Group covered it in England and John Lennon revealed that the Beatles' 'Day Tripper' was based on a variation of its main riff. In 1969 he toured England and recorded 'It's Hard But It's Fair' for Blue Horizon. Sessions for Lillian Clayborn's DC label and for producer Mitch Corday in the 60s are also rumoured to exist. Parker gave up music for five years during the 80s, but returned in 1989. *Bent Out Of Shape* showed that his talent was undiminished; *Livin' Blues* accurately described Parker's style of stringing notes together as 'tight as a suspension bridge'.

● ALBUMS: *Bent Out Of Shape* (Black Top 1993)★★★, *Shine Me Up* (Black Top 1995)★★★.

PARKER, ROBERT

b. 14 October 1930, New Orleans, Louisiana, USA. An accomplished saxophonist, this versatile musician was first heard on numerous recordings by pianist Professor Longhair. Parker also appeared on sessions for Irma Thomas, Ernie K-Doe and Joe Tex while at the same time embarking on a singing career. His early releases were largely unsuccessful until 'Barefootin'', an irresistible dance record, became a hit in the USA and the UK during 1966. The singer continued this instinctive blend of soul and New Orleans R&B on several further releases, but 'Tip Toe' (1967) was his only further chart entry.

● ALBUMS: *Barefootin'* (Island 1966)★★.
● COMPILATIONS: *Get Ta Steppin'* (1987)★★.

PARKER, SONNY

b. 5 May 1925, Youngstown, Ohio, USA, d. 1957. Raised in Chicago by the vaudeville act Butterbeans And Susie, Parker developed into an all-round entertainer specializing in singing and dancing, and his powerful voice lent itself well to blues shouting. Recording with trumpeter King Kolax for Columbia in 1948, he came to the attention of bandleader Lionel Hampton, and recorded as the latter's blues vocalist for Decca and MGM over the next three years, covering many of the top US R&B hits of the day ('Drinking Wine', 'Spo-Dee-O-Dee', 'For You My Love', 'Merry Christmas Baby', and 'I Almost Lost My Mind'). During the Hampton years, Parker recorded sessions in his own name for Aladdin, Spire and Peacock, usually featuring a contingent from the then-current Hampton orchestra. Later sessions were recorded in the

mid-50s for Brunswick, Ultima and Hitts, and Parker continued to tour sporadically with Hampton. In 1957, Hampton brought Parker to Europe, and it was while touring France that he became seriously ill and died.

● COMPILATIONS: including with Wynonie Harris, Jimmy Rushing, Big Joe Turner *The Best Of The Blues Shouters* (1970).

PATT, FRANK 'HONEYBOY'

b. 1 September 1928, Fostoria, Alabama, USA. After singing in church as a child, Patt taught himself guitar soon after emigrating to Los Angeles, California, in 1952. There he formed a musical partnership with pianist Gus Jenkins, also from Alabama. Two years later Patt made his first record, with Jenkins, issued on the Specialty label, a powerful blues evoking the scene of a murder, 'Blood Stains On The Wall'. Although years later this came to be regarded as something of a classic, it made little impact at the time, and he had only one more record issued, in 1957, again with Jenkins. Over the next decade, he worked mostly outside the music business, but his career enjoyed a revival in the 70s, with further recording work and live appearances.

● ALBUMS: *City Blues* (1973)★★★, *Give Me A Chance* (JSP 1996)★★★.

PATTON, CHARLEY

b. 1 May 1891, Bolton, Mississippi, USA, d. 28 April 1934, Indianola, Mississippi, USA. Charley Patton was small, but in all other ways larger than life; his death from a chronic heart condition at the age of 43 brought to an end his relentless pursuit of the good things then available to a black man in Mississippi - liquor, women, food (courtesy of women), music, and the avoidance of farmwork, which carried with it another *desideratum*, freedom of movement. By 1910, Patton had a repertoire of his own compositions, including 'Pony Blues', 'Banty Rooster Blues', 'Down The Dirt Road', and his version of 'Mississippi Boweavil Blues', all of which he recorded at his first session in 1929. He also acquired a number of spirituals, although the degree of his religious conviction is uncertain. By the time he recorded, Charley Patton was the foremost blues singer in Mississippi, popular with whites and blacks, and able to make a living from his music. He was enormously influential on local musicians, including his regular partner Willie Brown, in addition to Tommy Johnson and Son House. Bukka White, Big Joe Williams and Howlin' Wolf were among others whose music was profoundly affected by Patton. His own sound is characteristic from the first: a hoarse, hollering vocal delivery, at times incomprehensible even to those who heard him in person, interrupted by spoken asides, and accompanied by driving guitar played with an unrivalled mastery of rhythm. Patton had a number of tunes and themes that he liked to rework, and he recorded some songs more than once, but never descended to stale repetition. His phrasing and accenting were uniquely inventive, voice and guitar complementing one another, rather than the guitar simply imitating the rhythm of the vocal line. He was able to hold a sung note to an impressive length, and part of the excitement of his music derives from the way a sung line can thus overlap the guitar phrase introducing the next verse. Patton was equally adept at regular and bottleneck fretting, and when playing with a slide could make the guitar into a supplementary voice with a proficiency that few could equal.

He was extensively recorded by Paramount in 1929-30, and by Vocalion in 1934, so that the breadth of his repertoire is evident. (It was probably Patton's good sales that persuaded the companies to record the singing of his accompanists, guitarist Willie Brown and fiddler Henry Sims, and Bertha Lee, his last wife.) Naturally, Patton sang personal blues, many of them about his relationships with women. He also sang about being arrested for drunkenness, cocaine ('A Spoonful Blues'), good sex ('Shake It And Break It'), and, in 'Down The Dirt Road Blues', he highlighted the plight of the black in Mississippi ('Every day, seems like murder here'). He composed an important body of topical songs, including 'Dry Well Blues' about a drought, and the two-part 'High Water Everywhere', an account of the 1927 flooding of the Mississippi that is almost cinematic in its vividness. Besides blues and spirituals, Patton recorded a number of 'songster' pieces, including 'Mississippi Boweavil Blues', 'Frankie And Albert' and the anti-clerical 'Elder Greene Blues'. He also covered hits like 'Kansas City Blues', 'Running

Wild', and even Sophie Tucker's 'Some Of These Days'. It is a measure of Patton's accomplishment as a musician and of his personal magnetism that blues scholars debate furiously whether he was a clowning moral degenerate or 'the conscience of the Delta', an unthinking entertainer or a serious artist. It is perhaps fair to say that he was a man of his times who nevertheless transcended them, managing to a considerable degree to live the life he chose in a system that strove to deny that option to blacks. A similar verdict applies to his achievements as a musician and lyricist; Patton did not work independently of or uninfluenced by his musical environment, but considering how young he was when the blues were becoming the dominant black folk music, his achievements are remarkable. He was able to take the given forms and transmute them through the application of his genius.

● COMPILATIONS: *Founder Of The Delta Blues 1929-1934* (Yazoo 1988)★★★★, *Volume 1* (Document 1990)★★★, *Volume 2* (Document 1990)★★★, *Volume 3* (Document 1990)★★★, *King Of The Delta Blues* (Yazoo 1991)★★★★, *King Of The Delta: The Essential Recordings Of Charley Patton* (Indigo 1996)★★★★.

● FURTHER READING: *Charley Patton*, John Fahey. *Voice Of The Delta*, International Symposium. *King Of The Delta Blues*, Steven Calt & Gayle Wardlow.

PAYTON, EARLEE

b. 24 November 1923, Pine Bluff, Arkansas, USA. A minor figure who gave Freddie King his start, Payton took up the harmonica at the age of 15, inspired by the records and live performances of both John Lee 'Sonny Boy' Williamson and Rice Miller 'Sonny Boy' Williamson. He moved to Chicago in 1942 and was able to see John Lee 'Sonny Boy' Williamson at the Club Georgia. He was also inspired by Memphis Slim, James 'Yank' Rachell and Memphis Minnie. In the late 40s, he sat in with a number of bands, including Muddy Waters. In 1951, he formed a band with Otis Rush, playing a number of bars including the Club Alibi. He then put together a band with Robert 'Mojo' Elem and drummer Johnny Junior, who left to be replaced by T.J. McNulty. Payton also took on Freddie King as lead guitarist as the band moved from Ricky's Show

Lounge to the Zanzibar and the Cotton Club. In 1956, his band plus Robert Lockwood on rhythm guitar backed Freddie King's debut single, 'Country Boy', for El Bee. The same band also recorded a demo session for Al Benson's Parrot, which has remained undiscovered and unissued. After King's departure from the band, Payton continued for a short time, and also fronted Little Walter's band while Walter was recovering from a shooting incident. He then gave up music.

PEABODY, DAVE

b. 20 April 1948, Southall, Middlesex, England. One of the few British blues musicians to establish himself on the American club and festival circuit, Peabody combines an instrumental expertise with a burgeoning folio of photographs and interviews. He had already been playing the guitar for several years when he saw the multi-instrumentalist Jessie Fuller and discovered a penchant for the blues, which was soon reinforced by John Hammond III's debut British tour. During his college years, he played in a number of jug bands and in 1971 made his first recordings as a member of Tight Like That for the French Vogue label. After a pair of solo albums, he made *Come And Get It* with ex-Savoy Brown pianist Bob Hall. It was to become one of a number of enduring, if intermittent, partnerships that Peabody formed over the ensuing years. His occasional partners include David 'Honeyboy' Edwards, Big Boy Henry, Charlie Musselwhite, Rob Mason and 'Big' Joe Duskin. As well as drawing on these friendships in putting together his albums, Peabody is also the resident blues interviewer and photographer for *Folk Roots*, where his understanding of blues music inspires a forthright response from his subjects.

● ALBUMS: *Peabody Hotel* (Village Thing 1973)★★★, *Keep It Clean* (Matchbox 1974)★★★, *Come And Get It* (Matchbox/Appaloosa 1976/1981)★★★, *Blues In Brussels* (CL 1977)★★★, *Payday* (Waterfront 1979)★★★, *Americana* (Waterfront 1987)★★★, *Dream Of Mississippi* (Appaloosa 1991)★★★, *Hands Across The Sea* (Appaloosa 1993)★★★, *Down In Carolina* (Appaloosa 1996)★★★.

PEEBLES, ANN

b. 27 April 1947, East St. Louis, Missouri, USA. An impromptu appearance at the Rosewood Club in Memphis led to Peebles' recording deal. Bandleader Gene Miller took the singer to producer Willie Mitchell whose skills fashioned an impressive debut single, 'Walk Away' (1969). Anne's style was more fully shaped with 'Part Time Love' (1970), an irresistibly punchy reworking of the Clay Hammond-penned standard, while powerful original songs, including 'Slipped Tripped And Fell In Love' (1972) and 'I'm Gonna Tear Your Playhouse Down' (1973), later recorded by Paul Young and Graham Parker, confirmed her promise. Her work matured with the magnificent 'I Can't Stand The Rain', which defined the Hi Records sound and deservedly ensured the singer's immortality. Don Bryant, Peebles' husband and a songwriter of ability, wrote that classic as well as '99 lbs' (1971). Later releases, '(You Keep Me) Hangin' On' and 'Do I Need You', were also strong, but Peebles was latterly hampered by a now-established formula and sales subsided. 'If You Got The Time (I've Got The Love)' (1979) was the singer's last R&B hit, but her work nonetheless remains among the finest in the 70s soul canon. After a return to the gospel fold in the mid-80s, Peebles bounced back in 1989 with *Call Me*. In 1992 the fine back-to-the-Memphis-sound, *Full Time Love*, was issued. She appeared that summer at the Porretta Terme Soul Festival in Italy and her rivetting performance was captured on a CD of the festival, *Sweet Soul Music - Live!*, released by Italian label 103.

● ALBUMS: *This Is Ann Peebles* (Hi 1969)★★★, *Part Time Love* (Hi 1971)★★★, *Straight From The Heart* (Hi 1972)★★★, *I Can't Stand The Rain* (Hi 1974)★★★★, *Tellin' It* (Hi 1976)★★★, *If This Is Heaven* (Hi 1978)★★★, *The Handwriting On The Wall* (Hi 1979)★★★, *Call Me* (Waylo 1990)★★★, *Full Time Love* (Rounder/Bullseye 1992)★★★, *Fill This World With Love* (Bullseye 1996)★★★.

● COMPILATIONS: *I'm Gonna Tear Your Playhouse Down* (Hi 1985)★★★★, *99 lbs* (Hi 1987)★★★, *Greatest Hits* (Hi 1988)★★★★, *Lookin' For A Lovin'* (Hi 1990)★★★, *Straight From The Heart/I Can't Stand The Rain* (1992)★★★, *Tellin' It/If This Is Heaven* (1992)★★★, *This Is Ann Peebles/The*

Handwriting On The Wall (1993)★★★, *The Flipside Of ...* (1993), *U.S. R&B Hits* (1995)★★★.

PERFECT, CHRISTINE
(see Fleetwood Mac)

PERKINS, PINETOP
b. Joe Willie Perkins, 7 July 1913, Belzoni, Mississippi, USA. A barrelhouse blues pianist from his childhood, Perkins travelled through Mississippi and Arkansas, and north to St. Louis and Chicago, playing piano, and sometimes guitar, behind Big Joe Williams, Robert Nighthawk, John Lee 'Sonny Boy' Williamson and others. He recorded for Sun Records in 1953, although only 'Pinetop's Boogie Woogie' was issued, many years later. He also accompanied Earl Hooker and Boyd Gilmore on Sun, and Nighthawk on Aristocrat. From the early 60s, he settled in Chicago. In 1969, Perkins replaced Otis Spann in the Muddy Waters Band, with which he toured up to and after the leader's death, also working as a solo act.
● ALBUMS: *Chicago Boogie Blues Piano Man* (JSP 1986)★★★, *Boogie Woogie King* (Black & Blue 1986)★★★, *Chicago Blues Session, Volume 12* (1989)★★★, *The Ultimate Sun Blues Collection* (1991)★★★, *With Chicago Beau And The Blue Ice Band* (Earwig 1992)★★, *Solitare* (Lunacy 1995)★★, *Big City Blues* (Antones 1995)★★★, *Live Top* rec. 1982 (Deluge 1995)★★★, *On Top* (Deluge 1996)★★★, *Born In The Delta* (Telarc 1997)★★★.

PERRY, BILL
b. *c.*1962, Chester, New York, USA. Blues guitarist and singer Bill Perry grew up in a home dominated by music where his grandfather played organ for the local church and his mother was a percussionist. However, he took more interest in his father's records of Kenny Burrell's guitar playing, and he started to learn the guitar himself at the age of six. He appeared in his first talent show by the time he was 13, and by the time he started at high school he was regularly playing dance party shows. After school he travelled widely through California and Colorado, gradually increasing his confidence as a singer (previous employment had been as a guitarist only). Returning to Middletown in New York, his reputation had

preceded him and he began a long association with Richie Havens. This was followed by his debut solo album, *Love Scars*, released in 1995. Rather than relying on the Jimi Hendrix and B.B. King cover versions that are a fixture of his live shows, *Love Scars* drew on original compositions such as 'Down In My Lonely Room' and 'Fade To Blue' (which Havens also interpreted on his album *Cuts To The Chase*). Greeted with great enthusiasm, not least from fellow musicians, on its original release on Rave-On Records, by 1996 it had transferred to PointBlank, Virgin Records' new blues subsidiary.
● ALBUMS: *Love Scars* (Rave-On 1995)★★★.

PERRYMAN, RUFUS 'SPECKLED RED'
b. 23 October 1892, Monroe, Louisiana, USA, d. 2 January 1973. Although his singing and piano playing were barely adequate, Perryman's work has a rather endearing, basic earthiness to it. In this respect it is sometimes preferable to the more bland styles that developed as the blues became an acceptable part of popular entertainment. He played mostly in the south, achieving wider popularity as a result of recordings, and in the late 50s and early 60s he toured Europe. In 1970 he recorded music for the soundtrack of the film *Blues Like Showers Of Rain*. Perryman, who died in 1973, was the elder brother of William 'Piano Red' Perryman.
● ALBUMS: *The Dirty Dozen* (1961)★★★.

PETERSON, JAMES
b. 4 November 1937, Russell County, Alabama, USA. Blues guitarist and singer James Peterson spent much of his early musical career as a club owner in Florida. He is probably best known, however, for being the father of child prodigy Lucky Peterson. James's own father had run a 'juke-joint' club in the early 50s, on exactly the same site where James later established Club 49. In the early 50s he travelled with his brother Aaron, before marrying and settling in Buffalo. There he established the Governor's Inn: The House Of Blues - although when purchasing the site he had to pretend to be a construction worker because the original tenant, who desperately wanted to sell, did not want to be seen associating with a black man. Artists including Jimmy Reed, John Lee Hooker, Howlin' Wolf,

Junior Wells, Buddy Guy, and many others, appeared at the venue, usually for six-night residencies. Other local stars included Elmore Weatherspoon and organist Joe Madison, while Peterson himself contributed backing guitar when visiting artists did not supply their own bands. Soon, with Lucky's emergence as a guitar-playing prodigy, he played alongside his son on shows including *What's My Line* and *Sesame Street*. The pair's exposure originally came as a result of recording a single together, '1, 2, 3, 4'/'Good Old Candy'. That was also Peterson Snr.'s first release, though he quickly followed it up with 'Sing The Blues Till I Die' for Yambo Records, which, like '1, 2, 3, 4', was produced by Willie Dixon. His first album was another collaboration with his son, but at the same time he continued to finance his musical career with club management (the After Dark in St. Petersburg and the New Governor's Inn in Buffalo) and a job as a second-hand car salesman. In the 90s he concentrated more on his own music, recording two albums for Ichiban Records before moving over to the Malaco Records' subsidiary label Waldoxy for 1995's critically acclaimed *Don't Let The Devil Ride*.

● ALBUMS: with Lucky Peterson *The Father, The Son, And The Blues* (1981)★★★, *Too Many Knots* (Ichiban 1992)★★★, *Don't Let The Devil Ride* (Waldoxy 1995)★★★★, *Preachin' The Blues* (Waldoxy 1996)★★★.

PETERSON, LUCKY

b. Judge Kenneth Peterson, 13 December 1964, Buffalo, New York, USA. Peterson was an exceptionally gifted musician as a child, and this has left him with the problem of harnessing his natural gift to a definable personality. His father James owned a blues club, the Governor's Inn, and his son received frequent opportunities to play alongside visiting musicians, although a three-year-old playing organ and drums may have been as much a curiosity as a phenomenon. Two years later he recorded for Willie Dixon; the single, '1, 2, 3, 4', and a subsequent album brought him a degree of celebrity and he made appearances on *Tonight* and *The Ed Sullivan Show*. At the age of 17, Little Milton asked him to join his band and after three years, he moved on to spend another three years backing Bobby Bland. While on a European tour with Bland, he recorded his first album as an adult, *Ridin'*, in Paris. By this time, he had taken up the guitar and subsequent albums such as *Lucky Strikes!* emphasized his prowess on the instrument. Meanwhile, he became a frequent session musician for other King Snake and Alligator artists, usually as a keyboard player. His move to Verve and the release of *I'm Ready* and *Beyond Cool* perpetuated his image as a guitarist and allowed him to broaden the scope of his musicianship to include interpretations of Jimi Hendrix and Stevie Wonder songs. His work with French horn and trumpet has yet to make its debut on record, but in trying to become the complete musician, Peterson risks subordinating the depth of his talent to a veneer of display.

● ALBUMS: with James Peterson *The Father, The Son, And The Blues* (1981)★★★, *Ridin'* (Isabel 1984)★★★, *Rough And Ready* (King Snake 1988)★★★, *Lucky Strikes!* (Alligator 1989)★★★, *Triple Play* (Alligator 1990)★★★, *I'm Ready* (Verve/Gitanes, 1993)★★★, *Beyond Cool* (Verve/Gitanes 1994)★★★, *Lifetime* (Verve/Gitanes 1996)★★★, with Mavis Staples *Spirituals & Gospel* (Verve/Gitanes 1996)★★★, *Move* (Verve/Gitanes 1997)★★★.

PETTIS, 'ALABAMA' JUNIOR

b. Coleman Pettis Jnr., c.1935, Alabama, USA, d. April 1988. Pettis worked under a variety of pseudonyms including Daddy Rabbit, Alabama Junior, and Junior Pettis. He learned to play guitar at the age of eight and moved to Chicago in 1952. He was strongly influenced by Lee Jackson, with whom he worked as rhythm guitarist, and is best known for his spell working with Magic Slim from 1973-83. He can be heard on several of Slim's records, supplying excellent complementary work to the leader's tough playing, and he also provides occasional lead vocals and compositions. In 1987 he made his only album under his own name for the Wolf label, and he died of cancer at the beginning of April 1988.

● ALBUMS: *Chicago Blues Sessions Volume Four* (Wolf 1987)★★★.

PHILLIPS, BREWER

b. 16 November 1924, Coita, Mississippi, USA. Phillips was on the Chicago blues scene from the mid-50s, when he worked briefly with Memphis Minnie, and from 1957-75 he played rhythm guitar for Hound Dog Taylor, taking occasional solos, and contributing significantly to the Houserockers' brash, energetic sound. After Taylor's death he continued to work the Chicago clubs, making occasional wider forays, and recording tracks that had the unpretentious, funky drive of his former leader, and revealed him to be a capable blues singer. He often works with pianist Aaron Moore.

● ALBUMS: *Whole Lotta Blues* (JSP 1983)★★★, *Ingleside Blues* (Wolf 1988)★★★, with Ted Harvey *Good Houserockin* (Wolf 1995)★★★, *Home Brew* (Delmark 1996)★★★.

PHILLIPS, GENE

b. Eugene Floyd Phillips, 25 July 1915, St. Louis, Missouri, USA. Phillips learned to play ukulele and switched to guitar at the age of 11, after which he began playing and singing for tips and graduated through several obscure local bands. Between 1941 and 1943, he played guitar behind the Mills Brothers, relocating with them to Los Angeles, and later worked and recorded with Lorenzo Flennoy, Wynonie Harris, Johnny Otis and Jack McVea. Phillips' Charlie Christian-inspired guitar and jump-blues shouting began to be featured on his own recordings for Modern Records from 1945, supported by west coast stalwarts such as Maxwell Davis and Jack McVea. They produced such hits as 'Big Legs', 'Just A Dream' and 'Rock Bottom'. Phillips' later records for RPM, Imperial, Exclusive, Federal (with Preston Love) and Combo, were successful locally and he spent the 50s doing extensive session work with artists such as Percy Mayfield, who played on 'Please Send Me Someone To Love' and Amos Milburn, but retired from the music business with the advent of rock 'n' roll.

● ALBUMS: *Gene Phillips & His Rhythm Aces* (Ace 1986)★★★, *I Like 'Em Fat* (Ace 1988)★★★.

PHILLIPS, STEVE

b. Nicholas Stephen Phillips, 18 February 1948, London, England. The son of sculptor Harry Phillips, Steve first started playing guitar in 1961, at the time emulating rockabilly artists from the Sun label. From the age of eight he had been enthralled by Elvis Presley, when others of his age were just discovering Hank B. Marvin and the Shadows. Phillips was influenced by such artists as Robert Johnson and Scotty Moore, an influence that became apparent later in his country blues playing. Up until 1964, Phillips had played piano in a jug band, called Easy Mr. Steve's Bootleggers, but by 1965 he switched to blues. By the end of 1968, he was being booked regularly in the folk and blues clubs of his local area. During 1968, Phillips met Mark Knopfler, at the time a junior reporter in Leeds, and together they formed a duo, the Duolian String Pickers. This lasted until Knopfler moved to London, later to form Dire Straits. From 1974-76 Phillips fronted the Steve Phillips Juke Band, which included his brother on bass. He met Brendan Croker in 1976, and they played occasionally as a duo. During this time, Phillips had been supporting his music working as a guitar repairer and a furniture and picture restorer. Following a brief period of unemployment, he took up landscape painting until 1986. Long-time friend Croker coaxed Phillips out of his 'retirement' by organizing bookings. BBC disc jockey Andy Kershaw, using the growing popularity of 'roots music', helped create a demand that enabled Phillips to turn professional in 1986. Phillips achieved a higher profile with his appearances as support to acts such as the Blues Band and Nanci Griffith. He was then approached by Knopfler, who offered to produce an album by Phillips. The project developed into the Notting Hillbillies, which included Guy Fletcher from Dire Straits, and Brendan Croker. Steve Phillips' recorded output is limited and is no reflection on his obvious talent. In 1991, he recorded two tracks, 'Stones In My Passway' and 'When You Got A Good Friend', for a Robert Johnson compilation. *The Best Of Steve Phillips* consists of recordings made during the previous 10 years, but is not a compilation in the strict sense of the word.

● ALBUMS: *The Best Of Steve Phillips* (Unamerican Activities 1988)★★★, *Steel Rail Blues* (Unamerican Activities 1989)★★★, with the Notting Hillbillies *Missing Presumed Having A Good Time* (Vertigo 1990)★★★, *Just Pickin'* (Revival 1997)★★★.

PHILLIPS, WASHINGTON

b. *c*.1891, Freestone County, Texas, USA, d. 31 December 1938, Austin, Texas, USA. Phillips was unique on record in accompanying his plaintive gospel singing with the ethereal sounds of the dolceola, a zither equipped with a piano-like keyboard, of which only some 100 examples were made following its invention in 1902. Phillips recorded annually for Columbia from 1927-29, and his simple moral homilies were the work of a man who proclaimed his lack of education, preferring to trust in faith. His most famous song is the two-part 'Denomination Blues', an attack on the squabbling of black Christian sects, so titled because it uses the tune of 'Hesitation Blues'.

● COMPILATIONS: *Denomination Blues* (1980)★★★, *I Am Born To Preach The Gospel* (Yazoo 1992)★★★.

PIANO RED

b. William Lee Perryman, 19 October 1911, Hampton, Georgia, USA, d. 8 January 1985. The younger brother of blues artist Rufus 'Speckled Red' Perryman, this powerful keyboard player enjoyed several R&B bestsellers from 1950-51, including 'Rockin' With Red' and 'Red's Boogie'. He subsequently assumed another identity, Dr. Feelgood, and with his backing group, the Interns, secured further success with a series of pounding performances. His most influential releases included 'Right String Baby But The Wrong Yo Yo', the eponymous 'Doctor Feelgood', beloved of British beat groups, and 'Mister Moonlight', which was recorded by both the Beatles and the Merseybeats. Another of Perryman's whimsical offerings, 'Bald Headed Lena', was covered by the Lovin' Spoonful, but none of these versions matched the wry insistency of the originals. Perryman remained a popular live attraction, particularly in Europe, until his death in 1985.

● ALBUMS: *Piano Red In Concert* (Groove 1956)★★★, *Happiness Is Piano Red* (King 1970)★★★, *All Alone With His Piano* (1972)★★★, *Piano Red - Ain't Going To Be Your Low-Down Dog No More* (1974)★★, as Dr. Feelgood *All Alone* (1975)★★★, *Percussive Piano* (1979)★★, *Dr. Feelgood* (Black Lion 1979)★★★, with the Interns *What's Up Doc* (1984)★★, *Music Is Medicine* (1988)★★.

PIANO SLIM

b. Robert T. Smith, 1 August 1928, La Grange, Texas, USA. Slim began singing and playing saxophone in clubs in the late 40s, but after being shot in the chest he switched to drums, playing behind Lightnin' Hopkins for a spell. He became a pianist when working with a band in Odessa, Texas, and on moving back to Houston, Henry Hayes taught him about music; he also claims to have recorded around this time. Don Robey recommended Slim to Bobbin Records in St. Louis, and they released a single by him in the late 50s. He remains based in St. Louis, and has played in innumerable bars and clubs. In 1981 he recorded his first album, mostly solo, although with guitarist Amos Sandford on some titles, then two years later he made an album with a band that included two horns. Reviewing these two records, both issued by Swingmaster, *Living Blues* stated: 'whether you prefer solo piano blues or rocking horn-backed material, Robert T. Smith can deliver the goods'.

● ALBUMS: *Mean Woman Blues* (Swingmaster 1981)★★★, *Gateway To The Blues* (Swingmaster 1983)★★★, *That's Fat: The Best Boogie 'n' Blues* (Collectables 1996)★★★.

PIAZZA, ROD

b. 18 December 1947, Riverside, California, USA. Piazza heard the R&B records his brothers bought in the 50s and formed a blues band when he was mid-teens. He became friendly with George Smith, a huge influence on his vocals and harmonica playing. Piazza made two albums with the Dirty Blues Band for ABC-Bluesway, and in the late 60s formed Bacon Fat. In the mid-70s he was singer/harmonica player for the Chicago Flying Saucer Band, which became the Mighty Flyers, a goodtime blues group. In the 80s Piazza also recorded two solo albums to showcase his harder blues approach. He has also recorded on sessions for Jimmy Rogers, Big Joe Turner and Michelle Shocked.

● ALBUMS: *Harpburn* (Making Waves 1986)★★★, *So Glad To Have The Blues* (Special Delivery 1988)★★★, as Rod Piazza And The Mighty Flyers *Blues In The Dark* (1991)★★★, *Alphabet Blues* (Black Top 1992)★★★, *Live At BB King's* (Big Mo 1994)★★★, with the Mighty Flyers *Tough And Tender* (Tone Cool 1997)★★★★.

PICHON, WALTER 'FATS'

b. 3 April 1906, New Orleans, Louisiana, USA, d. 25 February 1967, Chicago, Illinois, USA. Pichon spent his musical career in the area between jazz, blues and pop, leading his own bands occasionally, and working as a pianist for artists including Luis Russell, Fess Williams, Ted Lewis, Mamie Smith, Elmer Snowden and Armand Piron. He recorded a few hokum vocals for Russell under his own name; the accompanists on the latter included Hawaiian guitarist King Benny Nawahi, for whom Pichon returned the compliment. In the 40s he began a long residency at the Absinthe House, New Orleans, also working in New York and the Caribbean. He was still active in the 60s, although treatment for failing eyesight interrupted his playing for long periods.

PICKENS, BUSTER

b. 3 June 1916, Hempstead, Texas, USA, d. 24 November 1964, Houston, Texas, USA. An early life as an itinerant musician, playing barrelhouses across the southern states, enabled Pickens to develop his down-home blues piano style, although it was firmly in the Texas idiom. Following military service in World War II, he settled back in Houston, and made his first record, supporting the vocals of Alger 'Texas' Alexander, along with guitarist Leon Benton. He also played regularly with Lightnin' Hopkins, and appeared as accompanist on some of that artist's records for Prestige/Bluesville in the early 60s. He also made a solo album in 1960, which demonstrated his deep knowledge of the Texas blues style. The possibilities of a successful new career in the blues revival, however, were tragically curtailed when he was murdered a few years later.
● ALBUMS: *Texas Barrelhouse Piano* (1960)★★★.

PICKETT, DAN

b. James Founty. Pickett was a singer and guitarist, whose August 1949 recordings prompted years of speculation. Many noted his stylistic links with the blues of the east coast, and it was through company files that critics discovered his real name. Pickett's repertoire was derived almost exclusively from 30s recordings, and his virtuosity went into the delivery, rather than the composition, of his songs, which sound as if they could have been recorded a decade or so earlier. However, the transformations to which he subjected many songs are the work of a true original. His guitar playing, influenced by Tampa Red, is complex but effortlessly fluent, and perfectly integrated with his intense but extrovert singing, which is often remarkable for the number of words crammed into a single line.
● ALBUMS: *Dan Pickett & Tarheel Slim* (Flyright 1991)★★★.

PIERCE, BILLIE

b. Wilhemina Goodson, 8 June 1907, Marianna, Florida, USA, d. 29 September 1974. After working for many years as singer or pianist (or both) in obscure southern clubs (with a brief moment of reflected glory as accompanist to Bessie Smith), Goodson married De De Pierce in 1935 and thereafter usually played in his company. After a long period of obscurity, in the mid-60s their joint careers were briefly revived.
● ALBUMS: including *Billie And De De* (Jazzology 1966/1988)★★★, *New Orleans Music* (Arhoolie 1981)★★★.

PITCHFORD, LONNIE

b. 8 October 1955, Lexington, Mississippi, USA. Through his adoption of the one-string 'diddley-bow' and tuition in the music of Robert Johnson from Robert Lockwood, Pitchford has risked being regarded as a museum curator rather than an active bluesman. He began constructing one-string guitars while still a child and his musical education as a guitarist and pianist remained in isolation until he was discovered by enthomusicologist Worth Long. He was introduced to Robert Johnson when he met Lockwood at the World's Fair in Knoxville, where Long arranged a concert appearance along with Sammy Myers and Theodis Morgan. He and Lockwood played together for three years thereafter. Pitchford's recreations of Johnson's 'Come On In My Kitchen' and 'Terraplane Blues' sound like self-conscious performance art alongside the band numbers on *All Around Man*, and asks of which format most nearly represents the man's talent.
● ALBUMS: *All Around Man* (Rooster 1994)★★.
● COMPILATIONS: *Mississippi Moan* (L + R 1988)★★★, *Roots Of Rhythm & Blues: A Tribute to the Robert Johnson Era* (Columbia 1992)★★★, *Deep Blues* (Anxious 1992)★★★.

POPA CHUBBY

b. Ted Horowitz, Bronx, New York, USA. Popa Chubby and his band came to light in the mid-90s after serving a long apprenticeship at New York's famed blues club, Manny's Carwash. The ebullient, cantankerous Chubby grew up in a home filled with music - Illinois Jacquet allegedly played at his parents' wedding. His father, who worked at a small candy store in the Bronx, took his son to see Chuck Berry when he was six years old and as a result Chubby took up the guitar. Later, as rock 'n' roll developed into more polished forms, his principle influences became Jeff Beck, Jimmy Page and Eric Clapton. In fact, his public statement that 'Jeff Beck made as big a contribution to the blues as Muddy Waters and Elmore James did', has offended many blues aficionados who see Chubby as an impostor and embarrassment. Previously he had also worked with the CBS Records punk band Chaos, before spending a brief period with Richard Hell And The Voidoids. In the late 80s he spent much of his time busking, re-learning the blues on New York subways. His performances at Manny's Carwash provided ample opportunity for Chubby to play with every visiting blues artist of note, and while journalists continued to criticize him for being 'white' he claims the only resistance he has ever encountered has been inverse racism. Indeed, he has toured with black blues artists of the stature of Earl King, Albert King and James Cotton. His 1995 debut for OKeh Records, Booty & The Beast, confused many blues commentators. While his physical demeanour and name led to many presuming he was a rap artist, the contents were far from the mainstream blues tradition, encompassing a strong element of hard rock derived from his affection for the Led Zeppelin and Black Sabbath recordings of the mid-70s.

● ALBUMS: Booty & The Beast (OKeh 1995)★★★, Hit The High Hard One (Prime 1997)★★★.

PORTNOY, JERRY

b. 25 November 1943, Evanston, Illinois, USA. Portnoy's father owned a rug store on Chicago's Maxwell Street, and every Sunday his son could drink in the wealth of music to be heard in the bustling street market. Blues was an early influence but he took little interest in the piano lessons that began when he was 10, nor in the accordion or the guitar that he adopted during the folk boom. Portnoy did not take up the harmonica until he was 24, but within two years he had formed a duo with mandolinist Johnny Young. After a two-year stint, he joined Johnny Littlejohn's band for a further two years before moving on to the Sam Lay Band. His career changed significantly in 1974 when Muddy Waters asked him to replace 'Mojo' George Buford. For the next six years, he toured the world and appeared on Waters' three Blue Sky albums, two of which received Grammy Awards. In 1980, along with Pinetop Perkins, Calvin Jones and Little Willie Smith, he left Waters, recruited Louis Myers and formed the Legendary Blues Band. The following year, they released Life Of Ease, followed in 1983 by Red Hot 'n' Blue. Portnoy left in 1986 and took a year off from music. He formed the Broadcasters with Ronnie Earl in 1987, but 18 months later left to form his own band, the Streamliners. That band made its recording debut, Poison Kisses, in 1991, the same year that Eric Clapton asked him to play the blues night at his annual Royal Albert Hall concert series. Portnoy returned in the same role in 1993 and took part in the sessions and subsequent tour for Clapton's 'return to the blues' album, From The Cradle.

● ALBUMS: Poison Kisses (Modern Blues Recordings 1991)★★★.

POWELL, EUGENE

b. 23 December 1909, Utica, Mississippi, USA. Powell made his first blues records by courtesy of Bo Carter, who set up a 1936 session for Bluebird. Carter heavily influenced his guitar playing, in sometimes discordant duets with Willie (Bill) Harris. Powell's singing, though warmer than Carter's, had a similar clarity. Powell recorded as 'Sonny Boy Nelson', Nelson being his stepfather's name, and besides his own titles accompanied his then wife, Mississippi Matilda, and the harmonica player Robert Hill. Powell and Matilda separated in 1952, and he retired from music soon after. In the 70s, he was still a skilful guitarist, and was persuaded by Bo Carter's brother Sam Chatmon to perform for white audiences, although it was not long before he retired again because of his second wife's

health problems, and subsequently his own.
● ALBUMS: *Police In Mississippi Blues* (1978)★★★, *Sonny Boy Nelson With Mississippi Matilda And Robert Hill* (1986)★★★.

POWER, DUFFY

Power was one of several British vocalists, including Marty Wilde, Billy Fury and Dickie Pride, signed to the Larry Parnes stable. Having completed a series of pop singles, including 'Dream Lover' and 'Ain't She Sweet', the singer embraced R&B in 1963 with a pulsating version of the Beatles' 'I Saw Her Standing There' on which he was backed by the Graham Bond Quartet. Power's later singles included 'Tired, Broke and Busted', which featured support from the Paramounts, but he later supplemented his solo career by joining Alexis Korner's Blues Incorporated. The singer appeared on *Red Hot From Alex* (1964), *Sky High* (1966) and *Blues Incorporated* (1967), during which time group members Jack Bruce (bass), Danny Thompson (bass) and Terry Cox (drums) assisted on several informal sessions later compiled on Power's *Innovations* set. Guitarist John McLaughlin also contributed to the album, before joining the vocalist's next project, Duffy's Nucleus. Power resumed his solo career late in 1967 when this short-lived attraction disbanded, but a subsequent fitful recording schedule did little justice to this underrated artist's potential.
● ALBUMS: *Innovations* aka *Mary Open The Door* (Transatlantic 1970)★★★, *Little Boy Blue* (1971)★★, *Duffy Power* (Spark 1973)★★, *Powerhouse* (Buk 1976)★★.
● COMPILATIONS: *Blues Power* (1992)★★★.

PRICE, 'BIG' WALTER

b. 2 August 1917, Gonzales, Texas, USA. Like many other aspects of society today, the blues features personalities famous for being famous. Big Walter Price is one. Raised from the age of three by his uncle, C.W. Hull, and aunt, he moved with them to San Antonio in 1928. Throughout his schooling, he also worked in cottonfields, sold newspapers, shined shoes and washed dishes. Taking an interest in music, he played with the Northern Wonders gospel group. After school, he worked on the railroad until, in 1955, he made three records for TNT Records, the first, 'Calling Margie', achieving local suc-

cess. Thereafter, he recorded 'Shirley Jean', on which his reputation rests, and four other singles for Peacock in Houston, several of them with Little Richard's old band, the Upsetters, masquerading as the Thunderbirds. In the next 10 years, he recorded for Goldband, Myrl, Jet Stream and Teardrop, while other tracks recorded for Roy Ames and featuring Albert Collins on guitar were issued later on Flyright and P.Vine. In July 1971, also for Ames, he recorded an album eventually issued in England 17 years later. His ebullient personality tended to minimize the effect of his rather wayward timing; although described as an exponent of classic Texas piano blues, the influence is more geographical than musical.
● ALBUMS: *Boogies From Coast To Coast* (1988)★★★.

PRIMER, JOHN

b. 3 March c.1946, Camden, Mississippi, USA. Primer recalls hearing the music of Muddy Waters as a youngster, and he played a one-string instrument before moving to Chicago in 1963 and acquiring a guitar. He initially played in Jimmy Reed's style. He began to take music more seriously around 1973 and played at the famed Chicago club Theresa's (1974-80), usually with Sammy Lawhorn, who gave Primer many tips on playing blues guitar. In the early 80s he was a member of the Muddy Waters band, and after Waters' death he replaced 'Alabama' Junior Pettis as second guitarist in Magic Slim's band the Teardrops. Slim allows his accompanist some of the spotlight, and Primer has recorded for Austrian label Wolf; he is highly rated for his pure blues playing (particularly slide guitar) and singing. Primer is a worthy standard-bearer of the old Chicago blues traditions.
● ALBUMS: *Chicago Blues Session, Volume Six - Poor Man Blues* (Wolf 1987)★★★, *Blue Behind Closed Doors* (Wolf 1994)★★★, *The Real Deal* (Code Blue 1995)★★★, *Mr. Freeze* (Flying Fish 1995)★★★, *Keep On Lovin' The Blues* (Code Blue 1997)★★★.

PROFESSOR LONGHAIR

b. Henry Roeland Byrd, 19 December 1918, Bogalusa, Louisiana, USA, d. 30 January 1980. Byrd grew up in New Orleans where he was part of a novelty dance team in the 30s. He also played piano, accompanying John Lee 'Sonny Boy' Williamson. After wartime service, Byrd gained a residency at the Caldonia club, whose owner christened him Professor Longhair. By now, he had developed a piano style that combined rumba and mambo elements with more standard boogie-woogie and barrelhouse rhythms. In 1949 he made the first record of his most famous tune, 'Mardi Gras In New Orleans', for the Star Talent label, which credited the artist as Professor Longhair And His Shuffling Hungarians. He next recorded 'Baldhead' for Mercury as Roy Byrd and his Blues Jumpers and the song became a national R&B hit in 1950. Soon there were more singles on Atlantic (a new version of 'Mardi Gras' and the well-known 'Tipitina' in 1953) and Federal. A mild stroke interrupted his career in the mid-50s and for some years he performed infrequently apart from at Carnival season when a third version of his topical song, 'Go To The Mardi Gras' (1958), received extensive radio play. Despite recording Earl King's 'Big Chief' in 1964, Longhair was virtually inactive throughout the 60s. He returned to the limelight at the first New Orleans Jazz & Heritage Festival in 1971 when, accompanied by Snooks Eaglin, he received standing ovations. (A recording of the concert was issued in 1987.) This led to European tours in 1973 and 1975 and to recordings with Gatemouth Brown and for Harvest. Longhair's final album, for Alligator, was completed shortly before he died of a heart attack in January 1980. In 1991 he was posthumously inducted into the Rock 'n' Roll Hall Of Fame.

● ALBUMS: *New Orleans Piano* reissue (Atco 1972)★★★★, *Rock 'N' Roll Gumbo* (1974)★★★★, *Live On The Queen Mary* (Harvest 1978)★★★, *Crawfish Fiesta* (Alligator 1980)★★★, *The London Concert* (JSP 1981)★★★, *The Last Mardi Gras* (Atlantic 1982)★★★★, *Houseparty New Orleans Style (The Lost Sessions 1971-1972)* (Rounder 1987)★★★, *Live In Germany* (1993)★★★, *Go To The Mardi Gras* (Wolf 1997)★★★.
● COMPILATIONS: *Fess: The Professor Longhair Anthology* (Rhino 1994)★★★★.
● FURTHER READING: *A Bio-discography*, John Crosby.

PRYOR, SNOOKY

b. James Edward Pryor, 15 September 1921, Lambert, Mississippi, USA. As a child he became drawn to the harmonica after watching an albino player, John Blissett, together with his friend Jimmy Rogers. When he was 13 he saw Rice Miller (Sonny Boy Williamson number 2) play. After settling in Chicago in 1945 after US Army service, Pryor joined the Maxwell Street group of blues singers which included Johnny Young, Floyd Jones and Moody Jones, with whom he recorded in 1948. Their records were harbingers of the amplified down-home sound of post-war Chicago blues, although at this time Pryor's singing and harmonica were heavily influenced by John Lee 'Sonny Boy' Williamson. Pryor made his first record, 'Telephone Blues', with guitarist Moody Jones in 1949. There were later singles for J.O.B. ('Boogy Fool', 1950), Parrot (1953), Blue Lake (1954) and Vee Jay Records ('Someone To Love Me', 1956). During the 50s Pryor also frequently toured the south. After making the dance novelty 'Boogie Twist', Pryor left the music business in 1963 but returned in the early 70s, touring and recording in Europe in 1973. A 1974 album was made with a New Orleans rhythm section including guitarist Justin Adams. In recent years he has benefited from the revived interest in blues, recording his 1992 album for Texas label Antone's, which has to date resulted in regular new albums, notably his 1997 release *Mind Your Own Business*.

● ALBUMS: *Snooky Pryor* (Flyright 1969)★★, *Snooky Pryor And The Country Blues* (1973)★★★, *Do It If You Want To* (1973)★★★, *Homesick James And Snooky Pryor* (1974)★★★, *Shake Your Moneymaker* (1984)★★★, *Too Cool To Move* (Antone's 1992)★★, with Johnny Shines *Back To The Country* (Black Pig 1993)★★★, *In This Mess Up To My Chest* (Antone's 1994)★★★, *Mind Your Own Business* (Antone's 1997)★★★★.
● COMPILATIONS: *Snooky Pryor - 1947 To 1960s* (Flyright 1990)★★★.

PUGH, JOE BENNIE

b. 10 July 1926, Hughes, Arkansas, USA, d. 3 April 1960, Horseshoe Lake, Arkansas, USA. An admirer of John Lee (Sonny Boy) Williamson, Joe Pugh aka Forest City Joe only recorded two sessions 11 years apart, but these were enough to create a significant reputation. He lived most of his life in Crittenden County, which encompasses the sites of his birth and death. Like many other harmonica players growing up in the 30s, his idolization of Williamson led to an imitation not only of his instrumental style but also of the speech impediment that affected his 'tongue-tied' vocals. In the late 40s he travelled north to Chicago several times, earning a reputation in the clubs where he played. On 2 December 1948, six months after Williamson had been murdered with an ice pick, Pugh recorded eight titles for Aristocrat with a guitarist tentatively identified as J.C. Cole. Only one single was issued at the time, combining 'Memory Of Sonny Boy' and 'A Woman On Every Street'. The complete session was released in the late 80s. Returning to Arkansas, nothing was heard of him until August 1959, when Alan Lomax recorded him for the *Southern Folk Heritage* series, both solo and with a band including guitarist Sonny Boy Rodgers, performing Williamson songs and 'Red Cross Store', a piano blues. Nine months later, he died when the lorry in which he was travelling home from a dance overturned, killing him instantly.

● ALBUMS: *Memory Of Sonny Boy* (1988)★★★.

QUALLS, HENRY

b. 8 July 1934, Cedar Grove, Elmo, Texas, USA. As nearly all the elder statesmen of Texas blues have died, it falls to individuals such as Qualls to represent, in a less than competent way, a tradition that has all but succumbed to the passage of time. While performing songs first recorded by artists such as Lightnin' Hopkins and Li'l Son Jackson, his faltering guitar technique, including a very wayward slide style, is more reminiscent of Smokey Hogg, an artist who built a reputation on his incapacity to observe the formalities of 12-bar blues. Taught as a youth by Emmitt Williams, Qualls supplemented his instruction by making regular visits to Dallas to watch Hopkins, Jackson and Frankie Lee Sims in action. Through most of his adult life, music was an intermittent hobby as he earned his living ploughing fields and mowing the lawns of the Dallas élite. Found by Dallas Blues Society men Scottie Ferris and Chuck Nevitt, Qualls became a reluctant local celebrity. His album contains the expected material from the Hopkins and Jackson songbooks, along with Big Boy Crudup's 'Death Valley Blues' and fumbled versions of 'Motherless Children' and 'I Shall Not Be Moved'. The touchstone of his importance as a Texas bluesman is his ability to place the Newbeats' 'Bread And Butter' alongside Lowell Fulson's 'Reconsider Baby'.

● ALBUMS: *Blues From Elmo, Texas* (Dallas Blues Society 1994)★★★.

QUATTLEBAUM, DOUG

b. 22 January 1927, Florence, South Carolina, USA. It was after moving to Philadelphia in the early 40s that Quattlebaum took up the guitar seriously, and toured with a number of gospel groups, claiming to have recorded with the Bells Of Joy in Texas. In 1952, he recorded solo as a blues singer for local label Gotham. By 1961, he was accompanying the Ward Singers but, when discovered by a researcher, was playing blues and popular tunes through the PA of his ice-cream van, hence the title of his album. *Softee Man Blues* showed him to be a forceful singer, influenced as a guitarist by Blind Boy Fuller, and with an eclectic repertoire largely derived from records. Quattlebaum made some appearances on the folk circuit, but soon returned to Philadelphia, where he recorded a single in the late 60s. He is thought to have entered the ministry soon afterwards.

● ALBUMS: *Softee Man Blues* (1962)★★★, *East Coast Blues* (1988)★★★.

QUILLIAN, RUFUS AND BEN

Rufus (b. 2 February 1900, Gainesville, Georgia, USA, d. 31 January 1946; piano, vocals) and Ben (b. 23 June 1907, Gainesville, Georgia, USA; vocals) worked in various combinations, but mostly in a group named the Blue Harmony Boys. This group, which also included other singers or musicians at various times, such as guitarist James McCrary, was notable in that the vocalists sang blues and related material in sweet, close harmonies. Ben was not with them at their first recording session in 1929, but was present at sessions in the following two years. The brothers were well-known as performers around Atlanta at this time and had a regular spot on a local radio station. Although their material on record was of a goodtime nature, Rufus was also known for composing religious songs.

● COMPILATIONS: *Complete Recordings In Chronological Order* (Matchbox 1985)★★★.

RACHELL, YANK

b. James Rachell, 16 March 1910, Brownsville, Tennessee, USA, d. 9 April 1997. Rachell learned mandolin from his uncle Daniel Taylor and later extended his talents to include guitar, harmonica and violin. He worked on the L&N railroad as a track hand in his early years, supplementing his income by playing local dances and parties in the company of local artists such as Hambone Willie Newbern. Rachell seems to have been doubling as a talent scout when he recorded with Sleepy John Estes in 1929. Later, he formed a partnership with Dan Smith and worked on record with John Lee 'Sonny Boy' Williamson. Recordings under his own name appeared on labels such as Victor, Vocalion and Banner and between 1938 and 1941 he recorded 24 titles for the famous Bluebird label. Despite all this activity Rachell was never able to survive as a full-time musician and often worked as a farmer. He returned to music, along with Estes and Hammie Nixon, with the revival of interest in blues in the early 60s. During that period he appeared at festivals, clubs and concerts, and recorded again for Delmark in 1964.

● ALBUMS: *Yank Rachell* (Blue Goose 1964)★★★, *Mandolin Blues* (Delmark 70s)★★★, *Chicago Style* (Delmark 70s)★★★.

● COMPILATIONS: *Complete Recordings In Chronological Order Volume 1 (1934-1938) Vol 2 (1938-1941)* (Wolf 1988)★★★.

RADCLIFF, BOBBY

b. 22 September 1951, Bethesda, Maryland, USA. Radcliff started to play guitar at the age of 12. In the 60s and 70s he worked on the Washington DC blues scene, associating with veterans such as Thomas 'TNT' Tribble and Bobby Parker. By the end of the 60s he spent some time in Chicago, meeting and absorbing the music of bluesmen such as Magic Sam, Otis Rush, and Jimmy Dawkins. Radcliff moved to New York in 1977 and in the early 80s he recorded a little edition album for the A-OK label. Towards the end of the decade he was recommended to his present label, Black Top Records, by Ronnie Earl, and his first album for them was highly acclaimed. Radcliff is a strong singer and a powerful, rhythmic guitarist who utilizes elements of soul and funk in his playing.

● ALBUMS: *Dresses Too Short* (Black Top 1989)★★★, *Universal Blues* (Black Top 1991)★★★, *There's A Cold Grave In Your Way* (Black Top 1994)★★★.

RAINER

b. Rainer Ptacek, 7 June 1951, East Berlin, Germany, d. 12 November 1997. A taste for seclusion and a penchant for unstructured, imaginative slide guitar playing made Rainer something of a cult figure before his records became generally available. His parents fled to West Berlin three years after his birth and in 1956 the family emigrated to America and settled in Chicago. While studying at the Saint Rita High School, Rainer heard blues players such as Muddy Waters, Paul Butterfield and Charlie Musselwhite at the Aragon Ballroom and the Electric Circus. He moved west in 1972 and settled in Tucson. For the next 20 years, his principal employment was as a guitar repairman after periods as a cab driver, janitor and cabinet maker. He was also a founding member of bands such as Naked Prey, the Giant Sandworms and the Band Of Blacky Ranchette. He formed Das Combo with Nick Augustine and Ralph Gilmore in 1984. A year later their initial cassette release, *The Mush Mind Blues*, was reviewed in *Rolling Stone* by Kurt Loder, followed in 1986 by *Barefoot Rock*, which was only released in England. *Worried Spirits* was a solo effort recorded in two days direct to DAT, incorporating natural sounds and effects machinery. *The Texas Tapes* was a long-standing project with Z.Z. Top guitarist Billy Gibbons. He also recorded with Robert Plant, who returned the favour on *The Inner Flame* in 1997, raising money for Rainer's medical bills following the diagnosis of an inoperable brain tumour.

● ALBUMS: with Das Combo *Barefoot Rock* (Making Waves 1986)★★★, *Worried Spirits* (Demon 1992)★★★, with Das Combo *The Texas Tapes* (Demon 1993)★★★, *Nocturnes (The Instrumentals)* (Glitterhouse 1995)★★★.

RAINEY, GERTRUDE 'MA'

b. Gertrude M. Pridgett, 26 April 1886, Columbus, Georgia, USA, d. 22 December 1939. After working as a saloon and tent show singer around the turn of the century, Rainey began singing blues. She later claimed that this occurred as early as 1902 and however much reliance is placed upon this date she was certainly among the earliest singers to bring blues songs to a wider audience. By the time of her first recordings, 1923, she was one of the most famous blues singers in the Deep South and was known as the 'Mother of the Blues'. Although many other singers recorded blues songs before her, she eschewed the refining process some of them had begun, preferring instead to retain the earthy directness with which she had made her name. Her recordings, sadly of generally inferior technical quality, show her to have been a singer of great power, while her delivery has a quality of brooding majesty few others ever matched. A hard-living, rumbustious woman, Rainey influenced just about every other singer of the blues, notably Bessie Smith whom she encouraged during her formative years. Although Rainey continued working into the early 30s her career at this time was overshadowed by changes in public taste. She retired in 1935 and died in 1939. In the late 80s a musical show, *Ma Rainey's Black Bottom*, was a success on Broadway and in London.

● COMPILATIONS: *Ma Rainey Vol. 1 (1923-24)* (Riverside 1953)★★★, *Complete Recordings Vol. 2 (1924-25)* (Riverside 1953)★★★, *Ma Rainey Volume 3* (Riverside 1953)★★★, *Broken Hearted Blues* (Riverside 1956)★★★.

● FURTHER READING: *Ma Rainey And The Classic Blues Singers*, Derrick Stewart-Baxter, *Mother Of The Blues: A Study Of Ma Rainey*, S. Lieb. *Ma Rainey's Black Bottom*, August Wilson.

RAITT, BONNIE

b. 8 November 1949, Burbank, California, USA. Born into a musical family, her father, John Raitt, starred in Broadway productions of *Oklahoma!* and *Carousel*. Having learned guitar as a child, Raitt became infatuated with traditional blues, although her talent for performing did not fully flourish until she attended college in Cambridge, Massachusetts. Raitt initially opened for John Hammond, before establishing her reputation with prolific live appearances throughout the east coast circuit, on which she was accompanied by long-time bassist Dan 'Freebo' Friedberg. Raitt then acquired the management services of Dick Waterman, who guided the careers of many of the singer's mentors, including Son House, Mississippi Fred McDowell and Sippie Wallace. She often travelled and appeared with these performers and *Bonnie Raitt* contained material drawn from their considerable lexicon. Chicago bluesmen Junior Wells and A.C. Reed also appeared on the album, but its somewhat reverential approach was replaced by the contemporary perspective unveiled on *Give It Up*. This excellent set included versions of Jackson Browne's 'Under The Falling Sky' and Eric Kaz's 'Love Has No Pride' and established the artist as an inventive and sympathetic interpreter. *Taking My Time* features assistance from Lowell George and Bill Payne from Little Feat and demonstrated an even greater diversity, ranging from the pulsating 'You've Been In Love Too Long' to the traditional 'Kokomo Blues'. Subsequent releases followed a similar pattern, and although *Streetlights* was a minor disappointment, *Home Plate*, produced by veteran Paul A. Rothchild, reasserted her talent. Nonetheless Raitt refused to embrace a conventional career, preferring to tour in more intimate surroundings. Thus the success engendered by *Sweet Forgiveness* came as a natural progression and reflected a genuine popularity. However its follow-up, *The Glow*, although quite commercial, failed to capitalize on this newfound fortune and while offering a spirited reading of Mable John's 'Your Good Thing', much of the material was self-composed and lacked the breadth of style of its predecessors. Subsequent releases, *Green Light* and *Nine Lives*, proved less satisfying and Raitt was then dropped by Warner Brothers Records, her outlet of 15 years. Those sensing an artistic and personal decline were proved incorrect in 1989 when *Nick Of Time* became one of the year's most acclaimed and bestselling releases. Raitt herself confessed to slight amazement at winning a Grammy award. The album was a highly accomplished piece of work, smoothing some of her rough, trademark blues edges for an AOR market. The emotional title track became a US hit single while the album, produced by Don

Was of Was (Not Was), also featured sterling material from John Hiatt and Bonnie Hayes. Raitt also garnered praise for her contributions to John Lee Hooker's superb 1990 release, *The Healer*, and that same year reached a wider audience with her appearance of the concert for Nelson Mandela at Wembley Stadium. She continued in the same musical vein with the excellent *Luck Of The Draw* featuring strong material from Paul Brady, Hiatt and Raitt herself. The album was another multi-million-seller and demonstrated Raitt's new mastery in singing smooth emotional ballads, none better than the evocative 'I Can't Make You Love Me'. Her personal life also stabilized following her marriage in 1991 (to Irish actor/poet Michael O'Keefe), and after years of singing about broken hearts, faithless lovers and 'no good men', Raitt entered the 90s at the peak of her powers. She was also growing in stature as a songwriter: on her 1994 album she displayed the confidence to provide four of the songs herself, her first nine albums having yielded only eight of her own compositions. Although that album, *Longing In Their Hearts*, spawned further US hits and achieved 2 million sales it was a record that trod water. Even her US hit version of Roy Orbison's 'You Got It' from the film *Boys On The Side* sounded weak. On her first ever live album, *Road Tested*, Raitt was joined by Bruce Hornsby, Jackson Browne, Kim Wilson, Ruth Brown, Charles Brown and Bryan Adams.

● ALBUMS: *Bonnie Raitt* (Warners 1971)★★★, *Give It Up* (Warners 1972)★★★, *Takin' My Time* (Warners 1973)★★★★, *Streetlights* (Warners 1974)★★★, *Home Plate* (Warners 1975)★★, *Sweet Forgiveness* (Warners 1977)★★, *The Glow* (Warners 1979)★★★, *Green Light* (Warners 1982)★★★, *Nine Lives* (Warners 1986)★★, *Nick Of Time* (Capitol 1989)★★★★, *Luck Of The Draw* (Capitol 1991)★★★★, *Longing In Their Hearts* (Capitol 1994)★★★, *Road Tested* (Capitol 1995)★★.

● COMPILATIONS: *The Bonnie Raitt Collection* (Warners 1990)★★★★.

● VIDEOS: *The Video Collection* (PMI 1992), *Road Tested* (Capitol 1995).

● FURTHER READING: *Just In The Nick Of Time*, Mark Bego.

RANKIN, R.S.

b. 22 February 1933, Royse City, Texas, USA. Rankin's uncle was 'T-Bone' Walker, who encouraged the youngster to play blues guitar and then took him on the road as a valet in the late 40s. He worked and recorded with Walker during the 50s, and was dubbed 'T-Bone' Walker Jnr. around 1955, and it was under this name that he recorded for the Midnite label in 1962. He has been less active on the music scene since the mid-60s but did surface to play at the T-Bone Walker Memorial Concert in Los Angeles, California, in May 1975, when *Blues Unlimited* reported that 'he did a fantastic job on his uncle's classics'.

● COMPILATIONS: one 1962 recording only *Texas Guitar - From Dallas To L.A.* (1972).

RAY, DAVE

As a member of Koerner, Ray And Glover, with 'Spider' John Koerner and Tony Glover, Dave 'Snaker' Ray was in the vanguard of the folk revival of the 60s. An accomplished 6- and 12-string guitarist, the artist pursued a concurrent solo career with two compulsive country blues albums. The first included interpretations of material by, among others, Muddy Waters, Robert Johnson and Lead Belly, while the follow-up featured a greater emphasis on original material. The rise of electric styles obscured Ray's progress and it was 1969 before he re-emerged in Bamboo, a country-based duo he had formed with pianist Will Donight. Their eccentric album made little impression and Ray's subsequent profile was distinctly low-key. However, in 1990 Ray and Glover teamed up to record *Ashes In My Whiskey* for the Rough Trade label, winning critical acclaim.

● ALBUMS: *Fine Soft Land* (1967)★★★. As Koerner, Ray And Glover *Blues, Rags And Hollers* (1963)★★★, *More Blues, Rags And Hollers* (1964)★★★, *The Return Of Koerner, Ray And Glover* (1965)★★★, *Live At St. Olaf Festival* (60s/70s)★★, *Some American Folk Songs Like They Used To Be* (1974)★★, with Tony Glover *Ashes In My Whiskey* (Rough Trade 1990)★★★, with Glover *Picture Has Faded* (Tim/Kerr 1994)★★★.

RAY, HARMON

b. 1914, Indianapolis, Indiana, USA. Ray grew up in St. Louis, where he took up blues singing in the 30s, adopting the vocal style of Peetie Wheatstraw, with whom he worked as a double act from 1935 until Wheatstraw's death in 1941. In 1942, Ray recorded as 'Peetie Wheatstraw's Buddy'. After military service he settled in Chicago, singing in clubs, and recording for J. Mayo Williams, who may have been the source of a Hy-Tone 78 release. Ray's last recordings were made in 1949, one song being in the manner of Charles Brown, and the other three in Wheatstraw's style; two of these were cover versions of Wheatstraw songs, but 'President's Blues' was an original tribute to Truman. Ray continued to work in Chicago clubs until the early 60s, when cancer forced him to retire.

● COMPILATIONS: *Chicago Blues* (1985).

REBENNACK, MAC

(see Dr. John)

RED DEVILS

Blues-influenced hard rockers the Red Devils were formed in Los Angeles, California, USA, in 1988. The band consisted of Lester Butler (vocals, harp), Jonny Ray Bartel (bass) and Bill Bateman (drums) among others, although only these three were in the 90s line-up which also featured Paul Size (lead guitar) and Dave Lee Bartel (rhythm guitar). They emerged from an informal jam session and Bateman recalls their first audience as 'nine champion skateboarders sitting at the bar'. Butler had first learned blues harp at the age of six, because the instrument was the only one within his budget. Later he became a pupil of urban blues guitar maestro Hollywood Fats, who contributed to groups including the Blasters and the James Harman Band. When Fats died in 1986 it gave Butler the impetus to enter the music industry. After performing regularly at high school parties and other informal events, he eventually made the acquaintance of Bateman and Bartel, both fellow travellers on the Los Angeles roots rock scene (Bateman had also played on three albums with the Blasters). The Red Devils finally came to the attention of Def American Records and Rick Rubin in the early 90s, who saw an opening for their dense, excitable blues rock sound. Rubin was also on hand to record the band's debut album, a glimpse of the Red Devils in their natural, live setting. The previous year they had appeared on sessions with Mick Jagger, though he did not include the results on his *Wandering Spirit* album.

● ALBUMS: *King King* (This Way Up/Def American 1993)★★★.

RED NELSON

b. Nelson Wilborn, 31 August 1907, Sumner, Mississippi, USA. Red Nelson was a Chicago-based vocalist, and possibly a guitarist, but not a pianist, despite frequent reports to that effect. He was given interesting and varied accompanists during his recording career, which began in 1935, and was a fine singer with a telling falsetto, although he often held himself emotionally in check, possibly to accommodate the 30s fashion for the laconic. His 1935/6 Decca recordings with Cripple Clarence Lofton, though less considered, are outstanding, with 'Crying Mother Blues' an unquestionable masterpiece, while his 1947 titles for Aladdin, with James Clark on piano, are almost as good. Last seen working with Muddy Waters in the 60s, Nelson was an amiable alcoholic with a penchant for *double entendres*, as might be inferred from the ebullient 'Dirty Mother Fuyer', which he recorded in 1947 under the pseudonym 'Dirty Red'.

● COMPILATIONS: *Blues Uptown* (1969)★★★, *The Piano Blues Vol. 9 Lofton/Noble* (1979)★★★, *Red Nelson* (1989)★★★.

REED, A.C.

b. Aaron Corthen Reed, 9 May 1926, Wordell, Missouri, USA. Reed was attracted to the saxophone by hearing a Jay 'Hootie' McShann record. On moving to Chicago at the age of 15, he bought a saxophone and studied music, although he was tutored in the blues by J.T. Brown. He spent much of the 50s touring the south-western states with blues musician Dennis Binder. The following decade he re-established himself in Chicago, recording in his own right for several small labels, even enjoying a minor hit with 'Talkin' 'Bout My Friends' on Nike Records in the mid-60s. He became an in-demand session musician for over three decades. He has had long spells in the bands of

Buddy Guy and Albert Collins but now has a successful solo career. Reed's vocals, powerful saxophone playing and often witty songwriting have been recorded for the white collector market by Alligator and Wolf, and he also runs his own Ice Cube label.

● ALBUMS: *Take These Blues And Shove 'Em* (1984)★★★, *I'm In The Wrong Business* (Alligator 1987)★★★, *I Want You To Love Me* (Ichiban 1995)★★★, *Can't Make It On My Own* (Ichiban 1996)★★★.

REED, JIMMY

b. Mathis James Reed, 6 September 1925, Leland, Mississippi, USA, d. 29 August 1976, Oakland, California, USA. Jimmy Reed was a true original: he sang in a lazy mush-mouthed ramble, played limited, if instantly recognizable, harmonica, and even more minimal guitar. He produced a series of hits in the 50s that made him the most successful blues singer of the era. He was born into a large sharecropping family and spent his early years on Mr. Johnny Collier's plantation situated near Dunleith, Mississippi. Here, he formed a childhood friendship with Eddie Taylor which was to have a marked effect on his later career. Reed sang in church and learned rudimentary guitar along with Taylor, but while the latter progressed Reed never became more than basically competent on the instrument. He left school in 1939 and found work farming around Duncan and Meltonia, Mississippi. Around 1943-44 he left the south to find work in Chicago where opportunities abounded due to the war effort. He was drafted in 1944 and served out his time in the US Navy. Discharged in 1945 he returned briefly to Mississippi before gravitating north once more to the Chicago area. Working in the steel mills, Reed gigged around in his leisure time with a friend named Willie Joe Duncan, who played a one-string guitar, or Diddley-bow. He also re-established contact with Eddie Taylor who had similarly moved north to try his luck. This led to Reed's becoming known on the local club scene and after appearances with John and Grace Brim, he secured a recording contract with Vee Jay Records in 1953. His initial sessions, though highly regarded by collectors, produced no hits and Vee Jay were considering dropping him from their roster when in 1955 'You Don't Have

To Go' took off. From then on, his success was phenomenal as a string of hits such as 'Ain't That Lovin' You Baby', 'You've Got Me Dizzy', 'Bright Lights Big City', 'I'm Gonna Get My Baby' and 'Honest I Do' carried him through to the close of the decade. Many of these timeless blues numbers were adopted by every white R&B beat group during the early 60s. Two of his songs are now standards and are often used as rousing encores by name bands; 'Baby What You Do You Want Me To Do' closed the Byrds' and Closer Than Most's live performances for many years and 'Big Boss Man' is arguably the most performed song of its kind - sung by the Merseybeats, Pretty Things, Grateful Dead and countless blues artists. Much of the credit for this success must be attributed to his friend Eddie Taylor, who played on most of Reed's sessions, and his wife, Mama Reed, who wrote many of his songs and even sat behind him in the studio reciting the lyrics into his forgetful ear as he sang. On some recordings her participation is audible. Reed's songs had little to do with the traditional blues, but they were eminently danceable and despite employing the basic blues line-up of harmonica, guitars and drums were generally classed as R&B. His hits were 'crossovers' appealing to whites as well as blacks. Perhaps this contributed to his continuing success as the blues entered its post-rock 'n' roll hard times. In his later days at Vee Jay, various gimmicks were tried, such as dubbing an album's worth of 12-string guitar solos over his backing tracks, faking live performances and introducing a commentary between album cuts; none were too successful in reviving his flagging sales. To counter the positive elements in his life, Reed was continually undermined by his own unreliability, illness (he was an epileptic) and a fascination for the bottle. He visited Europe in the early 60s, by which time it was obvious that all was not well with him. He was supremely unreliable and prone to appear on stage drunk. By the mid-60s his career was in the hands of the controversial Al Smith and his recordings were appearing on the Bluesway label. Inactive much of the time due to illness, Reed seemed on the road to recovery and further success, having attained control over his drink problem. Ironically, he died soon afterwards of respiratory failure, and was buried in Chicago. Reed is an important figure who has influenced countless artists through his songs. Steve Miller recorded *Living In The 20th Century* with a segment of Reed songs and dedicated the album to him. The Rolling Stones, Pretty Things and the Grateful Dead also acknowledge a considerable debt to him.

● ALBUMS: *I'm Jimmy Reed* (Vee Jay 1958)★★★★, *Rockin' With Reed* (Vee Jay 1959)★★★★, *Found Love* (Vee Jay 1960)★★★★, *Now Appearing* (Vee Jay 1960)★★★★, *At Carnegie Hall* (Vee Jay 1961)★★★, *Just Jimmy Reed* (Vee Jay 1962)★★★★, *T'ain't No Big Thing...But He Is!* (Vee Jay 1963)★★★, *The Best Of The Blues* (Vee Jay 1963)★★★, *The 12-String Guitar Blues* (Vee Jay 1963)★★★★, *Jimmy Reed At Soul City* (Vee Jay 1964)★★★, *The Legend, The Man* (Vee Jay 1965)★★★, *The New Jimmy Reed Album* (Bluesway 1967)★★★, *Soulin'* (Bluesway 1967)★★★, *Big Boss Man* (Bluesway 1968)★★★, *Down In Virginia* (Bluesway 1969)★★★, *As Jimmy Is* (Roker 1970)★★★, *Let The Bossman Speak!* (Blues On Blues 1971)★★★.

● COMPILATIONS: *The Best Of Jimmy Reed* (Vee Jay 1962)★★★★, *More Of The Best Of Jimmy Reed* (Vee Jay 1964)★★★★, *The Soulful Sound Of Jimmy Reed* (Upfront 1970)★★★, *I Ain't From Chicago* (Bluesway 1973)★★★, *The Ultimate Jimmy Reed* (Bluesway 1973)★★★★, *Cold Chills* (Antilles 1976)★★★, *Jimmy Reed Is Back* (Roots 1980)★★★, *Hard Walkin' Hanna* (Versatile 1980)★★★, *Greatest Hits* (Hollywood 1992)★★★, *Speak The Lyrics To Me, Mama Reed* (Vee Jay 1993)★★★, *Cry Before I Go* (Drive Archive 1995)★★★, *The Classic Recordings Volumes 1-3* (Tomato/Rhino 1995)★★★★, *Big Legged Woman* (Collectables 1996)★★★★.

REYNOLDS, BLIND JOE

b. 1900, Arkansas, USA, d. 10 March 1968, Monroe, Louisiana, USA. Reynolds also recorded as Blind Willie Reynolds. He was a wild and violent man with an extensive criminal record, who carried a gun even after he was blinded by a shotgun during an argument in the mid-20s. He played widely in Mississippi and Louisiana, and recorded in 1929 and 1930; the two 78s that he made feature fierce singing and slide guitar, closely allied to the blues styles of Mississippi.

His lyrics are caustic, misogynistic, bawdy and sometimes hastily self-censored. His signature tune, 'Outside Woman Blues', was recorded by Cream in the 60s, at which time Reynolds was still performing in his original milieu, perhaps the last important blues singer of his generation to do so.

● COMPILATIONS: *Son House And The Great Delta Blues Singers* (1990).

RHODES, EUGENE

Rhodes' blues singing and guitar were recorded in the Indiana State Penitentiary in the early 60s. As a youth, he had been a travelling one-man band, and claimed to have met Blind Lemon Jefferson, Buddy Moss and Blind Boy Fuller, being particularly impressed and influenced by the latter pair. Rhodes' repertoire consisted largely of the commercially recorded blues of the late 20s and the 30s, with a few well-known spirituals; his performances were marred by his erratic timing and uncertain pitch.

● ALBUMS: *Talkin' About My Time* (Collectors Issue 1963/1988)★★.

RHODES, SONNY

b. Clarence Edward Smith, 3 November 1940, Smithville, Texas, USA. Rhodes received his first electric guitar at the age of nine and began emulating 'T-Bone' Walker, Chuck Willis (Rhodes still wears a turban), Junior Parker and Bobby Bland. He first recorded in 1961 in Austin, then moved to California two years later and recorded for Galaxy in 1965. In the 70s and 80s he made several mediocre albums for European companies and some interesting singles for Blues Connoisseur, Cleve White's Cherrie label, and his own Rhodes-Way label. In 1991 Rhodes made the best album of his career for Ichiban, high-lighting his vocals and songwriting skills in addition to his prowess on both regular and lap steel guitars.

● ALBUMS: including *I Don't Want My Blues Colored Bright* (Amigo 1978)★★★, *Just Blues* (1985)★★★, *Disciple Of The Blues* (Ichiban 1991)★★★★, *Living Too Close To The Edge* (Ichiban 1992)★★★★, *Out Of Control* (King Snake 1996)★★★★.

RHODES, WALTER

Reportedly from Cleveland, Mississippi, USA, Rhodes was unusual, possibly unique, in coming from that state, to be a blues singing accordionist. He had one record issued, cut in 1927, and it seems certain that Charley Patton either knew Rhodes personally or his record, as Patton's 'Banty Rooster Blues' is a cover of Rhodes' 'The Crowing Rooster'. Rhodes played in a band that included two guitars and a fiddle, though only a guitar duo backs him on record. He is said to have died in the 40s after being struck by lightning.

● COMPILATIONS: *Memphis Blues* (1987)★★★, *Giving You The Blues* (Swingmaster 1989)★★★.

RIDDLE, LESLIE

b. 13 June 1905, Burnsville, North Carolina, USA, d. 1980. Although not discovered until the 60s, Riddle was one of the few remaining exponents of the music prevalent among black communities before the blues held sway. His association with the Carter Family during the 30s served to highlight the interaction of black and white musicians in the area bounded by Tennessee, Virginia and North Carolina. At the age of 10, Riddle learned to play guitar in open tuning from his uncle Ed Martin, who taught him traditional pieces such as 'John Henry', 'Casey Jones' and a train piece, 'KC'. Moving to Kingsport, Tennessee, he met another guitarist, John Henry Lyons, and also George McGhee, father of Brownie. In August 1927, Riddle lost his left leg in an accident at the cement plant where he worked. Thereafter, he turned increasingly to music, often partnering Brownie McGhee. In 1934, Lyons introduced him to A.P. Carter, who took him on trips around Tennessee and Virginia collecting songs. Riddle also taught about a dozen of his own pieces, including 'The Cannon Ball', to the Carter family, with whom he associated for several years. He moved to Rochester, New York, in 1942 where he remained until approached by Mike Seeger, then researching the Carter family. *Step By Step* consists of recordings made by Seeger between 1965 and 1978 which combine sacred and secular material encapsulating a bygone era.

● ALBUMS: *Step By Step* (Rounder 1994)★★★.

RIGGINS, J., JNR.
(see Dixon, Floyd)

RISING SONS
One of the most legendary unrecorded groups, the Rising Sons consisted of Taj Mahal (vocals, guitar), Ry Cooder (vocals, guitar), Gary Marker (bass), Ed Cassidy (drums) and Jesse Lee Kincaid (vocals, guitar). Kevin Kelley also deputized on drums during their brief recording period when Cassidy injured his wrist playing a frenetic version of 'Blind' Willie McTell's 'Statesboro Blues'. Formed in Los Angeles, California, USA, in 1965, the group was signed to Columbia Records but their album was never issued. One single, 'Candy Man'/'The Devil's Got My Woman', did surface, but the group had by then disbanded. Mahal became a prominent blues/folk performer, Cooder made his name playing sessions and later recorded successfully under his own name. Kelley briefly joined the Byrds and Cassidy became a mainstay in Spirit. Marker became a renowned journalist. Sessions from the album, produced by Byrds/Paul Revere associate Terry Melcher, became widely bootlegged due to interest in the various participants, and nearly two decades later they were given an official release by Columbia Records. Mahal contributed three new vocal takes for this project, but its patchwork quality finally laid to rest one of the great mysteries of the 60s.
● ALBUMS: *Rising Sons Featuring Taj Mahal And Ry Cooder* (Columbia/Legacy 1993)★★★.

ROBERTSON, SHERMAN
b. 27 October 1948, Breaux Bridge, Louisiana, USA. Already a veteran of zydeco, Texas R&B and swamp blues, Robertson is a seasoned entertainer who rarely writes his own material but knows how to sell a song. Like many of his generation, he was initially inspired by country music and asked his father for a guitar after watching Hank Williams on television. He learned about blues from Floyd London, who also lived in the Fifth Ward of Houston where Robertson grew up. Conrad Johnson was music director of his high school band and recruited him to play in his group, Connie's Combo. Later, Robertson formed the Crosstown Blues Band, with whom he made his first albums, but broke them up when Clifton Chenier, a friend of his father's, asked him to work with him. In the next five years, he visited Europe and recorded with Chenier for Arhoolie and Maison De Soul. He then joined Rockin' Dopsie's band and took part in the Paul Simon session that became part of Simon's *Gracelands* album. He next joined Terrence Simien's Mallet Playboys, where he stayed for two and a half years. In 1992 he was contacted by blues producer Mike Vernon, who eventually signed him to Indigo Records and recorded *I'm The Man* with him in February 1993. Robertson became a regular visitor to Europe, undertaking lengthy tours and appearing at most European blues festivals, where his energy regularly won over audiences. His album was re-released on Mike Vernon's Code Blue label in 1994 with a different cover and this was followed by his first proper Code Blue release, *Here And Now*, an album that once again failed to capture the excitement of his live performances. Taken out of context from a live gig it is an average collection of slow soulful tracks. Robertson's reputation continues to slowly build as a powerful live performer but on record to date he seems to fall short.
● ALBUMS: *Bad Luck And Trouble* (Lunar 2 1981)★★★, *Married Blues* (Lunar 2 1983)★★★, *Sherman & Friends* (Lunar 2 1985)★★, *I'm The Man* (Indigo/Code Blue 1993/4)★★★, *Here And Now* (Code Blue 1995)★★.

ROBEY, DON
b. 1 November 1903, Houston, Texas, USA, d. 16 June 1975, Houston, Texas, USA. Houston businessman and impresario Don Robey bought his nightclub, the Bronze Peacock, in 1945, and it soon became a centre for developing local talent as well as bringing in big names from across the country. Soon after, he opened a record shop, which eventually became the base of operations for his Peacock Records, one of the first ever labels in the USA to have a black owner. Peacock developed as one of the most important R&B and gospel labels, featuring artists such as Gatemouth Brown, Johnny Ace and Big Mama Thornton, as well as the Dixie Hummingbirds and Five Blind Boys. Robey then bought the Duke label from Memphis, which became another major outlet, especially for Bobby Bland and Junior Parker. Another label, Songbird, also issued gospel records for many years.

ROBILLARD, DUKE

b. Michael Robillard, 4 October 1948, Woonsocket, Rhode Island, USA. Although associated in most minds with Roomful Of Blues, the band he formed with pianist Al Copley in 1967, Robillard's ambitions reach beyond the rigorous guidelines of the blues. This is reflected in the number of times he has left blues-based bands in order to pursue more personal musical goals. In its first 12 years, Roomful Of Blues extended its gig sheet beyond Boston and Rhode Island and down the east coast to New York and Washington. After signing with Island Records and recording two albums, Robillard left the band in 1979 to form the Pleasure Kings with Thomas Enright and Tom DeQuattro. He also worked with Robert Gordon and the Legendary Blues Band. In 1990 he replaced Jimmie Vaughan in the Fabulous Thunderbirds, which at the time featured two ex-Roomful musicians, Preston Hubbard and Fran Christina. In 1992, he left the Thunderbirds to once again form a new band, this time with Marty Ballou and ex-Lonnie Mack drummer Jeff McAllister. *Temptation* featured a set of original songs (with the exception of Sugar Boy Crawford's 'What's Wrong?') that illustrated Robillard's creative potential without establishing a persona as convincing as that he assumes when playing blues. *Duke's Blues* was a throwback album that not only reprised numbers such as Roy Milton's 'Information Blues' and T-Bone Walker's 'Don't Leave Me Baby', but actually sounded as if the songs were recorded in the 50s. Robillard's own modern songs on the album had a similar 50s feel.

● ALBUMS: *Duke Robillard & The Pleasure Kings* (Rounder/Demon 1984)★★★, *Too Hot To Handle* (Rounder/Demon 1985)★★★, *You Got Me* (Rounder 1988), *Swing* (Rounder 1990)★★★, *Turn It Around* (Rounder 1991)★★★, *After Hours Swing Session* (Rounder 1992)★★★, *Temptation* (PointBlank 1994)★★★, *Duke's Blues* (PointBlank 1995)★★★, *Dangerous Place* (PointBlank 1997)★★★.

● COMPILATIONS: *Plays Jazz: The Rounder Years* (Bullseye 1997)★★★, *Plays Blues: The Rounder Years* (Bullseye 1997)★★★★.

ROBINSON, 'LONESOME' JIMMY LEE

b. 30 April 1931, Chicago, Illinois, USA. In the 40s, Robinson played blues guitar on Chicago's Maxwell Street, occasionally working with Eddie Taylor. In the 50s he worked in the clubs, associating with artists including Freddie King, Elmore James and Magic Sam. He became an in-demand session player, both as a bassist and guitarist, and recorded under his own name for the Bandera label in the early 60s. He toured Europe with the *American Folk Blues Festival* in 1965 and again in 1975 with the *American Blues Legends*, recording on both occasions.

● ALBUMS: *Chicago Jump* Bandera recordings (1979)★★★, two tracks, plus backing other artists *American Blues Legends '75* (1975).

ROBINSON, FENTON

b. 23 September 1935, Greenwood, Mississippi, USA. Although held in high regard by both his peers and audiences, Robinson's mellow voice and jazz-oriented guitar-playing remains a rare pleasure. Robinson took an interest in guitar on hearing T-Bone Walker's Black & White records in 1946 and was helped by local musician Sammy Hampton. In 1951 he moved to Memphis and received tuition from Charles McGowan, guitarist in Billy 'Red' Love's band. In 1953 he moved to Little Rock, Arkansas, to play with Love and Eddie Snow. He formed a band with Larry Davis, then a drummer but later a bass player and guitarist. Robinson made his recording debut in Memphis in 1955 with 'Tennessee Woman' for Lester Bihari's Meteor label. Two years later, he and Davis recorded for Duke Records in Houston, playing on each other's tracks. Robinson's four Duke records included a remake of 'Tennessee Woman', 'Mississippi Steamboat' and the first version of his most famous song, 'As The Years Go By'. In the 60s, he moved to Chicago and made singles for U.S.A., Palos (his other blues standard, 'Somebody Loan Me A Dime'), Giant and Sound Stage 7. During the 70s, he made two critically acclaimed albums for Alligator, *Somebody Loan Me A Dime* and *I Hear Some Blues Downstairs*, before personal problems and disillusionment kept him out of music. One album, *Blues In Progress* was made in 1984 with guitarist/arranger Reggie Boyd. In 1989, he headlined the Burnley Blues Festival and recorded the *Special Road* in Holland. Not just a bluesman, Robinson seems too individual a musician to pander to blunatic audiences and his career suffers thereby.

● ALBUMS: *Somebody Loan Me A Dime* (Alligator 1974)★★★, *I Hear Some Blues Downstairs* (Alligator 1977)★★★, *Blues In Progress* (Black Magic 1984)★★★, *Mellow Fellow* (Charly 1987)★★★, *Special Road* (1989)★★★.

ROBINSON, FREDDIE

b. c.30s, Arkansas, USA. As 'Fred Robertson' he recorded with Little Walter (Jacobs) in the late 50s and by the early 60s he had become a noted guitarist in Chicago, where he recorded for the Queen, M-Pac/One-Der-Ful and Chess labels. After moving to Los Angeles around 1968, he maintained his links with producer/musician Milton Bland (aka Monk Higgins) and recorded in a jazz context for World Pacific in 1969 and as a blues and soul guitarist for Enterprise (the Stax subsidiary label) a few years later. In 1977 he recorded for ICA, with which he also worked as a session guitarist, writer and arranger, mostly in a soul vein. In the 80s he toured and recorded with Louis Myers.

● ALBUMS: *The Coming Atlantis* (1969)★★★, *At The Drive-In* reissued as *Black Fox* (Enterprise 1972)★★★, *Off The Cuff* (1973)★★★.

ROBINSON, L.C. 'GOOD ROCKIN''

b. Louis Charles Robinson, 15 May 1915, Brenham, Texas, USA, d. 26 September 1976. Robinson began playing guitar at the age of nine, and was reputedly taught to play bottle-neck style by Blind Willie Johnson. Western swing musician Leon McAuliffe introduced him to the steel guitar; Robinson was also a blues fiddler of note and gave Sugarcane Harris some lessons on the instrument. He moved to the San Francisco area around 1939, where he often played together with his brother A.C. Robinson. They recorded for the Black And White label in 1945 as the Robinson Brothers. L.C. recorded for Rhythm Records in the early 50s, for World Pacific in the 60s, and for Arhoolie and Bluesway in the 70s, and also accompanied Mercy Dee Walton and John Lee Hooker on records. He died of a heart attack in 1976.

● ALBUMS: *Ups And Down* (Arhoolie

1971)★★★, *House Cleanin' Blues* (Bluesway 1974)★★★.
● COMPILATIONS: *Mojo In My Hand* (Arhoolie 1996)★★★.

ROCKET 88

This part-time attraction was drawn from the ranks of the UK's finest R&B/jazz musicians. Formed in 1979, the unit revolved around singer/guitarist Alexis Korner, bassist/vocalist Jack Bruce and three members of the Rolling Stones' circle, Ian Stewart (piano), Bill Wyman (bass) and Charlie Watts (drums). The unit took its name from a 1951 recording by Jackie Brenson, often cited as the first rock 'n' roll single, although the music offered by this *ad hoc* collective invoked the earlier boogie-woogie style of Meade 'Lux' Lewis. Their lone album, recorded live in Hannover, Germany, included versions of 'St. Louis Blues' and 'Roll 'Em Pete' and, while undeniably low-key, was nonetheless an enthralling glimpse into the artistic preferences of musicians freed from perceived commercial restraints. Korner's premature death ended speculation that Rocket 88 might blossom into a full-time commitment.

● ALBUMS: *Rocket 88* (Atlantic 1981)★★★.

ROCKIN' DOPSIE

b. Alton Rubin, 1932, Carenco, Lafayette, USA, d. 26 August 1993. Rubin taught himself accordion at the age of 14, and in 1955 teamed up with scrub-board player Chester Zeno to work the local club circuit, adapting his name from that of 'Doopsie', a Chicago dancer. In 1969-70 he recorded for the Bon Temps and Blues Unlimited labels, and in 1973 began a successful collaboration with Sonet Records and producer Sam Charters. Following the death of Clifton Chenier in 1987, Rubin, under his alter-ego guise of the Rockin' Dopsie, was hailed as the 'king of zydeco', and was crowned as such by the Mayor of Lafayette, Louisiana, in 1988. During that decade he worked alongside a number of gifted performers attempting to bring Cajun and zydeco to a broader, international audience, achieving substantial success in that pursuit. Numerous international tours were undertaken and Rubin's vivacious stage presence (singing and playing the accordion) became a familiar sight at folk and roots music festivals the world over. His less readily available early recordings tended towards blues-based material, with a more contemporary edge evident on subsequent releases for GNP and Atlantic Records, where he was backed by his full band, the Zydeco Twisters. His 1990 album for Atlantic, *Louisiana Music*, provided a good introduction to his later work, consisting almost entirely of highly rhythmic numbers such as 'Zydeco Two Step' and 'I'm In The Mood', aimed squarely at ballroom dancers. The recording was personally supervised by Atlantic Records founder Ahmet Ertegun. However, Rubin probably remained best renowned for appearing on Paul Simon's *Gracelands* album. Rubin's band, the Twisters, featured his sons Alton (drums) and David Rubin (rub-board), and the legendary zydeco saxophone player John Hart. After his father's death in 1993 from a heart attack, David became known as Rockin' Dopsie Jnr.

● ALBUMS: *Clifton Chenier/Rockin' Dupsee* (Flyright 1970)★★★★, *Hold On* (Sonet 1979)★★★, *Crown Prince Of Zydeco* (Sonet 1987)★★★★, *Big Bad Zydeco* (GNP 1988)★★★, *Good Rockin'* (GNP 1988)★★★, *Saturday Night Zydeco* (Maison De Soul 1988)★★★, *Zy-De-Co-In* (Sonet 1990)★★★, *Louisiana Music* (Atlantic 1990)★★★★.

ROCKIN' SIDNEY

b. Sidney Semien, 9 April 1938, Lebeau, Louisiana, USA. The full range of black south Louisiana music - blues, R&B, swamp pop and zydeco - can be found in the work of Rockin' Sidney, who was born and grew up in the French-speaking part of that state. Many of his records are characterized by a light approach - even his blues tracks frequently opt for melody rather than emotional expression. Nevertheless, he has recorded regularly for over 30 years, from early singles on the local Jin and Goldband labels to albums self-produced in his own studio. In the early 80s, he achieved a wider profile through the success of his song 'Toot Toot'. So far he has not managed to recapture its novelty appeal, despite evident hard work: his recent recordings have featured Semien playing all of the instruments. His infectious and accessible songs have done much to widen the appeal of zydeco music in Europe.

● ALBUMS: *They Call Me Rockin'* (Flyright

1975)★★★, *Boogie Blues 'N' Zydeco* (Maison De Soul 1984)★★★, *My Toot Toot* (Ace 1986)★★★★, *Creola* (ZBC 1987)★★★, *Crowned Prince Of Zydeco* (Maison De Soul 1987)★★★, *Give Me A Good Time Woman* (Maison De Soul 1987)★★★, *A Celebration Holiday* (ZBC 1987)★★★, *Hotsteppin* (JSP 1987)★★★, *My Zydeco Shoes* (Maison De Soul 1987)★★★★, *Live With The Blues* (JSP 1988)★★★, *Mais Yeah Chere* (1993)★★★★.

RODGERS, PAUL

b. 17 December 1949, Middlesbrough, England. The former Bad Company and Firm vocalist originally came to prominence as the stylist front man of the 60 heavy prog rock band Free. Until the mid-90s his solo career had never raised his profile above cult status, although few would deny he has one of the most powerful and recognisable voices in post 60s rock music. His solo career floundered until the release of *Muddy Waters Blues*, an excellent tribute album demonstrating Rodgers strong natural feeling for the blues. A new album, *Now*, co-produced by Eddie Kramer was released in 1996 to excellent reviews and healthy enough sales to put him back in the album charts. Although he will be requested to sing 'All Right Now' and 'Can't Get Enough of Your Love' for the rest of his performing life, Rodgers now has enough credibility as a solo artist to build a successful career.

● ALBUMS: *Cut Loose* (1983)★★, *10 from 6* (1985)★★, *Muddy Waters Blues* (London 1993)★★★★, *Paul Rodgers Live* (1996)★★★, *Now* (SPV 1997)★★★.

RODGERS, SONNY

b. Oliver Lee Rodgers, 4 December 1939, Hughes, Arkansas, USA, d. 7 May 1990. Rodgers learned guitar from his father and was influenced by B.B. King, Robert Nighthawk and Muddy Waters. After forming his first band at the age of 17, he recorded as accompanist to Forest City Joe Pugh in 1959. Two years later, Rodgers settled in Minneapolis, beginning a long association with Mojo Burford. He also recorded with Lazy Bill Lucas. In the early 70s Rodgers had a spell as guitarist in Muddy Waters' band, and after some years out of music, he formed his own band in the 80s, winning several music awards in Minnesota. His Blue Moon single 'Big

Leg Woman/Cadillac Blues' was voted 'Blues Single Of 1990' in the international W.C. Handy awards. Rodgers only made one full album, which was highly acclaimed on its release, and tragically coincided with his death on 7 May 1990, just prior to a tour of the UK.
● ALBUMS: *They Call Me The Cat Daddy* (1990)★★★★.

ROGERS, JIMMY

b. James A. Lane, 3 June 1924, Ruleville, Mississippi, USA. Self-taught on both harmonica and guitar, Rogers began working at local house parties in his early teens. He then followed an itinerant path, performing in Mississippi and St. Louis, before moving to Chicago in 1939. Rogers frequently took work outside of music, but having played for tips on the city's famed Maxwell Street, began appearing in several clubs and bars. Although he worked as a accompanist with pianist Sunnyland Slim, Rogers established his reputation with the Muddy Waters Band, with whom he remained until 1960. The guitarist thus contributed to many of urban blues' finest performances, including 'Hoochie Coochie Man', 'I Got My Mojo Workin'' and the seminal *At Newport*. Rogers also enjoyed a moderately successful career in his own right. 'That's All Right' (1950), credited to Jimmy Rogers And His Trio, featured Waters, Little Walter (harmonica) and Big Crawford (bass), and its popularity around the Chicago area engendered a new group, Jimmy Rogers And His Rocking Four. Several more sessions ensued over the subsequent decade, but the guitarist only enjoyed one natio·1al R&B hit when 'Walkin' By Myself' reached number 14 in 1957. By the 60s Rogers found himself eclipsed by a new generation of guitarists, including Buddy Guy and Magic Sam. Despite enjoying work supporting Sonny Boy Williamson and Howlin' Wolf, he spent much of the decade in seclusion and only re-emerged during the blues revival of the early 70s. He was signed to Leon Russell's Shelter label for whom he completed *Gold Tailed Bird*, a low-key but highly satisfying set. It inspired a period of frenetic live activity which saw Rogers tour Europe on two occasions, with the American Folk Blues Festival (1972) and the Chicago Blues Festival (1973). Appearances in the USA were also well received, but the artist

retired from music during the middle of the decade to work as the manager of an apartment building. However, Rogers rejoined Muddy Waters on *I'm Ready* (1977), one of the excellent selections recorded under the aegis of Johnny Winter. These releases brought Waters new dignity towards the end of his career and invested Rogers with a new-found confidence. He continues to perform on the contemporary blues circuit and his 1990 release, *Ludella*, named after the artist's guitar, was produced by Kim Wilson from the Fabulous Thunderbirds. *Blue Bird* was a raw Chicago blues album featuring Carey Bell on harmonica, Johnson's son, Jimmy D. Lane, on lead guitar and Johnnie Johnson (piano).
● ALBUMS: *Gold Tailed Bird* (Shelter 1971)★★★★, *That's All Right* i (1974)★★★, *Live: Jimmy Rogers* (JSP 1982)★★★, *Feelin' Good* (Blind Pig 1985)★★★, *Dirty Dozens* (JSP 1985)★★★, *Ludella* (Bedrock 1990)★★★, *Blue Bird* (Analogue Productions 1994)★★★★, with Rod Piazza *Feelin' Good* (Blind Pig 1995)★★★.
● COMPILATIONS: *Chicago Bound, Golden Years* (1976)★★★, *Chess Masters* (Chess 1982)★★★, *Chicago Blues* (JSP 1982)★★★, *That's All Right* ii (Charly 1989)★★★, *Jimmy Rogers Sings The Blues* (Sequel 1990)★★★, *Chicago Blues Masters* (Capitol 1996)★★★.

ROGERS, ROY

b. 28 July 1950, Redding, California, USA. Since producing a quartet of bestselling and award-winning albums with John Lee Hooker, Rogers' own career has become more of an indulgence than a necessity. By 13, he was playing guitar in a high school R&B band. A few years later, he began to study blues techniques and slide playing in particular. During the 70s, he formed a partnership with harmonica player David Bergin, making their recording debut with *A Foot In The Door*. In 1979, he formed the Delta Rhythm Kings, a trio that he has retained ever since; between 1982 and 1986, he divided his time between them and being a member of John Lee Hooker's Coast To Coast Boogie Band. Rogers financed his own album, *Chops Not Chaps*, in 1986, later reissued on Blind Pig. *Slidewinder*, released the following year, also featured Hooker and Allen Toussaint. Toussaint worked on *Slide Of Hand* six years later. Rogers teamed up with another harmonica player,

Steve Miller's sideman Norton Buffalo, on *R&B* and subsequently *Travelin' Tracks*. Hooker's *The Healer* was released in 1989, bringing both commercial success and a fistful of Grammy awards. *Mr Lucky* and *Boom Boom* followed in 1991 and 1992, but it was not until 1995's *Chill Out* that Rogers established a firm presence on both sides of the microphone. His Liberty albums contain a shrewd mixture of the entertaining and the edifying, showing that Rogers now combines an understanding of the music with a commercial ear.

● ALBUMS: *A Foot In The Door* (Waterhouse 1976)★★★, *Slidewinder* (Blind Pig 1987)★★★, *Blues On The Range* (Blind Pig 1989)★★★, with Norton Buffalo *R&B* (Blind Pig 1991)★★★, *Chops Not Chaps* (Blind Pig 1992)★★★, with Buffalo *Travelin' Tracks* (Blind Pig 1993)★★★, *Slide Of Hand* (Liberty 1993)★★★, *The Slide Zone* (Liberty 1994)★★★, *Rhythm And Groove* (PointBlank 1996)★★★.

ROLAND, WALTER

b. Birmingham, Alabama, USA, d. *c.*1970. Although a somewhat obscure character, Walter Roland saw something like 40 recordings issued under his own name during the period 1933-35. He is also justly famous for the work he did accompanying Lucille Bogan (Bessie Jackson) and Sonny Scott around the same time. Roland was a skilled pianist, capable of providing sympathetic support to his own and other people's vocal performances as well as displaying a considerable ability in the 'barrelhouse' style. His own voice was expressive and his blues ran the whole gamut from the deeply introspective through to the cheerfully obscene. Although often only discussed in relationship to the outstanding Bogan, Roland stands on his own as a blues singer and pianist of the first rank whose work deserves to be much better known and appreciated. His 1933 recording 'Jook It, Jook It', a piano solo issued under the name of the Jolly Jivers, has appeared on many anthologies.

● COMPILATIONS: *The Piano Blues Volume 6: Walter Roland* (1978)★★★, *Walter Roland 1933-1935 (The Remaining Sides)* (Document 1988)★★★, with Lucille Bogan *1927 - 35* (1993)★★★, *Complete Recorded Works In Chronological Order Vol 1 (1933)* (Document 1996)★★★, *Complete Recorded Works In Chronological Order Vol 2 (1934-1935)* (Document 1996)★★★.

ROOMFUL OF BLUES

Formed as a seven-piece band in the Boston, Massachusetts, area in the late 70s, Roomful Of Blues quickly established first a national reputation in the USA with their very authentic-sounding, swing big band R&B, and then broke through on the international scene in the 80s. The group honed their first-hand knowledge of the music by playing with many of the originators, as well as making numerous recordings in their own right. They also recorded behind 'Big' Joe Turner, Eddie 'Cleanhead' Vinson and Earl King. The group's main successful alumni included guitarists Duke Robillard (b. Michael Robillard, 4 October 1948, Woonsocket, Rhode Island, USA) and Ronnie Earl (b. Ronald Earl Horvath, 1953, New York City, USA), vocalist Curtis Salgado, pianist Al Copley, and saxophonist Greg Piccolo. Despite personnel changes, the group continues to work regularly, although their impact has lessened due to the many similar groups that have followed in their wake. Hopes for a new era of interest in the band rose in 1994 when they signed a three-album contract with the Bullseye Blues label under the leadership of Carl Querfurth (trombone). A stable line-up ensued for the excellent *Turn It On, Turn It Up* in 1995. Upon its release on 13 October 1995, the Governer of Rhode Island announced an official annual Roomful Of Blues day for the state of Rhode Island. The present band comprises Carl Querfurth (b. 3 February 1956, Camden, New Jersey, USA; trombone), John 'JR' Rossi (b. 13 November 1942; drums), Doug James (b. Douglas James Schlecht, 1953, Turlock, California, USA; saxophone), Matt McCabe (b. 6 June 1955, Devon, England; keyboards), Chris Vachon (b. 4 October 1957, South County, Rhode Island, USA; guitar), Sugar Ray Norcia (b. 6 June 1954, Westerly, Rhode Island, USA; vocals, harmonica), Kenny 'Doc' Grace (b. 11 March 1951, Providence, Rhode Island, USA; bass), Bob Enos (b. 4 July 1947, Boston, Massachussetts, USA; trumpet) and Rich Lataille (b. 29 October 1952, Providence, Rhode Island, USA; saxophone).

● ALBUMS: *The First Album* (Island 1977)★★, *Let's Have A Party* (Antilles 1979)★★, *Hot Little*

Mama (Blue Flame 1981)★★★, *Eddie 'Cleanhead' Vinson & Roomful Of Blues* (Muse 1982)★★★, *Blues Train/Big Joe Turner & Roomful Of Blues* (Muse 1983)★★★, *Dressed Up To Get Messed Up* (Rounder 1984)★★★, *Live At Lupo's Heartbreak Hotel* (Rounder 1986)★★★, with Earl King *Glazed* (Black Top 1988)★★★, *Dance All Night* (Rounder 1994)★★★, *Turn It On, Turn It Up* (Bullseye Blues 1995)★★★★, *Under One Roof* (Bullseye Blues 1997)★★★.
● COMPILATIONS: *Roomful Of Blues With Joe Turner/Roomful Of Blues With Eddie Cleanhead Vinson* (32 Blues 1997)★★★★.

ROTH, LILLIAN

b. Lillian Rutstein, 13 December 1910, Boston, Massachusetts, USA, d. 1980. Entering show-business while still a tiny child, she appeared on the stage and also in films. Billed as 'Broadway's Youngest Star', she sang and danced in shows staged by leading showmen such as Earl Carroll and Florenz Ziegfeld. She made silent films as early as 1918 but was invited to Hollywood when Paramount boss Jesse L. Lasky heard her sing the blues during a New York show designed to introduce Maurice Chevalier to American audiences before his film debut. She appeared with the Marx Brothers in *Animal Crackers* (1930), *Paramount On Parade* (1930) and *Ladies They Talk About* (1933), a feature for Barbara Stanwyck. Unfortunately, Roth's private life was in turmoil through failed relationships and drink, and by the end of the 30s she had succumbed to alcoholism and was soon a forgotten figure. Then, in 1953, she was featured on television's *This Is Your Life*. The show, together with the publication of Roth's autobiography, *I'll Cry Tomorrow*, convinced Hollywood that here was a story worth telling. The similarly titled film, released in 1955 and starring Susan Hayward as Lillian, was a rare example of a Hollywood biopic that told a tragic tale without unnecessary sensationalism. Roth was able to fashion a new career out of this appraisal of her life and she worked regularly in clubs and on television for the rest of her life. In 1977, half a lifetime after her last film, she appeared in a minor role in the Brooke Shields debut feature film *Communion (Holy Terror/Alice, Sweet Alice)*. Roth's singing of the blues was for the time a rarity for a white woman and she contrived to deliver this material with a fair degree of authenticity.

RUSH, BOBBY

b. Emmitt Ellis Jnr., 10 November 1936, Homer, Louisiana, USA. For most of his career, Rush has managed to forge an amalgam of blues, soul and R&B which allows him the widest scope for personal expression. The son of a preacher, he began performing in Pine Bluff, Arkansas, with a band that included guitarist Boyd Gilmore and Johnny 'Big Moose' Walker. Moving to Chicago, he led a series of bands that at times included Freddie King, Luther Johnson, Bobby King and Luther Allison. During the 60s, he made singles for small labels such as Jerry-O, Palos and Starville before recording 'Gotta Have Money' for ABC-Paramount, the earliest example of the Rush signature style. Six records for Salem made little impression before 'Chicken Heads' on Galaxy put Rush's name on the *Billboard* charts. Further singles for On Top, Jewel, Warner Brothers and London Records led to a contract with Gamble And Huff's Philadelphia International label. *Rush Hour* was the first significant release of Rush's career but 'artistic differences' precluded any further collaboration. Throughout the 80s Rush recorded for James Bennett's LaJam label a series of albums that highlighted his skill at adapting traditional blues themes for a contemporary audience. This continued with his switch to Urgent! in the 90s, although *Instant Replay: The Hits* perhaps denoted that his career was marking time. A move to Malaco Records' subsidiary Waldoxy produced *One Monkey Don't Stop No Show*, a much more impressive effort apart from an unnecessary reprise of the perennial 'Jezabel'.
● ALBUMS: *Rush Hour* (Philadelphia International 1979)★★★, *Sue* (LaJam 1982), *Wearing It Out* (LaJam 1983)★★★, *Gotta Have Money* (LaJam 1984)★★★, *What's Good For The Goose Is Good For The Gander* (LaJam 1985)★★★, *A Man Can Give It But He Can't Take It* (LaJam 1989)★★★, *I Ain't Studdin' You* (Urgent! 1991)★★★, *Instant Replay: The Hits* (Urgent! 1992)★★★, *Handy Man* (Urgent! 1993)★★★, *It's Alright* (Ronn 1995)★★★, *One Monkey Don't Stop No Show* (Waldoxy 1995)★★★, *Lovin' A Big Fat Woman* (Waldoxy 1997)★★.

RUSH, OTIS

b. 29 April 1934, Philadelphia, Mississippi, USA. A left-handed blues guitarist, Rush moved to Chicago where his impassioned singing and playing on 'I Can't Quit You Baby' brought a Top 10 R&B hit in 1956. He became one of the 'young turks' of the Chicago scene together with Buddy Guy, Freddie King and Magic Sam. 'I Can't Quit You Baby' and other Cobra recordings ('Double Trouble', 'All Your Love') from the same era inspired British guitarists such as Peter Green, Eric Clapton and Mick Taylor, who strived to recreate the starkly emotive quality of his solos. John Mayall opened the pivotal *Bluesbreakers* with 'All Your Love' and continued by making Rush more widely known in the UK with recordings of 'So Many Roads', 'I Can't Quit You Baby' (also recorded by Led Zeppelin) and 'Double Trouble'. In the early 60s, Rush recorded for Chess and Duke where 'So Many Roads' and 'Homework' became his best-known songs. As blues declined in popularity with black audiences, he turned increasingly to college concerts and collaborations with white blues artists such as Mike Bloomfield, with whom he made an album for Cotillion in 1969. During the 70s, Rush toured Europe and Japan, recording in Sweden, France and Japan as well as making two albums for Chicago-based label Delmark. *Right Place Wrong Time* had been made in 1971 for Capitol with producer Nick Gravenites, but was only issued on the independent Bullfrog label five years later. He performed and toured less frequently in the 80s, although an album made at the 1985 San Francisco Blues Festival showed him to be on top form. Rush's influence has always been greater than his commercial standing and like Buddy Guy, his former stablemate at Chess, he has become a guitarist's guitarist. In keeping with the recent blues boom Rush seems destined to benefit in a similar way to John Lee Hooker and Buddy Guy. John Porter, the producer of Guy's excellent *Damn Right I Got the Blues*, was enlisted to work on *Ain't Enough Comin' In*. On this, his best work in many years, Rush demonstrates total confidence and experience and is well supported by Mick Weaver (organ), Bill Payne (piano) and Greg Rzab (bass).

● ALBUMS: *Chicago - The Blues - Today !* (Chess 1964)★★★, *This One's A Good Un* (Blue Horizon 1968)★★★, *Mourning In The Morning* (Cotillion 1969)★★★, *Chicago Blues* (Blue Horizon 1970)★★★, *Groaning The Blues* (Python 1970)★★, *Cold Day In Hell* (Delmark 1975)★★★, *Right Place, Wrong Time* (Bulldog 1976)★★, *So Many Roads - Live In Concert* (1978)★★★, *Troubles, Troubles* (Sonet 1978)★★★, *Screamin' And Cryin'* (1979)★★, *Tops* (Blind Pig 1988)★★★, *Lost In The Blues* (Alligator 1991)★★★, *Ain't Enough Comin' In* (This Way Up 1994)★★★★, *Blues Interaction Live In Japan 1986* (Sequel 1996)★★★★, *Live And Awesome* (Genes 1996)★★.

● COMPILATIONS: *Blues Masters Vol. 2* (Blue Horizon 1968)★★★, *Double Trouble - Charly Blues Masterworks Vol. 24* (1992)★★★★.

RUSHING, JIMMY

b. 26 August 1902, Oklahoma City, Oklahoma, USA, d. 8 June 1972. Rushing began singing while still studying music at school in his hometown. By 1923 he was a full-time professional singer, working in California with, among others, Jelly Roll Morton and Paul Howard. Back home in the mid-20s he teamed up with Walter Page and then joined Bennie Moten, and by 1935 was a member of the Count Basie band. He remained with Basie until 1948 and then worked as a solo, sometimes leading a small band. During these later years he regularly worked with leading jazz artists including Benny Goodman, Buck Clayton, Basie, and, during tours of the UK, with Humphrey Lyttelton. Rushing's voice was a slightly nasal high tenor which carried comfortably over the sound of a big band in full cry. The fact that he sang at a somewhat higher pitch than most other male blues singers gave his performances a keening, plaintive quality. In fact, his singing style and repertoire made him far more than merely a blues singer and he was at ease with romantic ballads. Nevertheless, he tinged everything he sang, from love songs to up-tempo swingers, with the qualities of the blues. Despite his extensive repertoire, in later years he favoured certain songs, including 'Going To Chicago', 'Every Day I Have The Blues' and 'Exactly Like You', but even repeated performances at clubs, concerts and record dates were infused with such infectious enthusiasm that he never palled. Known because of his build as 'Mr Five By Five',

Rushing was at his best in front of a big band or a Kansas City-style small group, but even when he stepped out of character, as on his final formal record date, he could enchant listeners. By the early 70s, and his last date, his voice was showing signs of decades of wear and tear, but he retained his unflagging swing and brought to unusual material such as 'When I Grow Too Old To Dream' and 'I Surrender Dear', great emotional depth and a sharp awareness of the demands of both music and lyrics. An exceptionally gifted artist, Rushing was always unmistakable and never imitated.

● ALBUMS: *Sings The Blues* (Vanguard 1954)★★★★, *Goin' To Chicago* (1954)★★★★, *Listen To The Blues* (Vanguard 1955)★★★★, *The Jazz Odyssey Of James Rushing Esq* (Columbia 1957)★★★, *If This Ain't The Blues* (Vanguard 1957)★★★, *Listen To The Blues* (Fontana 1957)★★★, *Showcase* (Vanguard 1957)★★★, with Ada Moore, Buck Clayton *Cat Meets Chick* (Philips 1957)★★★, *Little Jimmy Rushing And The Big Brass* (Columbia 1958)★★★, with Clayton *Copenhagen Concert* (1959)★★★, *Rushing Lullabies* (Columbia 1959)★★★, *Two Shades Of Blue* (Audio Lab 1959)★★★, *The Smith Girls* (Columbia 1961)★★★, *Five Feet Of Soul* (Colpix 1963)★★★, *Blues I Love To Sing* (Ace Of Hearts 1966)★★★, *Gee, Baby, Ain't I Good To You* (1967)★★★, *Who Was It Sang That Song* (1967)★★★, *Every Day I Have The Blues* (Bluesway 1967)★★★, *Livin' The Blues* (Bluesway 1968)★★★, *The You And Me That Used To Be* (Bluebird 1971)★★★.

● COMPILATIONS: *The Essential Jimmy Rushing* (Vanguard 1978)★★★★, *Mister Five By Five* (Columbia 1980)★★★★, *The Classic Count* (Intermedia 1982)★★★.

S.O.B. BAND
(see Sons Of Blues)

SAFFIRE - THE UPPITY BLUES WOMEN

Gaye Adegbalola (b. 21 March 1944, Fredericksburg, Virginia, USA; guitar), Ann Rabson (b. 12 April 1945, New York, USA; piano) and Earlene Lewis (b. 31 January 1945, Avenal, California, USA; bass), replaced by Andra Faye McIntosh (b. Indianapolis, USA). Rabson grew up in Ohio, where she took up the guitar and began singing professionally at the age of 18. Moving to Fredericksburg, Virginia, in 1971, she met Gaye Adegbalola and gave her guitar lessons. As well as each performing solo, the pair began to gig together in 1984. Four years later, they gave up their jobs as a computer analyst and science teacher to form Saffire with Lewis, a real estate agent who played in a bluegrass band. A demo tape sent to Bruce Iglauer resulted in their signing with Alligator Records. Their debut album was one of the label's best-sellers for 1990 and Adegbalola won a W.C. Handy Award for Song Of The Year with 'Middle Aged Blues Boogie'. While recording *Broadcasting*, Lewis left the group, to be replaced by McIntosh, who already played guitar, violin and mandolin and thereafter took up the double bass. While benefitting from the heightened awareness of feminism, the group manages to combine a politically correct posture with humour and musicianship.

● ALBUMS: *Saffire - The Uppity Blues Women* (Alligator 1990)★★★, *Hot Flash* (Alligator 1991)★★★, *Broadcasting* (Alligator 1992)★★★, *Old, New, Borrowed & Blue* (Alligator 1994)★★★, *Cleaning House* (Alligator 1996)★★★.

Solo: Ann Rabson *Music Makin' Mama* (Alligator 1997)★★★.

SAIN, OLIVER

b. 1 March 1932, Dundee, Mississippi, USA. Working out of St. Louis, saxophonist Sain first established himself as a bandleader and producer, but later in his career made a name for himself as a disco star. After forming his band in St. Louis in 1960 he developed a considerable local reputation playing at all the clubs in the city and across the Mississippi in East St. Louis and other communities. Members of his band have included Fontella Bass, Bobby McClure and Little Milton. He made his first records in 1962 for the tiny Bobbin label, featuring Fontella Bass on vocals and piano and Little Milton on guitar. In 1966 he founded Archway Studio and occasionally recorded himself as well as a host of St. Louis/East St. Louis acts. Sain never achieved any national recognition, however, until the early 70s, when he began recording instrumentals for the Nashville-based Abet label, establishing himself as an unlikely disco star. His most renowned hits were 'Bus Stop' (number 47 R&B) in 1974 and 'Party Hearty' (number 16 R&B) in 1976. His last chart record a year later was 'I Feel Like Dancin'' (number 74 R&B). Sain's albums, unlike his singles, were broader than disco in appeal, containing besides rousing dance grooves some warm southern-style soulful saxophone playing. During the 80s and 90s he established himself as a producer of blues acts, notably Larry Davis, Eddie Kirkland, David Dee, and Johnnie Johnson.

● ALBUMS: *Main Man* (Abet 1973), *Bus Stop* (Abet 1974), *Blue Max* (Abet 1975), *So Good In The Morning* (Houston Connection 1981).
● COMPILATIONS: *Disco King* (Soul Posters 1976), *At His Best* (Abet 1977).

SANE, DAN

b. 22 September 1896, Hernando, Mississippi, USA, d. *c.*1971, Osceola, Arkansas, USA. Sane, sometimes identified as Dan Sain and also as Dan Sing, was an unobtrusive but important member of the Memphis blues community up to the 50s. He only ever sang on an unissued recording, and it was as a ragtime-influenced guitarist that he made his mark. He recorded as a member of the band led by Jack Kelly, accompanying the singing of violinist Will Batts, a fellow band member, and guitarist Frank Stokes. He recorded fairly extensively, with the latter

producing percussive but effortlessly nimble flat-picked figures that meshed with Stokes' rhythm guitar to form one of the most impressive series of two-guitar arrangements in blues.
● COMPILATIONS: *The Beale Street Sheiks* (1990), *Frank Stokes* (1990), *Jack Kelly & His South Memphis Jug Band* (1990).

SATAN AND ADAM

Sterling Magee (b. 20 May 1936, Mount Olive, Mississippi, USA) and Adam Gussow (b. 3 April 1958, Congers, New York, USA). Magee almost had a career in the 60s when, managed by Al Sears and Jesse Stone, he made one single for Sylvia Records, 'Get In My Arms Little Girlie', and a pair for Ray Charles's Tangerine label, 'Oh She Was Pretty' and 'I Still Believe In You'. By the mid-80s he had become a one-man band on 125th Street in Harlem, playing guitar, two hi-hats, tambourines and a sounding board. In October 1986, Gussow, a 1979 Princeton graduate who had busked in Paris and Amsterdam, happened by and asked to play. Since then, the pair have toured Europe on several occasions and appeared in U2's concert film *Rattle & Hum*. Their first album was nominated for a W.C. Handy award, but its sequel added nothing to the impression made by *Harlem Blues*. Their dynamic blend of funk, blues and R&B intrigues the ear on first listening but the hybrid nature of their music leaves little room for creative development.
● ALBUMS: *Satan and Adam* cassette (Duane Street Music Collective 1991)★★★, *Harlem Blues* (Flying Fish/Demon 1991)★★★, *Mother Mojo* (Flying Fish/Demon 1993)★★.

SAUNDERS, RED

b. Theodore Saunders, 2 March 1912, Memphis, Tennessee, USA, d. 4 March 1981, Chicago, Illinois, USA. One of Saunders' two claims to fame was his position as leader of the house band in Chicago's Club DeLisa, a tenure that lasted two decades up to 1958. During that time, the prevailing tastes in music ranged from jazz to blues and R&B and he worked with Albert Ammons, Louis Armstrong, Duke Ellington and Woody Herman. Saunders studied percussion at school in Milwaukee, principally drums, but also vibes and timpani. Before taking up his position at the Club DeLisa, he was with Tiny Parham's

Savoy Ballroom Orchestra. He recorded for Savoy, Sultan and Supreme before securing a contract with OKeh. The featured vocalist on his 1950/1 sessions was Jumpin' Joe Williams, some years and a coat of polish before his stint with Count Basie. Saunders' other claim to fame was a ramshackle 1952 novelty hit, 'Hambone'. The 'Hambone Kids', Sammy McGrier, Ronny Strong and Delecta Clark (who grew up to become Dee Clark), patted 'juba', slapping their bodies in syncopated rhythm, between singing childish verses that anticipated 'Bo Diddley', while Dolores Hawkins ejaculated 'Yeah!' at the end of each stanza.

● COMPILATIONS: *Okeh Rhythm & Blues* (Epic 1982), *The OKeh Rhythm & Blues Story 1949-1957* (Epic/Legacy 1993).

SAVOY BROWN

Formed in 1966 as the Savoy Brown Blues Band, this institution continues to be led by founding guitarist Kim Simmonds. The original line-up, comprising Simmonds (b. 6 December 1947), Brice Portius (vocals), Ray Chappell (bass), John O'Leary (harmonica), Bob Hall (piano) and Leo Mannings (drums), was featured on early sessions for producer Mike Vernon's Purdah label, before a second guitarist, Martin Stone, joined in place of O'Leary. The reshaped sextet then secured a recording contract with Decca. Their debut, *Shake Down*, was a competent appraisal of blues favourites, featuring material by Freddie King, Albert King and Willie Dixon. Unhappy with this reverential approach, Simmonds dismantled the group, retaining Hall on an auxiliary basis and adding Chris Youlden (vocals), Dave Peverett (guitar, vocals), Rivers Jobe (bass) and Roger Earl (drums). The new line-up completed *Getting To The Point* before Jobe was replaced by Tone Stevens. The restructured unit was an integral part of the British blues boom. In Youlden they possessed a striking frontman, resplendent in bowler hat and monocle, whose confident, mature delivery added panache to the group's repertoire. Their original songs matched those they chose to cover, while the Simmonds/Peverett interplay added fire to Savoy Brown's live performances. 'Train To Nowhere', from *Blue Matter*, has since become one of the genre's best-loved recordings. Youlden left the group following *Raw Sienna*, but

the inner turbulence afflicting the group culminated at the end of 1970 when Peverett, Stevens and Earl walked out to form Foghat. Simmonds, meanwhile, toured America with a restructured line-up - Dave Walker (vocals), Paul Raymond (keyboards), Andy Pyle (bass) and Dave Bidwell (d. 1977; drums) - setting a precedent for Savoy Brown's subsequent development. Having honed a simple blues-boogie style, the guitarist seemed content to repeat it, and the group's ensuing releases are not as interesting. Simmonds later settled in America, undertaking gruelling tours with musicians who became available, his determination both undeterred and admirable. The reintroduction of Walker to the group in the late 80s marked a return to the group's original sound, before the singer left again and was replaced by Pete McMahon (vocals/harp). This line-up toured in support of a new compilation and the re-release of their (remastered) Decca CDs, but *Bring It On Home*, released in 1995, failed to sell. However, the group continue to be a popular live attraction.

● ALBUMS: *Shake Down* (Deram 1967)★★★, *Getting To The Point* (Deram 1968)★★★, *Blue Matter* (Deram 1969)★★★★, *A Step Further* (Deram 1969)★★★, *Raw Sienna* (Deram 1970)★★★, *Looking In* (Deram 1970)★★, *Street Corner Talking* (Deram 1971)★★, *Hellbound Train* (Deram 1972)★★★, *Lion's Share* (Deram 1972)★★, *Jack The Toad* (Deram 1973)★★, *Boogie Brothers* (Deram 1974)★★, *Wire Fire* (Deram 1975)★★, *Skin 'N' Bone* (Deram 1976)★★, *Savage Return* (1978)★★, *Rock 'N' Roll Warriors* (1981)★★, *Just Live* (1981)★★★, *A Hard Way To Go* (Platinum 1985)★★★, *Make Me Sweat* (GNP 1988)★★, *Kings Of Boogie* (GNP 1989)★★, *Live And Kickin'* (GNP 1990)★★★, *Let It Ride* (1992)★★, *Bring It Home* (1995)★★★. Solo: Kim Simmonds *Solitaire* (1997). Chris Youlden *Chris Youlden And The Big Picture* (Matico 1993)★★★.

● COMPILATIONS: *The Best Of Savoy Brown* (Deram 1977)★★★, *Blues Roots* (Decca 1978)★★★, *Highway Blues* (See For Miles 1985)★★★, *The Savoy Brown Collection* (Polygram 1994)★★★.

SAYLES, CHARLIE

b. 4 January 1948, Woburn, Massachusetts, USA. Sayles only became acquainted with the blues when he heard a record by B.B. King during his US military service in Vietnam, and began to take a serious interest in playing harmonica in 1971. During the 70s he played frequently on the streets in cities across the country, and was put on the bill of several folk festivals. His original blues compositions, featuring raw, amplified harmonica and direct singing, were captured on vinyl in 1976 when he was playing in New York. Sayles began working with a small band around 1980, but he still remains largely an uncompromising street and solo performer.

● ALBUMS: *The Raw Harmonica Blues Of Charlie Sayles* (1976)★★★, *Night Ain't Right* (JSP 1990)★★★, *I Got Something To Say* (JSP 1995)★★★.

SCOTT, BUDDY

b. Kenneth Scott, 9 January 1935, Jackson, Mississippi, USA, d. 5 February 1994, Chicago, Illinois, USA. Scott is typical of the lesser-known Chicago bluesmen who played a supporting role to more famous names in the music's post-war heyday. With the increasing number of deaths of these more famous names, some of the attention has been focused upon men such as Scott in the twilight of their years. He was born into a large musical family which moved north to Chicago in 1940. John Lee 'Sonny Boy' Williamson was a frequent visitor and Scott's mother, Ida, played guitar behind him at the Piccadilly bar. He took up the guitar at 16 and joined his brother Howard's band, the Masqueraders. During the 50s and 60s, he worked live with jazz and blues bands and performed in a succession of family bands; he also recorded with Syl Johnson, Little Mack and Lee 'Shot' Williams, and made a number of singles for the Biscayne, PM and Capri labels. In 1978, Alligator recorded his band, Scotty And The Rib Tips, for its Living Chicago Blues series, after Queen Sylvia Embry requested his presence on her own session. Scott remained a jobbing musician for the rest of his life, usually in bands that featured one or more of his children. His son, Kenneth Jnr., played rhythm guitar on *Bad Avenue*, a collection of blues standards and two original songs, recorded in 1992 and released a year later. Entertaining, although hardly innovative, it illustrated Scott's enduring appeal.

● ALBUMS: as Scotty And The Rib Tips *Living*

Chicago Blues Vol. 3 (Alligator 1978/1991)★★★, *Bad Avenue* (Verve/Gitanes 1993)★★★.

SCOTT, ISAAC

b. 11 June 1945, Pine Bluff, Arkansas, USA. Scott's family moved to the west coast in the late 40s, settling in Portland, Oregon, and Isaac was exposed to both gospel music and blues as a youngster. Until the 70s he worked with gospel groups, but in 1974 he chose to concentrate on blues, while he was living in Seattle, Washington. His guitar playing reflects the influence of Albert Collins, and his singing and repertoire reveal strong elements of blues, soul, and gospel. Scott has had two albums released by Red Lightnin' and live material has been issued by Solid Smoke and Criminal.

● ALBUMS: *Isaac Scott Blues Band* (Red Lightnin' 1978)★★★, *Big Time Blues Man* (Red Lightnin' 1983)★★★.

● COMPILATIONS: *Lost And Found* (Sequel 1995)★★★.

SCOTT-ADAMS, PEGGY

b. Peggy Stoutmeyer, 25 June 1948, Opp, Alabama, USA. After forming her own gospel group, the Gospel Harmonettes, while still at school, Scott-Adams became the featured vocalist for Ben E. King's band. She then briefly sang with The Sextet, a trio formed by James and Bobby Purify, and survived a near-fatal car crash that threatened her career. Relocating to Jackson, Mississippi, Scott-Adams recorded a series of highly successful R&B singles with Jo Jo Benson for the SSS label in the late 60s, including 'Pickin' Wild Mountain Berries', 'Lover's Holiday' and 'Soul Shake'. In 1970 the duo moved to Atlantic Records, and recorded with Jerry Wexler at Muscle Shoals Studios, but their successful run of singles had by now dried up. Scott-Adams also released two solo singles for Atco, before the duo broke up in 1971. She went on to record for Old Town, Mercury and RCA, before reuniting with Benson and achieving moderate success with *Nothing Can Stand In Our Way* in the early 80s. She subsequently disappeared from the music business, working in her husband's funeral home, reappearing briefly to duet with Ray Charles on his *Would You Believe* and *Strong Love Affair* albums. She came out of her musical 'retirement' with the release of a new album, *Help Yourself*, in 1996. As she wryly told *Billboard* magazine shortly after its release: 'I had this quiet little life just five months ago. You know, being a mortician's wife, well, it's a very serene business. Then all hell broke loose.' Her breakthrough with *Help Yourself* had much to do with the success of the attendant single, 'Bill', on local blues and R&B radio stations. The song, which described the loss of a lover, not to another woman, but to a man, was written by Jimmy Lewis, the owner of Miss Butch Records. Scott-Adams had initially been reluctant to record such a potentially controversial single. However, she was pleased with the attendant publicity which helped to promote album sales. *Help Yourself* included other strong tracks, particularly the tender soul ballad 'I'll Take Care Of You', which reminded many of her late 60s peak.

● ALBUMS: with Jo Jo Benson *Soul Shake* (SSS International 1969)★★★, with Jo Jo Benson *Lover's Heaven* (SSS International 1969)★★, *Great Scott* (Old Town 1975)★★★, with Jo Jo Benson *Nothing Can Stand In Our Way* (Gulf Coast 1983)★★★, *Help Yourself* (Miss Butch/Mardi Gras 1996)★★★★.

SEALS, SON

b. Frank Seals Jnr., 11 August 1942, Osceola, Arkansas, USA. Son Seals was one of 13 children of Jim Seals, an entertainer and club owner in rural Arkansas. Son began his musical education on the drums and worked with many of the later famous musicians who travelled through the area. Having taught himself to play the guitar, he formed his own band to work around the city of Little Rock. He moved to Chicago in 1971, initially to work outside music, although he soon began to make appearances at local clubs. In 1973, he signed to the Alligator label and recorded his first album. Since then, he has become well known on the blues scene both in the USA and in Europe. Edging towards the 'soul blues' category his career has gained strength, particularly with the release of the well-received album *Bad Axe*, although he has not yet fully achieved the attention he deserves. *Living In The Danger Zone* was a bleak record, despite featuring uptempo horn charts. In 1997 he was shot in the face following an argument with his wife.

● ALBUMS: *The Son Seals Blues Band* (Alligator 1973)★★★★, *Midnight Son* (Alligator 1975)★★★★, *Live 'N' Burning* (Alligator 1978)★★★★, *Chicago Fire* (Alligator 1980)★★★, *Bad Axe* (Alligator 1984)★★★★, *Living In The Danger Zone* (Alligator 1991)★★★, *Nothing But The Truth* (Alligator 1994)★★★, *Live* (Alligator 1996)★★★.

SELLERS, BROTHER JOHN

b. 27 May 1924, Clarksdale, Mississippi, USA. Raised by his godmother after his family broke up in the aftermath of a terrible flood, Sellers moved to Chicago in the 30s, and began his professional music career in gospel. He subsequently toured with Mahalia Jackson in the 40s. His religious convictions did not prohibit him from singing blues music, and he recorded in both genres from 1945. He was quick to see the growing market among whites for black music, and was working festivals and white clubs by the early 50s. In 1957 he came to Europe with Big Bill Broonzy. After Broonzy's death his star began to wane as research uncovered more intuitive blues singers, whose approaches were regarded as more 'authentic' than Sellers' stagey and rather inflexible singing. He has continued to make solo appearances, and has been with the Alvin Ailey Dance Company (as a musician) since the early 60s.

● ALBUMS: *Brother John Sellers Sings Blues And Folk Songs* (1954)★★★, *In London* (1957)★★★, *Big Boat Up The River* (1959)★★★, *Baptist Shouts And Gospel Songs* (1959)★★★.

SEMIEN, 'IVORY' LEE

b. 13 September 1931, Washington, Louisiana, USA. Having played music from his early years, Ivory Lee settled in Houston in his teens and began to play in the blues clubs in that city, making his first records as a vocalist in the early 50s. He became drummer with the great slide guitarist Hop Wilson, and they made a number of records together, some with Wilson as leader, others - including his best-known song 'Rockin' In The Coconut Top' - with Semien himself on vocals. In the early 60s, he started his own record label, Ivory Records, whose best-known releases featured some magnificent blues by Wilson. He remained an active musician in Houston, at least on a semi-professional basis,

although making little impact outside that city.
● ALBUMS: *Rockin' Blues Party* (1987)★★★, *Steel Guitar Flash* (1988)★★★.

SEWARD, ALEC
b. 16 March 1902, Charles City, Virginia, USA, d. 11 May 1972, New York City, New York, USA. Raised in Newport News, Virginia, Seward was a semi-professional blues singer and guitarist from the age of 18. In 1923, he moved to New York, where he became an associate of Sonny Terry and Brownie McGhee. He recorded with Louis Hayes under a variety of colourful pseudonyms, including Guitar Slim & Jelly Belly, the Blues King and the Back Porch Boys, and with Terry and Woody Guthrie for the nascent folk audience. His music was typical of the southeast, being gentle, relaxed, and ragtime-influenced. By 1960, when mental illness ended Hayes' musical career, Seward also largely retired. He recorded again in the mid-60s, but was little heard of him thereafter.
● ALBUMS: *Creepin' Blues* (1965)★★★, *Carolina Blues* (1972)★★★, *Late One Saturday Evening* (1975)★★★.

SHADE, WILL
b. 5 February 1898, Memphis, Tennessee, USA, d. 18 September 1966, Memphis, Tennessee, USA. Although named after his father, Will Shade was raised by his grandmother Annie Brimmer and was often known around Memphis as Son Brimmer. He took an early interest in music and played guitar and harmonica. He worked as a musician in and around Memphis, sometimes joining the medicine shows that visited the city. During the 20s he formed the Memphis Jug Band, a shifting conglomeration of local talent that included, at different times, Charlie Burse, Will 'Casey Bill' Weldon, Furry Lewis, Jab Jones, and Ben Ramey. The popularity of this group, whose work ranged from knockabout, goodtime dance numbers to moving blues performances, was at its peak during the years 1927-34, after which they ceased to record but remained mainstays of the local scene. The group often supported singers such as Jenny Mae Clayton, Shade's wife, and Memphis Minnie, at one time married to Will Weldon. Shade enjoyed a brief second career when, in the company of Charlie Burse,

he recorded for the Folkways and Rounder labels in the early 60s. His death was the result of pneumonia.
● COMPILATIONS: *Memphis Jug Band 1927-1930 (3 volumes)* (1991), *Memphis Jug Band 1932-34* (1991).

SHAKEY JAKE
b. James D. Harris, 12 April 1921, Earle, Arkansas, USA, d. 2 March 1990, Pine Bluff, Arkansas, USA. A professional gambler when not playing harmonica (his nickname was derived from the crapshooters' call 'Shake 'em, Jake'), Harris began playing in Chicago blues bands during the late 40s. He recorded a single in 1958, on which his contribution was overshadowed by that of his nephew Magic Sam. During the 60s he recorded two albums that did not do him justice, as club recordings with Sam make evident. His encouragement of younger musicians brought about the recording debut of, among others, Luther Allison, with whom Jake recorded his best album after moving to Los Angeles. In later years, occasional recordings appeared, including some on his own label, and Harris ran a blues club for a while, but was dogged by poor health and isolated by neighbourhood gang violence.
● ALBUMS: *Good Times* (1960)★★, *Mouth Harp Blues* (1961)★★, *Further On Up The Road* (1969)★★★, *The Devil's Harmonica* (1972)★★★, *Magic Rocker* (1980)★★★, *Magic Touch* (1983)★★★, *The Key Won't Fit* (Murray Brothers 1985)★★★.

SHAKEY VICK
Formed in 1968 in Birmingham, England, Shakey Vick was a short-lived blues band fronted by Graham Vickery (vocals, harmonica). Bruce Langman (guitar), Nigel Tickler (bass) and Ned Balen (drums) completed the line-up. The group was signed by Pye Records in 1969 as the label embraced contemporary music in an attempt to rid itself of a staid, conservative image. *Little Woman You're So Sweet* was recorded live at Birmingham's Mother's club, a then-popular venue on the 'underground' circuit. The ensuing raw atmosphere enlivened a set comprising largely of tested blues standards, including 'Good Morning Little Schoolgirl' and 'Movin' To Chicago'. Imitators rather than pio-

neers, Shakey Vick split up on the demise of the British blues boom.

● ALBUMS: *Little Woman You're So Sweet* (Pye 1969)★★★.

SHANNON, MEM

b. 1954, New Orleans, USA. Mem Shannon moved to New Orleans, Missouri, USA, in 1959. As an amateur blues singer he discovered plenty of musical opportunities in the region, occasionally adding guitar and sometimes clarinet accompaniment to impromptu bar room sessions. The city's music circuit of that time demanded singers capable of copycat renditions of standards such as 'Hoochie Coochie Man' and 'Dust My Broom' rather than contemporary interpreters, but Shannon happily performed this function in bar bands and the occasional gospel group for several years while nurturing his own songwriting in private. However, when his father (also named Mem) passed away in 1981, Shannon was suddenly expected to become the household breadwinner. He put aside his music for nearly a decade while supporting the family as a taxi driver. Eventually, in 1990, he established his own group around a collective of musicians known as the Membership. Contributors included Peter Carter (bass), Barry Thomas (drums), Jackie Banks (keyboards) and Lance Ellis and Tim Green on saxophones. In 1991 they appeared in the Jazz Search contest organized by a New Orleans television station, before travelling to California to appear at the Long Beach Blues Festival. Later, saxophone player Green introduced Shannon to producer Mark Bingham. Together they recorded 10 songs, linked by studio dialogue, as the basis for *A Cab Driver's Blues*. Ranging from the comic domestic conflict of 'My Baby's Been Watching TV' to the incessant funk of 'Boogie Man', it was an inspirational achievement. Due to have been released on Bingham's regional label Gert Town, it was eventually housed on Joe Boyd's Hannibal Records. The title wryly reflected Shannon's long spell in the musical wilderness, which, given the evidence of his songwriting, was a substantial loss to the blues idiom. *2nd Blues Album* was released in 1997, which built on the first by embracing southern soul alongside regular blues. Shannon's gorgeously fruity voice is exquisite, with shades of Brook Benton

and Billy Eckstine - further confirmation of an immense vocal, guitar and songwriting talent.

● ALBUMS: *A Cab Driver's Blues* (Hannibal 1996)★★★, *2nd Blues Album* (Hannibal 1997)★★★★.

SHANNON, PRESTON

b. Memphis, Tennessee, USA. A contemporary soul singer whose songs are mixed with discernible elements of southern funk and blues, Preston Shannon made his Bullseye Blues Records debut in 1994 with *Break The Ice*. With a voice clearly modelled on Otis Redding, this saw him combine classic soul phrasing with guitar work drawing on the Delta blues style of Albert King. It won over numerous critics, many of whom saw his style as a powerful distillation of the traditions at work behind twentieth-century music in Memphis. The follow-up set, 1996's *Midnight In Memphis*, was recorded at Willie Mitchell's Royal Studio with brothers Ron and Willi Levy on production. Featuring a full horn section, the title-track was a joint Shannon/Levy composition. Once again, the album provoked an approving critical response.

● ALBUMS: *Break The Ice* (Bullseye Blues 1994)★★★, *Midnight In Memphis* (Bullseye Blues 1996)★★★.

SHAW, ALLEN

b. *c.*1890, Henning, Tennessee, USA, d. 1940, Tipton County, Tennessee, USA. A travelling man, remembered in western Tennessee and in Memphis, Shaw played forceful steel guitar, and sang the blues in an exultant voice on his one issued record, cut in 1934 with Willie Borum on second guitar. On one title, Shaw played impeccably sensitive, yet very powerful, slide guitar. Shaw and Borum also backed Hattie Hart at this session. Shaw's son, Willie Tango, considered to be a better guitarist than his father, never recorded (although he was the subject of a song recorded by Memphis Minnie).

● COMPILATIONS: *Memphis Blues* (1990).

SHAW, EDDIE

b. 20 March 1937, Benoit, Mississippi, USA. Shaw grew up in neighbouring Greenville and learned to play clarinet and trombone before choosing the saxophone. He played with local jump-blues bands (including one led by Ike

Turner) and sat in with Muddy Waters in 1957. Waters hired him immediately and he moved to Chicago. Once there he associated with Howlin' Wolf and Magic Sam, and recorded with both. He also fronted his own band on vocals and saxophone. Eddie also ran the 1815 Club in Chicago, wrote and arranged songs for other artists, learned to play blues harmonica, and has recorded as bandleader for Mac Simmons' label, for Alligator's *Living Chicago Blues* project, and for the Isabel and Rooster companies.

● ALBUMS: *Have Blues - Will Travel* (1979)★★★, *Movin' And Groovin' Man* (1982)★★★, *The Blues Is Good News* (1993)★★★, *Home Alone* (Wolf 1995)★★★.

SHAW, EDDIE 'VAAN'

b. 8 November 1955, Greenville, Mississippi, USA. When Howlin' Wolf is your babysitter and your father (Eddie Shaw) leads his band, it is hardly surprising if, like Vaan Shaw, you grow up to play the blues yourself. He spent his childhood in and around the band, learned the mechanics of guitar playing from Magic Sam and Hubert Sumlin, and actually backed Wolf at the tender age of 11, substituting for an absent Sumlin. The following year, he joined the house band when his father bought the 1815 Club (renaming it Eddie's Place) and backed Muddy Waters, Wolf, Freddie King and James Cotton. After Wolf's death, Eddie Shaw formed the Wolf Gang with his former sidemen and Vaan as guitarist. His first album, *Morning Rain*, would have been more impressive had there been less reliance upon standard Chicago fare. That was remedied by *The Trail Of Tears*, of which more than half consisted of songs written by Shaw *fils et père*.

● ALBUMS: *Morning Rain* (Wolf 1993)★★★, *The Trail Of Tears* (Wolf 1994)★★★★.

SHAW, ROBERT

b. 9 August 1908, Staffons, Texas, USA. One of the great Texas barrelhouse piano players, Shaw was raised on his father's cattle ranch. His mother played piano and guitar. From his mid-20s he started playing for local parties. Eventually he left home to work as an itinerant pianist in bordellos, juke-joints and barrelhouses throughout Texas and up as far as Kansas City, Missouri. In 1935 he settled in Austin, Texas,

working outside music running a food market, with occasional private party work, into the 70s. He played the Berlin Jazz Festival in 1974 and Montreux in 1975. Nat Hentoff referred to him as a 'gruff easeful blues singer telling stories that came out of his audience's lives'.

● ALBUMS: *Texas Barrelhouse Piano* (Arhoolie 1980)★★★, *The Ma Grinder* (1993)★★★.

SHAW, THOMAS

b. 4 March 1908, Brenham, Texas, USA, d. 24 February 1977, San Diego, California, USA. Shaw was taught harmonica and guitar by relatives while still quite young, developing his blues style through his collaborations with more famous artists of the day, Blind Lemon Jefferson and Ramblin' Thomas. Having spent much of his youth travelling throughout Texas, he settled in California in 1934. There he continued his musical activities, appearing on radio and setting up his own club, which ran for many years. In the 60s, he became a minister at a San Diego church, but he was also 'rediscovered' during the blues revival, and made his first recordings, in which the Jefferson influence was especially notable. He appeared at folk festivals and toured in Europe in 1972.

● ALBUMS: *Born In Texas* (Advent 1974)★★★.

SHEPHERD, KENNY WAYNE

b. c.1976, USA. A classically-styled blues rock guitarist, Shepherd recorded his debut album for Revolution Records in 1995 with the aid of singer Corey Sterling. Extracted from the album, 'Deja Voodoo' became a hit on mainstream rock radio and delivered an audience beyond blues purists, though they too were impressed with the guitarist's skill - the album stayed at the top of *Billboard*'s Blues chart for 20 weeks. As a result, Shepherd was able to play dates with his heroes, B.B. King and Buddy Guy. Later he also toured with celebrated rock guitarists including Steve Vai and Joe Satriani. By April 1997 and his second collection, Sterling had been replaced by fellow blues aficionado Noah Hunt. Shepherd again wrote all the lyrics, though this time his record label paired him with Talking Heads' alumni Jerry Harrison as producer. This unusual, seemingly incongruous partnership gelled immediately, resulting in a clean, reflective sound, augmented by the guest contribu-

tions of Chris Layton (Double Trouble), Tommy Shannon, Reese Wynans and James Cotton. As well as original material, the set included cover versions of Jimi Hendrix's 'I Don't Live Today', 'Voodoo Chile' and Bob Dylan's 'Everything Is Broken'.
● ALBUMS: *Ledbetter Heights* (Revolution 1995)★★, *Trouble Is ...* (Revolution 1997)★★★★.

SHIELDS, LONNIE
b. 17 April 1956, West Helena, Arkansas, USA. From some of his statements, it would be easy to cast Shields as a reluctant bluesman. His early musical experience centred around the church, although he never joined his church's choir. He was 11 when he acquired his first guitar and took some instruction from Eddie Smith, a local multi-instrumentalist. Two years later, he bought his first amplified model and joined a band that changed its name from the Checkmates to the Shades Of Black, to reflect its repertoire drawn from the Isley Brothers and Earth, Wind And Fire. He became a multi-instrumentalist himself, playing saxophones in school, and guitar, bass and harmonica with the band. In his late teens, he spent some time with a gospel group, the Christian Stars. His first exposure to blues came through drummer Sam Carr, who worked with Frank Frost and Big Jack Johnson as the Jelly Roll Kings. His major debut as a blues player came at the inaugural 1986 King Biscuit Blues Festival, where he met Jim O'Neal of Rooster Blues. Shields recorded a single for O'Neal, 'Strong Woman', the following year, but kept his job as a shoe repairman which he had had from the age of 15. *Portrait* was recorded over a number of years and featured artists such as Johnson, Lucky Peterson and Vaan Shaw. It showed Shields to be a capable songwriter and guitarist with the promise of development in future projects.
● ALBUMS: *Portrait* (Rooster Blues 1993)★★★, *Tired Of Waiting* (JSP 1996)★★★.

SHINES, JOHNNY
b. 26 April 1915, Frayser, Tennessee, USA, d. 20 April 1992. Johnny Shines was taught to play the guitar by his mother and sometimes worked the streets of Memphis for tips with a group of other youths. In 1932 he set up as a sharecropper in Hughes, Arkansas, but still worked part-time as a musician. During the 30s he hoboed around the work-camp and juke-joint circuit in the company of such men as Robert Johnson, with whom he appeared on a radio show in 1937. His ramblings took him as far as Canada. In 1941 he took the trail north to Chicago where he sometimes performed in the famous Maxwell Street market before forming his own group to play the clubs; he sometimes doubled as house photographer. Despite being respected by his fellow musicians and occasionally recording under the name Shoe Shine Johnny, his career did not take off until the 60s when his slide guitar and strong, emotive vocals were seen as a direct link with Delta blues, then much in vogue. From then on Johnny Shines went from strength to strength, touring the USA, Europe and Japan with great success, often in the company of Robert Lockwood. Shines was an intelligent and articulate man who was fully aware of his position in the blues world and made the most of his late opportunities. Concerned about the quality of life offered to his children in the northern cities, he moved back to the south where he suffered a heart attack that affected his playing. His recovery was slow and although he still played guitar, he was unable to return to the dazzling proficiency of his earlier days.
● ALBUMS: *Masters Of The Modern Blues* (1966)★★★, *Last Night Dream* (1968)★★★, *With Big Walter Horton* (1970)★★★, *Standing At The Crossroads* (1970)★★★, *Sitting On Top Of The World* (1972)★★★, *Nobody's Fault But Mine* (1973)★★★, *Johnny Shines And Company* (Biograph 1974)★★★, *Johnny Shines* (Advent 1974)★★, *Hey Ba-Ba-Re-Bop!* (Rounder 1978)★★★★, *Hangin' On* (Rounder 1980)★★★, *Mr Blues Is Back To Stay* (Rounder 1981)★★★, *Johnny Shines Live 1974* (Wolf 1988)★★★, *Traditional Delta Blues* (Biograph 1991)★★★, with Snooky Pryor *Back To The Country* (1993)★★★, *Masters Of The Modern Blues* (Testament 1994)★★★, with Big Walter Horton *Johnny Shines With Big Walter Horton* (Testament 1995)★★★, *Too Wet To Plow* 1974 recording (Blues Alliance 1996)★★★, *Worried Blues Ain't Bad* 1975 recording (Blues Alliance 1996)★★.

SHORT, J.D.

b. 26 December 1902, Port Gibson, Mississippi, USA, d. November 1962. Short grew up in various parts of Mississippi where he learned guitar from Willie Johnson and piano from Son Harris. In 1923, Short moved to St. Louis where he was discovered by Jessie Stone. He recorded country blues for Paramount (1930) and Vocalion (1932), but spent most of the 30s playing clarinet in a St. Louis jazz group. Short was crippled by a wartime injury but continued performing after 1945, often as a guitar/harmonica/bass drum one-man band and sometimes with his cousin Big Joe Williams. The duo worked together on Short's final recording for Sonet, recreating the music of their early years in the south on tracks such as 'Starry Crown Blues'. Short died a few months later, in November 1962.
● COMPILATIONS: *The Legacy Of The Blues Vol. 8* (1962)★★★.

SHOWERS, 'LITTLE' HUDSON

b. 6 September 1919, Anguilla, Mississippi, USA. Little Hudson (as he was known on record) had been playing guitar for some years when he moved to Chicago at the age of 20. There he began to play on the flourishing blues scene, and eventually started his own group, the Red Devils Trio. He made some records with his band, which included pianist Lazy Bill Lucas, in 1953 for the JOB label, but otherwise remained obscure. A very short recording, originally made as a radio advertisement, has been unearthed and issued in more recent years.
● ALBUMS: *John Brim And Little Hudson* (1981)★★★, *Southside Screamers* (1984)★★★.

SIEGAL-SCHWALL BLUES BAND

Corky Siegal (vocals, harmonica) and Jim Schwall (guitar, vocals) began working as a duo in April 1965. As such they made several appearances in Chicago's south-side clubs, prior to securing a date at the prestigious *Pepper's*. Here they used a temporary rhythm section, Bob Anderson (bass) and Billy Davenport (drums), before replacing them with Jos Davidson and Russ Chadwick. Although an electric ensemble, the group's early albums were less intense than those of contemporaries such as the Paul Butterfield Blues Band and Charlie Musselwhite's South Side Blues Band. Siegal-Schwall offered a lighter perspective, reliant on a collective effort rather than virtuoso soloing. Siegal was, nonetheless, an accomplished harmonica player and the group retained an in-concert popularity throughout the 60s. The two founder-members remained at the helm through several line-up alterations, but the band broke up in 1974 following the release of the highly unusual *Three Pieces For Blues Band And Orchestra* by William Russo. Siegal and Schwall were reunited 14 years later to celebrate the 15th anniversary of radio station WXRT-FM, on which the group had performed during its inauguration.
● ALBUMS: *The Siegal-Schwall Band* (1966)★★★, *Say Siegal-Schwall* (1967)★★★, *Shake!* (1968)★★★, *Siegal-Schwall 70* (1970)★★★, *Siegal-Schwall Band* (1971)★★★, *Sleepy Hollow* (1972)★★★, *953 West* (1973)★★★, *Three Pieces For Blues Band And Orchestra* (1973)★★★, *Live Last Summer* (1974)★★★, *RIP Siegal-Schwall* (1974)★★★, *Siegal-Schwall Reunion Concert* (Alligator 1988)★★★.
● COMPILATIONS: *The Best Of The Siegal-Schwall Band* (Vanguard 1974)★★★.

SIMMONS, 'LITTLE' MACK

b. 25 January 1934, Twist, Arkansas, USA. Simmons is one of the stalwarts of the Chicago club scene; he taught himself harmonica as a youngster and in the early 50s occasionally worked with bluesmen on the St. Louis, Missouri, club circuit, before settling in Chicago in 1954. Since the late 60s he has recorded for many small local labels, and sometimes larger companies such as Checker. He has run his own label and club from time to time and has recorded blues, gospel (he was known for a time as Reverend Mac Simmons) and soul. His version of 'Rainy Night In Georgia', performed as a harmonica instrumental, was a local hit in the early 70s. He toured Europe in 1975. His 90s album sounded like a 50s Chicago recording.
● ALBUMS: *Blue Lights* (1976)★★★, *High And Lonesome* (St George 1995)★★★.

SIMS, CLARENCE 'GUITAR'

b. c.1934, New Orleans, Louisiana, USA. Sims was initially inspired to sing the blues on hearing Tommy McClennan's recording of

'Bottle Up And Go', and later vocal influences included Nappy Brown, Fats Domino, Louis Jordan and Lloyd Price. In 1955 Sims moved to Los Angeles, where he appeared in talent shows and clubs. Two years later, he moved to San Francisco's Fillmore district, assuming the professional name 'Fillmore Slim', and recorded for the Dooto, Kent, and Dore labels. In the late 60s he also appeared on disc as 'Ron Silva'. However, Sims was imprisoned between 1980 and 1985, and it was during this time that he began to play guitar seriously. Following his release, he recorded a promising album for Troyce Keys' label in February 1987 and continues to play around the west coast.

● ALBUMS: *Born To Sing The Blues* (Eli Mile High 1987)★★★.

SIMPSON, MARTIN

b. 5 May 1953, Scunthorpe, South Humberside, England. Having started playing guitar at the age of 12, Simpson played the proverbial 'floor spots' at local folk clubs, and received his first paid booking at the age of 14. By the age of 18 he had become a full-time professional on the folk club circuit. He came to the attention of a number of influential people, one of whom was Bill Leader who recorded Simpson's debut, *Golden Vanity*, for his own Trailer label. The album mixed such folk standards as 'Pretty Polly' and 'Soldiers Joy' with contemporary works such as Bob Dylan's 'Love Minus Zero/No Limit'. That same year, Simpson opened for Steeleye Span on their UK tour, and shortly afterwards became an accompanist for June Tabor. In 1979 he joined the Albion Band at the National Theatre and played with them on two subsequent tours. *A Cut Above*, recorded with Tabor on Topic Records, is still highly regarded. There followed a succession of fine albums, but without a great degree of commercial success. Since 1987, Simpson has lived in the USA with his American wife Jessica Radcliffe Simpson (b. 18 February 1952, Los Angeles, California, USA). The two also work as a duo, having released *True Dare Or Promise* in 1987. *The Pink Suede Bootleg* was released as a limited edition. Noted for his style of playing, Simpson is not as often in the limelight as he was in the 70s and 80s, but a tour of the UK in 1991 showed that he was still a talent of great merit. In addition to solo and duo work, Simpson played briefly with Metamora in the USA, and has also been working with Henry Gray, the Louisiana-born blues pianist. Simpson also played on *Abbysinians* and *Aqaba* by June Tabor, and *Earthed In Cloud Valley* and *'Til The Beasts Returning* by Andrew Cronshaw. In 1991, Simpson was made honorary guitarist of the American Association of Stringed Instrument Artisans (ASIA). A new album from Martin and Jessica was released, featuring their New York-based band of Eric Aceto (violect), Hank Roberts (cello), Doug Robinson (bass) and Tom Beers (harmonica). *Smoke And Mirrors* was a successful excursion into acoustic blues with a notable version of Willie Dixon's 'Spoonful'.

● ALBUMS: *Golden Vanity* (Trailer 1976)★★★, with June Tabor *A Cut Above* (Topic 1981)★★★★, *Special Agent* (Topic 1981)★★★, *Grinning In Your Face* (Topic 1983)★★★, *Sad Or High Kicking* (Topic 1985)★★★, *Nobody's Fault But Mine* (Dambuster 1986)★★★, with Jessica Radcliffe Simpson *True Dare Or Promise* (Topic 1987)★★★, *Leaves Of Life* (Shanachie 1989)★★★, *When I Was On Horseback* (1991)★★★, *A Closer Walk With Thee* (Gourd 1994)★★★, with Radcliffe Simpson *Red Roses* (Rhiannon 1994)★★★, *Smoke And Mirrors* (Thunderbird 1995)★★★.

● COMPILATIONS: *The Collection* (Topic 1992)★★★★.

● VIDEOS: *The Acoustic Guitar Of Martin Simpson* (1994), *Acoustic Guitar Instrumentals* (1994).

SIMS, FRANKIE LEE

b. 30 April 1917, New Orleans, Louisiana, USA, d. 10 May 1970. Despite his birthplace, Sims' music is very much in the blues vein of Texas, where he lived in childhood. On his earliest records in 1947-48, for the Blue Bonnet label, he played a traditional finger-style guitar, but later developed an electric style of his own, riffing behind the vocals and filling the breaks with exciting, often distorted, flashes of lead. His best-known song was 'Lucy Mae', which he recorded several times, most successfully with Specialty in 1953. Later recordings on Ace and Vin developed his rocking style still further with a small band, but they marked the end of his brief period of success. A New York session in

1960 remained unissued until well after his death.

● COMPILATIONS: *Lucy Mae Blues* (1970)★★★, *Walking With Frankie* (Krazy Kat 1985)★★★.

SLIM HARPO

b. James Moore, 11 January 1924, Lobdel, Louisiana, USA, d. 31 January 1970. The eldest in an orphaned family, Moore worked as a longshoreman and building worker during the late 30s and early 40s. One of the foremost proponents of post-war rural blues, he began performing in Baton Rouge bars under the name Harmonica Slim. He later accompanied Lightnin' Slim, his brother-in-law, both live and in the studio, before commencing his own recording career in 1957. Christened 'Slim Harpo' by producer Jay Miller, the artist's solo debut coupled 'I'm A King Bee' with 'I Got Love If You Want It'. Influenced by Jimmy Reed, he began recording for Excello and enjoyed a string of popular R&B singles which combined a drawling vocal with incisive harmonica passages. Among them were 'Raining In My Heart' (1961), 'I Love The Life I Live', 'Buzzin' (instrumental) and 'Little Queen Bee' (1964). These relaxed, almost lazy, performances, which featured an understated electric backing, set the tone for Moore's subsequent work. His warm, languid voice enhanced the sexual metaphor of 'I'm A King Bee', which was later recorded by the Rolling Stones. The same group also covered the pulsating 'Shake Your Hips', which Harpo first issued in 1966, while the Pretty Things, the Yardbirds and Them featured versions of his songs in their early repertoires. Harpo enjoyed a notable US Top 20 pop hit in 1966 with 'Baby Scratch My Back' (also a number 1 R&B hit), which revitalized his career. Never a full-time musician, Harpo had his own trucking business during the 60s, although he was a popular figure in the late 60s blues revival, with appearances at several renowned venues including the Electric Circus and the Fillmore East; he suffered a fatal heart attack on 31 January 1970.

● ALBUMS: *Rainin' In My Heart* (Excello 1961)★★★, *Baby Scratch My Back* (1966)★★★, *Tip On In* (Excello 1968)★★.

● COMPILATIONS: *The Best Of Slim Harpo* (Excello 1969)★★★★, *He Knew The Blues* (Excello 1970)★★★, *Blues Hangover* (1976)★★, *Got Love If You Want It* (1980)★★★, *Shake Your Hips* (Ace 1986)★★★★, *I'm A King Bee* (Ace 1989)★★★★, *The Scratch: Rare And Unissued Vol 1* (Excello 1996)★★★★.

SMALL, DRINK

b. c.1934, Bishopville, South Carolina, USA. Small began playing guitar at the age of four and began his musical career while in high school, playing in secular groups and singing bass in a church choir. In the 50s he worked and recorded with the Spiritualaires of Columbia, and *Metronome* magazine voted him Top Gospel Guitarist during his time with the group. In 1959 he returned to South Carolina and began working as a blues musician, recording the same year for the Sharp label. He has since recorded for his own Bishopville label and for the Southland company, and he enjoyed a measure of attention following the release of a cassette album (from folk-blues to disco-blues); he followed it up with another well-received set a year later.

● ALBUMS: *The Blues Doctor* (1990)★★★, *Round Two* (1991)★★★.

SMITH, BESSIE

b. 15 April 1894, Chattanooga, Tennessee, USA, d. 26 September 1937. In her childhood, Smith sang on street corners before joining a touring black minstrel show as a dancer. Also in the show was Ma Rainey, and before long the young newcomer was also singing the blues. The older woman encouraged Smith, despite the fact that even at this early stage in her career her powerful voice was clearly heralding a major talent that would one day surpass Rainey. By 1920 Smith was headlining a touring show and was well on the way to becoming the finest singer of the blues the USA would ever hear. Despite changing fashions in music in the northern cities of New York and Chicago, Smith was a success wherever she performed and earned her billing as the Empress of the Blues. For all her successes elsewhere, however, her real empire was in the south, where she played theatres on the Theatre Owners' Booking Association circuit, packing in the crowds for every show. Although she was not among the first blues singers to make records, when she did so they sold in huge numbers, rescuing more than one recording company from the brink of bank-ruptcy. The records, on which her accompanists included Louis Armstrong and Joe Smith, con-solidated her position as the leading blues singer of her generation, but here too, fashion dictated a shift in attitude. By 1928 her recording career was effectively over, and personal problems, which stemmed from drink and poor judgement over her male companions, helped to begin a drift from centre stage. It was during this fallow period that she made her only film appearance, in *St Louis Blues* (1929), with James P. Johnson and members of the recently disbanded Fletcher Henderson Orchestra. She continued to per-form, however, still attracting a faithful, if diminished, following. In 1933 John Hammond Jnr. organized a record date, on which she was accompanied by, among others, Jack Teagarden and Coleman Hawkins, which proved to be her last. The following year she was in a highly suc-cessful touring show and in 1935 appeared at the Apollo Theatre in New York to great acclaim. In her private life she had a new companion, a showbiz-loving bootlegger named Richard Morgan, an uncle of Lionel Hampton, who brought her new stability. With the growing reawakening of interest in the earlier traditions of American music and another film planned, this should have been the moment for Smith's career to revive, but on 26 September 1937 she was fatally injured while being driven by Morgan to an engagement in Mississippi.

Smith's recordings range from uproarious vaudeville songs to slow blues; to the former she brought a reflection of her own frequently bawdy lifestyle, while the latter are invariably imbued with deeply felt emotions. All are deliv-ered in a rich contralto matched by a majestic delivery. Every one of her recordings is worthy of attention, but especially important to an understanding of the blues and Smith's para-mount position in its history are those made with Armstrong and Smith. Even in such stellar company, however, it is the singer who holds the attention. She was always in complete con-trol, customarily refusing to work with a drummer and determinedly setting her own, usually slow, tempos. Indeed, on some record-ings her entrance, after an opening chorus by her accompanists, noticeably slows the tempo.

On her final record date she makes a gesture towards compromise by recording with musi-cians attuned to the imminent swing era, but she is still in charge. Her influence is impossible to measure; so many of her contemporaries drew from her that almost all subsequent singers in the blues field and in some areas of jazz have stylistic links with the 'Empress of the Blues'. Many years after her death she was still the subject of plays and books, several of which perpetuated the myth that her death was a result of racial prejudice, or used her to promul-gate views not necessarily relevant to the singer's life. Fortunately, one of the books, Chris Albertson's *Bessie,* is an immaculately researched and well-written account of the life, times and music of one of the greatest figures in the history of American music.
● COMPILATIONS: *Any Woman's Blues (1923-30)* (Columbia 1970)★★★, *The World's Greatest Blues Singer* (Columbia 1971)★★★, *Empty Bed Blues* (Columbia 1971)★★★, *The Empress (1924-28)* (Columbia 1971)★★★, *Nobody's Blues But Mine (1925-27)* (Columbia 1972)★★★, *St Louis Blues (1929)* film soundtrack (Jazz Live 1981)★★★, *Jazz Classics In Digital Stereo* (1986)★★★, *Bessie Smith Story - The Collection* (Columbia 1989)★★★, *Do Your Duty* (Indigo 1994)★★★, *The Complete Recordings Vol. 1-5* (Columbia/Legacy 1991-96)★★★★.
● FURTHER READING: *Bessie Smith*, Paul Oliver. *Somebody's Angel Child: The Story Of Bessie Smith*, Carman Moore. *Bessie*, Chris Albertson. *Bessie Smith: Empress Of The Blues*, Elaine Feinstein.

SMITH, BYTHER

b. 17 April 1933, Monticello, Mississippi, USA. Smith began playing guitar in church, but after settling in Chicago in 1958 he started singing blues and was tutored on guitar by Herbert Sumlin and Freddie Robinson. He recorded for several local labels (including, reputedly, Cobra and Vee Jay), and worked with numerous gospel and blues groups, occasionally sitting in with his cousin J.B. Lenoir. In the late 60s he left music, returning in the early 70s as house guitarist at the famed Theresa's Lounge in Chicago, and enjoying a minor hit for CJ Records with 'Give Me My White Robe'. In 1983, Smith recorded an acclaimed album for Grits, with the follow-up two years later being reissued in 1991; Byther has also recorded for JSP. Smith is a modern, though traditionally rooted, Chicago bluesman with a very large repertoire.

● ALBUMS: *Tell Me How You Like It* (Grits 1983)★★★, *Addressing The Nation With The Blues* (JSP 1989)★★★, *Housefire* reissue (Bullseye Blues 1991)★★★, *I'm A Mad Man* (Bullseye Blues 1993)★★★, *Mississippi Kid* (Delmark 1996)★★.

SMITH, CLARA

b. *c.*1894, Spartanburg, South Carolina, USA, d. 2 February, 1935. Singing professionally from her mid-teens in theatres and tent shows throughout the Deep South, by 1923 Smith was a big name in New York. She sang in Harlem clubs, opening her own very popular and successful Clara Smith Theatrical Club. She was signed by Columbia to make records, on some of which she duetted with Bessie Smith. Her instrumental accompanists on record included Louis Armstrong, Lonnie Johnson and James P. Johnson. She worked constantly throughout the late 20s and into the early 30s, mostly in New York but with occasional short tours and residencies at clubs in other cities. She died suddenly from a heart attack on 2 February 1935. Smith sang the blues in a low-down, dragging manner, creating dirge-like yet often deeply sensual interpretations.

● COMPILATIONS: *Clara Smith, Vols. 1-7 (1923-32)* (VJM 1974)★★★.

SMITH, CLARENCE 'PINE TOP'

b. 11 January 1904, Troy, Alabama, USA, d. 15 March 1929, Chicago, Illinois, USA. Often considered to be the founder of the boogie-woogie style of piano playing, 'Pine Top' Smith was actually a vaudeville performer. From his mid-teens, Smith toured tent shows and theatres as a pianist and dancer. He gradually concentrated on piano and, encouraged by Charles 'Cow Cow' Davenport, made a handful of records. Smith's style was largely in the mould of humorous songs backed up by vigorous two-handed playing. His small list of recordings also included blues, but his fame rests, more than anything, on his recording of 'Pine Top's Boogie Woogie' (1928). This song possibly represents the first documented use of the term. His work

on the circuits took him all over the south in the company of such artists as Butterbeans And Susie and Ma Rainey, but it was in Chicago that his promising career was cut short when he was accidentally shot by a man named David Bell during a skirmish in a dancehall. He was 25 and left a wife and two children. His work has been covered by many artists over the years, and 'Pine Top's Boogie Woogie' remains as satisfying today as it was in 1928 when it made its initial impact.

● COMPILATIONS: *Compilation 1928-29-30* (Oldie Blues 1986)★★★, *Pine Top Smith And Romeo Nelson* (Oldie Blues 1987)★★★, *Compilation 1929-30* (Oldie Blues 1988)★★★.

SMITH, GEORGE

b. 22 April 1924, Helena, Arkansas, USA, d. 2 October 1983, Los Angeles, USA. A master of amplified and chromatic blues harmonica, Smith made a stunning debut in 1954 with 'Telephone Blues'/'Blues In The Dark', but failed to capture the audience that elevated Little Walter to stardom. This may have been because his west coast record label tended to back him with saxophones rather than the guitar-based sound of Chicago. Smith had worked in Chicago and Kansas City, but resided in Los Angeles from 1955, where he worked as a name act and accompanied Big Mama Thornton for many years. He continued to make recordings of variable quality, and was briefly a member of the Muddy Waters band. He toured Europe during the 70s, and was a member with J.D. Nicholson of the mainly white blues band Bacon Fat.

● ALBUMS: *Blues With A Feeling* (1969)★★★, *Arkansas Trap* (1970)★★★, *No Time For Jive* (1970)★★★, *Blowin' The Blues* (1979)★★★, *Boogiein' With George* (Murray Brothers 1983)★★★, *Harmonica Ace* (1991)★★★.

SMITH, J.B.

Johnnie B. Smith was recorded in the Texas State Penitentiary in the 60s while serving his fourth prison term, one of 45 years for murder. He was a powerful worksong leader, but his most important recordings were nine long, unaccompanied solos, which he approached as parts of a single song. Their 132 stanzas use essentially the same melody, at varying tempos, and with varying amounts of decoration. This melody, which appears to be unique to Smith, carries a four-line stanza, usually ABB'A' with B'A' a reversal of AB, leading to some striking poetic effects. Indeed, Smith was a remarkable poet of the prison experience, using some traditional lines and verses, but working them into songs that are largely original compositions, thematically coherent, and full of poignant images of confinement, loneliness and the slow passage of time. Smith was paroled in 1967, and did some preaching in Amarillo, but returned to prison owing to a parole violation.

● ALBUMS: *Ever Since I Have Been A Man Full Grown* (1970)★★★, *I'm Troubled With A Diamond* (1990)★★★, *Old Rattler Can't Hold Me* (1990)★★★.

SMITH, J.T. 'FUNNY PAPA'

b. *c*.1890, Texas, USA. Very little is known about the life of this blues guitarist and singer, although he reportedly played in New York in 1917, and worked in Texas and Oklahoma in the 20s and 30s, recording in 1930. One of his albums provided him with a nickname (or possibly reflected an existing one), 'The Howling Wolf', pre-dating the more famous blues artist of that name on record by about 20 years. His steady, rhythmic picking and warm baritone helped sell sufficient albums for him to record again the following year, including another 'Howling Wolf' track, and a dozen more. Following this, he served a prison sentence for murder. In 1935, he recorded at four long sessions in Fort Worth, Texas, along with Black Boy Shine and Bernice Edwards, although almost nothing from these was released. Smith's date of death is unrecorded.

● ALBUMS: *The Original Howling Wolf* (Yazoo 1988)★★★.

SMITH, JOE

b. 28 June 1902, Ripley, Ohio, USA, d. 2 December 1937. With his father, six brothers and a cousin all playing trumpet, it is hardly surprising that Smith also played the instrument. By his late teens, Smith was playing in New York, where he became a big attraction as musical director and featured soloist with a Noble Sissle and Eubie Blake show. He also established a reputation as a sensitive accompanist to singers, playing and recording with

Bessie Smith, Mamie Smith, Ma Rainey and Ethel Waters. He was hired by Fletcher Henderson in 1925, staying for three years, and later rejoining the band for occasional club and recording dates (during this period, his brother, Russell Smith, was Henderson's lead trumpeter). In the late 20s and early 30s, he was also frequently in and out of McKinney's Cotton Pickers. He was one of the first trumpeters to intelligently explore the possibilities of mutes other than to create barnyard effects. Despite a reputation for leading a wild lifestyle, Smith's playing was always tasteful and often deeply moving. Preferring to remain in the middle register, he rarely used the spectacular high notes with which his contemporaries pleased their audiences. In his introspective approach to his solos, and his habitually relaxed and unhurried accompaniments to singers, he prefigured the manner in which trumpet players of a later generation would utilize the instrument. In 1930, while touring with the Cotton Pickers, he was driving a car that was involved in an accident. A passenger in the car, his only close friend, George 'Fathead' Thomas, was killed. Subsequently, Smith's mental state deteriorated and in 1933 he was confined to an institution, where he died in December 1937.

● ALBUMS: including with Ethel Waters *Oh Daddy!* (1921-24), with Waters *Jazzin' Baby Blues* (1921-27), with Fletcher Henderson *A Study In Frustration* (1923-38), *The Bessie Smith Story* (1925-27), with Ma Rainey *Blame It On The Blues* (1920s).

SMITH, MAMIE

b. 26 May 1883, Cincinnati, Ohio, USA, d. 30 October 1940. Despite beginning her showbusiness career as a dancer, before the outbreak of World War I, Smith was established as a singer. Although she was essentially a vaudeville singer, in 1920 she recorded 'Crazy Blues', thus becoming the first black singer to record the blues as a soloist. The enormous success of this and her subsequent recordings established her reputation and thereafter she was always in great demand. Her accompanying musicians, on record and on tour, included Willie 'The Lion' Smith, Joe Smith, Johnny Dunn, Bubber Miley and Coleman Hawkins. She lived extravagantly, squandering the enormous amount of money

she earned, and when she died on 30 October 1940 after a long illness, she was bankrupt.
● COMPILATIONS: with others *Jazz Sounds Of The Twenties Vol. 4: The Blues Singers* (1923-31), *Complete Recorded Works 1920-1942 Vols. 1-4* (Document 1995)★★★.

SMITH, MOSES 'WHISPERING'

b. 25 January 1932, Union Church, Mississippi, USA, d. 19 April 1984, Baton Rouge, Louisiana, USA. Smith is more associated with the blues of Louisiana, where he settled in his 20s, than that of his birth state. He learned harmonica in his teens and was playing regularly while still in Mississippi, but it was following his relocation to Baton Rouge, and taking up with Lightnin' Slim, that he made his first records. His harmonica work was uncomplicated but effective, and his voice had a distinctive, almost hoarse quality, with an extraordinary power that gave him his sardonic nickname. The handful of singles recorded in 1963 and 1964 earned him a reputation on which he was able to capitalize during the blues revival some years later. There were a few more recordings on albums in the 70s, and a single in the early 80s showed he was still a convincing blues performer.
● ALBUMS: *Louisiana Blues* (1984)★★★.

SMITH, ROBERT CURTIS

b. *c.*1930, Mississippi, USA. This accomplished guitarist was influenced by Big Bill Broonzy. A wistful but committed blues singer, Smith was discovered by chance in Wade Walton's barber shop. Smith worked as a farm labourer, and raised a large family in considerable poverty. He was recorded again in 1962, but failed to achieve success with the new white audience. In 1969 he was reported to have joined the church and abandoned the blues.
● ALBUMS: *The Blues Of Robert Curtis Smith* (1963)★★★, *I Have To Paint My Face* (1969)★★★.

SMITH, TRIXIE

b. 1895, Atlanta, Georgia, USA, d. 21 September 1943. Unlike many of her contemporaries, Smith attended university before going on the road as a singer. She worked the vaudeville circuit, singing popular songs of the day interspersed with blues songs. By the early 20s she was making records and had embarked upon a parallel career as an actress. A highly polished performer, her records include several outstanding examples of the blues on which she is accompanied by artists such as James P. Johnson, Fletcher Henderson and Freddie Keppard.
● ALBUMS: including *Trixie Smith And Her Down Home Syncopators* (1925)★★★.

SMITHER, CHRIS

b. 11 November 1944, Miami, Florida, USA. Smither began his music career during the 60s, performing in the coffee-houses and clubs of New Orleans, where he had lived from the age of 2. His first real blues influence was a Lightnin' Hopkins recording, *Blues In My Bottle*, which he heard when he was 17. He moved to Boston, Massachusetts, in 1966, where he continued playing the lucrative coffee-house/folk circuit, and began associating with artists such as Bonnie Raitt, John Hammond and Mississippi Fred MacDowell. After a promising start, with two albums on the Poppy label, the label folded. He recorded *Honeysuckle Dog* for United Artists, which featured Raitt, but this was never released. Smither has had his songs covered by numerous performers, including Raitt, who included his 'Love Me Like A Man' and 'I Feel The Same' on two of her albums, and John Mayall, who used 'Mail Order Mystics' as the title track of his recent album. Smither has performed at various times with many musicians including Nanci Griffith, Jackson Browne, Van Morrison, and also at numerous major festivals throughout the USA.

Smither's smooth, lyrical guitar style encompasses elements of folk, blues, country and rock and his voice is capable of sounding soft one minute and gruff the next. Having fought off the demon alcohol, Smither faced the 90s as a survivor, fresh and enthusiastic towards his work. The live *Another Way To Find You* was recorded over two nights in a studio with an invited audience. *Happier Blue* shows the artist truly coming into his own; this excellent set includes Lowell George's 'Rock And Roll Doctor' and J.J. Cale's 'Magnolia', in addition to the original title track. The powerful lyric of the latter is but one example of his emotional talent: 'I was sad and then I loved you, it took my breath, now I think you love me and it scares me to death, cause now I lie awake and wonder, I worry I think about losing you, I don't care what you say, maybe I was happier blue'. Smither's guitar-playing is worthy of note (Bonnie Raitt calls him 'her Eric Clapton'), as he is able to be percussive and rhythmic, and plays in a fluid, busy style that is as breathtaking as it is effortless. His voice is another asset, equally effortless and with a floor-rumbling bass resonance.

● ALBUMS: *I'm A Stranger Too* (Poppy 1970)★★, *Don't It Drag On* (Poppy 1972)★★, *It Ain't Easy* (1984)★★★, *Another Way To Find You* (Flying Fish 1991)★★★, *Happier Blue* (1993)★★★★, *Up On The Lowdown* (Hightone 1995)★★, *Small Revelations* (High Tone 1997)★★★★.

SMOKEY BABE

b. Robert Brown, 1927, Itta Bena, Mississippi, USA, d. 1975, Louisiana, USA. Smokey Babe led a hard life of farmwork and migrant labour before and after settling in Baton Rouge, Louisiana. Here he entertained, and jammed with, his neighbours and friends, and was recorded in the early 60s. He was one of the most talented acoustic blues guitarists located by folkloric research, singing and playing both swinging, energetic dance music and moving, personal blues. However, he never achieved the acclaim and wider exposure that his talent merited.

● ALBUMS: *Country Negro Jam Session* (1960)★★★, *Hot Blues* (1961)★★★, *Hottest Brand Goin'* (Ace 1989)★★★.

SMOTHERS, LITTLE SMOKEY

b. Abraham Smothers, 2 January 1939, Tchula, Mississippi, USA. Ten years younger than his brother, Otis 'Big Smokey' Smothers, the teenage Abe arrived in Chicago in the mid-50s, and because of his 'younger brother' status, received help from many established bluesmen. His first gig was with Big Boy Spires, who had already helped his brother and his cousin, Lester Davenport. Magic Sam was also a major influence in the development of his guitar-playing. He spent two years in Howlin' Wolf's band and played on the July 1959 session that produced 'Mr Airplane Man' and 'Howlin' For My Darling'. Smothers then formed his own band, the

Wrench Crew, with another cousin, Lee 'Shot' Williams as vocalist. From 1962, he also nurtured the respective talents of Paul Butterfield and Elvin Bishop, giving tuition and allowing them to sit in at his gigs. When they were offered a recording contract, Smothers took to the road with Earl Hooker and then spent the 70s working with Jimmy Rogers. Although he appeared on the *American Blues Legends '79* album, his job as a construction worker prevented him from joining the ensuing tour. During the 80s, he worked with the Legendary Blues Band and guitarist Billy Flynn from the band was involved in the making of *Bossman*, along with Elvin Bishop, Lee 'Shot' Williams and Tony Zamagni. Typically, Smothers surrendered his spotlight to others on a record that displayed a worthy but minor talent.

● ALBUMS: *Bossman* (Black Magic 1993)★★★, *Second Time Around* (CrossCut 1996)★★★.

SMOTHERS, OTIS 'BIG SMOKEY'

b. 21 March 1929, Lexington, Mississippi, USA, d. 23 July 1993. Raised in the Tchula area, Smothers learned harmonica and guitar from an aunt before moving north to Chicago in 1946. His first stage appearance came five years later, with Johnny Williams and Johnny Young at the Square Deal Club. Other musicians with whom he played, on and off the street, included Big Boy Spires, Earl Hooker, Henry Strong and his own cousin, Lester Davenport. He also played with Bo Diddley, and claimed to have been on 'Bring It To Jerome'. In 1956 he joined Howlin' Wolf's band, playing second guitar on 'The Natchez Burning' and 'I Asked For Water'. Later, he was in a Muddy Waters junior band, along with Freddie King, Mojo Elem and drummer T.J. McNulty. Having been rejected by Chess Records, he recorded for Federal in August 1960. Encouraged by producer Sonny Thompson to emulate Jimmy Reed, he recorded 'Honey, I Ain't Teasin'' as part of a marathon 12-title session whose second half was immeasurably improved by the addition of Freddie King, the day before his own Federal debut. Another 1962 Federal session, with harmonica player Little Boyd, produced 'Twist With Me Annie', a bizarre updating of Hank Ballard's original. Some time later, while a member of Muddy Waters' band, he recorded 'I Got My Eyes On You' for the obscure Gamma label. By the 70s, he had almost forsaken music, saying with more equanimity than some in his position, 'Everybody can't be president'.

● ALBUMS: *The Complete Sessions* (Krazy Kat 1982)★★★.

SOLOMON, KING

b. 12 October 1940, Tallulah, Louisiana, USA. Solomon enjoyed singing in the local church choir and for 10 years he was a member of the popular Friendly Brothers Spiritual Quartet. It was while touring with them that he made the switch to blues singing, subsequently appearing on the same bills as artists such as B.B. King and Etta James. He made his first record in 1959 and he has appeared on numerous small labels since then, with records occasionally being leased to larger companies such as Checker and Kent. He has been based in California for most of his recording career and has made one album, although the Dutch label Diving Duck did release a well-received compilation of his older material. Solomon continues to sing occasionally in small clubs in Los Angeles.

● ALBUMS: *Energy Crisis* (1978)★★★.
● COMPILATIONS: *Non Support Blues* (Diving Duck 1988)★★★.

SON HOUSE

b. Eddie James House Jnr., 21 March 1902, Riverton, Mississippi, USA, d. 19 October 1988, Detroit, Michigan, USA. Brought up in a religious home, Son House was drawn to the ministry in his youth, and took up the guitar, and the blues, as late as 1927. Throughout his life there was to be a tension between his religious feelings and his secular way of life (including the playing of blues). In 1928 he served a year in jail for manslaughter (in self-defence). In 1930, he met Charley Patton at Lula, where he was spotted by a Paramount talent scout. House, Patton, Willie Brown and Louise Johnson travelled north to a memorable recording session, at which House recorded three two-part blues (together with one untraced record, and a test located in 1985). All were the work of an extraordinary musician. House was no virtuoso, but he brought total conviction to his performances: his ferocious, barking voice, driving bass ostinato, and stabbing bottleneck phrases blended

into an overwhelming totality that, for all its impact on the listener, was fundamentally introspective. In the 30s, House and Brown played widely through Mississippi, Arkansas and Tennessee, and House taught both Muddy Waters and Robert Johnson some guitar technique and the 'Walking Blues' theme. In 1941, following a tip from Waters, Alan Lomax of the Library of Congress located House at Lake Cormorant and made a number of recordings, including some hollers and three pieces which invaluably preserve House and Brown playing in a band with Fiddlin' Joe Martin (mandolin) and Leroy Williams (harmonica). Lomax returned the following year to supplement the single House solo recorded in 1941; the results document the breadth of House's repertoire, and catch him at the peak of his powers. In 1943, he moved to Rochester, New York, and had retired from music by 1948. When rediscovered in 1964, House was infirm, alcoholic, and barely able to play, but was fired by the admiration of his young white fans, and regained most of his abilities, recording a splendid album for Columbia Records, and providing an unforgettable experience for all who saw him in concert. All the intensity of his early recordings remained, and even when he was clearly in renewed physical and mental decline, it was a privilege to witness his music. He retired from performing in 1974, and lived in Detroit until his death.

● ALBUMS: *The Vocal Intensity Of Son House* (Saydisc 1965)★★★★, *The Legendary Father Of Folk Blues* (Columbia 1965)★★★★, *John The Revelator* (Liberty 1970)★★★★, *The Real Delta Blues* (Blue Goose 1974)★★★★, *Death Letter Blues* (Edsel 1985)★★★★, *Son House & The Great Delta Blues Singers* (Document 1990)★★★★, *The Complete Library Of Congress Sessions 1941-1942* (Biograph 1991)★★★★, *Delta Blues And Spirituals* (Capitol 1995)★★★★.

SONS OF BLUES

This young, Chicago-based band (aka S.O.B. Band) originally comprised Lurrie Bell, Billy Branch, bassist Freddie Dixon (son of Willie Dixon), and drummer Jeff Ruffin. They garnered international acclaim for their recordings on Volume Three of the Alligator label's groundbreaking *Living Chicago Blues* series. Bell left in the early 80s and so Branch assumed leadership.

Guitarist Carlos Johnson joined the group, before being replaced in turn by Carl Weathersby. The band's 1983 album for the Red Beans label included solid Chicago blues and some contemporary R&B. The line-up of Branch, Weathersby, bassist J.W. Williams and drummer Moses Rutues was augmented by several guests, including Jimmy Walker. In recognition of Williams' own former band, the group is now known as the Sons Of Blues/Chi-Town Hustlers, under which name they recorded in 1987. Weathersby, increasingly the band's focal point, left in 1997 to concentrate on his solo career.

● ALBUMS: *Where's My Money* (Red Beans 1983)★★★, *Live '82* (Bellaphon 1994)★★★.

SPAND, CHARLIE

Details on Spand's early history and later life is scant. What is known is that he recorded in excess of 20 tracks for the Paramount label between 1929 and 1931 and a further eight for OKeh Records in 1940. He was a friend and working partner of Blind Blake, with whom he recorded the classic 'Hastings Street' and appeared on the Paramount sampler disc 'Home Town Skiffle'. Spand's piano work was in the powerful Detroit style and his writing skills were considerable. His first recording, 'Soon This Morning', became something of a staple for blues pianists. Working mainly in Chicago he was known to artists such as Little Brother Montgomery and Jimmy Yancey but after the war he disappeared. It is speculated, by Francis Wilford Smith, that Spand was born around the turn of the century in Ellijay, Georgia, and retired to Los Angeles.

● COMPILATIONS: *Piano Blues, Vol. 1* (1977), *Piano Blues, Vol. 5* (1978), *Piano Blues, Vol. 16* (1981).

SPANN, LUCILLE

b. Mahalia Lucille Jenkins, 23 June 1938, Bolton, Mississippi, USA. Spann sang gospel to start with, both in Mississippi and later in Chicago, where she lived in her early teens. In the 60s, she met the great blues pianist Otis Spann, and they began a musical partnership and later married. They recorded together, but tragically their collaboration came to an end with Otis's early death in 1970. Lucille continued to work in music and made a number of further recordings.

● ALBUMS: *Cry Before I Go* (1974)★★★.

SPANN, OTIS

b. 21 March 1930, Jackson, Mississippi, USA, d. 24 April 1970, Chicago, Illinois, USA. One of the finest pianists of post-war blues, Spann learned the instrument as a child. He initially played in his stepfather's church, but by the age of 14 was a member of a small local group. Having pursued careers in football and boxing, Spann moved to Chicago where he returned to music through work with several established attractions, including Memphis Slim and Roosevelt Sykes, before fronting the house band at the city's Tick Tock club. In 1952 the pianist made his first recordings with Muddy Waters and the following year he became a permanent member of this seminal artist's group, with whom he remained for most of his professional life. Spann did complete a solo session in 1955 with the assistance of Willie Dixon and Robert Lockwood, but session appearances for Bo Diddley and Howlin' Wolf apart, he is recalled for the subtle yet complementary support he contributed to Waters' music. Spann supported the singer on his groundbreaking UK tour of 1958 and was an integral part of the group that appeared at the 1960 Newport Jazz Festival. He subsequently completed an album for the Candid label, before resuming his association with Waters with a series of successful tours. British concerts during 1963 and 1964 proved highly influential on the emergent R&B scene and on the second visit Spann recorded two tracks, 'Pretty Girls Everywhere' and 'Stirs Me Up', with Yardbirds guitarist Eric Clapton. Spann began a thriving solo career on returning to the USA, completing a series of albums for several different labels, including Prestige and Bluesway. These releases not only showcased his remarkable talent on piano, they also revealed a skilled composer and vocalist and featured sterling support from such contemporaries as Waters, James Cotton (harmonica) and S.P. Leary (drums). The latter also appeared on *The Biggest Thing Since Colossus*, Spann's collaboration with Fleetwood Mac stalwarts Peter Green, Danny Kirwan and John McVie. Barring contributions to a session by Junior Wells and the film *Blues Like Showers Of*

Rain, this excellent set was the artist's last significant work. Increasingly debilitated by illness, Otis Spann entered Chicago's Cook County Hospital, where he died of cancer in 1970.

● ALBUMS: *Otis Spann Is The Blues* (Bluesway 1960)★★★, *Blues Is Where It's At* (1963)★★★, *Portrait In Blues* (1963)★★★, *Piano Blues* (1963)★★★, *The Blues Of Otis Spann* (Decca 1964)★★★★, *Good Morning Mr Blues* (Storyville 1964)★★★, *Chicago Blues* (Testament 1964)★★★★, with Memphis Slim *Piano Blues* (Storyville 1964)★★★★, *Blues Now* (Decca 1965)★★★, *The Blues Never Die!* (Stateside 1965)★★★, *Blues Are Where It's At* (HMV 1967)★★★, *Nobody Knows My Troubles* (Polydor 1967)★★★, *Bottom Of The Blues* (Stateside 1968)★★★, *Raw Blues* (1968)★★★, *Fathers And Sons* (Chess 1969)★★★, *Cracked Spanner Head* (Deram 1969)★★★, with Robert Lockwood Jnr. *Raised In Mississippi* limited edition (Python 1969)★★★, *The Biggest Thing Since Colossus* (Blue Horizon 1969)★★★, *Blues Never Die* (1969)★★★, *Cryin' Time* (Vanguard 1970)★★★, *The Everlasting Blues* (1970)★★★, *Walking The Blues* (1972)★★★.

● COMPILATIONS: *Candid Spann, Volume 1* (Crosscut 1983)★★★★, *Candid Spann, Volume 2* (Crosscut 1983)★★★★, *Nobody Knows Chicago Like I Do* (Charly 1983)★★★, *Rarest* (JSP 1984)★★★, *Take Me Back Home* (Black Magic 1984)★★★, *Walking The Blues* (Candid 1987)★★★, *The Blues Of Otis Spann ... Plus* (See For Miles 1994)★★★★, *Otis Spann's Chicago Blues* (Testament 1994)★★★★, *Down To Earth: The Bluesway Recordings* (MCA 1995)★★★★, Otis with Muddy Waters and his band *Live The Life* (Testament 1997)★★★.

SPARKS BROTHERS

Twin brothers, Aaron 'Pinetop' Sparks (d. *c*.1938) and Marion (aka Milton) 'Lindberg' Sparks (b. 22 May 1910, Tupelo, Mississippi, USA, d. 25 May 1963, St. Louis, Missouri, USA) were constantly in trouble with the law for fighting, gambling and theft, although Milton gradually reformed after a jail sentence for manslaughter in 1937. Pinetop was an accomplished pianist, equally adept at slow numbers and mid-tempo boogies, in which his style recalls Big Maceo. Lindberg's singing was more nasal, but equally attractive. Pinetop and Lindberg played the rowdy house-parties of St. Louis, and recorded, separately and together, from 1932-35, leaving an impressive body of work, including what appear to be the original versions of '61 Highway' and 'Every Day I Have The Blues'. Their lyrics make poetry from the realities of their lives: travel, lowlife, prison and sex.

● COMPILATIONS: *Sparks Brothers* (1989)★★★.

SPIRES, ARTHUR 'BIG BOY'

b. 6 November 1912, Yazoo City, Mississippi, USA. One of eight children, Spires remembers watching Henry Stuckey perform around his home-town. Teaching himself guitar in his late teens, he accompanied Lightnin' Hopkins when the latter made forays into Mississippi in the early 40s, playing in Yazoo City's Beer Garden. Spires moved to Chicago in 1943, studied guitar with Eddie El, and played in a group with El and fellow guitarist Earl Dranes. In 1952 the group submitted demos to Leonard Chess, who made one single (Checker 752) with Spires' vocals; 'Murmur Low' is a faithful reworking of Tommy Johnson's 1928 recording of 'Big Fat Mama', the vibrato in Spires' voice akin to that of Arthur 'Big Boy' Crudup, indicating the provenance of his nickname. The following year, he recorded 'About To Lose My Mind' (Chance 1137) which featured John Lee Henley on harmonica. A further session for United was split between Spires and Willie 'Long Time' Smith. Abandoning music at the end of the 50s, Spires did not record again until 1965, taping a session for Pete Welding's Testament label with Johnny Young.

● COMPILATIONS: *Wrapped In My Baby* (1989)★★★.

SPIVEY, ADDIE 'SWEET PEAS'

b. 22 August 1910, Houston, Texas, USA, d. 1943, Detroit, Michigan, USA. Like her sister Elton ('The Za Zu Girl'), Addie probably owed her recording career to the success of the third sister, Victoria Spivey. A less mannered singer than Victoria, Sweet Peas possessed a big, rich voice that was deployed to good effect, accompanied by a quartet led by Henry 'Red' Allen. Later recordings were less successful, and in the late 30s Spivey retired from showbusiness.

● COMPILATIONS: *Henry 'Red' Allen Volume 2* (1975), *Blues Box 2* (1976), *Super Sisters* (1982).

SPIVEY, VICTORIA

b. 15 October 1906, Houston, Texas, USA, d. 3 October 1976, New York City, New York, USA. Spivey was recording at the age of 19, and enjoyed early hits with 'Black Snake Blues' and 'T.B. Blues', both sung in her unmistakable nasal, acidic tones. She recorded until 1937, appeared in the early black film musical *Hallelujah*, and worked in vaudeville until her retirement in the early 50s. In 1960, she made a comeback, still writing remarkable songs, which she usually accompanied on piano or - less happily - ukulele. She founded the Spivey label in 1962, issuing some valuable recordings, and the first featured Bob Dylan as an accompanist. Others were by inferior artists and/or poorly recorded. She was invaluable in coaxing contemporaries such as Lucille Hegamin and Alberta Hunter back to recording. Self-styled 'The Queen', Spivey was the Madonna of the blues, hyper-energetic, propelled by total self-belief, always performing, and drawn to themes of drugs, violence and sexual deviance.

● ALBUMS: *Idle Hours* (1961)★★★, *Songs We Taught Your Mother* (1962)★★★, *Basket Of Blues* (1962)★★★, *Victoria Spivey And Her Blues* (Spivey 1963)★★★, *Queen And Her Nights* (Spivey 1965)★★★, *The Victoria Spivey Recorded Legacy Of The Blues* (Spivey 1970)★★★, *Victoria Spivey With The Easy Riders Jazz Band* (GHB 1988)★★, with Roosevelt Sykes *Grind It!* (Sequel 1996)★★★.

● COMPILATIONS: *Victoria Spivey (1926-1937)* (Blues Document 1990)★★★.

STACKHOUSE, HOUSTON

b. 28 September 1910, Wesson, Mississippi, USA, d. 1981. Despite his colourful name and his reputation among his peers, Stackhouse only received interest and acclaim towards the end of his life, although he played a contributory role in the development of delta blues. He became an active musician in his teens, learning first harmonica, violin, then mandolin and guitar. Moving to Crystal Springs, Mississippi, he came under the influence of Tommy Johnson and his brothers, Clarence and Mager. He in turn taught his first cousin, Robert Nighthawk, and on one occasion the pair worked with Jimmy Rodgers in Jackson, Mississippi. During the 30s, with Carey 'Ditty' Mason and Cootsie Thomas, he worked in a band modelled on the Mississippi Sheiks, with whom he occasionally played. In April 1946, Nighthawk summoned him to Helena, Arkansas, where he was advertising *Mother's Best* flour on station KFFA, with a band that included Pinetop Perkins and Kansas City Red. Stackhouse then became a member of the King Biscuit Boys, led by Peck Curtis when Sonny Boy Williamson (Rice Miller) was out of town. A day job with Chrysler and gigs with the Biscuit Boys continued through the 50s. He was not recorded until August 1967, in a session that also included Nighthawk and Curtis. A week later, he recorded with 'Ditty' Mason. Tracks from these sessions appeared on anthologies released by Testament, Arhoolie, Matchbox and Flyright. During the 70s, Stackhouse became a regular participant in blues festivals throughout the USA. As befitted the station he had taken for himself, his death in 1981 went unrecorded.

● COMPILATIONS: *Mississippi Delta Blues Vol. 1* (1968)★★★, *Cryin' Won't Help You* (Edsel 1995)★★★, *Big Road Blues* (Wolf 1996)★★.

STAPLES, POPS

b. Roebuck Staples, 2 December 1914, Winona, Mississippi, USA. Despite spending most of his life (very successfully) performing gospel music, Pops Staples had a solid grounding in blues in his teenage years. Brought up on Will Dockery's Plantation outside Drew, he watched Charley Patton playing guitar on the boss's porch. He took up the guitar at 16, learning by ear and playing church songs for his father. However, at weekends, he sneaked off to chittlin' feasts to earn some change playing the blues. Married at 18, he moved his growing family to Chicago in 1935, taking menial jobs and at weekends singing with the Silver Trumpets. In 1952, he bought a cheap guitar and taught his children to sing gospel songs. Five years later, the Staples Singers went professional. Staples was 77 when he recorded his first solo album, which brought together Ry Cooder, Bonnie Raitt, Jackson Browne and Willie Mitchell. The songs ranged from Browne's title track to Cooder-produced versions of 'Down In Mississippi' and 'I Shall Not Be Moved'. *Father Father* continued in the same vein, combining 'Jesus Is Going To Make Up (My Dying Bed)' with Bob Dylan's 'You Got To Serve Somebody' and Curtis Mayfield's 'People Get Ready'. Though hardly blues, Pops Staples' music represents a gentle voice of reason in a strident world.

● ALBUMS: *Peace To The Neighborhood* (PointBlank 1992)★★★, *Father Father* (PointBlank 1994)★★★, *The Kershaw Session* (Strange Fruit 1995)★★★.

STIDHAM, ARBEE

b. 9 February 1917, Devalls Bluff, Arkansas, USA. In his childhood he learned to play harmonica, clarinet and alto saxophone and formed his own band. When Stidham moved to Chicago he met Lester Melrose who signed the young blues singer to RCA-Victor in 1947. His biggest hit, 'My Heart Belongs to You', was recorded at the first session in September of that year, and Stidham spent the rest of his career trying to emulate its success. After Victor (1947-50), he recorded for Sittin' In With (1951), Checker (1953), Abco (1956) and States (1957) as a vocalist, but took up the guitar in the 50s under the tutelage of Big Bill Broonzy. In 1960-61, Stidham recorded one album for Bluesville (which included a remake of his big hit) and two for Folkways, in which his singing was accompanied by his guitar. He also accompanied Memphis Slim on one of the pianist's Folkways sessions. In 1965 Stidham again re-recorded 'My Heart Belongs To You' for Sam Phillips. In the 70s a single was released on Blues City and a brace of albums on Mainstream and Folkways.

● ALBUMS: including *There's Always Tomorrow* (70s), *My Heart Belongs To You* (Crown Prince 1987)★★★.

STOKES, FRANK

b. 1 January 1888, Whitehaven, Tennessee, USA, d. 12 September 1955, Memphis, Tennessee, USA. Stokes was raised in Mississippi, taking up the guitar early in life. He worked on medicine shows, and in the streets of Memphis in the bands of Will Batts and Jack Kelly. By 1927, when Stokes and his fellow guitarist Dan Sane made their first records as the Beale Street Sheiks, they were one of the tightest guitar duos in blues, heavily influenced by ragtime, and also performing medicine show and minstrel songs. Stokes was the vocalist, and played second guitar. They recorded together until 1929.

However, Stokes also recorded solo, and with Will Batts on fiddle. Stokes' recorded personality is that of the promiscuous rounder, by turns macho or pleading for another chance. His singing is forthright, with impressive breath control. Stokes and Sane worked together until illness forced Stokes to retire from music in 1952.

● COMPILATIONS: *The Remaining Titles* (Matchbox 1984)★★★, *Creator Of The Memphis Blues* (Yazoo 1988)★★★, *Frank Stokes* (Roots 1988)★★★, *The Beale Street Sheiks* (1990)★★★, *The Victor Recordings* (Document 1992)★★★.

STORYVILLE

This blues- and soul-influenced rock band, formed in Austin, Texas, USA, features the highly regarded vocals of singer Malford Milligan. For the group's first release, on the now defunct November Records in 1994, Storyville was effectively just Milligan with friends and studio professionals, including former Stevie Ray Vaughan associates Chris Layton (drums) and Tommy Shannon (bass). Guitarists David Grissom and Dave Holt also contributed. After the album was released it won six 1995 Austin Music Awards, including that for Best Band, and Milligan opted to retain all four of the previously named musicians as permanent members of the unit. *A Piece Of Your Soul* was released via an agreement between the UK-based Code Blue label and Atlantic Records in 1996, Milligan commenting that much of its inspiration was based on recent listening to Sam Cooke and Otis Redding - although conversely, these approaches were grounded in more conventional rock song cycles. Few critics, meanwhile, bothered to look further than Hootie And The Blowfish for a suitable musical comparison.

● ALBUMS: *The Bluest Eyes* (November 1994)★★★, *A Piece Of Your Soul* (Code Blue/Atlantic 1996)★★★.

STOVALL, JEWELL 'BABE'

b. 4 October 1907, Tylertown, Mississippi, USA, d. 21 September 1974, New Orleans, Louisiana, USA. More properly regarded as a songster in the tradition of Mance Lipscomb, Stovall emerged in the blues revival of the mid-60s. The youngest of 12 children in a sharecropping family, he taught himself to play the guitar, encouraged by his schoolteacher. He learned his first tune, later twice recorded as 'Maypole March', from his eldest brother Myrt Holmes. During the 20s, Stovall became part of a group of musicians, congregated around an older man, Herb Quinn, that played for both black and white audiences. In the mid-30s, Tommy Johnson married a local girl, Rosa Youngblood, and stayed in the area for some years. Stovall, along with Arzo Youngblood, O.D. Jones and Roosevelt Holts, learned Johnson's 'Big Road Blues' and copied his style. Around this time, he married, and moved to Franklinton, Louisiana. In 1957, he began to play on the streets of New Orleans' French Quarter. He was recorded, twice in 1958, and once with brother Tom on mandolin in 1961, by Larry Borenstein, the tapes remaining unissued until 1988. A full session, with accompaniment from banjo and string bass, was recorded in 1964, but was poorly distributed by Verve. Stovall joined the folk circuit thereafter, appearing at the first five New Orleans Jazz & Heritage Festivals from 1970-74.

● COMPILATIONS: *Babe Stovall 1958 - 1964* (Flyright 1990)★★★.

STOVEPIPE NO.1

b. Sam Jones. Stovepipe was a Cincinnati-based, one-man band, playing guitar, rack harmonica, and the length of chimney pipe that gave him his nickname, which produced booming, fruity bass lines. He recorded as early as 1924, with a repertoire of gospel, blues, ballads and white dance tunes. Jones was associated with the guitarist and harmonica player David Crockett, who accompanied Jones on recordings in 1927, and led King David's Jug Band; Jones was the band's lead singer on its 1930 recordings, and his stovepipe provided the 'jug' sound.

● COMPILATIONS: *Stovepipe No. 1 & David Crockett* (1988)★★★, with David Crockett *Complete Recordings In Chronological Order 1924-1930* (Document 1994)★★★.

STREHLI, ANGELA

b. 22 November 1945, Lubbock, Texas, USA. A linchpin in the Austin blues scene from its inception in the 70s, Strehli had met up with Lubbockites Joe Ely and Jimmie Dale Gilmore and learned harmonica and bass before becoming a singer. As the Texas representative of the YWCA, she visited Chicago in 1966 and spent her free time visiting blues clubs to see Muddy Waters, Howlin' Wolf and Buddy Guy. In her final years at university, she formed the Fabulous Rockets with Lewis Cowdrey; an attempt to establish the band in California failed after a few months. Returning to Austin, she sang back-up for James Polk And The Brothers and sat in with Storm, formed by Cowdrey and Jimmie Vaughan. In 1972 she formed Southern Feeling with W.C. Clark and Denny Freeman. Three years later she took a job as stage manager and sound technician for the Antone's club. Strehli went back to full-time singing in 1982 and in 1986 recorded *Stranger Blues*, an EP that inaugurated the Antone's label. *Soul Shake* followed a year later. In 1992, along with Marcia Ball and Lou Ann Barton, she recorded *Dreams Come True*, an album of original songs, along with Ike Turner's 'A Fool In Love' and 'I Idolize You' and Etta James's 'Something's Got A Hold On Me'. In 1990, Strehli dissolved her band and moved to San Francisco. *Blonde And Blue* combined Little Walter and Elmore James songs with her own material and a duet with Don Covay on 'Um, Um, Um, Um, Um, Um'.

● ALBUMS: *Soul Shake* (Antone's 1987)★★★, with Marcia Ball, Lou Ann Barton *Dreams Come True* (Antone's 1990)★★★, *Blonde And Blue* (Rounder 1994)★★★.

● COMPILATIONS: *Antone's Women* (Antone's 1992)★★★.

STUCKEY, HENRY

b. 11 April 1897, Bentonia, Mississippi, USA, d. 9 March 1966, Jackson, Mississippi, USA. Stuckey is best known as the apparent originator of a local style of blues guitar playing and singing, mostly associated with Skip James, also from Bentonia. He had taught himself guitar in childhood, which may partly account for the rather odd uses of open tunings that James was to exploit so effectively on his records. The two men played together frequently in the 20s, but Stuckey did not make any records when James did so in 1931. He claimed later to have recorded in 1935, but no trace of any recordings has been found. He remained sporadically active in music, mainly on a local basis, although he also worked for a while in Omaha, Nebraska.

SUMLIN, HUBERT

b. 16 November 1931, Greenwood, Mississippi, USA. Renowned for his guitar work, particularly in support of his mentor Howlin' Wolf, Hubert Sumlin began his career in the Mississippi juke-joints. He joined Jimmy Cotton and met Wolf in Memphis where he worked with him briefly before following him to Chicago in 1954. His occasionally stormy relationship with Wolf lasted until the latter's death, although on Wolf's obsequies he is listed as a son. He was in Europe with Wolf on the AFBF of 1964 and later worked with other bluesmen including Eddie Taylor and Muddy Waters. Since Wolf's death Hubert has pursued his career under his own name, often working with alumni of Wolf's band. Never a strong singer, he has relied on his guitar-playing prowess to see him through, but his work has been patchy and some feel that he has yet to regain his original stature. It is significant that much of the sound created on Wolf's records was due in no small part to Sumlin's tremendous guitar playing. He can be heard on dozens of Chess sides throughout the 50s and 60s.

● ALBUMS: *Blues Party* (Demon 1987)★★, *Healing Feeling* (Black Top 1990)★★, *Blues Guitar Boss* (JSP 1991)★★, *My Guitar And Me* (Evidence 1994)★★, *Blues Anytime* 60s recording (Bellaphon 1994)★★★.

SUNNYLAND SLIM

b. Albert Luandrew, 5 September 1907, Vance, Mississippi, USA, d. 17 March 1995. A seminal figure in the development of the post-war Chicago blues, Sunnyland Slim taught himself piano and organ as a child in Mississippi and spent many years playing around the south, before settling in Chicago in 1942. There he established his reputation with older musicians such as Lonnie Johnson, Tampa Red and Peter J. 'Doctor' Clayton (some of his earliest records were issued under the pseudonym Doctor Clayton's Buddy), but more importantly with the new breed of blues singers and musicians that included figures such as Muddy Waters and Little Walter. In the company of artists such as these, his powerful piano work was to set the standard for underpinning the hard, electric sound associated with Chicago blues in the 50s. He recorded extensively under his own name for many important labels of the period, such as Chess, J.O.B., Vee Jay and Cobra, as well as smaller labels, producing such classic Chicago blues sides as 'Johnson Machine Gun', 'Going Back To Memphis' and 'Highway 51'. He was also to be heard accompanying many other important artists of the time, including Robert Lockwood, Floyd Jones and J.B. Lenoir, as well as those already mentioned. He is often credited as having helped younger musicians to get their careers started. Throughout the 60s and 70s, he recorded prolifically and toured widely both in the USA and overseas. In the 80s, although in ill health, he produced albums on his own Airway label, and lent assistance to young players such as Eddie Lusk and Lurrie Bell. He died in 1995 of complications from kidney failure.

● ALBUMS: *Slim's Shout* (Bluesville 1961)★★★★, *Give Me Time* (Delmark 1984)★★★, *Devil Is A Busy Man* (Charly 1989)★★★★, *Be Careful How You Vote* (Airway 1989)★★★, *House Rent Party* (1992)★★★, *Slim's Got His Thing* (BMG 1992)★★★, *Sunnyland Train* (Evidence 1995)★★★, *Chicago Jump* (Evidence 1995)★★★, *Live At The D.C. Blues Society* (Mapleshade 1995)★★.

● COMPILATIONS: *Legacy Of The Blues Volume Eleven* (Sonet 1975)★★★★.

SWEET PAIN

This UK studio group comprised several of the country's leading blues musicians. Saxophonist Dick Heckstall-Smith was a veteran of Blues Incorporated, the Graham Bond Organisation and John Mayall's Bluesbreakers before becoming a founder-member of Colosseum, while John O'Leary (harmonica) and Keith Tillman (bass) were concurrently members of the John Dummer Blues Band. Stuart Cowell (guitar), Sam Crozier (piano), Junior Dunn (drums) and vocalists Annette Brox and Alan Greed completed the line-up featured on the unit's lone album. Its tough blend of jazz-based R&B was marked by the free-playing associated with informal 'jam' sessions, and on its completion the individual members resumed their respective careers. This release, dubbed *England's Heavy Blues Super Session* for America, is a testimony to their short-lived collective ambition.

● ALBUMS: *Sweet Pain* aka *England's Heavy Blues Super Session* (1969)★★★.

SYKES, ROOSEVELT

b. 31 January 1906, Elmar, Arkansas, USA, d. 17 July 1983. Sykes learned piano at the age of 12 and by the early 20s was playing in local barrel-houses. He moved to St. Louis in 1928 and his first records for OKeh and Victor were made from 1929-31. During the 30s, Sykes recorded for Decca and acted as a talent scout for the label. Among his most popular compositions were 'Night Time Is The Right Time' and 'The Honeydripper', which was Sykes' nickname. He settled in Chicago in the early 40s, becoming the piano accompanist on numerous city blues records by artists such as St. Louis Jimmy and Lonnie Johnson. In 1954, he moved to New Orleans and continued to record prolifically for Decca, Prestige, Spivey, Folkways, Delmark and other labels. The Prestige album, *Honeydripper*, included King Curtis on saxophone. His versatility in different piano styles made Sykes well placed to take advantage of the increased European interest in blues and he made his first visit to the UK in 1961, performing with Chris Barber's jazz band. He returned in 1965 and 1966 with the Folk Blues Festival package and played many US blues and jazz festivals in the 70s. As a result of his popularity with these new audiences, much of his pre-1945 work was reissued in the 70s and 80s.

● ALBUMS: *Big Man Of The Blues* (1959)★★★, *Return Of Roosevelt Sykes* (Bluesville 1960)★★★, *Honeydripper* (Bluesville 1961)★★★, *Hard Drivin' Blues* (Delmark 1963)★★★, *Blues From Bar Rooms* (1967)★★★, *Feel Like Blowing My Horn* (Delmark 1973)★★★, *Dirty Double Mother* (1973)★★★, with Victoria Spivey *Grind It!* (Sequel 1996)★★★, *Music Is My Business* 1977 recording (Charly 1996)★★★.

● COMPILATIONS: *The Original Honeydripper* (Blind Pig 1988)★★★, *The Honeydripper 1945-1960* (Blues Encore 1992)★★★, *Roosevelt Sykes 1931-1941* (Best Of Blues 1996)★★★, *Blues By Roosavelt 'The Honeydripper' Sykes* (Folkways 1996)★★★.

● VIDEOS: *Roosevelt Sykes/Jay 'Hootie' McShann* (1992).

T.O.B.A.

The Theatre Owners Booking Association was an organization that booked black acts into US black theatres for black audiences between 1911 and 1930. Thus, TOBA was formed for reasons rooted in prejudice and racism and the majority of the people behind the organization were white. At the height of the era the organization had a circuit of some 80 theatres strung between Philadelphia and Dallas. The association was known among entertainers as 'Tobytime' although some thought that 'Tough On Black Acts' might be a more appropriate explanation of the acronym. An unfortunately large number who felt they had been badly treated considered 'Tough On Black Asses' to be even more apt. Among the entertainers who worked on the Tobytime circuit were the brilliant dance teams the Nicholas Brothers and the Berry Brothers, Bessie Smith, Bill 'Bojangles' Robinson, Ida Cox, Bert Williams, dancer Rubberlegs Williams, comedian Moms Mabley, Ethel Waters, Beulah 'Sippie' Wallace, Fletcher Henderson, Joe 'King' Oliver, Alphonso Trent, Bennie Moten, Luis Russell, Count Basie, dancers Buck and Bubbles, comedians and singers Butterbeans And Susie, Ma Rainey, Victoria Spivey, Sammy Price, Duke Ellington and Louis Armstrong. For all the deficiencies in management that prompted criticism from performers, TOBA was extremely important in providing a focus for the emerging sense of identity of Afro-American culture in the 20s. There is little doubt that it was also an invaluable organization in advancing, admittedly for its own profit, the development of performers of the highest quality. Those who saw the leading acts during their Tobytime days, also the time when many were at their peak, were convinced that those whose names are now forgotten were at least the equal of the tiny handful of black acts that broke through the barrier and entertained on white stages in the 20s.

T.V. SLIM

b. Oscar Wills, 10 February 1916, Houston, Texas, USA, d. 21 October 1969, Kingman, Arizona, USA. A musician from the late 30s, Wills was resident and recording in Louisiana during the 50s, playing guitar (and harmonica, though not on record), and singing blues in a voice that was rich and laid-back on slow songs, hoarse and exciting on up-tempo ones. He operated his own Speed label, but recorded the humorous tale of 'Flat Foot Sam' ('always in a jam') for Cliff; when Cliff went out of business, Slim acquired the tape and leased it to Checker, for whom it was a novelty hit. Wills moved to California in 1959, and did some touring and recording, but was chiefly occupied running the television repair shop that gave him his nickname. He died in a car crash while returning from a gig in Chicago.
● ALBUMS: *Goin' To California* (1979)★★★, *Flat Foot Sam* (Moonshine 1989)★★★.

TAGGART, BLIND JOE

Joel 'Blind Joe' Taggart was second in popularity only to Blind Willie Johnson as a 'guitar evangelist'. Like Johnson, he often employed a female voice on his sessions and although he did not possess Johnson's vocal range or his guitar skills, he did produce many recordings that are as effective today as when they were recorded. These range from his early, often unaccompanied duets with his wife Emma (some made before Johnson even recorded) to his later days when his own guitar work had much improved and he was sometimes aided by a very young Josh White. He also used the voices of his son James and daughter Bertha, and had his work issued under the pseudonyms Blind Jeremiah Taylor, Blind Tim Russell and Blind Joe Donnell. It is generally accepted that the singer who recorded 'C and O Blues' at one of his sessions in 1927 under the name of Blind Joe Amos was also Taggart disguising his involvement with the 'devil's music'.
● COMPILATIONS: *Blind Joe Taggart 1926 - 1934* (Wolf 1987)★★★, *Blind Joe Taggart: A Guitar Evangelist* (Herwin 1988)★★★.

TAJ MAHAL

b. Henry Saint Clair Fredericks, 17 May 1940, New York City, New York, USA. The son of a jazz arranger, Mahal developed his early interest in black music by studying its origins at university. After graduating, he began performing in Boston clubs, before moving to the west coast in 1965. The artist was a founder-member of the legendary Rising Sons, a respected folk rock group that also included Ry Cooder and Spirit drummer Ed Cassidy. Mahal resumed his solo career when the group's projected debut album was shelved. His first solo album, *Taj Mahal*, released in 1968, was a powerful, yet intimate, compendium of electrified country blues that introduced an early backing band of Jesse Davis (guitar), Gary Gilmore (bass) and Chuck Blakwell (drums). A second album, *The Natch'l Blues*, offered similarly excellent fare while extending his palette to include interpretations of two soul songs. This early period reached its apogee with *Giant Steps/The Ole Folks At Home*, a double album comprising a traditional-styled acoustic album and a vibrant rock selection. Mahal continued to broaden his remarkable canvas. *The Real Thing*, recorded in-concert, featured support from a tuba section, while the singer's pursuit of ethnic styles resulted in the African-American persuasion of *Happy Just To Be Like I Am* and the West Indian influence of *Mo Roots*. He has maintained his chameleon-like quality over a succession of cultured releases, during which the singer has remained a popular live attraction at the head of a fluctuating backing group, known initially as the Intergalactic Soul Messengers, then as the International Rhythm Band. In the 90s Mahal veered more closely towards soul and R&B. His interpretations of Doc Pomus's 'Lonely Avenue' and the Dave Bartholomew/Fats Domino classic 'Let The Four Winds Blow' were particularly noteworthy on *Phantom Blues*, as was the work of sessionmen Jon Cleary (piano) and Mick Weaver (organ).
● ALBUMS: *Taj Mahal* (Columbia 1968)★★★★, *Giant Steps/De Ole Folks At Home* (Columbia 1969)★★★★, *The Natch'l Blues* (Columbia 1969)★★★★, *The Real Thing* (Columbia 1971)★★★, *Happy Just To Be Like I Am* (Columbia 1972)★★, *Recycling The Blues And Other Related Stuff* (Columbia 1972)★★★, *The*

Sounder (1973)★★, *Oooh So Good 'N' Blues* (Columbia 1973)★★★, *Mo' Roots* (Columbia 1974)★★★, *Music Keeps Me Together* (Columbia 1975)★★, *Satisfied 'N Tickled Too* (Columbia 1976)★★, *Music Fuh Ya'* (Warners 1977)★★, *Brothers* (Warners 1977)★★, *Evolution* (Warners 1977)★★, *Taj Mahal And The International Rhythm Band Live* (1979)★★★, *Live* (1981)★★, *Take A Giant Step* (Magnet 1983)★★★, *Taj* (Sonet 1987)★★★, *Live And Direct* (Teldec 1987)★★★, *Big Blues - Live At Ronnie Scott's* (Essential 1990)★★★, *Mule Bone* (Gramavision 1991)★★★, *Like Never Before* (Private Music 1991)★★★, *Dancing The Blues* (Private Music/BMG 1994)★★★, *An Evening Of Acoustic Music* (Tradition & Moderne/Topic 1995)★★★, *Phantom Blues* (Private 1996)★★★★, *An Evening Of Acoustic Music* (Ruf 1997)★★★, *Señor Blues* (Private Music/BMG 1997)★★★.
● COMPILATIONS: *Going Home* (Columbia 1980)★★★★, *The Taj Mahal Collection* (Castle 1987)★★★.
● VIDEOS: *At Ronnie Scott's 1988* (Hendring 1989).

TAMPA RED

b. Hudson Woodbridge aka Whittaker, *c.*8 January 1904, Smithville, Georgia, USA, d. 19 March 1981, Chicago, Illinois, USA. Tampa Red was raised in Tampa, Florida, by his grandmother Whittaker's family, hence his nickname. By the time of his 1928 recording debut for Vocalion, he had developed the clear, precise bottleneck blues guitar style that earned him his billing, 'The Guitar Wizard'. He teamed with Thomas A. Dorsey in Chicago in 1925, and they were soon popular, touring the black theatre circuit. 'It's Tight Like That', recorded in late 1928, was a huge hit, fuelling the hokum craze. They recorded extensively, often in a *double entendre* vein, until 1932, when Dorsey finally moved over to gospel. Tampa also recorded with his Hokum Jug Band, featuring Frankie Jaxon, and alone, in which capacity he cut a number of exquisite guitar solos. By 1934, when Tampa signed with Victor, he had ceased live work outside Chicago. He was with Victor for nearly 20 years, recording a great many titles. During the 30s, many of them were pop songs with his Chicago Five, often featuring his kazoo. Usually a live solo act, he worked on record with various

piano players. He was also an accomplished pianist, in a style anticipating that of Big Maceo, who became his regular recording partner in 1941. In the late 40s, Tampa was still keeping up with trends, leading a recording band whose rhythmic force foreshadows the post-war Chicago sound. His wife Frances was his business manager, and ran their home as a lodging house and rehearsal centre for blues singers. Her death in the mid-50s had a devastating effect on Tampa, leading to excessive drinking and a mental collapse. In 1960, he recorded two under-produced solo albums for Bluesville, also making a few appearances. However, he had no real wish to make a comeback, and lived quietly with a woman friend, and from 1974 in a nursing home. In a career that ranged from accompanying Ma Rainey to being backed by Walter Horton, he was widely admired and imitated, most notably by Robert Nighthawk, and wrote many blues standards, including 'Sweet Black Angel', 'Love Her With A Feeling', 'Don't You Lie To Me' and 'It Hurts Me Too' (covered, respectively, by B.B. King, Freddy King, Fats Domino and Elmore James, among others).
● ALBUMS: *Don't Tampa With The Blues* (Bluesville 1961)★★★, *Don't Jive Me* (Bluesville 1962)★★★.
● COMPILATIONS: *Bottleneck Guitar* (1974)★★★, *Guitar Wizard* (RCA 1975)★★★, *The Guitar Wizard 1935 - 1953* (Blues Classics 1977)★★★, *Crazy With The Blues* (1981)★★★, *Tampa Red i* (1982)★★★, *Tampa Red ii* (1983)★★★, *Midnight Blues* (1988)★★★, *Get It Cats'* (1989)★★★, *Volume 2* (1990)★★★, *Bottleneck Guitar 1928 - 1937* (1993)★★★, *Complete Recorded Works 1934-53 Vol. 6* (Document 1994)★★★, *It Hurts Me Too* (Indigo 1994)★★★.

TARHEEL SLIM

b. Alden Bunn, 24 September 1924, Bailey, North Carolina, USA, d. 21 August 1977. Tarheel Slim was a blues, gospel and doo-wop singer and guitarist who took his sobriquet from the popular nickname of North Carolina - Tarheel State. Bunn learned guitar at the age of 12 and sang in church by the age of 20. He began working with the Gospel Four following World War II and then joined the Selah Jubilee Singers, with whom he first recorded, in the late 40s. As the gospel

group could not record secular music, they also worked under the names the Four Barons and the Larks, recording the R&B hits 'Eyesight To The Blind' and 'Little Side Car' for Apollo Records in 1951. Bunn recorded under his real name for Apollo and also with the group the Wheels in 1956 on Premium Records. That was followed by a partnership with his wife as the Lovers for Lamp Records in 1958. They then recorded for the Fire label as Tarheel Slim And Little Ann, a name they kept until 1962. After a spell outside the music business, Slim returned in 1970, when he recorded for Trix Records, an association that lasted until his death.
● ALBUMS: *Lock Me In Your Heart* (1989)★★★, *No Time At All* (Trix 1994)★★★.

TATE, BABY

b. Charles Henry Tate, 28 January 1916, Elberton, Georgia, USA, d. 17 August 1972, Columbia, South Carolina, USA. Tate moved to Greenville, South Carolina, at the age of 10, and there took up with Blind Boy Fuller. He learned guitar, and his music developed along similar lines to Fuller's, in the distinctively south-eastern style. He continued to play, at least on a part-time basis, in the local area, interrupted only by military service in World War II. He partnered Pink Anderson for several years and this connection led to his making an album in 1962, in which he demonstrated a wide tradi-tional repertoire, although the Fuller sound also came across strongly. He recorded again 10 years later, with harmonica player Peg Leg Sam.
● ALBUMS: *See What You Done* (Prestige 1962)★★★.

TAYLOR, EDDIE

b. 29 January 1923, Benoit, Mississippi, USA, d. 1985. A self-taught musician, Eddie 'Playboy' Taylor found early inspiration in the work of Charley Patton, Son House and Robert Johnson. His formative years were spent playing guitar at local social gatherings and clubs but in 1948 he travelled to Chicago to pursue a full-time career. Taylor's combo became a popular attraction and in 1953 he auditioned for the city's Vee Jay label. Paradoxically, the company preferred the style of back-up guitarist Jimmy Reed and their roles were consequently reversed. Taylor appeared on the majority of masters Reed

recorded between 1953 and 1964, including 'You Don't Have To Go' (1955), 'Ain't That Lovin' You Baby' (1956) and 'Honest I Do' (1957), each of which reached the R&B Top 10. Taylor's sessions as a leader commenced in 1955 and he later achieved a local hit with 'Big Town Playboy'. Despite such success, further recordings were sporadic, and only six more titles were issued, the last of those in 1964. Taylor, meanwhile, sought employment as an accompanist with other Vee Jay acts, including John Lee Hooker and Sunnyland Slim. In 1968 he joined Hooker and Reed on a successful European tour, but positive reviews did not engender a new recording deal. The guitarist continued sporadic studio work until 1972 when he completed *I Feel So Bad* for a west coast independent label. This in turn inspired a second transatlantic tour, during which Taylor recorded *Ready For Eddie* for the Birmingham-based Big Bear company. He then endured a further low-key period, but a collection of masters from the Vee Jay era, released in 1981, rekindled interest in this accomplished, yet underrated, bluesman's career. Eddie Taylor was never a self-promoter and he has probably sold more records since his death in 1985 than while he was alive.
● ALBUMS: *I Feel So Bad* (1972)★★★, *Ready For Eddie* (Big Bear 1972)★★★, *My Heart Is Bleeding* (L&R 1988)★★★, *Still Not Ready For Eddie* (Antone's 1988)★★★, *Stormy Monday* (Blues Beacon 1994)★★★, with Floyd Jones *Masters Of Modern Blues* (Testament 1994)★★★, *Long Way From Home* (Blind Pig 1995)★★★.
● COMPILATIONS: *Big Town Playboy* (Charly 1981)★★★, *Bad Boy* (Wolf 1993)★★★.

TAYLOR, EVA

b. Irene Gibbons, 22 January 1895, St. Louis, Missouri, USA, d. 31 October 1977, Mineola, New York, USA. On stage from the age of three, Taylor had toured the Antipodes and Europe before her teens. In 1921 she settled in New York and married the bandleader, pianist and composer Clarence Williams. She pursued a pro-lific career in musical theatre, recording and especially appearing on radio until 1942, when she virtually retired, although she made a few European appearances in the late 60s and 70s. Taylor's singing lacked much jazz or blues feeling; it seems likely that her husband's position as 'race' records manager for OKeh Records accounts for the frequency with which Taylor recorded. Not surprisingly, it was often a Clarence Williams composition that was selected.

● COMPILATIONS: *Sidney Bechet Memorial Album* (c.1960), *Jazz Sounds Of The Twenties, Volume 4* (c.1962), *Clarence Williams* (c.1962), *Eva Taylor & Clarence Williams 1925-26* (Fountain 1988).

TAYLOR, JOHNNIE

b. 5 May 1938, Crawfordsville, Arkansas, USA. Having left home at the age of 15, Taylor surfaced as part of several gospel groups, including the Five Echoes and the Highway QCs. From there he joined the Soul Stirrers, replacing Sam Cooke on the latter's recommendation. Taylor switched to secular music in 1961; releases on Cooke's Sar and Derby labels betrayed his mentor's obvious influence. In 1965 he signed with Stax Records and had several R&B hits before 'Who's Making Love' (1968) crossed over into *Billboard*'s pop Top 5. Further releases, including 'Take Care Of Your Homework' (1969), 'I Believe In You (You Believe In Me)' and 'Cheaper To Keep Her' (both 1973), continued this success. Taylor maintained his momentum on a move to Columbia. The felicitous 'Disco Lady' (1976) was the first single to be certified platinum by the RIAA, but although subsequent releases reached the R&B chart they fared less well with the wider audience. Following a short spell with Beverley Glenn, the singer found an ideal niche on Malaco Records, a bastion for traditional southern soul. Taylor's first album there, *This Is The Night* (1984), reaffirmed his gritty, blues-edged approach, a feature consolidated on *Wall To Wall*, *Lover Boy* and *Crazy 'Bout You*. It is *Wanted: One Soul Singer*, *Who's Making Love* and *Taylored In Silk* that best illustrate his lengthy period at Stax. Taylor had one of the great voices of the era: expressive graceful and smooth, and yet it is a mystery why he failed to reach the heights of the likes of Otis Redding, Marvin Gaye and Wilson Pickett. *Somebody's Gettin' It* compiles several Columbia recordings while Taylor's early work on Sar can be found on *The Roots Of Johnnie Taylor*. In 1996 Taylor experienced something of a revival when his Malaco album *Good Love* became a huge hit and reached the top of the Billboard blues chart.

● ALBUMS: *Wanted One Soul Singer* (Stax 1967)★★★★, *Who's Making Love?* (Stax 1968)★★★★, *Looking For Johnny Taylor* (Stax 1969)★★★★, *The Johnnie Taylor Philosophy Continues* (Stax 1969)★★★, *Rare Stamps* (Stax 1970)★★★, *One Step Beyond* (Stax 1970)★★★, *Taylored In Silk* (Stax 1973)★★★, *Super Taylor* (Stax 1974)★★★, *Eargasm* (1976)★★★, *Rated Extraordinaire* (1977)★★, *Disco 9000* (1977)★★, *Ever Ready* (1978)★★, *Reflections* (197)★★, *She's Killing Me* (1979)★★, *A New Day* (1980)★★, *Just Ain't Good Enough* (1982)★★, *This Is Your Night* (Malaco 1984)★★★, *Best Of The Old And The New* (1984)★★★, *Wall To Wall* (Malaco 1985)★★★, *Lover Boy* (Malaco 1987)★★★, *In Control* (1988)★★, *Crazy 'Bout You* (Malaco 1989)★★★, *Little Bluebird* (Stax 1991)★★★, *Just Can't Do Right* (90s)★★★, *Real Love* (90s)★★★, *Good Love!* (Malaco 1996)★★★★.

● COMPILATIONS: *The Roots Of Johnnie Taylor* (Star1969)★★★, *The Johnnie Taylor Chronicle (1968-1972)* (Stax 1978)★★★★, *The Johnnie Taylor Chronicle (1972-1974)* (Stax 1978)★★★, *Somebody's Getting It* (1989)★★★, *Raw Blues/Little Bluebird* (1992)★★★, *The Best Of ... On Malaco Vol. 1* (1994)★★★.

TAYLOR, KOKO

b. Cora Walton, 28 September 1935, Memphis, Tennessee, USA. Taylor is one of the few major figures that post-war Chicago blues has produced. Her soulfully rasping voice has ensured her popularity in the Windy City, and latterly further afield, for over 30 years, since she recorded her first single for the local USA label. Signed by the leading black music independent label Chess, she attained their last blues hit in 1966 with the Willie Dixon song 'Wang Dang Doodle', whose cast of low-life characters suited her raucous delivery (guitarwork supplied by Buddy Guy). In the 70s and 80s a series of well-produced and sometimes exciting albums with her band the Blues Machine, as well as such prestigious gigs as Carnegie Hall and the Montreux International Jazz Festival, have confirmed her position as the world's top-selling female blues artist. She opened her own blues club in Chicago during 1995. Although she admits that 'It's not easy to be a woman out there', she has succeeded on her own terms and without compromising the raunchy, bar-room quality of her music. Taylor married for a second time in 1996 at the age of 61, given away by Buddy Guy.

● ALBUMS: *Koko Taylor* (Chess 1968)★★★★, *Basic Soul* (Chess 1972)★★★★, *Chicago Baby* (1974)★★★, *I Got What It Takes* (Alligator 1975)★★★, *The Earthshaker* (Alligator 1978)★★★, *From The Heart Of A Woman* (Alligator 1981)★★★, *Queen Of The Blues* (Alligator 1985)★★★, *An Audience With The Queen - Live From Chicago* (Alligator 1987)★★★, *Blues In Heaven* (Vogue 1988)★★★, *Jump For Joy* (Alligator 1990)★★★, *Force Of Nature* (Alligator 1993)★★★.

● COMPILATIONS: *Koko Taylor rec. 1965-69* (Chess 1987)★★★★.

TAYLOR, MELVIN

b. 13 March 1959, Jackson, Mississippi, USA. At three years old Taylor moved with his family to Chicago, and began playing guitar around the age of six, inspired by an uncle who played blues. He was influenced by a variety of guitarists, including B.B. King, Albert King, Jimi Hendrix, and particularly Wes Montgomery. In the early 70s Taylor played on Maxwell Street, Chicago's open-air street market, and in his mid-teens was with a group call the Transistors. He has also worked with Carey Bell (and son Lurrie Bell), and was a member of Eddie Shaw's group (he also recorded with Shaw) and the Legendary Blues Band. He made his debut recording for the French label in 1982, and a follow-up appeared in 1984. He also recorded on Alligator's 'New Bluebloods' anthology. Taylor is a fleet-fingered player who now plays with feel and technique.

● ALBUMS: *Melvin Taylor Plays The Blues For You* (1984)★★★, *Melvin Taylor And The Slack Band* (Evidence 1995)★★★.

TAYLOR, MICK

b. Michael Taylor, 17 January 1948, Welwyn Garden City, Hertfordshire, England. A rock and blues guitarist, much influenced by B.B. King, Muddy Waters and jazz saxophone giant John Coltrane, Taylor taught himself to play after leaving school at 15. His first band, the Welwyn-based Gods, also featured Ken Hensley (later of Uriah Heep) and John Glascock (Jethro Tull). In August 1965, Taylor deputized for absentee Eric Clapton in John Mayall's Bluesbreakers, and joined the band on a permanent basis from June 1967. He was the longest-serving of Mayall's guitarists by the time he left to join the Rolling Stones in 1969, as a replacement for Brian Jones. Taylor had minimal involvement with their *Let It Bleed*, but his controlled and tasteful blues playing brought a rare lyricism to the band's early 70s releases. He left the Stones in December 1975, working initially with Jack Bruce and Carla Bley, and appearing on two albums by jazz-rockers Gong. The well-received *Mick Taylor* put him back in the limelight temporarily; he spent much of the early 80s as part of Bob Dylan's band, appearing on three albums and touring with him in 1984. *Stranger In This Town* met with little success, and Taylor subsequently joined informal band the Bluesmasters (with Junior Wells and Steve Jordan) on *Win Or Lose* (1991), the debut release by American Brian Kramer. Taylor was reunited with John Mayall, guesting on his excellent *Wake Up Call* in 1993. Those wishing to hear him at his best should listen to albums with John Mayall: *Crusade* (1967), *Diary Of A Band Vol. 1* (1968), *Diary Of A Band Vol 2* (1968), *Bare Wires* (1968), *Blues From Laurel Canyon* (1969) and *Back To The Roots* (1971); the Rolling Stones: *Let It Bleed* (1969), *Get Yer Ya-Ya's Out* (1970), *Sticky Fingers* (1971), *Exile On Main Street* (1972), *Goat's Head Soup* (1973) and *It's Only Rock 'N' Roll* (1974); and some interesting work on Bob Dylan's *Infidels* (1983) and *Real Live* (1984).

● ALBUMS: *Mick Taylor* (Columbia 1979)★★, *Stranger In This Town* (Maze 1990)★★, with Carla Olson *Mick Taylor And Carla Olson Live* (Demon 1990)★★★, *Live At 14 Below* (Backtrip 1996)★★★.

TAYLOR, MONTANA

b. Arthur Taylor, 1903, Butte, Montana, USA. Nicknamed after his birthplace, Taylor was raised in Indianapolis, where he learned piano in 1919. He played at cafés and rent parties there and in Chicago, before recording two 78s for Vocalion in 1929. Although one record was partially spoiled by the vocal antics of the Jazoo Boys, Taylor's percussive, inventive piano playing was of the highest order. Shortly afterwards he stopped playing, discouraged by the absence of royalties. Located by jazz fans in

1946, Taylor made a series of recordings that not only showed he retained all his instrumental abilities, both solo and as accompanist to Bertha 'Chippie' Hill, but also revealed him to be a moving singer, particularly on slow, introspective pieces such as 'I Can't Sleep'. Discouraged anew, however, Taylor dropped out of sight once more, and his subsequent whereabouts are unknown.

● COMPILATIONS: *Montana's Blues* (Oldie Blues 1988)★★★.

TAYLOR, THEODORE 'HOUND DOG'

b. 12 April 1917, Natchez, Mississippi, USA, d. 17 December 1975, Chicago, Illinois, USA. Taylor had an apprenticeship playing guitar in Mississippi with musicians such as Elmore James and John Lee 'Sonny Boy' Williamson. In 1942 he moved to Chicago where he worked the clubs as well as the market on Maxwell Street. Two singles from the early 60s underlined the vitality of his music, especially the high-energy 'Five Take Five'. He won a following among young blues fans and toured Europe as well as North America. In 1971 he made an album for Alligator Records and this helped establish a reputation for intense bottleneck guitar blues and R&B. He did not live long enough to exploit this reputation.

● ALBUMS: *And His Houserockers* (Alligator 1971)★★★, *Beware Of The Dog* (Alligator 1975)★★★★, *Natural Boogie* (Alligator 1978)★★★.

TEMPLE, JOHNNY

b. 18 October 1906, Canton, Mississippi, USA, d. 22 November 1968, Jackson, Mississippi, USA. Johnny Temple learned guitar from his stepfather Slim Duckett, a well-known performer from the Jackson area who later recorded for OKeh Records in 1930. Temple could also play the mandolin and often worked at house parties and juke-joints. In 1932 he moved to Chicago where he worked as a general all-round musician and recorded blues for both Decca and Vocalion. He worked with the famous McCoy brothers and recorded as part of the knockabout jazz group the Harlem Hamfats. He continued to work in Chicago until well into the post-war period, appearing with artists such as Billy Boy Arnold and Walter Horton, as well as forming his own

group, the Rolling Four. In the mid-60s he returned to Jackson where, after a period of ill health, he died from cancer at the age of 62.

● COMPILATIONS: *Chicago Blues* (1985)★★★, *Johnny Temple 1935 - 1939* (Document 1987)★★★, *Johnny Temple 1937 - 1949* (Best Of Blues 1991)★★★.

TERRY, SONNY

b. Saunders Terrell, 24 October 1911, Greensboro, North Carolina, USA, d. 12 March 1986, New York City, New York, USA. By the age of 16, Sonny Terry was virtually blind following two accidents, which encouraged his concentration on music. After his father's death, Terry worked on medicine shows, and around 1937 teamed up with Blind Boy Fuller, moving to Durham, North Carolina, to play the streets with Fuller, Gary Davis and washboard player George Washington (Bull City Red). Terry made his recording debut in December 1937 as Fuller's harmonica player. His vocalized tones were interspersed with a distinctive falsetto whoop, and he continued in this fashion until Fuller's death in 1941. By Terry's good fortune, Fuller was in jail when John Hammond Jnr. wished to recruit him for the 1938 *Spirituals To Swing* concert, and Terry took his place. His inextricably interwoven harmonica playing and singing were a sensation, but had little immediate effect on his career, although OKeh Records did record him as a name artist. In 1942, Terry was to appear at a concert in Washington DC, and J.B. Long, who managed them both, suggested that Brownie McGhee should lead Terry. This led to a booking in New York, where both men relocated, and to the formation of their long-term musical partnership. In New York Terry recorded, as leader and sideman, for many black-orientated labels, but his first New York sides were made for Moses Asch of Folkways with accompaniment by Woody Guthrie, and this was a pointer to the future. By the late 50s, Terry and McGhee had effectively ceased to perform for black audiences, and presented their music as 'folk-blues'. This was seen as a sell-out by those who demanded uncompromisingly 'black' music from blues singers. However, an objective examination of their repertoire reveals a large number of songs that had been recorded for black audiences in an R&B setting, while the children's songs and country dance music Terry recorded for Asch remain a valuable documentation. Even so, Terry's singing voice (now no longer falsetto) was rather coarse, and sometimes badly pitched. McGhee and Terry were not close friends, and in the later days they actively disliked one another even to the point of bickering on stage; nevertheless, their partnership brought the blues to a vast audience worldwide.

● ALBUMS: *Sonny Terry's Washboard Band* (Folkways 1950)★★★, *Sonny Terry And His Mouth Harp* (Stinson 1950)★★★★, *Harmonica And Vocal Solos* (Folkways 1952)★★★★, *Folk Blues* (Elektra 1954)★★★★, *City Blues* (Elektra 1954)★★★★, *Harmonica And Vocal Solos* (1958)★★★★, *Sonny Terry's New Sound* (1958)★★★★, *On The Road* (1959)★★★, *Sonny's Story* (Bluesville 1961)★★★★, *Sonny Is King* (Bluesville 1963)★★★, *Washboard Band Country Dance Music* (1963)★★★, *Hometown Blues* (1969)★★★, *Wizard Of The Harmonica* (1972)★★★, with Johnny Winter and Willie Dixon *Whoopin'* (Alligator 1985)★★★.

● COMPILATIONS: *Old Town Blues Vol. 1* (1986)★★★, *Sonny Terry* (Krazy Kat 1987)★★★, *Toughest Terry And Baddest Brown* (Sundown 1987)★★★, *Sonny Terry* (Document 1988)★★★, *Brownie McGhee & Sonny Terry Sing* (1990)★★★★, *The Folkways Years* (Smithsonian/Folkways 1991)★★★★, *Whoopin' The Blues: The Capitol Recordings 1947-1950* (Capitol 1995)★★★★.

● VIDEOS: *Whoopin' The Blues 1958-1974* (Vestapol 1997).

THACKERY, JIMMY

b. 1953, Pittsburgh, Pennsylvania, USA. Raised in Washington DC, blues-rock guitarist Thackery is a raw live player who has earned favourable comparisons to Stevie Ray Vaughan. With Mark Wenner he formed the blues-based Nighthawks in 1972, recording 20 albums over 15 years and touring extensively. Tired of the endless touring schedule, Thackery left the band in 1987 and formed the six-piece Assassins, recording three R&B-based albums on his own Seymour label. Financial problems led to Thackery dissolving the Assassins in 1991 to form the trio, Jimmy Thackery And The Drivers, with Mark Sutso (drums) and Wayne Burdette (bass). A recording

contract with Blind Pig Records ensued, leading to 1992's *Empty Arms Motel* album. Thackery has released three more albums for Blind Pig (with Burdette replaced by Michael Patrick), recording with in-demand producer Jim Gaines. Although his albums have become gradually less blues-oriented since *Empty Arms Motel*, Thackery still attracts the aficionados on account of his dynamic live shows.

● ALBUMS: With the Nighthawks: *Rock & Roll* (Aladdin 1974)★★★, *Open All Night* (Adelphi 1975)★★★, *Live At Kuba Koda Hall, Tokyo* (Columbia 1975)★★★, *Psyche Delly* (Adelphi 1976)★★★, *Live* (Adelphi 1976)★★★, *Side Pocket Shot* (Adelphi 1977)★★★, *Jacks And Kings I* (Adelphi 1978)★★★, *Jacks And Kings II* (Adelphi 1978)★★★, *The Nighthawks* (Mercury 1980)★★★, *10 Years Live* (Rounder 1982)★★★, *Rock & Roll* (Rounder 1983)★★★, *Hot Spot* (Rounder 1984)★★★, *Direct Current: DC Bands Collective* (1985)★★★, *Hard Living* (Rounder 1986)★★★, *Living In Europe* (Rounder 1987)★★★. With the Assassins: *No Previous* (Seymour 1988)★★★, *Partners In Crime* (Seymour 1989)★★★, *Cut Me Loose* (Seymour 1990)★★★. Jimmy Thackery And John Mooney *Sideways In Paradise* (Blind Pig 1993)★★★. Jimmy Thackery And The Drivers: *Empty Arms Motel* (Blind Pig 1993)★★★, *Trouble Man* (Blind Pig 1994)★★★, *Wild Night Out* (Blind Pig 1995)★★★, *Drive To Survive* (Blind Pig 1996)★★★.

● COMPILATIONS: Jimmy Thackery And John Hammond *Hot Tracks* (Vanguard 1982)★★★. With the Assassins *Backtrack* (Rounder 1988)★★★, *The Best Of The Nighthawks - Blues* (Adelphi 1988)★★★, *The Best Of The Nighthawks - Rock* (Adelphi 1988)★★★.

THARPE, SISTER ROSETTA

b. 20 March 1915, Cotton Plant, Arkansas, USA, d. 9 October 1973. After first singing in a church choir, Tharpe quickly became a solo singer. In addition to her deeply held religious views, she was influenced by blues singers and musicians and took up the guitar to help broaden her repertoire. By the late 30s she was a popular performer at sacred and secular functions, happily switching from gospel to jazz. She was featured at John Hammond's 'Spirituals To Swing' concerts at Carnegie Hall and also worked at the

Cotton Club with Cab Calloway. In the early 40s she spent a year with the Lucky Millinder band, recording several bestselling numbers that included 'I Want A Tall Skinny Papa' and a marvellous rendition of 'Trouble In Mind'. Apparently conscience-stricken at this venture into the seamier side of life, she returned to the safety of the church, rocking congregations to the roots of their souls with her ecstatic and sometimes frenzied singing. She continued to record and her duets with fellow gospel singer Marie Knight are classics of the form. Later in her career, she continued to sing in churches but returned regularly to the jazz scene, making enormously successful tours of Europe and the UK with Chris Barber and others in the 50s and 60s. One of the few gospel singers to become an effective jazz performer, her vitality and zeal won her a substantial following in both fields. She died in October 1973.

● ALBUMS: *Live In Paris, 1964* (Concert 1988)★★★.
● COMPILATIONS: with Lucky Millinder *Apollo Jump* (rec. 1941-42), *Complete Recorded Works 1938-44 Vols. 1* and *2* (Document 1995)★★★★.

THEM

Formed in Belfast, Northern Ireland, in 1963, Them's tempestuous career spawned some of the finest records of the era. The original line-up - Van Morrison (b. 31 August 1945, Belfast, Northern Ireland; vocals, harmonica), Billy Harrison (guitar), Eric Wrixen (keyboards), Alan Henderson (bass) and Ronnie Millings (drums) - were stalwarts of the city's Maritime Hotel, where they forged a fiery, uncompromising brand of R&B. A demo tape featuring a lengthy version of 'Lovelight' engendered a management agreement with the imposing Phil Solomon, who persuaded Dick Rowe to sign the group to Decca Records. The group then moved to London and issued their debut single, 'Don't Start Crying Now', which flopped. Brothers Patrick and Jackie McAuley had replaced Wrixen and Millings by the time Them's second single, 'Baby Please Don't Go', was released. Although aided by session musicians, the quintet's performance was remarkable, and this urgent, exciting single - which briefly served as the theme song to the influential UK television

pop programme *Ready Steady Go* - deservedly reached the UK Top 10. It was backed by the Morrison-penned 'Gloria', a paean to teenage lust hinged to a hypnotic riff, later adopted by aspiring bar bands. The follow-up, 'Here Comes The Night', was written and produced by R&B veteran Bert Berns. It peaked at number 2, and although it suggested a long career, Them's internal disharmony undermined progress. Peter Bardens replaced Jackie McAuley for the group's debut album, which matched brooding original songs, notably the frantic 'Mystic Eyes' and 'You Just Can't Win', with sympathetic cover versions. Further defections ensued when subsequent singles failed to emulate their early success and by the release of *Them Again*, the unit had been recast around Morrison, Henderson, Jim Armstrong (guitar), Ray Elliott (saxophone, keyboards) and John Wilson (drums). This piecemeal set nonetheless boasted several highlights, including the vocalist's impassioned reading of the Bob Dylan composition, 'It's All Over Now, Baby Blue'. Dave Harvey then replaced Wilson, but this version of Them disintegrated in 1966 following a gruelling US tour and a dispute with Solomon. Posthumous releases included the extraordinary 'The Story Of Them', documenting the group's early days at the Maritime in Belfast. Morrison then began a highly prolific solo career, leaving behind a period of confusion that saw the McAuley brothers re-emerge with a rival unit known variously as 'Them', 'Them Belfast Gypsies', the 'Freaks Of Nature', or simply the 'Belfast Gypsies'. Meanwhile, ex-Mad Lads singer Kenny McDowell joined Henderson, Armstrong, Elliott and Harvey in a reconstituted Them, who moved to Los Angeles following the intervention of producer Ray Ruff. *Now And Them* combined garage R&B with the *de rigueur* west coast sound exemplified by the lengthy 'Square Room', but the new line-up found it hard to escape the legacy of its predecessors. Elliott left the group in 1967, but the remaining quartet completed the psychedelic *Time Out, Time In For Them* as a quartet before McDowell and Armstrong returned to Belfast to form Sk'Boo. Henderson then maintained the Them name for two disappointing albums, on which he was supported by anonymous session musicians, before joining Ruff for a religious rock-opera, *Truth Of*

Truths. He subsequently retired from music altogether, but renewed interest in his old group's heritage prompted a reunion of sorts in 1979 when the bassist recruited Billy Harrison, Eric Wrixen, Mel Austin (vocals) and Billy Bell (drums) for *Shut Your Mouth*. True to form, both Harrison and Wrixen were fired prior to a tour of Germany, after which the Them appellation was again laid to rest.

● ALBUMS: *Them* aka *The Angry Young Them* (Decca 1965)★★★★, *Them Again* (Decca 1966)★★★★, *Now And Them* (Tower 1968)★★★, *Time Out, Time In For Them* (Tower 1968)★★★, *Them* (Happy Tiger 1970)★★★, *In Reality* (Happy Tiger 1971)★★★, *Shut Your Mouth* (Teldec 1979)★★★.
Solo: Billy Harrison *Billy Who?* (Vagabound 1980)★★.

● COMPILATIONS: *The World Of Them* (Decca 1970)★★★★★, *Them Featuring Van Morrison, Lead Singer* (Decca 1973)★★★, *Backtrackin' With Them* (London 1974)★★★, *Rock Roots: Them* (Decca 1976)★★★★, *One More Time* (Decca 1984)★★★, *The Them Collection* (Castle Communications 1986)★★★, *The Singles* (See For Miles 1987)★★★★.

● FURTHER READING: *Van Morrison: A Portrait Of The Artist*, Johnny Rogan.

THOMAS, CHRIS

b. 14 October 1962, Baton Rouge, Louisiana, USA. The son of bluesman Tabby Thomas, Chris grew up with the music of his father and other local artists including Slim Harpo, Silas Hogan, and Henry Gray, although he includes Prince, Jimi Hendrix, and Bob Marley among his major influences. He has toured and recorded with his father, and material under his own name has appeared on Bluebeat (his father's label), Arhoolie and Wolf. Currently under contract to Hightone/Warner Brothers Records, his combination of Hendrix-styled guitar lines and rap/reggae vocals in a blues setting is refreshingly original.

● ALBUMS: *The Beginning* (Arhoolie 1986)★★★, with various artists *Louisiana Blues Live At Tabby's Blues Box* (1989)★★★, *Cry Of The Prophets* (Sire 1990)★★★, *21st Century Blues - From Da 'Hood* (Private 1995)★★★.

THOMAS, EARL

b. Earl Thomas Bridgeman, 1950, Pikeville, Tennessee, USA. With a navy officer for a father, Thomas grew up in Seattle, Guam and San Diego, before returning to Pikeville in 1965. He grew up listening to his father play blues guitar and harmonica. In 1983, he moved to Arcata, California, where he studied dentistry at Humboldt State University, but before he had completed his studies, he had begun to sing at open-mike nights in local clubs. In 1987, he and co-writer Phillip Wooten moved to San Diego, where Thomas joined the Rhumboogies, performing 40s jump band music. In 1989, he recorded *I Sing The Blues*, which he released on his own Conton label. He also formed a band, the Blues Ambassadors, which has featured musicians such as Zach Zunis, Joel Foy, Christopher Crepps and Michael Cherry in the line-up. A copy of his album reached Herb Cohen, who signed him to Bizarre Records. *Blue ... Not Blues* consisted of remixed versions of the original album plus three new songs. Thomas has toured Europe with Buddy Guy and appeared at the Montreux Jazz Festival. A life-long fan of Ike Turner, his second album reflected his growing interest in both rhythm and the blues.

● ALBUMS: *I Sing The Blues* (Conton 1990)★★★, *Blue ... Not Blues* (Bizarre/Demon 1992)★★★, *Extra Soul* (Bizarre/Demon 1994)★★★.

THOMAS, GEORGE

b. c.1885, Houston, Texas, USA, d. March 1930, Chicago, Illinois, USA (1936, Washington DC, USA, is also cited). Thomas was the pianist head of an important Texas blues clan that included his daughter Hociel Thomas, his siblings Beuluh 'Sippie' Wallace and Hersal Thomas, plus Bernice Edwards, not a blood relative, but raised with the family. Thomas was an important composer (of 'New Orleans Hop Scop Blues' and 'Muscle Shoals Blues', among other tunes) and publisher, for a time in partnership with Clarence Williams. On disc, he made 'The Rocks' in 1923 (as Clay Custer), a solo that contains the earliest recording of a walking bass; he also accompanied Sippie's friend Tiny Franklin, and made one record under his own name, in addition to several with his jazz group, the

Muscle Shoals Devils.

● COMPILATIONS: *The Thomas Family* (1977)★★★.

THOMAS, HENRY

b. 1874, Big Sandy, Texas, USA, d. *c*.1930. One of the oldest black folk artists to record during the 20s, Thomas's highly individual repertoire of rags, breakdowns, church songs and ballads is of considerable importance to musicologists seeking to document the milieu from which the blues developed. Born to ex-slaves on a share-cropping farm in east Texas, Thomas was more than 50 when he first recorded in Chicago in July 1927. Thus, the songs from that and two other 1927 sessions, and single sessions in 1928 and 1929, were already some decades out of date. Although seven of his 23 issued sides were labelled 'blues', very few conformed to any of the established metrical patterns. His nickname of 'Ragtime Texas' defined more nearly the nature of his music than it did his penchant for constant travelling. He sometimes supplemented his loud voice with Pan-pipes, though his technique was far more rudimentary than that of men such as Sid Hemphill, who recorded for the Library of Congress in 1942. One of his most noted songs was 'Railroadin' Some', in which he detailed the stops on several Texas and Louisiana railway lines. 'Don't Ease Me In' and 'Don't Leave Me Here' were both variants on 'Alabama Bound'. His 'Bull Doze Blues' was the basis for Canned Heat's 1969 hit, 'Goin' Up The Country'.

● COMPILATIONS: *Texas Worried Blues* (Yazoo 1989)★★★.

THOMAS, HERSAL

b. 1910, Houston, Texas, USA, d. 3 July 1926, Detroit, Michigan, USA. A child prodigy on piano, Thomas was tutored by his brother George, but soon surpassed him for invention. In mid-20s Chicago, his reputation for technique and feeling made other pianists wary of playing at parties where he was present. He recorded 'Hersal Blues' and his celebrated 'Suitcase Blues', an enduring standard of blues piano, in 1925, and was accompanying his sister Beuluh 'Sippie' Wallace (with Joe 'King' Oliver and Louis Armstrong) before he was 15. In 1925/6 he was heavily in demand for recording, backing

his niece Hociel Thomas, among others. He was working at Penny's Pleasure Inn in Detroit, an engagement arranged by Sippie, when he died of food poisoning, aged only 16.

● COMPILATIONS: *The Thomas Family* (1977)★★★.

THOMAS, HOCIEL

b. 10 July 1904, Houston, Texas, USA, d. 22 August 1952, Oakland, California, USA. Sister of George Thomas, and niece of Beuluh 'Sippie' Wallace and Hersal Thomas, Hociel Thomas was a direct and effective blues singer, as she showed when she recorded during 1925-26; her records always featured Hersal on piano, and his sudden death in 1926 devastated Hociel, who abandoned her musical career. Discovered in California by jazz fans, she recorded some fine sides in 1946 with her own capable Texas piano and Mutt Carey on trumpet, and appeared with Kid Ory in 1948, but soon retired again. In about 1950, she was acquitted of manslaughter after a fight with a sister, in which the sister died and Hociel was blinded.

● COMPILATIONS: *Hot Society LP 1001* (untitled) (1970)★★★, *Louis And The Blues Singers* (1972)★★★, *The Piano Blues, Vol. 4* (1977)★★★, *The Thomas Family* (1977)★★★.

THOMAS, JAMES 'SON'

b. 14 October 1926, Eden, Mississippi, USA, d. 26 June 1993. Until his discovery by a blues music researcher in 1967, Thomas had never travelled more than 100 miles from Leland, Mississippi. As such, he was a valuable source of lore on the creative processes of delta blues, and made a number of satisfying recordings, accompanying his dark singing with the typically hypnotic guitar of the region. In subsequent years, he travelled more widely, including Europe, and recorded again. This recognition enabled him to afford to give up his various jobs including those of gravedigger and removal man. Greater exposure revealed him to be a likeable performer, but one with few original themes, as is often typical of blues singers of his generation. Thomas was also a storyteller and folk sculptor, working with clay he dug from his local river. In 1991 he had an operation to remove a brain tumour. Two years later, while recovering from a stroke, he suffered a fatal cardiac arrest.

● ALBUMS: *The Blues Are Alive And Well* (1970)★★★, *Down On The Delta* (1981)★★★, *Plays And Sings Delta Blues Classics* (Swing Master 1982)★★★, *Highway 61 Blues* (1983)★★★, *Good Morning School Girl* (1986)★★★, *Bottomlands* (1990)★★★.

THOMAS, JESSE 'BABYFACE'

b. 3 February 1911, Logansport, Louisiana, USA, d. 13 August 1995, Shreveport, Louisiana. Although he was the younger brother of blues guitarist Willard Ramblin' Thomas, Jesse was not influenced by his style. On his 1929 debut records, he imitated Lonnie Johnson and Blind Blake, but by the time of his next recordings in 1948, he had developed an individual electric guitar style of great fluency. This stemmed from formal training, an acquaintance with jazz, and his serious attempts to transfer his piano playing to the guitar. His singing and playing were still placed firmly within Texan blues traditions. Thomas recorded intermittently on the west coast until 1957, when he returned to Louisiana. While there, he occasionally released records on his self-operated Red River label, a successor to Club, which had briefly traded in the early 50s. A mid-60s soul recording was less successful than a blues single released on Red River in 1989. This showed that Thomas remained a capable and sophisticated musician.
● ALBUMS: including *Down Behind The Rise* (1979)★★★, *1948-53* (1993)★★★, *Lookin' For That Woman* (Black Top 1996)★★★.

THOMAS, KID

b. Louis Thomas Watts, 20 June 1934, Sturgis, Mississippi, USA, d. 13 April 1970, Beverly Hills, California, USA. Watts was also known as Tommy Lewis/Louis. Chicago-based from 1941, he played harmonica and sang blues from the end of the 40s, recording for Federal in 1955, and seeing occasional releases on small labels until the end of his life. This came shortly after his location by a music researcher in California, where Thomas had settled in 1960. He had killed a child in a road accident and was shot by the boy's father after manslaughter charges were dismissed. The strong feelings this aroused among blues enthusiasts should not be allowed to mask the fact that Thomas was a minor and derivative performer, albeit an impressively energetic one, especially when imitating Little Richard.
● ALBUMS: *Rockin' This Joint Tonite* (1979)★★★, *Here's My Story* (1991)★★★.

THOMAS, LAFAYETTE JERL

b. 13 June 1928, Shreveport, Louisiana, USA, d. 20 May 1977, Brisbane, California, USA. One of the few post-war guitarists to develop a personal style from an early admiration of 'T-Bone' Walker, Thomas was encouraged by his uncle, Jesse 'Babyface' Thomas. The family moved to San Francisco soon after his birth and there he learned to play both piano and guitar. His first gig in 1947 was with Al Simmons' Rhythm Rockers. In 1948 he replaced guitarist Robert Kelton in Jimmy McCracklin's band, with whom he remained intermittently for the rest of his career. He made his first record while on tour with McCracklin. 'Baby Take A Chance With Me', recorded in Memphis in 1951 for Sam Phillips, was issued on Chess under the name of L.J. Thomas And His Louisiana Playboys. He also worked with Bob Geddins, playing on many Jimmy Wilson sessions leased to Aladdin, 7-11, Big Town and Irma. His own records were made for small labels such as Jumping, Hollywood (unissued) and Trilyte, but more often he cut odd titles at McCracklin's 50s sessions for Modern, Peacock and Chess, discovered and issued on album three decades later. Moving briefly to New York in 1959, he made 'Lafayette's A-Comin'' for Savoy with pianist Sammy Price, before returning to the west coast. He worked outside music for most of the 60s, sharing one album session with pianist Dave Alexander and L.C. 'Good Rocking' Robinson in September 1968. The comeback was brief and he spent his last years working as a hose assembler. His best work is to be found on the records of McCracklin and Wilson, providing the biting solos for which he will be remembered.
● ALBUMS: *Everybody Rock! The Best Of Jimmy McCracklin* (1989)★★★.

THOMAS, RAMBLIN'

b. Willard Thomas, 1902, Logansport, Louisiana, USA, d. c.1945, Memphis, Tennessee, USA. According to his younger brother, Jesse 'Babyface' Thomas, Willard Thomas was nicknamed by Paramount when he recorded in 1928.

He was peripatetic and spent much of his time between Dallas (where he played with Blind Lemon Jefferson) and Shreveport, where he probably acquired the slide guitar technique heard on many of his records. Thomas also travelled east of Shreveport into Louisiana, where he associated with King Solomon Hill. Although echoes of Jefferson, Blind Blake and Lonnie Johnson are audible, both Thomas's sour-edged playing and his cynical, hard-bitten singing are instantly recognizable. Thomas was an inventive lyricist who drew on his life for his songs, singing of being locked up for 'Vag', of 'Hard Dallas', and of the alcoholism that may have hastened his death from tuberculosis.
● ALBUMS: *Ramblin' Thomas* (1983)★★★.

THOMAS, RUFUS

b. 26 March 1917, Cayce, Mississippi, USA. A singer, dancer and entertainer, Thomas learned his trade as a member of the Rabbit's Foot Minstrels, a vaudeville-inspired touring group. By the late 40s he was performing in several Memphis nightclubs and organizing local talent shows. B.B. King, Bobby Bland and Little Junior Parker were discovered in this way. When King's career subsequently blossomed, Thomas replaced him as a disc jockey at WDIA and remained there until 1974. He also began recording and several releases appeared on Star Talent, Chess and Meteor before 'Bear Cat' became a Top 3 US R&B hit. An answer to Willie Mae Thornton's 'Hound Dog', it was released on Sun in 1953. Rufus remained a local celebrity until 1960 when he recorded with his daughter, Carla Thomas. Their duet, ''Cause I Love You', was issued on the fledgling Satellite (later Stax) label where it became a regional hit. Thomas secured his reputation with a series of infectious singles; 'Walking The Dog' (1963) was a US Top 10 entry, while several of his other recordings, notably 'Jump Back' and 'All Night Worker' (both in 1964), were beloved by aspiring British groups. His later success with novelty numbers – 'Do The Funky Chicken' (1970), '(Do The) Push And Pull, Part 1' (1970) and 'Do The Funky Penguin' (1971) – has obscured the merits of less brazen recordings. 'Sophisticated Sissy' (1967) and 'Memphis Train' (1968) are prime 60s R&B. Thomas stayed with Stax until its 1975 collapse, from where he moved to AVI. His releases there included *If There Were No Music* and *I Ain't Getting Older, I'm Gettin' Better*. In 1980 Thomas re-recorded several of his older songs for a self-named collection on Gusto. In the 80s he abandoned R&B and recorded some rap with *Rappin' Rufus*, on the Inchiban label, and tackled blues with *That Woman Is Poison*, on the Alligator label. Bob Fisher's Sequel Records released a new album from Thomas in 1996. *Blues Thang* proved to be an unexpected treat from a man celebrating his 79th birthday at the time of release. He continues to perform regularly.
● ALBUMS: *Walking The Dog* (Stax 1963)★★★★, *Do The Funky Chicken* (Stax 1970)★★★★, *Doing The Push And Pull Live At PJs* (Stax 1971)★★★, *Did You Heard Me?* (Stax 1973)★★★, *Crown Prince Of Dance* (Stax 1973)★★★, *Blues In The Basement* (1975)★★★, *If There Were No Music* (AVI 1977)★★★, *I Ain't Gettin' Older, I'm Gettin' Better* (AVI 1977)★★★, *Rufus Thomas* (Gusto 1980)★★, *Rappin' Rufus* (Ichiban 1986)★★, *That Woman Is Poison* (Alligator 1989)★★, *Timeless Funk* (1992)★★, *Blues Thang* (Sequel 1996)★★★.
● COMPILATIONS: *Jump Back - A 1963-67 Retrospective* (Edsel 1984)★★★, *Can't Get Away From This Dog* (Ace/Stax 1991)★★★, *The Best Of - The Singles* (Ace/Stax 1993)★★★★.

THOMAS, TABBY

b. 5 January 1929, Baton Rouge, Louisiana, USA. Thomas's first musical influences came from radio and records, and he started to play music himself while in the airforce. He sang with an R&B band during the early 50s and his first records were in that style, with strong touches of Roy Brown's sound. A release on the Feature label in 1954 marked the beginning of a long, if intermittent, association with producer Jay Miller, during which they tried a wide range of styles, including blues and soul. Their most successful collaboration was 'Hoodoo Party', on Excello in 1962. In 1981, Thomas opened the Blues Box in Baton Rouge to showcase local artists; this has achieved an international reputation for regular appearances by Silas Hogan, Henry Gray and Thomas's own son Chris.
● ALBUMS: *25 Years With The Blues* (1979)★★★, *Hoodoo Party* (1990)★★★.

THOMAS, WILLIE B.

b. 25 May 1912, Lobdell, Mississippi, USA. Thomas was permanently disabled by a back injury he received in his early teens during his family's migration to Louisiana. He partnered the fiddler James 'Butch' Cage on kazoo for 10 years before taking up the guitar, on which he recorded with Thomas after their discovery in 1959. Thomas was unusual in seeing no conflict between his secular music and his activities as a street preacher. His guitar playing, though limited, was an ideal complement to Cage's fiddle, and they formed an unmistakable, raucous vocal duo.
● ALBUMS: *Country Negro Jam Session* (1960), *I Have To Paint My Face* (1969), *Raise A Rukus Tonight* (1979).

THOMPSON, JOE AND ODELL

b. 9 December 1918 and 9 August 1911, respectively, Mebane, North Carolina, USA. Joe (fiddle) and Odell Thompson (banjo) were first cousins whose fathers were musicians on the same instruments. Odell took up blues and the guitar in the 20s, but continued to play the older repertoire with his cousin in local stringbands until the 40s. As this style lost popularity, they retired until the early 70s, when a folklore researcher persuaded them to perform in public once more. Much of their repertoire was derived from their fathers, so that they preserved the music of the pre-World War I black string band; as possibly the last black fiddle-banjo duo performing, it was an unexpected bonus that they were still vigorous and skilful musicians.
● ALBUMS: *Old Time Music From The North Carolina Piedmont* (1989).

THOMPSON, SONNY

b. Alphonso Thompson, 22 August 1916, Centreville, Mississippi, USA, d. 11 August 1989. This long-time Chicago-based R&B bandleader and pianist first recorded boogie-woogies in 1946 for the Detroit-based Sultan label. After signing for the Miracle label in Chicago, he succeeded with 'Long Gone', which went to number 1 on the R&B chart in 1948. The gently rolling instrumental set the tone for later hits, 'Late Freight' (R&B number 1, 1948), 'Blue Dreams' (R&B number 10, 1949) and 'Mellow Blues' (R&B number 8, 1952). His later chart records fea-

tured the vocals of his wife, Lulu Reed, notably 'I'll Drown In My Tears' and 'Let's Call It A Day', both from 1952. He worked largely as a session musician during the 50s, and in 1959 succeeded Ralph Bass as an A&R director for King Records' Chicago office. After the closure of the King office in 1964, Thompson continued session work and made occasional tours of Europe.
● ALBUMS: *Moody Blues* (King 1956)★★★, *Mellow Blues For The Late Hours* (King 1959)★★★, with Freddy King, Lulu Reed *Boy, Girl, Boy* (1962)★★, *Swings In Paris* (Black & Blue 1974)★★.
● COMPILATIONS: *Cat On The Keys* (Swingtime 1988)★★★, *Jam Sonny Jam* (Sequel 1996)★★★★.

THORNTON, WILLIE MAE 'BIG MAMA'

b. 11 December 1926, Montgomery, Alabama, USA, d. 25 July 1984, Los Angeles, California, USA. Thornton was the daughter of a minister and learned drums and harmonica as a child. By the early 40s she was singing and dancing in Sammy Green's Hot Harlem Revue throughout the southern states. Basing herself in Texas, she made her first records as Big Mama Thornton for Peacock in 1951. Two years later she topped the R&B charts with the original version of 'Hound Dog', the Leiber and Stoller song that Elvis Presley would later make world famous. The backing was by Johnny Otis's band with Pete Lewis contributing a memorable guitar solo. Thornton toured with Otis and recorded less successfully for Peacock until 1957 when she moved to California. There she made records for Bay-Tone (1961), Sotoplay (1963) and Kent (1964). Her career took a new turn when she joined the 1965 Folk Blues Festival troupe. The next year, Arhoolie recorded her in Chicago with Muddy Waters, James Cotton and Otis Spann. A 1968 live album for the same label included 'Ball And Chain' which inspired Janis Joplin's notable version of the song. She sang some pop standards on the 1969 Mercury album and in the 70s she recorded for Backbeat, Vanguard and Crazy Cajun. On *Jail*, recorded before prison audiences, she performed new versions of 'Hound Dog' and 'Ball And Chain'.
● ALBUMS: *In Europe* (1965)★★★, *Big Mama Thornton, Vol. 2* (1966)★★★, *With Chicago Blues*

(Arhoolie 1967)★★★, *Ball & Chain* (Arhoolie 1968)★★★, *Stronger Than Dirt* (Mercury 1969)★★★, *The Way It Is* (1970)★★★, *Maybe* (1970)★★★, *She's Back* (Backbeat 1970)★★★, *Saved* (1973)★★★, *Jail* (Vanguard 1975)★★★, *Sassy Mama* (Vanguard 1975)★★★, *Mama's Pride* (Vanguard 1978)★★★, *Live Together* (1979)★★★.
● COMPILATIONS: *The Original Hound Dog* (Ace 1990)★★★, *Hound Dog: The Peacock Recordings* (1993)★★★, *The Rising Sun Collection* (Just A Memory 90s)★★★.

THOROGOOD, GEORGE

b. 31 December 1952, Wilmington, Delaware, USA. White blues guitarist George Thorogood first became interested in music, notably Chicago blues, when he saw John Paul Hammond performing in 1970. Three years later he formed the Destroyers in Delaware before moving them to Boston, where they backed visiting blues stars. The Destroyers comprised Thorogood (guitar), Michael Lenn (bass) and Jeff Simon (drums). Schoolfriend Ron Smith played guitar on-and-off to complete the quartet. In 1974 they recorded some demos that were released later. They made their first album in 1975 after blues fanatic John Forward spotted them playing at Joe's Place in Cambridge, Massachusetts, and put them in touch with the folk label Rounder Records. The album was not released immediately, as Blough replaced Lenn and his bass parts had to be added. It was eventually released in 1978 (on Sonet Records in the UK) and the single 'Move It On Over' was Rounder's first release. Smith left in 1980 and was replaced by saxophonist Hank Carter. Thorogood, a former semi-professional baseball player, took time away from music that season to play, but by 1981 was back in the fold as the band opened for the Rolling Stones at several of their American gigs. The venues were unfamiliar to Thorogood as he customarily shunned large arenas in favour of smaller clubs, even going to the extent of playing under false names to prevent the smaller venues becoming over-crowded. After three albums with Rounder they signed to Capitol Records and continued to record throughout the 80s and 90s. In 1985 they appeared at Live Aid playing with blues legend Albert Collins.

● ALBUMS: *George Thorogood And The Destroyers* (Rounder 1977)★★★, *Move It On Over* (Rounder 1978)★★★, *Better Than The Rest* (Rounder 1979)★★, *More George Thorogood And The Destroyers* (Rounder 1980)★★, *Bad To The Bone* (Capitol 1982)★★★, *Maverick* (Capitol 1985)★★, *Live* (Capitol 1986)★★, *Born To Be Bad* (Capitol 1988)★★, *Boogie People* (Capitol 1991)★★, *Killer's Bluze* (1993)★★, *Haircut* (1993)★★, *Let's Work Together* (EMI 1995)★★, *Rockin' My Life Away* (EMI 1997)★★.

TIBBS, ANDREW

b. Melvin Andrew Grayson, 2 February 1929, Columbus, Ohio, USA, d. 5 May 1991, Chicago, Illinois, USA. Although little-known now, Tibbs was an important contributor to the early success of the Aristocrat record label, the precursor of Chess and Checker Records. His father, Rev. S.A. Grayson, was one of Chicago's most prominent Baptist ministers and the young Tibbs sang in choirs directed by Mahalia Jackson and Ruth Jones (who later married his brother, Robert, and changed her name to Dinah Washington). He based his blues singing style on Roy Brown, Ivory Joe Hunter and Gatemouth Moore. He was spotted while singing at the Macomba Lounge by owner Leonard Chess, who was in the process of buying Aristocrat Records. Still aged only 18, both sides of his first single, 'Bilbo Is Dead' and 'Union Man Blues', caused controversy; the first was seen as a criticism of the recently deceased Mississippi segregationist senator, Theodore Bilbo, while local Chicago teamster unions objected to the b-side. Tibbs recorded another six singles for Aristocrat, including 'Married Man Blues', and 'You Can't Win' for Chess and 'Rock Savoy Rock' for Peacock. After an unissued session for Savoy, he and his brother Kenneth recorded a single for Atco in 1956, which featured King Curtis on his first Atlantic session. Tibbs' last single, 'Stone Hearted Woman', was recorded for M-Pac! in 1965. He retired from singing thereafter and worked for West Electric for the rest of his life.
● ALBUMS: *Strutting At The Bronze Peacock* (Ace 1987)★★★.
● COMPILATIONS: *Chess Blues* (MCA/Chess 1992)★★★.

TINSLEY, JOHN

b. 10 February 1920, Chestnut Mountain, Virginia, USA. Tinsley learned guitar when he was 11, and from the age of 18 played at social events. He acquired much of his repertoire from, and was stylistically influenced by, the records of Blind Boy Fuller and Buddy Moss. He also composed personal blues, including one arising from a 1949 incident when he shot and wounded his stepfather. In 1952 Tinsley recorded a 78 with Fred Holland for a local label, but its failure to sell induced him to stop playing blues by 1955. In 1977, he resumed playing with the encouragement of blues music researchers, made some likeable recordings and visited Europe a couple of times, despite a dispute with a Danish promoter on the first occasion.

● ALBUMS: *Country Blues Roots Revived* (1978)★★★, *Home Again Blues* (1980)★★★, *Sunrise Blues* (1982)★★★.

TOSCANO, ELI

b. Elias P. Toscano. Toscano was of Mexican and Italian descent and lived on the near west side of Chicago. He began his career in the music business operating a television repair and record shop, which he expanded into a one-stop distributorship and then a record company. He ran three important record labels, issuing blues and R&B in Chicago in the 50s. The first was Abco, on which, with co-owner Joe Brown, he issued eight releases, most notably by Arbee Stidham and Louis Myers. Then he began his Cobra label, which issued more than 30 discs including classic tracks by Otis Rush, Ike Turner, Harold Burrage and Magic Sam. A subsidiary label was Artistic, whose five issues included two by Buddy Guy and another by Turner. Toscano reportedly died in a boating accident in the early 60s, but rumours continued for decades afterwards that it was a gangland slaying, reputedly over an unpaid gambling debt.

TOWNSEND, HENRY

b. 27 October 1909, Shelby, Mississippi, USA. Townsend was raised in Cairo, Illinois, then moved to St. Louis in the late 20s. He took up guitar at about the age of 15, and was a forceful and accomplished player by the time of his recording debut in 1929. He was closely associated with Walter Davis, touring with him and providing accompaniment on his recordings. In the early 30s, Townsend added piano to his skills. He worked and recorded with Robert Lee McCoy, John Lee 'Sonny Boy' Williamson and Big Joe Williams, as well as making further records under his own name. After World War II, he appeared on Davis's last sessions (playing imaginative electric guitar), and teamed with Roosevelt Sykes for a time. Following his retirement Townsend was discovered by a new, white audience and recorded intermittently. He continued to develop his music and compose new songs, concentrating on piano, and sometimes duetting with his wife, Vernell.

● ALBUMS: *The Blues In St Louis* (1961)★★★, *Mule* (1980)★★★, *Hard Luck Stories* (1981)★★★, *Henry Townsend & Henry Spaulding* (Wolf 1988)★★★.

TRADITION RECORDS

Before the emergence of Tradition Records in the 50s, American folk and blues had often been poorly recorded and packaged. Tradition changed all that, establishing a catalogue of fine recordings which also engaged with flamenco, Irish and jazz music. Arguably the most pivotal release on the label was Odetta's *Sings Ballads & Blues*, which was later cited by Bob Dylan as 'the first thing that turned me on to folk singing'. Lightnin' Hopkins released two groundbreaking live albums, *Autobiography In Blues* and *Country Blues*, for the label, drawn from a Houston, Texas, performance in 1959. 'Big' Bill Broonzy's *Treat Me Right* was also recorded live in Paris in 1951, and the label was additionally responsible for the first release of Lead Belly sessions conducted in New York between 1943 and 1944. Irish folk legends Liam Clancy and Tommy Makem (from Clancy Brothers And Tommy Makem) also recorded their first album, *The Lark In The Morning*, for Tradition. Other artists on the roster included Carlos Montoya, Errol Garner, Woody Herman and Coleman Hawkins. A series of reissues in 1996 on the Rykodisc Records label helped to reinstate Tradition's role in the emergence of popular music.

TRICE, RICHARD

b. 16 November 1917, Hillsborough, North Carolina, USA. Born into a very musical family, Trice learned guitar early, and was partnering his brother Willie Trice, playing blues for dances by his early teens. In the 30s, he took up with Blind Boy Fuller, and his music developed very much in Fuller's mould. In the late 30s he made records, two sides solo and two supporting his brother, very much in the eastern states style of the time. In the 40s, he moved to Newark, New Jersey, and not long afterwards made a solo record under the pseudonym Little Boy Fuller. In the 50s he moved back south, and his music moved in a religious direction when he joined a gospel quartet. He was interviewed by researchers in the 70s, but refused to play blues guitar again.

● ALBUMS: *Bull City Blues* (1972)★★★.

TRICE, WILLIE

b. 10 February, 1910, Hillsborough, North Carolina, USA, d. 10 December, 1976, Durham, North Carolina, USA. Trice's parents played music and he learned guitar from an uncle, but one of his principal influences as a blues guitarist was Blind Gary Davis. In the 30s he formed a partnership with his younger brother, Richard Trice, playing the ragtime-influenced blues style prevalent in the Carolinas at that time. In 1937 he made a record, with Richard playing second guitar, but it can have had little success as he did not record again until the 70s. He lived his whole life in the same area, and continued to play music. In his retirement he made some new recordings, and saw an album released shortly before his death at the age of 66.

● ALBUMS: *Bull City Blues* (1972)★★★, *Blue And Rag'd* (1975)★★★.

TROUT, WALTER, BAND

b. 6 March 1951, Atlantic City, New Jersey, USA. This highly talented and experienced blues guitarist finally formed and recorded with his own band in 1989 after a lengthy spell with John Mayall and Canned Heat. With a line-up of Jim Trapp (bass), Leroy Larson (drums) and Dan Abrams (keyboards), he debuted with *Life In The Jungle* in 1990. This showcased Trout's remarkable feel and dexterity and courted Jimi Hendrix, Robin Trower and Gary Moore comparisons. Klas Anderhill took over on drums for *Prisoner Of A Dream*, on which the band moved into a more commercial mainstream rock direc-

tion. Much of the soulful passion was replaced for a heavier approach more akin to bands such as Europe, Whitesnake and Bon Jovi. Trout moved away from his blues roots with *Transition*, although his remarkable ability as a guitarist shone through an album of patchy songs. Following a live album Trout moved to Silvertone Records, presumably in the hope of expanding his market to a wider audience. *Tellin' Stories* was an exciting set of crisply recorded rock/blues yet surprisingly it was not the anticipated commercial success. A year later he was back with Provogue, having now replaced Larson and Abrams with Bernard Pershey and Martin Gerschwitz, respectively. *Breaking The Rules* was a quieter and more introspective album with Trout's contentment with life seemingly apparent from the lyrics. *Positively Beale Street* mixed together all of Trout's previous styles, and his guitar playing is exemplary. The slow, gospel-influenced ballad 'Let Me Be The One', written by Dave Williams and Mick Parker, is the album's highlight.

● ALBUMS: *Life In The Jungle* (Provogue 1990)★★★★, *Prisoner Of A Dream* (Provogue 1991)★★★, *Transition* (Provogue 1992)★★, *Live, No More Fish Jokes* (Provogue 1992)★★, *Tellin' Stories* (Silvertone 1994)★★★, *Breaking The Rules* (Provogue 1995)★★★, *Positively Beale Street* (Provogue 1997)★★★.

TUCKER, LUTHER

b. 20 January 1936, Memphis, Tennessee, USA, d. 17 June 1993, San Rafael, California, USA. Tucker moved to Chicago, Illinois, at the age of nine and was probably best known as one of Little Walter's backing guitarists both on stage and on record in the 50s. He was heavily influenced by his mother who played piano and guitar, but Tucker started playing himself after hearing Robert Lockwood Jr. Lockwood became his mentor, together with his mother. He also worked with other musicians such as J.T. Brown, Junior Wells, Muddy Waters and Sonny Boy 'Rice Miller' Williamson in the same decade. Tucker remained an in-demand backing guitarist and recorded with numerous blues artists, including James Cotton, Otis Rush and John Lee Hooker. He settled in California in 1969 and occasionally led a group under his own name. He was known for the speed of his playing and recorded in his own right for Messaround and Paris Albums. He lived in the Netherlands for some years but returned to live in California. Tucker died in 1993 from a heart attack.

● COMPILATIONS: *Blue Bay* three tracks only (1976), *San Francisco Blues Festival European Sessions* three tracks only(1980), *Sad Hours* (Antone's 1994)★★★, with the Ford Blues Band *Luther Tucker And The Ford Blues Band* (Cross Cut 1995)★★★.

TUCKER, TOMMY

b. Robert Higginbotham, 5 March 1933, Springfield, Ohio, USA, d. 22 January 1982. Renowned as an R&B performer, Tucker began his career as a jazz musician playing piano and clarinet for the Bob Woods Orchestra. He led his own group, the Dusters, recorded under the name Tee Tucker for Atco in 1961 and worked with saxophonist Roland Kirk prior to recording 'Hi-Heel Sneakers' in 1964. This simple, but compulsive 12-bar blues song established the singer's reputation when it was consistently covered by other acts. This one song contained a pot-pourri of references, the bizarre 'hi-heel sneakers' and 'wig hats on her head.' The casually understated delivery of the line: 'You better wear some boxing gloves, in case some fool might want to fight', gave the song great subtle humour. Further excellent singles in a similar style, including 'Long Tall Shorty', were less successful and forced Tucker to revert to club work. He visited Britain during the 70s as part of the *Blues Legends* package and, inspired by an enthusiastic response, began recording again. This irrepressible performer, sadly, died from poisoning in 1982.

● ALBUMS: *Greatest Twist Hits (Rock And Roll Machine)* (Atlantic 1961)★★★, *Hi-Heel Sneakers & Long Tall Shorty* (Checker 1964)★★★★, *Mother Tucker* (Red Lightnin' 1974)★★★, *Rocks Is My Pillow, Cold Ground Is My Bed* (Red Lightnin' 1982)★★, *Memphis Badboy* (Zu Zazz 1987)★★★, *Tommy Tucker And His Californians* (Circle 1988)★★, *Tommy Tucker And His Orchestra* (Circle 1988)★★★.

TURNER, 'BIG' JOE

b. Joseph Vernon Turner, 18 May 1911, Kansas City, Missouri, USA, d. 24 November 1985, Los Angeles, California, USA. 'Big' Joe Turner (aka Big Vernon) began singing in local clubs in his early teens upon the death of his father, and at the age of 15 teamed up with pianist Pete Johnson. Their professional relationship lasted on-and-off for over 40 years. During the late 20s and early 30s, Turner toured with several of Kansas City's best black bands, including those led by George E. Lee, Bennie Moten, Andy Kirk and Count Basie. However, it was not until 1936 that he left his home ground and journeyed to New York City. Making little impression on his debut in New York, Turner, with Johnson, returned in 1938 to appear in John Hammond Jnr.'s *From Spirituals To Swing* concerts and on Benny Goodman's *Camel Caravan* CBS radio show, and this time they were well received. Johnson teamed up with Albert Ammons and Meade Lux Lewis as the Boogie Woogie Boys and sparked the boogie-woogie craze that subsequently swept the nation and the world. Turner's early recordings depicted him as both a fine jazz singer and, perhaps more importantly, a hugely influential blues shouter. He appeared on top recording sessions by Benny Carter, Coleman Hawkins and Joe Sullivan as well as his own extensive recording for Vocalion (1938-40) and Decca (1940-44), which featured accompaniment by artists such as Willie 'The Lion' Smith, Art Tatum, Freddie Slack or Sammy Price, when Johnson, Ammons or Lewis were unavailable. After World War II, Turner continued to make excellent records in the jazz-blues/jump-blues styles for the burgeoning independent labels - National (1945-47), Aladdin (1947, which included a unique *Battle Of The Blues* session with Turner's chief rival, Wynonie Harris), Stag and RPM (1947), Down Beat/Swing Time and Coast/DooTone (1948), Excelsior and Rouge (1949), Freedom (1949-50), and Imperial/Ba'you (1950), as well as a west coast stint in 1948-49 with new major MGM Records. As the 40s wore on, these recordings, often accompanied by the bands of Wild Bill Moore, Maxwell Davis, Joe Houston and Dave Bartholomew, took on more of an R&B style which began to appeal to a young white audience by the early 50s. In 1951 'Big' Joe started the first of 13 years with the fledgling Atlantic Records, where he became one of the very few jazz/blues singers of his generation who managed to regain healthy record sales in the teenage rock 'n' roll market during the mid to late 50s. His early Atlantic hits were largely blues ballads such as 'Chains Of Love' and 'Sweet Sixteen', but 1954 witnessed the release of Turner's 'Shake Rattle And Roll' which, covered by artists such as Bill Haley and Elvis Presley, brought the 43-year-old blues shouter some belated teenage adoration. This was maintained with such irresistible (and influential) classics as 'Hide And Seek' (1954), 'Flip, Flop And Fly', 'The Chicken And The Hawk' (1955), 'Feelin' Happy' (1956) and 'Teenage Letter' (1957). At the height of rock 'n' roll fever, Atlantic had the excellent taste to produce a retrospective album of Turner singing his old Kansas City jazz and blues with a peerless band, featuring his old partner Pete Johnson. The album, *The Boss Of The Blues*, has since achieved classic status.

In the late 50s, Atlantic's pioneering rock 'n' roll gave way to over-production, vocal choirs and symphonic string sections. In 1962 Turner left this fast-expanding independent company and underwent a decade of relative obscurity in the clubs of Los Angeles, broken by the occasional film appearance or sporadic single release on Coral and Kent. The enterprising Bluesway label reintroduced 'Big' Joe to the general public. In 1971 he was signed to Pablo Records, surrounded by old colleagues like Count Basie, Eddie Vinson, Pee Wee Crayton, Jay McShann, Lloyd Glenn and Jimmy Witherspoon. He emerged irregularly to produce fine one-off albums for Blues Spectrum and Muse, and stole the show in Bruce Ricker's essential jazz film *The Last Of The Blue Devils*. Turner's death in 1985 was as a result of 74 years of hard living, hard singing and hard drinking, but he was admired and respected by the musical community and his funeral included musical tributes by Etta James and Barbara Morrison.

● ALBUMS: *Sings Kansas City Jazz* (Decca 1953)★★★, *The Boss Of The Blues* (Atlantic 1956)★★★★, *Joe Turner And The Blues* (Savoy 1958)★★★★, *Joe Turner* (Atlantic 1958)★★★★, *Big Joe Rides Again* (Atlantic 1959)★★★★, *Rockin' The Blues* (Atlantic 1959)★★★★, *Big Joe Is Here* (Atlantic 1959)★★★★, *Careless Love* (Savoy 1963)★★★, *Big Joe Singing The Blues* (Bluesway 1967)★★★, *Texas Style* (Black & Blue 1971)★★, with Count Basie *The Bosses* (1975)★★★, with Pee Wee Crayton *Every Day I Have The Blues* (1976)★★★, with Jimmy Witherspoon *Nobody In Mind* (Pablo 1976)★★★, *Things That I Used To Do* (Pablo 1977)★★★, with Basie, Eddie Vinson *Kansas City Shout* (1978)★★★, *The Midnight Special* (Pablo 1980)★★★, *Have No Fear, Joe Turner Is Here* (Pablo 1981)★★★★, *In The Evening* (Pablo 1982)★★★, *The Trumpet Kings Meet Joe Turner* (Pablo 1982)★★★, *Boogie Woogie Jubilee* (1982)★★★, *Big Joe Turner & Roomful Of Blues* (1983)★★★★, *Life Ain't Easy* (Pablo 1983)★★★, *Blues Train* (Muse 1983)★★★, *Kansas City Here I Come* (Pablo 1984)★★★, with Witherspoon *Patcha, Patcha All Night Long: Joe Turner Meets Jimmy Witherspoon* (Pablo 1986)★★★, *I Don't Dig It* (Jukebox 1986)★★★, *Honey Hush* (Magnum Force 1988)★★★, *Steppin' Out* (Ace 1988)★★★, with Basie *Flip, Flop & Fly* rec. 1972 (Pablo 1989)★★★, with 'Big' Joe Turner *Bosses Of The Blues* (Bluebird 1989)★★★, *I've Been To Kansas City* (1991)★★★, *Every Day In The Week* (1993)★★★, with the Memphis Blues Caravan *Jackson On My Mind* (Mystic 1997)★★.

● COMPILATIONS: *The Best Of Joe Turner* (Atlantic 1953)★★★★, *Jumpin' The Blues* (Arhoolie 1981)★★★, *Great R&B Oldies* (Carosello 1981)★★★, *Boss Blues* (Intermedia 1982)★★, *The Very Best Of Joe Turner* (Intermedia 1982)★★★, *Roll Me Baby* (Intermedia 1982)★★, *Rock This Joint* (Intermedia 1982)★★★, *Jumpin' With Joe* (Charly 1984)★★★, *Jumpin' Tonight* (Pathé Marconi 1985)★★★, *Big Joe Turner Memorial Album: Rhythm & Blues Years* (Atlantic 1987)★★★★, *Big Joe Turner: Greatest Hits* (Atlantic 1987)★★★★, *The Complete 1940-1944 Recordings* (1990)★★★★, *Shouting The Blues* (Specialty/Ace 1993)★★★★, *Jumpin' With Joe - The Complete Aladdin And Imperial Recordings* (EMI 1994)★★★★, *Greatest Hits* (Sequel 1994)★★★★.

TURNER, IKE AND TINA

Ike Turner (b. 5 November 1931, Clarkdale, Mississippi, USA) and Tina Turner (b. Annie Mae Bullock, 26 November 1938, Brownsville, Tennessee, USA). The commercial rebirth of singer Tina Turner, coupled with revelations about her ex-husband's unsavoury private life, has obscured the important role Ike Turner played in the development of R&B. A former piano player with Sonny Boy Williamson and Robert Nighthawk, Turner formed his Kings Of Rhythm during the late 40s. This influential group was responsible for 'Rocket 88', a 1950 release often named as the first rock 'n' roll recording but confusingly credited to its vocalist, Jackie Brenston. Turner then became a talent scout for Modern Records where he helped develop the careers of Bobby Bland, B.B. King and Howlin' Wolf. Now based in St. Louis, his Kings Of Rhythm were later augmented by a former gospel singer, Annie Mae Bullock. Originally billed as 'Little Ann', she gradually became the core of the act, particularly following her marriage to Ike in 1958. Their debut release as Ike And Tina Turner came two years later. 'A Fool In Love', a tough, uncompromising release featuring Tina's already powerful delivery, preceded several excellent singles, the most successful of which was 'It's Gonna Work Out Fine' (1961). Highlighted by Ike's wry interjections, this superior performance defined the duo's early recordings. Although their revue was one of the leading black music touring shows, the Turners were curiously unable to translate this popularity into record sales. They recorded for several labels, including Sue, Kent and Loma, but a brief spell with Philles was to prove the most controversial. Here, producer Phil Spector constructed his 'wall-of sound' around Tina's impassioned voice, but the resultant single, 'River Deep Mountain High', was an unaccountable miss in the USA, although in the UK charts it soared into the Top 3. Its failure was to have a devastating effect on Spector. Ike, unhappy at relinquishing the reins, took the duo elsewhere when further releases were less successful. A support slot on the Rolling Stones' 1969 North American tour introduced the Turners to a wider, generally white, audience. Their version of John Fogerty's 'Proud Mary' was a gold disc in 1971, while the autobiographical 'Nutbush City Limits' (1973) was also an international hit. The group continued to be a major in-concert attraction, although Tina's brazen sexuality and the show's tried formula ultimately paled. The Turners became increasingly estranged as Ike's character darkened; Tina left the group in the middle of a tour and the couple were finally divorced in 1976. Beset by problems, chemical or otherwise, Ike spent some 18 months in prison, a stark contrast to his ex-wife's very public profile. In *What's Love Got To Do With It?* (1993), a film biography of Tina Turner, Ike was portrayed as a 'vicious, womanising Svengali'. Since his return Turner has attempted to redress the balance of his past with little success. Other than 'Rocket 88' there is little in the Ike Turner solo catalogue to excite. An embarrassing 'I Like Ike' campaign was undertaken by the UK purist fanzine *Juke Blues*, which also failed to convince the outside world that Ike had anything to offer musically.

● ALBUMS: *The Soul Of Ike And Tina Turner* (Sue 1960)★★, *Dance With The Kings Of Rhythm* (Sue 1960)★★★, *The Sound Of Ike And Tina Turner* (1961)★★★, *Dance With Ike And Tina Turner* (Sue 1962)★★★, *Festival Of Live Performances* (Kent 1962)★★, *Dynamite* (Sue 1963)★★★★, *Don't Play Me Cheap* (Sue 1963)★★★, *It's Gonna Work Out Fine* (Sue 1963)★★★★, *Please Please Please* (Kent 1964)★★★, *The Soul Of Ike And Tina Turner* (Kent 1964)★★★, *The Ike And Tina Show Live* (Loma 1965)★★★★, *The Ike And Tina Turner Show Live* (Warners 1965)★★★★, *River Deep - Mountain High* (London 1966)★★★★, *So Fine* (Pompeii 1968)★★★★, *In Person* (Minit 1968)★★★★, *Cussin', Cryin' And Carrying On* (Pompeii 1969)★★★, *Get It Together!* (Pompeii 1969)★★★, *A Black Man's Soul* (Pompeii 1969)★★★, *Outta Season* (Liberty 1969)★★★, *In Person* (Minit 1969)★★★, *River Deep - Mountain High* (A&M/London 1969)★★★★, *Come Together* (Liberty 1970)★★★, *The Hunter* (Harvest 1970)★★★★, *Workin' Together* (Liberty 1971)★★★, *Her Man, His Woman* (Capitol 1971)★★★, *Live In Paris* (Liberty 1971)★★★★, *Live At Carnegie Hall - What You Hear Is What You Get* (Liberty 1971)★★★, *'Nuff Said* (United Artists 1972)★★, *Feel Good* (United Artists 1972)★★, *Let Me Touch Your Mind* (United Artists 1973)★★, *Nutbush City Limits* (United Artists 1973)★★★★, *Strange Fruit* (1974)★★★, *Sweet Island Rhode Red* (United Artists 1974)★★, *Delilah's Power* (United Artists 1977)★★, *Airwaves* (1978)★★.

Solo: Ike Turner *Blues Roots* (United Artists 1972)★★, *Bad Dreams* (United Artists 1973)★★, *Funky Mule* (DJM 1975)★★, *I'm Tore Up* (Red Lightnin' 1978)★★, *All The Blues All The Time*

(Ember 1980)★★. His early work with the Kings Of Rhythm and as a talent scout is represented on *Hey Hey* (1984)★★★, *Rockin' Blues* (1986)★★★, *Ike Turner And His Kings Of Rhythm Volumes 1 & 2* (1988)★★★, *Talent Scout Blues* (Ace 1988)★★★, *Rhythm Rockin' Blues* (Ace 1995)★★★, *Without Love I Have Nothing* (Juke Blues 1996)★★, *My Blues Country* (Mystic 1997)★★.
● COMPILATIONS: *Ike And Tina Turner's Greatest Hits* (Sue 1965)★★★, *Ike And Tina Turner's Greatest Hits* (Warners 1969)★★★★, *Tough Enough* (Liberty 1984)★★★, *The Ike And Tina Turner Sessions* (1987)★★★, *The Best Of Ike And Tina Turner* (1987)★★★★, *Fingerpoppin' -The Warner Brothers Years* (1988)★★★, *Proud Mary: The Best Of Ike And Tina Turner* (EMI 1991)★★★★, *Live!!!* (1993)★★★.
● FURTHER READING: *I Tina*, Tina Turner with Kurt Loder.

TURNER, OTHER

b. 2 June 1907, Jackson, Mississippi, USA. A sharecropper most of his life, from 1970 Turner managed to buy some land of his own. A player of the fife, and of the bass and snare drums that accompany the fife, Turner kept up the practice of singing while working in the fields, which dates from slavery, and was uncommon by the time he was recorded. His guitar-accompanied blues singing was derived from his field hollers, and was both overwhelmingly intense and remarkably uninfluenced by commercial recordings. Turner's daughter Bernice continued the tradition as a player of the drum.
● ALBUMS: *Traveling Through The Jungle* (1974)★★★, *Afro-American Music From Tate And Panola Counties, Mississippi* (1978)★★★.

TURNER, TITUS

A US, Georgia-born singer and songwriter, he made his first records for OKeh in 1951, but his first big success came in 1955 when Little Willie John had a Top 10 R&B hit with the Turner composition 'All Around The World'. The song was revived as 'Grits Ain't Groceries' by Little Milton in 1969. Turner made other singles for Wing and Atlantic before he had his first hits in 1959 with a pair of 'answer' songs to current bestsellers by Lloyd Price, a singer with a similar style to Turner's. 'The Return Of Stag-O-Lee' (King) was a follow-up to 'Staggerlee' while Turner's 'We Told You Not To Marry' (Glover), was a riposte to 'I'm Gonna Get Married'. In 1961, Turner had a minor pop hit with a revival of 'Sound Off', produced by Al Gallico on Jamie, but this was overshadowed by Ray Charles' success with 'Sticks And Stones', the powerful gospel blues that is Turner's best-known composition. During the 60s, Turner discovered blues singer Tommy Tucker and worked with producer Herb Abramson. He continued to record a range of blues, soul, novelty and disco material for such companies as Josie, Atco, Philips and Mala.
● ALBUMS: *Sound Off* (1961)★★★.

VALENTINE, CAL

b. 28 May 1937, Dallas, Texas, USA, d. 1 January 1997. In a musical career spanning four decades, Valentine went through a number of incarnations before his most recent apotheosis as a Texas bluesman. While at school he befriended Al Braggs, who later added 'TNT' to his name and had a successful singing career during the 60s. Together, they formed the Five Notes, who in 1955 recorded 'Park Your Love' for Chess. Later, as the Five Masks, they recorded 'Polly Molly' for the Jan label, and as the Five Stars, 'Juanita', for B.B. King's short-lived Blues Boy Kingdom. Influenced by the Five Royales' Lowman Pauling and local bluesmen Cal Green and Frankie Lee Sims, Valentine took up the guitar in 1958. After working in a showband with Braggs, Valentine joined his younger brother Robert to form the Valentines, who recorded three singles for King, including 'Hey

Ruby' and 'I Have Two Loves'. With the Texas Rockers, he recorded 'Boogie Twist' for Lyons, before moving to Oakland to work in the house band of the Showcase Club. In 1962 he spent three months in Jimmy McCracklin's touring band, after which he formed the Right Kind with Ron Lewis, Bobby Reed and Frank Samuels. The band made a number of singles for Galaxy and backed visiting artists in the Oakland area. For much of the 70s and 80s, Valentine worked outside the music business in Dallas before returning to Oakland and forming another band. Although he performed an entertaining selection of blues and R&B perennials in his latter days, a weak voice and an unoriginal guitar style cannot raise Valentine beyond the limitations of his journeyman background.
● ALBUMS: *The Texas Rocker* (Black Magic 1994)★★.

VAN WALLS, HARRY

b. Harold Eugene Vann Walls, 24 August 1918, Millersboro, Kentucky, USA. Van Walls was raised in Charleston, West Virginia, by his music teacher mother, and learned to play piano at a very early age, accompanying the local church choir. His attention switched to blues and jazz in his teens with Jay McShann becoming a particularly potent influence. Soon he began playing dates locally, both with bands and as a solo pianist and vocalist. In 1949 Van Walls and his band travelled to New York to back tenor saxophonist Frank 'Floorshow' Culley at his debut session for the fledgling Atlantic label, and there he remained to provide the distinctive piano part to the famed Atlantic R&B Sound on the records of Granville 'Stick' McGhee, Ruth Brown, Joseph 'Joe' Morris, the Drifters, the Clovers and Big Joe Turner. In 1954 Van Walls eased up on the session work to join a band, the Nite Riders, who had a solid career recording for Grand, Apollo (for whom they recorded the classic 'Women And Cadillacs'), Teen/Sound and a host of other licensees. In 1963 Van Walls left the group to settle in Canada, but was rediscovered by *Whiskey, Women And Song* magazine in 1987 and was persuaded to record again.
● ALBUMS: *They Call Me Piano Man* (1989)★★★.

VAUGHAN, JIMMIE

b. 20 March 1951, Dallas, Texas, USA. Vaughan began playing rock music as an adolescent and worked with several local bands, moving nearer to the blues with each one, finally establishing a formidable reputation as a guitar player. In 1968 he saw Muddy Waters, and from then on concentrated almost exclusively on blues. He moved to Austin, Texas, in 1970 and formed the Fabulous Thunderbirds in 1975. The band were often cited as one of the prime movers in the blues revival in 80s America, with Vaughan's stylish, pared-down and economical guitar a major factor in their success. He recorded on many sessions and left the Thunderbirds in 1990 to work with his brother Stevie Ray Vaughan, shortly before the latter's death.
● ALBUMS: with Stevie Ray Vaughan as the Vaughan Brothers *Family Style* (Epic 1990)★★★★, *Strange Pleasure* (Epic 1994)★★★.

VAUGHAN, MAURICE JOHN

b. 10 May 1952, Chicago, Illinois, USA. A self-taught blues musician, Vaughan began playing at the age of 12. Although he was primarily known as a guitarist and saxophonist, he also played piano and bass guitar. His influences include Howlin' Wolf, Elmore James and particularly Albert King. After appearing on several sessions (including Phil Guy's), he released his debut album on his own Reecy label in 1984. It was later picked up by Alligator; he also recorded for that label's *New Bluesblood* anthology in 1987, as well as for the French label Blue Phoenix. In 1988 *Guitar Player* magazine included him in its listing of the greatest working blues musicians.
● ALBUMS: *Generic Blues* (Reecy 1984)★★★, *In The Shadow Of The City* (Alligator 1993)★★★.

VAUGHAN, STEVIE RAY

b. 3 October 1954, Dallas, Texas, USA, d. 27 August 1990, East Troy, Wisconsin, USA. This blues guitarist was influenced by his older brother Jimmie (of the Fabulous Thunderbirds), whose record collection included such key Vaughan motivators as Albert King, Otis Rush and Lonnie Mack. He honed his style on his brother's hand-me-down guitars in various high school bands, before moving to Austin in 1972. He joined the Nightcrawlers, then Paul Ray And

The Cobras, with whom he recorded 'Texas Clover' in 1974. In 1977 he formed Triple Threat Revue with vocalist Lou Ann Barton. She later fronted Vaughan's most successful project, named Double Trouble after an Otis Rush standard, for a short period after its inception in 1979. The new band also featured drummer Chris Layton and ex-Johnny Winter bassist Tommy Shannon. Producer Jerry Wexler, an early fan, added them to the bill of the 1982 Montreux Jazz Festival, where Vaughan was spotted and hired by David Bowie for his forthcoming *Let's Dance* (1983). Vaughan turned down Bowie's subsequent world tour, however, to rejoin his own band and record *Texas Flood* with veteran producer John Hammond. *Couldn't Stand The Weather* showed the influence of Jimi Hendrix, and earned the band its first platinum disc; in February 1985, they picked up a Grammy for their contribution to the *Blues Explosion* anthology. *Soul To Soul* saw the addition of keyboards player Reese Wynans; Vaughan, by this point a much sought-after guitarist, could also be heard on records by James Brown, Johnny Copeland, and his mentor, Lonnie Mack. The period of extensive substance abuse that produced the lacklustre *Live Alive* led to Vaughan's admittance to a Georgia detoxification centre. His recovery was apparent on *In Step*, which won a second Grammy. In 1990 the Vaughan brothers worked together with Bob Dylan on their own *Family Style*, and as guests on Eric Clapton's American tour. Vaughan died in 1990, at East Troy, Wisconsin, USA, when, anxious to return to Chicago after Clapton's Milwaukee show, he switched helicopter seats and boarded a vehicle that crashed, in dense fog, into a ski hill. Vaughan was a magnificent ambassador for the blues, whose posthumous reputation continues to increase. Plans to erect an 9-foot bronze statue to the guitarist in his home-town of Austin went ahead in October 1992.

● ALBUMS: *Texas Flood* (Epic 1983)★★★★, *Couldn't Stand The Weather* (Epic 1984)★★★★, *Soul To Soul* (Epic 1985)★★★★, *Live Alive* (Epic 1986)★★★, *In Step* (Epic 1989)★★★★, as the Vaughan Brothers *Family Style* (Epic 1990)★★★★, *The Sky Is Crying* (Epic 1991)★★★★, with Double Trouble *In The Beginning* rec. 1980 (Epic 1992)★★★, *Live At*

Carnegie Hall (Epic 1997)★★★.

● VIDEOS: *Live At The El Mocambo* (Epic 1992), *Live From Austin Texas* (Epic Music Video 1995).

● FURTHER READING: *Stevie Ray Vaughan: Caught In The Crossfire*, Joe Nick Patoski and Bill Crawford.

VAUGHN, JIMMY

b. 20 March 1925, Chicago, Illinois, USA, d. 9 March 1991, Alton, Illinois, USA. Pianist Vaughn spent most of his life as a sideman and had just made his first recordings as a leader before his sudden death. His family moved to Alton, Illinois, in 1934 and he took up the piano while at school. His interest in blues and boogie music came from a local pianist, Barrelhouse Buck MacFarland, who recorded for Paramount and Decca in the late 20s/early 30s. After three years in the army during World War II, he returned to Alton and played locally for some 10 years before joining Albert King's band as pianist and arranger. In the early 60s, he held the same position in Little Milton's band before moving to California. Over the next 15 years, he worked with T-Bone Walker, Ike And Tina Turner and Phillip Walker (also recording with the latter). In the mid-80s, he returned to Alton. His four titles on *Rockin' Eighty-Eights* include two instrumentals, 'Hey! Come 'Ere' and 'Ida's Song', along with 'Ripple Wine Dream', his adaptation of Big Bill Broonzy's 'Just A Dream'. Vaughn died of a stroke just before the album was issued in 1991.

● ALBUMS: with Johnnie Johnson, Clayton Love *Rockin' Eighty-Eights* (Modern Blues Recordings 1991)★★★.

VERNON, MIKE

b. 20 November 1944, Harrow, Middlesex, England. Vernon's early interest in blues, R&B and jazz inspired *R&B Monthly*, an influential publication he founded with fellow-enthusiast Neil Slaven in 1964. Having secured a position at Decca Records as a production assistant, Vernon worked with such disparate artists as Kenneth McKellar, Benny Hill and David Bowie, but he is renowned for his relationship with the company's blues acts. He oversaw sessions by John Mayall, Savoy Brown and the Artwoods and, in partnership with Slaven, established several independent labels including Purdah, Outasite and the original Blue Horizon. The latter was established as a fully fledged concern in 1967 when Vernon secured a distribution agreement with CBS Records on the strength of their early signing, Fleetwood Mac. This exceptional group was the producer's major attraction and he drew just commercial desserts when their 1968 single 'Albatross' sold in excess of one million copies. Further success with Chicken Shack and Duster Bennett accompanied a series of judicious reissues from B.B. King, Elmore James and Otis Rush which together consolidated Blue Horizon's role as a premier blues outlet. The loss of Fleetwood Mac in 1969 prompted Vernon's departure from Decca. Free to concentrate fully on his label, he began planning to expand its repertoire and, having switched distribution to Polydor in 1971, enjoyed hits with Dutch progressive rock band Focus. Vernon also nurtured British talent, including Mighty Baby and Jellybread, as well as recording in his own right, but latterly dissolved the company to pursue a career as an independent producer. 'Natural High' became a million-selling single for protégés Bloodstone; he later enjoyed fruitful partnerships with Freddy King and Jimmy Witherspoon. Vernon drew plaudits for his work with Pete Wingfield and the Olympic Runners while his studio at Chipping Norton in rural Oxfordshire was another successful venture. A series of demos recorded there by Level 42 helped launch this highly popular group. Mike retained his affection for blues with recordings for Dana Gillespie, and he relaunched the Blue Horizon name during the late 80s with releases by Charlie Musselwhite and Blues And Trouble. This respected entrepreneur has since continued to forge his independent path by forming a new label, Indigo, on which one of the first releases was Jimmy Witherspoon's *The Blues, The Whole Blues And Nothin' But The Blues*.

● ALBUMS: *Bring It Back Home* (Blue Horizon 1971)★★★, *Moment Of Madness* (1973)★★★.
● COMPILATIONS: *The Blue Horizon Story* 3-CD set (Sony 1997)★★★★.

VINCENT, JOHNNY
b. John Vincent Imbragulio, 3 October 1925, Hattiesburg, Mississippi, USA. Johnny Vincent

owned a successful record company operating in Jackson, Mississippi, from the 40s to the 60s. His first label was Champion, which issued an obscure disc by Arthur Crudup. Better known was the Ace label, responsible for a large number of excellent blues, R&B and rock 'n' roll by artists such as Frankie Lee Sims, Sammy Myers, Earl King and Huey 'Piano' Smith. Vincent resurrected the label in later years, but in 1997 he concluded the sale of the masters to Castle Communications for reissue under their Sequel Records label.

VINCENT, MONROE
b. 9 December 1919, Woodville, Mississippi, USA, d. April 1982, Oakland, California, USA. Also known throughout his career as Vince Monroe, Polka Dot Slim and Mr. Calhoun, Vincent was 40 years old and living in Baton Rouge, Louisiana, before he made his first records, although he had been playing harmonica and singing blues since his youth in Mississippi. Having developed a style that mixed elements of Sonny Boy 'Rice Miller' Williamson and Louisiana R&B, he seems to have been something of an all-purpose performer at J.D. 'Jay' Miller's Crowley studio in the late 50s, recording in slightly different styles and using two different names, with the resulting records appearing on two different labels. He was resident in New Orleans for many years, playing in local bars and clubs, and making more records, under yet another pseudonym, in the early 60s. Later in his life, he moved to the west coast.
● COMPILATIONS: *Gonna Head For Home* (1976)★★★.

VINSON, EDDIE 'CLEANHEAD'
b. 18 December 1917, Houston, Texas, USA, d. 2 July 1988, Los Angeles, California, USA. Taking up the alto saxophone as a child, his proficiency at the instrument attracted local bandleaders even while young Vinson was still at school, and he began touring with Chester Boone's territory band during school holidays. Upon his graduation in 1935, Vinson joined the band full-time, remaining when the outfit was taken over by Milton Larkins the following year. During his five-year tenure with the legendary Larkins band he met T-Bone Walker, Arnett Cobb, and

Illinois Jacquet, who all played with Larkins in the late 30s. More importantly the band's touring schedule brought Vinson into contact with Big Bill Broonzy, who taught him how to shout the blues, and Jay 'Hootie' McShann's Orchestra whose innovative young alto player, Charlie Parker, was 'kidnapped' by Vinson for several days in 1941 in order to study his technique. After being discovered by Cootie Williams in late 1941, Vinson joined the Duke Ellington trumpeter's new orchestra in New York City and made his recording debut for the OKeh label in April 1942, singing a solid blues vocal on 'When My Baby Left Me'. With Williams' orchestra, Vinson also recorded for Hit Records (1944), Capitol Records (1945) and appeared in a short film, *Film-vodvil no 2* (1943), before leaving to form his own big band in late 1945 and recording for Mercury Records. At Mercury he recorded small-group bop and blasting band instrumentals, but his main output was the fine body of suggestive jump-blues sung in his unique wheezy Texas style. Hits such as 'Juice Head Baby', 'Kidney Stew Blues' and 'Old Maid Boogie' were the exceptions, however, as most of Vinson's no-holds-barred songs, including 'Some Women Do', 'Oil Man Blues' and 'Ever-Ready Blues', were simply too raunchy for airplay. After the 1948 union ban, Vinson began recording for King Records in a largely unchanged style ('I'm Gonna Wind Your Clock', 'I'm Weak But Willing', 'Somebody Done Stole My Cherry Red'), often with all-star jazz units. However, his records were not promoted as well as King's biggest R&B stars, such as Wynonie Harris and Roy Brown, and he left to return to Mercury in the early 50s, rejoining Cootie Williams' small band briefly in the mid-50s. In 1957 he toured with Count Basie's Orchestra and made some recordings with a small Basie unit for King's jazz subsidiary, Bethlehem Records, after which he retired to Houston. In 1961 he was rediscovered by Cannonball Adderley, and a fine album resulted on Riverside Records with the Adderley brothers' small band. From then until his death in 1988, Vinson found full-time employment at worldwide jazz and blues festivals and dozens of credible albums on jazz and blues labels such as Black & Blue, Bluesway, Pablo, Muse and JSP.

● ALBUMS: *Cleanhead's Back In Town* (Bethlehem 1957)★★★, *Back Door Blues* (Riverside 1961)★★★★, *Cherry Red* (Cherry Red 1967)★★★, *Wee Baby Blues* (1969)★★★, *Kidney Stew* (1969)★★★, *Live!* (1969)★★★, *The Original Cleanhead* (1969)★★★, *You Can't Make Love Alone* (1971)★★★, *Jammin' The Blues* (1974)★★★, *Eddie 'Cleanhead' Vinson In Holland* (1976)★★★, *Cherry Red Blues* (Bellaphon 1976)★★★, *Live In Blue Note, Göttingen* (1976)★★★, *Great Rhythm & Blues Volume 2* (1977)★★★, *The Clean Machine* (Muse 1978)★★★, *Hold It Right There!* (1978)★★★, *Live At Sandy's* (1978)★★★, *Fun In London* (JSP 1980)★★, *I Want A Little Girl* (Pablo 1982)★★, with Count Basie, 'Big' Joe Turner *Kansas City Shout* (1982)★★★, *Eddie 'Cleanhead' Vinson And A Roomful Of Blues* (1982)★★★★, *Mr Cleanhead's Back In Town* (Mole 1982)★★★, *Kidney Stew* (1984)★★, *Mr Cleanhead Steps Out* (Saxophonograph 1985)★★★, *Cleanhead And A Roomful Of Blues* (Muse 1986)★★★, *Sings The Blues* (Muse 1987)★★, with Etta James *Blues In The Night: The Early Show* (1988)★★★, with Cannonball Adderley *Cleanhead & Cannonball* (Landmark 1988)★★★, *The Real 'Mr Cleanhead'* (Official 1989)★★, *Meat's Too High* (JSP 1989)★★★, *Midnight Creeper* (Blue Moon 1989)★★★, with James *Blues In The Night: The Late Show* (1989)★★★, *Meat's Too High* (JSP 1994)★★.

VINSON, MOSE

b. 7 August 1917, Holly Springs, Mississippi, USA. Vinson's piano playing was a time capsule of blues and boogie techniques learned in the 30s and 40s. As a five-year-old, he sat on his mother's lap to play piano in church. At 15, influenced by meeting Sunnyland Slim, he decided to move to Memphis, where he worked barrelhouses and bars, broadening his repertoire to play for white audiences, where the real money was. In the late 40s he played at the Parlor Club, accompanying the young B.B. King. Working as a plumber and janitor by day, in 1953 Vinson took a job as caretaker at Sam Phillips' Sun studio. Between sessions, he would sit at the piano and run through various pieces. Phillips decided to record him and cut two versions of '44 Blues', one retitled 'Worry You Off My Mind', and 'My Love Has Gone', also known as 'Come See Me'. Musicians on the two sessions included Walter Horton, Joe Hill Louis and Joe Willie Wilkins. The following year, Vinson played on James Cotton's *Cotton Crop Blues*. When his style of music fell out of fashion, he continued to play in church and at home until he was taken up by the Center for Southern Folklore. Under their auspices, he played for schoolchildren and at various cultural functions. His contributions to *Memphis Piano Today* were recorded at his home in 1990.

● ALBUMS: with Booker T. Laury *Memphis Piano Today* (Wolf 1991)★★★, with Joe Hill Louis *The Be-Bop Boy* (Bear Family 1992)★★★.
● COMPILATIONS: *Sun Records - The Blues Years* (Charly 1985)★★★.

VINSON, WALTER

b. 2 February 1901, Bolton, Mississippi, USA, d. 22 April 1975, Chicago, Illinois, USA. An accomplished blues guitarist in his teens, Vinson became a close associate of the Chatman family, and especially of fiddler Lonnie Chatman. Vinson and Chatman issued most of their records under the name the Mississippi Sheiks. Vinson had a high regard for his partner's playing, but unfortunately his view that the guitar was merely a back-up instrument led him to oversimplify his playing. As well as recording with Chatman, Vinson made records under his own name up to 1940. His career was interrupted from 1936-40 from the effects of a stroke. In the early 70s, he was briefly a member of a re-formed Mississippi Sheiks that included Sam Chatman.

● ALBUMS: *The New Mississippi Sheiks* (1972)★★★, *Rats Been On My Cheese* (Agram 1988)★★★.

VON BATTLE, JOE

Von Battle was a record store owner in the Detroit ghetto, recording local black talent in 1948 and issuing material intermittently on a confusing variety of labels. Artists included himself (backed by two out-of-tune harmonicas, piano and bass), Iverson 'Louisiana Red' Minter, L.C. Green and One String Sam. However, Von Battle's most important recordings were early blues tracks by John Lee Hooker, gospel by Rev. C.L. Franklin and the first recordings of Franklin's 14-year-old daughter, Aretha Franklin. Like much other material, the Franklin recordings were leased to Chess to bring in some cash, as Von Battle operated on a shoestring, which meant poor distribution and often poor sound quality for his own releases which, although sometimes superb, are usually very rare. Modern, King and Gotham also benefited from Von Battle material. By the 70s he had retired from recording, but was still operating a shop.

WALKER, CHARLES

b. 26 July 1922, Macon, Georgia, USA, d. 24 June 1975, New York City, New York, USA. Walker's career as a blues singer and guitarist began in Newark, New Jersey, in 1955, and he recorded for a number of small labels in the late 50s and early 60s. Changing audience tastes and marriage prompted him to retire from music in 1962, but after his wife's death in 1968 he began to perform and record again, and was just beginning to be promoted to white audiences at the time of his death.

● ALBUMS: *Blues From The Apple* (1974)★★★, *New York Rhythm 'N' Blues* (1974)★★★, *Blow By Blow* (1980)★★★.

WALKER, EDDIE

b. 31 October 1948, England. This singer, guitarist and songwriter specialized in ragtime and country blues. His work encompasses the styles of artists such as 'Big' Bill Broonzy, Mississippi John Hurt and Rev. Gary Davis. Between 1977 and 1982 Walker released four albums, the second of which was a compilation of residency appearances at the Cutty Wren Folk Club in Redcar, Cleveland. This included Walker's song

'Candy'. Another Walker original, 'Stolen My Heart Away', was joint winner of the Tyne Tees television programme *Songwriter* in 1982. Walker has now teamed up with the highly respected guitarist John James in the duo Carolina Shout. James was earlier featured playing guitar on Walker's 1985 release *Picking My Way*. The album included a tribute to songwriter Steve Goodman. Walker has played the Hong Kong Folk Music Festival, in addition to regular dates in Europe, and continues to play the folk circuit, though more often these days as part of Carolina Shout.

● ALBUMS: *Everyday Man* (1977)★★, *Folk At The Wren* (1978)★★★, *Castle Cafe* (1981)★★★, *Red Shoes On My Feet* (Ragged 1983)★★★, *Picking My Way* (Ragged 1985)★★★. As Carolina Shout *Carolina Shout* (1989)★★★.

WALKER, JIMMY

b. 8 March 1905, Memphis, Tennessee, USA. Raised in Chicago, Walker learned piano in his teens, and later played for dances and house rent parties. He abandoned blues in the mid-30s, as he felt it to be incompatible with playing in church. However, he resumed playing blues in the early 50s, working in the clubs as a name act, and as accompanist for Homesick James, Billy Boy Arnold, Elmore James and Little Walter. He made occasional recordings from the 60s onwards, usually in duet with Erwin Helfer, his own 'rough and ready piano' being somewhat affected by his age and inherent limitations.

● ALBUMS: *Rough And Ready Piano* (1964)★★, *Jimmy Walker & Erwin Helfer* (1974)★★, *Original South Side Blues Piano* (Wolf 1988)★★★, *Small Town Baby* (1993)★★.

WALKER, JOE LOUIS

b. 26 December 1949, San Francisco, California, USA. Although born in the city and raised during the era of 'flower power', Joe Louis had a strong and realized sense of the blues tradition. He was also a guitarist of considerable accomplishment. His albums are superior examples of modern blues, generally consisting of songs that are fluent and witty and sacrifice none of their 'bluesiness' in their awareness of contemporary trends. Formal musical training allows him to write and arrange his own material, including the horn charts. He usually produces lyrics alone or in various combinations made up from the impressive team of Amy and (Dennis) Walker and Henry Oden. On one of his finest songs, 'I'll Get To Heaven On My Own', he performs solo, accompanying himself with some delta-styled slide guitar. Yet even this number, which has the pure feel and power of the early blues, does not take refuge in recycling traditional verses. In an interview with M.K. Aldin he expressed his ideas about other people's material: 'I don't do cover songs (on recordings). I do some of them live. I have a real theory about 'em. I can't do 'em any better than they've been done but . . . I change them'. Another statement: 'And my style is not all playing 90 miles-an-hour,' indicates another reason why, in the heavily rock-influenced modern scene, Joe Louis Walker is a man to watch. *Blues Of The Month Club* or *Great Guitars* would make an excellent starting point, although the latter features other major artists, who tend to overcrowd the star of the show.

● ALBUMS: *Cold Is The Night* (Ace 1987)★★, *The Gift* (Ace 1988)★★★, *Blue Soul* (Demon 1989)★★★, *Live At Slim's* (Demon 1991)★★, *Live At Slims, Volume Two* (Demon 1992)★★, *Blues Survivor* (Verve 1993)★★★, *JLW* (Verve 1994)★★★, *Blues Of The Month Club* (Verve 1995)★★★★, *Great Guitars* (Verve 1997)★★★.

WALKER, JOHNNY 'BIG MOOSE'

b. 27 June 1929, Greenville, Mississippi, USA. Walker learned to play several instruments in his teens but is known primarily as a pianist. He began touring with blues bands from 1947, playing piano and organ, and worked with many Mississippi artists in the 40s and early 50s, including Ike Turner, Sonny Boy 'Rice Miller' Williamson, Lowell Fulson and Choker Campbell. Walker's most enduring associations were with Elmore James and Earl Hooker, to whose recordings he made telling contributions on piano, although his organ work was less successful. He served in the US Army between 1952 and 1955 and recorded in his own right for Ike Turner in 1955, though the results were not released until the late 60s. Tracks that Walker made the same year for the Ultra label were released under the name 'Moose John'. In the late 50s he settled in Chicago, and became an in-demand session player (most notably recording with Elmore James as 'Bushy Head'), and is widely regarded as one of the best blues pianists still active.

● ALBUMS: *To Know A Man* (1969)★★★, *Rambling Woman* (1970)★★★, *Some Old Folks Boogie* (1978)★★★, *Going Home Tomorrow* (1980)★★★, *Blue Love* (Evidence 1996)★★★.
● COMPILATIONS: *Swear To Tell The Truth* (JSP 1991)★★★, *The Rising Sun Collection* (Just A Memory 1995)★★★★.

WALKER, PHILLIP

b. 11 February, 1937, Welsh, Louisiana, USA. Originating from the Port Arthur area of Louisiana, Walker worked in many bands building a reputation as a performer of note. Moving to Los Angeles, he recorded for the small Elko label before finally having an album made up from tracks recorded for producer Bruce Bromberg during 1969-72. These were released on Hugh Hefner's Playboy label. Later albums confirmed his initial promise and Walker has become one of the most effective of the 'modern' blues performers. His varied background renders him capable of playing in many styles, from the Texas blues of Lightnin' Hopkins, through the Louisiana 'swamp' sound, up to the most sophisticated offering of writers like Dennis Walker. He is married to blues singer Ina Beatrice 'Be Bop' Walker.

● ALBUMS: *Blues* (Playboy 1973)★★★, *Someday You'll Have These Blues* (Alligator 1977)★★★, *Tough As I Want To Be* (Black & Blue 1984)★★★, *The Bottom Of The Top* (Demon 1990)★★★, with Otis Grand *Blues From Texas* (1992)★★★, *Working Girl Blues* (Black Top 1995)★★★.
● COMPILATIONS: *All Night Long They Play The Blues* (1979)★★★, *Mr. Fullbright's Blues, Volume 1* (1990)★★★.

WALKER, T-BONE

b. Aaron Thibeaux Walker, 28 May 1910, Linden, Texas, USA, d. 16 March 1975, Los Angeles, California, USA. Walker, whose T-Bone acronym is a corruption of his middle name, was raised in Dallas where his parents operated an 'open house' to all the touring blues musicians. During his childhood, Walker was brought into contact with artists such as Blind Lemon Jefferson, and in fact he became Jefferson's 'eyes' around the streets of Dallas whenever the blind musician was in town. Inspired by the more sophisticated blues and singing style of pianist Leroy Carr, Walker took up the guitar, and began performing himself. During the mid-20s he toured Texas as a musician/comedian/dancer with Dr. Breeding's Big B Tonic Show, before joining a travelling revue led by singer Ida Cox. By 1929 he had made a solitary country blues record for Columbia Records as 'Oak Cliff T-Bone'. His recording career may very well have started and finished there, had he not travelled to Oklahoma City and met Chuck Richardson, the man who was teaching young Charlie Christian (a boyhood friend of Walker's) to play single string solos on the new electrified instrument - 'T-Bone' began his instruction alongside Christian that same day. Developing his act as a singer and dancer in the style of Cab Calloway (with whose band he toured for a week in 1930 as first prize in a talent contest), Walker was introduced to the slick world of jazz and big band swing. He moved to Los Angeles in 1934 and obtained a job with 'Big' Jim Wynn's band in Little Harlem. Walker's popularity steadily grew throughout the late 30s and in 1940 he took a job with Les Hite's Orchestra. His amplified guitar, still a novelty, brought a distinctive touch to the ensemble's overall sound while an undoubted showmanship increased the attention lavished upon the artist. Upon arriving in New York with Hite, Varsity Records recorded the orchestra, and Walker's feature, 'T-Bone Blues', became a great success - although Frank Pasley and not 'T-Bone' played the electric guitar accompaniment. Leaving Hite, upon his return to California, Walker co-led a band with Big Jim Wynn at the top Los Angeles nightspots, honing his provocative act which included playing the guitar behind his head while doing the splits - a sense of showmanship that would later influence Chuck Berry and Jimi Hendrix.

In 1942-44 Walker recorded for Capitol Records with Freddie Slack's band. Slack repaid the compliment by supporting Walker on the first release under the guitarist's name. The two tracks, 'Mean Old World' and 'I Got A Break Baby', rapidly became standards for the next generation of electric blues guitarists. During 1945-46 Walker was in Chicago, starring at the

Rhumboogie Club with Milt Larkins' or Marl Young's Orchestras (Young's band accompanied Walker on the recordings he made in Chicago for the club's own Rhumboogie label and for disc jockey Al Benson's Swingmaster Records). Upon his return to the west coast, Walker was in great demand, both in concert and with his new records released on the Black & White label and its jazz subsidiary Comet (1946-47 - later purchased and released by Capitol Records). These included classics such as 'I'm Gonna Find My Baby', 'T-Bone Shuffle' and 'Call It Stormy Monday'. The latter melancholic ballad, also known as 'Stormy Monday' and 'Stormy Monday Blues', has since been the subject of numerous interpretations by artists as disparate as Chris Farlowe, Bobby Bland and the Allman Brothers. In the late 40s the second musician's union ban and a heavy touring schedule with his old partner Big Jim Wynn prevented Walker from recording, but in 1950 he secured a four-year contract with Imperial Records where he demonstrated a harder, funkier style of blues, with sessions utilizing T.J. Fowler's band in Detroit and Dave Bartholomew's band in New Orleans, as well as his own working unit from Los Angeles. These experiments continued after moving to Atlantic Records from 1955-59, where he teamed up with blues harmonica player Junior Wells in Chicago and modern jazz guitarist Barney Kessel in Los Angeles. Although nominally versed in blues, Walker often sought the accompaniment of jazz musicians who allowed free rein for the guitarist's fluid style. He continued to record prolifically throughout the early 50s, but gradually eased such strictures in favour of regular concert appearances. He visited Europe on several occasions and performed successfully at many large-scale jazz and blues festivals. Later albums, including *The Truth* and *Funky Town*, showcased a virtually undiminished talent, still capable of incisive playing. However, by the early 70s his powers were diminished through ill health, and at personal appearances he often played piano instead of his guitar. In 1974 he suffered a severe stroke from which he never made a recovery. T-Bone Walker died of bronchial pneumonia in 1975, his reputation as a giant of blues music assured.

● ALBUMS: *Classics In Jazz* (Capitol 1953)★★★, *T-Bone Walker* i (1956)★★★★, *Sings The Blues* (Imperial 1959)★★★, *T-Bone Blues* (Atlantic 1960)★★★★, *Singing The Blues* (Imperial 1960)★★★★, *I Get So Weary* (Imperial 1961)★★★★, *The Great Blues, Vocals And Guitar* (1963)★★★★, *T-Bone Walker* ii (Capitol 1964)★★★★, *I Want A Little Girl* (Delmark 1967)★★★, *Stormy Monday Blues* (Wet Soul 1967)★★★★, *The Truth* (Brunswick 1968)★★★, *Blue Rocks* (1968)★★★, *Funky Town* (Bluesway 1968)★★★, *Feeling The Blues* (1969)★★★, *Very Rare* (Reprise 1973)★★★, *Dirty Mistreater* (1973)★★★, *T-Bone Jumps Again* (Charly 1981)★★★★, *Good Feelin'* 1968 recording (Polydor 1982)★★★, *Plain Ole Blues* (Charly 1982)★★★, *Hot Leftovers* (Pathé Marconi 1985)★★★, *Low Down Blues* (Charly 1986)★★★★, with 'Big' Joe Turner *Bosses Of The Blues* (Bluebird 1989)★★★.

● COMPILATIONS: *The Blues Of T-Bone Walker* (1965)★★★★, *Stormy Monday Blues* (1968)★★★★, *Classics Of Modern Blues* (1975)★★★★, *T-Bone Walker Jumps Again* (1980)★★★, *Plain Ole Blues* (1982)★★★, *The Natural Blues* (Charly 1983)★★★, *Collection - T-Bone Walker* (Déjà Vu 1985)★★★, *I Don't Be Jivin'* (Bear Family 1987)★★★, *The Inventor Of The Electric Guitar Blues* (Blues Boy 1983)★★★★, *The Bluesway Sessions* (Charly 1988)★★★★, *The Talkin' Guitar* (Blues Encore 1990)★★★, *The Hustle Is On: Imperial Sessions, Volume 1* (Sequel 1990)★★★★, *The Complete 1940 - 1954 Recordings Of T-Bone Walker* (Mosaic 1990)★★★★, *The Complete Imperial Recordings, 1950-54* (EMI 1991)★★★★, *T-Bone Blues* rec. 1955-57 (Sequel 1994)★★★★, *The Complete Capitol Black And White Recordings* 3-CD set (Capitol 1995)★★★★.

● FURTHER READING: *Stormy Monday*, Helen Oakly Dance.

WALKER, WILLIE

b. 1896, South Carolina, USA, d. 4 March 1933, Greenville, South Carolina, USA. Blind from birth, Walker worked only as a musician, and was playing guitar in a string band with Rev. Gary Davis by 1911. Josh White said that 'Blind Blake was fast but Walker was like Art Tatum.' This is no exaggeration, as Walker's issued 1930 recordings, especially the two takes of 'South Carolina Rag', ably confirm. He was a strong singer, but it is his guitar that immediately

astonishes: lightning-fast but impeccably clear (and admirably accompanied by Sam Brooks). At least some of Walker's playing appears to be a transfer to the guitar of mandolin figurations. It has been speculated that on 'Dupree Blues' he flatpicks the bass strings and simultaneously fingerpicks the treble; certainly his abilities were held in awe by former associates even 40 years after his death from congenital syphilis.
● COMPILATIONS: *Ragtime Blues Guitar* (1982)★★★.

WALLACE, BEULAH 'SIPPIE'

b. Beulah Thomas, 1 November 1898, Houston, Texas, USA, d. 1 November 1986, Detroit, Michigan, USA. Blues singer Sippie Wallace was a sister to Hersal and George Thomas (both piano players of some renown), and an aunt of George's blues-singing daughter Hociel Thomas. Wallace left Houston to join George in Chicago in 1923 and recorded her first single, 'Up The Country Blues', in October of that year. It was a hit and led to a career that, intermittently, spanned four decades. Her initial period of success on record and in vaudeville came to a close when she moved to Detroit in 1929 to work in the church. Wallace did not work in music again until 1937 when she sang with Jimmy Noone's Orchestra. In 1946, she recorded again and later began working on the revived blues circuit playing colleges and clubs. In 1966 she toured Europe with the AFBF. In 1983 she saw her last album nominated for a Grammy award.
● ALBUMS: *Sippie Wallace* (Atlantic 1982)★★★, *Sings The Blues* (Storyville 1988)★★★, *Women Be Wise* rec. 1966 (Storyville 1993)★★★.
● COMPILATIONS: *The Piano Blues, Volume 4* (1977)★★★.

WALLACE, WESLEY

Wallace was a blues pianist who recorded a few accompaniments to St. Louis singers in 1929, and made one 78 rpm record under his own name, on which his fame rests. 'Fannie Lee' is an excellent instrumental, but 'No. 29' has a good claim to being one of the finest of all train/railroad tunes. Wallace plays an absolutely even, unaccented 6/4 bass, and has a dazzling right hand.
● COMPILATIONS: *The Piano Blues Vol. 1 Paramount* (1977).

WALTON, WADE

b. 10 October 1923, Lombardy, Mississippi, USA. Walton is best known as a musical barber, entertaining visitors to his shop in Clarksdale, Mississippi, but he started in music in his youth, and was touring with minstrel shows in his teens. He formed the Kings Of Rhythm with Clarksdale's most famous R&B artist, Ike Turner, but preferred to stay with his steady work when Turner moved on to a career as a professional musician. Paul Oliver recorded Walton in his shop in 1960, singing and playing or stropping his razor in rhythm, and he made an album two years later. Since then he has made a number of recordings, and appeared in short films, and often acts as unofficial host for blues fans visiting the town.
● ALBUMS: *The Blues Of Wade Walton* (1962)★★★.

WARD, ROBERT

b. 15 October 1938, Luthersville, Georgia, USA. Ward's rediscovery in 1990 is a rare instance of a 'legend' returning from more than a decade of obscurity with his talent undiminished. A self-taught guitarist, he formed his first band, the Brassettes, in Avon Park, Florida, in 1959 after two years' army service. Returning to Georgia, he pawned a Gibson Les Paul in order to afford the move to Dayton, Ohio, where he lived with an aunt. His next group, the Ohio Untouchables, was the quintessential R&B garage band, its celebrity owing, in large part, to Ward's use of a Magnatone amplifier with its distinctive vibrato effect. The group made a number of singles for the Detroit-based Lupine label, most famously 'Forgive Me Darling', an extended guitar showcase loosely based on Bo Diddley's 'I'm Sorry'. Producer Robert West used them to back the Falcons' 'I Found A Love', with Wilson Pickett as lead vocalist. When Pickett set out on a solo career, Ward went with him, while the other Untouchables eventually mutated into the Ohio Players. Further live and session work for the Temptations and the Undisputed Truth kept Ward out of the public eye. Following the deaths of his wife and mother in 1977, he abandoned music and returned to Dry Branch, Georgia. He was rediscovered by Black Top producer Hammond Scott after a two-year search. *Fear No Evil*, featuring re-recordings of 'Forgive Me

Darling' and 'Your Love Is Real', was a resounding critical success, bringing Ward a measure of international celebrity and established him as a popular artist at festivals in America and Europe. *Rhythm Of The People* is slightly less focused but did introduce his wife Roberta, who regularly appears singing gospel songs with him. *Black Bottom* was a mixture of regular blues with redolent 60s soul music, featuring Mark 'Kaz' Kazanoff (tenor and baritone saxophone), Ward Smith (tenor and baritone saxophone), Ernest Youngblood Jr. (tenor saxophone), Steve Howard (trumpet), Rick Trolsen (trombone) and Jimmy Weber (trumpet). This brass section perfectly complements Ward's frequently thin-sounding Fender Telecaster.

● ALBUMS: *Three Shades Of Blue* (Lupine 1984)★★★, *Fear No Evil* (Black Top 1990)★★★, *Blues Cocktail Party!* (Black Top 1991)★★, *Black Top Blues-A-Rama Vol. 7* (Black Top 1993)★★★, *Rhythm Of The People* (Black Top 1993)★★★, *Black Bottom* (Black Top 1995)★★★, *Hot Stuff* (Relic 1995)★★★.

● COMPILATIONS: *Twiggs Country Soul Man* (Black Top 1997)★★★.

WARREN, BABY BOY

b. Robert Henry Warren, 13 August 1919, Lake Providence, Louisiana, USA, d. 1 July 1977, Detroit, Michigan, USA. Baby Boy Warren made exactly 10 records, mostly for tiny storefront labels, but the quality of his lyrics and plaintive vocal sincerity made them all memorable. The youngest of eight children (hence the sobriquet), Robert was raised in Memphis by his mother, Beulah, after his father, Lee, died in March 1920. Learning guitar from older brothers Jack and Willie, Robert spent his weekends working the Arkansas joints with Howling Wolf and Sonny Boy Williamson (Rice Miller). Moving to Detroit in 1941, Warren made his first records with pianist Charley Mills for Staff; 'My Special Friend', 'Nervy Woman' and 'Don't Want No Skinny Woman' revealed affinities with John Lee (Sonny Boy) Williamson. 'Please Don't Think I'm Nosey' was later recorded by Eddie Kirkland. Rice Miller was a frequent visitor and recorded with Warren and Washboard Willie for Joe Von Battle; 'Hello Stranger', 'Sanafee' and the instrumental 'Chicken' are Warren's most famous tracks and hark back to the musicians'

country origins. The first two tracks were also recorded for Blue Lake, with Calvin Frazier on second guitar. Warren retired through ill health and disillusionment during the 60s. He was rediscovered in 1967, and spent the decade before his death appearing at blues festivals, and, with Boogie Woogie Red (Vernon Harrison), he toured Europe in 1972.

● COMPILATIONS: *Baby Boy Warren* (1991)★★★.

WASHBOARD DOC

b. Joseph Doctor, 8 September 1911, Charleston, South Carolina, USA, d. 16 September 1988, New York City, New York, USA. A street musician from his arrival in New York in 1935, Washboard Doc was on the fringes of black musical life thereafter, claiming to have recorded alongside Ralph Willis and Sonny Terry. He certainly provided backing for Alec Seward, and played, with varying degrees of appropriateness, on many Victoria Spivey albums. Full albums by his trio led to a European visit in 1980.

● ALBUMS: *Washboard Doc And His Hep 3* (1978)★★★, *Early Morning Blues* (L&R 1979)★★★.

WASHBOARD SLIM

b. Robert Young, 5 June 1900, Marshall, Texas, USA, d. 2 June 1990, Philadelphia, Pennsylvania, USA. Young was a trumpeter, trombonist, guitarist, drummer, singer and comedian on travelling circuses and medicine shows, settling in North Carolina in the 30s. A stroke temporarily limited his musical scope, and he concentrated on the washboard, which he adorned with frying pans and cowbells. He played with Blind Boy Fuller, Buddy Moss, Sonny Terry and Brownie McGhee, recording behind the last three in 1941. He settled in Philadelphia in the 40s, playing in the streets and occasionally at coffee-houses and festivals.

WASHBOARD WILLIE

b. William Paden Hensley, 24 July 1909, Phoenix City, Alabama, USA. Raised in Georgia, where he began drumming at the age of six, Washboard Willie moved to Detroit in 1945, and soon became a fixture on the city's blues scene, playing the bars with his Super Suds Of Rhythm, and making occasional records for independent record producer Joe Von Battle. These are of limited interest, as Von Battle could only fund minimal accompaniment (guitar, piano and bass guitar), rather than the horn section that Willie's jump-blues needed. His back-up work on 'Brother Will' Hairston's 'Alabama Bus', about the Montgomery bus boycott in the Civil Rights movement of the early 60s, is a demonstration of what the washboard and its associated kitchen implements can achieve. In 1973 he appeared in Europe, confirming in person that he was a lively and extrovert entertainer.

● ALBUMS: *Detroit Blues - The Early 1950s* (1966)★★★, *Whuppin' That Board* (1969)★★★, *American Blues Legends '73* (1973)★★★, *Motor Town Boogie* (JSP 1982)★★★.

WASHINGTON, ISIDORE 'TUTS'

b. 24 January 1907, New Orleans, Louisiana, USA, d. 5 August 1984, New Orleans, Louisiana, USA. Raised by his aunt, Rosetta Howard, and exposed to music from childhood, Washington was fluent in the old barrelhouse-blues styles, but as his aunt was determined he should not to be limited to them, he also played pop, jazz, boogie and ragtime. He claimed to have influenced all the New Orleans pianists, from Professor Longhair to Fats Domino and James Booker, and was certainly much respected by them. In the 30s he played in jazz bands, and in the 40s and 50s, he was closely associated with Smiley Lewis, later joining Oscar 'Papa' Celestin. Reluctant to record, he was only finally persuaded to do so shortly before his death (which occurred at a concert).

● ALBUMS: *New Orleans Piano Professor* (Rounder 1983)★★★.

WASHINGTON, WALTER 'WOLFMAN'

b. Edward Washington, 20 December 1943, New Orleans, Louisiana USA. Washington began his musical career singing gospel music in church and was a self-taught guitarist. He had a very long association with singer Johnny Adams, who gave him music and singing advice. Washington's music tended towards the silky-smooth, soulful side of the blues. In the 60s, he spent over two years touring with Lee Dorsey, and met up with B.B. King and Jimi Hendrix during this time; both of them were to influence him. After this he worked with Irma Thomas

and several other bands before forming his own group. He recorded a few singles and made his first album in 1981 and has had regular album releases since, signing with Rounder Records in 1985. In 1991, he recorded for PointBlank.

● ALBUMS: *Leader Of The Pack* (1981)★★★, *Wolfman* (Rounder 1987)★★★, *Wolf Tracks* (Rounder 1987)★★★, *Out Of The Dark* (Rounder 1988)★★★, *Rainin' My Life* (Maison De Soul 1988)★★★, *Good And Juicy* (Charly 1989)★★★, *Wolf At The Door* (Rounder 1991)★★★, *Sada* (PointBlank 1991)★★★.

WATERFORD, CHARLES 'CROWN PRINCE'

b. 21 October 1919, Jonesboro, Arkansas, USA. Waterford's parents, who were both musicians, taught him to sing. His first professional jobs were with Andy Kirk's 12 Clouds Of Joy and Leslie Sheffield's Rhythmaires. Waterford became known as 'the Crown Prince Of The Blues' during his brief stay with Jay McShann's Orchestra, during which time he recorded for Philo/Aladdin and Premier/Mercury. Usurped by Jimmy Witherspoon, Waterford went solo in 1946 to record in Chicago for Hy-Tone, and the following year recorded his most celebrated tracks in Los Angeles for Capitol Records with Pete Johnson's band. These included the salacious 'Move Your Hand Baby'. Waterford rejoined McShann at a 1949 recording session for Jack Lauderdale and made four superb tracks for King with young Harold Land And His All-Stars, and another four with the Joe Thomas Orchestra. A mid-50s session for Excello resulted in two tracks of prime blues shouting, but later records for Orbit and Stampede tried to appeal to the twist craze and sank into obscurity. By contrast, Waterford's earlier sides show him to be an original blues singer; most of his songs were self-penned and featured highly original and evocative lyrics. It is reported that Waterford is still alive and his time is now devoted to the church.

● COMPILATIONS: *Shoutin' The Blues* (Oldie Blues 1988)★★★.

WATKINS, JOHN 'MAD DOG'

b. 19 July 1953, Chicago, Illinois, USA. As a youngster, Watkins was exposed to his parents' blues record collection and later taught himself to play bass and drums. Around 1967-68 his mother finally bought him a guitar and by 1969 he was playing with Buddy Guy at Theresa's Lounge in Chicago. From there, he went on to play with Koko Taylor, Son Seals, Junior Wells and others. He toured with Willie Dixon for seven years and then joined James Cotton's band, recording with both artists. He made his own debut album in France in 1984 and also recorded one track for Alligator's *New Bluebloods* anthology in 1987. He spent two years working with his uncle, blues guitarist Jimmy Johnson, but formed his own band in 1987 to showcase his crisp guitar-playing and soulful blues singing.

● ALBUMS: *Here I Am* (1984)★★★.

WATSON, JOHNNY 'GUITAR'

b. 3 February 1935, Houston, Texas, USA, d. 17 May 1996, Yokohama, Japan. Before Watson made a name for himself in the 70s playing funk R&B, he had a long career stretching back to the early 50s. Watson's father played piano, which also became Watson's first instrument. On seeing Clarence 'Gatemouth' Brown perform, he convinced himself that he had to play guitar. He inherited a guitar from his grandfather, a sancti-fied preacher, on the condition that he did not play the blues on it - 'that was the first thing I played', Watson later said. In the early 50s his family moved to Los Angeles, where he started playing piano in the Chuck Higgins band and was billed as 'Young John Watson'. Switching to guitar, he was signed to Federal and recorded 'Space Guitar', an instrumental far ahead of its time in the use of reverberation and feedback. He also played 'Motorhead Baby' with an enthu-siasm that was to become his trademark. He recorded the same track for Federal with the Amos Milburn band in tow. Watson became in demand as a guitarist and in the late 50s toured and recorded with the Olympics, Don And Dewey and Little Richard. Johnny 'Guitar' Watson was from the same mould of flamboy-ance that motivated another of Little Richard's guitarists: Jimi Hendrix. Watson later stated: 'I used to play the guitar standing on my hands, I had a 150 foot cord and I could get on top of the auditorium - those things Jimi Hendrix was doing, I *started* that shit!'. Moving to the Modern label in 1955, he had immediate success with a

bluesy ballad, 'Those Lonely, Lonely Nights' (US R&B Top 10), but failed to follow up on the label. In 1957 the novelty tune 'Gangster Of Love' (later adopted by Steve Miller) gave him a minor hit on the west coast. A partnership with Larry Williams was particularly successful and in 1965 they toured England and recorded an album for Decca. Watson did not return to the charts until 1962, when on the King label he hit with 'Cuttin' In' (US R&B number 6), which was recorded with string accompaniment. The following year he recorded *I Cried For You*, a 'cocktail-lounge' album with hip renditions of 'Polkadots And Moonbeams' and 'Witchcraft'. The Beatles inva-sion signified hard times for the inventors of rock 'n' roll. Watson recorded two soulful funk albums for the Fantasy label (*Listen* and *I Don't Want To Be Alone, Stranger*) with keyboardist Andre Lewis (who later toured with Frank Zappa). As if to repay his enthusiasm for Watson's guitar playing, which Zappa had often admitted to admiring, Watson was recruited for Zappa's *One Size Fits All* in 1975. In 1976 Watson released *Ain't That A Bitch* on DJM Records, a brilliant marriage of 50s rockin' R&B, Hollywood schmaltz and futuristic funk. Watson produced, played bass, keyboards and drums on the album, which went gold; a further six albums appeared on DJM to the same formula. In 1981 he left the label for A&M Records, but the production diluted Watson's unique sound and the record was a failure. One positive side effect was a characteristic solo on Herb Alpert's *Beyond*. Watson retired to lick his wounds, emerging with *Strike On Computers* at the end of the 80s and an appearance at London's Town & Country Club in 1987.

● ALBUMS: *Gangster Of Love* (King 1958)★★★★, *Johnny Guitar Watson* (King 1963)★★★, *The Blues Soul Of Johnny Guitar Watson* (Chess 1964)★★★★, *Bad* (Chess 1966)★★★★, with Larry Williams *Two For The Price Of One* (1967)★★★★, *Johnny Watson Plays Fats Waller In The Fats Bag* (OKeh 1968)★★★, *Listen* (Fantasy 1974)★★★, *I Don't Want To Be Alone, Stranger* (Fantasy 1975)★★★, *Captured Live* (1976)★★★, *Ain't That A Bitch* (DJM 1976)★★★, *A Real Mother For Ya* (DJM 1977)★★, *Funk Beyond The Call Of Duty* (DJM 1977)★★, *Gangster Of Love* (DJM 1977)★★★, with the Watsonian Institute *Master Funk*

(1978)★★, *Giant* (DJM 1978)★★, with Papa John Creach *Inphasion* (DJM 1978)★★, with the Watsonian Institute *Extra Disco Perception* (1979)★★, *What The Hell Is This?* (DJM 1979)★★, *Love Jones* (DJM 1980)★★, *Johnny 'Guitar' Watson And The Family Clone* (DJM 1981)★★, *That's What Time It Is* (A&M 1981)★★, *Strike On Computers* (Valley Vue 1984)★★, *Bow Wow* (M-Head 1996)★★.
● COMPILATIONS: *The Very Best Of Johnny 'Guitar' Watson* (DJM 1981)★★★★, *I Heard That!* (Chess 1985)★★★★, *Hit The Highway* (Ace 1985)★★★★, *Gettin' Down With Johnny 'Guitar' Watson* (Chess 1987)★★★, *Three Hours Past Midnight* (Flair 1991)★★★, *Gangster Of Love* (Charly 1991)★★★★★, *Listen/I Don't Want To Be Alone, Stranger* (Ace 1992)★★★, *Bow Wow* (Wilma/Bellmark 1994)★★★, *Gangster Of Love: The Best Of Johnny 'Guitar' Watson* (Castle 1995)★★★★, *Hot Just Like TNT* (Ace 1996)★★★★.

WAYNE, WEE WILLIE

b. New Orleans. Wayne was a blues singer and drummer who was discovered by Stan Lewis. As James Waynes, he recorded for Bob Shad's Sittin In With label in Houston in 1950. Among the titles released by Shad were 'Junco Partner' and 'Tend To Your Business', a big R&B hit in 1951. Wayne next joined Imperial, recording with Lee Allen's studio band in New Orleans from 1951-52. These tracks, including 'When Night Falls' and 'Two Faced Woman', were issued under the name Wee Willie Wayne. After a 1954 session in Los Angeles for Aladdin where he sang 'Crying In Vain', Wayne recorded 'Travelin' Mood' (Imperial 1955), which became popular in the New Orleans area. He continued to perform locally and in 1961 made a new version of 'Tend To Your Business' for Imperial, who issued an album of his work the following year. Wayne subsequently left the music business and in the late 60s was reported to be hospitalized, suffering from a mental illness.
● ALBUMS: *Travelin' Mood* (Imperial 1962)★★★, *Travelin' From New Orleans* (Sundwon 1982)★★★.

WEATHERSBY, CARL

b. Carlton Weathersby, 24 February 1953, Jackson, Mississippi, USA. Signed to a multi-album contract by Evidence Records in 1996, Weathersby is an intensely physical guitar player with a talent for writing some of contemporary soul/blues' most distinctive songs. Moving to the urban environment of East Chicago as a teenager, he was brought up listening to classic-era Motown alongside blues giants such as Little Milton and Albert King. Service in Vietnam and various dead-end jobs followed before King, a friend of the family, hired Weathersby as a backing guitarist between 1979 and 1981, during which period he also worked with Milton. Weathersby then joined the acclaimed Sons Of Blues in 1982 as a replacement for the unreliable Carlos Johnson, his distinctive, soul-tinged voice and guitar-playing adding a greater diversity to their traditional blues repetoire. After 15 years with the band, during which time he became their main focal point, Weathersby left in January 1997 to concentrate on his solo career. He has released two acclaimed albums to date, featuring a powerful mix of Weathersby originals and cover versions that confirm a talent that has been crying out to be heard.
● ALBUMS: *Don't Lay Your Blues On Me* (Evidence 1996)★★★★, *Looking Out My Window* (Evidence 1997)★★★★.

WEAVER, CURLEY JAMES

b. 25 March 1906, Covington, Georgia, USA, d. 20 September 1960, Almon, Georgia, USA. Weaver's mother taught him his first lessons on guitar, and he moved to Atlanta in the 20s, where he played with musicians such as Charlie and Robert Hicks (aka Charley Lincoln and Barbecue Bob). He made his first records in 1928, and recorded frequently up to 1935 as a solo artist, and also as an accompanist to other artists including Eugene 'Buddy' Moss and 'Blind' Willie McTell. He also appeared in the groups the Georgia Cotton Pickers and the Georgia Browns. These show him as a versatile and skilled musician, whose work encompassed a range of styles from ragtime-flavoured numbers to tough bottleneck blues. In the 40s and early 50s, Weaver made a few more records, which rank among the best country blues recordings of the period.
● COMPILATIONS: *Georgia Guitar Wizard* (1988)★★★, *1933-1950* (1990)★★★.

WEAVER, SYLVESTER

b. 25 July 1897, Louisville, Kentucky, USA, d. 4 April 1960, Louisville, Kentucky, USA. Though little is known of his life and his influences, Weaver has the distinction of being the first country bluesman to have been recorded, almost a year before Papa Charlie Jackson and three before Blind Lemon Jefferson. His first sessions, as a solo instrumentalist and accompanying Sara Martin, were cut for OKeh in October and November 1923, with further sessions in March and May 1924. OKeh also used him as a talent scout and three years later, Weaver took Walter Beasley and the 14-year-old Helen Humes to New York for the series of sessions that marked the end of his recording career. He also made his debut as a vocalist and banjo soloist at an earlier April 1927 session. 'Guitar Rag', which he recorded in 1923 and 1927, was later used by Bob Wills' guitarist Leon McAuliffe (without acknowledgement) as the basis for 'Steel Guitar Rag', becoming the exhibition piece of all steel guitarists. Weaver was thus denied the one significant achievement of his career, and since nothing further is known about him except for his death from cancer in 1952, he may never have known what his talent had wrought.
● COMPILATIONS: *Smoketown Strut* (Agram 1982)★★★, *The Slide Guitar: Bottles, Knives & Steel* (Columbia 1990)★★★, *Great Blues Guitarists: String Dazzlers* (Columbia 1991)★★★, *Complete Recorded Works In Chronological Order* (Document 1992)★★★.

WEBB, 'BOOGIE' BILL

b. 1924, Jackson, Mississippi, USA, d. 23 August 1990, New Orleans, Louisiana, USA. Among Webb's first guitar teachers was Roosevelt Holts, and he later played with Tommy Johnson and Ishmon Bracey. He retained the ability to play in the south Mississippi blues style throughout his life, but in the 40s he extended his musical points of reference when he teamed up with a young Chuck Berry, and later in New Orleans, when he played with Fats Domino's band. In 1952, he recorded four tracks, of which only two were issued, and he did not record again until the 60s. In the meantime, he lived for a period in Chicago, where he played with some of the big names of the time, including Muddy Waters. In 1966, he made the first of a number of record-

ings aimed at the blues revival, although his album was not released until 1989.
● ALBUMS: *Drinkin' And Stinkin'* (1989)★★★.

WEBB, STAN

(see Chicken Shack)

WEBSTER, KATIE

b. Kathryn Thorne, 1 September 1939, Houston, Texas, USA. Webster learned to play the piano as a child, playing hymn tunes when her mother was within earshot and Fats Domino and Chuck Berry tunes when she was not. She developed, in her words, 'A funky left hand and a rollin' right', which talent led to her becoming house pianist at Jay Miller's studio in Crowley, Louisiana, from 1959-66. During that period, she backed Excello Records' swamp blues artists such as Lazy Lester, Lonesome Sundown and Lightnin' Slim. She also recorded under her own name, or with billing shared with Ashton Conroy (Ashton Savoy). These recordings showed her to be a versatile performer, covering tough, down-home blues, rocking R&B, soul and pop ballads, and revealed a sweet, but sassy voice. She played with Otis Redding's touring band from 1966 until Redding's death the following year, after which her career took a downturn and she played only local gigs during the 70s. In 1982 she toured Europe, the first of many such tours. Currently, her career is on the upturn as she continues to tour with her band, Silent Partners, and to lay down her two-fisted playing and no-nonsense singing on a succession of fine albums.
● ALBUMS: *Katie Webster Has The Blues* (1979)★★★, *You Can Dig It* (1981)★★★, *Live And Well* (1982)★★★, *200% Joy* (1984)★★★, *You Know That's Right* (Arhoolie 1985)★★★, *The Swamp Boogie Queen* (Alligator 1988)★★★, *Two Fisted Mama* (Alligator 1989)★★★★, *No Foolin'!* (Alligator 1991)★★★★, *I Know That's Right* (1993)★★★.
● COMPILATIONS: *Whooee Sweet Daddy* (1977)★★★, *The Many Faces Of Katie Webster* (Schubert 1988)★★★, *Katie Webster* Excello material (Flyright 1989)★★★.

WELCH, MIKE

b. c.1980, Austin, Texas, USA. While Austin continues to enjoy a contemporary blues boom, few of the city's residents have the vibrancy and enthusiasm demonstrated by 'Monster' Mike Welch. The recipient of great praise for his 1996 debut album, which paired him with three seasoned local musicians, Welch was only 16 when he recorded *These Blues Are Mine*. He had first discovered the blues via an old album of Albert King's at the age of nine, by which time he had already spent two years learning guitar. As a precocious 11-year-old he was invited to join local blues jams, working alongside Ronnie Earl, Luther 'Guitar Junior' Johnson, Matt Murphy and Johnny Copeland. At 13 Welch opened the bill at the Cambridge House Of Blues, sharing a stage with Junior Wells, Joe Walsh and actor Dan Aykroyd. It was the latter who gave him his nickname, 'Monster Mike'. His debut album for Tone-Cool Records followed the presentation of the 1995 Boston Music Award. Despite such widespread recognition, the majority of his performances remain confined to weekends and holidays owing to his ongoing studies at high school. However, a follow-up album was not long in appearing.

● ALBUMS: *These Blues Are Mine* (Tone-Cool 1996)★★★★, *Axe To Grind* (Tone-Cool 1997)★★★.

WELDON, CASEY BILL

b. 10 July 1909, Pine Bluff, Arkansas, USA. Weldon was briefly married to Memphis Minnie in the 20s, and made his recording debut with the Memphis Jug Band in 1927, also recording under the name of Will Weldon. He sang in a high, straining voice, and played chugging guitar, which, in duet with Vol Stevens, emulated the playing of Charley Jordan. Weldon reappeared in Chicago in 1935, having allegedly made his way there via Kansas City (hence his nickname, a version of 'K.C.'). His singing became deeper and warmer, embellished with falsetto, while his guitar-playing had changed even more radically. Sometimes billed as 'the Hawaiian Guitar Wizard', he now played steel guitar with a slide. He was evidently influenced by Hawaiian players such as Sol Hoopii (and possibly by western swing guitarists such as Leon McAuliffe), but he remained firmly rooted in blues. Extensively recorded, Weldon composed the standards 'Gonna Move To The Outskirts Of Town' and 'Somebody Changed The Lock On My Door'. His songs often featured a trademark melody, but when he broke away from this he played highly inventive, swinging guitar. He disappeared from the music scene after 1938, reportedly moving to California, and later to Detroit.

● COMPILATIONS: *Bottleneck Guitar Trendsetters Of The 1930s* (1975)★★★, *Casey Bill Weldon (1935-37)* (Old Tramp 1988)★★★, *Complete Recorded Works 1936-38 Vols. 1-3* (Document 1994)★★★.

WELLINGTON, VALERIE

b. Valerie Eileen Hall, 14 November 1959, Chicago, Illinois, USA, d. 2 January 1993, Maywood, Ilinois, USA. Wellington trained as an opera singer at Chicago's American Conservatory of Music for three years. She learned piano as a youngster and played with local bluesman Lee 'Shot' Williams at the age of 15. In 1982 she came to the notice of the blues audience as a singer by portraying Ma Rainey in a local musical stage play and, two years later, she recorded her debut album for the Rooster label, which received 'rave' reviews from the critics, all of whom commented on the power of Wellington's voice. In 1987 she contributed one track to Alligator Records' *The New Bluebloods*, an anthology of younger blues artists, as well as providing music to several television commercials. She died from a brain aneurysm at the age of 33.

● ALBUMS: *Million Dollar Secret* (Rooster Blues 1984)★★★, *Life In The Big City* (GBW 1992)★★★.

WELLS, JUNIOR

b. Amos Blackmore, 9 December 1934, Memphis, Tennessee, USA. Having eschewed parental pressure to pursue a career in gospel music, Wells began playing harmonica on the streets of west Memphis, inspired by local heroes Howlin' Wolf and Junior Parker. Having followed his mother to Chicago in 1946, the young musician won the respect of senior figures of the blues fraternity, including Tampa Red, Big Maceo and Sunnyland Slim. Wells formed a trio, initially known as the Little Chicago Devils, then the Three Deuces, with Louis Myers (guitar) and David Myers (bass). Later known as the Three Aces, the group became a popular attraction, especially with the addition of drummer Fred Below. Their reputation reached Little Walter, harmonica player with Muddy Waters, who was about to embark on a solo career. Walter appropriated the Aces as his backing group, while Wells joined Waters on tour. The exchange was not irrevocable as the Aces accompanied Wells on his first solo sessions, credited to Junior Wells And His Eagle Rockers, which included the original version of 'Hoodoo Man', a song the artist would return to over the years. A spell in the US Army then interrupted his progress, but Wells resumed recording in 1957 with the first of several releases undertaken for local entrepreneur Mel London. These included 'Little By Little' (1960) and the excellent 'Messin' With The Kid' (1960), the latter of which featured guitarist Earl Hooker, but Wells' most fruitful partnership was forged in 1965 when he began a long association with Buddy Guy. *Hoodoo Man Blues* consummated their relationship and this superb set, one of the finest Chicago blues albums, featured Wells' sterling harmonica work and Guy's exemplary, supportive guitar playing. Subsequent releases, including *On Tap*, *Southside Blues Jam* and *It's My Life Baby*, although less fiery were nonetheless impressive, and the group became popular with both black and white audiences, the latter through appearances on the rock circuit. In the *Billboard* R&B chart he had successes with 'Up In Heah' (1966) and 'You're Tuff Enough' (1968). By the end of the 60s Wells and Guy were sharing top billing, while a release as Buddy And The Juniors denoted their association with pianist Junior Mance. However, Guy's growing reputation resulted in a diminution of this democratic approach and the harmonica player's role was increasingly viewed as supportive. By the early 90s, the partnership was dissolved. Wells is still an impressive stylist and he remains, with Little Walter and Sonny Boy 'Rice Miller' Williamson, a leading practitioner of post-war blues harmonica. *Ebony* magazine aptly described his talent: 'Wells plays the harp like most of us breathe'. Wells became seriously ill in 1997 and his condition remains critical.

● ALBUMS: *Hoodoo Man Blues* (Delmark 1966)★★★, *On Tap* (Delmark 1966)★★★, *It's My Life Baby!* (Vanguard 1966)★★★★, *Southside Blues Jam* (Delmark 1967)★★★, *Comin' At You* (Vanguard 1968)★★★, *You're Tuff Enough* (Blue Rock 1968)★★★, *Junior Wells Sings At The Golden Bear* (Blue Rock 1968)★★★, *Blues Hit Big Town* (Delmark 1969)★★★, *Buddy And The Juniors* (1970)★★★, *Buddy Guy And Junior Wells Play The Blues* (1972)★★★★, with Buddy Guy *Alone And Acoustic* , reissued in 1991 with extra tracks (1981)★★★★, with Guy *Drinkin' TNT 'N' Smokin' Dynamite* (Red Lightnin' 1982)★★★, with James Cotton, Carey Bell, Billy Branch *Harp Attack* (1991)★★★, *Better Off With The Blues* (Telarc 1993)★★★, *Everybody's Gettin' Some* (Telarc 1995)★★★, *Come On In This House* (Telarc 1996)★★★, *Live At Buddy Guy's Legends* (Telarc 1997)★★★.

● COMPILATIONS: *Blues Hit Big Town* (1969)★★★, *In My Younger Days* (1971)★★★, *Chiefly Wells* (Flyright 1986)★★★, *Universal Rock* (Flyright 1986)★★★, *Messing With The Kid 1957-1963* (Flyright 1986)★★★, *Undisputed Godfather Of The Blues* (1993)★★★.

WELLS, VIOLA 'MISS RHAPSODY'

b. 14 December 1902, Newark, New Jersey, USA, d. 22 December 1984, New York City, USA. Touring the TOBA circuit as a classic blues singer in the 30s Wells met and married guitarist Harold Underhill. She was a much-admired jazz and blues singer in her day, winning substantial respect, and envy, from her fellow singers and musicians. In the early to mid-40s, billed as 'The Ebony Stick Of Dynamite', she became a huge success at Harlem's Apollo Theatre on 125th Street, and had her own radio shows as both performer and disc jockey. Despite such exposure she recorded only three times in her heyday (for Savoy Records in 1944-45) and retired from music in 1946 as a result of diabetes. In the mid-60s she was rediscovered by blues historian Sheldon Harris, who persuaded her to test for Columbia Records and reunited her with Victoria Spivey, who recorded a handful of sides by 'Miss Rhapsody'. She remained in obscurity until April 1972 when she was again brought out of retirement to record a jazz-blues album for the Saydisc-Matchbox label in New York City. Her last years were, happily, employed touring as singer with Clyde Bernhardt's Harlem Blues & Jazz Band.

● ALBUMS: *Miss Rhapsody* (Matchbox 1972)★★★, with Little Esther Phillips, Albinia

Jones, Linda Hopkins *Ladies Sing The Blues* (1977)★★★.

WESTON, JOHN

b. 1927, Lee County, Arkansas, USA. If Weston is a somewhat diffident musician, it may be because he did not perform in public until after his 60th birthday. Nevertheless, his debut album consists of original and accomplished material, in stark contrast to a number of other late developers who struggle to interpret rather than invent. Weston has a childhood memory of Sonny Boy Williamson (Rice Miller) cutting across his parents' farm on his way to country suppers and juke-joints, with a belt of harmonicas strapped across his chest. Later, he heard Miller's *King Biscuit Time* on KFFA out of Helena, while he pursued a number of jobs as a farmer, butcher, car mechanic and carpenter. His own harmonica technique was developed with the assistance of Willie Cobbs. Weston made his public debut during the 70s, as a member of the Speckled Rhythms, a family band led by Jobie Kilzer. After his 1988 solo debut, Weston received the Blues Foundation's Lucille Award the following year. Two members of his band Blues Force, guitarist Troy Broussard and bassist James 'Famous' Jones, also spent time in bands led by Cobbs. Weston sings in a gently inflected style reminiscent of Little Milton and essays undemonstrative solos on both chromatic and diatonic harmonicas.
● ALBUMS: *So Doggone Blue* (Fat Possum 1993)★★★, *I'm Doin' The Best I Can* (Appaloosa 1996)★★★.

WHEATSTRAW, PEETIE

b. William Bunch, 21 December 1902, Ripley, Tennessee, USA, d. 21 December 1941, East St. Louis, Illinois, USA. Wheatstraw, also known as the Devil's Son-In-Law, was an influential and popular blues artist of the 20s and 30s. He opened a club with 'Big' Joe Williams in 1929. An accomplished guitarist, pianist and singer, he was tragically killed in a car accident at a comparatively young age. Throughout his recordings, usually with Vocalion or Decca, he was accompanied by musicians such as James 'Kokomo' Arnold, Lonnie Johnson and Lil Armstrong. Although he recorded many tracks, little of his work has been available for some time, giving fuel to the argument that his importance and influence is on the wane.
● COMPILATIONS: *Peetie Wheatstraw And Kokomo Arnold* (Blues Classics 1988)★★★.
● FURTHER READING: *The Devil's Son-In-Law*, Paul Garon.

WHEELER, BIG

b. Golden Wheeler, 15 December 1929, Beaconton, Georgia, USA. Wheeler's first encounter with a harmonica came about through Buster Brown, whom he heard on WALB, a local radio station. He left Georgia in 1941 and after spending time in New Jersey and Ohio, he arrived in Chicago at the time that Muddy Waters and Little Walter were first making their presence known. Wheeler formed his own band in 1956 with Walter 'Big Red' Smith, Donald Griffin and Johnny Swan. Others with whom he worked in clubs and at house parties included Little Eddie King, Willie Black and his brother James. Although he continued to play over the next three decades, he always kept his job as a mechanic. His first recordings were made in 1990 and illustrated his debt to Little Walter. *Bone Orchard* was recorded in two sessions in August 1992 and February 1993, accompanied by the Ice Cream Men, led by disc jockey and drummer Steve Cushing. The band, normally including harmonica player Scott Dirks, was formed in 1980 to back Little Smokey Smothers. Wheeler sings and plays harmonica unadventurously but well, although the deliberate air of recreation is hard to dispel.
● ALBUMS: with A.C. Reed *Chicago Blues Session Vol. 14* (Wolf 1990)★★★, *Big Wheeler's Bone Orchard* (Delmark 1993)★★★.

WHEELER, GOLDEN

b. 16 December 1929, Baconton, Georgia, USA. Wheeler became interested in the blues during the 30s and learned to play harmonica from Buster Brown in the early 50s. Wheeler moved to Chicago in 1954 and began to play seriously the following year, inspired by Junior Wells and Little Walter. He formed his first band, but after a few years of low pay and problems with other musicians, he performed less and less, and did not resume an active musical career until 1987. Wheeler is a solid Chicago blues singer and player, and has recorded for the Mr. Blues label

in 1976 (issued by Rooster in 1988) and for Wolf Records under his own name and as accompanist to Eddie King and Artie 'Blues Boy' White.
● COMPILATIONS: *Low Blows: An Anthology Of Chicago Harmonica Blues* two tracks by Wheeler (1988), *Chicago Blues Session, Volume 14* four tracks by Wheeler (1989).

WHITE, 'SCHOOLBOY' CLEVE

b. 10 June 1928, Baton Rouge, Louisiana, USA. White taught himself to play harmonica as a youngster and received his stage-name because of his youthful appearance. In the mid-50s he recorded with Lightnin' Slim and in his own right for J.D. 'Jay' Miller's Feature label, and in 1957 for Ace Records. In 1960 he moved to Los Angeles, California, and retired from music, although in 1970 he relocated to San Francisco and began to perform again. He has since recorded for Blues Connoisseur and his own Cherrie label, whose roster also includes J.J. Malone.
● ALBUMS: *Lightnin' Slim Volume Three: The Feature Sides 1954* , although credited to Lightnin' Slim, the title includes compositions and backings by White (1981).

WHITE, ARTIE 'BLUES BOY'

b. 1937, Vicksburg, Mississippi, USA. White began singing gospel at the age of 11 and, after moving to Chicago in 1956, he sang with the Full Gospel Wonders. He began singing blues in the early 60s and later recorded singles for small labels such as Gamma, World-Wide, PM and Sky Hero (both owned by 'Little' Mac Simmons), and Altee ('Leanin' Tree' was a local hit for the latter company). For some time he ran a Chicago club called Bootsy's Lounge and in 1985 he made his debut album for the Ronn label. In 1987 he signed with Ichiban and has had regular album and single releases since that time, all of a consistently high standard and spotlighting White's soul-drenched blues singing, which, transferred to the stage, reveals White to be a dynamic performer although on his 1997 release *Home Tonight* the Muscle Shoals rhythm section outshines the singer.
● ALBUMS: *Nothing Takes The Place Of You* (Ichiban 1987)★★★, *Where It's At* (Ichiban 1988)★★★, *Thangs Got To Change* (Ichiban 1989)★★★, *Tired Of Sneaking Around* (Ichiban

1990)★★★, *The Bluesmaker - Hit And Run* (1993)★★★, *Home Tonight* (Waldoxy 1997)★★.
● COMPILATIONS: *The Best Of Artie White* (Ichiban 1992)★★★★.

WHITE, BUKKA

b. Booker T. Washington White, 12 November 1906, Houston, Mississippi, USA, d. 26 February 1977, Memphis, Tennessee, USA. White learned guitar and piano in his teens, and hoboed from 1921, playing blues with artists such as George 'Bullet' Williams. In the mid-30s White was a boxer and baseball pitcher. He recorded for Victor in 1930, a largely unissued session including spirituals and the first of his breakneck train imitations. Returning to Vocalion in 1937, he recorded his composition 'Shake 'Em On Down' and was given the misspelt billing which he always disliked. By the time 'Shake 'Em On Down' was a hit, White had been imprisoned in Parchman Farm for assault. There, he recorded two songs for the Library of Congress, and claimed to have had an easy time as a prison musician. However, when he recorded commercially again in 1940, he was clear that he had been traumatized by his experience. The result was a remarkable series of recordings obsessed with prison, trains, drink and death. The songs were poetic, complete and coherent, often with deep insights into their topics, their heavy vocal delivery perfectly complemented by fierce, percussive slide guitar. After his US Navy service during World War II, White settled in Memphis from 1944 onwards. In 1946, his second cousin, B.B. King, lived with him, learning perhaps less about music than about the blues singer's life. As white interest in blues increased, 'Fixin' To Die Blues' and 'Parchman Farm Blues' became cult songs. Rediscovered in 1963, White had retained most of his abilities, and was extensively recorded (including, for the first time, on piano). He joined the folk club and festival circuit, performing across the USA, Canada, Mexico and Europe until the mid-70s, when illness enforced his retirement.
● ALBUMS: *Sky Songs* (Fontana 1966)★★★, *Bukka White* (Columbia 1966)★★★, *Memphis Hot Shots* (Blue Horizon 1969)★★★, *Big Daddy* (Biograph 1974)★★★, *Shake 'Em Down* (1993)★★★.
● COMPILATIONS: *The Legacy Of The Blues*

Volume One (Sonet 1969)★★★, *Aberdeen Mississippi Blues (1937-40)* (Travellin' Man 1985)★★★, *The Complete Sessions 1930-1940* (Travellin' Man 1990)★★★, *The Complete Bukka White* (Columbia Roots 'N' Blues 1994)★★★, *1963 Isn't 1962* (Genes/Edsel 1995)★★★.

WHITE, GEORGIA

b. 9 March 1903, Sandersville, Georgia, USA. The birth date was supplied by Big Bill Broonzy and, at the time of writing, it is not known whether Georgia White is still alive. Her first record was recorded for Vocalion in 1930 in the company of Jimmie Noone, but she enjoyed considerably greater success during the late 30s when she recorded almost 100 tracks for the Decca label. An excellent blues singer with an easy style, she was also a competent pianist and may, indeed, have worked for Decca as a house musician at one time. She worked, but did not record, with Bumble Bee Slim and during the late 40s formed an all-girl band. Around 1950 she was working as pianist in Big Bill's Laughing Trio and her last recorded appearance was at a Chicago club in 1959. Her blues were often humorous and she could play first-rate boogie-woogie, but she also had a more sober side and blues pundits do not seem to have afforded her the attention that her talent deserves.
● ALBUMS: *Georgia White Sings And Plays The Blues* (Rosetta 1984)★★★.
● COMPILATIONS: *Complete Recorded Works Vols. 1-4* (Document 1995)★★★.

WHITE, JOSH

b. Joshua White, 11 February 1915, Greenville, South Carolina, USA, d. 5 September 1969, Manhasset, New York, USA. A grounding in church music stood Josh White in good stead, as it was something to which he returned at various points in a long career as a blues singer and, later, folk entertainer. He learned guitar while acting as a guide for blind street singers, and began his recording career at a young age. Between 1932 and 1936, he recorded prolifically. The results often demonstrated a notable versatility, covering blues in local or more nationally popular idioms (sometimes under the pseudonym Pinewood Tom) or sacred material as the Singing Christian. In the mid-30s he moved to New York, where he found a new audience

interested in radical politics and folk music. In retrospect, it seemed as if he was diluting as well as tailoring his music for the consumption of white listeners, who were at this time unused to hearing authentic black music. As the years went on, he learned a lot of new material, and turned his repertoire into an odd mixture, encompassing everything from traditional ballads such as 'Lord Randall' to popular songs like 'Scarlet Ribbons', as well as protest songs and blues. He toured overseas in the post-war years and recorded extensively.
● ALBUMS: *Josh White Sings Blues* (Mercury 1949)★★★, *Ballads And Blues* (Decca 1949)★★★, *Josh White Sings* (Stinson 1950)★★★, *A Josh White Program* (London 1951)★★★, *Ballads Vol. 2* (Decca 1952)★★★, *Strange Fruit* (EmArcy 1954)★★★, *A Josh White Program Vol. 2* (London 1956)★★★, *Josh White Comes A Visiting* (Period 1956)★★★, *Josh At Midnight* (Elektra 1956)★★★, *Josh Sings Blues* (Elektra 1957)★★★, *25th Anniversary Album* (Elektra 1957)★★★, *The Josh White Stories Vols 1 & 2* (ABC 1957)★★★, *Chain Gang Songs* (Elektra 1958)★★★, *Josh White Live* (ABC 1962)★★★, *The Beginning* (Mercury 1963)★★★, *The World Of Josh White* (1969)★★★, *Josh White With Molly Malone* (1974)★★★, with the Ronnie Sisters *Blues And Spirituals* (Joker 1981)★★★, *Blues And...* rec. 1956 (Wooded Hill 1997)★★★.
● COMPILATIONS: *Joshua White 1936-41* (Best Of Blues 1989)★★★, *Joshua White (Pinewood Tom) Vol. 2* (Earl Archives 1989)★★★, *Blues Singer 1932-1936* (Columbia 1996)★★★.

WHITE, LAVELLE

b. 3 July c.1928, Amite, Louisiana, USA. Blues singer Lavelle White moved with her mother to Murphy, Mississippi, as a baby. Here, she learned to sing by accompanying the family's sharecropping activities, performing alongside her piano-playing mother at church. At the age of 15 she moved from Mississippi to Houston, where she began to work as a singer on the club circuit before securing engagements with local artists such as Clarence Green, Clarence Hollimon and Guitar Slim. She then joined a travelling rodeo that travelled through Oklahoma and neighbouring states. On her return to Houston she was introduced to producer Don Robey by Johnny Copeland; her first records for the Duke label were cut in 1957 and credited to 'Miss La-Vell'. Her singles for Duke included the self-composition 'Stop Those Teardrops', plus a version of Joe Medwick's 'Yes, I've Been Crying' and 'Just Look At You Fool'. However, Robey never considered her an artist of sufficient standing to release a full album. From then on she became a regular touring companion to blues and R&B artists, including James Brown, B.B. King, Bobby Bland, Junior Parker, the Drifters, Otis Redding and Gladys Knight And The Pips, as a popular opening act. She had already begun to write her own songs, one of which, 'Lead Me On', later appeared on Bland's 1974 album *Two Steps From The Blues*, though it was credited to a third party. In the 70s and 80s she became a fixture at Chicago's Kingston Mines club, working alongside Koko Taylor and Lonnie Brooks, before returning to Texas. There she was eventually offered the opportunity to record her first solo album by Clifford Antone of Antone's Records.

● ALBUMS: *Miss Lavelle* (Antone's 1994)★★★, *It Haven't Been Easy* (Antones 1997)★★★.

WHITE, LYNN

b. 6 August 1953, Mobile, Alabama, USA. Having trained her voice in church, when White took a part-time job at bluesman Big Ike Darby's record store, she sang along with the records as they played. She had become store manager before her boss realized her ability. Already aware of her brother Larry Saunders' ability as a soul singer, Darby nurtured her talent, releasing an album and a number of singles, including 'Blues In My Bedroom' and her answer to B.B. King's hit, 'I Didn't Make My Move Too Soon', on his Darby and Sho Me labels. Her 1982 single, 'I Don't Ever Wanna See Your Face Again', was picked up for national distribution by Willie Mitchell's Waylo label. Mitchell acquired her contract and re-recorded 'Blues In My Bedroom'. Despite showing a strong talent, White's subsequent records bore too many resemblances to Mitchell's previous work with Ann Peebles, although each album contained worthwhile examples of an original style.

● ALBUMS: *Am I Too Much Woman For You?* (Darby 1979)★★★, *Blues In My Bedroom* (Waylo 1983)★★★, *Slow & Easy* (Waylo 1986)★★★,

Love & Happiness (Waylo 1988)★★, *Yes I'm Ready* (Waylo 1990)★★, *At Her Best* (Blues Works 1996)★★★.

WIGGINS, PHIL

b. 8 May 1954, Washington DC, USA. Though partnered since 1976 by fellow Washingtonian John Cephas, Wiggins first developed his harmonica style playing with street singer Flora Molton. Having learned the basics on a plastic harmonica, he appropriated his sister's instrument and, having watched Molton play, the 14-year-old Wiggins went to her house to jam. Through her festival appearances, he met musicians like Johnny Shines and Wilbert 'Big' Chief Ellis. He first met Cephas in 1974 and the pair joined up with Ellis to form the Barrelhouse Ramblers, a band that lasted until Ellis's death in 1977. Cephas and Wiggins have worked as a duo ever since, touring throughout America and Europe on a regular basis. Although he claims to have learned from most of the musicians with whom he has played, Wiggins attributes particular importance to Sonny Terry's complex style. Both *Dog Days Of August* and *Guitar Man* won Handy Awards in their respective years.

● ALBUMS: *Bowling Green John Cephas & Harmonica Phil Wiggins From Virginia, USA* (L + R 1981)★★★, *Sweet Bitter Blues* (L + R 1983)★★★, *Dog Days Of August* (Flying Fish 1986)★★★★, *Guitar Man* (Flying Fish 1990)★★★, *Flip, Flop & Fly* (Flying Fish 1992)★★★.

● COMPILATIONS: *Roots Of Rhythm And Blues: A Tribute To The Robert Johnson Era* (Columbia 1992)★★★.

WIKSTRÖM, ROLF

b. Sweden. Considered to be among Sweden's finest blues guitarists, Rolf Wikström has recorded almost 20 albums in a career that began in the mid-70s. He hardly matches the preferred image of the bluesman - tall and blonde with a middle-class background including a stint as an economist - yet his records tell a different story. That story began as a child when he borrowed his first guitar from his uncle and practised solos he heard on the radio. However, it was only when a television repairman visited that he was informed that he had been playing a totally untuned guitar.

Having re-learned the instrument he bought his first guitar, a Fenton Vail, at the age of 14, which he played through a battery-driven radio that served as his amplifier. In his late teens he joined a Stockholm blues band. Such was this group's legendary capacity for alcohol intake, that they were credited with ending the long-held Swedish tradition of supplying bar bands with free beer. Inspired by Jimmy Page, Wikström then purchased lighter banjo strings for his guitar to give it a distinctive tonal quality and embarked on solo recordings, beginning in 1975 with *Sjung Svenska Folk* (Sing Swedes!). Since then he has broadened his repertoire from raw, primal blues to encompass ballads and jazz flourishes. He has carved out a successful career in a country noted for the keen reception it affords high quality blues, though in truth he has not been able to export his reputation abroad save for small clusters of supporters in mainland Europe and America. This is of little concern to Wikström, who continues to play live as often as possible, often in support of visiting blues greats such as Charles Brown and Albert Collins.

● ALBUMS: including *Sjung Svenska Folk* (MNW 1975)★★★, *Blues Är Allt Jag Har* (MNW 1992)★★★.

WILKINS, JOE WILLIE

b. 7 January 1923, Davenport, Mississippi, USA, d. 28 March 1979, Memphis, Tennessee, USA. His reputation as a guitarist, higher among his fellow musicians that it is with even those possessed examples of his work, Wilkins has apologists who maintain that his influence reached further and deeper than is currently recognised. His father, Frank, bought him a guitar when he was 12 and already proficient on the harmonica. He learned more from Bob Williams, Pat Rhodes and Sam Harris, members of a string band that included his father. Soon he took to the road, working in cottonfields and playing on street corners, earning the name 'Joe Willie The Walking Seeburg'. He encountered Sonny Boy Williamson (Rice Miller) and Robert Lockwood during his travels, trading ideas with the latter. He linked up with them in 1942 in Helena, Arkansas, broadcasting on station KFFA. He was one of the King Biscuit Boys with Sonny Boy, and promoted Mother's Best Flour alongside

Lockwood. He also met and worked with Robert Nighthawk and B.B. King in West Memphis. In Jackson, Mississippi in 1951, he played on sessions for Sonny Boy and Willie Love, and in Memphis in 1953 was on Albert Williams' session for Sun. He continued to work with Sonny Boy until the latter's death in 1965. During the 70s, despite being hampered by illness, he worked the Memphis area with his own King Biscuit Boys and recorded a single and album, though neither are currently available.

● ALBUMS: *Goin' In Your Direction* (1991)★★★.

WILKINS, ROBERT, REV.

b. 16 January 1896, Hernando, Mississippi, USA, d. 30 May 1987, Memphis, Tennessee, USA. Wilkins moved to Memphis during World War I, and by the 20s was playing his guitar and singing in the blues joints of Beale Street. Between 1928 and 1934, he made a series of excellent recordings, which showed a carefully crafted approach, tailoring his fingerpicked accompaniments to suit the lyrics as well as the tunes. Some of his records were issued under his middle name, Tim. There was a 30-year gap before he recorded again, following rediscovery in the days of the folk/blues boom. By this time he had renounced blues and played only religious music, having been ordained a minister in 1950. His overall style was much the same, and 'Prodigal Son' was later covered by the Rolling Stones.

● ALBUMS: *Memphis Gospel Singer* (1964)★★★, *Before The Reverence* (Magpie 1976)★★★, *The Original Rolling Stone* (Herwin 1980)★★★, *Remember Me* (Edsel 1994)★★★.

WILLIAMS, BIG JOE

b. Joe Lee Williams, 16 October 1903, Crawford, Mississippi, USA, d. 17 December 1982, Macon, Mississippi, USA. Big Joe Williams was one of the most important blues singers to have recorded and also one whose life conforms almost exactly to the stereotyped pattern of how a 'country' blues singer should live. He was of partial Red Indian stock, his father being 'Red Bone' Williams a part Cherokee. 'Big Joe' took his musical influences from his mother's family, the Logans. He made the obligatory 'cigar box' instruments when a child and took to the road when his step-father threw him out around

1918. He later immortalized this antagonist in a song that he was still performing at the end of his long career. Joe's life was one of constant movement as he worked his way around the lumber camps, turpentine farms and juke joints of the south. Around 1930 he married and settled, in St. Louis, Missouri, but still took long sweeps through the country as the rambling habit never left him. This rural audience supported him through the worst of the depression when he appeared under the name 'Poor Joe'. His known recordings began in 1935 when he recorded six tracks for Bluebird in Chicago. From then on he recorded at every opportunity. He stayed with Bluebird until 1945 before moving to Columbia Records. He formed a loose partnership on many sessions with John Lee 'Sonny Boy' Williamson which have been likened to that of Muddy Waters and Little Walter. In 1952, he worked for Trumpet in Jackson, Mississippi, then went back to Chicago for a session with Vee Jay. Other recordings made for smaller companies are still being discovered. During 1951-52, he also made recordings of other singers at his St. Louis base. Williams found a wider audience when blues came into vogue with young whites in the 60s. He continued to record, and tour, adding Europe and Japan to his itinerary. He still used cheap, expendable guitars fixed up by himself with an electrical pick-up and usually festooned with extra machine heads to accommodate nine strings. With his gruff, shouting voice and ringing guitar he became a great favourite on the club and concert circuit. He had come full circle and was living in a caravan in Crawford, Mississippi, when he died. The sheer volume of easily accessible albums recorded during his last years tended to obscure just how big a blues talent Joe's really was.

● ALBUMS: *Piney Woods Blues* (1958)★★★, *Tough Times* (Fontana 1960)★★★, *Nine String Guitar Blues* (1961)★★★, *Blues On Highway 49* (Esquire 1961)★★★, *Mississippi's Big Joe Williams And His Nine-String Guitar* (Folkways 1962)★★★, *Big Joe Williams At Folk City* (Bluesville 1962)★★★, *Blues On Highway 49* (Delmark 1962)★★★, *Blues For Nine Strings* (Bluesville 1963)★★★, *Studio Blues* (Bluesville 1964)★★★, *Starvin' Chain Blues* (Delmark 1966)★★★, *Classic Delta Blues* (Milestone 1966)★★★, *Back To The Country* (Bounty 1966)★★★, *Hellbound And Heaven Sent* (Folkways 1967)★★★, *Don't You Leave Me Here* (Storyville 1969)★★★, *Big Joe Williams* (Xtra 1969)★★★, *Hand Me Down My Old Walking Stick* (Liberty 1969)★★★, *Crawlin' King Snake* (RCA 1970)★★★, *Legacy Of The Blues, Volume 2* (Sonet 1972)★★★, *Tough Times* (1981)★★★, *Thinking Of What They Did* (1981)★★★, *Big Joe Williams 1974* (1982)★★★.

● COMPILATIONS: *Field Recordings 1973-80* (1988)★★★, *Malving My Sweet Woman* (1988)★★★, *Complete Recorded Works In Chronological Order Volumes 1 & 2* (1991)★★★, with Luther Huff, Willie Love *Delta Blues - 1951* (1991)★★★, *The Final Years* (Verve 1995)★★★.

WILLIAMS, 'UNCLE' JOHNNY

b. 15 May 1906, Alexandria, Louisiana, USA. Williams learned guitar in 1918, and divided his time between Mississippi and Chicago until 1938. He moved north permanently, and became a professional musician in 1943. He worked with many Chicago blues singers, most closely with Theodore 'Hound Dog' Taylor, Big Boy Spires and his cousin Johnny Young. In the late 40s, Williams played guitar behind Young on an Ora-Nelle 78, singing on one side. He and Young also recorded for Al Benson's Planet/Old Swingmaster labels, and Williams shared a 1953 session with Spires for the Chance label, on which his serious delivery is pehaps indicative of the Baptist minister he became in 1959.

● ALBUMS: *Chicago Boogie* (1974), *Going Back Home* (1984).

WILLIAMS, BILL

b. 28 February 1897, Richmond, Virginia, USA, d. 6 October 1973, Greenup, Kentucky, USA. Williams claimed to have played 'Yankee Doodle Dandy' within 15 minutes of picking up a guitar in 1908, and his awesome abilities when aged over 70 with an arthritic wrist lend his claim credibility. By 1922, he had settled in Greenup to work as a trackliner after a period of wandering, and played thereafter for the local white audience. His repertoire included the 'blues, rags and ballads' of his posthumous album, songster material such as 'Chicken' and 'Railroad Bill', white fiddle pieces transposed to guitar, and pop songs such as 'Darktown

Strutters' Ball' and 'Up A Lazy River'. There was even a ragtime version of 'The Star-Spangled Banner'. Discovered in 1970, he had a brief, and professedly reluctant, career playing concerts and television shows.

● ALBUMS: *Low And Lonesome* (1971)★★★, *Blues, Rags And Ballads* (1974)★★★.

WILLIAMS, BLIND CONNIE

b. *c*.1915, Florida, USA. Williams was recorded in 1961 in Philadelphia, having been found by a folklorist singing spirituals to his accordion accompaniment. He proved also to have a repertoire of the better-known blues, and to be an accomplished guitarist. As a result of studying at the St. Petersburg School for the Blind, he had a sophisticated grasp of harmony, and used many passing notes and altered chords. Williams' technique was also influenced by an association with Rev. Gary Davis in New York (though his dating of it to the late 30s is confusing, since Davis did not move to New York until 1944). Williams was also a quartet singer, though not recorded as such. He was still known to be alive in 1974, though frail and seldom performing in the streets.

● COMPILATIONS: *Philadelphia Street Singer* (1974)★★★.

WILLIAMS, GEORGE 'BULLET'

(see Coleman, Burl C. 'Jaybird')

WILLIAMS, J. MAYO

b. 1894, Monmouth, Illinois, USA, d. 2 January 1980, Chicago, Illinois, USA. A college graduate, Williams was nicknamed 'Ink' by musicians; he was the first, and in his time the most successful, black executive in the US record industry. In 1924, he joined Paramount, which he made perhaps the most successful of all 'race' labels in terms of both quality and quantity of output, recording Blind Lemon Jefferson, Papa Charlie Jackson and Ma Rainey, among others. Williams was careful to find out what black purchasers wanted; when replies to market research indicated overwhelming demand for blues, he abandoned his own preference for the likes of Paul Robeson. In 1927, Williams resigned to found the short-lived Black Patti label, moving on immediately to Vocalion, to whom he brought Georgia Tom, Tampa Red and Jim Jackson. In 1934, he became responsible for black A&R at Decca, recording Mahalia Jackson's debut sides. After World War II, Williams operated a series of small labels, all of which suffered from undercapitalization and a loss of touch by Williams. As an executive, his income came from a share of publishing royalties and from padding his expense accounts; he said: 'I was better than 50% honest, and in this business that's pretty good'.

WILLIAMS, JODY

b. Joseph Leon Williams, 3 February 1935, Mobile, Alabama, USA. This legendary Chess studio guitarist was the leader of one of Howlin' Wolf's early bands. More people are familiar with Jody Williams' guitarwork than they are with his name. Anyone with Bo Diddley's 'Who Do You Love' or Billy Boy Arnold's 'I Wish You Would' (Williams wrote 'I Was Fooled', the b-side of the original Vee Jay single) or Billy Stewart's 'Billy's Blues' (the trial run for 'Love Is Strange'), has a sample of his ringing, nervy guitarwork. Though making only a handful of singles, few of them under his own name, he was an extremely busy session and house musician throughout the 50s. He arrived in Chicago in 1941, first taking up the harmonica before learning guitar with Ellas McDaniel (Bo Diddley), but to greater effect than the future star. By 1951, they and tub bass player Roosevelt Jackson, had formed a band. Williams quickly became a proficient and in-demand musician, touring the USA in Charles Brown's band before he was 20. That year (1955), he played on Diddley's 'Diddy Wah Diddy', Arnold's 'I Wish You Would' and soloed alongside B.B. King on Otis Spann's 'Five Spot'. Inevitably, his own career was incidental to his other work. Singles appeared on Blue Lake, Argo and Herald as Little Papa Joe or Little Joe Lee or Sugar Boy Williams, since Joe Williams already sang with Count Basie's band. In the mid-60s, he abandoned music to study electronics, and later, computer maintenance. He has made sporadic appearances since then but has not been tempted back to performing.

WILLIAMS, JOHNNY

b. 15 January 1942, Tyler, Texas, USA, d. December 1986. Williams was one of those myriad R&B singers that probably has a greater impact in the clubs than on record, because in Chicago - where he moved in 1956 - he was acclaimed for his full-bodied, deep soul style, yet his legacy on record is small. He began his career in gospel, singing with the Royal Jubilees. Williams first recorded in 1966, when he achieved a small local hit with 'My Baby's Good' for Chess Records. It was not a great record but two of his best, 'The Breaking Point', recorded for Twinight Records in 1967, and 'I Made A Mistake', recorded for Carl Davis's Bashie label in 1969, inexplicably never found an audience. In 1972, he finally reached the national charts with 'Slow Motion (Part 1)' (number 12 R&B, number 78 pop), which was recorded in Philadelphia for Gamble And Huff's Philadelphia International Records label. Unable to repeat this achievement, he went back to working the Chicago clubs. He had some local success with a single on the Babylon label, 'You're Something Kinda Mellow', in 1974. His death in December 1986 went unnoticed.

WILLIAMS, JOSEPH 'JO JO'

b. 1920, Coahoma, Mississippi, USA. One of a legion of musicians whose name and record follow one another with Pavlovian accuracy, Williams played in bands whose members sometimes worked with better-known artists. Raised in north-west Mississippi and on the outskirts of Memphis, his first steps in music were with baling wire strung on the wall. During the 30s he witnessed Son House and Willie Brown playing for country suppers. He developed his guitar-playing in Memphis in the early 40s before moving on to Chicago. In 1953 he played his first professional gig, with pianist William 'Lazy Bill' Lucas. Two years later, Williams formed his own group with Lucas, drummer Johnny Swanns and Lucas's niece, 'Miss Hi Fi', singing. He then teamed up with harmonica player Mojo Buford in a band with Dave Members and Cadillac Sam Burton. With Buford, he became a member of Muddy Waters' Junior Band, playing Smitty's Corner when Waters was out of town. In 1959, he made two records, the first unnumbered, for the Atomic-H label. 'All Pretty Wimmens' epitomizes raucous, impromptu blues at its best, all the better for being obscure, as was the follow-up, 'Afro Shake Dance'. In 1962, he moved, with Lucas and

Buford, to Minneapolis, playing bass in a group that recorded as Mojo & The Chi Fours, the material released on Folk Art and Vernon. Two years later, the band had two singles released on Adell. Williams recorded with Lazy Bill for Lucas's own label in 1970, and retired from music some time in the 70s.
● ALBUMS: *Lazy Bill And His Friends* (1970)★★★.

WILLIAMS, L.C.

b. 12 March 1930, Crockett, Texas, USA, d. 18 October 1960, Houston, Texas, USA. Another artist whose given names are initials, Williams grew up in Mullican, Texas, before moving to Houston around 1945. There he worked in dancehalls and bars as both singer and dancer. He also learned to play drums. Having made the acquaintance of Lightnin' Hopkins, he recorded for Bill Quinn's Gold Star label, nicknamed 'Lightnin' Jr.', with Hopkins backing him on guitar and piano on three singles, and pianists Leroy Carter and Elmore Nixon on one side each of a fourth, all subsequently reissued. He also recorded for Freedom, another Houston label owned by Solomon Kahal, making six records, one combining 'My Darkest Hour' and 'I Want My Baby Back' reissued on Imperial, mostly with Conrad Johnson's Conney's Combo. In 1951 he recorded at least four titles, including 'Baby Child' and 'Fannie Mae', for Sittin In With, owned by New Yorker Bob Shad. Shad probably produced Williams' final commercial session, made the same year for Mercury with backing by saxophonist Henry Hayes And His Rhythm Kings. Williams, addicted to cheap wine, also suffered from tuberculosis. Just prior to his death, he recorded one title with Hopkins and harmonica player Luke 'Long Gone' Miles. When asked the significance of his initials, Williams' reply was 'love crazy'. Ironic, then, that his death was from lung collapse.
● ALBUMS: *Texas Blues - The Gold Star Sessions* (1992)★★★, *The Big Three* (1992)★★★.

WILLIAMS, LEE 'SHOT'

b. Henry Lee Williams, 21 May 1938, Tchula, Mississippi, USA. For most of his career, Williams has been a journeyman singer on the chitlin circuit, eschewing identification with the blues scene until recently. He grew up with his cousins, Little Smokey Smothers and Otis 'Big Smokey' Smothers. When his mother died in the mid-50s, he was adopted by the family of singer Arlean Brown. After spending time in Detroit, he moved to Chicago in 1958 and worked in a bakery until the pressure of gigging every night led to a full-time singing career. He made his first single, 'Hello Baby', for Foxy in 1961. Two years later, he signed to Federal and released three singles, including 'You're Welcome To The Club', later covered by Little Milton. Other records emerged during the 60s, on labels such as Palos, Gamma, Shama and Sussex. During much of that time, he toured the south with Earl Hooker's band. In the 70s, he indulged a talent for cooking by opening Lee's Diner on Chicago's West Side. Early in the 80s, he moved to Memphis, where in 1991 he recorded *I Like Your Style* at Otis Clay's studio. The following year, *Shot Of Rhythm And Blues* was recorded for the Japanese Soul Trax label. In 1993, he sang on four tracks of Little Smokey Smothers' *Bossman*, which led to a contract with Black Magic and *Cold Shot*.

● ALBUMS: *I Like Your Style* (4 Way 1991)★★★, *Shot Of Rhythm And Blues* (Soul Trax 1992)★★★, *Cold Shot* (Black Magic 1995)★★★, *Hot Shot* (Ecko 1996)★★★.

WILLIAMS, LESTER

b. 24 June 1920, Groveton, Texas, USA, d. 13 November 1990, Houston, Texas, USA. Raised in Houston on the records of Blind Lemon Jefferson and Lonnie Johnson, Williams was inspired to take up the electric guitar after hearing fellow Texan 'T-Bone' Walker. His debut recording on the small local Macy's Records - 'Wintertime Blues' - was his biggest hit. His last records were made for Imperial Records in 1956, although he continued to perform locally, and was rediscovered in 1986 for a tour of Europe.

● ALBUMS: *Dowling Street Hop* (Krazy Kat 1982)★★★, *Texas Troubador* (Ace 1987)★★★, *I Can't Lose With The Stuff I Use* (1993)★★★.

WILLIAMS, LIL' ED

b. 18 April 1955, Chicago, Illinois, USA. Williams' first exposure to the blues was through the records of Elmore James and Muddy Waters, and his uncle J.B. Hutto taught him to play slide guitar when he was 13 years old. Williams also taught himself bass and drums. He played with Hutto, whose stinging playing is echoed in his own raunchy style, and also worked for tips in west side Chicago clubs with his half-brother James 'Pookie' Young. A three-hour session for Alligator Records in 1986 resulted in Williams' debut album and one track on the ground-breaking *New Bluesblood* compilation the following year. These recordings garnered international acclaim for Williams and his group the Blues Imperials, who have rapidly become a major attraction.

● ALBUMS: *Roughhousin'* (Alligator 1986)★★★, *Chicken, Gravy And Biscuits* (1989)★★★.

WILLIAMS, ROBERT PETE

b. 14 March 1914, Zachary, Louisiana, USA, d. 31 December 1980, Rosedale, Louisiana, USA. Although he had been playing and singing blues since he was a young man, Williams first came to wider notice when he was recorded in 1958 by folklorist Harry Oster. At the time, Williams was serving a sentence for murder at the penitentiary at Angola. His sombre vocals and gentle, understated guitar accompaniments were impressive in themselves, but more significant was his unique ability to sing long, partially extemporized songs, sometimes based around a traditional formula, sometimes remarkably original and intensely personal. This exposure led to his being taken up by a younger audience, and on his release from prison he made many appearances at concerts and festivals in the USA and overseas. He also made many more records, most of which testify to his great creative imagination and artistry.

● ALBUMS: *Angola Prisoners Blues* (1958)★★★, *Blues From Bottoms* (1973)★★★, *Those Prison Blues* (Arhoolie 1981)★★★, *Live* (Wolf 1988)★★★, *With Big Joe Williams* (Storyville 1988)★★★, *Robert Pete Williams And Roosevelt Sykes* (77 Records 1988)★★★.

● COMPILATIONS: *Legacy Of The Blues Volume Nine* (Sonet 1973)★★★, *Vol. 1 - I'm Blue As A Man Can Be* (Arhoolie 1994)★★★★, *Vol. 2 - When A Man Takes The Blues* (Arhoolie 1994)★★★★.

WILLIAMS, ROOSEVELT THOMAS

(see Grey Ghost)

WILLIAMSON, JOHN LEE 'SONNY BOY'

b. 30 March 1914, Jackson, Tennessee, USA, d. 1 June 1948, Chicago, Illinois, USA. Williamson learned harmonica as a child, and as a teenager in Tennessee was associated with the group of musicians around Sleepy John Estes. 'Sonny Boy' had been in Chicago for three years when he came to record in 1937, but his early records retained the plaintive sound, and often the songs, of Estes' circle. From the first, however, Williamson was an unmistakable musician, partly through his 'tongue-tied' singing style (probably a controlled version of his stammer), but chiefly for his harmonica playing. He worked almost invariably in 'cross-note' tuning, in which the key of the harmonica is a fourth above that of the music. This technique encourages drawn rather than blown notes, thus facilitating the vocalization, slurring and bent notes that are basic, in conjunction with intermittent hand muting and various tonguing and breath control effects, to most blues harmonica playing. In his time, Williamson was the greatest master of these techniques, and of blending voice and harmonica into a continuous melodic line; he reached a peak of technical and emotional perfection that sets the standard and defines the aesthetic for blues harmonica players to this day. Williamson recorded prolifically, as both leader and accompanist. His music developed continuously, and by the end of his life featured a powerful ensemble sound with amplified guitar. Williamson was equally adept at the expression of emotional intensity and the provision of rocking, exuberant dance music; in the musically rather bland years of the 40s, he preserved these qualities in the blues of Chicago, as if to prophesy the changes that were taking place by the time of his death. Universally liked, despite his enthusiasm for fighting when drunk, Williamson was greatly respected by his fellow musicians; he was enormously influential on more than one generation of harmonica players, from his contemporaries such as Walter Horton and Drifting Slim, to youngsters like Junior Wells and Billy Boy Arnold, and a remarkable proportion of his songs became blues standards. In Forrest City Joe, he acquired a devoted imitator, but perhaps the best indication of John Lee Williamson's importance, notwithstanding the monetary considerations that were doubtless his initial motivation, was the stubborn insistence of Sonny Boy 'Rice Miller' Williamson, a harmonica genius in his own right, that he was 'the original Sonny Boy Williamson'. On 1 June 1948, Williamson's life came to a tragic end following a serious assault.

● COMPILATIONS: with Big Bill Broonzy *Big Bill & Sonny Boy* (1964)★★★, *Blues Classics Volume 1* (Blues Classics 1965)★★★, *Blues Classics Volume 2* (Blues Classics 1968)★★★, *Blues Classics Volume 3* (Blues Classics 1972)★★★, *Bluebird, Number. 1* (1982)★★★, *Bluebird, Number. 15* (1985)★★★, *Sonny Boy Williamson* (1986)★★★, *Rare Sonny Boy* (RCA 1988)★★★, *Blues In The Mississippi Night* oral history (Rykodisc 1990)★★★★, *Sugar Mama: The Essential Recordings Of Sonny Boy Williamson* (Indigo 1995)★★★.

WILLIAMSON, SONNY BOY 'RICE MILLER'

b. Aleck/Alex Ford, 5 December 1899, Glendora, Mississippi, USA. d. 25 May 1965, Helena, Arkansas, USA. Being a man who would never compromise a good story by affording undue attention to veracity, and mischievous to boot, Sonny Boy's own various accounts of his life were never to be trusted and led to much confusion. Often referred to as 'Sonny Boy Williamson II' he was, in fact, older than John Lee 'Sonny Boy' Williamson, whose name, and associated glory, he appropriated some time in the late 30s or early 40s. Why he felt the need to do so is odd in light of the fact that he owed John Lee Williamson nothing in terms of style or ability, and alongside the latter and Little Walter Jacobs, was one of the most innovatory and influential exponents of the blues harmonica. He was the illegitimate child of Millie Ford, but he took to using his stepfather's name and by common association became 'Rice Miller'. He mastered his chosen instrument (he could also play guitar and drums) early in his life and seems to have taken to the road as soon as he was able, relying on his skill for a livelihood. His wanderings throughout the south brought him into contact with many blues artists. The list includes Robert Johnson, Robert Lockwood, Elmore James and Howlin' Wolf, whose half sister, Mary, he married in the 30s. During this period Williamson used many names, working as 'Little Boy Blue', Willie Williamson, Willie Williams and Willie Miller (after his brother) and known to his friends as 'Foots' because of his habit of razoring his shoes, no matter how new they might be, to make them comfortable. He was cashing in on the popularity of John Lee Williamson (safely out of the way in Chicago) when he secured a job broadcasting over KFFA radio out of Helena on the *King Biscuit Show* in 1941. The show was heard all over the south and made Williamson famous. He continued to travel but now sought radio stations to advertise his activities. In the early 50s he recorded for Lillian McMurray's Trumpet label in Jackson, Mississippi, along with friends Willie Love and Elmore James. His work on this label includes many outstanding performances, with 'Mighty Long Time' being perhaps the greatest of all. On the strength of his popularity he extended his area of work and began to appear in the bars of Detroit, where he worked with Baby Boy Warren, and in Chicago (John Lee Williamson was dead by this time). He began his career with Chess Records of Chicago in 1955 with his hit 'Don't Start Me Talkin'' and became a mainstay of the label almost until his death. In 1963, he took Europe by storm as a result of his appearances with the AFBF. His impressive appearance - tall and stooped in his famous grey/blue suit (quartered like a jester's doublet) and sporting a bowler hat and umbrella, along with his hooded eyes and goatee beard - hypnotized audiences as he weaved back and forth, snapping his fingers and clicking his tongue in a display of perfect rhythmic control. His skill on the harmonica was augmented by many tricks of showmanship such as playing two instruments at once (one with his large and plastic nose) or holding the harp end in his mouth and manoeuvring it with his tongue. He stayed in Europe after the tour had ended and played his way around the burgeoning blues clubs. He recorded for the Storyville label in Denmark and with Chris Barber in Britain, then returned to mainland Europe, often stating his intention to take up permanent residence. He never lived to see the days when Chess tried to convert their roster of blues singers into pop stars by uniting them with the most unlikely material and musical support, but in earlier days he had been quite happy to follow a similar route, by recording with such groups as the Yardbirds and the Animals, and a jazz band led by Brian Auger. Some of these efforts stand up better than others but Williamson did not care - as long as he was paid. Despite moving around extensively, he still maintained a home in the USA with his second wife Mattie Lee Gordon. He was back in Helena, appearing on the *King Biscuit Show* once more, when he died in his sleep in 1965. Apart from his skill as a harmonica player and singer Sonny Boy Williamson was also a 'character' and anecdotes about him are legendary, both among the blues fraternity and his fans in Europe. If he was difficult, contentious, and unreliable, he was also a charming man who played upon his reputation as an evil, dangerous, hard-living blues troubadour. His music reveals that he was also capable of being both sensitive and humorous. He will always remain something of a conundrum, but as an artist his stature is recognized and his fame deserved.

● ALBUMS: *Down And Out Blues* (Checker 1959)★★★★, *Portraits In Blues Vol. 4* (Storyville 1964)★★★★, *The Real Folk Blues* (Checker 1965)★★★★, *In Memoriam* (Chess 1965)★★★, *More Real Folk Blues* (Checker 1966)★★★, *Sonny Boy Williamson And The Yardbirds* (Mercury 1966)★★, *Bummer Road* (Chess 1969)★★★, *One Way Out* (MCA 1976)★★★, *The Animals With Sonny Boy Williamson* rec. 1963 (Charly 1982)★★★, *King Biscuit Time* (Arhoolie 1989)★★★, *Goin' In Your Direction* (Trumpet 1992)★★★, *The EP Collection* (See For Miles 1994)★★★★.

WILLIS, AARON 'LITTLE SONNY'
(see Little Sonny)

WILLIS, CHICK
b. Robert L. Willis, 24 September 1934, Atlanta, Georgia, USA. Willis's primary influence was Eddie 'Guitar Slim' Jones, whom he saw numerous times in Atlanta. As a guitarist he toured with many R&B acts in the 50s, including Nappy Brown, Ray Charles and Big Joe Turner, and for several years he was on tour with his cousin Chuck Willis. In the 60s he began fronting his own band. He had made his recording debut around 1956, but for many

years was confined to working for small singles companies. In 1972, he had a huge hit with the risqué 'Stoop Down Baby', achieved without any airplay, and he is still often billed as 'the Stoop Down Man'. He can still produce pure 50s style blues and R&B from time to time.

● ALBUMS: *Stoop Down Baby, Let Your Daddy See* (1972)★★★, *Chick Sings Chuck* (Ichiban 1987)★★★, *Now!* (Ichiban 1988)★★★, *Footprints In My Bed* (Ichiban 1990)★★★, *Back To The Blues* (Ichiban 1991)★★★.

WILLIS, CHUCK

b. 31 January 1928, Atlanta, Georgia, USA, d. 10 April 1958. R&B singer Willis made his recording debut in 1951. The following year he reached number 2 in the black music charts with 'My Story', the first of several hits the artist enjoyed while signed to the OKeh label. In 1956 he had his first hit for Atlantic Records when 'It's Too Late' reached the US R&B Top 3, and the following year he topped the same chart with 'C.C. Rider'. In April 1958, the singer succumbed to peritonitis, in the wake of which his posthumous single, 'What Am I Living For', sold in excess of one million copies. The ironically titled b-side, 'I'm Gonna Hang Up My Rock 'N' Roll Shoes', also reached the R&B Top 10, and despite his brief life and career, Willis remained an influential stylist in the development of R&B. He composed many of his best-known recordings, and cover versions by acts as disparate as Derek And The Dominos, the Animals, Buddy Holly, Jerry Lee Lewis, the Band, Ted Taylor and Otis Redding are a tribute to their longevity.

● ALBUMS: *Chuck Willis Wails The Blues* (Epic 1958)★★★, *The King Of The Stroll* (Atlantic 1958)★★★.

● COMPILATIONS: *Tribute To Chuck Willis* (Epic 1960)★★★, *I Remember Chuck Willis* (Atlantic 1963)★★★, *His Greatest Recordings* (Atlantic 1971)★★★, *My Story* (Official 1980)★★★, *Keep A Drivin'* (Charly 1984)★★★, *Be Good Or Be Gone* (Edsel 1986)★★★.

WILLIS, RALPH

b. 1910, Alabama, USA, d. 1957, New York City, New York, USA. Ralph Willis moved to North Carolina in the 30s, and met Blind Boy Fuller, Eugene 'Buddy' Moss and Brownie McGhee; he was closely associated with McGhee in New York after he relocated there in 1944, and his recordings often have McGhee on second guitar. They range from delicate guitar duets to driving dance music, although he could also be lazily wistful, as on his solo cover of Luke Jordan's 'Church Bells'. Despite his connection with McGhee and Sonny Terry, Willis did not capitalize on the burgeoning folk revival. He was known as 'Bama' for his rural ways; he perhaps lacked the drive or the self-confidence to achieve mainstream success.

● ALBUMS: *Faded Picture Blues* (1970)★★★, *Carolina Blues* (1974)★★★, *East Coast Blues* (1988)★★★.

WILSON, 'KID' WESLEY

b. 1 October 1893, Jacksonville, Florida, USA, d. 10 October 1958, Cape May Court House, New Jersey, USA. With his wife, Leola B. 'Coot' Grant, Wilson formed a long-established and very popular black vaudeville team, who were on stage from 1912 to the mid-30s. They recorded extensively, using a number of pseudonyms, and featuring comic dialogues of marital strife in the manner of Butterbeans And Susie. Both also recorded solo, and Wilson duetted with Harry McDaniels (as Pigmeat Pete & Catjuice Charlie). As important as their performing was their songwriting, which produced over 400 numbers, including 'Gimme A Pigfoot', and the other three songs recorded at Bessie Smith's last session. They reappeared briefly in the late 40s, recording and writing for Mezz Mezzrow's King Jazz label and playing a few concerts, but had retired by the decade's end.

● ALBUMS: including *Great Blues Singers Vol. 1* (1970), *Leola B. Wilson & 'Kid' Wesley Wilson* (Document 1989)★★★.

WILSON, EDITH

b. 6 September 1896, Louisville, Kentucky, USA, d. March 1981. Wilson was a blues-singing stage star whose career credits include a long list of revues beginning with *Put And Take* in 1921. In the same year she made her first records in with Johnny Dunn And His Original Jazz Hounds. She continued to work after the initial interest in the so-called classic blues had declined, appearing on stage and films, both as a singer and as an actress. She later appeared advertising cookies in the assumed role of 'Aunt Jemima'.

She never really retired and took advantage of the increased interest in blues during the 60s to embark on a second career that saw her recording an album for the Delmark label in 1970 and performing at the Newport Jazz Festival in 1980. As a blues singer, what she lacked of the rawness and power associated with performers such as Bessie Smith and Ma Rainey, she made up for in urbanity and wit.

● COMPILATIONS: *Edith Wilson With Johnny Dunn's Jazz Hounds* (Fountain 1979)★★★.

WILSON, HARDING 'HOP'

b. 27 April 1921, Grapeland, Texas, USA, d. 27 August 1975, Houston, Texas, USA. Although his nickname is a corruption of 'Harp', reflecting his early prowess on the harmonica, it is as a slide guitarist that Wilson will be remembered. As well as playing conventional guitar, he played steel guitar placed horizontally on a stand, a style usually associated with C&W musicians. He played and sang with great skill and expression, encompassing a range of rhythms and moods from rocking R&B to tormented slow blues. Working in east Texas and Louisiana, he made singles for the Goldband company in 1958, and the small Ivory label (owned by drummer 'Ivory' Lee Semien) in 1960 and 1961. These, plus a handful of tracks unissued at the time but released on an album after his death, account for his entire recorded legacy; however, they are sufficient to establish Wilson as one of the most original blues artists of his time.

● ALBUMS: *Steel Guitar Flash* (Ace 1988)★★★, *Houston Ghetto Blues* (Bullseye 1995)★★★★.

WILSON, JIMMY

b. 1921, Louisiana, USA, d. 1965, Dallas, Texas, USA. Wilson was singing in California with a gospel quartet when his distinctive, bluesy lead was noticed by impresario Bob Geddins, who recorded Wilson as the blues singer with his band, Bob Geddins' Cavaliers, and in his own right, for his Cava Tone label, often in the company of legendary Bay Area guitarist Lafayette Thomas. Some of these tracks created enough of a stir for Aladdin Records to take an interest and purchase some of Wilson's masters from Geddins, and later during 1952, Wilson began recording for Aladdin and its small subsidiary 7-

11. In 1953 Wilson again signed with Geddins to record for his new Big Town label, and the first release, 'Tin Pan Alley', although not a Wilson original, was a tremendous success and has since become synonymous with his name. Most of Wilson's mid-50s output was issued on Big Town, although occasional releases appeared on Irma and Elko (the latter under guitarist Jimmy Nolan's name), and four tracks were issued on the Chart label. Later recordings did not match up to the doomy Bay Area sound of his Geddins tracks, despite a couple of attempts at the 'Tin Pan Alley' sound and a good local seller, 'Please Accept My Love' on Goldband, which was covered successfully by B.B. King. Wilson died in 1965 of drink-related problems, virtually forgotten by the record-buying public.

● COMPILATIONS: *Trouble In My House* (Diving Duck 1985)★★, *Jimmy Wilson - San Francisco 1952-53* (1985)★★★.

WILSON, KIM

b. 6 January 1951, Detroit, Michigan, USA. Kim Wilson is a member of the blues band the Fabulous Thunderbirds. *Tigerman*, his first solo album, predominantly consisted of cover versions, performed by various combinations of ex- and current Thunderbirds, including Duke Robillard, Preston Hubbard, Fran Christina, Gene Taylor and Rusty Zinn, and also Derek O'Brien, Calvin Jones and George Rains. For much of the time, Wilson forsook his harmonica and chose to interpret songs by Johnny 'Guitar' Watson, T-Bone Walker and Bobby Bland. *That's Life* was a similarly disparate collection, containing tracks left over from the original sessions and newer recordings, including soul songs, 'Time Is On My Side' and 'I've Been Searchin''. During this time, the Thunderbirds remained without a recording contract, leaving a question mark over Wilson's future as a solo artist or a bandleader. Admirably equipped for either eventuality, the challenge for Wilson to reclaim old ground remained to be met.

● ALBUMS: *Tigerman* (Antone's 1993)★★★, *That's Life* (Antone's 1994)★★★.

WILSON, SMOKEY

b. Robert Lee Wilson, 11 July 1936, Greenville, Mississippi, USA. Wilson was eight when his father bought him his first guitar. His teenage years were spent developing his singing and playing skills. In 1961 he became a member of Junior Green And His Soul Searchers Band, which, after some years, he left to join Roosevelt 'Booba' Barnes, with whom he played for four years. In 1970, he moved to Los Angeles, hoping that his down-home style would be popular. He played in a number of clubs and became part-owner of the Casino Club, where he worked on a regular basis. In 1972, he sold his interest in the club and bought the Pioneer Club in south central Los Angeles. Artists such as Percy Mayfield, George Smith, Lowell Fulson and Big Mama Thornton played alongside Wilson. His first two albums featured an uncredited Rod Piazza on harmonica alongside a flashy rock guitarist, and inappropriate accompaniment marred the 1982 Murray Brothers outing. He fared better four years later, when he was accompanied by harmonica player William Clarke's band. Smoke N' Fire had guest appearances by Larry Davis and Jimmy McCracklin, effectively flattering Wilson's modest talent.

● ALBUMS: Blowin' Smoke (Big Town 1977)★★, Smokey Wilson Sings The Blues (Big Town 1978)★★★, 88th Street Blues (Murray Bros 1982)★★, Smokey Wilson & The William Clarke Band (Black Magic 1990)★★★, Smoke N' Fire (Bullseye Blues 1993)★★, 88th Street Blues (Blind Pig 1995)★★, The Real Deal (Bullseye Blues 1995)★★, The Man From Mars (Bullseye 1997)★★.

● COMPILATIONS: Hard Times - L.A. Blues Anthology (Black Magic 1991)★★★.

WILSON, U.P.

b. Huary Wilson, 4 September 1935, Shreveport, Louisiana, USA. Wilson learned to play on his grandmother's guitar, and after moving to Dallas, Texas, in the early 50s, he became acquainted with local bluesmen Mercy Baby, Zuzu Bollin and Frankie Lee Sims. Around 1954 he recorded behind Bollin, though the tracks remain unissued. In the late 50s Wilson played on a regular basis with Robert Ealey. During the 70s and early 80s he only occasionally played professionally, due to family commitments. In 1988 he recorded a session for Pee Wee Records, who released one single, 'Red Lightnin''. They later released a full album, On My Way. Blues And Rhythm magazine called Wilson's music

'superb Texas blues from one of the discoveries of the 80s'. Blueprint magazine disagreed when it reviewed his 1996 album: '(he) affects a curiously expressionless falsetto throughout, sounding like nothing so much as Skip James on Mogadon'.

● ALBUMS: On My Way (Pee Wee 1988)★★★★, Wild Texas Guitar (1989)★★★, Attack Of The Atomic Guitar (1992)★★★, Texas Blues Party Vol. 1: The Texas Tornado Live At Schooner's (Wolf 1995)★★★, Boogie Boy, The Texas Guitar Tornado Returns (JSP 1995)★★★, This Is U.P. Wilson (JSP 1996)★★★, Whirlwind (JSP 1997)★★★.

WINTER, EDGAR

b. 28 December 1946, Beaumont, Texas, USA. Although at times overshadowed by his brother, Johnny Winter, Edgar has enjoyed an intermittently successful career. The siblings began performing together as teenagers, and were members of several itinerant groups performing in southern-state clubs and bars. Edgar later forsook music for college, before accepting an offer to play saxophone in a local jazz band. He rejoined his brother in 1969, but the following year Edgar released Entrance. He then formed an R&B revue, Edgar Winter's White Trash, whose live set Roadwork was an exciting testament to this talented ensemble. Winter then fronted a slimmer group - Dan Hartman (vocals), Ronnie Montrose (guitar) and Chuck Ruff (drums) - which appeared on the artist's only million-selling album, They Only Come Out At Night. This highly successful selection included the rousing instrumental 'Frankenstein', which became a hit single in its own right. Guitarist Rick Derringer, who had produced Winter's previous two albums, replaced Montrose for Shock Treatment, but this and subsequent releases failed to maintain the singer's commercial ascendancy. He rejoined his brother in 1976 for Togethe, since which time Edgar Winter's professional profile has been considerably lean. Together with his brother Johnny, he sued DC Comics for depicting the brothers in a comic book as half-human, half-worm characters. The figures were illustrated by the creator of Jonah Hex; the Winter brothers were shown as 'Johnny And Edgar Autumn'.

● ALBUMS: Entrance (Epic 1970)★★, Edgar

Winter's White Trash (Epic 1971)★★★, *Roadwork* (Epic 1972)★★★★, *They Only Come Out At Night* (Epic 1972)★★★★, *Shock Treatment* (Epic 1974)★★★, *Jasmine Nightdreams* (Blue Sky 1975)★★★, *Edgar Winter Group With Rick Derringer* (Blue Sky 1975)★★★, with Johnny Winter *Together* (Blue Sky 1976)★★★★, *Recycled* (Blue Sky 1977)★★★, *The Edgar Winter Album* (Blue Sky 1979)★★, *Standing On The Rock* (1981)★★, with Rick Derringer *Live In Japan* (Thunderbolt 1992)★★★, *Mission Earth* (1993)★★, *I'm Not A Kid Anymore* (L + R 1994)★★★.
● COMPILATIONS: *Rock Giants* (1982)★★★.
● VIDEOS: *Live In Japan* (MMG Video 1992).

WINTER, JOHNNY

b. 23 February 1944, Leland, Mississippi, USA. Raised in Beaumont, Texas, with younger brother Edgar Winter, Johnny was a child prodigy prior to forging a career as a blues guitarist. He made his recording debut in 1960, fronting Johnny and the Jammers, and over the next eight years completed scores of masters, many of which remained unreleased until his success prompted their rediscovery. By 1968 the guitarist was leading Tommy Shannon (bass) and John Turner (drums) in a trio entitled Winter. The group recorded a single for the Austin-based Sonobeat label, consigning extra tracks from the same session to a demonstration disc. This was subsequently issued by United Artists as *The Progressive Blues Experiment*. An article in *Rolling Stone* magazine heaped effusive praise on the guitarist's talent and led to lucrative recording and management contracts. *Johnny Winter* ably demonstrated his exceptional dexterity, while *Second Winter*, which included rousing versions of 'Johnny B. Goode' and 'Highway 61 Revisited', suggested a new-found emphasis on rock. This direction was confirmed in 1970 when Winter was joined by the McCoys, a group struggling to shed their teeny-bop image. Billed as Johnny Winter And - with guitarist Rick Derringer acting as a foil - the new line-up proclaimed itself with a self-titled studio collection and a fiery live set. These excellent releases brought Winter much-deserved commercial success. Chronic heroin addiction forced him into partial retirement and it was two years before he re-emerged with *Still Alive And Well*. Subsequent work was bedevilled by indecision until the artist returned to his roots with *Nothing But The Blues* and *White Hot And Blue*. At the same time Winter assisted Muddy Waters by producing and arranging a series of acclaimed albums that recaptured the spirit of the veteran blues artist's classic recordings. Winter's recent work has proved equally vibrant and three releases for Alligator, a Chicago-based independent label, included the rousing *Guitar Slinger*, which displayed all the passion apparent on those early, seminal recordings. His career may have failed to match initial, extravagant expectations, but his contribution to the blues should not be underestimated; he remains an exceptional talent. Together with his brother Edgar, he sued DC Comics for depicting the brothers in a comic book as half-human, half-worm characters. The figures were illustrated by the creator of Jonah Hex; the Winter brothers were shown as 'Johnny And Edgar Autumn'.
● ALBUMS: *Johnny Winter* (Columbia 1969)★★★★, *The Progressive Blues Experiment* (Sonobeat/Imperial 1969)★★, *Second Winter* (Columbia 1969)★★★, *Johnny Winter And* (Columbia 1970)★★★★, *Johnny Winter And Live* (Columbia 1971)★★★, *Still Alive And Well* (Columbia 1973)★★★, *Saints And Sinners* (Columbia 1974)★★★, *John Dawson Winter III* (Blue Sky 1974)★★★, *Captured Live!* (Blue Sky 1976)★★★, with Edgar Winter *Together* (Blue Sky 1976)★★★★, *Nothin' But The Blues* (Blue Sky 1977)★★★, *White Hot And Blue* (Blue Sky 1978)★★, *Raisin' Cain* (Blue Sky 1980)★★, *Raised On Rock* (Blue Sky 1981)★★, *Guitar Slinger* (Alligator 1984)★★★, *Serious Business* (Alligator 1985)★★★, *Third Degree* (Alligator 1986)★★★, *Winter Of '88* (MCA 1988)★★, *Let Me In* (Virgin/PointBlank 1991)★★★, *Jack Daniels Kind Of Day* (1992)★★★, *Hey, Where's Your Brother?* (Virgin/PointBlank 1992)★★★, with Jimmy Reed *Live At Liberty Hall, Houston* (1993)★★★.
● COMPILATIONS: *The Johnny Winter Story* (GRT 1969)★★★, *First Winter* (1970)★★★, *Early Times* (1971)★★, *About Blues* (1972)★★, *Before The Storm* (Janus 1972)★★★, *Austin Texas* (United Artists 1972)★★★, *The Johnny Winter Story* (1980)★★★, *The Johnny Winter Collection* (Castle 1986)★★★★, *Birds Can't Row Boats* (1988)★★★, *Scorchin' Blues* (Epic/Legacy

1992)★★★, *A Rock N'Roll Collection* (Columbia/Legacy 1994)★★★.
● VIDEOS: *Johnny Winter Live* (Channel 5 1989).

WITHERSPOON, JIMMY

b. 8 August 1923, Gurdon, Arkansas, USA, d. 18 September 1997. Witherspoon crossed over into rock, jazz and R&B territory, but his deep and mellow voice placed him ultimately as a fine blues singer. He sang in his local Baptist church from the age of seven. From 1941-43 he was in the Merchant Marines and, during stopovers in Calcutta, he found himself singing the blues with a band led by Teddy Weatherford. In 1944, he replaced Walter Brown in the Jay McShann band at Vallejo, California, and toured with it for the next four years. In 1949 he had his first hit, 'Tain't Nobody's Business If I Do', which stayed on the *Billboard* chart for 34 weeks. Other recordings at the time with bands led by Jimmy 'Maxwell Street' Davis are fine examples of rollicking west coast R&B (collected as *Who's Been Jivin' You*). Witherspoon's popularity as an R&B singer faded during the course of the 50s, but he made a great impression on jazz listeners at the Monterey Jazz Festival in October 1959, performing with a group that included Ben Webster. Other collaborations with jazz artists included *Some Of My Best Friends Are The Blues*, with horns and strings arranged and conducted by Benny Golson, and a guest performance on Jon Hendricks' *Evolution Of The Blues Song*. He won the *Downbeat* critics' poll as a 'new star' in 1961. Frequent tours of Europe followed, beginning in 1961 with a Buck Clayton group and later with Coleman Hawkins, Roy Eldridge, Earl Hines and Woody Herman. He also did community work, including singing in prisons.

In the early 70s he gave up touring for a sedentary job as a blues disc jockey on the radio station KMET in Los Angeles, but resumed active music thanks to the encouragement of Eric Burdon. During his touring with Burdon he introduced a young Robben Ford as his guitarist and toured Japan and the Far East. In 1974 his 'Love Is A Five Letter Word' was a hit, though some fans regretted his neglect of the blues. A record with the Savoy Sultans in 1980 was a spirited attempt to recall a bygone era. *The Blues, The Whole Blues And Nothin' But The Blues* was

the first album release for Mike Vernon's new label Indigo. Witherspoon has been revered by generations during different eras, and his name often cited as a major influence during the 60s beat boom; his work is destined to endure.
● ALBUMS: *New Orleans Blues* (1956)★★★, *Goin' To Kansas City Blues* (RCA Victor 1957)★★★★, with Eddie Vinson *Battle Of The Blues, Volume 3* (1959)★★★, *At The Monterey Jazz Festival* (Hifi 1959)★★★★, with Gerry Mulligan *Mulligan With Witherspoon* (1959)★★★, *Jimmy Witherspoon* (Crown 1959)★★★, *Feelin' The Spirit* (1959)★★★★, *Jimmy Witherspoon At The Renaissance* (Hifi 1959)★★★, *Singin' The Blues* (World Pacific 1959)★★★, *Sings The Blues* (Crown 1960)★★★, *There's Good Rockin' Tonight* (World Pacific 1961)★★★★, *Spoon* (Reprise 1961)★★★, *Hey, Mrs. Jones* (Reprise 1962)★★★, *Roots* (Reprise 1962)★★★, *Baby, Baby, Baby* (Prestige 1963)★★★, *Evenin' Blues* (Prestige 1964)★★★, *Goin' To Chicago Blues* (Prestige 1964)★★★, *Blues Around The Clock* (1964)★★★, *Blue Spoon* (Prestige 1964)★★★, *Some Of My Best Friends Are The Blues* (Prestige 1964)★★★, *Take This Hammer* (Constellation 1964)★★★, *Blues For Spoon And Groove* (Surrey 1965)★★★, *Spoon In London* (Prestige 1965)★★★, *Blues Point Of View* (Verve 1967)★★★, with Jack McDuff *The Blues Is Now* (Verve 1967)★★★, *Blues For Easy Livers* (Prestige 1967)★★★, *Ain't Nobody's Business* (1967)★★★, *A Spoonful Of Soul* (Verve 1968)★★★, *The Blues Singer* (Stateside 1969)★★★, *Back Door Blues* (Polydor 1969)★★★, *Hunh!* (1970)★★★, *Handbags & Gladrags* (Probe 1970)★★★, *Blues Singer* (Stateside 1970)★★★, with Eric Burdon *Guilty* (MGM 1971)★★★, *Love Is A Five Letter Word* (1975)★★★, *Jimmy Witherspoon And Ben Webster (That's Jazz)* (1977)★★★, with New Savoy Sultans *Sings The Blues* (Muse 1980)★★★, with Buck Clayton *Live In Paris, Big Blues* (Vogue 1981)★★★, *Call My Baby* (1991)★★★, *The Blues, The Whole Blues And Nothin' But The Blues* (Indigo 1992)★★★, with Robben Ford *Live At The Notodden Blues Festival* (1993)★★★★, *Spoon's Blues* (Stony Plain 1995)★★★, with Howard Scott *American Blues* (Avenue/Rhino 1995)★★★, with Robben Ford *Ain't Nothin' New But The Blues* 1977 recording (AIM 1996)★★★★, with Robben Ford *Live At*

The Mint (On The Spot 1996)★★★, *Spoonful* (ARG Jazz 1997)★★★.
● COMPILATIONS: *The Best Of Jimmy Witherspoon* (Prestige 1969)★★★★, *Never Knew This Kind Of Hurt Before: The Bluesway Sessions* rec. 1969-71 (Charly 1988)★★★, *Meets The Jazz Giants* rec. 1959 (1989)★★★, *Blowin' In From Kansas* (Ace 1991)★★★★, *Jimmy Witherspoon & Jay McShann* rec. 40s (1992)★★★.

WOODFORK, 'POOR' BOB

b. 13 March 1925, Lake Village, Arkansas, USA, d. June 1988, Chicago, Illinois, USA. Woodfork learned guitar as a youngster, but his musical career began in the US Army during World War II, when the USO spotted him in Swansea, Wales. Back in Chicago, he worked as a sideman for Otis Rush, and later for Jimmy Rogers, Howlin' Wolf, George Smith and Little Walter. Some mid-60s recordings under his own name were released on albums for the new European blues audience, but did not advance his career. Woodfork continued to work as a sideman and occasional leader in the Chicago clubs.
● ALBUMS: including *Blues Southside Chicago* (1966)★★★, *Have A Good Time* (1971)★★★.

WOODS, JOHNNY

b. 1 November 1917, Looxahoma, Mississippi, USA, d. 1 February 1990, Olive Branch, Mississippi, USA. Like his sometime partner, Mississippi Fred McDowell, Woods was not discovered until he was in his fifties and it was through McDowell that he had his first chance to record, although they had not seen one another for eight years at that time. A self-taught harmonica-player, he developed his technique, which relied upon rhythmic figures, by adapting the work hollers he heard in the fields in which his family worked. Because of that, Woods was at his best when performing solo on 'So Many Cold Mornings' and 'Going Up The Country', or playing a one-chord traditional Mississippi piece such as 'Long-Haired Doney' (also known as 'My Jack Don't Need No Water'), which he recorded with both McDowell and R.L. Burnside.
● ALBUMS: *Mississippi Delta Blues Vol. 1* (Arhoolie 1967/1994)★★★, *So Many Cold Mornings* rec. 1981 and 1984 (Swingmaster 1988)★★★, *The Blues Of Johnny Woods* (Swingmaster 1989)★★★.

WOODS, OSCAR

b. 1900, Shreveport, Louisiana, USA, d. c.1956, Shreveport, Louisiana, USA. Little is known about Oscar 'Buddy' Woods, who was one of the most impressive of the pre-war slide guitar blues stylists. He was closely associated with Ed Schaffer with whom he recorded as the Shreveport Home Wreckers in Memphis in 1930. In 1932, he and Schaffer took part in what was probably one of the first integrated sessions when they lent their vocal and instrumental talents to support risqué country singer Jimmie Davis, later governor of Louisiana and famous for 'You Are My Sunshine'. Woods recorded some master sole tracks in 1936, in New Orleans, under the pseudonym of the Lone Wolf and later featured with Kitty Gray and others as the Wampus Cats. Finally, in 1940, he recorded five tracks for Alan Lomax of the Library Of Congress. He also worked with B.K. Turner, 'The Black Ace', and was last heard of working in the Shreveport area around the late 40s/early 50s.
● COMPILATIONS: *Complete Recordings: Oscar 'Buddy' Woods 1930-1938* (Document 1987)★★★.

WRENCHER, BIG JOHN

b. 12 February 1924, near Sunflower, Mississippi, USA, d. 15 July 1977, Clarksdale, Mississippi, USA. A self-taught harmonica player and singer, Wrencher recalled seeing many leading bluesman during his teens. He left Mississippi in 1947, though he returned frequently and on one trip was involved in a car crash that resulted in the loss of his left arm. He lived in Detroit, Michigan, and St. Louis, Missouri, before settling in Chicago during 1962, where he often worked for gratuities on Maxwell Street. He recorded for the Testament, Ja-Wes and Barrelhouse labels in the 60s and toured Europe in the early 70s, establishing a loyal following for his excellent harmonica playing and mellow vocals; he also recorded for Big Bear Records.
● ALBUMS: *Big John's Boogie* (Big Bear 1974)★★★, *Maxwell St. Alley Blues* (1978)★★★.

WYNN, 'BIG' JIM

b. 21 June 1912, El Paso, Texas, USA, d. 1976, Los Angeles, California, USA. After moving to Los Angeles as a child, Wynn began his musical tuition on clarinet before switching to tenor sax and playing professionally with the band of Charlie Echols. In 1936, Wynn had his own band and began to link up with the young 'T-Bone' Walker; this association would last until the end of the famous blues musician's life, with the Wynn band regularly touring and recording with him. The Wynn band's own recording career lasted through R&B's golden years, when records were released on 4 Star/Gilt Edge (1945 - including his biggest hit 'Ee-Bobaliba', which was lucratively covered in various disguises by the likes of Helen Humes and Lionel Hampton), Modern (1946), Specialty and Supreme (1948), Mercury and Recorded In Hollywood (1951) and Million (1954). By the late 40s, Wynn increasingly eschewed his tenor in place of a beefy baritone saxophone, and its deep honking, coupled with his own histrionic stage act, was the role model for the next generation of west coast R&B saxophonists. A respected session musician from the late 50s into the 70s, Wynn often played with the bands of his good friends 'T-Bone' Walker and Johnny Otis.

● COMPILATIONS: *Blow Wynn Blow* (Whiskey 1985)★★★.

YANCEY, MAMA

b. Estella Harris, 1 January 1896, Cairo, Illinois, USA, d. 19 April 1986, Chicago, Illinois, USA. Raised in Chicago, the young Estella took an early interest in music by singing in church and learning to play the guitar. She married pianist Jimmy Yancey in 1919 and over the next two decades frequently sang with him at informal parties. Yancey first recorded with her husband for Session in December 1943; 'Make Me A Pallet On The Floor' became her virtual signature tune thereafter. They recorded a long session for Atlantic Records in July 1951, just two months before Jimmy Yancey's death. Mama Yancey more or less retired from music after that but was persuaded to make the occasional appearance and recording session. *South Side Blues* and, to a lesser extent, *Mama Yancey Sings*, were the last occasions when her bellowing church-based singing style was heard at its best. Her last album, *Maybe I'll Cry*, was recorded when she was 87 years old, three years before her death.

● ALBUMS: with Little Brother Montgomery *South Side Blues* (Riverside 1961)★★★, *Mama Yancey Sings, Art Hodes Plays Blues* (Verve-Folkways 1965)★★★, with Jimmy Yancey *Chicago Piano Vol. 1* (Atlantic 1972)★★★, *Maybe I'll Cry* (Red Beans 1983)★★★.

YOUNG, 'MIGHTY' JOE

b. 23 September 1927, Shreveport, Louisiana, USA. Blues guitarist 'Mighty' Joe Young grew up in the northern state of Wisconsin but later relocated to Louisiana before settling in Chicago in the 50s. There he briefly joined a group called Joe Little And His Heart Breakers before joining harmonica player Billy Boy Arnold in his band. He next went to guitarist Jimmy Rogers' blues band in 1959, meanwhile recording several unsuccessful singles on his own. Young played with guitarist Otis Rush from 1960-63, still recording solo with no luck. He built a reputation as a session guitarist in the 60s, recording with artists such as Magic Sam, Willie Dixon and Tyrone Davis. Young recorded several albums in the early 70s and became a popular blues nightclub act in Chicago. Since 1976 he has been absent from the recording scene.

● ALBUMS: *Blues With A Touch Of Soul* (Delmark 1970)★★★, *Chicken Heads* (Ovation 1974)★★, *Mighty Joe Young* (Ovation 1976)★★, *Live At The Wise Fools Pub* (1990)★★★.

● COMPILATIONS: *Legacy Of The Blues Volume Four* (Sonet 1972)★★★.

YOUNG, ERNIE

Based in Nashville, USA, Young was a jukebox operator, record retailer and disc jockey. A move into production was therefore logical, given his access to retail outlets. Nashboro was founded in

1951 to record gospel, and Excello in 1952. Using the band led by Skippy Brooks for backing, Excello recorded many local blues artists, while Nashboro acquired a distinguished roster, including Edna Gallmon Cooke, Morgan Babb, the Consolers and the Swanee Quintet. Although there was occasional national chart success, Excello's predominant market was in the south. In 1955, Young finalized an agreement with Jay Miller whereby Miller recorded blues in his Crowley studio for Excello. A steady stream of classics was released, Excello's greatest chart success being Slim Harpo. In 1966, due to his age and ill health, Young sold the label and retired.

YOUNG, JOHNNY

b. 1 January 1918, Vicksburg, Mississippi, USA, d. 18 April 1974, Chicago, Illinois, USA. Although he was a more than competent guitarist, Young regarded mandolin as his main instrument. He learned both instruments, as well as harmonica, from uncle Anthony Williams, while living with him in Rolling Fork, birthplace of Muddy Waters. When he returned to Vicksburg, he played house parties with cousin Henry Williams, influenced by the records of Charlie McCoy and the Mississippi Sheiks. He also claimed to have worked with Robert Nighthawk and Sleepy John Estes before moving to Chicago in 1940. He joined the musicians who frequented the Maxwell Street market area, with Floyd Jones, Snooky Pryor and another cousin, Johnny Williams. In 1947 he made his first record, 'Money Takin' Woman', with Williams, for Ora Nelle, run by Maxwell Radio Shop owner Bernard Abrams. A year later, with Williams and Pryor, he recorded 'My Baby Walked Out' and 'Let Me Ride Your Mule' for Planet, as Man Young. Apart from two unissued songs for JOB, Young did not record again until the 60s, when he taped a number of sessions for Testament, Arhoolie, Vanguard, Milestone, Blues On Blues, Bluesway and Blue Horizon, in the company of artists such as Otis Spann, Walter Horton, Little Walter and James Cotton. From 1969 until his death, he was a member of the Bob Riedy Chicago Blues Band. In 1972 he toured Europe as a part of the American Folk Blues Festival.
● ALBUMS: *Johnny Young & His Chicago Blues Band* (Arhoolie 1965)★★★, *Fat Mandolin* (1969)★★★, *Chicago Boogie!* (1974)★★★, *Chicago Blues* (1993)★★★, *Johnny Young And Friends* (Testament 1994)★★★.

YOUNG, ZORA

b. 21 January 1948, Prairie, Mississippi, USA. A third cousin of Howlin' Wolf, Young has sufficient talent not to have to dwell on the fact. Singing in church from an early age helped her to develop both flexibility and control in her vocal technique. That continued after her family moved to Chicago in 1956, although she did not take up blues singing until 1971. During the 80s, she toured Europe on numerous occasions, while at home she played Bessie Smith in the stage show *The Heart Of The Blues*, alongside Valerie Wellington. In 1988, Young financed the recording of her first album, released on her own Black Lightning label. Three years later, she re-recorded its title track as part of *Travelin' Light*, an album of largely original material on which she was backed by members of the Legendary Blues Band.
● ALBUMS: *Stumbling Blocks & Stepping Stones* (Black Lightning 1988)★★★, *Travelin' Light* (Deluge 1992)★★★.
● COMPILATIONS: *Chicago Blues Ladies* (Wolf 1990)★★★.

BIBLIOGRAPHY

Allen, William Francis, Ware, Charles Pickard, and Garrison, *Slave Songs Of The United States*, New York, 1951.

Arnaudon, J.C., *Dictionnaire Du Blues*, Paris, 1977.

Baker, Houston A., *Blues: Ideology And Afro-American Literature*, University Of Chicago Press (USA), 1987.

Balliett, Whitney, *Dinosaurs In The Morning*, J.B. Lippincot, 1962.

Bane, Michael, *White Boy Singin' The Blues: The Black Roots Of White Rock*, Penguin (USA), 1982.

Barlow, William, *Looking Up At Down: The Emergence Of Blues Culture*, Temple University Press, Philadelphia, 1989.

Bastin, Bruce, *Crying For The Carolines*, Studio Vista (UK), 1971.

Bastin, Bruce, *Red River Blues: The Blues Tradition In The South East*, University Of Illinois Press (USA), 1986.

Bourgeois, Anna Stong, *Blues Women*, McFarland & Co. (USA), 1996.

Bradford, Perry, *Born With The Blues*, Oak Publications (USA), 1965.

Broven, John, *Rhythm And Blues In New Orleans*, Spa Books (UK), 1992.

Broven, John, *Walking To New Orleans*, Blues Unlimited, 1974.

Brunning, Bob, *Blues: The British Connection*, Blandford Press (UK), 1986.

Burley, Dan, *Dan Burley's Original Handbook Of Harlem Jive*, New York, 1944.

Campbell, James, *The Picador Book Of Blues And Jazz*, Picador (UK), 1995.

Carruth, Hayden, *Sitting In: Selected Writings On Jazz, Blues, And Related Topics*, University Of Iowa Press, 1994.

Charters, Samuel B., *Sweet As The Showers Of Rain: The Bluesmen Vol. 11*, Oak Publications (USA), 1977.

Charters, Samuel B., *The Blues Makers*, Da Capo (USA), 1991.

Charters, Samuel B., *The Bluesmen*, Oak Publications (USA), 1967.

Charters, Samuel B., *The Country Blues*, Da Capo (USA), 1977.

Charters, Samuel B., *The Legacy Of The Blues: Art And Lives Of 12 Great Bluesmen*, Da Capo (USA), 1977.

Charters, Samuel B., *The Poetry Of The Blues*, Oak Publications (USA), 1963.

Charters, Samuel B., *The Roots Of The Blues: An African Search*, Da Capo (USA), 1981.

Cohn, Lawrence (ed.), *Nothing But The Blues: The Music And Musicians*, Abbeville Press, 1993.

Cone, James H., *The Spirituals And The Blues*, Seabury Press, 1972.

Cook, Bruce, *Listen To The Blues*, Da Capo (USA), 1995.

Courlander, H., *Negro Folk Music, USA*, New York and London, 1963.

Courlander, H., *Negro Songs From Alabama*, New York, 1963.

Cowley, John, and Oliver, Paul (ed.), *The New Blackwell Guide To Recorded Blues*, Blackwell (UK), 1996.

Davis, Francis, *The History Of The Blues: The Roots, The Music, The People*, Hyperion (USA), 1995.

Davis, Stephen, *The History Of The Blues*, Secker (UK), 1995.

Deffaa, Chip, *Blue Rhythms: Six Lives In Rhythm And Blues*, University Of Illinois Press (USA), 1996.

Demetre, Jacques, and Chauvard, Marcel, *Voyage Au Pays Du Blues 1959*, Levallois-Perret: Editions Clarb (France), 1994.

Dennison, S., *Scandalize My Name: Black Imagery In American Popular Music*, New York, 1981.

Dixon, R.M.W., and Godrich, John, *Recording

The Blues, Studio Vista (UK), 1970.

Driggs, F., and Shirley, K., *The Book Of The Blues*, New York, 1963.

Dunbar, Tony, *Delta Time: A Journey Through Mississippi*, Pantheon (USA).

Evans, David, *Big Road Blues: Traditions And Creativity In The Folk Blues*, Berkeley Books (USA), 1982.

Fancourt, Leslie, *Blue Horizon Records 1965-1972*, Retrack Books (UK), 1992.

Fancourt, Leslie, *British Blues On Record*, Leslie Fancourt (UK), 1989.

Feather, Leonard, *The History Of Blues*, Charles Hansen Music & Books, 1972.

Ferris Jnr., William, *Blues From The Delta*, Studio Vista (UK), 1970.

Garon, Paul, *Blues And The Poetic Spirit*, Da Capo (USA), 1977.

Gart, Galen, *The History Of Rhythm And Blues: Volume 1-8*, Big Nickle, Milford (USA).

Gellert, L., *Me And My Captain*, New York, 1939.

Gellert, L., *Negro Songs Of Protest*, New York, 1936.

Godrich, John and Dixon, Robert M.W., *Blues And Gospel Records 1902-1942*, Storyville (USA), 1983.

Govenar, Alan, *Meeting The Blues: Rise Of The Texas Sound*, Da Capo (USA), 1995.

Green, Stephen, *Going To Chicago: A Year On The Chicago Blues Scene*, Woodford Publishing (USA), 1990.

Groom, Robert, *The Blues Revival*, Studio Vista (UK), 1970.

Guralnick, Peter, *Feel Like Going Home: Portraits In Blues And Rock 'N' Roll*, New York, 1971.

Guralnick, Peter, *Lost Highway: Journeys & Arrivals Of American Musicians*, Harper Collins, 1989.

Guralnick, Peter, *Searching For Robert Johnson*, Dutton (USA), 1988.

Guralnick, Peter, *The Listener's Guide To The Blues*, New York, 1979.

Hadley, Frank-John, *Grove Press Guide To The Blues*, Grove Press (USA), 1993.

Handy, W.C., (ed.), *Blues: An Anthology*, Da Capo (USA), 1985.

Handy, W.C., *A Treasury Of The Blues*, New York, 1925.

Handy, W.C., *The Father Of The Blues*, Da Capo (USA), 1991.

Hannusch, Jeff, *I Hear You Knockin': The Sound Of New Orleans Rhythm And Blues*, Ville Platte, Louisiana (USA), 1985.

Haralambos, Michael, *Right On: From Blues To Soul In Black America*, Da Capo (USA), 1979.

Harris, Michael W., *The Rise Of Gospel Blues*, Oxford University Press (UK), 1993.

Harris, Sheldon, *Blues Who's Who*, Da Capo Press (USA), 1989.

Harris, Sheldon, *Blues Who's Who: A Biographical Dictionary Of Blues Singers*, Arlington House, New York, 1979.

Harrison, Daphne Duval, *Black Pearls: Blues Queens Of The 1920s*, Rutgers University Press (USA), 1990.

Harrison, David, *World Of Blues*, Studio Edns., 1993.

Hart, Mary L., and Eagles, Brenda M., *The Blues: A Bibliographic Guide*, Garland Publications (USA), 1989.

Hatch, David and Millward, Stephen, *Blues To Rock*, Manchester University Press, 1989.

Herzhaft, Gerard, *Encyclopedia Of The Blues*, University Of Arkansas Press (USA), 1992.

Herzhaft, Gerard, *Encyclopedie Du Blues*, Lyons (France), 1979.

Herzhaft, Gerard, *Long Blues In A Minor*, University of Arkansas, 1991.

Hildebrand, Lee, and Vignes, Michelle, *Bay Area Blues*, Pomegranate Artbooks (USA), 1993.

Hughes, Langston, and Meltzer, Milton, *Black Magic: A Pictorial History Of The African-American In The Performing Art*, Da Capo (USA), 1990.

Jackson, B., *Wake Up Dead Man: Afro-American Worksongs From Texan Prisons*, Cambridge, Massachusetts (USA), 1972.

James, C.L.R., *Beyond A Boundary*, Pantheon, 1983.

Jones, Hettie, *Big Star Fallin' Mama: Five Women In Black Music*, Viking (USA), 1974.

Jones, LeRoi, *Black Music*, William Morrow (USA), 1971.

Jones, LeRoi, *Blues People: Negro Music In White America*, Payback Press, 1995.

Joseph, Pleasant, and Ottenheimer, Harriet J., *Cousin Joe; Blues From New Orleans*, University Of Chicago Press (USA), 1987.

Keil, Charles, *Urban Blues*, University Of Chicago Press (USA), 1966.

Kriss, E., *Barrelhouse And Boogie Piano*, New

York, 1974.

Larkin, Colin (ed.), *Guinness Who's Who Of Blues 2nd Edition*, Guinness Publishing (UK), 1995.

Larkin, Colin (ed.), *Guinness Who's Who Of Blues*, Guinness Publishing (UK), 1993.

Leadbitter, Mike, and Leslie Fancourt, *Blues Records Vol 2, 1943-1970*, Record Information Services, 1995.

Leadbitter, Mike, and Slaven, Neil, *Blues Records: A Complete Guide To 20 Years Of Recorded Blues: 1943-1966*, Oak Publications, 1968.

Leadbitter, Mike, and Slaven, Neil, *Crowley, Louisiana Blues*, Blues Unlimited, 1968.

Leadbitter, Mike, and Slaven, Neil, *Nothing But The Blues: An Illustrated Documentary*, Hanover Books, 1971.

Lomax, Alan, *Land Where The Blues Began*, Methuen (UK), Pantheon (USA), 1993.

Lomax, J. A., *Adventures Of A Ballad Hunter*, New York, 1947.

Lornell, Kip, *Happy In The Service Of The Lord (Afro American Gospel Quartets In Memphis)*, University Of Illinois Press (USA), 1988.

Lornell, Kip, *Virginia Blues: Country And Gospel Records 1902-1943*, University Of Kentucky Press (USA), 1989.

Lovell Jnr., John, *Black Song: The Forge And The Flame*, Macmillan, 1972.

Macleod, R. R., *Document Blues 1*, Pat Publications (UK), 1994.

Mann, Woody, *Six Black Blues Guitarists*, Oak Publications (USA), 1973.

McKee, Margaret, and Chisenhall, Fred, *Beale Black And Blue: Life And Music On America's Main Street*, Louisiana State University Press, 1993.

Mezzrow, Milton Mezz and Wolfe, Bernard, *Really The Blues*, Random House, 1946.

Mitchell, George, *Blow My Blues Away*, Da Capo, 1983.

Morgan, Thomas L., and Barlow, William, *From Cakewalks To Concert Halls: African American Popular Music*, Elliott & Clark, 1992.

Murray, Albert, *Stomping The Blues*, McGraw-Hill (USA), 1976.

Murray, Charles Shaar, *Blues On CD: The Essential Guide*, Kyle Cathie, 1993.

Myrus, Donald, *Ballads, Blues And The Big Beat*, Macmillan, 1966.

Napier, Simon A., *Back Woods Blues*, Blues Unlimited (UK), 1968.

Neff, Robert, and Connor, Anthony, *Blues*, Godine Publications (USA), 1975.

Nicholas, A. X., *Woke Up This Mornin': Poetry Of The Blues*, Bantam (USA), 1973.

Oakley, Giles, *The Devil's Music: A History Of The Blues*, BBC (UK), Harcourt Brace (USA), 1976.

Odum, H.W., and Johnson, G.B., *The Negro And His Songs*, Chapel Hill, 1925.

Oliver, Paul (ed.), *The Blackwell Guide To Blues Records*, Basil Blackwell (UK), 1991.

Oliver, Paul, *Aspects Of The Blues Tradition*, Oak Publications (USA), 1970.

Oliver, Paul, *Blackwell Blues Guide*, Basil Blackwell (UK), 1989.

Oliver, Paul, *Blues Fell This Morning: The Meaning Of The Blues*, Cambridge University Press, 1990.

Oliver, Paul, *Blues Off The Record: Thirty Years Of Blues Commentary*, Da Capo (USA), 1984.

Oliver, Paul, *Conversation With The Blues*, Horizon Press (USA), 1983.

Oliver, Paul, *Gospel, Blues And Jazz*, Macmillan (USA), 1990.

Oliver, Paul, *Savannah Syncopators: African Retentions In The Blues*, Madison Books (USA), Studio Vista (UK), 1970.

Oliver, Paul, *Screening The Blues: Aspects Of The Blues Tradition*, Da Capo (USA), 1989.

Oliver, Paul, *Songsters And Saints: Vocal Traditions On Race Records*, Cambridge University Press, 1989.

Oliver, Paul, *The Meaning Of The Blues*, Collier Books (USA), 1963.

Oliver, Paul, *The Story Of The Blues*, Chilton Books, 1969.

Oliver, Paul; Harrison, Max; Bolcom, W., *New Grove Gospel, Blues & Jazz, With Spirituals And Ragtime*, Norton (USA), 1986.

Olsson, Bengt, *Memphis Blues And Jug Bands*, Studio Vista (UK), 1970.

Oster, Harry, *Living Country Blues*, Folklore Associates, 1969.

Palmer, Robert, *Deep Blues*, Penguin Books, 1982.

Pearson, Barry Lee, *Virginia Piedmont Blues: The Lives And Art Of Two Virginia Bluesmen*, University Pennsylvania Press (USA), 1990.

Price, Sammy, *What Do They Want?*, Bayou

Press, 1989.

Raichelson, Richard M., *Beale Street Talks: A Walking Tour Down The Home Of The Blues*, Arcadia Press (USA), 1994.

Ramsey Jnr., F., *Been Here And Gone*, Brunswick, New Jersey, 1960.

Roach, Hildred, *Black American Music: Past And Present*, Krieger Publishing Company, 1992.

Rowe, Mike, *Chicago Breakdown*, Da Capo (USA), 1981.

Rowe, Mike, *Chiucago Blues: The City And The Music*, Da Capo (USA), 1981.

Russell, Tony, *Blacks, Whites And Blues*, Studio Vista (UK), Stein And Day (USA), 1970.

Ryan, Marc, *Trumpet Records - An Illustrated History With Discography*, Big Nickel Publications (USA), 1993.

Sackheim, Eric (ed.), *The Blues Line: A Collection Of Blues Lyrics*, New York, 1969.

Sackheim, Eric (ed.), *The Blues Line: A Collection Of Blues Lyrics From Leadbelly To Muddy Waters*, Ecco Press (USA), 1993.

Santelli, Robert, *The Big Book Of Blues*, Penguin Books, 1994.

Santoto, Gene, *Dancing In Your Head: Jazz, Blues, Rock, And Beyond*, Oxford University Press, 1994.

Scott, Frank, *The Down Home Guide To The Blues*, A Cappella Books (USA), 1991.

Seeger, M., *Anthology Of American Folk Music*, New York, 1973.

Shaw, Arnold, *Honkers And Shouters: The Golden Years Of Rhythm And Blues*, Macmillan (USA), 1978.

Sidran, Ben, *Black Talk*, Da Capo (USA), 1988.

Silverman, Jerry, *Folk Blues*, Macmillan (USA), 1967.

Smith Michael P., *A Joyful Noise: A Celebration Of New Orleans Music*, Taylor, 1990.

Sonnier, Austin Jr., *A Guide To The Blues: History, Who's Who, Research Sources*, Greenwood Press (USA), 1994.

Southern, Eileen, *The Music Of Black Americans*, W. W. Norton (USA), 1983.

Spencer, John Michael, *Blues And Evil*, University Of Tennessee Press (USA), 1993.

Springer, Robert, *Authentic Blues: Its History And Its Themes*, Edwin Mellen Press (Canada), 1995.

St. Pierre, Roger, *The Best Of The Blues: The Essential CD Guide*, Collins (UK), 1993.

Surge, Frank, *Singers Of The Blues*, Lerner (USA), 1969.

Sylvester, Peter, *A Left Hand Like God: A History Of Boogie Woogie Piano*, Da Capo (USA), 1989.

Taft, Michael, *Blues Lyric Poetry: An Anthology*, Garland (USA), 1983.

Titon, Jeff Todd, *Downhome Blues Lyrics: An Anthology From The Post-World War 11 Era*, Boston (USA), 1981.

Titon, Jeff Todd, *Early Downhome Blues: A Musical And Cultural Analysis*, University Of Illinois Press (USA), 1977.

Titon, Jeff Todd, *Early Downhome Blues: Second Edition*, University Of North Carolina (USA), 1994.

Tracy, Steven C., *Going To Cincinnati: A History Of Blues In The Queen City*, University Of Illinois Press (USA), 1995.

Traum, Happy, *The Blues Bag*, New York, 1968.

Trynka, Paul, and Wilmer, Val, *Portrait Of The Blues: America's Blues Musicians In Their Own Words*, Hamlyn (UK), Da Capo (USA), 1996.

Walton, Ortiz M., *Music: Black, White And Blue*, William Morrow (USA), 1972.

Webb, Stan, *Will You Dance With Me*, G C P, 1990.

Whitcomb, Ian, *Legends Of Rhythm And Blues Repercussions*, London, 1984.

White, N.I., *American Negro Folk-Songs*, Cambridge, Massachusetts (USA), 1928.

Wilcock, Donald E., and Guy, Buddy, *Damn Right I've Got The Blues: Buddy Guy And The Blues Roots Of Rock 'N' Roll*, Woodford Press, 1994.

Williams, Paul, *Blues And Outlaw*, E.P. Dutton (USA), 1969.

Wilson, Christine, *All Shook Up: Mississippi Roots Of American Popular Music*, Museum Of Mississippi (USA), 1996.

Work, John Wesley, *American Negro Songs & Spirituals*, Bonanza Books (USA), 1940.

INDEX

Humes, Helen, 176, 366, 386
Hunt, Billy, 179
Hunt, Chris, 134
Hunt, Noah, 315
Hunter, 'Long John', 176
Hunter, Alberta, 14, 37, 71, 177-178, 328
Hunter, Ellis, 122
Hunter, George, 67
Hunter, Ivory Joe, 15, 100, 346
Hunter, Joe, 15, 100, 346
Hunter, John, 176
Hunter, Lloyd, 277
Hurley, Bill, 180
Hurston, Zora Neale, 53, 204, 270
Hurt, Mississippi John, 33, 71, 115, 133, 141, 178, 187, 217, 251, 357
Hutchinson, Frank, 115
Hutto, J.B., 36, 38, 40, 99, 113, 165, 179, 184, 229, 248, 253, 268, 377
Hymas, Tony, 21

I

Ice Cube, 297
Icehouse, 167
Ichiban Records, 83, 100, 285
Iglauer, Bruce, 7, 84, 161, 231, 270, 308
Immediate Records, 122
Imperial Records, 12, 18, 74, 104, 113, 135, 199, 261, 360, 377
Impressions, 70, 157
In Crowd, 78-79, 206, 253
Ink Spots, 122, 279
Inmates, 180, 224
Innes, Dick, Jnr., 14
Iron Butterfly, 161
Iron Curtain, 247
Ironing Board Sam, 180
Island Records, 44, 58, 90, 185, 247, 301
Isley Brothers, 157, 316
Ivory Records, 312

J

J., Peter, 81, 210, 235, 331
Jack, Steve, 78-79
Jackson, 'New Orleans' Willie, 180
Jackson, Armand 'Jump', 180
Jackson, Arthur, 183
Jackson, Bessie, 41, 305
Jackson, Bo Weavil, 181
Jackson, Bud, 68
Jackson, Bullmoose, 181
Jackson, Calvin, 62
Jackson, Charlie, 37, 49, 182, 366, 375
Jackson, Cliff, 198
Jackson, Franz, 262
Jackson, George, 232
Jackson, J.J., 180
Jackson, Jack, 177
Jackson, Janet, 220
Jackson, Jim, 44, 65, 182, 228, 375
Jackson, John, 115, 182, 204
Jackson, Lee, 225, 285
Jackson, Lil Son, 25, 114, 182, 192, 292
Jackson, Mahalia, 83, 312, 346, 375

Jackson, Melvin, 182
Jackson, Michael, 123
Jackson, Millie, 130
Jackson, Papa Charlie, 37, 49, 182, 366, 375
Jackson, Peg Leg Sam, 183
Jackson, Roosevelt, 375
Jackson, Son, 25, 114, 182, 192, 292
Jackson, Stonewall, 250
Jackson, Tony, 204
Jackson, Willie, 180
Jacobs, 'Boogie Jake', 183
Jacobs, Marion Walter, 234
Jacobs, Matthew, 183
Jacques, Jean, 64
Jacquet, Illinois, 151-152, 277, 289, 356
Jagger, Mick, 108, 120, 216, 297
Jamail, Randall Hage, 23
James, Bennett, 306
James, Billy, 358
James, Charlie, 62
James, Chris, 221
James, Colin, And The Little Big Band, 183-184
James, Curley, 365
James, David, 186, 251, 272
James, Doug, 305
James, Eddie, 325
James, Elmer, 93
James, Elmore, 25, 28, 48, 53, 70, 76-77, 122, 135, 146, 166, 179, 184-185, 196-197, 199-200, 207, 219, 239, 249, 262, 269, 273, 289, 301, 330, 334, 338, 353, 355, 358-359, 377-379
James, Etta, 19, 28, 38, 76, 83, 97, 185-186, 248-249, 261, 277, 325, 330, 350, 356
James, Frank 'Springback', 186
James, Harry, 176
James, Jesse, 186
James, Jimmy, 48, 157, 193, 251, 304
James, John, 184, 186, 214, 338, 358
James, Lewis, 365
James, Milton, 232, 239
James, Nehemiah Curtis, 186
James, Scott, 135
James, Skip, 27, 71, 132-133, 141, 186-187, 278, 330, 382
James, Sonny, 197
James, Steve, 187
James, Sue, 184
James, Sylvester, 365
James, Willie, 66, 186-187, 207, 240, 277
Jammin' The Blues, 356
Jano, Johnny, 260
Jansch, Bert, 187-188
Jarmusch, Jim, 153
Jarrett, Pigmeat, 188-189
Jarvis, Felton, 105
Jason And The Scorchers, 101
Jaxon, Frankie, 164, 189, 334
Jay, Jimmy, 385
Jazz Festivals, 119, 330, 332
Jazz On A Summer's Day, 26
Jean, Shirley, 290
Jefferson Airplane, 92, 158
Jefferson Starship, 29, 92
Jefferson, Alex, 189
Jefferson, Benny, 163
Jefferson, Blind Lemon, 32, 37, 115, 144, 162, 170, 188-190, 208, 210, 222, 225-226,

234, 299, 315, 344, 359, 366, 375, 377
Jefferson, John, 115
Jeffery, Robert, 190
Jeffries, Mike, 157
Jelly Roll Kings, 191, 316
Jellybread, 35, 355
Jenkins, Bobo, 190
Jenkins, Clarence, 279
Jenkins, Gus, 190, 281
Jenkins, John, 190
Jenkins, John Pickens, 190
Jenkins, Mahalia Lucille, 326
Jennings, Ian, 28
Jesters, 101
Jeter, Claude, 224
Jethro Tull, 5, 337
Jewel Records, 24, 127-128, 150
Jim, Country, 68, 90
Jiminez, Flaco, 86
Jo Jo Gunne, 203
Joe, Cousin, 242, 317, 389
Joe, Monkey, 83
Joe, Tampa, 12
John And Johnny, 45
John, Chris, 108, 120
John, Elton, 16
John, Little Willie, 122, 130, 172, 352
John, Mable, 295
John, Maurice, 8, 353
John, Robert, 284
Johnny And Jack, 286
Johnny And John, 45, 236
Johnny And Walter, 227
Johns, Glyn, 273
Johnson, 'Big' Jack, 63, 127, 191, 316
Johnson, 'Blind' Willie, 86, 191-192, 302, 333
Johnson, Alan, 197
Johnson, Alfred 'Snuff', 192
Johnson, Alonzo, 194
Johnson, Arnold, 369
Johnson, Bessie, 192
Johnson, Buddy, 192
Johnson, Bunk, 259
Johnson, Carlos, 326, 365
Johnson, Charley, 56
Johnson, Charlie, 265
Johnson, Conrad, 300, 376
Johnson, David, 197, 244
Johnson, Earl, 212
Johnson, Eddie, 7
Johnson, Edith, 192
Johnson, Ella, 192
Johnson, Ernie, 218
Johnson, Gordie, 26
Johnson, Gus, 254
Johnson, Henry, 193
Johnson, Jack, 63, 127, 191, 316
Johnson, James 'Stump', 193
Johnson, James P., 176, 320-321, 323
Johnson, James, 27, 127, 176, 193, 320-321, 323
Johnson, Jesse, 192-193, 225
Johnson, Jimmy, 193, 239, 244, 364
Johnson, John, 9, 107
Johnson, Johnnie, 193, 214, 239, 304, 309, 354
Johnson, Leslie, 221
Johnson, Lonnie, 7, 10, 38, 51, 98, 134, 194-195, 208, 210, 321, 331-332, 343-344,